A Legacy Greater Than Words

A Legacy Greater Than Words

STORIES OF U.S. LATINOS & LATINAS OF THE WWII GENERATION

Maggie Rivas-Rodriguez
Juliana A. Torres
Melissa DiPiero-D'Sa
Lindsay Fitzpatrick

U.S. Latino & Latina WWII Oral History Project • *Austin*

Second paperback printing, 2007

Requests for permission to reproduce material from this work should be sent to
    U.S. Latino & Latina WWII Oral History Project
    University of Texas at Austin, School of Journalism
    1 University Station A1000, Austin, TX 78712-0113

The paper used in this book meets the minimum requirements of ANSI.NISO Z39.48-1992 (R1997)
(Permanence of Paper).

Library of Congress Control Number: 2006921082

ISBN 0-292-71418-1

For all the Latinos and Latinas of the WWII generation

Contents

Contents

Illustrations

Maps

Foreword

The Latinos of the United States are as new as the most recently arrived immigrant and as old as San Augustine, San Antonio, Santa Fe or San Francisco. The true character of the Hispanic people can only become clear if you hold these two ideas in focus at the same time: a population of newcomers and a population with a long history in this country. Because immigration has accounted for so much of the population growth for the past few decades and because it is so controversial, it is easy to lose sight of that other aspect: the past. To think of Latinos only as people just now in the process of defining their place in American society is a mistake. Even in trying to understand the newcomers, it would be misleading to forget those who had been here already when the current wave of immigration began. This book is a remedy.

In the middle of the 20th Century a much-extolled generation of Americans overcame the Great Depression, triumphed in World War II and laid the groundwork for extraordinary political, social and economic gains that followed at home and abroad. One need not admire everything that has transpired in their lifetimes to acknowledge that the Americans of the World War II generation had an extraordinary influence on mankind's course, arguably more than any generation, of any one nation, before or since, and that on the whole it was a positive influence. The presence of Latinos in that generation, however, is easy to overlook — and it usually is. Hispanics were then a very small share of the population and were comprised primarily of people of Mexican ancestry living in Texas, the Southwest and California. The autobiographical stories collected in this volume by the U.S. Latino & Latina WWII Oral History Project remind us that Hispanics did play a role in the larger narrative of that

era; that they did participate in the sacrifices and the accomplishments. This volume then is both U.S. history and Latino history. It depicts what was a small but distinctive cast of characters in the story of the World War II generation, and it offers a rich portrait of Hispanic lives during that important period. Those lives, moreover, have a significance that goes beyond the war years and still resonates today.

Like other Americans of their generation, the Latinos of the World War II era authored political and social orientations and created institutions which endured through the rest of the 20th Century. Like other Americans of their day, these Latinos began to move off the land into cities and towns and to adopt new ways. They were part of a generation that benefited from the GI Bill and other public investments in education, a generally rising economy and a drive for self-improvement spurred by the challenges of the 1930s and 1940s. As a result, many made quantum gains in economic and social status that produced a new, broader middle class and new cohorts of leadership. This was a generation of shifting mores and expectations, and especially so for Hispanics. They served the war effort in many ways and in disproportionately high numbers, and when the conflict ended, they claimed their due. And, they had special claims. One need only recall the story of Macario Garcia, an Army staff sergeant who won the Congressional Medal of Honor. Returning home to Sugarland, Texas, after a White House ceremony, he was refused service at a diner that did not feed Mexicans or blacks. Many of the protagonists of this volume, though less heralded, had similar experiences.

In a variety of initiatives, both collective and individual, Latinos fought discrimination in the aftermath of the war. Barriers to education, to political participation and to economic opportunity, which had been enforced by public policy and common custom, fell one after another in the 1950s, 60s and 70s. Though still incomplete, the Hispanic civil rights struggle launched by the World War II generation utterly transformed the position of Latinos in American society. And it created the context into which the new Latino immigrant population has flowed.

At the end of World War II about half of the Hispanic population was made up of people whose family roots in this country went back at least to their grandparents, i.e. they had been born in the United States and their parents had been born here as well. Such Latinos of long tenure make up less than a third of the total population today as the Hispanic population had changed both in number and character. The size of the Hispanic population doubled between 1970 and 1990 and since 1990 it has nearly doubled again due to immigration and high fertility rates among immigrants. The wave of Latino immigration that began in earnest in the 1970s is unlike previous immigrant waves in many ways. But, one of the most significant differences is that these newcomers join a population of co-ethnics who have a long history here. And, by coincidence, the Latino wave of immigration arrived just as the Hispanic civil rights struggle had become mature, influential and institutionalized. That history, especially the status of Hispanics as a minority group asserting its identity and claiming redress of grievances, undoubtedly influences the way Latino newcomers look at themselves and their new land.

These are two substantially different groups of people—the Latino newcomers and those of old stock. They have different origins, different trajectories and sometimes different interests. But they are now substantially intertwined by shared culture and ancestry and by a social system of managing racial and ethnic differences that puts them together into one category.

The growing Latino presence in the United States will be shaped by the interaction of the two. The new Hispanic identities now evolving in many different ways in many different places across the nation are drawing on both the new and the old. The legacies of the Latino World War II generation now play out in many millions of households where immigrant parents and their native-born children are inventing new ways to be Americans and new ways to be Latinos.

With this book and its other publications, the U.S. Latino & Latina WWII Oral History Project offers an invaluable resource for understanding the present and the future by chronicling the past. Through the lives portrayed here, we get the essential prologue to the journeys of the Hispanic population today and tomorrow. The United States can not be understood now without knowing this population. This book is Latino history. It illuminates the American future.

—*Roberto Suro*
Director, Pew Hispanic Center
Washington, D.C.

Preface

Please note that this preface is a detailed explanation of our methodology, perhaps more than is common. Our intent is to offer our experience to any other similar oral history project that may wish to consider publishing interviews as either news stories, as we have in the past, or in a book, as we do here. We have arrived at this point after taking our own guidance from many other oral history projects, credited in the acknowledgement section of this volume, as well as from much trial and error. If others can benefit from our experience, so much the better.
—*Maggie Rivas-Rodriguez*

We have undertaken the work of publishing *A Legacy Greater Than Words* with two goals in mind: to provide interested readers summaries of our stories and to turn over to the repository, where the archives will be held, as much, and as accurate, information as possible. Our hope is that once the files reside at the Nettie Lee Benson Latin American Collection, they will be available for public viewing as soon as possible, rather than require the time-consuming processing that would delay their use.

We have had, since the beginning of the U.S. Latino & Latina WWII Oral History Project, a way to demonstrate the richness of our interviews: a newspaper, Narratives, which was dedicated to the interviews. Eight issues of the newspaper were published between 1999 and 2004, courtesy of the Austin American-Statesman and the San Antonio Express-News. *A Legacy Greater Than Words* could not exist without the groundwork provided by Narratives. *A Legacy Greater Than Words* has followed the process developed through the publication of Narratives:

1. The interview is conducted by a volunteer.

2. A story is written by a journalism student, often not the person who conducted the interview.

3. A side-by-side edit session is held with the student and a professional journalist. Additional questions for the Interview Subject are listed within the story.

4. The story is sent via e-mail to two volunteer military historians, who verify military information, such as location of the person's military unit and dates.

5. The story is sent to the Interview Subject, with any additional questions from the student writer, the editor and the military historians.

The Interviews

The Project put together an interviewer training manual and a video early on, to guide volunteers unfamiliar with oral history interviewing. That manual was later posted on the Project's Web site. Among the admonishments: record with external microphones where at all possible for the best audio, try to use ear phones attached to the camera so that you can hear what the camera is picking up, remember to ask for as much detail as possible, always use a tripod, and make sure to get a signed permission form from the Interview Subject—allowing the interview to become public. A list of guideline questions was included, as was, in the hard copy, chapters from helpful readings on oral history interviewing.

Interviews have been conducted by people with varying degrees of experience. For some, this interview represented a first time. For others, such as our journalist friends and college professors, as well as a small band of repeat volunteer interviewers, interviewing was familiar territory. A list of all our interviewers is available at the end of this volume.

To the extent that they could, we encouraged interviewers to help the Interview Subject fill out a pre-interview form, provide military discharge papers, photographs, and any other documentation to augment the Subject's file.

Interviews were generally about two hours long and were videotaped in a variety of formats: Hi-8 in the early days, mini-digital video later, with only a handful in professional beta format. A few, mostly those conducted by interviewers in connection with other research and later donated to the Project, were only audio recorded. And in a very few cases, there are only testimonials handwritten by Subjects. This Project also includes Tributes, information provided by loved ones of WWII-era people who have passed on and were not interviewed.

Narratives

Housed within the University of Texas at Austin, School of Journalism, the Project has had access to journalism students who, as part of their training, must be able to synthesize large blocks of information and make it understandable, place it within its historical context and then write clearly and succinctly. Students time and again rose to the challenge of writing 800 to 1,000 word stories from interviews conducted by another. A list of the original story writers is available at the end of this volume.

Most stories were part of an assignment for a reporting class, J320D, taught by various journalism professors. All stories, however, were edited by Project editors in side-by-side edit sessions in front of a computer screen, a process that requires at least one hour per story. The editors were able to add, on top of the story file and throughout the story, questions not asked in the interview, or for clarification of unclear answers, or additional information not touched upon in the interview. The story would eventually be returned to the Interview Subject, who was asked to address the various additional questions.

The stories were then e-mailed to volunteer fact-checkers Richard Brito and Bill Davies, who added their questions and comments in red and blue type and sent them back to the Project. This procedure was adopted in the spring of 2001.

In Austin, the Project printed out the final version of the story and wrote a short note to the Interview Subject, asking him or her to answer the questions and make any and all corrections to the story and to mail the story back in the attached self-addressed stamped envelopes.

This procedure, of pre-publication review by the Interview Subject was adopted in the fall of 2000, at the recommendation of Interview Subject Virgilio Roel.

Interview Subjects' responses, and in some cases, a completely rewritten autobiography by the Subject, are included in the Subjects' files, to clearly delineate the "provenance" of the information, in the terms used by archivists: that is, to let future researchers understand where the information came from, particularly if it is information not included in the taped interview.

Finally, if the story wasn't returned promptly, students working for the Project often called the Interview Subjects to remind them to send in their corrections.

In publishing Narratives, the Project developed a simple system of spreadsheets and a new prefix for the electronic story file at the end of each of the steps.

Post-Narratives

In 2004, the Project published issue number 8 of Narratives. The newspaper had become a year-round production for the small Project Staff. The Project would turn attention to consolidating and processing the material already gathered. Interviews will continue to be conducted, as resources allow, and always accepted. But new interviews would be featured in the quarterly newsletter, Narratives Insider.

The Project had received numerous requests for all eight issues of the newspaper; as supplies of those older issues dwindled. It was apparent there was a demand for a publication that included all the stories. After considering several different models, we decided on a volume that summarizes the interviews, with the longer versions available on the Web, or on a CD or DVD later, as resources became available.

To get there, we would give all Interview Subjects an opportunity to make any and all corrections to their stories—from those that had been published in the first issue of Narratives until some of the more recent interviews. In a few cases, after the publication of their story in Narratives, we had heard back that there had been an error, but that the Subject chose not to correct it because they didn't want to hurt our feelings.

The Project hired two journalism students who had done superb jobs writing stories for the Project in the past: Juliana Torres and Lindsay Fitzpatrick. Lindsay excelled at combing the files, finding what was missing in each and then customizing a form letter to each Interview Subject in our database, asking them to review their story and send us the material missing. After they wrote the stories, Sara Hernando, one of the Project's work-studies students, sent the packets out, complete with forms that would have to be filled out by the Subject. Sara also later made phone calls to the Subjects to answer questions that came up in summarizing their stories. She was assisted by journalism student Kathryn Gonzales, whose Spanish-speaking ability was key.

The corrected stories, 800 to 1,000 words long, were summarized into 250 words, seeking to emphasize the aspect of the story that related to the chapter it would be placed into. By early December, the *Legacy* Team included Juliana Torres, Lindsay Fitzpatrick, Sara Hernando, Kathryn Gonzales, Jenny Achilles (a journalism graduate student), Jaime Margolis, (a journalism undergraduate student), Tino Mauricio (a photojournalism graduate student), Melissa DiPiero-D'Sa, Richard Brito, Bill Davies, Guillermo Torres and myself, Maggie Rivas-Rodriguez.

Organizing the Book

How best to help readers understand the extent of Latino involvement in World War II? In Narratives, the only concern about organization was to find a compelling story and attractive photograph for the cover—not easy, considering that all of them were compelling—as well as trying to get married couples on facing pages. But now, combining all those stories, the decision was made to organize the stories around whatever most distinguished the story. The vast majority of the stories would center on the Subjects' activities during WWII: whether they were in the military or not. That helped to organize the first two parts of the book.

In a few instances, even when the Subject had a distinguished military service, it was what came after the war that seemed to identify them, to place them in Part Three, dealing with post-war activities.

There has been a great deal of judgment involved here: in many cases, the Subject fit into more than one category. Heads were put together to resolve any questions; there was not always unanimous agreement and there was occasional second-guessing.

Chapters were organized around various themes and individual stories in those chapters are generally, but not always in alphabetical order. In a few cases, the stories that focused on events as they unfolded, most especially the war years, the order was changed and stories were arranged chronologically.

Melissa DiPiero-D'Sa and Juliana Torres teamed up to create the system of manila folders and excel spreadsheets that were used repeatedly to keep track of chapters, lengths, interview subjects' names. Without that basic structure, we soon would have foundered, especially as we added more writers.

The old issues of Narratives were ripped up, placed into manila envelopes by chapter, or subchapter. A team of writers grew as the deadline for publication loomed. The conference table in the Project office became a mass of (borrowed) laptop computers, manila envelopes, printouts of stories, bags of pretzels and other snacks.

A Legacy Greater Than Words could not have been completed had it not been for an online database built by Ajit D'Sa, husband of Melissa DiPiero-D'Sa, so that all the writers could keep track of which stage the various stories were in, and what chapter they would fit into, and whether a photograph was available. It also could not have been completed without a secure computer network that allowed all the participants to access the 500-plus text files and the thousands of photo files necessary to complete the work, without worrying that outsiders might tamper with and destroy our work.

After the stories were written, there was often additional information needed. Sometimes, the Interview Subject had moved to a retirement home, or, in some cases, had passed away since the interview. To ensure a link to the next-of-kin, the Project had begun soliciting contact information from the Interview Subjects with a form that included the relationship of the Subject to the contact persons, the contact persons' telephone numbers and mailing addresses. These contacts were crucial as phone calls were placed throughout the two week period around Christmas-New Year's 2005-2006 season. The most common missing element were the discharge papers which would have complete information about military service, including in which unit the Subject served, where he or she served, what medals were awarded. In some instances, it was not possible to get the unit information, despite our best efforts. The units are crucial to verifying the location of military servicemen during the war; without that information, military historians Bill Davies and Richard Brito's efforts are hampered.

Finally, the stories were returned, corrected by Project Staff, and laid out in the book by Melissa DiPiero-D'Sa, and hand-delivered to UT Press.

Photos and Maps

Where possible, the stories include wartime head shots of each Subject. In some cases, those older photographs were unavailable we chose to use available contemporary photographs of the Subjects. In several instances, no photographs were available within the time needed.

The Project used available maps. They were used to provide readers a general background of geographic locations during WWII. Our Interview Subjects may or may not be in the units shown on the various maps. Where we thought it appropriate and helpful, we have revised those maps to suit our specific needs. We hope we have maintained the integrity of the original map.

All but one of the photographs used through out the book, the one of Braceros—Chapter 8, are from the Project's own database, just a sample of the wealth of photographs available, perhaps for a later book.

Style

We blended two different styles—the journalistic Associated Press style with the academic Chicago style—to create this book. Where it made sense to use Chicago, we did; where it made more sense to use AP, we went that route. In a few instances, we created our own individual style practice.

For the most part, we used the WWII-era identities of geographic locations and institutions: countries, military installations, colleges.

We also used the terms Hispanic and Latino interchangeably. In instances where the context was specific to an ethnic group, such as Mexican American or Cuban American or Puerto Rican, we included the nationality.

Acknowledgements

How to thank the hundreds of people who have made this book a reality?

It's neither an easy nor a quick task, and I will take as much space as needed to do it, so here goes.

First and foremost, we must thank the hundreds of men and women whose stories we have recorded for the U.S. Latino & Latina WWII Oral History Project over the past six years. Of course, we couldn't have done this without their cooperation. They agreed to the interview and again and again were called on to answer a few more questions, send us some photographs to scan, read over their story and make any and all corrections. They have been patient and gentle with us. Those of us fortunate enough to interview them have learned much, not only about WWII and the social history of their times, but also about life in general. They have truly lifted us up.

To date, we have collected files for 532 people — mostly interviews, but a few "Tributes" to people who have passed on. Most of those stories are on the following pages.

However, not all the people who have been interviewed are included here. Some were interviewed after work began on this volume and we were forced to limit our book to interviews that had already been conducted and published. If there is enough demand — and funding — we will have another, updated volume, with the additional interviews, all of them important in telling the story of Latinos and Latinas of the World War II generation.

Also, thanks to the families of our Interview Subjects, who in many cases have been the ones to actually send us the material, and have sometimes been the ones organizing the interviews or driving their parents to the interview.

And then there are the interviewers. From the spring of 1999 to the present, there have been 215 different interviewers, a few conducting multiple interviews. Many have been relatives or friends of the interview subjects — conducting an interview for the first time. And some were college professors, like Joanne Sanchez of St. Edwards University in Austin, Mario Barrera of the University of California, Berkeley, Silvia Alvarez-Curbelo and Humberto García Muñoz, of the University of Puerto Rico, Río Piedras campus. They have been people such as Rea Ann Trotter of Colorado, who had already begun interviewing men as part of her own master's thesis in history and who later donated her material to us, including newly acquired permissions from the Interview Subjects. There is Paul R. Zepeda of Houston, who started out interviewing three of his WWII-veteran brothers and then took off from there. He later formed an interviewing partnership with WWII veteran Ernest Eguía and the two have continued to send us excellent work. My brother, Robert Rivas, in El Paso, specializes in extensive research before the interview and then in asking detailed follow-up questions. That explains why he has conducted our longest interview: eight hours over several days. Bill Luna, of Chicago, sends us interviews from the Midwest, while also carrying out numerous other volunteer activities.

All the interviews have been the subject of a story, written by one of 272 different writers. Many were UT students enrolled in a class dedicated to the Project, as well as journalism students in other classes. Thank you to my colleagues, George Sylvie, Griff Singer and Dave Garlock, for stepping in and assigning their students to write some of the stories. And thank you to all of the student writers. I hope the writers believe they benefited from the exchange: that they learned a little bit about history, about social justice, about the sacrifices made by this generation. I also hope they learned from the intensive side-by-side edits with tough, veteran journalists, one of the best techniques I know for teaching journalism.

Richard Brito, a retired colonel living in Austin, and Bill Davies, a Vietnam veteran/librarian in Sacramento, have handled our historical/military fact-checking with alacrity, skill and good humor. If we have any mistakes on the following pages and in any of our material, those errors are despite Richard and Bill's best efforts.

One person we could not have lived without has been San Antonio Express-News copy editor Guillermo Torres, who edited like a crazy person around his usual workload, on his own time, so that we could look good. Guillermo has edited more than commas and AP style, he has also tried to make sure our content worked. Where there are any errors in our copy, we take full responsibility—it is not Guillermo's fault.

Here and there people gave us wonderful in-kind contributions that provided us with the high quality professional services we could not have otherwise. They include:

Roland Hartzog and Cindy Cuellar of Creative Media Productions in Houston, for producing a 10-minute promotional video; María Elena Salinas, an anchor with Univision in Miami, for doing the voice-overs, in both Spanish and English, for that video; Gerald Rueda of Quinto Sol Productions in San Antonio, for videotaping two of our interviews.

But we couldn't rely solely on volunteers. We needed paid staff to handle the daily workload. Fortunately, each semester we have assembled a team of capable and cheerful young women and men to attend to the many details. They include: Jenny Achilles; Chrystel M. Akakpo; Nicole Cruz; Melissa DiPiero-D'Sa; Violeta Dominguez; Claudia Farías; Lindsay Fitzpatrick; Raquel

C. Garza; Antonio Gilb; Karla E. Gonzalez; Kathryn R. Gonzalez; Kristen E. Hatfield; Sara P. Hernando; Yazmin Lazcano; Ruth Lopez; Jaime B. Margolis; Thomas S. Meredith; Lynn (Maguire) Walker; Erika L. (Martinez) Rizo; Ismael Martinez; Valentino Mauricio; Julio C. Ovando; Laura M. Querubin; Rajesh Reddy; Denise Rocha; Israel Saenz; Brenda Sendejo; Kristian Stewart; Kelly Tarleton; Juliana Torres; Christina Tran; Miguel Valdievieso; Myers Vasquez; Lilly Velazquez and Joel Weickgenant.

Narratives

Our friends at the Austin American-Statesman gave our Project a remarkable gift in 1999, by agreeing to handle the production of Narratives. They went on to publish four issues of our newspaper, which provided our Project with a visual demonstration of the wealth it had to offer. Many thanks to Rich Oppell (editor), Kathy Warbelow (then-managing editor); Sharon Roberts (assistant managing editor); Robert Quigley (copy editor); G.W. Babb (layout designer); Emily Quigley (copy editor).

Our other friends in San Antonio, at the Express-News, published the other four issues of our newspaper, alternating with the Statesman. Thank you to: Bob Rivard (editor); Hallie Paul, (assistant managing editor); Monte Bach (layout design).

Although initially the Statesman and the Express-News provided design and layout, our UT students also stepped in and did that in the later issues. They were:

Leila Armush, Lucy Quintanilla, Beth Butler, Melissa DiPiero-D'Sa. Each of these young women deserves a huge ovation for their dedication to the cause.

Over the past six years, my best friends and a few family members have stepped in to help, sometimes with editing, sometimes by writing a story after the semester was over and all the students were gone, sometimes by correcting proofs. I give them a warm hug: Frank Trejo, Robert Montemayor, Anna Macias, Henry Mendoza and my mother, Henrietta Lopez Rivas, and sister, Lupe Rivas, in San Antonio.

We also were able to rely on emergency help from a few people. They include: Spanish copy-editing from Alfredo Carbajal Madrid, asst. managing editor of Al Día, in Dallas; for emergency fact-checking: Richard Koone, of the National Museum of the Pacific War in Fredericksburg; and Bruce Ashcroft, of the HQ AETC History Office at Randolph Air Force Base, near San Antonio; Cheryl Brownstein-Santiago, of the Los Angeles Times, for copy-editing.

Partnerships

Early on, our Project was able to form partnerships at the national and local level. Our deepest thanks to some of the best friends our Project has.

At the national level, the Department of Veterans Affairs Readjustment Counseling Centers, or Vet Centers, where veterans and their families can get assistance with counseling. Through the Vet Centers, we were able to hold what we called "Multiple Individual Interview Sessions" in 14 U.S. cities. Our deepest thanks to Al Batres, the director of the Vet Centers and to Hilario "Lalo" Martinez, the chair of the Hispanic Working Group, as well as to the staffs of the Vet Centers in San Antonio; Austin; Houston; El Paso; McAllen; Laredo; Kansas City, Mo.; Los Angeles; Miami; Phoenix; Tucson; Santa Fe; Albuquerque; San Juan, P.R. Some of them, like the San Antonio center, hosted our group numerous times, as we arrived loaded down with equipment and people in a flurry of history-making. Staff members at these centers have worked as volunteers on Saturdays and Sundays to make these interview sessions a source of healing for families.

The National Association of Hispanic Journalists, as well as its sister organization, the California Chicano News Media Association, on several occasions provided expert interviewers throughout the country. Many thanks to each of them for lending their special "journalist's ears" to make those interviews some of the best in oral history. The NAHJ's Board of Directors and the CCNMA's officers and executive director, Julio Moran, and president Efraín Hernandez, have been a tremendous help in soliciting volunteers. Our other national partners included Univision and Entravasión and those two entities were able to record some of our best interviews—with professional equipment.

On the local/regional level, our partners were many and leveraged their own resources to benefit this work. Those include:

- San Diego State University's Office of Educational Opportunities/Ethnic Affairs
- Michigan State University's School of Journalism
- St. Edward's University's New College
- University of California, Riverside
- Ernesto Galarza Applied Research Center, University of California
- San Diego State University's Department of Ethnic Studies
- University of New Mexico's Center for Regional Studies and the Southwest Hispanic Research Institute
- University of Puerto Rico, Río Piedras, Institute of Caribbean Studies and Centro de Investigaciones en Comunicación (Center for Communication Research)
- University of South Florida, Department of History
- University of Texas at El Paso's Institute of Oral History, Chicano Studies Program and Center for Communication Studies
- Museum of Mexican American Culture and History, Chicago

Guidance

We have been fortunate to have many exemplary oral history project models to study and oral history experts to advise us. Those involved in oral history understand the challenges posed and we have enjoyed tremendous cooperation and support from our friends in oral history, almost all in the Oral History Association. Thank you to our friends at the Shoah Foundation in Universal City, Calif., who generously allowed us to model our own pre-interview form after theirs. Thank you to J. Todd Moye, former director of the Tuskegee Airmen Oral History Project in Alabama, for his constant encouragement. Thank you, as well, to our friends at the Veterans History Project at the Library of Congress who have been glad to help in any way they could.

Ron Grele, former director of the Columbia University Oral History Institute spent several days in Austin in 2002 with us, as part of a scholar's workshop, and continues to be an important resource.

Our most sincere thanks to our Advisory Committee, which has stepped in to offer suggestions, always at the last minute, as we put together grant proposals. That committee includes: Silvia Alvarez Curbelo, professor, Center for Communication Studies, University of Puerto Rico, Río Piedras Campus; Albert Armendariz, Sr., attorney, El Paso; Alfonso R. Batres, Chief Officer of Readjustment Counseling Service, Department of Veterans Affairs; Dennis Bixler-Marquez, director, Chicano Studies Program at University of Texas at El Paso (UTEP); Don Carleton, director of UT-Austin's Center for American History; Jaime Chahín, Dean of the College of Applied Arts at Texas State University in San Marcos; Jorge Chapa, Professor and Founding Director of Latino Studies at Indiana University Bloomington; Augustine Chavez, former Director of the San Diego State University Office of Educational Opportunities and Ethnic Affairs; Gil Coronado, former director of the Selective Service System; Tobías Duran, Director, Center for Regional Studies, University of New Mexico; Miguel Encinias, WWII veteran, Albuquerque; Ivelisse Estrada, Senior Vice President of Corporate and Community Relations Univision Communications Inc., Los Angeles, CA; Yolette Garcia, Assistant Station Manager/Director of News and Public Affairs, KERA FM radio, Dallas; Humberto García Muñiz, professor of history at the University of Puerto Rico, Rio Piedra campus; Phillip Gonzales, Professor of Sociology, University of New Mexico; David B. Gracy II, School of Information, UT-Austin; Richard Griswold del Castillo, professor of Chicana and Chicano Studies, San Diego State University; Margo Gutierrez, assistant head librarian, Nettie Lee Benson Latin American Collection; Efraín Hernandez, member, National Association of Hispanic Journalists; George A. Martinez, professor, Dedman School of Law, Southern Methodist University; David Montejano Associate Professor of Ethnic Studies at the University of California, Berkeley; Julio Moran, executive director, California Chicano News Media Association; Kristine Navarro, of the Oral History Institute at the University of Texas at El Paso (UTEP); Chon Noriega, Professor of Critical Studies and Associate Director of the UCLA Chicano Studies Research Center; Joanne Rao Sanchez, Professor of History in the New College Program at St. Edward's University in Austin; Mario L. Sánchez, historian and registered architect, Austin; Otto Santa Ana, associate professor, César Chávez Center for Chicana and Chicano Studies at the University of California, Los Angeles; Carlos Vélez-Ibáñez, director, Chicana and Chicano Studies, Arizona State University; Pat Witherspoon, director, Department of Communication, UTEP.

Advisory Committee member David Gracy has played a special role—he has boiled down his decades of experience and study in the area of archival preservation into patient explanations of what we need to do, and why. Largely because of his recommendations, our archives will be available to the public sooner rather than later.

There are many other people who have been generous in writing letters of support that we have included in major grant proposals. Many of these people are scholars whose research areas include this generation of Latinos and Latinas, or, more generally of Americans. What is most heartening is that in many cases we have solicited these letters from men and women we've never met, but whose research is important in this area of Latinos and WWII, or just WWII. So, without even knowing us personally, they have taken the time to write thoughtful letters on our behalf so that we can include them in our information packets. I know I am committed to showing the same courtesy and spirit of cooperation toward others who seek my help.

UT Campus Resources

We have been fortunate to be part of a University so large that it can encompass a vast array of research projects, including ours. The resources within UT have been essential. Among our earliest and strongest supporters have been the faculty associates, staff and students affiliated with the Center for Mexican American Studies (CMAS), first under the directorship of Professor David Montejano, and more recently under Professor José Limón. CMAS and its wonderful CMAS staff have helped us organize events, supported one graduate student part-time, and linked us more closely to the larger Austin Hispanic community.

We've been extremely fortunate to have administrators in our department and college who believe in our goals. Our home department, the School of Journalism, and its parent, the College of Communication, has provided us with a support system that includes an office, access to services, such as the dubbing of thousands of hours

of videotape, the expert technical advice of our top-notch computer team and suggestions from the development (fund-raising) staff. Thank you to former journalism director Steve Reese and current director Lorraine Branham, former dean Ellen Wartella and current dean Rod Hart. Each of these individuals has applauded the Project and supported it, as they could.

A special thanks to the two journalism staff members that we keep far busier than they otherwise would be: Janice Henderson, office manager, and Sonia Reyes Klempner, accountant.

Financial Resources

UT Austin has a reputation as being a well-resourced campus and it is. But when it comes to a project like this, the actual costs of things like tapes, student salaries, printing, postage, overnight services, travel, etc., must be raised from external sources. It was no coincidence that we had bumper crop years of interviews right after we received major funding. Our Project has received support from the State of Texas, as a special item appropriation; the A.H. Belo Corp. Foundation in Dallas; the Anheuser-Busch Corp.; the Cain Foundation in Austin; Goya Foods, in Secaucus, N.J.; the Pew Hispanic Center in Washington, D.C.; Univision; Coors Brewing Co.; the Houston Chronicle; Southwestern Bell Corp. Foundation; University of California, Riverside; the University of New Mexico; Block Distributing Co.; the UT School of Journalism; the UT Center for Mexican American Studies and the UT College of Communication. In most cases, the support was for special events, such as major conferences or workshops, or for special reports.

There have also been hundreds of smaller private donations, which of course add up and pay for staff salaries and other costs. But the importance of the smaller private donations also represent the significant public support the Project has received. Many times that encouragement has had a positive effect far beyond the monetary value.

The Book

Although our Project self-published this book, we did enter into a distributing arrangement with the University of Texas Press. Many thanks to our friends there: Theresa May, who has been a valued supporter of our Project since its inception, and David Cavazos, for teaching us, via e-mails, in meetings, and telephone calls, about the technical side of compiling this book. Leslie Tingle, Teresa Wingfield and Nancy Bryan have also helped us on some of the other major questions we had about our cover and other publishing issues. The beauty of our relationship with UT Press has been that we have tried to meet the Press' own exacting standards, and its staff have been available to guide us.

Thanks to the good friends who provided us with maps for this book: Frank Martini at the Department of History, United States Military Academy, Westpoint; the United States Holocaust Memorial Museum, Washington, D.C.; the Perry-Castañeda Library Map Collection at the University of Texas at Austin; and the Center of Military History, United States Army; also to Mike Reagan, who provided the Bataan map; and the CIA World Fact Book. Although we were able to rely on the thousands of photographs we've scanned over the past six years, we did need one additional photograph from the Institute of Texan Cultures at the University of Texas at San Antonio. Thank you, in particular, to Patrick Lemelle at the Institute.

We also asked a couple of people to take a look at this book in its final stages, in particular Aric and Megan DiPiero, of Lehigh Acres, Fla., Ajit D'Sa, Richard Brito and Lynn Walker.

And I must acknowledge our book team. Our core group was Juliana Torres, Melissa DiPiero-D'Sa, Lindsay Fitzpatrick and me. Juliana and Lindsay were the main writers.

Juliana and Lindsay worked daily in the fall 2005 semester, juggling their classes and schoolwork as I'm sure they have never done in their lives. But, as usually happens, it was taking longer than we had expected; we wouldn't make our deadline without more help. We brought in two more writers: Jenny Achilles, a journalism graduate student, and Jaime Margolis, another journalism undergraduate student. Both Jenny and Jaime also edited and did some preliminary copy-editing, which I'm sure our professional copy editor Guillermo Torres will thank us for, since they edited the copy before he got it.

And we simply would not have as complete information without the diligence of Sara Hernando, Kathryn Gonzales, Yazmin Lazcano and Lynn Walker. Sara is a sociology undergraduate; Kathryn is a journalism undergraduate who could have written stories, except we needed her for this other work; Yazmin is our former full-time manager who in the fall of 2005 worked only part-time so that she could study and become a high school English teacher; Lynn Walker is a journalism graduate who worked part-time in the fall. All four of these young women undertook the chore of calling people at home repeatedly to nail down as many missing details as possible: dates of birth, places of birth, offspring's names, photos, etc. Finally, Tino Mauricio, a photojournalism graduate student, who has immense patience with our many photographic needs, has performed daily miracles in scanning yet dozens more photographs and making sure our images were as high quality as possible.

Lastly Melissa DiPiero-D'Sa. She is our graphic design person on the Project and has approached this assignment of laying out and designing *A Legacy Greater Than Words* as if it was the golden opportunity that she believes it is. She has helped organize the system we used and brought her husband in to develop an online database for this task. She has elevated our book and demanded the best of all of us. We are very fortunate that she has cared so deeply.

Richard Brito and Bill Davies, mentioned above, have been essential throughout—they were even involved in proofing pages.

The point is, the four names on the cover certainly deserve to be there. But this book owes much to the entire *Legacy* team. I have been immensely privileged and blessed to have been working with these remarkable people to make this book as good as we knew how.

Finally, a very personal thank you to the three dearest people in my life: my two sons, Ramón and Agustín, and my husband Gil. They have lived with this Project and endured my occasional absences, sporadic long hours, and constant preoccupation. There have been few family vacations over the past six years that haven't included something Project-related (but oh, the places we've been!). I thank my sons for their unconditional and sweet love and for keeping me grounded. And I thank Gil for the many tasks he has completed for the Project, as well as those he has assumed in our home life because I've been busy working on the Project. But more important, he has shared my dreams and has always believed in me. So long as he's in my corner, I know all is well.

—*Maggie Rivas-Rodriguez*
Director, U.S. Latino & Latina
WWII Oral History Project

My first thanks is to the families of the WWII veterans who manned the front lines of recording their family history. Without your encouragement and confidence in the importance of your loved ones' legacy, their stories would be forever lost.

Thank you to all the lovely Project staff who made this book possible.

This book would fall far short without the help of our military historians, Bill Davies and Richard Brito, who, in their spare time, reviewed every inch of these stories and spent hours researching obscure facts. I cannot thank you two enough for your willingness to answer my every silly question and your invaluable adherence to the detail few of us would have picked up on.

Thanks to my parents, who created more confidence and purpose in me than they know. To my siblings, grandparents and family, who are proud of me no matter what I do and always inspire me to continue forward. To Emily, Jenny, MK and Katie, upon whose support and encouragement I can always rely.

To Dr. Maggie, who, through her somewhat random recruiting process, decided to hire me and gave me the opportunity to be involved in her truly unique project. Thank you for being a role model, for the inspiration that created this project to begin with, for leadership that carried it through and for trusting me to try something I had never done.

Finally, to the Latino WWII generation. No matter how many times I read your stories, I will never fully appreciate the effort you invested and sacrifices you underwent to ensure that your children would live better lives. Generations will continue to be indebted to you for the foundation you laid for our future. I hope that our efforts even begin to recall the legacy you've created.

—*Juliana A. Torres*

First, I would like to thank both of my sets of Grandparents—Carl and Lorraine Seegmiller and John and Margaret DiPiero. I didn't have a true understanding of what it was like to live during the Depression and war-struck 1940s prior to joining this Project. I now have a deep and humble respect for you and your generation—I love you and miss you.

Thank you to all the men and women who served during WWII, again thank you grandpas Carl and John, and a very special and heartfelt thanks to those whose worth and citizenship was called into question by the very nation under which they served. I only hope we do your stories justice, and I thank you not only for serving, but also for persevering against such overwhelming odds—before, during and after the war.

To the Project Director, Dr. Maggie Rivas-Rodriguez, thank you. You gave me wings. I am so blessed to have been brought into such a worthy cause.

To all the past, current, and future staff members and volunteers of the U.S. Latino & Latina WWII Oral History Project—God bless you.

To my wonderful, amazing husband, Ajit, thank you for your patience, your words of encouragement, and your never-ending support.

To my parents.

John C. DiPiero is the most indomitable man I have ever known. He served two tours in Vietnam; survived colon cancer at the tender age of 32; graduated from college with the GI Bill, later passed the CPA exams, started his own CPA firm; and managed to support a family of five, including paying for my two brothers' and my college education. And I've never seen him complain. In fact no one loves life more than my Dad, and despite his life-altering asthma, cancer scars, and over 20 years of hard work there is always a smile on his face. Dad, you are my hero.

Konni Lee DiPiero, Mom, your caring and warm heart shines through all that you do. You stayed home with three kids when it was unfashionable to do so. You kept us out of trouble. You took me to all of my dance lessons for 10 years and supported all of my creative endeavors, and never dwelled on my failures. When I say, "I'm going home" what I mean is, "I'm going home to see my mother."

Finally, to my niece and nephew, Ashlee J. Leann and Koan John: the future will be bright. You have the opportunity to learn from our past mistakes and accomplishments—through education you will know the difference.

—Melissa DiPiero-D'Sa

To my mother and father, Elliott, Ian and the entirety of my beautiful family; Dr. Maggie, for this invaluable, enriching opportunity; my incredible co-workers, each of you made my job easier and infinitely more enjoyable; our relentlessly hard-working military historians; my supportive, amazing friends. And finally, the men and women of America's armed forces, whose valor I will never comprehend but will forever deeply respect. Thank you.

—Lindsay Fitzpatrick

A Legacy Greater Than Words

Introduction

For Americans of the WWII generation, the attack on Pearl Harbor represents that quintessential common experience—they can tell you exactly where they were and where they were going when they first heard the news. In their innocence of what was to come, no one could have predicted how the United States' entry into the war would transform the nation and its people, if not the world.

When the war first began, it seemed so remote, so abstract. Soon, there were more than 12 million men and women serving in the military. Ernest Montoya, of Avondale, Colo., would later note that the war experience touched virtually all Americans.

"During World War II, everybody knew about the war," Montoya said. "Everybody had somebody in it!"

Before long, there were newsreels at the movie theaters and stories and photographs, as well as government posters, which helped Americans comprehend the magnitude of the U.S. involvement. The war seemed to make everything speed up, recalled Antonio Moreno, of Gulf, Texas. Moreno's small town, a company town that produced sulfur for various purposes, was now in overdrive. His father, who worked in the sulfur production, began putting in longer days, sometimes as long as 22 hours at a stretch.

"I started noticing that everything was in more of a hurry because of the war," Moreno said.

Latinos and Latinas of this generation were part of those experiences, sometimes acted upon, sometimes exercising their own agency. In many ways, they were no different from their other American contemporaries, but at that time, in an era where people of color were not generally afforded many opportunities, WWII would represent an upheaval. Once they had enjoyed "a taste of equality," as WWII veteran Pete Moraga of Arizona would put it 60 years later, there was no turning back.

There was not only one type of life experience for these WWII Latinos and Latinas. Generally, the men's experiences were vastly different than that of women. And then there were the differences between the different ethnic groups that make up Latinos. And there were other differences between those from rural areas and those from cities.

Men and women interviewed on these pages often describe a childhood of poverty, of responsibilities, of hardship. They say that they matured early, far earlier than their children or grandchildren. And often, they say, they are grateful for that: those childhood challenges toughened them, made them able to withstand the vagaries of life later.

Some experiences they all lived through and which would define them:

• Most Latinos and Latinas of the WWII generation grew up poor during the Great Depression. Repeatedly, in interviews, they have said that they were poor, but didn't realize it: everyone around them was equally poor.

• Many lost one parent, or even both, during their childhood.

• Like many Americans, education was often a luxury and most got paying jobs in their teenage years or even earlier. The difference for many WWII-era Latinos was that they were schooled in segregated facilities, generally sub-par, compared to that of white children.

• Many grew up speaking Spanish as their first language, only learning English in school. It was commonplace to be punished for speaking Spanish at school.

• Many public facilities, such as swimming

pools, toilets, movie theaters, were segregated and either did not allow Latinos in, or had separate, marked, areas for them.

• Many of the men enjoyed the benefits of the Civilian Conservation Corps.

• The war afforded them new opportunities for travel, for jobs and for a new worldview.

• In employment, some plum jobs were off-limits. For females, the white-collar secretarial jobs were reserved for Anglo women. For men, earning managerial or supervisory positions were similarly unrealistic expectations.

• The war experience imbued in them a sense of entitlement: they were Americans and no longer just Mexicans living on American soil.

Poverty

In the late 20s and the 30s, America suffered its worst economic Depression. In Texas, most of the labor Mexicans did was in the fields. Living conditions were poor for these migrant workers of the era. Fred Davalos, of Clovis, N.M., recalled that families with many children had better prospects.

"Those were tough times," Davalos said. "In those years, the more people you had in your family, the more work you did. And the more work you did, the more income you got."

Eliséo Lopez of Ganado, Texas, was the middle child in a family of 13. His hard-working parents were self-sufficient.

"We raised our own cattle, we raised a lot of vegetables," he said. "Sometimes I think that a lot of people would be better off in the country now, than in town, 'cause every time we turn around, you have to take your hand out of your pocket to pay for something."

Alvino Mendoza's family lived in the fields.

"Sometimes we would build a fire, next to a tree, and sleep on our bags of cotton we had filled the day before. No shack, just under a tree," he said.

Another man who recalled the harsh, dehumanizing working conditions was Joseph Alcoser

of Melvin, Texas, a small town in Central Texas.

"Some [employers] would not supply clean water. The barrels they used to bring water were rusty and dirty. They were also placed far from the field where we were working. We had to walk a long way to get a drink of water," Alcoser recalled. "By the time we walked back to where we were working we were already thirsty again."

Although their childhoods were often poor, they would say, they witnessed the generosity and compassion of their own parents. Growing up in New Mexico, Delfina Josepha Lujan Cuellar recalled people coming to her family's door, asking for a handout.

"There were some people who had a very hard time," she said. "Once in a while people would come and ask Mother for a cup of this and a cup of that. My mom would help people that needed food and whatever."

They grew up at a time of poverty, a difficult educational system, in which it was commonplace for young people to leave school before graduating from high school.

Parents

It was commonplace for these WWII-era men and women to lose one, or even both parents in their youth. Sixty years later, those men and women considered that one of the great tragedies of their lives.

Joe Arambula was the second oldest of six children. His mother died when he was 15.

"I've always said that the mother is always the backbone of the family," Arambula said. "And my family is a perfect example of that. ... After that [his mother's death] my oldest brother went off to work, and I went to live with one of my aunts, and my brother and sister went to live with another aunt. And that broke up the family."

Federal Work Programs

For Joe Arambula and other men, two federal programs, the National Youth Administration (NYA) and the Civilian Conservation Corps (CCC) would play major roles in their youth. The CCC camps, in particular, gave the raw young men the discipline they would need later in the military. President Franklin D. Roosevelt enacted both federal works programs after he began his first term in office in March 1933, seeking to provide income and industry to the estimated 13 million unemployed Americans.

The NYA funded part-time jobs for high school and college students, with the intention of keeping them in school. The CCC was another program, which took on public works in parks facilities and forests, and became a sort of intermediary step for the Latino men who later served in the military.

Roberto Chapa, of the Rio Grande Valley of Texas, joined the Civilian Conservation Corps in 1940 and went to Colorado for his training. He would work in soil conservation.

"The training that they gave me ... getting up at 4 in the morning ... it's just like being in the Army," Chapa said.

Pablo Segura, of El Paso, and the members of Company E, 141st Infantry Regiment, 36th Infantry Division, went to combat training at Camp Bowie near Brownwood, Texas.

"We went to Brownwood, and it was just cantonments, tents that were half wood and half canvas," Segura said. "We had to go through six weeks of basic training. Those of us who had been in the CCC didn't have any trouble adjusting to Army life."

Besides the discipline, the men in the CCC also met young men from other parts of the country. Roberto Chapa, for instance, befriended young men from around the country.

When he went to Camp Adair, Oregon, for his Army basic training he had already developed more confidence and a better sense of himself, which would be key during his time on the front lines.

New Opportunities

The war afforded many of WWII-era Latinos and Latinas unprecedented opportunity. For Latina women, who could hardly aspire to a profession and few to higher education, new jobs opened up—making much higher salaries than they had ever made before.

Henrietta Lopez Rivas, of San Antonio, Texas, failed first grade because she spoke little English. But later Spanish became an asset when Civil Defense was in need of Spanish speaking interpreters. Rivas went from making $1.50 a week to $90 a month. Despite its many hardships, the war had given her something that she had not experienced before: a sense of equality. She was valuable because she was able to offer services that "Anglos" could not. She was valuable because of her heritage.

"It made me feel equal, more intelligent because what I did, very few Anglos could do," Rivas said.

Latina women had different strictures than their brothers. In many cases, Latinas of the WWII generation who served in defense plants far from their homes note that they were only permitted to do so because they would be accompanied by one of their sisters. Such was the case of María Isabel Solis Thomas and her sister, Elvia Solis, of Brownsville, Texas. The two young women got jobs for a ship building plant in Richmond, Calif. The Cooremans sisters of San Antonio, Delfina and Wilhelmina, would also leave home; these two young women traveled to Seattle to work for Boeing.

Different Perspectives

Discrimination and bigotry against other groups was also present. In Los Angeles, Richard Dominguez watched as Japanese-American classmates were taken away to detention camps.

"It was my first close-up experience with racial discrimination, although at the time, I guess I didn't recognize it as such, since it didn't happen to me," Dominguez said.

For Mexican Americans in the Southwest where there were few blacks, they saw prejudice in a different light. Betty Muñoz Medina, of Arizona, was working for the U.S. Army in Washington, D.C. When her supervisor called her on the carpet for assigning a black officer to a white unit, she realized that race would need special consideration.

"I didn't know anything about discrimination. This was the first time I had heard the word," she said.

This Book

This book is organized in three parts: the military experience, the home front experience and post-war. Part One of this book examines the WWII military experiences of Latinos and Latinas looking at each theater of war. Most notably the Pacific Theater, European Theater and other areas, beyond the main fronts, that may have garnered few headlines, but were essential nonetheless.

It also includes the role of Latinas in the military, many of whom served as nurses, but also in other capacities.

In the fifth chapter, Brothers in Arms, discusses only a few of the examples of several brothers serving in the military during the war. Those stories of families contributing several sons to the effort can be found throughout this volume.

Part Two looks at the home front experience: civilian women who served at military defense plants, younger men and women who viewed the war effort in a more youthful way, as well as that of Mexicans who came to the U.S. to bolster the sagging labor pool. This group included skilled workers, such as aircraft mechanic Abraham Moreno in Brownsville, Texas, as well as the

thousands of *braceros*—laborers who became "soldiers of the furrows," by planting and harvesting in the agricultural fields, as well as in the railways.

Part Three includes the stories of individuals whose lives after the war were particularly compelling. Some became involved in civil rights, especially in desegregating public institutions in the Southwest. Among that group are men like Ed Idar, Jr., Pete Tijerina, Jr., and Albert Armendariz. Others made their changes on a smaller, but no less significant scale, by working to desegregate their own home town schools, or by filing protests against racist businesses.

It is fitting to include a chapter on education, as many of the Latinos and Latinas of this generation aggressively pursued educations and thus were able to secure better jobs, more ways to contribute to society. Not noted here is that many of the Latinas postponed their entry into education only after raising their own children. As Felicitas Cerda Flores would say, "If I went to college at the age of 52, you can too." The most common bit of advice proferred by these men and women to younger generations is to get as much education as possible.

Chapter 11 on community notables includes individuals who made their marks in a variety of ways: by being ordained into the priesthood, by becoming active in veterans affairs, by becoming successful businessmen, or judges. It must be noted that many others whose stories are included elsewhere in this book, could have also fit into this chapter.

Finally, Chapter 12 features interviews with men who served in the military beyond WWII, many in Korea and then, later, in Vietnam. We even have one man, Julius V. Joseph, of Monterrey, Mexico, who served in WWI, WWII and Korea. Later, during the Vietnam war, Joseph would try to volunteer again.

U.S. LATINOS AND LATINAS IN THE MILITARY

Rudy Acosta, third from left on front row, with fellow crew members during World War II.

The European Theater

The United States had been watching developments in Europe from afar, while studiously maintaining its own neutrality. Not that there was not deep concern at the events unfolding in Germany. First, it watched as the government of Adolf Hitler forced the capitulation of the Rhineland in March of 1936, and the absorption of Austria two years later.

Then, on Sept. 1, 1939, when Germany invaded Poland, Britain and France were obligated, because of previous treaties, to declare war against Germany. World War II had begun and still U.S. public sentiment was largely against involvement—a spirit of isolation left over from World War I.

The U.S. did what it could to support the Allies, "short of war." This form of support consisted of selling armaments to the Allies, eventually through the Lend-Lease Act. Through this program, the U.S. could provide the Allied forces with arms and equipment, without requiring payment until after the war.

By the summer of 1941, the U.S. had gradually become involved by patrolling the Atlantic, searching for German U-Boats, and later by authorizing U.S. destroyers to attack German submarines.

Finally, in the fall of 1941, President Franklin D. Roosevelt approved of the arming of Merchant Marine ships to deliver materiel to Allied ports.

U.S. direct involvement in WWII was ushered in by the Japanese attack on Pearl Harbor on Dec. 7, 1941. Both Germany and Italy declared war on the U.S. four days later, in accordance with the Tripartite Pact, which called on the three Axis Powers to assist one another in the event of war.

Germany's war declaration opened the door to U.S. involvement in the European Theater. It was apparent that the United States war efforts would be aimed at "Europe First."

President Roosevelt was keenly aware that his country had limited resources, and he felt that Germany represented the larger threat. Japan, it was reasoned, could not sustain the war effort indefinitely: it had less manpower and industrial output than the United States could muster. Also, war in the Pacific required occupation of small islands in a vast expanse of ocean. Considering these logistical challenges and the more imminent threat from Germany, the U.S. decided to concentrate more of its effort in Europe, while putting up a respectable front in the Pacific.

Many Latinos in the Army, the Army Air Corps and the Navy would see action in the European Theater. Jesús Armendariz, of El Paso, Texas, arrived in Casablanca, Morocco, North Africa, on Nov. 21, 1943. From Africa, Armendariz's 88th Infantry Division arrived in Naples, Italy, on Dec. 6, 1944. "The war kept moving north," Armendariz said.

Others would serve as paratroopers in Normandy, and in the Battle of the Bulge—a battle in which many prisoners of war were taken. Throughout the European Theater, Latino men, and a few Latina women, served.

THE SECOND WORLD WAR

THE EUROPEAN THEATER, 1942 - 1945

N

Cartographia Cell of Excellence
Department of History, United States Military Academy

| 0 | 100 | 200 | 300 |
SCALE OF MILES

TIMELINE

Sept.
1939
- Germany invades Poland, 1 Sept.
- Great Britain & France declare war on Germany, 3 Sept.

1940
- Germany invades Denmark & Norway, 9 Apr.
- Germany invades Low Countries, 10 May
- Italy declares war on Great Britain & France, 10 June
- France signs armistice with Germany, 22 June
- Battle of Britain, July-10 Oct.
- 1st peacetime draft law in U.S. history, Sept.
- Wavell's 1st Libyan offensive, 9 Dec.- 7 Feb., 1941

1941
- Rommel's 1st offensive, 31 March
- Germany invades Greece & Yugoslavia, 6 Apr.
- German airborne assault on Crete, 20 May
- Germany invades U.S.S.R., 22 June
- U.S.S.R & Great Britain sign mutual aid pact, 13 July
- Siege of Leningrad, 8 Sept.- Jan. 1944 700,00 deaths estimated
- U.S. declares war on Japan after attack on Pearl Harbor, 8 Dec.
- Germany & Italy declare war on U.S., 11 Dec.

1942
- Battle of Stalingrad, 23 Aug.-2 Feb. 1943
- Battle of El Alamein, 23 Oct.
- Allied troops land at Morocco & Algeria, 8 Nov.

1943
- Battle of Tunis, 7 May
- Axis forces in N. Africa surrender, 13 May
- Battle of Kursk, 4 July-1 Aug.
- Allies land at Sicily, 10 July
- Italians secretly surrender, 3 Sept.
- Allies land at Salerno,10 July
- Allies land at Anzio, 22 Jan.

1944
- Allies invade Normandy, 6 June (D-Day)
- Soviets push Germans into Poland, mid-July
- Paris liberated, 25 Aug.
- Polish Resistance revolts against Germans in Warsaw, Aug.-Oct.
- Battle of the Bulge, 16 Dec.- 7 Feb. Last significant German offensive
- Yalta Conference, 4-11 Feb.
- Soviets launch attack on Berlin, 16 April
- Hitler commits suicide 30 Apr.
- Germany surrenders, WWII in Europe ends, 7 May

June
1945

NORMANDY LANDING

Roosevelt and Churchill decided at the Trident Conference (May 1943) to conduct a major cross-Channel invasion of Europe in June 1944. General Eisenhower was designated to command Operation OVERLORD. The greatest amphibious assault yet known to history began on the Normandy coast in complete tactical surprise on D-Day, 6 June 1944. To protect Eisenhower's flank, the U.S. Seventh Army landed in southern France (Operation DRAGOON) on 15 August 1944.

NORTH AFRICA

The Americans wanted to invade continental Europe in 1943, but this idea was deemed premature and was cancelled in favor of an Allied invasion of French North Africa. Operation TORCH consisted of three task forces which landed on 8 Nov. 1942. Moving east, these forces linked up with General Montgomery's Eighth Army in Apr. 1943, becoming 18th Army Group under the overall command of General Alexander. By 12 May 1943 this unit had forced the surrender of all Axis forces in North Africa

IRELAND

GREA

L
EIS

English Channel

Normandy Invasion,
D-Day, 6 June 1944

ATLANTIC OCEAN

PYRENEES MTN

PORTUG

Madrid ✪

SPAIN

From Great Britain

From U.S. PATTON (Nov. 1942)

Gibraltar (Great Britain)

RYDER (Nov. 1942)

SPANISH MOROCCO (SPAIN)

Oran

Algiers

Casablanca Mazagan Port Lyautey

Safi

FREDENALL (Nov. 1942)

ALGERI (FRANCE)

MOROCCO (FRANCE)

Legend

- ○ City or Town
- ✪ National Capital
- --- National Boundaries
- ✷ Battle Site
- → Axis Advance
- → Allied Advance (American & British)
- ---► Allied Advance (Soviet)
- ▢ Allies
- ▢ Axis
- ▢ Neutral Countries
- ▢ Axis Controlled (Max. Exte

NORTH SEA

NORWAY

Oslo ✶

SWEDEN

FINLAND

✶ Helsinki °   ○ Leningrad

Stockholm ✶

(Jan.-Dec. 1944)

BALTIC SEA

ESTONIA

DENMARK
Copenhagen ✶

Riga ✶

LATVIA

Memel   LITHUANIA

Smolensk ○

SOVIET UNION

Amsterdam ✶

(BELGIUM)

NETHERLANDS

Hamburg   Elbe

Von Rundstedt
(Dec. 1944-Jan. 1945)   Berlin

Rhine

Danzig
(Gdansk)

EAST
PRUSSIA
(GER.)

(June 1944-Feb. 1945)

Minsk ○

Gomel ○

Kursk, 1943 ✶

NTGOMERY
g. 1944-May 1945)

GERMANY

(Dec. 1944-May 1945)

Vistula

Warsaw ✶

Brest ○ (July 1943-Dec. 1944)

BRADLEY ○ Remagen

Torgau

POLAND

s   (Aug. 1944)
May 1945)

Battle of the Bulge

River

(June 1944-May 1945)

(July 1943-June 1944)

Kiev ○

Kharkov ○

Prague ✶

Auschweitz ○

Lvov ○

ANCE

DEVERS
(Sept. 1944-
May 1945)

Munich

CZECHOSLOVAKIA

Vienna ✶

Carpathian Mountains

WORLD WAR TWO IN EUROPE

World War II began in Europe on 1 Sept.
1939 with Germany invading Poland. U.S.
involvement started on 11 Dec. 1941, only four
days after Japan's attack on Pearl Harbor, when
Germany and Italy unexpectedly declared war on
the U.S. British Prime Minister Churchill met
with President Roosevelt in Washington D.C.
22 Dec. 1941-Jan. 1942, and decided to defeat
Germany first.

chy

SWITZERLAND

ALPS MTNS.

AUSTRIA

Budapest ✶

Lyons

River

CLARK
(Jan.-May 1945)

Trieste

HUNGARY

(June 1944-May 1945)

(June 1944-May 1945)

ROMANIA

Sevastopol ○

Yalta

PATCH
Aug.-Sept. 1944)

Po   River

Belgrade ✶

Bucharest ✶

Danube   River

BLACK SEA

ANDORRA

St. Tropez, 1944

CORSICA

ADRIATIC SEA

YUGOSLAVIA

Sofia ✶

BULGARIA

ITALY

Rome ✶

Anzio, 1943

Naples ○

Salerno, 1943

ALBANIA

Istanbul ○

TURKEY

SARDINIA

LEXANDER
1942-May 1943)

Palermo ○

GREECE

AEGEAN
SEA

Bizerte ○

Tunis, 1944

Bône ○

sserine Pass, 1943

Sicily Invasion, 1943

MALTA
(GREAT BRITAIN)

ITALIAN LANDINGS

Operation HUSKY the invasion of Sicily, began on 9 July
1943, and after that island was cleared, the mainland of Italy
was assaulted on 3 Sept. 1943. Allied forces continued to
"slog" their way up the Italian peninsula until 2 May 1945.
Amphibious operations at Salerno and at Anzio were
attempts to outflank the Germans in Italy.

CRETE

DODECANESE ISLAND
(ITALY)

CYPRUS
(GREAT BRITAIN)

TUNISIA
(FRANCE)

Mareth, 1943

MEDITERRANEAN   SEA

Tripoli ✶

Benghazi ○

Tobruk, 1942 ○

Cairo ✶

LIBYA
(ITALY)

SAHARA   DESERT

EGYPT

Nile   River

RED SEA

Map courtesy of the Department of History, United States Military Academy

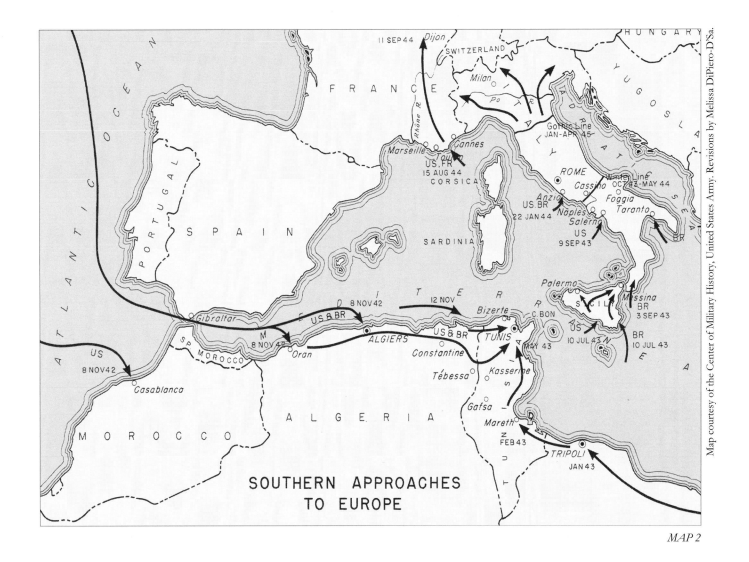

Map courtesy of the Center of Military History, United States Army. Revisions by Melissa DiPiero-D'Sa.

MAP 2

NORTH AFRICA AND ITALY

As early as spring 1941, American military leaders agreed that if the United States were to be drawn into the war raging in both Europe and the Pacific, it would be necessary to concentrate on a defeat of Germany first.

At the close of WWI, the American public had been weary of war and held firm to an isolationist policy. Attempts by the U.S. military to upgrade equipment were time and again rebuffed. In the summer of 1940, the likelihood of war was recognized by the administration. The National Guard was activated and federal-ized and industry was mobilized for war. Even so, on the day of the Pearl Harbor attack, the U.S. Armed Forces were generally unprepared to contend with the Axis military forces.

The U.S. considered, but discarded, the idea of a direct attack on German forces in continental Europe. Instead, it favored an indirect approach at the German forces supporting Benito Mussolini in Italy and the Mediterranean. President Roosevelt ordered that an invasion of northern Africa begin before the end of 1942. Troops were hurriedly trained in amphibious warfare, which combined land and sea forces to effectively invade the coastline. The Allies landed first in Morocco and Algeria during Operation Torch in December 1942. By May 1943, the Allies had neutralized the Axis presences in Africa. Bases in Casablanca, Oran and Algiers, among others, were used to train and prepare American troops during the rest of the war.

The Battle of Salerno

The Italian island of Sicily was taken by Aug. 17 and mainland Italy was first invaded in the Battle of Salerno on Sept. 9, 1943. The 36th Infantry Division was the first American division to invade continental Europe. Originally a Texas National Guard unit, the 36th boasted a large number of Latinos within its ranks, including the all-Latino Company E of the 141st Regimental Infantry Regiment. They landed on the beaches of Paestum near Salerno.

"When we got there, there was no resistance," said Tony Aguilera, a native of Los Angeles, and a member of the 36th Division. "We stopped and got all our ammo out. When the fog lifted, we were surrounded. Everyone was shooting us. You stood up and they knocked you down."

It was not the first time U.S. forces had confronted the Germans, who had taken control over the Italian Army for fear that the Italians might join the Allies following the fall of Sicily. However, the landing—coordinated with a simultaneous British landing farther north—was disorganized and, for many of the troops, it was their first experience in combat.

"After I saw my friend die, we were getting more cautious," said Ernesto Padilla, of Puerto de Luna, N.M., serving with the 45th Infantry Division. "We learned quite a bit in that first battle."

Despite heavy casualties, the invasion successfully launched the Allied campaign into southern Italy. By Sept. 16, British and American troops took Naples and turned northward.

To Rome

After crossing the Volturno River in October, the Allied Forces advanced to the Winter Line, where German forces set up their defense around the town of Cassino. The battle in the mountainous area progressed until the Allies reached the Garigliano and Rapido Rivers in early January 1944.

"The river was right there and we couldn't cross it," said Tony Olivas, a native of La Salle, Colo., with the 2d Field Artillery Observation Battalion.

It was decided that another amphibious attack behind the enemy's main front and closer to Rome could break up the German defenses and prevent another long and difficult campaign in the mountains. After another attempt to cross the Rapido River only cemented the stalemate in that area, U.S. forces landed at Anzio on Jan. 22. There, they fought a long and difficult campaign for the beachhead.

The German forces retreated from Anzio on June 2, leaving the path to Rome scantily guarded. Forces farther south, after fighting for five months in the Battle of Monte Cassino, linked up with their successful comrades in the north. Rome was captured on June 4, 1944.

AGUILERA, TONY. When the Germans captured Tony Aguilera, he was already a survivor of Los Nietos, an East Los Angeles barrio. He and his 13 siblings had lived off their father's wage of 25 cents an hour by working wherever they could and by learning survival on the streets. It was nonetheless a happy childhood, complete with marbles, tops and nickel shows, records and streetcar rides.

When he was drafted, Aguilera thought he wouldn't make it back.

"I thought we were going to go over there and get killed. I went; it was my duty," he said.

On Sept. 9, 1943, in the middle of the fog, Aguilera and the 36th Infantry Division landed on the Italian beach at Salerno. They were the first American division to land on the European continent.

"When we got there, there was no resistance," he said "We stopped and got all our ammo out. When the fog lifted, we were surrounded. Everyone was shooting us. You stood up and they knocked you down."

Shrapnel hit Aguilera in his left leg and he crawled into a trench to stay out of the line of fire. When the Germans found him several hours later, they took his weapons and transported him in a tank to a hospital. He spent three months there before he was moved to POW camp Stalag II-B near Hammerstein, Germany. He was rescued 16 months later.

"I did my share. ... That's something you never forget; you don't want nobody else to go through [similar experiences]," he said. "I used to have nightmares. ... I'd get up in the night and yell."

After the war, Aguilera returned to East Los Angeles. He married Molly Leon who had five children from a previous marriage. The couple would have one child together. Aguilera worked 40 years at Kal Kan Foods. Upon his retirement, he enjoyed a comfortable life, surrounded by grandchildren.

ARMENDARIZ, JESÚS LEYVA. A medic in the 1st division into Rome at its liberation, Jesús Leyva Armendariz said that the war changed his "way of being."

"When you're over there, you realize that you have someone who you love and you have a reason to stay alive and come back," he said.

Early on, Armendariz decided against enlisting in order to continue to provide for his family, who he had helped support since he was 9, by selling discarded crates of fruit in the market.

"I didn't know we were poor because everyone else around us was," he said of his childhood.

He met Celia Ceballos on March 19, 1942, and they married four months later, on July 3.

Not long after the wedding, Armendariz was drafted. The couple packed their bags and lived on bases stateside for 14 months while Jesús trained to be a medic.

Eventually, Armendariz was sent overseas. He arrived in Casablanca, Morocco, in North Africa, on Nov. 21, 1943—just five days after his first son, Jesús Jr., was born. From there he would go on to Naples, Italy. He began to treat the wounded in February 1944.

By the time Italy had surrendered, Armendariz had been wounded twice, but it was nothing the Army's makeshift medical practices could not manage.

"If I could fix a man with a wire and safety pins, I can fix myself," he said.

Armendariz was discharged on Feb. 12, 1946, and worked as a carpenter until his retirement. He and Celia had nine more children, all of whom married, went to college and have successful careers. Armendariz remained active in the community, becoming a member of the Veterans of Foreign Wars (VFW), for which he served as local post commander from 1987 to 1988.

Tony Aguilera

Date of Birth
23 SEPTEMBER 1923
Los Angeles, CA

Interviewed by
Milton Carrero
Galarza
23 MARCH 2003
Los Angeles, CA

WWII Military Unit
143d Infantry
Regiment,
36th Infantry
Division

Jesús Leyva
Armendariz

Date of Birth
10 MARCH 1921
El Paso, TX

Interviewed by
Maríel Garza
23 MARCH 2002
Los Angeles, CA

WWII Military Unit
Company C,
313th Medical
Battalion,
88th Infantry
Division

Eloy D. Baca

Date of Birth
24 DECEMBER 1921
Mosquero, NM

Interviewed by
Brian Lucero
24 JANUARY 2002
Rio Rancho, NM

WWII Military Unit
120th Engineer
Combat Battalion,
45th Infantry
Division

BACA, ELOY D. He had only known life on the ranch when he enlisted, but more than half a century later, Eloy Baca's memories of the war still played like a vivid film in his mind.

After landing in Oran, North Africa, the 45th Infantry Division invaded Sicily on July 10, 1943. The engineers were sent ahead of the infantry to clear the beach of the barbed wire entanglements that would stop the troops.

"I remember we were running and I'd see guys. ... It looked like they were stumbling. But they didn't stumble. They were shot," Baca said.

After a day of combat, he was assigned the task of clearing the bodies of the fallen men. For a week he toiled in the hot Sicilian sun, which quickly decomposed the bodies. Disgusted by the horrible smell, Baca couldn't eat for about a week.

Baca later participated in the initial amphibious assault in Italy at Salerno Bay on Sept. 20, 1943, and at Anzio on Jan. 22, 1944. Memories of the battlefield continued to haunt him later in life.

"But you know, when you're a unit, it's really not that bad," he said. "You think, having all these people with you, you're much safer. ... It's like a family."

On August 15, 1944, they landed at Ste. Maxime, France, fighting north to join the Allied forces in Normandy. In the mountains near Epinal, France, Baca and two other engineers were using dynamite to blow trees into the roads to block the German advance, when he slipped in the snow and was hurt as the TNT exploded. Baca was injured again, by mortar shells in the legs and head, while crossing the Danube River on April 26, 1945. He was discharged on July 15, 1945.

Baca earned a business degree at Abilene Business College and later ran his own liquor store. He married Flora Montaña on Jan. 1, 1948, and had four children: Herman, Dolores, Thomas and Paul.

Abner Carrasco

Date of Birth
1 FEBRUARY 1921
San Pedro, CA

Interviewed by
Steven Rosales
30 JUNE 2004
Palm Springs, CA

WWII Military Unit
Company E,
2d Battalion,
141st Infantry
Regiment,
36th Infantry
Division

CARRASCO, ABNER. During the landing at Salerno, Abner Carrasco was shooting at a German Panzer, a heavily armored tank, when its turret suddenly pivoted and pointed directly at him. Facing his potential death, he kept firing and was surprised when the tank drove off.

Carrasco had spent his childhood working odd jobs, from picking tomatoes to caddying at country clubs to setting up pins in bowling alleys. He joined the Texas National Guard in 1938 "for fun," not thinking that the United States would ever go to war.

In 1940, the 36th Infantry Division was mobilized and Carrasco was sent to Camp Boyd, Texas, for training as a machine gunner.

In 1943, Carrasco and his division were sent overseas to Morocco. From there, they participated in the Battle of Salerno, which Carrasco said was difficult not only because the Germans were well-trained soldiers with superior weaponry, but also because the American troops were not accustomed to the hilly terrain and were making their debut into combat. "Everything was so disorganized," he said. "The first plane we shot down was a British Spitfire."

Later, as his unit fought into Italy—San Pietro, Anzio and Battipaglia—Carrasco was struck in the right leg by a mortar shell. He spent two months in a hospital in North Africa. When he was sent back to Italy, he re-injured his leg and was sent back home to the United States and received a medical discharge.

Back home, Carrasco took advantage of the GI Bill and learned how to be a tool and die maker.

After a few years in that trade, he formed a new interest and began to work as a quality-control engineer at Hughes Aircraft. Later, a job at Lockheed Martin sent him to Iran for two years.

He retired at 68 and loved spending time with his four children and his grandchildren.

CONDE, GUADALUPE "LUPE" HUERTA. Even after 60 years of marriage, Lupe Conde still serenades his wife, María, who restored the sense of peace he lost in battle.

When the Civilian Conservation Corps discharged him in 1940, Conde enlisted in the Army for lack of better job opportunities. Conde had worked since he quit his segregated school at age 10 to help his father, José Conde, in the fields. His mother, Teofila Huerta, had died when he was 7, leaving three sons and two daughters behind.

In the Army, Conde spent a year at Camp Bowie, Texas, and it was there that he heard of the bombing of Pearl Harbor. He found himself in North Africa less than a year and a half later.

As he had done in the Civilian Conservation Corps, Conde served as a cook. He was the only Latino in his company, having declined an offer to transfer to the all-Latino Company E. His comrades in Company F fondly treated him affectionately. He fed 130 soldiers in North Africa and 140 later in Italy, taking pride in the fact that the men never left anything on their plates.

During the invasion of Salerno, Italy, Conde ran water, blankets and ammunition to the soldiers and offered them corned beef, hard crackers, coffee and C-rations. Later, he was ordered to collect dog tags from the fallen soldiers; some of the bodies were still warm when he got to them.

In Naples, Italy, he injured his legs when he jumped from a truck, but—not wanting to slow down the company—Conde did not report the injury until he couldn't bend his knees to sit. He was eventually sent to the hospital, where severe anxiety attacks prompted his return to the States.

Back in San Benito, a doctor advised Conde that marriage would sooth his unsteady nerves. He married María Gallegos on Jan. 23, 1945. The two had four children—Lupita, Alicia, Norma and Juan—and 12 grandchildren.

Guadalupe "Lupe" Huerta Conde

Date of Birth
20 APRIL 1918
San Benito, TX

Interviewed by
Carlos Condé
7 SEPTEMBER 2002
San Benito, TX

WWII Military Unit
Company F,
2d Battalion,
141st Infantry
Regiment,
36th Infantry
Division

CORDERO, FRANK. While he was stationed in Fort Sam Houston, Texas, Frank Cordero—drafted on Sept. 23, 1942—encountered people opposed to his involvement in the U.S. Army. The accusations of one Mexican woman in particular stood out in his memory.

"You're Mexican," she said, "You're not supposed to be in an American uniform."

"You know what?" he responded "I was born and raised in this country. That's why I'm wearing this uniform."

Later, he was sent to Louisiana for maneuvers. One night, using sheets of toilet paper draped over tree branches to mark a path through the swamp, Cordero and a friend set out to find the nearest town, where Cordero could wire to his wife in Los Angeles the $600 he had won in a game of dice. In the wee hours of the morning, they came to their destination. Unfortunately, the toilet paper trail was a failure and the two soon became lost. A rope bridge broke under Cordero and he was almost bitten by an alligator, but they made it back just in time for 6 a.m. roll call.

In December 1943, Cordero, a corporal, was sent to North Africa. The 88th Infantry Division relieved the British troops along the Garigliano River in Italy on March 5, 1944. Cordero took part in the capture of a monastery at Minturno and the division moved inland to liberate Rome.

In late 1944, Cordero sustained serious injuries to his right leg and hip. He was carried down the mountain where his battalion had come under fire. At an Army field hospital only a few miles from the front, he underwent surgery to remove the shrapnel.

He was discharged on account of his injuries and, by Christmas 1944, was on his way back to the States. After more surgery and about a year of recovery, he returned to his wife and daughter in Los Angeles.

Frank Cordero

Date of Birth
2 APRIL 1919
Alamogordo, NM

Interviewed by
Veronica García
23 MARCH 2002
Los Angeles, CA

WWII Military Unit
3d Battalion,
350th Infantry
Regiment,
88th Infantry
Division

Santiago Brito
Craver

Date of Birth
1 APRIL 1920
El Paso, TX

Interviewed by
Robert Rivas
6 NOVEMBER 2003
El Paso, TX

WWII Military Unit
57th Station
Hospital

CRAVER, SANTIAGO BRITO. For 33 months, Santiago Brito Craver drove ambulances and cared for the wounded at hospitals in Algeria, Tunisia, and Casablanca, Morocco. He later returned from the war to begin and care for a family.

Craver had been raised solely by his mother since he was 5, until his mother's death in 1937. He joined the Civilian Conservation Corps that same year, dropping out of high school to support his younger siblings. He eventually got a job working as an orderly at William Beaumont Army Hospital in El Paso, Texas.

Craver was walking out of a movie theater when he first heard of the attack on Pearl Harbor, and he was drafted just a few months afterward. He had six months of basic training at Camp Barkeley, Texas, and six more in medic training at Camp Gruber, Okla. He boarded the USS *Dorthea L. Dix*, for a nine-day trip through the Strait of Gibraltar, bound for Oran, Algeria. "I was seasick most of the time," he said. "I had a 104 temperature and we were crammed in there like a bunch of sardines. To vomit, you had to run or use your helmet. The restrooms were always full."

During his time overseas, he employed recent medical advances, such as penicillin, that gave wounded soldiers a better chance at survival. On one of his rounds driving the ambulance, Craver recognized an old friend from Beaumont Hospital and jumped at the chance to help him.

In nearly three years in North Africa, Craver picked up some French and Italian from the locals, who treated him well. He returned to El Paso on Dec. 9, 1945, and soon married Francisca Saenz. He got a job as a truck driver in New Mexico and worked hard to support his three daughters.

"We wanted them to have as much education as we could give them," he said, proud to provide a luxury he never had.

Santos Deliz

Date of Birth
24 SEPTEMBER 1923
New York, NY

Interviewed by
Lucy Guevara
10 FEBRUARY 2001
San Juan, PR

WWII Military Unit
Battery D,
216th Anti-Aircraft
Artillery Gun
Battalion (Mobile)

DELIZ, SANTOS. During fighting in Germany, Santos Deliz and a few other men from his unit crept into an abandoned house, seeking refuge and respite from the battle, and soon fell asleep.

"When I woke up there were five dead Germans around me. The explosion of a shell must have killed them," he said, unsure how he escaped the incident.

Deliz grew up in New York City. His early life was marked by his mother's death at age 8 and four years in orphanages with his three siblings while their father fought for custody. At age 15, Deliz used his deceased older brother's name and birth date to join the Civilian Conservation Corps for six months. Afterwards he had several jobs in New York—binding books, working at a nightclub and as a milling machinist—until he was drafted in 1943.

During training at Camp Edwards, Mass., Deliz grew restless while learning to set up phone lines. He went absent without leave, but felt remorseful and returned to his post after 12 days. His sergeant gave him kitchen police duty for the remainder of the war.

He was sent to North Africa on May 11, 1943, with the 216th Anti-Aircraft Battalion under Gen. George S. Patton's 2d Corps. Patton demanded the best from everyone and once scolded Deliz for giving away unused rations instead of discarding them.

The battalion invaded Sicily on Aug. 9, 1943, and Italy in September. They landed in southern France on Aug. 15, 1944, and advanced into Rhineland until the close of the war.

Upon his discharge Deliz discovered that his girlfriend had married someone else. Earning money became a priority, and he enrolled in a vocational school to learn the skills of a jeweler and watch repairman. He married Nivia Reyes in 1964 and had a daughter two years later. In 1976, he moved his business from New York City to Puerto Rico, where he lived from then on.

DIAZ, JOSEPH JOHN. He was the only Mexican American in his company and in a division that saw some of the most intense fighting in WWII. Time in the service gave Joseph Diaz a new perspective on life that he said younger generations can't understand.

"Enjoy it while you can because there is no such day as tomorrow," he advised.

As a boy growing up in a Latino community on the south side of Chicago, one of Diaz's favorite memories was of the World's Fair in 1933-34. He joined Paco Pera Juan's traditional Mexican dance group and though he never made much money, he enjoyed participating in the festivities.

He met his future wife, Juanita Cruz, in Indiana in 1939 and the couple had two daughters by the time he received his draft notice in late 1941.

With the 3d Infantry Division, Diaz assaulted Casablanca, Morocco, during Operation Torch in 1942. From there, they moved into Tunisia, where the fighting slowed and Diaz thought he might be heading home. Unfortunately, the division was moved quickly into Palermo, Italy. On the beaches of Naples, Italy, they barely escaped on boats as Mount Vesuvius erupted.

The fast pace rarely allowed the soldiers time to set up their guns, much less grieve for their fallen comrades. Their location was always secret, but Diaz still sent letters home to his family. Juanita would get news of his supposed whereabouts and follow his route on a map.

Eventually, the 3d Division invaded Rome, made it into France and Belgium, swept through Germany and was preparing to invade Berlin when Germany's surrender came.

Diaz was on his way to Japan when the atomic bombs ended the war. He met his third child when he returned home to Chicago on Aug. 25, 1945. Diaz worked in several factories until his retirement in 1983, and later enjoyed the company of his great-great grandchildren.

Joseph John Diaz

Date of Birth
11 AUGUST 1918
Kansas City, MO

Interviewed by
William Luna
3 MARCH 2003
Chicago, IL

WWII Military Unit
3d Infantry Division

ELIZONDO, RAYMON. Twenty years after his service, a film was made depicting Raymon Elizondo's unit in WWII. Coincidentally, Elizondo was hired to help paint the movie set, which transported him back to his days on the battlefields of Italy.

One of 12 children, Elizondo traveled around the country for much of his childhood as his parents looked for farm work, until his father found steady work with a mine in Utah. Elizondo was determined to get an education, but left school at age 17 to work for a railroad company. He was unfulfilled by the work and enlisted in the Army in 1942. After training in Montana, he was sent to the Aleutian Islands. Elizondo remembered the need to learn quickly during his training.

"They gave us a day's training [for a skill] and were supposed to be professional," he said. "They didn't horse around. They taught you how to kill."

From Alaska he was sent to Italy. He served there from November 1943 until August 1944.

The 1st Special Service Force was dissolved by the War Department, and Elizondo was sent to Company E, 505th Parachute Infantry Regiment, 82d Airborne Division. He went to Belgium to reinforce the troops fighting there, and it was there he learned that both of his brothers had died in combat.

Elizondo was discharged in 1945. He earned a Bronze Star and Paratrooper's Wings, as well as two Purple Hearts.

"It was quite an experience," Elizondo said of war. "But I went through it and thank the good Lord that I came back."

He married Eliza Esparza in 1948 and the couple had three children: Adrian, Elsa and Mark. The two later divorced.

Raymon Elizondo

Date of Birth
6 APRIL 1921
Salt Lake City, UT

Interviewed by
Israel Saenz
6 DECEMBER 2003
West Valley, UT

WWII Military Unit
3d Company,
2d Regiment,
1st Special
Service Force

José Blás Garcia

Date of Birth
3 FEBRUARY 1921
Vega Alta, PR

Interviewed by
Doralís Pérez-Soto
6 FEBRUARY 2003
San Juan, PR

WWII Military Unit
Company L,
3d Battalion,
65th Infantry
Regiment

GARCIA, JOSÉ BLÁS. In December 1940, José Garcia, with four other friends, left Santurce, P.R., for Fort Buchanan, P.R. When asked why he enlisted, Garcia just shrugged and responded that he had nothing better to do. His time in the service would allow him to see the world and use the money he earned to buy his own house back home in Puerto Rico.

Garcia joined the 65th Infantry Regiment, an all-volunteer Puerto Rican National Guard unit. After being stationed on several bases in Puerto Rico, he was shipped to Panama for a year. There, he took shifts of guard duty along the locks of the Panama Canal and transported soldiers inland.

He returned to the States for training in Camp Patrick Henry, Va., before leaving again. He arrived in North Africa on April 5, 1944.

His battalion joined the 12th Air Force on the island of Corsica and was then sent to the Maritime Alps and Monte Cassino in Italy.

From there, they landed in France and ascended into the snowy French Alps, where he developed a debilitating infection in his right hand and was hospitalized.

In Heidelberg, Germany, Garcia shot a German who was trying to rob a warehouse he was guarding. When the German died, a Puerto Rican general decided to bring charges against Garcia. Garcia contacted the American military authorities and, using body language to explain himself despite the language barrier, was exonerated.

He was in Germany when he heard of the end of the war. He returned home in December 1945. Garcia used the GI Bill to finish high school and later sold insurance. He married María Crespo in 1947. The couple had one daughter and two adopted children.

Guadalupe Garza

Date of Birth
28 DECEMBER 1919
Maverick County, TX

Interviewed by
Domingo Marquéz
20 SEPTEMBER 2002
Houston, TX

WWII Military Unit
Battery B,
58th Field Artillery
Battalion

GARZA, GUADALUPE. In all, Guadalupe Garza experienced 480 days of combat and participated in many of the major battles in Europe.

As the oldest of four brothers, Garza was able to attend school for the longest before enlisting in the Civilian Conservation Corps in October 1937. Despite being poor, Garza knew his family was lucky to have a cow and chickens to provide food during the Depression.

He was drafted in January 1942. At Fort Sam Houston, Texas, his cousin persuaded him and 10 other Latinos to choose an artillery assignment in hopes that they would all end up in the same unit.

"Once I got overseas, I never saw them again," said Garza, who joined the 58th Field Artillery Battalion. "I was the only Latino within 10 miles of my unit."

The battalion was sent to Tunisia. Garza first saw combat when the Germans began bombing Casablanca, Morocco, on New Year's Eve night 1942.

On Aug. 14, 1943 during the invasion of Sicily, Garza and a fellow soldier found themselves surrounded by Germans after landing behind enemy lines near Licata. They hid in the water off the beach and swam around Cape Orlando, surviving seven days with only grapes to eat, before finally reaching their own troops.

Garza also stormed Omaha Beach on D-Day and fought at Bastogne, Belgium, during the Battle of the Bulge. In Belgium, a shell exploded right by him and he was hit with shrapnel.

"I was lucky it hit me in my helmet," he said. "Any lower and I would have been dead."

He spotted a foxhole where some medics were tending the wounded. They dressed the gash in his head and Garza returned to battle. When the war in Europe ended, his unit was in Austria.

Back home, Garza married María Mauricio in 1947 and they had two children, José and María.

GOMEZ, FRED. Before going into battle, Frank Gomez made a pact with Sgt. Raymond Valencia. If one of them did not make it back, the other would name his first son after his fallen comrade.

"I respected him a lot," Gomez said of his friend. "He was just a very beautiful role model."

Sgt. Valencia died in battle. Gomez kept his promise and named his first son Raymond.

The son of Mexican immigrants and one of 12 siblings, Gomez grew up in a Mexican-American neighborhood in Chicago. He quit high school and his job at the Chicago Daily Times to enlist in the Army.

He was in a training camp in Pennsylvania when he found out he would be sent overseas. He joined the 45th Infantry Division and was sent by ship from New York City to North Africa.

With his division, Gomez fought against the German troops in the invasion of Sicily and pursued them through Italy.

He was struck in the back with shrapnel but, in two weeks, had recovered enough to rejoin his unit as they continued to push north into Germany.

With the constant advance, Gomez had little time to write letters back to his family. He was eager to return home to them, and did so upon his discharge.

After the war, he worked as a journeyman pressman for 24 years at the Chicago Daily Times, which later became the Chicago Sun. He married Margaret in 1946. The couple had three children.

Gomez believed that it was important to tell the stories of those who lost their lives, and to tell his own, because the war changed his perspective.

"It's an experience you definitely can never buy," he said, reflecting on how he was able to travel the world. "It was beautiful to see."

Fred Gomez

Date of Birth
1 DECEMBER 1923
Fort Worth, TX

Interviewed by
William Luna
17 SEPTEMBER 2002
Chicago, IL

WWII Military Unit
45th Infantry
Division

GOMEZ, MARCUS LOPEZ. Throughout his life, Marcus Gomez experienced many levels of discrimination but said that Latinos today are making good progress and are "really getting up there."

His father, who ran a business as a plastering contractor, found it difficult to get people who would work for him.

"He couldn't get white plasterers to work for him because they didn't want to work for a Mexican," Gomez said.

His mother died when he was 12, and he and his seven siblings were split up. Gomez started learning plastering from his father after his mother died. In high school, he walked seven miles to attend school two days per week and worked for his father the other three weekdays.

His future wife's father, Juan Gonzalez, was influential in the Lemon Grove Incident, the first successful legal challenge against segregation in schools.

He married Elisa Gonzalez in 1942, which—combined with a clerical mistake—delayed his draft notice until 1943. Gomez served in the Army Air Corps as a cook. He was stationed in southern France and then in Ancona, Italy.

"While the war was moving, we were moving behind it," he said.

He noted the racial tension abroad and back at home in California, where he was ignored at a bar until several Navy sailors and Marines backed him up, threatening the staff until he was served.

Five days after his return, Gomez returned to the family plastering business, where he worked until retirement. He and Elisa raised 11 children: Marcus Jr., Phillip, Beatrice, Elizabeth, Christine, Elaine, Susan, Andrew, Ralph, Lorraine and Louise. Gomez was an active member of the San Diego VFW chapter.

Marcus Lopez
Gomez

Date of Birth
24 MARCH 1924
El Paso, TX

Interviewed by
René Zambrano
30 JUNE 2000
San Diego, CA

WWII Military Unit
57th Fighter Group,
12th Airforce

Leon "Jack" Leura

Date of Birth
19 APRIL 1922
Durarte, CA

Interviewed by
Frank O.
Sotomayor
23 MARCH 2002
Los Angeles, CA

WWII Military Unit
Company A,
111th Combat
Engineers,
36th Infantry
Division

LEURA, LEON "JACK." A boxer turned Army engineer, Jack Leura was fortunate to have survived the experience of fighting along two lines of combat and being a prisoner of war.

Leura attended a segregated school and worked odd jobs starting in eighth-grade. After joining the Civilian Conservation Corps at age 17, Leura began his career as a featherweight boxer.

As an amateur, he made $4 to $5 a fight and only lost one out of 25 fights. At 19, he fought and won $30 for his first professional fight. His career was put on hold when he was drafted.

In June 1943, Leura was shipped to North Africa, where he trained for three months. As a Tech 5th grade, his task was to find and destroy mines.

The 36th Infantry Division invaded Italy and fought in Monte Cassino, Anzio and into Rome.

While serving with his unit protecting a small town in France, he was wounded in the left shoulder and taken prisoner by the Germans. For six months in a POW camp, he consumed nothing but coffee and a bowl of soup each day, until Russian shells destroyed the camp, allowing Leura and 40 others to escape.

Headed toward Poland, the group found an abandoned store of bicycles to aid their journey. Later, they hopped on trucks in a Russian convoy. In Poland, they caught a train to Russia and traveled to the port of Odessa, Ukraine.

He eventually made it back to the American headquarters in Italy. From there, he returned home on April 14, 1945, and started working in the heating and air-conditioning industry. Leura continued his boxing career until 1949, winning 29 out of 35 fights.

He married Betty Gil and had two children. She died in 1966 and he married Rose Velasco in 1975. He served as the local commander of the Ex-Prisoners of War Organization.

**Herbierto
Longoria Sr.**

Date of Birth
8 NOVEMBER 1918
Abram, TX

Interviewed by
Minette Hernandez
9 OCTOBER 1999
McAllen, TX

WWII Military Unit
Company F,
6th Armored
Infantry Division

LONGORIA, HERBIERTO SR. The youngest of seven children, Herbierto Longoria Sr. was the only one of his siblings who did not graduate from high school, instead he dropped out to work on his family farm in Mission, Texas. "Betito," as his family called him, was also the only member of his family to serve in WWII. In 1941, after hearing about the bombing of Pearl Harbor, he went to San Antonio, Texas, to join the Army at the age of 22.

Longoria was stationed in Italy, where he fought on the front lines, sometimes for two weeks straight. In 1944, he had fought in Italy for little over a year when he was wounded, shot just below the left knee. The young soldier waited about 12 hours until he could be transported behind the lines to a makeshift tent hospital. It took him three months to get out of bed and try to walk, one year to heal from his wound, and another year to fully recover.

Shortly before his own injury, Longoria had watched as a friend of his from Brownsville, Texas, was killed by a shell in a foxhole right in front of him. At the time, he was barely affected by what happened to his friend.

"You think that you are going to die right away because they are shelling," he said.

However, his wife, María Louisa Rincones—whom he married four years after his discharge—said that memories like these later kept her husband up at nights.

Longoria received a medical discharge in 1946 and returned home to Mission, where he continued working on the family farm. He and María Louisa had five children. Though he said that he is proud of his grandson who became a Marine, Longoria maintained no romantic notions of combat.

"Nobody should have to fight," he said. "They call it hell. War is hell."

MARTINEZ, RAUL MATA. For his skills as a machine gun specialist, Raul M. Martinez earned a sharpshooter medal and a Silver Star for gallantry in action. "I learned to shoot from the hip running, without aiming. ... You get to be an expert," he said. "I don't like to brag about it."

Raul Mata
Martinez

Date of Birth
17 MAY 1924
San Antonio, TX

Interviewed by
Robert Mayer
13 OCTOBER 2001
San Antonio, TX

WWII Military Unit
Company F,
7th Infantry
Regiment,
3d Infantry
Division

Martinez grew up in Cementville, Texas, a small village populated primarily by workers at the nearby cement factory. When he began to work at the factory, he followed in the footsteps of his father and grandfather. He was drafted in 1943.

"We were scared," he said, "We'd never seen anyone shoot someone else with real bullets."

In Casablanca at the beginning of his time overseas, he and a friend were hungry and bought some dry meat from a street vendor and realized, only after starting to eat it, that it was dog meat.

"Well, now it's too late," he said, finishing the tasty meat. "We already had some in our stomach."

Later, Martinez and the 3d Infantry Division invaded Sicily, then Italy and southern France. They fought across Germany and remained in Austria until the war's end.

At one point, his captain was giving him orders to create crossfire when Martinez was shot in the foot by a sniper, who was later discovered to be a woman. The captain didn't make it.

When news of Germany's surrender came, Martinez was not among those who celebrated.

"Some of the guys did, but not this Mexican here. I was still scared," he said.

Martinez declined an offer to stay longer in exchange for a 90-day furlough and a rank higher than his rank of master sergeant. He returned to work at the cement plant, where he worked for another 40 years.

On Nov. 18, 1945, he married Beatrice Bustos and the couple had four children: Raul, Dianne, Elaine and Audrey. Martinez said he and Beatrice are still newlyweds "in our heads."

NEGRÓN, OCTAVIO. Machismo and a need to escape problems at home caused Octavio Negrón to leave Puerto Rico in the rain on Dec. 17, 1940, and enlist in the U.S. military.

Octavio Negrón

Date of Birth
27 JANUARY 1922
Naranjito, PR

Interviewed by
Carlos I.
Hernandez
30 JANUARY 2003
San Juan, PR

WWII Military Unit
Company G,
2d Battalion,
65th Infantry
Regiment

He had grown up in a tiny Puerto Rican village, where he enjoyed sports—especially volleyball. He attended school until fourth grade when he began to work in his family's agricultural business.

The 65th Infantry Regiment was sent to Panama. From there, the troops were sent to Camp Patrick Henry, Va., for further training. There, the soldiers received their military identification number, which Negrón remembered many decades later.

They landed in North Africa on April 4, 1944, and in France shortly after, fighting their way across the country and into Rhineland. Afterward, Negrón was stationed in Germany for 10 months.

The few letters that Negrón sent to his family in Puerto Rico were censored for fear that they would reveal confidential information.

As a scout, Negrón most feared being killed by friendly fire. Two of his comrades had been killed that way. In a tense encounter in Germany, Negrón knocked a soldier to the ground and held him at gunpoint until it was proved he was an American.

While stationed in France, Negrón reported feeling hungry, cold, scared and sick.

"They told me I wasn't sick, but I was scared," he said.

The doctor prescribed soup and plenty of water to ease his battle anxiety and fatigue.

Negrón was discharged after 11 months in the Army. Back in Puerto Rico, he went on to study while working at a factory.

He married Julia Nieves less than a year after returning. They had seven children.

Anthony "Tony" Olivas

Date of Birth
16 JANUARY 1923
La Salle, CO

Interviewed by
Rea Ann Trotter
15 DECEMBER 2000
Avondale, CO

WWII Military Unit
2d Field Artillery
Observation
Battalion

OLIVAS, ANTHONY "TONY." As a witness to the devastation of war, Tony Olivas recommends that young people should strive for peace.

"I would like that: peace in the world, the whole world," he said.

The ninth of 11 children, Olivas attended school until eighth grade. Afterward, he worked on farms, earning a quarter per hour.

Olivas was drafted in March 1943, following two of his brothers—Joe and Paul—who were drafted the year before. As a member of a three-man forward observer team, he was one of the first on the field, laying telephone lines that the unit would use to direct the artillery fire.

His first battle experience came in San Pietro, Italy. He remembers most vividly, however, the Battle of Cassino, in which a river stood between American and German forces.

"The river was right there and we couldn't cross it," he said.

He directed the artillery to fire blindly across the river. In the end, the troops went around the area because it was booby-trapped. His unit also participated in the Battle of Anzio and ended up in Luxembourg for the Battle of the Bulge. In the sub-zero temperatures of Ardennes, Olivas said soldiers used frozen bodies left on the battlefield as chairs. For him, one of the most difficult aspects of the war was the lack of time to grieve for fallen comrades.

He was able, however, to meet up with his brother, Paul, in Salerno, Italy; in France; and in Germany, where he was given a ride to his brother's camp in Munich, and his brother was allowed to visit him in Augsburg.

He married Mary Rose Rael after he got out of the service in January 1946. They had six children: James, Delbert, John, Agetta, Sharon and Deborah.

Ernesto Padilla

Date of Birth
18 MAY 1922
Puerto de Luna, NM

Interviewed by
Brian Lucero
26 FEBRUARY 2002
Albuquerque, NM

WWII Military Unit
Company F,
120th Engineer
Combat Battalion,
45th Infantry
Division

PADILLA, ERNESTO. When he joined the National Guard to earn a paycheck of $50 and keep himself busy during high school summers, Ernesto Padilla knew about Germany's mobilization. He just didn't realize how much that bit of news would affect his life.

The 45th Infantry Division was federalized in September 1940—months after Padilla graduated high school. He spent a year training in Fort Sill, Okla., with the mostly Latino outfit. His enlistment was almost up when Pearl Harbor was bombed, canceling Padilla's discharge.

At bases in Massachusetts, New York and Virginia, Padilla trained and practiced bridge building. In July 1943, his division left for Oran, Africa, to prepare for the invasion of Sicily.

Not far out from Salerno, heavy naval gunfire boomed over the heads of Padilla's division for almost three hours before they shoved off. They used small craft to make their way across the water and waded in waist-deep water onto an empty beachhead. The troops marched about a quarter of a mile before they were met with a shower of bullets.

"After I saw my friend die, we were getting more cautious," Padilla said, "We learned quite a bit in that first battle."

Later—assured that the Germans had already retreated from the path from Callabria to Bevento—Padilla was surprised to hear an 88-mm artillery whistle over his head. Shrapnel injured his left hand and took out his left kneecap. In Algiers, his leg was amputated. Padilla, out of the war for good, was fitted with an artificial leg back in the States.

Padilla used the GI Bill to build a career in the aircraft industry. He married Gloria Sharp in 1948 and together they raised four children: Nancy, David, Charlie and Judy.

PRADO, EDWARD LOPEZ. On Sept. 14, 1943, Edward Prado watched as the waves rolled over the body of a fallen soldier. The day before, American troops had fought to gain this beach near Salerno, Italy. The day before, three of Prado's friends had been alive. Now they were dead.

Prado enlisted on Jan. 8, 1941, to escape the inevitability of being drafted and to turn his life around. As a child, he had picked cotton with his parents and three siblings. He dropped out of school in eighth grade and sold vegetables door-to-door from his Model "T" car. After his parents died when he was 19, he worked at an electric company, a furniture upholsterer and a pool hall until he joined the military.

When the five Latinos at Camp Bowie, Texas, were assigned the same tent, Prado realized he would have to earn respect among his fellow non-Latino comrades. He joined preparations for a Golden Gloves boxing tournament to showcase his skills in the ring.

"I knew that I could take care of some of the guys that were boxing in there. I went in there ... and I knocked that guy out," he said. "They all opened their eyes."

Prado refused the offer to join the tournament, but noticed less discrimination against him.

After the bombing of Pearl Harbor, Prado trained for two more years. He married Bertha Cadena on Dec. 9, 1942, and on April 2, 1943, left for Oran, Algeria, to prepare for the Salerno invasion.

Prado reiterated that he was one of the lucky ones to return home, though operating 105 Howitzers affected his hearing. Prado felt that fighting in the war was his duty. Along with his brother, Pete, he is a member of the VFW, "to remember the ones that didn't make it and honor them."

He and Bertha had three children: Mary, Edward and Robert.

Edward Lopez Prado

Date of Birth
13 OCTOBER 1915
San Antonio, TX

Interviewed by
Ruben Ali Flores
26 FEBRUARY 2000
San Antonio, TX

WWII Military Unit
Company C,
131st Field Artillery
Battalion,
36th Infantry
Division

TAMAYO, ANDREW SIDONA. The day after Japan bombed Pearl Harbor, Andrew Tamayo proudly enlisted in the U.S. Army. Yet while in combat in Sicily, he wondered why he was fighting so hard for a country that discriminated against him.

"I began changing my mind about helping these gringos," he said. "I remember how they treated us over here [in the States]."

He remembered that his mother, Brigida Sidona, could not find a better job because she was viewed as a Mexican, though she was a mix of Italian and Spanish. Growing up in San Antonio, he worked as a paperboy to supplement his mother's wages as a maid.

When he was 14, Tamayo moved to Houston to live with his father, Andrew Martinez Tamayo, who promised to quit drinking. When he did not follow through, young Tamayo lived on his own, until his mother joined him in 1938. Among other jobs, he worked as an assistant to an auto mechanic.

In the Army, Tamayo discovered a few Mexican Americans in his unit who became like family to him. On Nov. 8, 1942, the unit assaulted Fedala, Morocco, and later participated in the campaign in Tunisia. They landed in Sicily on July 10, 1943.

Despite the doubts he experienced in Sicily, Tamayo was transferred to the 100th Infantry Division to serve in France for three more years. Near the German border, he was struck by fragments of a mortar shell.

His tour ended shortly thereafter. He returned to the States in May 1945 and was discharged.

Back home in Houston, Tamayo attended the University of Houston, courtesy of the GI Bill, and worked as an auto mechanic.

Andrew Sidona Tamayo

Date of Birth
13 JUNE 1921
San Antonio, TX

Interviewed by
Ernest Eguía
18 SEPTEMBER 2002
Houston, TX

WWII Military Unit
39th Field Artillery
Battalion,
3d Infantry Division

Transferred to
100th Infantry
Division

Refugio Miguel
"Mike" Vasquez

Date of Birth
17 JANUARY 1920
Laredo, TX

Tribute Provided by
Wilhelmina
Cooremans-
Vazquez (Wife)

WWII Military Unit
756th Tank
Battalion

Transferred to
1st Reconnaissance
Troop (Mechanized),
1st Infantry Division

VASQUEZ, REFUGIO MIGUEL "MIKE." One Valentine's Day, Mike Vasquez knocked on the door to the Cooremans' house with three boxes of chocolates for the daughters still living at home. Fourteen-year-old Wilhelmina, the youngest, answered the door. She was so shocked that the biggest box was for her, that she slammed the door and left Mike outside until her mother reminded her of her manners. Though Wilhelmina was too young for a relationship, the two kept in contact.

"It was during this time that World War II started and suddenly he and all the other boys were gone," Wilhelmina said. Vasquez was inducted into the Army on Feb. 2, 1942.

Vasquez was assigned to the 756th Tank Battalion. During his time in the military, Vasquez kept a notebook to record important dates, where he was stationed and people he met along the way.

His first stop overseas was Casablanca on Jan. 26, 1943. From there he would travel to other parts of Morocco, Algeria and Tunisia. Vasquez and the 756th Tank Battalion—attached to the 45th Infantry Division—first saw combat on Sept. 17, 1943, landing in full pack at Paestum, Italy. The battalion fought on and Vazquez was wounded by shrapnel southwest of Oliveto Citra, Italy, on Sept. 22, 1943. He returned to combat on Jan. 29, 1944, in time for his battalion, traveling with the 45th Division, to cross the Rapido River and become the first Allied unit into Cassino.

He was shipped back to the States on March 27, 1944, to have the shrapnel removed. When he was deemed well enough to serve, Vasquez was again sent to Europe on April 25, 1945—this time with the 1st Reconnaissance Troop in the 1st Infantry Division. Since the war was already over, Vasquez served in the occupation of Germany until his discharge.

Vasquez and Wilhelmina Cooremans wrote letters during his time overseas. Shortly after his return, on Jan. 17, 1946, they married. The couple had two children, Michael and Rene.

Gonzalo Villanueva

Date of Birth
10 JANUARY 1919
Arecibo, PR

Interviewed by
Doralís Pérez-Soto
28 MARCH 2003
Arecibo, PR

WWII Military Unit
Company C,
2d Battalion,
65th Infantry
Regiment

VILLANUEVA, GONZALO. Though his time in the service allowed him to see Africa and Europe, Gonzalo Villanueva was happy to return to his native Puerto Rico.

"I remember that when I arrived in San Juan—when I arrived on solid ground—the first thing I did was kiss it," he said.

Villanueva had only worked in the sugar cane fields when he enlisted in September 1943. By October he was shipped to Panama. After passing back through the States, he and the 65th Infantry Regiment were sent to North Africa, where Villanueva contracted typhus. He received treatment in Italy.

Upon his return to Africa, he was reassigned to the Cannon Company of the 2d Battalion. After six months, the 65th Infantry Regiment was sent to France. There, the Regiment was divided. Villanueva's company was stationed in the Alps between France and Italy.

For 90 days in the Alps, Villanueva didn't take off his shoes and eventually developed trench foot, a condition that affects the skin, muscles, and eventually, the nerves of the feet—because they are kept wet for a long period of time. His comrades had to cut his shoes from him and clean his infected feet with cold water and lotion. He later was stationed in Manheim, Germany, from October 1944 to October of the following year before it was announced that the war was over.

Two months after meeting her, on Aug. 31, 1946, Villanueva married Josefina González Guzman. They had four children.

Using the GI Bill, he finished eighth grade and graduated from high school. He worked as a guard at the Río Piedras State Penitentiary in Puerto Rico. Later, he worked at the office of the Nutritional Assistance Program.

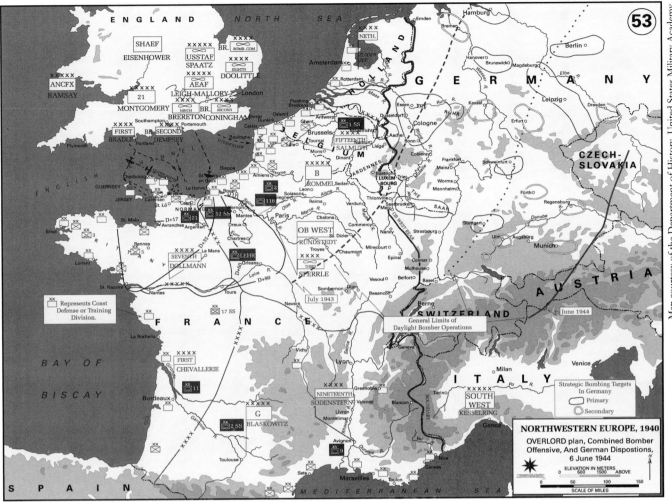

NORTHWESTERN EUROPE, 1940
OVERLORD plan, Combined Bomber Offensive, And German Dispostions, 6 June 1944

MAP 3

FIGHTING FROM THE AIR AND THE SEA

Prior to the United States' entry into WWII, the U.S. government recognized a need to improve its Armed Forces. This included a massive expansion of the Air Corps, which was part of the Army.

As early as 1938, President Franklin D. Roosevelt announced the Civilian Pilot Training Program. The program would utilize colleges and universities to train its students as pilots, potentially for use in the military. When Germany invaded Poland in September 1939, the possibility that the United States would have

to fight in an aerial war was taken more seriously. With pilots and crewmen still in short supply, the Civilian Pilot Training Program was put under control of the military and more specifically targeted to facilitate the country's need.

As improvements to its forces were made, the significance and influence of the Army Air Corps grew during WWII. Later, in 1947, the United States Air Force was created, becoming an independent entity and a new branch of the Armed Forces.

Becoming a Pilot

To be trained as a pilot in the Army Air Corps, one had to have at least two years of college. For many Latinos, that was a difficult requirement to meet.

"It was hard to aspire to things like that because being a pilot was considered kind of elite," said Miguel Encinias, of Tucumcari, N.M., who flew 40 missions and shot down three enemy planes as a fighter pilot in WWII. "All the time I was in training, I never met another pilot who was Hispanic."

Hank Cervantes—who dreamed of becoming a pilot even as a child, working in the fields as a migrant worker in California—eventually found a place in the Army Air Corps as a pilot flying over Germany.

Los Angeles native William Carrillo proved that a college education was arbitrary to becoming a pilot, eventually flying 25 missions over Europe. In the initial paperwork to apply for pilot training, Carrillo wrote that he went to the "College of Hard Knox." He was well on his way to becoming a B-17 bomber pilot before anyone noticed.

Nonetheless, there was still pressure to excel beyond what his Anglo counterparts were required. In addition to his time in the air as a pilot, Carrillo volunteered to crew on another 30 bombing missions.

"Deep down I wanted to prove to some of my comrades that I was not a cowardly Mexican," Carrillo admitted.

The college education requirement to become a pilot was officially dropped in 1941 and the minimum age lowered from 22 to 18, making it easier for people like Hector Santa Anna, of Miami, Ariz., to enlist in the Army and complete flight training. However, of the 97 cadets who received their wings at Brooks Air Field, Texas, on July 29, 1943, Santa Anna was the only Latino. "It wasn't easy being the only one," he said. "They would always single you out."

Flying over Europe

In the air, American bombers and fighter planes faced opposition from fighter planes of the Luftwaffe, the German Air Force, as well as anti-aircraft artillery fired from the ground. The exploding shells from the artillery guns were called "flak."

"This is what scared the hell out of me more than the fighters: those bursts of flak that get so close," said bomber Rudy Acosta, who grew up in El Paso, Texas, and California. "I hated flak."

Pilots and crew members were required to fly at least 25 combat missions overseas before they were either discharged or returned to serve stateside. As the war wore on, the minimum was increased to 35.

The Navy in Europe

Most of the fighting in Europe took place on land, freeing up the vast majority of the Navy to fight in the Pacific. However, accompanied by the British Fleet, the U.S. Navy did have a presence in Europe: battling against German U-boats and submarines in the Atlantic Ocean.

Luis Reyes Davila of El Paso, Texas, was part of this force. Assigned to the Composite Squadron 13, a squadron of Avenger bombers and Wildcat fighters aboard the USS *Tripoli*, Davila went on a nine-month tour hunting submarines which provided fuel and provisions for the U-boats in the South Atlantic.

Starting off as a translator, Delmiro Elizondo, a San Antonio native, soon ascended to a similar role, tracking enemy ships and planes using top-secret radar technology in the Mediterranean Sea aboard the USS *Catoctin*.

The U.S. Navy also played a key role in the amphibious landings onto the beaches of Normandy. Aboard a ship in the English Channel, Cayetano Casados of Carrillos, N.M., was a member of the Naval crew that experienced the first rounds of enemy fire during the D-Day invasion.

ACOSTA, RUDOLFO "RUDY." During a bombing raid over Budapest, Hungary, on April 13, 1944, Rudy Acosta first faced enemy gunfire. Flak cracked like thunderclaps, making him jump every time.

Rudolfo "Rudy" Acosta

Date of Birth
21 JANUARY 1923
El Paso, TX

Interviewed by
Louis Sahagun
14 NOVEMBER 2000
Upton, CA

WWII Military Unit
15th Air Force

"This is what scared the hell out of me more than the fighters: those bursts of flak that get so close," he said. "I hated flak."

He was in his last year at Lincoln High School in Los Angeles, Calif., when the war began for the United States with the bombing of Pearl Harbor. He took a job as a mechanic at Lockheed Aircraft, for a few months before being drafted in 1942.

He was nervous about serving in the military. "I was afraid I was going to end up in the infantry," he said. "I remembered the old movies you see with the guy sloshing through the mud and foxholes. I said, 'That's not for me.'"

In the Army, Acosta was first assigned to the Signal Corps, but was accepted into gunnery school and became a gunner on B-17 and B-24 bombers at Nellis Air Force Base, Nev.

Acosta traveled with the 15th Air Force through Brazil and Africa before they landed in Italy in April 1944. In all, Acosta flew 36 missions until his discharge in Oct. 4, 1945.

"I think I aged 10 years in knowledge in those three years," he said. "All the places I was stationed and all the things I witnessed. ... I would have never been able to learn if I just stayed home."

Acosta was born in El Paso, Texas; his parents divorced when he was 11 and his mother took her seven children to California. After the war, Acosta held many jobs, settling into a construction job for 25 years and later working at the Santa Anita Race Track. He married Irene Acosta in 1954 and had three children with her: Debra, Rudy Jr. and Monica. His first great-grandchild was born on Sept. 15, 2003.

AUTOBEE, JOSEPH "JOE" MARION. As part of the 8th Air Force, Joe Autobee was among the last groups to bomb Germany. Afterward, he was given whiskey and a sandwich, as he had been given after every other raid.

Joseph "Joe" Marion Autobee

Date of Birth
16 FEBRUARY 1924
Avondale, CO

Interviewed by
Rea Ann Trotter
24 JULY 2001
Avondale, CO

WWII Military Unit
448th Bomb Group,
2d Air Division,
8th Air Force

"I think whiskey's good for your nerves," he said, unable to guess another reason for the custom.

Autobee graduated high school in 1942. He was working at Pueblo Army Air Base in Colorado when he was drafted. It was the second time his country called him to the induction center at Fort Logan, Colo., though his name was one of the few not called the first time he showed.

For a year and a half, Autobee was in training, including basic training at Buckley Air Field, gunnery training at Harlingen Army Gunnery School, Texas, and flight training at March Field, Calif. In southern California, he remembered feeling scorched while training 500 feet over the Mojave Desert.

Autobee and the 448th Bomb Group touched down in Liverpool, England, on Dec. 18, 1944. Autobee flew 21 missions as a gunner in a B-24 bomber, and he enjoyed the view from his post. For every mission, he recorded temperature, altitude, ammunition, target, time over Germany, and flak in a book, which he kept long after the war ended.

He also carried a little prayer book with him, and became more religious because of the war.

Autobee remembered how most soldiers in the Air Corps volunteered for as many missions as possible, wanting to finish their quota so they could go home. "Not me," he said. "I took my time."

After the war, Autobee was stationed stateside in Connecticut and Nebraska. When he was discharged, he and a friend hitchhiked from Lincoln, Neb., to Denver, Colo. Autobee returned home to Pueblo, Colo., and was a foreman for the Pueblo Army Depot for 36 years.

Richard G.
Candelaria

Date of Birth
14 JULY 1922
El Paso, TX

Interviewed by
Mario Barrera
16 FEBRUARY 2003
Las Vegas, NV

WWII Military Unit
435th Fighter
Squadron,
479th Fighter
Group,
8th Air Force

CANDELARIA, RICHARD G. In 1945, Richard G. Candelaria was flying apart from his squadron when he encountered two jet fighters and 15-16 ME-109s. As he radioed for help, he engaged the lead and single-handedly shot down four aircraft before his squadron arrived.

Less than a week later, Candelaria, making a second pass over an enemy airfield in Rostock, Germany, was struck by anti-aircraft artillery. Candelaria guided his burning plane as far as he could and then bailed out. He buried his parachute and hid in nearby woods to wait for nightfall. For four days, he evaded capture while heading south. German civilians discovered and reported him. Candelaria was a prisoner of war for 31 days until he and a few others hijacked a car and took a German captain hostage to get back to Allied territory.

Being a pilot was his life's dream. As a boy, he read about WWI pilots and biplanes and watched fighters take off and land at a nearby base near his home in Southern California. "I wanted to be a fighter pilot," he said. "That was my one wish."

He was born in El Paso, Texas, but his family moved to Southern California when he was a child. After graduating from high school in 1939, Candelaria passed the entrance exams for the Army Air Corps pilot training program and studied at the University of Southern California. He was accepted into the flying program in January 1943 and graduated as second lieutenant. For four months, Candelaria served as a flight instructor in Arizona. In May 1944, the call came for more fighter pilots, and Candelaria rushed to sign up.

He flew P-38 and P-51 Mustangs in Europe, escorting heavy bombers to their targets and back. Candelaria shot down six enemy planes in WWII, earning the title "Fighter Ace," and earned the rank of captain. He married Betty Jean Landreth in 1953; they had two daughters, Camdelyne and Calia.

William Carrillo

Date of Birth
11 FEBRUARY 1919
Los Angeles, CA

Interviewed by
Mario Barrera
6 JULY 2001
Daly City, CA

WWII Military Unit
100th Bomb Group,
3d Division,
8th Air Force

CARRILLO, WILLIAM. Though he knew he wanted to be in the Air Corps when he enlisted in 1942, William Carrillo did not have the required college degree. On the application for the Air Corps cadet program, he wrote that he had attended the "College of Hard Knox." By the time anyone noticed that Hard Knox wasn't an accredited institution, Carrillo was on his way to becoming a pilot.

Carrillo flew a B-17 bomber out of England in 25 missions. Often, he flew with other crews as well, filling in gaps where they were missing members. Altogether, he participated in 55 missions.

"I did not have a death wish or anything," he wrote. "I guess deep down I wanted to prove to some of my comrades that I was not a cowardly Mexican."

The raids took him over France and Germany. On May 24, 1944, Carrillo's plane was shot down over Berlin. Carrillo bailed out and landed into the slate roof of a Berlin home, his legs stuck in the attic. He felt sure he was going to die when the man who lived there pulled him down and held him at the point of a rifle bayonet. He was handed over to the Gestapo, who, for two weeks, beat him to try to learn about the impending Allied invasion. When they could get no information out of him, Carrillo was sent to a Luftwaffe-run POW camp in Poland. There, his interrogators produced a notebook of information on the 100th Bomb Group and tried to entice him into joining the Luftwaffe. Carrillo was rescued in Munich, Germany, in 1945.

Back in the States, he returned to his job as a janitor at MJB Coffee in San Francisco. However, when his boss discovered he had been an officer in the war, Carrillo was promoted to a management position and worked as a general manager until his retirement in 1995. Carrillo married Veronica Alves in 1948 and the couple had five children: Karen, Kristine, Kim, Kent and Kirk. Carrillo and his wife were kept busy by their 12 grandchildren.

CASADOS, CAYETANO. Aboard a ship in the English Channel, Cayetano Casados watched as more and more vessels crowded the water, sure that something huge was about to begin. Casados was a member of the Naval crew that experienced the first rounds of enemy fire during the D-Day invasion, but remembered his crew's good fortune in the invasion: they lost only one man.

As the only Latino on his ship, Casados said he never experienced discrimination, but was sometimes surprised by his fellow soldiers' lack of knowledge. Some would ask him why he was fighting in the war since Mexico was not involved.

"I felt sorry for these college-educated guys," he said. "At that time I could name every capital and every state and yet one guy with two years of college experience from Duke didn't even know where New Mexico was."

Growing up in Cerillos, N.M., Casados remembered his family's struggles to make ends meet. He began working full time after 11th grade.

He was drafted in 1943. After boot camp and gunnery school in San Diego, Calif., he attended firefighting school and English classes in Boston, Mass. He then boarded the USS *Quincy*, where he would stay during his entire tour of duty.

After the Normandy invasion, Casados stayed with his ship in the south of France. He then traveled to the Pacific, where he helped demilitarized Izo Island and the Japanese mainland. He was later told that his ship was a mere 50 miles from the bombings at Hiroshima and Nagasaki.

Casados was discharged on Jan. 9, 1946. He then returned to New Mexico. There he married Aurora Garcia, with whom he had two children, Paulina and Fernando. Casados worked as general manager for Empire builders for 32 years.

Cayetano Casados

Date of Birth
7 AUGUST 1923
Carrillos, NM

Interviewed by
Norman L. Martinez
3 NOVEMBER 2002
Santa Fe, NM

WWII Military Unit
USS *Quincy* (CA-71)

CASTRO, LADISLAO CATALINO "L.C." As he bailed out of the spiraling bomber within sight of England's shores on March 18, 1944, L.C. Castro resolved not to be taken prisoner. For six months, he evaded capture in German-controlled France.

Castro had graduated from high school in Austin, Texas, in 1942 and enlisted in the Army Air Corps in November 1942. After training, he joined the crew of a B-24 Liberator as an assistant engineer and aerial gunner. They were deployed to England in October 1943.

Castro participated in a total of 21 missions. In Norway, his unit bombed a plant that was manufacturing "heavy water" for use in production of nuclear weapons. On his last mission over Friedrichshafen, Germany, the 506th Squadron was severely crippled by anti-aircraft fire. Castro was struck in the right leg and his bomber was losing fuel, but the crew decided to try to make it back to England. They were shot down over occupied France.

Castro opened his parachute close to the ground, landing hard and limping to a haystack to hide. He could hear the Germans, who had found the rest of his 10-man crew, searching for him. His wounded right leg was broken from his parachute jump, but Castro was able to hide from authorities with the help of French civilians. In Amiens, he moved from house to house, until the French Underground took him to the home where 16 other Allied airmen were hiding.

The Canadian Army liberated Amiens on Sept. 1, 1944. After the war, Castro became a member of the Air Force Reserves and was called into active duty during the Korean War.

He married Sallie Castillo in 1948 and had two sons, James and Juan. Though he had planned to be an auto mechanic before the war, Castro studied business using the GI Bill. After seven years with the U.S. Postal Service, he became an accountant at Bergstrom AFB, until his retirement in 1989.

Ladislao Catalino
"L.C." Castro

Date of Birth
13 FEBRUARY 1924
Austin, TX

Interviewed by
Alan K. Davis
1 MARCH 2001
Austin, TX

WWII Military Unit
44th Bomb
Group (Heavy),
506th Bomb
Squadron (Heavy),
8th Air Force

Enrique "Hank" Cervantes

Date of Birth
10 OCTOBER 1923
Fresno, CA

Interviewed by
Maggie Rivas-Rodriguez and
Bruce Ashcroft
30 MAY 2004
Washington, D.C.

WWII Military Unit
349th Squadron,
100th Bomb Group,
13th Combat Wing,
3d Air Division

CERVANTES, ENRIQUE "HANK." A card given to Hank Cervantes on his eighth birthday sparked his first aspiration to become a pilot. Despite the difficulty of breaking into a field where there were very few Mexican Americans, he eventually achieved his dream.

He was given an English name in school and discouraged from speaking Spanish outside of his home. For the son of a migrant farm laborer, his ambitions for flight often seemed unrealistic.

"I shared [my dream] with my mother one day when we were picking prunes and she smiled and said, 'Good for you, now get back to work,' " he said.

After Cervantes graduated from high school in 1941, he tried to join pre-flight Navy school but was rejected because one recruiter said, they didn't accept "Filipinos, spics or niggers." He was drafted in January 1943.

It wasn't until later that Cervantes took a test and was accepted into the Air Corps. The required college classes were difficult, yet he persevered and made his family, especially his mother, proud. The tragedy that awaited him as he graduated flight school on June 27, 1944, was difficult to face. Cervantes returned home to find his mother in a mental institution, unable to recognize him.

As a B-17 pilot during WWII, he flew 25 combat missions over Germany. He also served in Greenland during the Korean War. His career as a pilot was full of strife, as Cervantes advanced past Anglos who questioned his capacity to lead. He experienced the Air Force's evolution from B-17s to B-58s, which were phased out six months after his retirement in 1965, as a lieutenant colonel. As a civilian, Cervantes worked at the Department of Defense and served on the staff of Los Angeles Mayor Tom Bradley. He headed personnel boards for the city. He wrote an autobiography titled *Piloto: Migrant Worker to Jet Pilot* to share his experiences.

Luis Reyes Davila

Date of Birth
15 DECEMBER 1924
El Paso, TX

Interviewed by
Liliana Velazquez
2 FEBRUARY 2002
El Paso, TX,

WWII Military Unit
Composite
Squadron, VC-66,
USS *Tripoli*
(CVE-64)

Transferred to
Composite
Squadron, VC-13

DAVILA, LUIS REYES. Equipped with Avenger bombers and Wildcat fighters, Luis Reyes Davila and his squadron departed for nine months of South Atlantic anti-submarine and convoy protection on March 15, 1944. He and Composite Squadron 13 would go for 30 days at a time chasing "mother submarines," those providing fuel and provisions for smaller German U-boats. Throughout the war, Davila sailed on the USS *Tripoli* as a member of the air division, responsible for making sure planes were in good condition and ready to use.

It was not long before Davila was confronted by the stark realities of war. In the South Atlantic, a plane landed on his ship and the crew parked it on the side. They were unable to tie the plane down and the plane somehow caught on fire. The propeller never stopped running. Davila watched as a friend standing in front of him "put his head in the propeller." Davila recalled: "It was just like when you shuffle a deck of cards. I looked up and passed out."

Sights such as this instilled a death-defying mentality in the young sailor: He was more willing to take chances, to risk his life. "I figured I was going to get killed during the war," he said, "so I figured my time is coming up." Originally assigned to Composite Squadron VC-66, Davila was separated from the squadron—his unit transferred to another ship while he remained on the *Tripoli*. His replacement in Composite Squadron 66 was killed in action in the Pacific.

His travels across two oceans took him far from his home in El Paso, Texas, where he was born Dec. 15, 1924, to Gonzalo Reyes and Concepción Ortega. His parents divorced and both died before Davila was 8; his uncle and aunt, José L. and Remedios G. Davila, raised him.

Davila was discharged in 1946, and returned home. He met Flora Ortega at a dance club in Ciudad Juarez, Mexico. They married in 1947 and had two sons, José Luis and Miguel.

ELIZONDO, DELMIRO ISIDRO. Though he had earned his pilot's license, Delmiro Elizondo became a sailor in 1942, when recruiters assigned him to the Navy. While he was initially disappointed, Elizondo's patriotism was unflappable, and he embraced his assignment.

During basic training in San Diego with 100 other Mexican Americans from San Antonio, Elizondo translated for his captain. Eager to ascend the ranks of the military, he applied for a higher position. He was placed in a top-secret radar school to learn new technology.

His new skills in tow, he reported to the Mediterranean Sea on the USS *Catoctin*. Working in the Combat Information Center, he tracked enemy ships and planes and plotted the vessel's course. He was also responsible for assigning crews to land missions. Even with his authority, he was against putting others' lives in danger before his own and refused to stay aboard the ship during the crew's invasion of southern France in August 1944.

"I turned to my superior and asked how I could possibly send 10 men to risk their lives and not risk mine," he said. "It was at this point that I put my second-in-command in charge and went with the men ashore."

Elizondo said that amid the chaos, he sometimes saw glimmers of humanity, such as a small house he saved from destruction. He told his men that it was surrounded by mines so they would not destroy the pristine hilltop home.

Elizondo was en route to the Pacific when the war ended. He was discharged in 1946 and returned to Spicewood, Texas, his childhood home, and found a job as a salesman. He married Yolanda Garza, and the couple had two children, Diana Maria and Mary Alice. After the death of his first wife in 1968, he married Nelwyn Ruth Dodd in 1970.

Delmiro Isidro
Elizondo

Date of Birth
15 MAY 1925
San Antonio, TX

Interviewed by
Kevin Klauber
17 APRIL 2002
Spicewood, TX

WWII Military Unit
USS *Catoctin*
(AGC-5), Flagship
for Commander,
8th Fleet

ENCINIAS, MIGUEL. As a pilot, Miguel Encinias was shot down on two occasions—once over Europe during WWII and then again during the Korean War.

Encinias had joined the New Mexico National Guard at age 16, along with many of his Hispanic friends, many of whom spoke no English. After Pearl Harbor, he was accepted into the pilot training program.

"It was hard to aspire to things like that because being a pilot was considered kind of elite," he said. "All the time I was in training, I never met another pilot who was Hispanic."

He flew 40 missions over Tunisia, Sicily and Corsica, France. He shot down three enemy planes. Encinias was shot down in northern Italy. He spent 15 months at a POW camp near the Polish border in Germany. There, the prisoners half-jokingly hoped to be home by Christmas 1963; they passed news of the outside world on notepads given to them by the Red Cross.

"We knew about the Normandy landing the day it happened," he said. "We could have never believed the Normandy landing could have taken place so quickly."

Finally, the prisoners could hear the shattering of cannons in the east, and cheered the Russian invasion. They escaped when the Germans abandoned the camp.

He returned to service during the Korean War and was again shot down, but was rescued by U.S. forces. He retired from the Air Force as a lieutenant colonel in 1971.

After earning his doctorate, Encinas taught French and Spanish at New Mexico Western University and at the University of Albuquerque. He married French-born, Jeannine Henriette Blondel, in 1963. The couple had three daughters: Ana-María, Valerie and María-Isabel, and a son, Juan Pablo.

Miguel Encinias

Date of Birth
8 APRIL 1923
Tucumcari, NM

Interviewed by
Brian Lucero
3 DECEMBER 2001
Albuquerque, NM

WWII Military Unit
45th Infantry
Division

Transferred to
52d Bomb
Squadron (Heavy),
29th Bomb Group,
20th Air Force

Enrique "Henry" Rodriguez Falcón

Date of Birth
6 DECEMBER 1921
Austin, TX

Interviewed by
Paul R. Zepeda
24 OCTOBER 2003
Houston, TX

WWII Military Unit
447th Bomb
Squadron,
321st Bomb Group,
12th Air Force

FALCÓN, ENRIQUE "HENRY" RODRIGUEZ. After three years in the war, having flown combat missions as an aerial gunner, Enrique "Henry" Falcón came back to Texas physically unscathed. Nonetheless, he was a victim of the after-effects of the war, until he met the woman who would be his wife.

Falcón did not hesitate when his draft notice came. He had been working as a tailor after leaving high school in the 10th grade. Two of his brothers had already volunteered.

Falcón chose to join the Army Air Corps. "They asked me if I wanted to fly, and I said 'Absolutely,'" he said.

After basic training, Falcón began gunnery training in De Ridder, La. He was sent overseas before he finished training and served as waist gunner in Tunisia, Sicily, Naples, Rome and North Africa.

Falcón had flown 12 missions before anyone realized that he was not fully trained. He was reassigned to the ordnance department, where he maintained the ammunition for B-25 bombers.

He was in Italy when the war ended and still remembers the huge celebration in the streets. Returning home to Austin, Texas, was difficult. His father had died of a heart attack while he was away, and a close childhood friend had been killed in the war. Falcón decided that peace was too sharp a contrast to the intense aerial combat he had experienced. He moved from Austin to Houston.

"When I came home, I couldn't find myself," he said. "It was hard."

That changed when Falcón met Gloria Felán. They married in December 1947 and had three children: Cynthia, Ronald and Richard. Today, the children live near their parents in Houston.

Falcón attended watch repair school and then worked as a salesman for American Bakers in Houston until his retirement in 1980.

Leonard Vara Fuentes

Date of Birth
6 NOVEMBER 1922
Laredo, TX

Interviewed by
Maggie Rivas-Rodriguez
6 NOVEMBER 2004
San Antonio, TX

WWII Military Unit
87th Fighter
Squadron,
79th Fighter Group,
12th Air Force

FUENTES, LEONARD VARA. Even after flying several successful missions over Italy during WWII, Leonard Fuentes was prepared to continue serving his country, and remained in the military after the war, serving in Korea.

Fuentes graduated from high school and wanted to attend trade school, so he began working odd jobs near Kelly Field and began saving for his education. After Pearl Harbor, Fuentes was compelled to join the war effort. Fuentes enlisted in 1943 and began training as an airplane mechanic and then as a pilot. The military sent him to Texas A&M University as part of the College Training Detachment Program, where he was one of only two Latinos in his class.

He then started his tour of duty overseas and flew eight successful missions over Italy during the war with the 87th Fighter Squadron. He also tested planes to assess damages. He hungered for more combat, so after fighting had subsided in Europe with Germany's surrender, he volunteered to join the 345th Fighter Group to fly missions in the Pacific.

"I felt like I hadn't done hardly anything to help with the war effort," he said modestly. "I was fine and felt like I could still help."

His ship had made a stop in Panama en route to Japan when the war ended and he returned to the States. He remained in the military, working as an electronic specialist and serving as a fighter pilot during the Korean War. Fuentes married Eva Cerda in 1946 and the couple had three children: Leonard, Robert and Linda.

He was discharged from the Army in 1953 with the rank of 1st lieutenant. He eventually returned to school, graduating from San Antonio College in 1974. He then worked as a liaison between Kelly Field and Lockheed-Martin.

GARCIA, NARCISO. The mission over Corsica, Italy, should have been easy, with the target completely unguarded. But as Narciso Garcia and the 488th Bomb Group approached, they were met by the highest concentration of anti-aircraft batteries that they had yet encountered.

The engine on Garcia's plane was damaged, and the plane was losing fuel, but the crew decided to try to make it back to base instead of crash-landing in nearby Switzerland. They survived the trip to England and waited for news of the other planes. Of a squadron of 24, only 11 made it back.

Garcia served as a tail gunner in a B-25 Mitchell bomber and flew tactical missions in Northern Italy. "We were called 'bridge busters,'" he said, "We kept the Brenner Pass closed." The Brenner Pass lies on the border between Austria and Italy and is the lowest and easiest pass through the Alps. Garcia and the 448th Bomb Squadron were constantly bombing the area, destroying German bridges, ammo dumps, railroad yards and fuel tank farms to keep traffic through the area to a minimum. Garcia flew in 41 combat missions.

Garcia was drafted during his last year in high school and accepted into the Air Cadet Program. Growing up, he was known in his neighborhood in El Paso, Texas, as "el inventór." His innovations included a tiny mechanical carnival and repairs on bicycles, phonographs and sewing machines. But because of the expense, college was never a practical consideration.

"It was only after the war and the advent of the GI Bill that everyone knew I was destined to go to college," he said. Garcia was discharged on Nov. 6, 1945, and attended Texas Western College, where he graduated with a bachelor's degree in civil engineering in 1951. Later, he worked for the U.S. Corps of Engineers at White Sands Missile Range, N.M., until his retirement.

Garcia married Frances Najera and they had two children: Michael and Loretta.

Narciso Garcia

Date of Birth
22 FEBRUARY 1924
El Paso, TX

Interviewed by
Maggie Rivas-
Rodriguez
17 MARCH 2001
El Paso, TX

WWII Military Unit
488th Bomb
Squadron,
340th Bomb Group,
57th Bomb Wing,
12th Air Force

GUERRA, JUVENTINO. Raised in small towns and on ranches, Juventino Guerra never went far from home. Then WWII opened new opportunities to travel and learn other perspectives. He enlisted on Jan. 8, 1941, in San Antonio, Texas. Initially, he was promised two weeks to say goodbye to his family before leaving Texas. But the two weeks were reduced to a phone call in New Jersey just before shipping out with the 324th Material Squadron, bound for Buenos Aires, Argentina.

Guerra's squadron was responsible for readying planes for flight. Guerra, who had experience in clerical work with his job at Cavazos Tourist and Insurance Agency in Laredo, Texas, before the war, was responsible for keeping records of the members in his squadron. From South America, the squadron traveled around Africa, up to Madagascar and to the Red Sea. They spent five months in Egypt, during which Guerra worked with the Air Force Service Command and his squadron supported the British 8th Army. They went on to Tunisia, Libya, Sicily and Italy. His camp was bombed in Corsica, and Guerra was wounded in his left knee.

During his time in the service, Guerra corresponded with Elena Pimentel, who he had met at a train station before enlisting. He missed her so much that he proposed to her in a letter. She insisted he come home and meet her family before they started to make plans. Guerra returned home on Oct. 9, 1945, declining a commission to stay on and fight in Japan.

He married Elena on April 6, 1946, and the couple had four children: Cristina, Juventino Jr., Olga and Victor.

Guerra worked as an accountant. He opened his own accounting business which he ran for 30 years. He later became a real estate broker.

Juventino Guerra

Date of Birth
18 JUNE 1917
Hebbronville, TX

Interviewed by
Markel Riojas
6 NOVEMBER 2004
San Antonio, TX

WWII Military Unit
324th Air Material
Squadron

Transferred to
941st Air Engineer
Squadron

Joe Hernandez

Date of Birth
22 FEBRUARY 1924
San Antonio, TX

Interviewed by
Brenda Sendejo
18 JULY 2004
Austin, TX

WWII Military Unit
330th Bomb
Squadron,
93d Bomb
Group (Heavy),
2d Air Division,
20th Combat Wing,
8th Air Force

HERNANDEZ, JOE. During the 22 months Joe Hernandez was in Europe, he flew 35 bombing missions as top turret gunner on a B-24.

The raids over Germany were particularly difficult. As Hernandez's plane and crew approached their target, they were met with a barrage of anti-aircraft fire.

"It was like driving on a bumpy road," he said, explaining how flak exploding next to them would shake the whole plane. On three different occasions, the damage was bad enough to force the B-24 to an emergency landing.

Yet it was planes in Hernandez's own squadron that triggered his closest brush with death. While flying in tight formation, the B-24 was caught in the violent turbulence created by the nearby planes, a condition called propeller wash. The whirlwind plunged the crew into a tailspin.

"The pilot gave the order to bail out, but there was so much centrifugal force that you couldn't move," he said.

The plane dropped 5,000 feet before the pilot was able to right it. Fortunately, the crew was able to land safely. Hernandez was awarded the Air Medal in late 1944. On his birthday, he was shipped back to the States. He became an aerial gunnery instructor in Boise, Idaho, until his discharge in September.

After the war, he returned to San Antonio, Texas, where his parents had immigrated and raised him. Hernandez had dropped out of high school just short of graduation to help his parents run the family restaurant. He and his brother were both drafted in 1943.

Hernandez married Aurora Zapata; during their more than 50 years of marriage, the couple raised five children: Christine, Daniel, Eleanor, Marshall and George.

Francisco "Frank"
Xavier Jacques

Date of Birth
14 JULY 1917
Tankersley, TX

Tribute Provided by
Hiram Jacques
(Son)

WWII Military Unit
338th Bomb
Squadron,
96th Bomb Group,
8th Air Force

JACQUES, FRANCISCO "FRANK" XAVIER. When Francisco "Frank" Jacques tried to enlist after the U.S. declared war on Japan, he was turned away for having only a fourth-grade education. He had grown up on a small family farm and attended a one-room schoolhouse for Mexican Americans, where the students were taught as one large class.

He was drafted in 1942 and qualified for training as a side gunner for a B-17 Bomber by exaggerating his education level and doing well on an exam.

Shortly before shipping out to England, Jacques found himself in Pyote, Texas, close to his West Texas hometown of Sweetwater, but unable to visit. Saddened, he threw one of his dog tags next to the railroad tracks, never guessing that a boy would find the tag and bring it to Jacques' mother.

At first, Jacques served in a B-17 ground crew, later acting as guard on the runway. He was finally assigned as a side gunner on a B-17 and, during the next two months, flew on six bombing missions over Berlin. Jacques was wounded on the last raid, after flak ripped through oxygen hoses and traumatized his lungs. He was re-assigned to ground crew upon his recovery.

Jacques participated in the invasion of Normandy and then served in Morocco, France, Belgium and Germany as a rifleman. Shortly before D-Day, he received news that his father had died.

Upon his discharge on Oct. 5, 1945, Jacques returned home to persistent discrimination, most obvious as he watched his cousin get shot and killed by a sheriff for using a gas station bathroom.

He held several jobs in the Sweetwater area, as a sheep shearer and construction worker, in the loading docks and at local manufacturers. Jacques married Argentina Galán in 1948 and raised three children: Jerry, Ruth and Hiram. Jacques later enjoyed backpacking, dancing and traveling around the United States and Mexico.

MARQUEZ, ALBERTO OCHOA. On an autumn day in 1942, Alberto Marquez and a friend were on their way to lunch when they spotted the now-famous Uncle Sam poster, "I WANT YOU!" The friends began to jokingly argue which of them he was pointing at.

"Well, let's go find out who they want!" Marquez said and the two headed to the local Navy recruiting office. Marquez was rejected because he had two missing molars. He apologized to have to leave his friend and left to try a different branch. When both the Army and Army Air Corps had the same problem with his enlistment, he decided to visit a local dentist office, where he had worked for three years. He finally was accepted into the Air Corps on Oct. 5, 1942.

"I wanted to get away from Houston, but you know what they did?" He said, "They sent me to Ellington Field!"

Marquez worked as a file clerk at the military airfield in Houston, where his grandmother had raised him and several of his cousins. Unsatisfied with the assignment, Marquez applied for Officer Candidate School and Gunnery. After training, Marquez was assigned to a plane named "No Love, No Nothing." He developed a camaraderie with the 10-member crew and, at age 29, the oldest crew member, often undertook the responsibility of maintaining order.

Marquez flew 33 missions as nose gunner over England, Germany and France. His most painful memories are of American planes being shot out of the air. His own plane was hit many times and sometimes had to limp back to base.

Upon his discharge, Marquez resumed work at the dental office. He married his first wife, Ester Martinez, in 1935 and had a son, Albert, and daughter, Sylvia. After their divorce, he married Sarah Ramón in 1950 and they had two sons, Adrian and James.

Alberto Ochoa
Marquez

Date of Birth
24 MAY 1913
Sanderson, TX

Interviewed by
Ernest Equia and
Paul R. Zepeda
22 APRIL 2003
Houston, TX

WWII Military Unit
713th Bomb
Squadron,
448th Bomb Group,
8th Air Force

NAJERA, MANUEL. As the sole surviving son of his family, Manuel Najera had an option to stay out of the service. Instead, he reported for assignment and flew 35 missions as a B-17 gunner.

"If I would have died, it would have ended my family," he said.

Najera dropped out of school at 16 to help his single mother. He was 18 when his draft papers came. "I told them I didn't care what I did," Najera said. The recruiters decided to make him a flyer. After basic training and gunnery school, he was sent to Salt Lake City for assignments. "They pointed me into a corner with nine others and that was our crew," he said. "From then on, we were going to sleep together, eat together, everything together."

The crew shipped out July 4, 1944, and was based in Salisbury, England, for the duration of their tour of duty. On his first mission, Najera thought that the experience was fun until he realized the Germans were shooting at his plane, too.

Though they were never shot down, Najera's crew had a few close calls. Once, the radio operator in front of him was wounded when a shell exploded near the plane and, with one of their engines gone, the return trip was nearly a failure. Another time, the crew was forced to throw everything overboard to keep the damaged plane in the air.

When he fulfilled his required number of missions, Najera was transferred to Lubbock, Texas. At the news of the war's end, he was in charge of keeping the festivities in the dry county free of alcohol. Najera said later he was lousy at the assignment and told the men to hide their drinks.

He married Consuelo Guerra on June 23, 1951, and lived in Saginaw with her and their five children: Gabriel, Nancy, Patricia, Lawrence and Daniel. Najera worked for a Chevrolet parts plant for 40 years until his retirement.

Manuel Najera

Date of Birth
22 MARCH 1925
Saginaw, MI

Interviewed by
Juan Marinez
12 OCTOBER 2002
Saginaw, MI

WWII Military Unit
487th Bomb Group,
8th Air Force

Hector Santa Anna

Date of Birth
26 FEBRUARY 1923
Miami, AZ

Interviewed by
Lorena Ruley
31 MAY 2003
Millersville, MD

WWII Military Unit
832d Bomb
Squadron,
486th Bomb Group,
8th Air Force

SANTA ANNA, HECTOR. The great-great-nephew of a famous Mexican general, Hector Santa Anna flew 35 missions as a B-17 bomber pilot over Europe, taught hundreds of pilots how to fly, and eventually rose to the rank of lieutenant colonel over the course of a 22-year military career.

After Santa Anna graduated from Miami (Ariz.) High School, he wanted to join the military, but his father objected, persuading him to instead pursue a college education. Santa Anna left for California to earn money as a miner to finance his schooling. In Oxnard, Calif., he visited the Army Air Corps training field outside of town and decided he wanted to become a pilot.

He returned home to Miami, Ariz., and enlisted. He completed flight training at Brooks Air Field, Texas, on July 29, 1943. Of the 97 cadets to receive their wings that day, Santa Anna was the only Latino.

"It wasn't easy being the only one. They would always single you out," he said. "With a name like Santa Anna, you stood out. Some would accept you, and others would not."

Because he was bilingual, he was assigned to basic flight training school in Waco, Texas, where he taught other Latinos to fly. His later assignment to a base in Sudbury, England, allowed him to log more than 250 hours of flight time over Europe from Nov. 16, 1944, to March 3, 1945. He completed his quota of missions faster than anyone in his bomber group.

"The most pleasant thing was to come back in and land that last mission," he said.

After the war, Santa Anna was sent to train pilots in Lubbock, Texas, where he met Olive Allen. They married in November 1945, and had two daughters, Sylvia and Cynthia. Santa Anna served for three years as special assistant to the secretary of defense for public affairs before retiring from the military in 1985. He worked as a flight instructor for the Air Force, Navy and Army until 2002.

Paul Lopez Solis

Date of Birth
23 AUGUST 1919
Victoria, TX

Interviewed by
Paul R. Zepeda
and Ernest Eguía
22 JANUARY 2003
Houston, TX

WWII Military Unit
18th Troop Carrier
Squadron,
64th Troop
Carrier Group,
18th Air Force

SOLIS, PAUL LOPEZ. Though the war allowed Paul Solis to hitchhike through the United States and see parts of the world he probably would have never experienced, it also made him appreciate what he had at home.

"From going all around the world and seeing all these other countries, there's no place like the United States," he said.

Before the war, Solis worked mostly as a waiter. Life had been difficult for his mother, two sisters and two brothers after their father died in 1933. Solis dropped out of 11th grade to support his mother. In December 1941, he tried to enlist but was advised to wait and spend one more Christmas at home.

Though his brothers were already in the Navy, Solis joined the Army Air Corps. After training, he and a friend saved money by hitchhiking from the radio school in Illinois to Massachusetts, from there they would ship out.

He was first sent to North Africa for about a year. Solis and his crew flew in a C-47, dropping supplies to troops on the front lines. The 18th Troop Carrier Squadron consisted of about 28 similar crews and their planes. During Solis' nearly four years in the military, he also served in Italy, France and the China-Burma-India Theater.

Solis and his brothers all came home safely after the war. He returned to the restaurant business, but unsure what he wanted to do, attended the University of Houston and then an art vocational school. He married Emma Torres in 1948 and, in need of immediate income, settled into a 34-year career at the U.S. Postal Service.

The couple had three children: Maria Theresa, Robert and John.

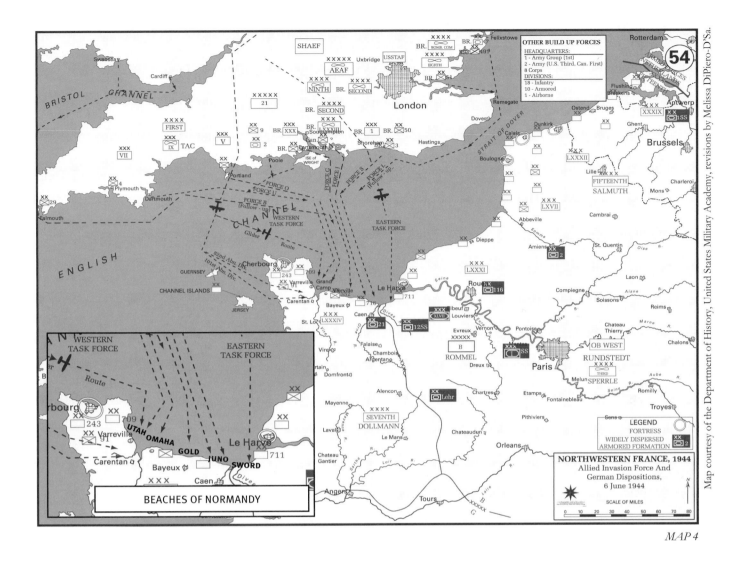

MAP 4

NORMANDY

In England on June 4, 1944, Lauro Vega, of Southern California, and the members of his unit were given a delicious home-style meal of fried chicken, potatoes and gravy. One of his fellow soldiers brought the reality of the dinner to Vega's attention.

"It was a good meal—the best meal we had," he said. "A buddy of mine said, 'We're not getting this meal for nothing; I bet you we're gonna go to the invasion already.' By God, he was right."

On the morning of June 6, 1944, 100,000 men prepared to cross the English Channel to storm the beaches of Normandy, France, in the largest amphibious invasion in history. After British soldiers had been forced out of France by German troops in 1940, the Allies began planning a return to the continent, hoping for a decisive victory that would turn the tide of the war in the European Theater. On D-Day that plan was set into motion, and so began one of the bloodiest invasions in military history. Code named Operation Overlord, the invasion involved a total of nearly 3 million troops from 12 Allied nations.

Poor weather conditions delayed the initial invasion, scheduled for June 5. Heavy winds and choppy waters motivated General Dwight D. Eisenhower, Supreme Allied Commander, in Europe, who oversaw the Allied troops, to push back the attack. The weather had improved little by the next day, but the invasion was set into motion nonetheless. The inclement weather was perhaps to the Army's advantage, as few could have guessed the troops would begin an assault during that dismal, dark morning.

The invasion began on the eve of June 5th, with airborne troops landing behind the beaches near the Orne River and Sainte Mere-Eglise and Carentan in hopes of securing road junctions and key crossings before the waterborne invasion began.

As morning came, bombers flew over the coast of France, and the 101st and 82d Airborne Divisions dropped paratroopers and landed in gliders. Neither division had a good drop; many soldiers did not land at their intended destinations and were left wandering through the French countryside attempting to find their units and reach their objectives.

"We were hooked on the back of the airplane like a trailer hooks to a car," said Joe Uriegas, of Austin, Texas. More than three hundred gliders were used on D-Day. Gliders were towed behind aircraft on a 300-ft. nylon rope, 1 inch in diameter, and were used to carry light artillery, vehicles and supplies. Each glider normally carried 15 troops and, although many were lost, proved to be a great asset during the operation.

The invasion of Normandy occurred on five beaches dotting the coast of Normandy, with American troops coming ashore at Utah and Omaha Beaches. Utah was on a considerably smaller scale than Omaha, and U.S. troops came ashore to establish a port for the Allies. Fewer casualties occurred at Utah, as American troops were met with fewer defensive forces as they came ashore.

Omaha, the better known of the beaches at Normandy, was the site of the greatest bloodshed. Violent tides prevented half of the amphibious tanks from completing the 10-mile trek from the mother ships to the beachhead. Once the soldiers reached the shore, soaking wet and exhausted, they found a perilous mix of fortifications, steel poles and other obstructions. Land mines also dotted the beach. The cliffs along the shore served as excellent locations for German snipers, who picked off soldiers as they made landfall.

Approximately 2,500 men were killed at Omaha Beach, most during the initial hours of the invasion. Chaos reigned, but the soldiers pressed forward on the beach and clawed up the steep cliffs along the shore en route to Saint-Lô.

The horrific conditions of the invasion were a shock to the troops, many of whom were in combat for the first time. Wading through the cold waters to the shore, terrifying anticipation gripped many soldiers. Still, those who made it to shore persevered.

"We ran like hell when we got to the beaches," said Mike Gomez, of Phoenix, who fought with the 837th Ordnance Combat Depot. "It's a matter of survival, but you always have a little fear in you. It's their life or yours." *(See Mike Gomez' story in Chapter 1, Witnesses to the Nazi Concentration Camps.)*

As the battle raged around them, medics dodged gunfire and land mines, scrambling to help legions of fallen soldiers.

The survivors of the dangerous invasion fought on, in the hedgerows of France. The Allies eventually took Normandy and continued on to the interior of the country, liberating Paris on August 25, 1944. Following that victory troops fought in campaigns throughout Europe. Many soldiers, such as Pablo Gonzales, of Saginaw, Mich., a tank commander and Silver Star recipient, participated in the Battle of the Bulge before returning home for a hero's welcome.

ARMIJO, CEPRIAN. Even a wound dangerously close to his lung could not keep Ceprian Armijo away from the battlefield. While fighting in France in November 1944, Armijo was struck in his upper back by shrapnel. He was transferred to Amsterdam and then Belgium for treatment, returning to his unit less than three months later in February 1945.

Ceprian Armijo

Date of Birth
26 SEPTEMBER 1920
Avondale, CO

Interviewed by
Rea Ann Trotter
15 DECEMBER 2001
Avondale, CO

WWII Military Unit
Company E,
116th Infantry
Regiment,
29th Infantry
Division

"My wound was so close to the lung and they didn't have the equipment to probe," he said of Army physicians at Amsterdam. "They were afraid to puncture a lung or something."

Armijo was drafted in July 1942 and barely passed his medical exam because of astigmatism in his right eye. However, doctors believed he was feigning injury to avoid the draft, and passed him, despite the problems his vision could cause when firing his rifle. He trained at Fort Carson, Colo., near his hometown of Avondale, for 15 months before he went to training at Fort Meade, Md. From there he went to New York, where he boarded a ship for Europe. Once there, he said the fear was constant.

"You knew you were in battle because you could see German soldiers laying by the road or something," Armijo said. "Anybody that says it doesn't scare you. ... [They're] lying."

At war's end, Armijo was guarding ammunition dumps in Germany and, at age 24, was the oldest man in his company.

He arrived in New York City on Oct. 11, 1945. He returned to Avondale unannounced to surprise his parents. Not long after, he married Eliza Autobee, a childhood friend. The couple had three children: David, Gloria Jean and Timothy. Armijo and his family remained in Colorado, where Armijo worked for the Army Depot, working his way up to shipping and receiving supervisor before his retirement in 1979.

BARBOSA, AMADOR. After losing a team of five men, Amador Barbosa refused to continue sending soldiers to the shores of Normandy to clear the mines before the invasion on D-Day. Instead, the sergeant told his superiors if any other mines needed to be cleared, he would do it himself.

Amador Barbosa

Date of Birth
26 OCTOBER 1921
Kansas City, MO

Interviewed by
Manny López
3 AUGUST 2003
Kansas City, MO

WWII Military Unit
112th Engineer
Combat Battalion

"I can't tell others to get killed," he said, even though he was faced with a demotion for defying superior officers. "I can live without the stripes, but I cannot live with this."

Barbosa was stripped of his title, given the rank of private 1st class and ordered to continue preparing for the invasion. His duty was to take loads of explosives to the shore. He recalled the cold, turbulent waters when he waded through with a single life preserver and a load of TNT.

"It seemed like hours and hours," Barbosa said of the trek to the shore at Omaha Beach. "All the dead soldiers floating in the sea as you're going in. ... That didn't help any."

His motivation came from the explosives strapped to his back. "I really just wanted to get rid of that thing!" he said.

Danger was constant during Barbosa's tour of duty. He remembers forcing his way into a burning trailer full of grenades and bullets to remove the ordnance to prevent an explosion.

Even with the ever-present peril, Barbosa said he tried to remain resilient and positive to keep his spirits high. "You couldn't let it get the best of you; that didn't help and it might be worse."

He finally returned to his hometown of Kansas City, Mo., following his discharge on Oct. 26, 1945. He continued his work at a plastics factory, where he stayed until his retirement.

Barbosa married twice, first to Aura Perez and then Joann Hundley. He had two children, Florence and Edward. Barbosa became active in the American Legion and the Guard of Honor, which helps arrange military funerals.

Eduardo Botello

Date of Birth
19 MAY 1925
Laredo, TX

Interviewed by
Xochitl Salazár
9 OCTOBER 2003
Austin, TX

WWII Military Unit
Company C,
1st Battalion,
313th Infantry
Regiment,
79th Infantry
Division

BOTELLO, EDUARDO. After he was wounded three times, Eduardo Botello's combat days ended, but not before he had crossed France to participate in the invasion of Germany. He scaled dikes, dug foxholes and trekked 15 miles a day through the French countryside between hospital stays.

Raised in Laredo, Texas, Botello went to work at age 17, following the death of his father, Anastacio. He attended classes at Martin High School part-time, and worked at Herring-Price Lumber Co. to help support his mother Abelina and five siblings.

Botello was drafted on Sept. 7, 1943, and assigned to the 79th Infantry Division following basic training at Camp Phillips, Kan. He was one of two Mexican Americans in his company of 200. Though he was sometimes called derogatory names, he said he was "just like any other soldier."

On June 12, 1944, his company landed at Utah Beach in France. After he survived a collapsing house, Botello's final, combat-ending injury came in Duisenberg, Germany. When a mortar round exploded nearby, he suffered a severe concussion.

"I had blood coming out of my ears, mouth and nose," he said.

He was assigned to a military government office in Germany, where he worked for five months until his discharge on December 23, 1945.

He earned his high school diploma in 1946 and spent two years studying accounting.

He decided to leave college and returned to public service, working for the U.S. Customs Office for 40 years. He worked at the U.S.-Mexican border and in 1972 he was part of one of the largest drug seizures at Laredo, Texas, earning him the Sustained Superior Performance Award.

In 1950 he married Carlota Perez, and the couple had five children, Eduardo Jr., Ruben, Carlos, Nydia and Marissa. All of his children graduated from college.

Manuel Martinez Castillo

Date of Birth
3 AUGUST 1922
Austin, TX

Interviewed by
Chandler Race
14 OCTOBER 1999
Austin, TX

WWII Military Unit
Company C,
60th Infantry
Regiment,
9th Infantry
Division

CASTILLO, MANUEL MARTINEZ. After shrapnel was lodged into his helmet during fighting in Belgium, Manuel Castillo was unsure if he could recover. But the valiant actions of a fellow soldier saved his life, something Castillo remembered some 60 years later. After Castillo was hit, the other soldier dragged Castillo to safety while the battle raged on, and later returned to the trench to bring Castillo back to his company.

"He told me his name but he was in another part of the company," Castillo said of the man who saved his life. "I never got to talk to him. He took me back ... those are some of the things you never forget."

Castillo was temporarily blinded by his injury and spent time in hospitals in Europe, Staten Island, New York and Los Angeles. He credits the Veterans Administration in Waco, Texas, and the diligent care of his second wife, Velia, for his recovery.

Castillo was drafted in 1942 and left for Europe the same year. His barge made landfall at Omaha Beach on June 10, 1944, and from there he traveled through France to Belgium. He participated in direct combat in Belgium, and assisted in the capture of nearly 30 German prisoners of war before he sustained his combat-ending injury on Oct. 13, 1945. Following his formal medical discharge in June 1945, he returned to Texas where he began working as a house painter, and later segued into tile work, a job that allowed him to collaborate with his relatives.

Castillo credits his war experience with opening his eyes and teaching him an array of things about himself and the world. "I, myself, learned a lot of things that, if I would have stayed, had not gone into the service, I don't think I would have learned," he said.

He married Margaret Ramirez and later Velia Ledezma, with whom he shared much of his life.

CERVANTES, VALENTINO "SMOKEY." One of eleven siblings born to a father who pressed his children to graduate high school, Valentino "Smokey" Cervantes was married and working at a shipyard in Houston, Texas, when the war interrupted his life. Cervantes left behind his wife, Rosemary Yramateguer, two sons—his youngest was born 13 years later—when his draft notice came to their home on Aug. 18, 1944.

Though he'd never been away from home and assumed he was the only Hispanic in his company, Cervantes got along well with the men in his unit. The 801st Tank Destroyer Battalion landed at Normandy with the 4th Infantry Division and fought in the Battle of the Bulge with the 99th Infantry Division. It later supported the 30th and 83d Infantry Divisions and ended the war with the 13th Armored Division.

On an M1 Tracked Recovery Vehicle, Cervantes picked up disabled half-tracks—lightly armored military vehicles—after each battle. Once, a bomb fell 20 yards away from his vehicle while the company was crossing the Ruhr River in Germany.

"We heard the whistling sound, but we couldn't move. We just had to wait until the bomb hit," he said, "That's the closest I ever came to getting hit."

Cervantes spent 13 months in Germany before he was sent home in February 1946.

"It's terrible. War is not funny," he said, "They glorify it on TV, but it's not like that when you see your buddies all shot up; it's different. I saw a lot of dead soldiers. We would always move forward to different towns, and when we got there, the bodies were still on the ground, all shot up."

Cervantes earned the Sharpshooter's Medal for the 45 mm pistol. Though he would never want to repeat it, his war experience was one he "wouldn't trade for the world."

Valentino "Smokey" Cervantes

Date of Birth
13 FEBRUARY 1920
Houston, TX

Interviewed by
Celina Moreno
3 MARCH 2002
Houston, TX

WWII Military Unit
Headquarters Company, 801st Tank Destroyer Battalion

CORREA, MARGARITO. Even after grueling combat in Europe, Margarito Correa was ready to fight in the Pacific Theater, eager to see more of the world.

"Me and three other Mexicans signed up to go fight in Japan," he said. "But we received notice the war has ended. I wanted to go fight again to see how it was over there. I wasn't afraid. I liked it."

His battalion landed in Normandy and there Correa used his skills as a gunner to protect members of the infantry, firing at airplanes.

As his battalion moved through the countryside toward Germany, they fended off enemy forces. At one point, before crossing the Rhine River, Correa became trapped in a small Belgian town where food and gasoline were dropped from planes. Correa remembers the leaflets dropped by the Germans, full of brutal images and harsh words.

"The German would drop papers saying 'You'll never get to see your father again,' " he said.

Correa remembered the day he was drafted. His father delivered the draft letter to him while he was working on the railroad in Pflugerville, Texas.

"I threw aside the pickaxe and shovel, and off I went," he said. "I was never afraid to go. I wanted to go to another country."

Correa and his company eventually reached Germany, and he was there when he received news the war had ended. His division was in combat for 147 consecutive days during his time in Europe. He was discharged on November 29, 1945.

After the war, he returned to central Texas. He married his first wife, Celia Perez, in 1946. They later divorced, and Correa married Eva Salazar. Correa has six children and stepchildren: Ruth, Margarito Jr., Roberto, Pete, Serefino and Josie.

Margarito Correa

Date of Birth
21 NOVEMBER 1920
Pflugerville, TX

Interviewed by
Ismael Martinez
20 AUGUST 2002
Round Rock, TX

WWII Military Unit
Battery D, 377th Coast Artillery Battalion

Fred Davalos

Date of Birth
26 JANUARY 1925
Clovis, NM

Interviewed by
Maggie Rivas-
Rodriguez
2 NOVEMBER 2002
Albuquerque, NM

WWII Military Unit
551st Parachute
Infantry Regiment

Transferred to
887th Engineer
Company

Transferred to
517th Parachute
Infantry Regiment
Combat Team

DAVALOS, FRED. Even with his eye gouged out by shrapnel, Fred Davalos realized many others were more severely wounded, and walked a mile through the dismal Rhineland back to camp for treatment.

"I didn't want to take up any space, so I chose to walk," Davalos said. "I could barely see anything, and it was 2 o'clock in the morning."

The injury cost him his eye. Davalos returned to complete his tour of duty after an operation in Paris. "I was going to go back into combat," he said. "They told me that since I still had one eye, I could do it."

Davalos fought in Sicily with the 551st Parachute Infantry Regiment and the 887th Engineer Company during the invasion of France and with the 517th Parachute Infantry Regiment Combat Team at the Battle of Ardennes.

He said he was primed for the difficulties of war by the poverty of his youth. Davalos left school after the ninth grade to help support his family.

"We were poor," he said. "I got tired of wearing the same clothes every day. I came from a large family, and feeding us was hard for our parents."

Drafted in 1943 while working as a bellman in his native Clovis, N.M., Davalos was one of five sons in his family, each of whom served in the military. Davalos left New Mexico for the first time to train in Texas, Georgia and North Africa before he entered combat in Sicily.

Davalos was discharged on Jan. 16, 1946. He then returned to Clovis, marrying Sophie Olona in 1951. The couple had five children: Ella, Fred Jr., David, Donald and Arthur. Davalos continued in government service, working as a clerk in the U.S. Postal Service until his retirement.

Johnnie W. Flores

Date of Birth
10 FEBRUARY 1910
Somerset, TX

Tribute Provided by
Fred A. Flores
(Nephew)

WWII Military Unit
Company B,
36th Armored
Infantry Regiment,
3d Armored
Division

FLORES, JOHNNIE W. The fifth of seven children born to José María and Teresa Huizar Flores near San Antonio, Johnnie W. Flores was working in Los Angeles when he was drafted in 1941. After his unit left for Liverpool, England on Sept. 5, 1943, José and Teresa never saw their son again.

"My generation is the last to have seen or known Johnnie, though only through short, fleeting, youthful memories," said Fred Flores, Johnnie's nephew, who was 7 when news of his uncle's death came. "It is for this reason that I have gathered all that I could of Johnnie's life, to provide it for the next generations of this family."

In affectionate letters to his parents and sister, Stella F. McGee, Johnnie sent his regards, asked for family news and made sure they had received the money he wired home. One letter is dated June 25, 1944—the day he and the 3d Armored Division landed in Normandy.

"[France is] very green and beautiful but most of the towns are destroyed flat to the ground by bombs and heavy shelling," Johnnie wrote in August 1944. "It's terrible for these French people and all of us but it has to be done to drive the Germans out."

On Sept. 1, 1944, Johnnie was shot in the left hand while fighting in Belgium and spent the month in a hospital. He rejoined his outfit in Germany in October. On the morning of December 12, they invaded the towns of Echtz and Hoven, and Johnnie died in combat. It wasn't until Dec. 31, 1944 that a telegram arrived in Poteet, Texas, to inform Johnnie's parents that he was missing in action.

"As far as anyone was concerned, he was gone," Fred wrote, "I recall all of us going to grand-mother's house. I remember her crying pretty much nonstop."

Their fears were confirmed some days later. Johnnie was buried first in Belgium and in 1947 was re-interred at Fort Sam Houston in San Antonio.

GALINDO, JOSÉ. Relying heavily on the power of faith and prayer, José Galindo found ways to bear the intense strain of war. He prayed each night before sleeping, and he said that this truly helped alleviate the fear associated with combat.

José Galindo

Date of Birth
3 MAY 1919
Carerada, Mexico

Interviewed by
Lisa Cummings
21 OCTOBER 1999
Austin, TX

WWII Military Unit
982d Ordnance
Depot Company

"I remember when we got on this English boat getting ready to go on the invasion," he said. "I knelt down and prayed to the good Lord."

Born in Mexico, Galindo moved to Austin, Texas, in 1921. He graduated from Austin High School in 1938, one of only two Mexican Americans in his class. He enrolled in the College of Fine Arts at the University of Texas at Austin, but interrupted his education when he enlisted in the Army.

He received training in Scotland and eventually participated in the invasion of Normandy. The ties that developed among the soldiers helped him through the long days and lonely nights. He never felt he was treated differently or unfairly within his company.

"Actually when it came down to the brass tacks, we were all one family," he said.

His passion for music, which he studied before he left for the war, allowed him to bond with other musicians in his company. He also remembers playing baseball and horseshoes in his free time.

Despite the family he was growing close to overseas, nothing could replace the happy, comfortable home life he had left behind. When he was discharged on Dec. 25, 1945, he was thrilled to return home in time for a special Christmas dinner.

After the war, Galindo married a teacher. Emma H. Galindo Elementary School in South Austin is named after her. Galindo remembered Emma's work to get bilingual education implemented in local schools. They had one son, Joseph Paul, and shared 26 years together. After Emma's death, Galindo married Norma Govea. He worked in the tortilla business until his retirement in 1999.

GAMEZ, CIPRIANO. On the eve of D-Day, paratrooper Cipriano Gamez was dropped off-target and spent five days searching for his regiment with only a small box of food to sustain him while he wandered through the French countryside. Hidden enemy forces compounded the uncertainty and confusion he faced alone.

Cipriano Gamez

Date of Birth
15 DECEMBER 1922
Belmont, IA

Interviewed by
William Luna
9 MAY 2002
Highland, IN

WWII Military Unit
508th Parachute
Infantry Regiment

Transferred to
Company A,
342d Infantry
Regiment,
86th Infantry
Division

"It was terrible because there are a ton of hedge walls and the Germans had already taken over the entrances and exits," Gamez said. "Once I found my way back, I spent 31 days on the line."

Gamez was one of only six in his platoon of 30 who survived. He was promoted to staff sergeant and continued on to invade the Netherlands on Sept. 17, 1944. The 508th Parachute Infantry Regiment was dropped north of the Rhine River to secure the bridge at Arnhem. German armored units were waiting for them, and only 2,500 of the 10,000 men managed to escape across the Rhine. During this operation, Gamez was wounded when he encountered a group of Germans. He spent two weeks in the hospital recovering from a wound to his left arm. Soon after his release from the hospital, Gamez began a journey to Belgium for the Battle of the Bulge. His regiment was assigned to take the Thierdu-mont Ridge.

"After the ridge was taken, we were sent to look for the wounded," he said. "I have never known so much fear. It was terrible slaughter for us and most of the men were dead or frozen."

Though he had trained to liberate prisoners, he was rotated home to the States. He was discharged on Nov. 9, 1945. He married Carmen Negrette in 1946 and the couple had two children, Dwight and Richard. Following his first wife's death in 1985, Gamez married Esperanza Teserina who had three children: John, Lou and Mary. He worked at a steel mill in Indiana as a foreman until his retirement.

Pablo B. Gonzales

Date of Birth
26 JULY 1921
D'Hanis, TX

Interviewed by
Jeffrey K. Watanabe
19 OCTOBER 2002
Saginaw, MI

WWII Military Unit
30th Infantry
Division

GONZALES, PABLO B. A strong faith kept Pablo Gonzales focused and steady during the hectic fighting at Normandy. He remembered the shock of guns firing and soldiers dying, something his previous training left him unprepared to face.

"In maneuvers, people do not get shot, but with the battalion, you hear guns going off," he said. "The main thing on my mind was my faith in God. I thought if these college kids and *gueros* [whites] were ready to sacrifice their life for their country, then I was ready, too."

After his older half-brother enlisted, Gonzales' mother was reluctant to have another son join the armed forces. Gonzales decided to wait to be drafted, despite his desire to enlist. In December 1942, he was called to serve. He soon left for Boston and finished training in England, before charging the shores of Normandy.

He fought in the Battle of the Bulge and for his efforts in that battle, earned a Silver Star. His unit defended a bridge against German Panzers and successfully destroyed four tanks.

On January 28, 1945, Gonzales earned the rank of sergeant and became a tank destroyer commander.

"It was an honor as a Mexican to become a tank commander. It made me feel prouder," he said.

He was discharged on October 31, 1945, and left the service with a Purple Heart for wounds he sustained in Holland.

Returning home to Michigan, Gonzales began working for General Motors. He married Nicolasa Contreras in 1946. The couple had seven children. After his retirement, Gonzales was involved in the music industry and was an active member of the American Legion Post 500, having served as post commander eight times.

Julian Gonzalez

Date of Birth
16 FEBRUARY 1917
Edinburg, TX

Interviewed by
Nancy Acosta
13 OCTOBER 2000
San Antonio, TX

WWII Military Unit
Company F,
2d Battalion,
9th Regiment,
2d Infantry Division

GONZALEZ, JULIAN. Proud of his dual heritage, Julian Gonzalez wrote "Viva Mexico" on the playground during elementary school, but also jumped at the chance to serve his adopted country during WWII. His military journey led him through the ranks and around the world, from the castles of Belfast, Ireland, to the shores of Normandy.

Gonzalez was initially motivated by emotion; he remembered his reaction to Pearl Harbor.

"I was real mad, and, I don't know, I was excited," he said. "I wanted to go in and fight."

Gonzalez arrived in Ireland in October 1943 and began a grueling seven-month training session to prepare for the invasion of Normandy.

Landing at Omaha Beach one day after D-Day, Gonzalez's regiment was assigned to destroy hedgerows in the French countryside, as the hedges provided excellent cover for German snipers. As a staff sergeant, he led his men through dangerous, mine-ridden fields as they disabled sniper points. He often charged ahead of his men, hurling grenades at enemy targets to ensure the safety of his soldiers.

He eventually sustained major injuries when he detonated a land mine coming back from a patrol. He lost toes and shrapnel riddled his leg. He was treated by doctors on the front line and sent to England to recover. He later received the Distinguished Service Cross, the military's second highest honor, for his service.

At war's end, Gonzalez returned to south Texas, where he met and married his first wife, Severa Treviño. Gonzalez began a career in home remodeling. Following the death of Severa from tuberculosis, he married Rose de Rosa, and helped raise her two children. The couple later had three children of their own: Nancy, Chris and Larry.

GUERRA, HENRY MARTINEZ. From the fields of West Texas to the beaches of Normandy, Henry Guerra fought adverse conditions to succeed. He spent much of his young life under the scorching Texas sun, picking cotton, spinach and radishes, and later participated in some of the most gruesome battles of WWII.

Guerra left school to help support his family. A year later he was drafted and in November 1940, he was inducted into the Army as an infantry soldier. After training at Camp Bullis, Texas, Fort Sam Houston, Texas, and Camp McCoy, Wis., Guerra was then deployed to Europe, landing near Belfast, Ireland. He landed on Omaha Beach on June 7, 1944, the day after D-Day.

He remembered hearing the order from Eisenhower over the radio, and preparing to invade France. As they approached the shore, soldiers were told to keep their heads down, but some disobeyed orders to gaze out toward the shore.

The troops saw explosions and carnage everywhere as they approached the beach.

Normandy, however, was only the beginning, and Guerra continued fighting with the 38th Infantry Regiment until the war's end.

Guerra kept a journal detailing his service. Though filled with horrific, graphic images of death and destruction, a Bible passage urging faith and love is on the cover. Memories of the war haunted Guerra well into his civilian life.

He was discharged in June 1945, with a Purple Heart, three Bronze Stars and a host of other medals.

He returned to Texas and earned his GED. He then began a career in civil service. He worked as a storekeeper and later as an industrial engineer.

Henry Martinez
Guerra

Date of Birth
5 MAY 1923
Kennedy, TX

Interviewed by
Brenda Sendejo
6 NOVEMBER 2004
San Antonio, TX

WWII Military Unit
Company L,
38th Infantry
Regiment,
2d Infantry
Division

JUAREZ, ANASTACIO PEREZ. From the cotton fields of Staples, Texas, to the battlefields of Europe, Anastacio Juarez's life led him to all corners of the world, but his heart always remained with his family. During his service, he regularly wrote letters to his future wife, Rafaela Navarro, and kept a photo of her tucked in his wallet as he trudged through Italy and France.

Drafted in January 1942, Juarez trained in Missouri, Louisiana and New Jersey before he set sail for Europe. He remembered having to overcome a deficiency in English to succeed in the military. During his basic training, Juarez spent 30 days practicing commands after dinner, so he could keep up with the other soldiers. His unwavering dedication paid off, eventually earning him the rank of corporal.

Juarez's and the 177th Signal Replacement Company—attached to the 3d Infantry Division—invaded the south of France in Aug. 15, 1944. Juarez reached the beaches and jumped into water that reached his neck. Even with the mounting fear and uncertainty during the frenzied invasion, Juarez was always mindful of his patriotic duty. "I can't tell you that we were never afraid, or that a person doesn't cry," he said. "But you do what you have to do."

Juarez was discharged on Oct. 8, 1945, and returned to the States. He married Rafaela, and the couple had eight children: Mary Alice, Susana, Josefina, Ramon, Gilberto, Rosemary, Irma and Eduardo. Juarez stressed the importance of education to his children, and all eight pursued post-secondary degrees or certifications.

When he returned to Texas, Juarez chose to stop farming, instead taking a job at the Kelly Air Force Base in San Antonio, Texas. There he worked as a mechanic for 10 years, and later spent 20 years as an aircraft sheet metal worker.

Anastacio Perez
Juarez

Date of Birth
2 MAY 1918
Staples, TX

Interviewed by
Alicia Perez
30 JUNE 2000
San Antonio, TX

WWII Military Unit
177th Signal
Replacement
Company

Transferred to
563d Signal
Company,
63d Infantry
Division

Gilbert Lopez

Date of Birth
30 SEPTEMBER 1919
Azusa, CA

Interviewed by
Jack Steingart
28 AUGUST 2002
Los Angeles, CA

WWII Military Unit
114th Infantry
Regiment,
44th Infantry
Division

LOPEZ, GILBERT. Despite the discrimination and racism he faced in his youth, including segregated sections in movie theaters and signs reading "No Mexicans or dogs allowed," Gilbert Lopez was proud to defend his country.

He asked himself why he fought for a country that practiced discrimination. "Is this what I am going over there giving up my life for? And die for these kinds of people?

"But then I thought 'Well all these people are not bad, there are good people.'"

When he was drafted in 1944, Lopez was already a married man with three children; Gilbert Jr., Eileen and Susan. His wife, Jennie Padilla, remained at home raising the children while he served.

Initially stationed at Camp Robertson, Ark., Lopez was given permission to leave training when his daughter became seriously ill.

He eventually landed in France in September 1944, and then continued on to Frankfurt, Germany, and Austria. His responsibilities in the regiment included rifle handling and transporting and carrying ammunition.

In Austria, four days before the war's end, a bullet from his own men ended Lopez's time in combat. A miscommunication about the password in a foxhole led to a bullet to the thigh for Lopez. He was taken to a hospital, where he encountered a surprise: his brother, Roger, was in the same hospital, being treated for a concussion.

Lopez was discharged in 1946 and built a house in Irwindale, Calif. He used the GI Bill to attend shoe repair school and welding school and later focused primarily on construction work. Lopez and his wife had four more children: Evelyn, John, Monica and Robert.

José Ángel Lopez

Date of Birth
18 JULY 1924
Jourdanton, TX

Interviewed by
Rea Ann Trotter
5 JANUARY 1996
Houston, TX

WWII Military Unit
80th Infantry
Division

LOPEZ, JOSÉ ÁNGEL. After experiencing the horrors of war firsthand, José Ángel Lopez stowed many of the memories of hellish combat in the back of his mind, but never forgot the valuable lessons he learned during his service.

Lopez enlisted in the Army in 1941 and began training, first at Camp Forrest, Tenn., and later at Camp Phillips, Kan., before completing maneuvers in Arizona and California. He reported to Fort Dix, N.J., in July 1944 and boarded the *Queen Mary*, bound for Northwich, England.

The 80th Division arrived on the shores of Normandy on August 3, 1944. After landing at Utah Beach, the division continued through Europe, participating in campaigns in Northern France, the Rhineland and Ardennes.

As he began combat in the Battle of the Bulge, he remembered worrying that each day on the front lines might be his last.

"It's a terrible thing going into battle thinking, 'Maybe this will be it,'" he said. "Don't be afraid to say you are afraid because you will be afraid in life. Being afraid, that's what keeps you alive."

Lopez and his division began liberating concentration camps near the war's end. He remembered the gaunt faces of the prisoners inside the walls of the camps.

"They [the prisoners] just smiled when they saw us," he said. "All you could see was jaws and teeth, walking skeletons, nothing but bones and skin."

Lopez was discharged and returned to the States in 1946. He finished high school and then trained as a machinist, eventually opening his own machine shop.

Though he preferred not to revisit his memories of the war, he cherished the maturity he gained while serving his country.

LOPEZ, JOSÉ M. As an American who celebrated his Mexican heritage, decorated veteran José Lopez earned the highest military honors in both the United States and Mexico. He received the Medal of Honor in the States, and he was later awarded la Condecoración del Mérito Militar during his pilgrimage to the Basilica in Mexico City.

José M. Lopez

Date of Birth
10 JULY 1910
Veracruz, Mexico

Interviewed by
Manuel Medrano
6 OCTOBER 2001
San Antonio, TX

WWII Military Unit
Company K,
23d Infantry
Regiment,
2d Infantry
Division

"I prayed a lot to the Virgen de Guadalupe," Lopez said. "And she allowed me to succeed, and I finished with combat."

Lopez was a successful lightweight boxer when he met a group of men from the Merchant Marines after a match in Melbourne, Australia. He joined their ranks in 1936 and spent five years traveling to Pacific islands such as Fiji and Tahiti. He returned to Brownsville, Texas, in 1942 and married Emilia Herrera. That year, he was drafted and began basic training at Camp Roberts, Calif. He went to Europe, and landed at Omaha Beach on June 7, 1944, one day after D-Day.

On Dec. 17, 1944, Lopez demonstrated his bravery on the Belgian battlefield. He single-handedly shot 100 German soldiers, which allowed his company to construct a line of defense, while he kept the approaching troops at bay. This valiant act secured the Medal of Honor and a hero's welcome when he returned home.

"Oh boy, they gave me a welcome! I met the mayor, the Italian guy," Lopez said, referring to famous New York Mayor Fiorello LaGuardia.

He moved to San Antonio to work as a contact representative for the Veteran's Administration.

Lopez volunteered in the Korean War, retrieving the bodies of fallen soldiers. However, when President Harry S. Truman discovered Lopez was overseas again, he ordered him home.

Lopez has five children and stepchildren: Candida, Virginia, Maggie, Beatrice and Juanito.

MARINO, JOHNNIE. In October 1940, an overwhelming desire to serve his country motivated Johnnie Marino to give a false birth date to enlist without parental approval. Three days later, he left for Fort Sam Houston, Texas.

Johnnie Marino

Date of Birth
24 JUNE 1922
Colorado City, TX

Interviewed by
Paul R. Zepeda
22 MAY 2001
Houston, TX

WWII Military Unit
Service Battery,
38th Field Artillery
Battalion,
2d Infantry
Division

In October 1943, Marino left for Europe on an uneasy voyage. His ship dodged German U-boats as it crossed the Atlantic. "I swore I'd never get into a boat again," Marino said.

He landed at Omaha Beach in the third wave of troops. His landing craft stopped 250 feet from the shore, forcing the troops to wade to shore. The chaos was compounded by the German's high position on the bluffs, allowing the enemy forces excellent aim.

"They told us, 'If you see someone hit or is laying there, don't stop. If you stop, you're going to be with him,' " he said. "We were like sitting ducks."

Afterward, Marino fought in the Battle of the Bulge, and drove a truck in Operation Red Ball Express, to re-supply the Army. At one point during a drive, he stepped out of his truck to stretch and watched as a German rocket tore through the doors of his truck just moments later.

"We were pretty shaken up after that," he said.

Adding to the horrors of war Marino witnessed were the concentration camps of Hadamar and Belsen. On May 8, 1945, Marino was in Pilsner, Czechoslovakia, when he received word that the war had ended. He later returned to the States.

He married his first wife, Mamie Cavazos, in October 1945. He later married Josephine Gonzalez in 1965. Marino had five children: Gloria, Esther, John, Jon and Jason. He worked as a truck driver, and eventually a supervisor of South West Freight, Inc. until his retirement.

Luis Martinez

Date of Birth
19 AUGUST 1915
Laredo, TX

Interviewed by
Nicole Cruz
28 SEPTEMBER 2002
Laredo, TX

WWII Military Unit
362d Fighter
Squadron,
357th Fighter Group,
8th Air Force

MARTINEZ, LUIS. The Civilian Conservation Corps jump-started Luis Martinez's passion for the military, which would eventually lead him to the invasion at Normandy.

"I took part in D-Day—the longest day in history, they call it," he said. "It was June the sixth. I don't forget that. It was my wife's birthday, too."

Martinez met and married his English wife, Kathleen Maud Feeke, while serving overseas.

"It was one of those things," he said. "We danced, and we got friendly, and we started seeing each other. We finally agreed to marry."

In addition to finding the love of his life while serving in Europe, Martinez found considerable success as a soldier, and excelled in his work repairing vehicles and serving in the Army's fire department.

After D-Day, Martinez served as part of the American occupation in Germany. While there, he attended the funeral of General George Patton.

When he was discharged in 1946, Martinez had earned the rank of corporal. He stayed an active member of the Army Reserves for 25 years, but was never called to duty again.

Following the war, Martinez and his wife settled in Martinez's hometown of Laredo, Texas. The couple had seven children: Teresa, Luis, Robert, Richard, Chester, George and Brenda. Four served in the military.

Martinez attended community college, becoming a refrigeration specialist. He opened his own air-conditioning business in 1980. His wife ran the L&K grocery store, named for the couple's first initials, until her death in 2000. Martinez continued to work with his local chapters of the American Legion and VFW and served as a commander in both organizations.

Tomás Martinez

Date of Birth
21 DECEMBER 1923
La Mesa, NM

Interviewed by
Marcello Salcido
1 APRIL 2001
Penn Valley, CA

WWII Military Unit
261st Medical
Battalion,
1st Engineer
Brigade

MARTINEZ, TOMÁS. Constantly putting the needs of wounded soldiers before his own, Army medic Tomás Martinez sometimes went as far as to disobey orders to help his fellow soldiers. He said that during combat, instinct dictated his response.

"When you're in combat ... you weren't afraid of anything," Martinez said. "As long as you know what to do, orders don't really mean much to you."

Martinez was wounded during the D-Day invasion, when his landing craft hit a water mine and was blown in half. After 2 1/2 months of rehabilitation in an English hospital, Martinez rejoined his unit. He tended to wounded men by day and often volunteered for additional shifts of nighttime watch to prove he wasn't "a chicken" to his Anglo counterparts.

Martinez was wounded again during a drive to cut off a major supply route highway between France and Germany. This time shrapnel was lodged in his knee. He spent three weeks recovering and again rejoined his unit. During combat at the Battle of the Bulge, Martinez was wounded for the third time.

"The infantry was withdrawing, when I and the crew of medics went to pick up the wounded left behind," he said. "... A piece of shrapnel hit me inside the arm near the elbow, sending me to the hospital for three weeks."

Martinez was discharged on Sept. 28, 1945. He returned to his hometown but soon left for Los Angeles and then northern California, where he found a job picking grapes. There, he met his wife, Celia Salcido, with whom he had three children: Vivian, Chris and Tommy.

Martinez then put himself through barber school and went on to own a grocery store and build a home for his family, a testament to his pride in being a self-made man.

MEJÍA, MANUEL SALAZAR. Enlisting at age 18, during his sophomore year of high school, Manuel Mejía began his military career at Fort Benning, Ga., a career that would take him across the Atlantic as a paratrooper in the 82d Airborne Division.

Raised in Kansas City, Kan., by Mexican parents, Mejía was a voracious reader in his youth. He used newspapers to track the war in Europe and the military careers of friends. In 1942, Mejía began his own list of military achievements, which culminated with a promotion to staff sergeant.

After basic training, Mejía received jump training at Fort Bragg, N.C., and maneuver training in Yuma, Ariz. He left from New York harbor, landing in Belfast, Ireland 14 days later. He completed training in Nottingham, England.

Mejía's first mission was to jump behind enemy lines and disable "pillboxes," gun emplacement surrounded by concrete and steel. Their pilot miscalculated the jump, and Mejía and his men landed in an apple orchard. There, Mejía used aluminum noisemakers to round up his men. The troops continued and destroyed six pillboxes that day.

"We beat the daylights out of them," Mejía said. "We climbed on top of that [pillbox] and started throwing grenades inside of them holes."

Mejía then fought in the Battle of the Bulge, and was training troops in Munich when the war ended. He was discharged with two Presidential Citations.

Following the war, Mejía returned to Kansas City in March 1946. He married Beatrice Marie Muñoz in June of that year, and the couple had three children: René, Ronald and Bea Marie. He worked for the Simmons Mattress Co. for 45 years and was the chief inspector of the box spring department. He retired to Green Valley, Ariz.

MORALES, BENITO. After completing his basic training at Fort Sheridan, Ill., in 1943, Benito Morales was given a choice of the military branch he wanted to join. He selected the Army—a choice that would lead him to the beaches of France less than a year later.

Arriving a few days after D-Day, Morales reached Omaha Beach after German forces had been pressed inland. He could still hear the battles raging in the distance years later and he was thankful he completed his service unharmed.

"When I was going overseas, I thought I would never come back," Morales said. "I don't consider myself a hero. I consider myself lucky."

Though he downplayed his bravery, the military did not overlook his actions, awarding Morales the Bronze Star for assisting in the evacuation of 11 wounded soldiers at the Ludendorff Bridge in Germany. The certificate that accompanied his award explained that he helped the injured soldiers with no regard for his own safety.

Raised in South Texas and Chicago, Morales overcame discrimination at school, where students threw rocks at him and his six siblings.

Morales was forced to leave his classes to support his family during the Great Depression. He began working on farms, and later found a job in a large candy factory, where he was employed when his draft notice arrived.

Morales was discharged in November 1945 and returned to the Chicago area. He took a job at Sunbeam as a machine operator.

He married Frances Carica in 1950 and the couple had seven children: Rose, Rosy, Paula, Tom, Norma, Arlene and Felicia.

Manuel Salazar
Mejía

Date of Birth
4 APRIL 1925
Kansas City, KS

Interviewed by
Joe Olague
5 JANUARY 2003
Tucson, AZ

WWII Military Unit
80th Infantry
Division

Transferred to
102d Infantry
Division

Transferred to
82d Airborne
Division

Benito Morales

Date of Birth
9 JUNE 1923
Flatonia, TX

Interviewed by
William Luna
5 DECEMBER 2002
Cicero, IL

WWII Military Unit
39th Infantry
Regiment,
9th Infantry
Division

William R. Ornelas

Date of Birth
2 FEBRUARY 1924
Santa Ana, TX

Interviewed by
Maggie Rivas-
Rodriguez
25 OCTOBER 1999
San Antonio, TX

WWII Military Unit
101st Airborne
Division

ORNELAS, WILLIAM R. It was snowing when the train first dropped William Ornelas at Camp Grant, Ill., in April 1943. There, he started basic training. "I was used to hard work so I went through it real easy. We used to go march 30 miles with a full pack," Ornelas said.

One of seven brothers who served in WWII, Ornelas joined the Army and was initially trained to be a medic. Bored with the assignment, he volunteered to join the 101st Airborne Division as they were being shipped overseas and received paratrooper training after they reached England in September 1943. The 101st Airborne Division parachuted into Normandy behind Utah Beach on D-Day. They fought in Holland, Belgium and France and served in the occupation of Germany.

"All I wanted to do was come home. Get it over with and get back," Ornelas said.

After the war, he found work on a ranch and then on the railroad. "I decided, one day, that there was no future in that," he said. The GI Bill allowed him to attend the Brown County Vocational School in Texas, where he learned welding and woodworking.

With his new skills, Ornelas went to work for Convair, an aircraft company, and made twice as much as he had in previous jobs. His career as an aircraft mechanic included working on a Boeing B-52 and Navy rescue helicopters and a job at the International Airport in San Antonio, Texas.

"I worked on a lot of aircraft," he said, "I learned about an airplane from wing to wing, from the front to the rear. Anything they wanted, it could be done."

After joining the reserves to work at Kelly Air Force Base, Ornelas served in the Vietnam War for three months at the end of the conflict.

He married Carmen Benavides and they had five children: Rodolfo, Suzanne, Samuel, Jimmy and Deborah Ann.

Fernando I. Pagán

Date of Birth
16 DECEMBER 1921
Canóvas, PR

Interviewed by
Doralís Pérez-Soto
20 FEBRUARY 2003
San Juan, PR

WWII Military Unit
Company A,
293d Combat
Engineering
Battalion

PAGÁN, FERNANDO I. Arriving at Normandy four days after the D-Day invasion, Fernando Pagán saw the horrific remnants of the invasion firsthand.

"I saw dead paratroopers dangling from the trees," he said. "I saw mutilated corpses. ... They didn't have time to take them away."

Pagán was drafted in December 1942. During basic training, Pagán was selected to complete engineer training. He completed the training in Nashville, New Orleans, La.; and Virginia Beach, Va.; before leaving for Liverpool, England, in 1943.

He was assigned to the 293d Combat Engineer Battalion. The battalion built bridges across rivers and embankments to increase the flow of U.S. troops, and transported soldiers by the unit's two boats. They also played a crucial role in constructing different kinds of bridges for different purposes, usually infantry footbridges or pontoon bridges.

Pagán and his unit spent time in Paris, where he celebrated with the French; Belgium, where he encountered many grateful Belgians; and Germany, where U.S. soldiers were forbidden to interact with German citizens.

During his staying in Germany, Pagán had his closest call of the war.

"I was shot at by a sniper, and my truck saved me," he said.

The sniper's bullet became lodged in a piece of metal on the truck that served as a shield. Following the attack, Pagán completed his 18-month tour of duty, and returned to the States in 1945. He held a variety of jobs, from taxi driver to upholsterer to bartender.

He returned to his native Puerto Rico in 1967. He had a daughter, Denise, with his first wife. He had a second daughter, Eunice, with his wife Ruth, whom he married in 1983.

RAMIREZ, OSWALDO V. Trudging through the freezing waters toward Omaha Beach, Oswaldo Ramirez was surrounded by fallen soldiers. He survived the trek to the shore, and once on land, began to rescue soldiers who had been shot, dodging enemy fire as he risked his life to bring wounded men to safety.

Oswaldo V. Ramirez

Date of Birth
13 OCTOBER 1915
Mission, TX

Interviewed by
Robert Mayer
20 SEPTEMBER 2001
Austin, TX

WWII Military Unit
81-mm Mortar
Section,
16th Infantry
Regiment,
1st Infantry Division

"That experience was hell," Ramirez said. "It was a big mess."

Ramirez landed at the shores of Normandy when he was nearly 30 years old. He had already graduated from the University of Texas at Austin and was working as a mapmaker in McAllen, Texas, when he enlisted in 1941. He was originally told he would be working stateside in public relations. However, his assignment changed, and after training at Camp Roberts, Calif., Fort Benning, Ga., and Camp Howze, Texas, Ramirez left for Europe. He was assigned to the 16th Infantry Regiment.

After the landing at Normandy, Ramirez working with the 3d Battalion in the 16th Regiment as a liaison officer using his expertise with maps. "I had to contact division corps commanders, colonels, generals and find out the bigger picture," he said. "They liked my work because I was a good artist, I got good information and could communicate well."

Ramirez went on to fight in the Battle of the Bulge, where he was wounded. He was discharged with the rank of first lieutenant.

After the war, Ramirez used the GI Bill to attend Loyola College in New Orleans, and then focused his career on labor relations. His assignments allowed him, his wife, Lillian Hollingsworth, and their seven children—John, Paul, James, Margaret, Mary, Catherine and Barbara—to travel throughout Latin America, including Honduras, Panama and Cuba. After his retirement, Ramirez coordinated rosary services for inmates at Travis County (Texas) jails.

REYNA, ANTONIO "TONY" RAMOS. As a "clean up" man during the days after the D-Day invasion, Tony Reyna helped restore order to the villages and towns shaken by the fighting in Normandy and throughout the French countryside. He was eager to help others during his tour of duty, but also said that the experience abroad helped him expand his perspective.

Antonio "Tony"
Ramos Reyna

Date of Birth
17 JANUARY 1922
Austin, TX

Interviewed by
Matthew Trana
11 OCTOBER 2000
Austin, TX

WWII Military Unit
29th Infantry
Division

"I saw a lot of countries, I saw a lot of cultures," he said. "I learned one thing from that. There [are] good people anywhere and there [are] bad people too. You can't judge one for all of them."

Reyna was drafted on December 7, 1942. He completed basic training at Fort Benning, Ga., and later practiced maneuvers in Massachusetts and South Carolina. He was then shipped to Iceland and from there, traveled to Southampton, England; Liege, Belgium; and the shores of France.

He braved the beaches of Normandy, where he saw the shore littered with fallen soldiers, and continued to the Battle of the Bulge. In the battlefronts of Ardennes, miscommunication and the chaos of uncertainty reigned.

"Sometimes it [got] a little disorganized because they would bomb a place where you are," he said. "You don't know what to do right away."

After that battle, Reyna was transferred to Frankfurt, Germany, where he remained until the war's end. He was discharged on April 15, 1946, and remembers his homecoming as one of the happiest moments of his life.

Reyna met and married Connie Loera in 1948. The couple had six children: Carolina, Antonio Jr., Christina, Julianne, Mary Alice and Fernando. He found work as truck driver and later worked for Economy Furniture, initially as an assembler, and eventually rising through the ranks to supervisor in the shipping department.

Reginald Rios

Date of Birth
28 JULY 1925
Austin, TX

Interviewed by
Christopher Nay
20 FEBRUARY 2001
Austin, TX

WWII Military Unit
Company C,
314th Infantry
Regiment,
79th Infantry
Division

RIOS, REGINALD. In the freezing, damp foxholes of France, Reginald Rios fought as an infantryman, constantly on the front line, dodging bullets and firing rounds across the battlefield. In one particularly jarring moment in northern France in December 1944, U.S. Sherman tanks faced off against German Panzers. Rios watched helplessly as soldiers fell to enemy fire.

Rios had joined the Texas State Guard in 1941, but soon drafted. In 1942, he left his home state to prepare for his overseas assignments.

He trained at Camp Gruber, Okla., and Camp Phillips, Kan. In March 1944, Rios left for Manchester, England. While training in preparation for D-Day, he and the 79th Infantry Division came under nightly German bombings. After participating in the invasion at Normandy, Rios and his division fought across France. They participated in Operation Nordwind, the last German offensive, from Dec. 31, 1944, to Jan. 5, 1945. The division was relieved of battle duty four months later. "It was so pretty to see the Americans winning," Rios said. The war ended shortly after, and he was given security duties in small towns in Czechoslovakia.

At last, on Christmas Eve, 1945, Rios was put on a ship home. He spent six months in Monterrey and Nuevo Laredo, Mexico, with an uncle before returning to Austin, Texas, in June 1946. There, he started working for the Reynolds-Penland Department Store and used the GI Bill to attend classes at the Nixon-Clay Business School.

Rios became a successful tailor, retiring from the business in 1990. He married Amelia Riojas in 1956 and they had a daughter, Rosanna, in 1961. Rios was active in the Knights of Columbus, the Century Club and Our Lady of Guadalupe Church in Austin.

Mike Silva

Date of Birth
8 JULY 1924
Socorro, NM

Interviewed by
Violeta Dominguez
2 NOVEMBER 2002
Albuquerque, NM

WWII Military Unit
1674th Engineer
Detachment

SILVA, MIKE. The gruesome images of war engrained themselves permanently in Mike Silva's memory, some 50 years after he was discharged from the Army.

"I am still in the war now," he said. "How do you think it feels to see a head there, a leg there and pure blood in the water? It's haunting. I can't get it out of my head."

He enlisted in the Army and said that at the time, he was young and foolish.

"I wanted to go because I was a dummy," Silva said. However, he did not regret his decision, and said that if he lived his life a second time, he would still enlist.

After training at Fort Bliss, Texas, for six months, he was deployed to Europe. While the men knew the mission that lay ahead, a sense of playfulness and calm pervaded the voyage.

"On the ship, we talked and laughed," Silva remembered. "We were not thinking about the war."

However, the harsh realities of WWII came into sharp focus when he landed at the body-strewn beaches of Omaha.

Silva's life was spared when a bullet aimed at him struck another soldier, but close calls drove fear into Silva's heart. He remembers waking up one evening, terrified that all the other soldiers were dead, though they were only sleeping. The mental effects of the war stayed with Silva long after his discharge. However, the military helped him learn English and taught him lessons a classroom never could.

He returned to Albuquerque, N.M., where he married Betty Chavez in 1948. They had four children: Michael, William, Philip and Melissa.

Silva worked at Kirtland Air Force Base, in Albuquerque, N.M., and as a janitor. He was also active in the Knights of Columbus and American Legion.

TAFOYA, ARTHUR. As a medic on the front lines at Normandy, it was the hail of bullets, not the gory, sometimes morbid work, that Arthur Tafoya found most difficult.

"Bullets don't discriminate," he said. "It didn't matter that we had red crosses [on our uniform]. We were always under fire."

Drafted in 1943, Tafoya believed it was his duty to serve the country, and he left for Camp Barkeley, Texas, for basic training. When he arrived in England, Tafoya began training as a medical corpsman for three weeks in preparation of the invasion of France. He was assigned to the 393d Infantry Regiment.

"We were on the front line and dealt with injured soldiers on the spot," he said.

Tending to soldiers on the front lines, he learned to dodge enemy fire, a skill that was useful on Christmas Day 1944, when he ran across the battlefield to claim a holiday lunch.

"We got our turkey," he said. "I hit the ground I don't know how many times, but I never let go of that turkey."

After fighting in France, Tafoya continued on to Frankfurt, Germany. There he sustained an injury that ended his tour of duty, when the jeep he was riding in overturned. He was discharged as a corporal and returned to the U.S. in 1945.

He enrolled in college, but re-enlisted in 1950 and served in the Korean War.

Tafoya later used his skills as a medic at the Pentagon in U.S. Army Dispensary for three years, before returning to Las Vegas, N.M., where he worked at the Las Vegas Medical Center. He stayed at the Medical Center for 33 years, eventually becoming the manager of the brain-retraining unit, working with patients who had suffered brain damage.

Arthur Tafoya

Date of Birth
24 OCTOBER 1924
Las Vegas, NM

Interviewed by
Norman L. Martinez
3 NOVEMBER 2002
Santa Fe, NM

WWII Military Unit
393d Infantry
Regiment,
99th Infantry
Division

TORRES, GILBERTO. A long scar running the length of Gilberto Torres' forearm serves as a reminder of his service in Europe during WWII. After landing at Normandy on June 19, 1944, he continued fighting in the war-torn French countryside until Aug. 7, 1944, when he sustained the injury that left the scar.

Before he was wounded, Torres trekked through swamps, minefield and rivers as his regiment moved through France. Though the country was known for its rich history and beautiful sights, Torres said that during the war, he saw a very different France.

"Nothing was beautiful in France," he said. "The whole place was a mess."

Torres was hit by machine gun fire outside the French city of St. Malo. While the injury was serious enough to end Torres' days in combat, he still counts himself lucky.

"I saw one of them [soldiers] with no arms or legs," he said. "Just a torso."

Torres was sent to hospitals in England; Charleston, S.C.; and El Paso, Texas before he was formally discharged from the Army on March 1, 1947, with the rank of corporal, a Purple Heart, Bronze Star and various other decorations.

He began working on farms in Texas before securing a position as a mechanic, a job he held for 17 years until his retirement in 1969. He married Olivia Reyna in 1949 and the couple had three children. They divorced and in 1971 Torres married Rosa Valencia, with whom he also had three children.

Torres became one of the first members of the G.I. Forum, aiding in the fight for equal rights for Mexican Americans. He has encouraged his grandchildren to take advantage of the opportunities that were lacking during his youth.

Gilberto Torres

Date of Birth
1 SEPTEMBER 1925
Brady, TX

Interviewed by
Israel Saenz
7 FEBRUARY 2004
San Angelo, TX

WWII Military Unit
Company B,
331st Infantry
Regiment,
83d Infantry
Division

David Pineda
Towns

Date of Birth
17 SEPTEMBER 1917
Eagle Pass, TX

Tribute Provided by
David Raphael
Towns (Son)

WWII Military Unit
237th Engineer
Combat Battalion

TOWNS, DAVID PINEDA. Letters from loved ones were the highlight of David Pineda Towns' tour of duty in Europe, a tour cut tragically short during fighting in France. His wife had even relayed the news via mail that his son, David, had been born.

"It's letters, and letters only, that bring up the morale of a soldier," Towns wrote to his wife, Lilia.

Serving as a platoon leader in the invasion of Normandy two days after D-Day, Towns was a fearless leader, confronting enemy forces head-on. His determination and tireless service led to a shot to the head that ended his life on the battlefields of France. He met German troops in the vicinity of St. Come du Mont (near Carentan), and it was there that he suffered his fatal wound.

Born in the small border town of Eagle Pass, Texas, Towns was one of eight children born to Pedro Towns and Luz Pineda. He was a fiery, energetic young man.

"His energy, vitality and love of life were outstanding. I wanted to imitate him in many ways," brother Pedro Towns said.

Towns was studying architecture at the University of Texas when the war began. Two days after the attack on Pearl Harbor, he withdrew from the University and enlisted in the Army. He completed his basic training at Camp Barkeley, Texas, and then received training as a medic at Fort Ord, Calif.

He traveled to Hawaii for more training and it was there that he was selected for Officers Candidate School. Towns trained with the U.S. Army School of Engineers at Fort Belvoir, Va., before leaving for Europe.

Towns' final letter was addressed to his sister, Ruth. In it, he wrote that if killed in battle, he would have no regrets because he had lived a full 27 years.

Dominick Tripodi

Date of Birth
21 NOVEMBER 1925
Los Angeles, CA

Interviewed by
Luz Villareal
23 MARCH 2002
Los Angeles, CA

WWII Military Unit
Company C,
20th Engineer
Combat Battalion

TRIPODI, DOMINICK. After the attacks of Sept. 11, 2001, Dominick Tripodi quickly volunteered to fight terrorism abroad. Though he was denied, at 76 years old, the U.S. Army applauded the unwavering patriotism of the decorated veteran.

Tripodi's military journey began in 1943, when he lied to enlistment officials about his age. At 17 years old, he was unwilling to wait another moment before beginning his service, and was inducted into the U.S. Army on Oct. 23, 1943. While training at Camp Roberts, Calif., he returned home on weekends, and his parents tried to persuade him to leave the military.

It was to no avail, and in April 1944, Tripodi left for Dover, England, and began preparing for the D-Day invasion. His unit was responsible for clearing land mines and unexploded ordnance to make way for ground troops. He remembered casting aside his heavy pack to make a run for shore, attempting to avoid the hail of bullets and moving to avoid falling to enemy fire.

After campaigns in France and Luxembourg, Tripodi was captured by German forces and taken as a POW. He hid a large wound in his shoulder as he trudged to the camp to avoid being killed. Tripodi and 16 others were held captive from December 1944 to May 1945. They lived in a 16x16-foot cage with a stove and a bucket for a restroom. Tripodi dropped to 98 pounds before he was freed by British troops.

"We were only given small amounts of potatoes to eat," Tripodi recalled. "You could feel lice biting your skin at night. It was such a horrible experience."

Tripodi was discharged on Nov. 23, 1945, after receiving treatment for the problems he experienced while a prisoner. He returned to California, and worked for a dairy in East Los Angeles. He married Evangelina Ayala on July 14, 1946. The couple had two children: Nancy and Gary.

URIEGAS, JOE MORENO. His unshakable Catholic faith sustained Joe Uriegas during his tour of duty in Europe, during which he fought in some of WWII's most dangerous battles. Uriegas regularly held Sunday Mass for soldiers, and constantly prayed for his fellow troops.

Drafted in 1942, Uriegas trained in Oklahoma and Georgia before departing for Europe. Over the shores of Normandy, Uriegas, sitting in a rickety, 38-ft.-long, plywood glider tethered to the back of a plane, was dropped into the battle.

"We were hooked on the back of the airplane like a trailer hooks to a car," he said. "I thought and still think the gliders are one of the stupidest things the U.S. ever came up with to fight a war with."

Immediately after landing, Uriegas, who had been promoted to staff sergeant, began to secure and sort rations that had been dropped along with the men. He also scouted the front lines for enemy positions, strategy and strength. The dangerous mission killed three of Uriegas' eight companions.

"I got scared all the time," he said. "I was thinking I would be next. You see men falling all over."

Uriegas was honorably discharged on Nov. 4, 1945, and returned to his young wife, Ysidra Avila, in Austin, Texas. The couple had a daughter, Mary Ellen.

He worked at the University of Texas for 35 years, retiring as inventory warehouse supervisor.

Uriegas became active in the Democratic Party, serving as a delegate to conventions at the local and state levels.

While the scars of war battered Uriegas mentally and he was plagued by nightmares, he again relied on his faith. He helped to establish the first Texas post of the Catholic War Veterans at St. Mary's Church in Austin, which later moved to San José Church in South Austin. The post still exists today and raises funds for its college scholarships for local students.

Joe Moreno
Uriegas

Date of Birth
1 JULY 1915
Oak Hill, TX

Interviewed by
Cody Morris
27 MARCH 2001
Austin, TX

WWII Military Unit
Service Battery,
188th Field
Artillery Battalion

VEGA, LAURO. On June 4, 1944, Lauro Vega and the members of his unit were given a delicious home-style meal of fried chicken, potatoes and gravy. An astute observation from one of the members of his regiment brought the reality of the meal to Vega's attention.

"It was a good meal—the best meal we had," he said. "A buddy of mine said, 'We're not getting this meal for nothing, I bet you we're gonna go to the invasion already.' By God, he was right."

During the invasion at Normandy, Vega's battalion gave anti-aircraft support to the 16th Infantry Regiment, 1st Infantry Regiment. He remembered the sea of men wading through the choppy ocean waters to approach the beach, and took comfort in the size of the invasion, with thousands of men hitting the beaches. "Before we landed you could look back and as far as your could see there was all kinds of landing crafts," Vega said. "I was just one of thousands of guys that were landing. I wasn't by myself and that way I didn't think anything could happen to me."

The son of Mexican immigrants, Vega left high school at 17 to join the Civilian Conservation Corps. There he earned $30 a month, $22 of which was immediately sent home to his family. He then began working for Consolidated Aircraft, helping to build B-24 bombers. In 1943, he was drafted, and in February of that year, he left for basic training. Because of his experience with bombers, he specialized in anti-aircraft training at Fort Bliss near El Paso, Texas.

He left for Europe in December 1944. Following D-Day, he continued through Europe, escaping death several times, including an instance when he suffered a concussion from an exploding shell. He was discharged in November 1945 and returned to California.

Vega worked in construction, carpentry and as a truck driver. He married Saturnina Villalobos in 1951 and the couple had five children: Angelica, Lauro, Daniel, Sonia and Francisco.

Lauro Vega

Date of Birth
12 APRIL 1923
National City, CA

Interviewed by
René Zambrano
8 OCTOBER 2000
Chula Vista, CA

WWII Military Unit
197th Anti-Aircraft
Artillery Battalion

Martín Vega

Date of Birth
10 FEBRUARY 1915
East Chicago, IN

Interviewed by
William Luna
20 JULY 2002
East Chicago, IN

WWII Military Unit
105th Combat
Engineer Battalion,
30th Infantry
Division

VEGA, MARTÍN. With an unshakable work ethic instilled in him during childhood, Martín Vega's tireless efforts during his military service were already second nature. Before the war he often rose at 4 a.m. to pick cotton with his father, and was always eager to work. He constantly looked for ways to assist his family financially.

"When I was 12 years old, I used to shine shoes," he said. "I'd go into pool halls, stores, taverns, asking to shoe shine."

Vega was working as a blacksmith when he was drafted in 1943. In his battalion, he was the only Latino, but said he was treated well by officers and fellow soldiers.

Four days after the D-Day invasion, Vega and his unit landed at Omaha Beach.

"Fortunately, I was not in the first, second or third wave," Vega said. "I was in the ninth wave."

After landing at Normandy, Vega continued through Europe, traveling through Belgium, the Netherlands, and Luxembourg before reaching Germany.

During fighting in Germany in Sept. 1944, Vega was wounded in the head and leg, and earned a Purple Heart. He was sent to England to recover and then returned to the battlefield in France.

He spent most of his remaining time in the service as a mechanic, a job that proved dangerous, as Vega spent his days on railroad tracks and trains. In efforts to hinder transportation of Allied troops and supplies, German forces often attacked the railroads.

"The train got bombed all to hell," Vega remembered. "We scattered like chickens. Luckily, it was hurting the cars and not the soldiers."

After his discharge on Aug. 8, 1945, Vega began working at a steel mill. He married Antonia Rivas on September 6, 1947. The couple had four children: Steve, Nora, Sandra and Annette.

Andres Ybarra

Date of Birth
16 AUGUST 1921
San Marcos, TX

Interviewed by
Shamiso Masowsue
8 DECEMBER 2002
Austin, TX

WWII Military Unit
29th Infantry
Division

YBARRA, ANDRES. Inexperienced in combat, Andres Ybarra was often terrified that each battle would be his last. He was so scared that he stopped sending letters home, deciding that bad news would be easier on his family if they had not heard from him recently. Unfortunately, his plan backfired, leading to an embarrassing encounter with the Red Cross.

"My aunt told my mother that the Red Cross could find out if something had happened to me," he said. "I was never more embarrassed then when the Red Cross tracked me down. They found my unit and made me sit down right there and write a letter home to say I was all right."

His family's concerns were warranted. Ybarra landed on the beaches of Normandy a few days after the initial D-Day invasion, and moved through France, Luxembourg, the Netherlands and Germany. He said that throughout the war he became desensitized to death, but he does not feel any less lucky to have made it back safely.

When the war ended, Ybarra was offered the opportunity to train as an officer. He refused the position, opting to return home with the rest of his company.

He remembered the warm welcome he received as his ship sailed into New York Harbor in early summer 1945.

"Everyone was celebrating and giving us a salute," he said.

Ybarra then enrolled at Southwest Texas State University and earned a bachelor's degree in history. He taught at schools throughout Texas for 33 years before retiring.

He wed Vilma Turnine. The two were married for 39 years. After his first wife's death, Ybarra remarried, this time to Margie Sandoval. Ybarra had five children: Virginia, Andy, Frank, Sandra and Juanita.

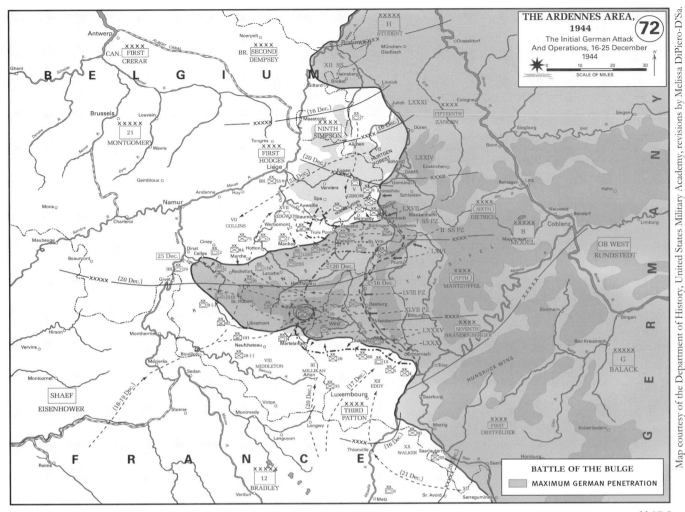

Map courtesy of the Department of History, United States Military Academy, revisions by Melissa DiPiero-D'Sa.

MAP 5

THE BATTLE OF THE BULGE

During the cruel, punishing winter of 1944, Adolf Hitler ordered a last gasp offensive that, had it been successful, would have split the Allies and allowed Germany to sue for terms more favorable than unconditional surrender.

The German attack would surprise the Allies, but Gen. Dwight D. Eisenhower, Supreme Allied Commander, was able to interpret the attack on the Ardennes, a region of Belgium and Luxembourg, on December 16, 1944, for what it was: a major offensive. Eisenhower quickly responded by marshalling forces to that area.

The Battle of the Bulge—so called because the German offensive had created a large bulge in the battleline—would become known as the toughest battle fought by the U.S. Army in WWII. During the Battle of the Bulge, two-thirds of the 106th Infantry Division were captured and the adjacent divisions were severely tested. The infantry weakness was corrected by the transfer of tens of thousands of soldiers from rear area support units. The soldiers of the 82d and 101st Airborne Divisions distinguished themselves fighting as light infantry. The Germans were defeated by a northward attack into their flank by Patton's 3d Army.

Hitler felt that if successful, the Ardennes Offensive would end the fighting in the West and allow Germany to move its military strength to the East in its war with Russia.

The German campaign to seize the strategically important port city of Antwerp and divide the Allied armies might have succeeded, but the German lead tank units could not be refueled. The Germans had expected to seize Allied fuel depots but were stopped short. When the weather cleared, allowing Allied air strikes and the dropping of supplies by parachute to surrounded Bastogne, the Germans' last Western front campaign was defeated.

It would last 41 days and cost 81,000 American casualties, including 19,000 killed and 15,000 captured. With far fewer men — 55,000 — the British had casualties of 1,400; including 200 men killed. The Germans, however, were thoroughly routed, with at least 100,000 casualties.

Among those who survived unhurt was Joe A. Arambula, a native of Bison, Okla., who recalls "complete chaos."

"We had a lot of casualties," said Arambula, who served with Company G, 110th Infantry Regiment, 28th Infantry Division. "I don't remember the names, but I recognized faces, and when we reorganized, they just weren't there."

Pete Dimas, of Ojito Frio, N.M., was serving with the 106th Infantry Division. Dimas arrived in France in early December and quickly boarded trucks en route to Luxembourg. On Dec. 16, he heard what he would later understand were "Screaming Meemies" rockets. "They seemed like they were tearing up the sky," Dimas said.

His company was captured and, as the men were led through a devastated city, someone sang *God Bless America*. "We kept on singing," he said. "We just wanted to let the Germans know we weren't licked yet."

Several of the men had already fought at Normandy before the Battle of the Bulge.

California native Alfred "Fred" Castro, with the 84th Division, 333d Infantry Regiment, was wounded at the Bulge when a land mine shattered his right knee. Castro was so disoriented, however, that he wasn't aware he was hurt until his finger sank into a gaping hole on his leg.

"I didn't get killed, by the [grace] of God. He just wants me to be here, that's it," Castro said.

It wasn't until two months later that Castro was able to get back to the United States where adequate facilities existed for his needed surgery, released on a medical discharge. His body twice rejected an artificial kneecap, so bolts were used to keep his leg together.

The Battle of the Bulge demonstrated the resolve of the Allied soldiers to ensure Germany's defeat. George Vasquez, a native of Texas, serving with the 106th Infantry Division, earned his Silver Star during the Battle of the Bulge for single-handedly destroying an enemy machine gun post.

Despite the overwhelming odds, compounded by weather and weakened troops, the Allies were able to successfully complete their counter attacks during the Battle of the Bulge. This victory was crucial to the Third Reich's defeat, and cleared the way for an Allied invasion on German soil. The Allies began sealing their victory in the European Theater.

ADAMÉ, JOSÉ "JOE" ERIBERTO. Despite the horrors of war he witnessed while fighting in Normandy, Joe Adamé remained patriotically committed to his country. "I would do it over again," he said. "If I were 18 years old, I would go fight for the United States."

Raised in El Paso, Texas, by Mexican parents, Adamé enlisted in the Army at age 20. He left for Europe in 1943—full of nervous anticipation and uncertainty—and trained in Liverpool, England. On June 29, 1944, his company's ship sprang a leak while crossing the English Channel with the rest of the 86th Chemical Mortar Battalion, and they had to turn around. They waited in England for two more weeks before landing in Normandy, where the destruction of D-Day was still evident.

"All those young men buried in Omaha Cemetery had no chance to learn what life was really about," he said, reflecting on his trip to Normandy for the 50-year anniversary of the battle.

Adamé's battalion fought across the Brittany peninsula to the Siegfried Line and participated in the Battle of the Bulge. They were in Bischofteinitz, Czechoslovakia, when the war ended.

Adamé was discharged in October 1945. After a warm welcome home at New York Harbor, Adamé returned to El Paso. He brought with him a new sense of discipline and independence along with an appreciation for his hometown and the family he left behind while serving.

He also saw changes in his home community with the adoption of the GI Bill.

"A lot of Latino war veterans started going to college," Adamé said. "It changed the whole setup of El Paso in a way, because more Hispanics were advancing."

In 1950, he married Ana Maria Arguelles. Proud of his dual heritage, he raised his family to speak English and Spanish. He also stressed the value of education to his children: María Christina, Irma, José, Eduardo, Antonio and Margarita. All six pursued degrees.

José "Joe"
Eriberto Adamé

Date of Birth
22 MARCH 1922
El Paso, TX

Interviewed by
Christina Perkins
8 DECEMBER 2001
El Paso, TX

WWII Military Unit
Company B,
59th Signal
Battalion

Transferred to
Company C,
86th Chemical
Mortar Battalion

ARAMBULA, JOE A. Unable to contain his patriotism, 17-year-old Joe Arambula tried to enlist in the armed forces, but his father refused to allow it.

"My dad wouldn't sign the consent form," Arambula remembered. "Because I was too young and didn't know what I was doing, so he said. He saved my life."

Arambula instead began working as a welder through a National Youth Association program in the shipyards of Seattle. He found the work fulfilling and was reluctant to answer the draft notice that came in early 1944. He was first trained in anti-aircraft, switching to infantry upon his arrival in England as he joined the 28th Infantry Division. He first saw battle in Ardennes.

"We had a lot of casualties. I don't remember names, but I recognized faces, and when we reorganized, they just weren't there," Arambula said. "Battle of the Bulge was especially hard. Complete chaos."

On January 19, 1945, he lost his closest friend, Amos Brasheers, in a truck accident prior to combat. Arambula broke his arm as he was thrown from the rolling truck. After six weeks in recovery, he boarded a train to return to the front but was stopped on the way, by the military police. He believes that because he had already lost two brothers—Manuel and Joaquin—while fighting in Italy and Germany, respectively, the military removed him from combat in Europe.

He returned to Texas, and was stationed at Camp Swift, where he met Nora Ramirez at a festival. He began training to be sent to the Pacific Theater with the 2d Infantry Division but the war ended and he was discharged in May 1946. Arambula married Nora on May 23, 1948, and worked for the U.S. Postal Service, striving to give his children—Michael, Joseph and Rubyann—a good education. All three of his children earned their degrees.

Joe A. Arambula

Date of Birth
2 AUGUST 1924
Bison, OK

Interviewed by
Michael Taylor
13 OCTOBER 2001
San Antonio, TX

WWII Military Unit
Company G,
110th Infantry
Regiment,
28th Infantry
Division

Transferred to
Company A,
9th Infantry
Regiment,
2d Infantry
Division

Benerito "Bennie"
Seferino Archuleta

Date of Birth
9 MARCH 1926
Las Vegas, NM

Interviewed by
Brian Daugherty
3 NOVEMBER 2002
Santa Fe, NM

WWII Military Unit
99th Infantry
Division

ARCHULETA, BENERITO "BENNIE" SEFERINO. Six months in Europe was enough to impact Bennie Archuleta's life forever. His time overseas began in October 1944.

"We were on the move from the day I hit the ground till the day I came back," he said.

On Nov. 9, 1944, after marching through France, the 17-year-old and the 99th Infantry Division joined the fighting in Belgium. They later fought in the Battle of the Bulge and in Germany. Though he said he was too young to appreciate religion before the war, his perspective quickly changed.

"I learned to pray pretty damn fast," he said. He befriended fellow Catholic William Baker and the two would pray at every opportunity. "At the time, we didn't know if that was going to be the last time we were going to pray."

News of the surrender reached him at a campsite in Bavaria, Germany, where his commanding officers began listing those who would be returning to the States. At first, Archuleta was excited when he was called, but soon realized he would be reassigned to the war that was still raging in the Pacific. A tropical-weight uniform replaced Archuleta's winter clothing. Three days before he reported to San Francisco, Archuleta was getting a haircut "when all the bells and sirens cut loose" signaling the end of the war in Japan. The man cutting his hair never finished.

Archuleta was discharged in May 1946. He earned his GED and pursued business administration at Highlands University in Las Vegas, N.M. However, after 14 months of school, he still jumped at the sound of car backfire and airplanes passing overhead and could not concentrate. He decided to work full time, and was eventually hired by the U.S. Forest Service, which allowed him to travel and satisfy his restlessness. He married Eva Marie Rains on June 24, 1946. The couple had four sons: Toby, Bennie, Ruben and Anthony.

Andres Arredondo

Date of Birth
26 FEBRUARY 1916
Laredo, TX

Interviewed by
Juan de la Cruz
28 SEPTEMBER 2002
Rio Bravo, TX

WWII Military Unit
NOT AVAILABLE

ARREDONDO, ANDRES. The most vivid memories of the war for Andres Arredondo were of his time in a German prisoner of war camp near Luxembourg.

"I remember having to work in the winter when the ground was covered in ice," he said. "There were days I couldn't move because the pain was so great. Most of the time, my hands and feet were black and blue while I worked."

Hard work was not foreign to Arredondo. After his father had died when he was 8, he took on the responsibility of sustaining his family. He immediately dropped out of school and began to work. His draft papers came in 1940, when he was 24 years old.

"My mother was scared," he said. "But she also knew that it was something I had to do."

He was sent to basic training in San Antonio, Texas, and left the continent from New York, bound for combat on European mainland.

He frequently forgot the possibility of death, knowing that he could only rely on his rifle and his desire to live.

In mid-December, during the Battle of the Bulge, Arredondo and a group were on a patrol near Luxembourg, when they were suddenly surrounded and captured by the Germans. Arredondo was interrogated through a translator, which proved difficult given his limited English skills. Later, in the POW camp, he would eat a meager breakfast of bread and cheese, work all day and eat a dinner of horsemeat and coffee. He was finally liberated at the end of the war.

"Our bodies were covered completely in lice. [It seemed like] we hadn't bathed in a year," he said.

Arredondo was sent to San Antonio until his discharge. After the war, he worked as a policeman. He and his wife, Margarita, raised nine children.

AZIOS, ARNULFO D. "A.D." The tower bells at the University of Texas at Austin played "You're in the Army Now" as more than a hundred members of the Organized Reserve Corps were called to active duty. A.D. Azios was among them.

As the youngest of six boys born to immigrant parents, Azios learned to speak English in first grade. He graduated from high school in 1939 and worked for three years to earn tuition for college. However, the man who hitchhiked to Austin to enroll at UT put his academic goals on hold when he enlisted in the Army in 1943. During training, Azios qualified for a program that taught him German for four months. His division was sent to Europe in 1944.

Azios was hit by shrapnel during the Battle of the Bulge. He found protection in the basement of 19 Grande Rue, Beauford, Luxembourg—an address he will never forget. As his injury had affected his sight, Azios could only hear the clicks of his enemies' boots as they came closer. He called out in German and kept himself and the other soldiers alive by answering their captors' questions.

In April, as the POWs were continually moved out of Allies' reach, Azios organized an escape.

"I was desperate, brave or stupid for thinking about escaping," he said. "We didn't know that we were about 100 yards from a long line of German machine guns. We were caught between Americans and Germans. It was one of the worst experiences of the whole war."

The escapees found protection in a barn. Before American troops caught up with them on April 13, 1945, Azios was responsible for taking 10 Germans as POWs.

The war ended while he was en route to Fort Bliss, Texas. Azios returned to his pre-law studies and married Lauren Cuellar on Aug. 23, 1947. They had two daughters, Norma and Diana. Azios became a state district judge in the 232d Criminal District Court before retiring.

Arnulfo D. "A.D." Azios

Date of Birth
5 FEBRUARY 1921
Laredo, TX

Interviewed by
Paul R. Zepeda
13 DECEMBER 2002
Houston, TX

WWII Military Unit
75th Infantry Division

Transferred to
9th Armored Division

BOSSOM, NATHAN EDGAR. Fluent in Spanish, Nathan Edgar Bossom always had an appreciation for Hispanic culture, acquired in part from his father whose job in construction took him throughout Mexico and Central America. After his participation in WWII and the Korean War, the Alabama native married a Mexican-American woman and made the Rio Grande Valley his home.

He was drafted just weeks out of high school. After 18 weeks of grueling preparation, Bossom was shipped to Scotland. He was issued his first gun in France and sent into battle in Belgium via railroad cars that still smelled like the livestock they carried before the war.

Between the bitter cold and waist-high snow, Bossom's feet froze in his poorly insulated boots. Both feet and images of the violent battle would continue to bother him after the war.

"During the Battle of the Bulge, any time you closed your eyes, you had a good chance of getting killed," he said. "So you never went to sleep unless there was another soldier with you and one was able to stay on guard while the other slept." Bossom's wife, Mary, said that he would suddenly wake wide-eyed in the middle of the night, as if the atrocities he experienced still haunted him.

Ammunition, food and fuel for vehicles ran low on the front lines. Through letters, Bossom and others heard that the shortages were due to labor unions that had gone on strike for a pay raise. Even years later, Bossom maintained that "our own local citizens ... hurt us most when we were at war."

Bossom returned to Harlingen, Texas, after the war and found a job at a wholesale newspaper company. He was called into service three years later for the Korean War.

He married Mary Ramirez when he returned from Korea. The couple settled in Brownsville, Texas and had three children: Alan, James and Brenda. Bossom had two children—Terry and Carole—from a previous marriage.

Nathan Edgar Bossom

Date of Birth
19 DECEMBER 1925
Birmingham, AL

Interviewed by
Yudith Vargas
6 APRIL 2002
McAllen, TX

WWII Military Unit
Company C, 60th Infantry Regiment, 9th Infantry Division

Luis Aguilar
Calderon

Date of Birth
25 AUGUST 1925
El Paso, TX

Tribute Provided by
George Calderon,
(Son)

WWII Military Unit
Company I,
3d Battalion,
290th Infantry
Regiment,
75th Infantry
Division

CALDERON, LUIS AGUILAR. Fighting in temperatures that plummeted well below zero, Luis Calderon remained in combat despite frostbite on his feet and little in his stomach.

The eldest son in his family, Calderon hoped to stay in school, but when the Great Depression presented trying times for the family, he was forced to leave school at 8, after only completing the third grade.

He was 16 when Pearl Harbor was bombed, and he received his draft notice in August 1943. Calderon trained in Texas and Kentucky before being shipped to England. He entered battle on Christmas Eve 1944, and participated in campaigns in the Rhineland and Ardennes.

He was later sent on a reconnaissance mission with a radio operator and an officer, and fought in the Battle of the Bulge.

During that battle, Calderon developed frostbite, but the medics simply sprayed his feet and he returned to fighting. He was also hit in the chest with the butt of a rifle during hand-to-hand combat and was given a handful of painkillers. Again, he returned to battle.

Calderon remembered how they were forced to scavenge for food, often in the bombed out homes in the countryside — raw potatoes or spoiled food, whatever they could find.

Calderon returned to the States in November 1945. He married Amelia "Molly" Hidalgo and the couple had six children: José Luis "Sonny," Domingo Arturo "Tury," Carmen, Ruben, George and Esmeralda Elaine "Essie."

Calderon worked for the city of El Paso, Texas, as a heavy equipment operator, following the war. A strict father, he garnered admiration and respect from those who knew him. His son Sonny said, "If dad had played football, he would have been first string."

Diego Campa

Date of Birth
3 NOVEMBER 1922
Florence, KS

Interviewed by
Maggie Rivas-
Rodriguez
1 AUGUST 2003
Newton, KS

WWII Military Unit
166th Engineer
Combat Battalion

CAMPA, DIEGO. Drafted in 1943, Diego Campa saw the Army as a way to see the world and escape the racism that often plagued him at home in Kansas. His experience as a solider taught him many things, and he is still unable to describe exactly how the war changed him.

"I always thought that whoever goes into war doesn't come back," Campa said. "So I never really thought about what life would be like after the war."

Though he was drafted, Campa was excited when he received his call to service.

"I always wanted to go into the military," he said. "The only time I ever got out of Florence [Kansas] is when the Army took me."

Despite his excitement and high expectations for the Army, Campa says there was still some racism within the ranks. He remembers white soldiers receiving better treatment and says that sometimes, he felt unwanted in his unit.

However, Campa found a family with other Mexican-American soldiers while serving. He also took comfort in the letters he regularly received from his mother, Benita, and young wife, Ventura Terrones, whom he had married in September 1942.

His battalion landed in England on July 3, 1944, and Campa's military tour of Europe began in France on Aug. 7, 1944. From there, he fought in the campaigns in Ardennes, Central Europe, Northern France and the Rhineland. He was discharged on October 24, 1945 and returned to Florence, moving to Newton, about 28 miles south, shortly after.

Campa returned to work at the Santa Fe Railway Company, where he was employed prior to WWII. He stayed with the company until his retirement in 1982. Campa and his wife had 10 children who remained nearby in Newton and Wichita, Kan.

CARAVEO, EPIMENIO. After growing up an orphan on a ranch in Van Horn, Texas, Epimenio Caraveo joined the legendary 101st Airborne Division and was proclaimed a hero in Bastogne, Belguim, where schoolchildren asked to have their picture taken with him.

He was drafted just three days after Pearl Harbor and by 1943, left for combat in North Africa. In 1944, he said he "got crazy" and volunteered for a 90-day paratrooper training program on the Italian island of Sardinia. Becoming a member of the 101st Airborne Division was one of Caraveo's most cherished accomplishments.

"That's a tough outfit. You're a different kind of fighter all together. You die like any other soldier, but you train to be a little tougher than the rest," he said.

Caraveo jumped into Normandy on D-Day with his unit and fought until the capture of Saint-Lô. Shortly after, he participated in Operation Market Garden. During the Battle of the Bulge, the 101st was surrounded by the Germans in the town of Bastogne but held out for nine days until they were relieved. Caraveo suffered leg and head wounds but was one of seven survivors in the regiment's Company F. Yet difficulties and discrimination still awaited him back in the States.

"When we came back to our country, we didn't know which way to go. There were no jobs," he said. "I came home, but didn't have a home."

Caraveo married Lilia Ramirez in 1946 and spent the little money he had on a wedding dress and a makeshift home: a two-door Ford sedan with the back seats removed to make a bed. He used the GI Bill to finance an apartment and body shop classes in El Paso, Texas. The Caraveos bought a home in 1958, where they raised their children: Leo, Isabel and Cynthia. Caraveo worked as a truck driver for 30 years. All three of his children attended college and had successful business careers.

CASTRO, ALFRED "FRED." During basic training at Camp Howze, Texas, Fred Castro and 10 other soldiers went to a restaurant and waited an hour without being offered even water. Finally, a waitress told them the restaurant wouldn't serve Mexicans. The men vented their frustrations and military police were summoned but looked the other way as the men tore apart the restaurant.

"They said as long as we have the uniform on, we're American citizens," Castro said.

After waiting for a month in New York for the weather to clear up, Castro was crammed into a leaky fishing boat on June 6, 1944, with 100 other men destined for combat in Europe.

"They used anything that sailed to get over there. We were up on tables so we wouldn't get wet but when we had to jump into the water, we went," he said.

The 84th Infantry Division landed on Omaha Beach in Normandy in early November. With the Germans already retreating, they pursued them through Paris, Marseilles, and other French towns.

After fighting in the Netherlands, Castro's unit was allowed to rest, as many of the men suffered from combat fatigue. One night, the division received orders to leave for Luxembourg and joined the forces fighting in the Battle of the Bulge.

During the battle, a land mine shattered Castro's right knee. Disoriented, he did not realize he was injured until he reached down and sank his fingers into a gaping hole in his leg. After initial treatment, he waited two months to return to the States on a medical discharge for surgery. His body rejected an artificial kneecap twice, and bolts were used to keep his leg together.

Castro returned to LaVerne after the war and was hired at a welding company, where he stayed for 30 years. On April 16, 1945, he married Alicia Ayon Lopez, whom he had met at a dance before he was sent to training. They had five children: Robert, Eulalia, Diane, Clifford and Darrel.

Epimenio Caraveo

Date of Birth
15 FEBRUARY 1920
Candelaria, TX

Interviewed by
Celina Moreno
2 FEBRUARY 2002
El Paso, TX

WWII Military Unit
Company F,
327th Glider
Infantry Regiment,
101st Airborne
Division

Alfred "Fred"
Castro

Date of Birth
22 JANUARY 1922
LaVerne, CA

Interviewed by
Laura Loh
23 MARCH 2002
Los Angeles, CA

WWII Military Unit
Company B,
333d Infantry
Regiment,
84th Infantry
Division

Pete Dimas

Date of Birth
21 OCTOBER 1920
Ojito Frio, NM

Interviewed by
Norma Gallegoz
4 JANUARY 2003
Phoenix, AZ

WWII Military Unit
Company B,
423d Infantry
Regiment,
106th Infantry
Division

DIMAS, PETE. During the Battle of the Bulge, Pete Dimas cooked food for his company in holes and trenches. His task changed drastically, overnight, when Germans took them as prisoners of war and "cooking" was reduced to dividing up bread among his fellow POWs.

When he heard about the bombing of Pearl Harbor on the radio, Dimas agreed with his friends that they would have to go and fight. He enlisted on July 8, 1942, and attended cooking school. He had served meals to the officers in the Civilian Conservation Corps earlier. After about a year in the Army Air Corps, Dimas volunteered to transfer to a unit going overseas.

The 106th Infantry Division arrived in France on Dec. 5, 1944, and was packed into trucks, headed north to the front lines in Luxembourg. On Dec. 16, 1944, Dimas heard the haunting sound of "Screaming Meemies," rockets launched from truck beds and tanks.

"They seemed like they were tearing the sky up," Dimas said. The Battle of the Bulge had begun. His company was forced to surrender and was taken prisoner by the Germans. Dimas and a soldier were allowed to make a litter out of branches and an overcoat for a wounded comrade. That night, as they walked through a ruined city, someone began singing *God Bless America*. "We kept on singing," Dimas said. "We just wanted to let the Germans know we weren't licked yet."

For six months Dimas divided a loaf of bread among seven men each day, and sometimes a spoon of sugar or marmalade and occasionally soup, with worms.

At the end of the war, Germans took them as far as the Elbe River where they were stopped by Russians. American soldiers rode across in a canoe to liberate Dimas and his comrades.

He was discharged on Oct. 10, 1945. Dimas married Dilia Irene Basurto, and the couple had five children: Alice, Sylvia, Pete, Richard and Patricia.

Leon Eguía

Date of Birth
13 NOVEMBER 1921
Houston, TX

Interviewed by
Liliana Velazquez
2 MARCH 2002
Houston, TX

WWII Military Unit
Company C,
307th Combat
Engineer Battalion
(Airborne),
82d Airborne
Division

EGUÍA, LEON. For many years, Leon Eguía did not share his war experiences with anyone.

"I saw a lot of things," he said, opening up for the first time in 2002. "So I put a wall between myself and my feelings. Otherwise, I would become crazy."

Eguía was drafted at age 20 and trained as a paratrooper. He said that even though he was in an Army uniform, a drugstore clerk in Lockhart, Texas insisted, "We don't serve Mexicans here." He landed in England on Aug. 12, 1944, and later fought in Belgium in the Battle of the Bulge.

"We were baptized into battle on Christmas Eve, 1944, and spent the next six weeks living and sleeping in snow-covered foxholes and eating K and C rations," he said. In crossing the Rhine River in Dusseldorf, Germany, he saw many paratroopers "blown out of the sky" and crashing into trees. He watched a German tank run over a soldier's head. Experiences in battle caused him to block emotions and develop a stoic, single-minded focus despite the constant risks and threats to his life.

"You don't think about those things," he said. "What's going to happen is going to happen."

By the end of the war, Eguía's battalion had fought across the Ruhr industrial area in Germany and met up with Russian forces on the banks of the Elba River. He was discharged on Dec. 19, 1945, and returned to Houston. He found work in Corpus Christi as a tailor in a clothing store.

Eguía married Antonia Ramirez on June 23, 1949. They settled in Houston and had four children: Gloria Jean, Alice, Leon Jr. and Edward James. Eguía became an active member of the community as a firefighter for 55 years and member of League of United Latin American Citizens (LULAC), the Knights of Columbus and the VFW.

Today, he serves as a eucharist minister at Houston's St. Patrick's Catholic Church and enjoys traveling the U.S., Europe and Mexico with his wife.

GARZA, JOSÉ GUADALUPE. Though he was the only Mexican American in his company, José Garza remembers little discrimination, save for a few jealous soldiers who envied his rank, a position he earned after the stress of war proved too much for another soldier.

"In the first combat we had, our sergeant went crazy," Garza said. "So they put me in as sergeant to guide the squad."

After being drafted in 1942, Garza landed in France with the 80th Infantry Division on Aug. 3, 1944. They advanced toward Saarbrucken, Germany and fought on the Siegfried Line at Zweibrucken. As they were called to Luxembourg for the Battle of the Bulge, Garza injured his leg in northeastern France and was sidelined for two months. He returned to a much tamer war on the German front.

"When I went back, the Germans didn't fight a lot any more," he said. "The soldiers were very young and they were there not because they wanted, but because they forced them."

Letters home to his wife, Concepción, helped him to remain close to the life he left behind and missed so much. Upon returning to the States, he utilized the GI Bill to attend vocational school for furniture repair. Garza then became a migrant worker, traveling throughout the U.S. picking vegetables. During his time as a migrant worker, his daughter María Perla was born. After the birth of his second child, José Guadalupe Jr., Garza decided to settle in the Texas border town of Brownsville, where he worked for the Brownsville Navigation District as a craftsman.

Reflecting on his time in WWII, Garza says that while the sacrifices he made to keep the U.S. safe were worth it, he remains hesitant to discuss the details of the horrors of war he witnessed.

"I don't really talk about that, not even with my wife," he said. "I mean, it's not pretty. It's something sad. Even though they were enemies ... they were human beings."

José Guadalupe
Garza

Date of Birth
18 JULY 1921
Brownsville, TX

Interviewed by
Vanesa Salínas
17 MARCH 2001
Brownsville, TX

WWII Military Unit
Company E,
2d Battalion,
318 Regiment,
80th Infantry
Division

GARZA, MOISES. When his grandson joined the Army in 2001, Moises Garza told him that he had fought in the Battle of the Bulge. The veteran had avoided discussing the war and though his family always considered him a war hero, the comment renewed their interest in his experiences.

"Now everybody knows," he said. "They made copies of my discharge and the telegram sent to my mother about my wounds. Now they know what happened to me."

On June 14, 1942, Garza left his simple farm life in La Joya, Texas, and—without telling his parents—enlisted in the Army. His first mission, at the end of August 1944, was to back up the infantry already in Normandy, France. Allied forces pushed the Germans from France and into the Netherlands. Garza and his unit fought from there to Belgium and finally into Germany, where he stood in the stadium where Adolf Hitler once delivered speeches.

During the Battle of the Bulge, Garza was wounded in his wrist. He was sent to a hospital in Southampton, England, in February 1945. There, he learned that one of his cousins had been killed. He yearned to avenge his death, but as the war was coming to an end, he never returned to battle.

Back in the States after his discharge, Garza was angered to see posted signs that banned minorities from using buses, public bathrooms and swimming pools.

"They did not have any appreciation for what we did," he said.

Within six months of his return, Garza earned his high school diploma. He worked a number of different jobs, including 33 years with the U.S. Postal Service. He married Emma Guerra on Sept. 20, 1951 and they had 10 children: Rosana, Martha, Alma, Emma, José, Moises, Orlando, Nelda, Jesús and Minerva. Garza was a member of the Disabled American Veterans, VFW and the Catholic War Veterans.

Moises Garza

Date of Birth
4 SEPTEMBER 1924
La Joya, TX

Interviewed by
Yudith Vargas
6 APRIL 2002
McAllen, TX

WWII Military Unit
Battery B,
755th Field Artillery
Battalion

Abelardo Martinez Gonzales Sr.

Date of Birth
29 JUNE 1923
Falfurrias, TX

Interviewed by
Trinidad "Tito"
Aguirre
8 SEPTEMBER 2000
San Antonio, TX

WWII Military Unit
Medical
Detachment,
507th Parachute
Infantry Regiment,
17th Airborne
Division

GONZALES, ABELARDO MARTINEZ SR. After serving as a paratrooper and medic, Abelardo M. Gonzales Sr. still provides for his fallen comrades of war. In 2000, he was given an award for more than 2,000 hours invested into providing burials with full military honors for all veterans.

Part of the 507th Parachute Infantry Regiment, Gonzales made his first jump into Normandy on the dawn before D-day. It was dark, cloudy and difficult for Gonzales to see where he was falling.

"Of all the places for me to land, I end up landing on my knees—on the only paved road for miles around," Gonzales said. "Both of my knees were injured. I couldn't walk."

He and other wounded soldiers hid in a farmhouse. From the front door keyhole, Gonzales watched the Germans advance past them into battle and return in retreat 24 hours later. One full-length cast and a mended kneecap later, Gonzales returned to his unit just as the 82d, 101st and 17th Airborne Divisions sent in trucks to stop the German tank offensive in the Ardennes.

"Three divisions, they put them right in front of the advancing Germans," Gonzales said. "We stopped them right there. They didn't go no further. ... That was the Battle of the Bulge."

Bullets whizzing by and flying shards of jagged bomb shrapnel faded to background noise as Gonzales answered the cries of "Medic!" on the battlefield. Many times, all he could offer was a shot of morphine and a helmet hung on a rifle to signal that below lay a wounded soldier.

After three cold months on the front lines, the 17th Airborne Division was given leave in France. They returned to the air on March 24, 1945, this time jumping over the Rhine River in full visibility.

"As we floated down, we acted like we were dead, so that maybe the Germans would not shoot at us," he said, "Up there, there is no place to hide."

The war ended the next month and Gonzales returned home to his mother and sisters.

Catarino Hernandez

Date of Birth
15 AUGUST 1924
Seguin, TX

Interviewed by
Antonio Gilb
13 NOVEMBER 2001
San Antonio, TX

WWII Military Unit
Company C,
61st Battalion,
13th Infantry
Regiment,
28th Infantry
Division

HERNANDEZ, CATARINO. In the first days of the Battle of the Bulge in Schmidt, Germany, U.S. scouts reported that a division of German tanks and soldiers lay in wait on the outskirts of town. Officers ordered the 28th Infantry Division to abandon the area. In their haste a handful of soldiers—including Catarino Hernandez, a 19-year-old from Seguin, Texas—were left behind.

Hernandez and his comrades took shelter in a basement as American fighter planes bombed the city. On the third day, one of the bombs hit the house where they were hiding, and he blacked out.

He woke to German guns pointed straight at him. Hernandez spoke a little German and could understand that the soldiers wanted to kill him. The 28th Division had fought against those very troops just days before. A German officer made sure Hernandez was unharmed, though he was taken prisoner.

For the next six days, Hernandez was unsuccessfully interrogated for military intelligence in a small prison behind German lines. Afterward he traveled for a week without food on a railroad car. He ended up at a prison camp, where his weight dropped from 125 to 100 pounds from the meager rations and hard work. Prisoners were lucky to sleep three hours in beds covered with bugs.

"I kept praying that God would bring me back home," Hernandez said. "I never lost hope of coming home." He was released in May 1945, but would suffer from nightmares and post-traumatic stress disorder (PTSD) decades later.

Hernandez had married Elvira H. Valdez just months before being drafted in November 1943. When he came home in 1945, jobs were difficult to find, and Hernandez worked whenever he could to make ends meet. Eventually he got a job in construction, from which he retired in 1984.

He and Elvira had three daughters: Guadalupe, Olga and Teresa.

HERNANDEZ, JOEL R. Although he enlisted only because he couldn't find a job, Joel Hernandez looked back on his time in the Army as a blessing that enabled him to lead a fulfilling life.

He grew up attending school in the morning and working on his father's ranch for the rest of the day. In 1936, he married Rosela Black and moved in with her parents on a ranch outside Katy, Texas. She died giving birth to their first daughter, Barbara Rosela, who was adopted by Rosela's parents. Hernandez decided to enlist in the Army shortly after, on June 4, 1940.

He trained as a horseman in the 1st Cavalry Division at Fort Bliss, Texas, for two years. He and one other soldier were the only other Mexican Americans on base. The man who gave them the hardest time eventually became Hernandez's good friend. However, Hernandez was shunned by some Mexican-American civilians, who thought he was a traitor for joining the U.S. Army.

When the U.S. entered the war, Hernandez was reassigned to the 691st Tank Destroyer Battalion. They departed from Boston to Europe in 1944. Hernandez was part of the occupational forces that followed the invasion through Luxembourg and Belgium, winding up in Germany in 1945 at the end of the war. Although he saw no combat, Hernandez nonetheless participated in the campaigns in northern France, the Ardennes, Battle of the Bulge and Rhineland.

In November 1945, he moved back to Houston, which was still starved for jobs.

"When I came back, I didn't know what to do," he said. "All I learned in the Army was combat and I couldn't find a job in that."

He became an automotive paint and body repairman and retired from the career 36 years later. He married Gloria Mayorga on Dec. 30, 1950. They had two children — Gilda and Mario — and credit the success of their marriage and family to their strong faith in God.

Joel R. Hernandez

Date of Birth
27 JULY 1917
Mackay, TX

Interviewed by
**Paul R. Zepeda
and Ernest Eguía**
3 OCTOBER 2002
Houston, TX

WWII Military Unit
**691st Tank
Destroyer Battalion**

MEMBRILA, EMILIO MUÑOZ. The two of the three regiments in the 106th Infantry Division had been "wiped out" during the first days of the Battle of the Bulge, Emilio Membrila said. His squad was ordered to defend a crossroad near Winterspelt and shoot anything in sight, but the darkness, rain and fog hindered their vision.

"It was the worst barrage ... U.S. troops ever encountered," he said of the historic battle. "It was supposed to have been a quiet sector."

On Dec. 17, 1944, the U.S. Army reported Membrila missing in action. A telegram was sent to his wife on Jan. 19, 1945, but by that time Membrila, captured by a German Panzer division, was already in Limburg, Germany, at POW camp Stalag XII-A.

The Germans forced the prisoners to march for three days without food or water to Oflag III-A in Lukenwalde. Only 35 miles from the city, Membrila and his fellow prisoners could watch U.S. bombers fly over Berlin.

He was sent to a labor camp in Salzweder, Germany, where the 7th Armored Division liberated him and his comrades. He returned to the States in June 1945 and reunited with his wife. Membrila had married Vincenta Mena during his leave in January 1944 and she had joined the Women's Army Corps Medical in December 1944. For the remainder of the war, Membrila was stationed at Camp Beale, Calif., and visited Vincenta where she served in San Francisco.

Membrila worked as a refractory builder — building and maintaining furnaces for the smelting of copper ore — for Phelps Dodge Corp until his retirement in 1983. After Vincenta died of a stroke in 1993, Membrila lived in a small community in Thatcher, Ariz., with this only son, Michael, who was born in June 1946.

Emilio Muñoz
Membrila

Date of Birth
12 SEPTEMBER 1921
Clifton, AZ

Interviewed by
Violeta Dominguez
5 JANUARY 2003
Tucson, AZ

WWII Military Unit
**Company A,
424th Infantry
Regiment,
106th Infantry
Division**

José Navarro

Date of Birth
17 MAY 1922
Asherton, TX

Interviewed by
Veronica Franco
13 OCTOBER 2001
San Antonio, TX

WWII Military Unit
99th Infantry
Division

NAVARRO, JOSÉ. Unlike most soldiers, José Navarro preferred the conditions of his basic training to his hometown of Asherton, Texas, because the camp had electricity and indoor plumbing. Ever mindful of the opportunities that the military afforded its veterans, he saw the draft as a way to better himself and achieve his lifelong goal of attending college and finding work as a teacher.

After leaving school after sixth grade, Navarro worked in the fields of South Texas, picking crops to help support his family.

He worked in the fields until he was drafted on Nov. 12, 1942, promptly leaving for training in Mississippi. Navarro was part of the Allied invasion of Normandy and later fought in the Battle of the Bulge. Despite earning a Bronze Star for his valiant service, heroic acts were never the focus of Navarro's service.

"You were not looking to do outstanding things," he said. "You did what you needed to do, what you were trained to do: fight and win."

Navarro's tour of duty ended when he was wounded in the Ardennes by a "buzz bomb," a pilotless aircraft that German troops launched at Allied targets. The planes were designed to crash upon the depletion of their fuel supply. The crafts carried warheads full of explosives, and the buzz bomb that wounded Navarro also injured several other members of his squad. He stayed in French hospitals and narrowly escaped amputation of his leg.

Despite the difficult time abroad, Navarro is grateful for his military tour. He said he was exposed to new points of view and that serving with English speakers helped his language skills.

Navarro married Angelita Martinez in 1946 and had five children: Mary Olga, Antonio, Carmen, Yolanda and Silvia.

Jessie Ortiz

Date of Birth
16 JUNE 1922
Fresno, CA

Interviewed by
Cindy Cárcamo
6 MAY 2001
San Luis Obispo, CA

WWII Military Unit
84th Infantry
Division

ORTIZ, JESSIE. The war taught Jessie Ortiz firsthand that Anglos bleed red, just like Latinos.

"It was a source of education for all of us in the sense that we could look in the eye of each other," he said. "It brought us to an understanding that we are all human beings."

Ortiz enlisted in December 1942, became a combat engineer, and landed in England on Oct. 1, 1944. The 84th Infantry Division marched across France, fought through the Netherlands and reached Germany by Nov. 17, 1944. They helped take Gelenkirchen, then the second-largest town in Germany to fall to the Allies, and settled into battle on the Siegfried Line.

Ortiz was once awakened at midnight and ordered to retreat when the Germans broke through the lines in the Ardennes. For three days, his division traveled behind the enemy troops and made a stand against them in Belgium, beginning their involvement in the Battle of the Bulge.

"We were supposed to stop everything," he said. "The orders were: 'They will not pass.'"

A group of Germans, dressed in American uniform and speaking English, once tried to infiltrate their lines. Ortiz and his comrades stopped them, provoking a battle. They were warned later of the threat over the radio. At another point during the battle, Ortiz was laying mines as fast as he could, to delay the Germans who were fighting just over the hill, when he heard Christmas music. He discovered a Catholic church and obtained permission from his captain to attend the service. He and a few others were rushed through communion, which he later described as a beautiful experience.

After fighting back into Germany, Ortiz and his division were sent home in December 1945.

Ortiz became a tool-and-die maker and retired after 31 years with the Vendo Manufacturing Co. in Pinedale, Calif. He married Elena Luz Flores on July 4, 1948. They had eight children: Dominic, Maria, Christine, Caroline, Gregory, Catherine, Jude and Socorro.

URIAS, LEOVA TELLEZ "L.T." In late 1943, the 106th Infantry Division was one of the newest and untried divisions in the U.S. Army. After arriving in France, they received orders to relieve the 2d Infantry Division on the line in a quiet zone near St. Vinh, Belgium.

"We had been there about four days," L.T. Urias said. "That's when the Germans made that push that was known as the Battle of the Bulge."

Most of the division was surrounded and forced into surrender. Only Urias' regiment, the 424th, was able to draw back and fight into the fourth week against the Germans.

"They were superior in arms," he said. "They had machine-gun fire a whole lot faster than ours."

After about two weeks in heavy battle, the 2d Division relieved Urias and his comrades. With the backup holding strong on the front lines, Urias and a few other soldiers were given orders to infiltrate the enemy lines and capture German troops to interrogate them.

"We ... were stopped by machine gun power," he said. "Instead of capturing them, they got us."

The Germans confiscated the Americans' rifles, valuables and snowshoes. For the next two weeks, Urias and the others were interrogated and fed "maybe a thin slice of bread and sometimes muddy soup." They were transferred to Limburg, Germany, where conditions did not improve.

"I remember when we were marching toward the camp, I swapped my knit sweater for about a half a loaf of bread and a jar of marmalade jelly," he said. The 6th Armored Division liberated Urias and his fellow prisoners on March 29, 1945 and he was taken to a hospital in Paris. Since entering the service, until his release as a POW, Urias had gone from 190 to 140 pounds.

On Sept. 5, 1948, he married Anita Chavez. They had four children: Rebecca, Cynthia, Loida and Wilma.

Leova Tellez "L.T." Urias

Date of Birth
28 SEPTEMBER 1925
Sonora, TX

Interviewed by
Kevin and
Sharon Bales
10 MARCH 2001
Fort Worth, TX

WWII Military Unit
Company K,
424th Infantry
Regiment,
106th Infantry
Division

VASQUEZ, GEORGE S. On Dec. 23, 1944, the 424th Regiment of the 106th Infantry Division—which had been holding the German offensive at the onset of the Battle of the Bulge—was finally forced to fall back. At night, the commander of Company K ordered his troops to march out of the area. George Vasquez and five other soldiers were exhausted and stopped briefly to rest. "The whole company just vanished in the dark," Vasquez recalled. A fellow infantryman woke him up, "Everybody's gone, George. What are we going to do?"

For a month, the six soldiers drank from streams and snuck into villages for bread and raw potatoes. They had to keep running from German troops and avoid any civilians who might turn them in. The weather gave them frostbite and froze the water in their canteens. One man just gave up and sat in the road to wait for his captors to find him. Vasquez never found out what happened to him. By the time they caught up with their unit, he had lost 41 pounds and developed trench foot, but rejoined the fighting.

On their way into Germany, Vasquez's squad rescued a group of POWs—including one man from their own unit who used to tease Vasquez—from a house they were about to destroy. Vasquez was awarded a Silver Star for single-handedly destroying an entire enemy machine gun position. After the war, he and 20 other recipients of the award were honored in a parade in Paris in April 1945. He was promoted to staff sergeant and served in reconnaissance missions, traveling ahead of tanks from Frankfurt, Germany, to Salzburg, Austria, and to Munich, Germany.

Vasquez earned his GED after the war and started working for the Chicago, Burlington and Quincy Railroad. He married Esperanza Gonzales on Jan. 22, 1949. They had two sons, George and John, and a daughter, Christine.

George S. Vasquez

Date of Birth
3 SEPTEMBER 1925
San Antonio, TX

Interviewed by
Angela Macias
11 AUGUST 2002
Grove Heights, MN

WWII Military Unit
Company K,
424th Infantry
Regiment,
106th Infantry
Division

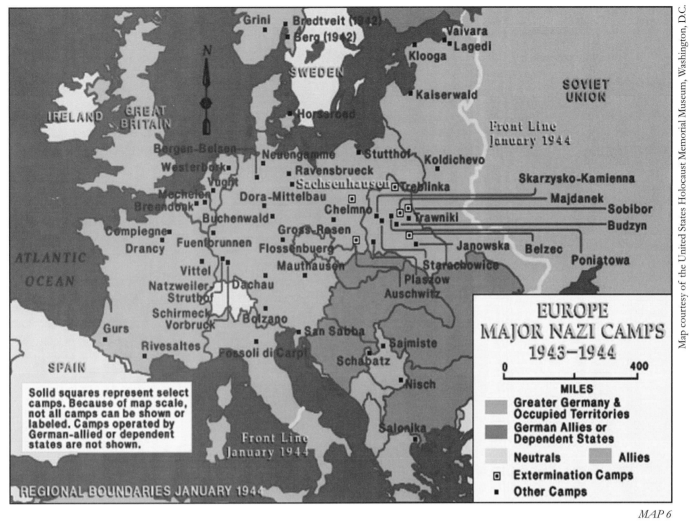

MAP 6

WITNESSES TO THE NAZI CONCENTRATION CAMPS

The gruesome horrors of war were not limited to the battlefield during WWII. Throughout Germany and Poland, Nazi Germany set up concentration camps which imprisoned civilians.

The camps were initially used as labor camps, with prisoners working in coal mines and producing rubber. Many became death camps, with massive gas chambers and ovens to cremate bodies. Workers unable to keep up were executed and buried in huge trenches or burned in ovens. Frail women, children and the elderly went directly from the trains to the gas chamber.

By 1939, there were six concentration camps; more followed throughout the early 1940s. Besides race (Jews and Gypsies), people were also sent to death camps for anti-Nazi activity, homosexuality and mental defects.

Many American soldiers witnessed the inhumane conditions of the camps as they moved into the interior of Germany.

Ubaldo Arizmendi, a Brownsville, Texas, soldier with the 47th Infantry Division, arrived at Dachau to help the skeleton-like prisoners. He called Dachau "the most horrible place."

Salomon Abrego

Date of Birth
24 FEBRUARY 1923
Laredo, TX

Interviewed by
Juan de la Cruz
28 SEPTEMBER 2002
Laredo, TX

WWII Military Unit
Company D,
Battalion A,
68th Medical
Regiment

ABREGO, SALOMON. During the Battle of the Bulge, Salomon Abrego and his fellow soldiers suffered through one of the coldest winters to hit the area in more than 20 years. As a medic, he watched helplessly as the cold ruined some of the crucial supplies.

"It was so cold that the plasma was freezing," he said. "Soldiers were going into shock because we couldn't use it. ... My friends were dying all around me. It was depressing at night, when you had a chance to feel that way."

Abrego had wanted to join the Army since he was a little boy growing up in Laredo, Texas. Following his brother, Abrego enlisted in 1942. He was assigned and trained as a medic, though he had wanted to join the front lines with the infantry. "They saw where I excelled. I knew about biology. I wanted to be a surgical technician," he said.

On his way to Scotland from New York, he suffered a terrible case of seasickness and said he felt as if he wanted to die. He arrived with his unit in London at 4 a.m. during an air raid.

After the Battle of the Bulge, Abrego's unit was sent to help liberate concentration camps. He helped clean and feed the victims they were able to save. At the end of the day, Abrego said his unit would be white with DDT insecticide powder that was thought to be harmless to humans and used to clean lice off the victims.

The greatest tragedy Abrego endured was when his brother, Guillermo, was killed in July 1945, while he was trying to land a B-24 Liberator after the crew had parachuted out.

Abrego returned to the States and earned a pharmacy degree at the University of Texas at Austin. He became a pharmacist in Laredo, and married Evelyn Newell on July 10, 1948. They had four children, all of whom were involved in the medical field.

Ubaldo Arizmendi

Date of Birth
26 JUNE 1923
Brownsville, TX

Interviewed by
Andrea Shearer
6 APRIL 2002
McAllen, TX

WWII Military Unit
7th Infantry
Regiment,
3d Infantry Division

ARIZMENDI, UBALDO. Witness to some of the most devastating images of WWII, from the invasion of Normandy to the liberation of the prisoners at the infamous concentration camp at Dachau, Ubaldo Arizmendi said that the war changed his life forever.

"I was happy being able to work and feed myself instead of someone giving me food," he said. "That makes a difference ... to anybody who has been through what we [had] gone through."

Enlisting in 1941 after his father unwittingly signed the consent form, a 17-year-old Arizmendi left Brownsville, Texas, on Nov. 7 for Camp Roberts, Calif., to begin his basic training. He was sent to Alaska and Blackstone, Va., before he boarded the *Queen Elizabeth* and set sail for England in November 1944. There, he was part of the Normandy invasion, where he witnessed some of the most intense fighting of WWII. He worked as an airplane mechanic while in France, and because of his anti-aircraft training he was a lookout for enemy planes at night.

His unit continued into Germany, and, as they moved through small towns, he was responsible for finding vacant homes for men to sleep in. Arizmendi remembers one home where he found a safe. Inside were piles of German money, and desperate to stay warm, the men burned the paper notes.

Arizmendi arrived at the concentration camp in Dachau, where he and other soldiers covered themselves in grease and taped their clothes to them to avoid lice infestations. Inside the walls of the camp, they helped liberate hundreds of prisoners, many clinging to life, starving and sick.

"It was the most horrible place you can ever think," Arizmendi said.

He was discharged on Nov. 18, 1945, though he re-enlisted from 1950 to 1953 for the Korean War. Arizmendi married Guadalupe "Lupita" Coronado in 1951. The couple had five children: Mary, Ubaldo, Belinda, Edward and Alberto.

CORDOVA, ALFREDO. About five years ago, Alfredo Cordova was describing how he was part of a unit during WWII that liberated a concentration camp. Then a surprise: the psychologist informed Cordova that he had been a 6-year-old boy when Cordova's Army unit freed him.

"The smell in the camps was horrible," Cordova said. "If I saw them today, I would be more horrified than I was then, but war changes you. You are in a different mind."

Drafted in April 1944, Cordova left his home in New Mexico on May 23, 1944, on a train bound for El Paso, Texas. Already the married father of two when he was called to serve, Cordova remembered the sting of leaving his family.

"I was standing on the back of the train," he said. "And I remember Lina standing with our two children, and she was crying."

After training in Texas, Cordova continued to Fort Robinson, Ark. He then spent 31 days on a ship headed for England. He fought in the Battle of the Bulge, and in campaigns in Austria, France and Germany.

Cordova's unit was in the Austrian Alps when the war ended. They then helped liberate concentration camps in the area.

Cordova earned a Bronze Star for his participation in the taking of the Siegfried Line. He was discharged on January 1, 1946.

Upon his return to the United States, Cordova began working in water conservancy, where he eventually served as foreman. He later attended trade school, learning upholstering and finishing. He opened his own furniture business, Al's Upholstery. Cordova retired in 1970. He and his wife, Lina Martinez, had three children: Naida, Alfred and Dorothy.

Alfredo Cordova

Date of Birth
4 MAY 1923
Albuquerque, NM

Interviewed by
Iliana Limon
2 NOVEMBER 2002
Albuquerque, NM

WWII Military Unit
Company A,
1st Battalion,
142d Regiment,
36th Texas Division

CORTEZ, HERMAN R. After surviving brutal combat the day after D-Day, Herman Cortez was about to begin fighting in the Battle of the Bulge at Ardennes, France, when an explosion robbed him of his sight for three days. Doctors were preparing to send Cortez to England for medical treatment, but the young private was undeterred by his injury and refused to leave the battlefield.

Cortez told the doctor, "No sir. I'm not going to a hospital. I got my eyesight. If I quit now, I won't be good to myself or anybody else. I'm gonna lose my nerve. I want to go back and face what I had to face. I won't be free until the end."

He instead continued his work as part of the 37th Field Artillery Battalion. It was his responsibility to locate the enemy on the front lines and then report the artillery range to others in his battalion.

He eventually traveled through France to Germany, where he saw the horrors of the Nazi regime firsthand, and he later remembered the stale smell of death at the concentration camps.

At war's end, Cortez was in Czechoslovakia. His battalion was flown back to the States on July 20, 1945.

Cortez returned to his childhood home in Houston, Texas, where he had served as a member of the Civilian Conservation Corps before enlisting in 1940. He married Aurora Solis in 1949 and had one daughter, Carol, and a son, Herman.

Cortez's passion for the military continued after the war, as he worked in the engineering department of the Houston VA Hospital. He remained there for 30 years, retiring in 1978. He says that if he were able, he would enlist again, a testament to his unflappable patriotism.

"I'll salute anyone who puts on a uniform," Cortez said. "Because they are doing for their country what somebody has to do, whether they like it or not."

Herman R. Cortez

Date of Birth
19 NOVEMBER 1920
Victoria, TX

Interviewed by
Paul R. Zepeda
1 MARCH 2002
Houston, TX

WWII Military Unit
37th Field Artillery
Battalion,
2d Infantry
Division

Mike C. Gomez

Date of Birth
9 JANUARY 1925
Phoenix, AZ

Interviewed by
Ricardo Pimentél
4 JANUARY 2003
Phoenix, AZ

WWII Military Unit
837th Ordnance
Combat Depot
Company

GOMEZ, MIKE C. Descending the ropes that hung from the sides of his ship, Mike Gomez prayed aloud as he prepared to storm the shores of Omaha Beach at Normandy on D-Day.

"We ran like hell when we got to the beaches," he said. "It's a matter of survival, but you always have a little fear in you. It's their life or yours."

As he dodged enemy fire on the beach, Gomez and his fellow soldiers ducked into shell holes to shield themselves from the hail of German bullets. In one instance, Gomez found a childhood friend from Phoenix, Ariz., hiding in the same shell hole. The reunion was a moment of comfort amid the chaos of the invasion.

Following the invasion, Gomez's unit delivered supplies to the front line, riding in tanks to ensure safe transport.

Raised in Arizona, Gomez was living in Phoenix—married and soon to be a father—when he was drafted in 1943. He trained in California, Washington and New Jersey before sailing to Europe. While abroad, he saw the horrors of war, from the waters of Normandy littered with the bodies of fallen soldiers, to the concentration camps at Dachau, the saddest sight Gomez had even seen, but a sight that reminded him of his purpose in the military.

"They wanted us to travel through the concentration camp," he said. "Possibly to make us realize why we were fighting."

Gomez was discharged on Nov. 21, 1945, and retuned to his wife, Dora Mendoza, and young son, Michael, in Arizona. There he attended Arizona Teacher's College—now Arizona State University—and earned a degree in accounting. He worked as the chief real estate negotiator for the Arizona Bureau of Reclamation until his retirement.

Joe G. Lerma

Date of Birth
17 DECEMBER 1922
El Paso, TX

Interviewed by
René Zambrano
11 APRIL 2001
San Diego, CA

WWII Military Unit
95th Infantry
Division

LERMA, JOE G. Even before arriving at the European concentration camps in 1945, Joe Lerma and his Army division could smell the dead.

"The sight and smell of human death is terrible," he recalled. While his division's job was to inform camp survivors the war had ended, they had difficulty convincing the men and women conditions were safe. "The people were afraid to come out," he said.

Lerma was born in El Paso, Texas, but work for the railroad company took his father Ramón and the family to San Diego, Calif., that same year.

Following the American entry into WWII, Lerma worked at an air base construction site outside of San Diego for 2 1/2 years—workdays were 10 hours long, seven days a week—until he received his draft notice. He went through basic training at Camp Roberts, Ark., and then joined the 95th Infantry Division at Fort Sam Houston, Texas. His division boarded the USS *Mariposa* and left for England in August 1944.

Lerma acted as scout and sniper for the division until his discharge in 1945.

In an act of unsurpassed courage, Lerma single-handedly captured a German bunker and machine gun during a battle, a story reported in the Sun Harbor Packing Co.'s Catch and Can News in April 1945. The newsletter reported that Lerma, a former employee, "without ammunition, had bluffed his way into the capture." A German officer, humiliated, "promptly tore a medal from his own uniform" and gave it to Lerma. Lerma's act of courage earned him a Silver Star.

Trench foot, rheumatic fever and wounds took their toll and Lerma received a medical discharge and spent all of 1946 in veterans' hospitals in Santa Fe, N.M., and Pasadena, Calif. He spent the next three years mastering the once-simple task of walking.

MARTINEZ, ASCENCIÓN "CHON." While in Germany in 1945, Chon Martinez and his unit passed a Nazi concentration camp. There, Martinez and his fellow soldiers witnessed the horrors of war, from mass graves to people "dead on their feet."

For him, however, one terrifying image stuck in his memory. "There was a big tree with ... dead bodies over it ... children and adults," he said. "We were too late, except for the walking skeletons around us."

Another time Martinez said God's hand guided him through the war; he and another soldier went for a walk and stumbled upon what seemed to be a camp with shacks and tents. There was a guard at the gate, though he didn't appear to be military personnel. Martinez and his comrade walked through the gate and were suddenly crowded by many Czechs and Polish, mostly young people. One of the many girls began talking to Martinez and he noticed her looking at the guard in a worried way.

"I decided the guard was threatening her, not me," he said. "I told my friend, who was closest to the guard, 'Disarm that guard and I'll cover you.'"

Martinez and his friend, later accompanied by a U.S. Army officer, discovered that the guard was a German living with two other members of Hitler's elite guard. As they rounded up the men, one tried to escape, but made the mistake of running in Martinez's direction. When the German saw Martinez's rifle pointing at him, he broke down and fell on his knees, crying.

Martinez never found out exactly what happened to the people within the fences.

"I believe they would've had a very bad fate, if we had not stumbled into that," he said with a tear, grateful to been able to help. "God bless America for being so good to me."

Martinez married Elizabeth Lopez on Dec. 7, 1946.

Ascensión "Chon" Martinez

Date of Birth
1 MAY 1921
Villa Acampo, Mexico

Testimonial by
Ascensión Martinez

WWII Military Unit
546th Anti-Aircraft Artillery Automatic Weapons Battalion (Mobile)

MARTINEZ, PORFIRIO ESCAMILLA. The horror of dead soldiers littering the beaches of Normandy and the feeling of bullets whizzing past are Porfirio Martinez's most prominent memories of WWII. Martinez left the States for the first time, when he boarded a ship for Europe as part of the 99th Chemical Mortar Battalion.

His battalion also participated in Operation Torch, securing the port cities of Oran and Algiers in Algeria, before continuing into France, Italy, Poland and Germany.

Martinez launched 26-pound mortar shells, hitting targets up to 3,800 yards away. Martinez and his partner alternated launching and firing shells to distance themselves from the extremely loud explosions. Each deafening blast left a constant ringing in the soldiers' ears, and contributed to Martinez's hearing loss.

In addition to grisly sights he saw on the battlefield, Martinez also remembers passing through a Polish concentration camp and witnessing the gruesome reminders of Nazi rule. He saw the long, cramped barracks and the stacks of charred bones.

"They would burn the bodies of the Jewish prisoners and then take out the bones and stack all of them up there," he said.

Martinez finished his tour of duty in 1945 and was discharged. He returned to Texas and has remained in the Austin area ever since. In 1946, he married Naomi Perez. The couple had eight children: Yolanda, Juanita, Porfirio Jr., Andres, Luis, Margarita, Rudolpho and Dolores. Martinez worked as a chef at the Fiesta Restaurant in Austin for 20 years.

Martinez never dwells on the hardships he has experienced, but prefers to highlight the positive. He said he still thanks God that he returned from his service abroad unharmed.

Porfirio Escamilla Martinez

Date of Birth
15 NOVEMBER 1913
Round Rock, TX

Interviewed by
Yazmin Lazcano
15 NOVEMBER 2000
Austin, TX

WWII Military Unit
99th Chemical Mortar Battalion

Xavier Pelaez

Date of Birth
20 DECEMBER 1925
Los Angeles, CA

Interviewed by
Luis Torres
23 MARCH 2002
Los Angeles, CA

WWII Military Unit
279th Infantry
Regiment,
70th Infantry
Division

Transferred to
3d Division

PELAEZ, XAVIER. As he scouted ahead of the 70th Infantry Division, Xavier Pelaez was often afraid—like the time his squad accidentally crossed a minefield, killing two men. But Pelaez never allowed himself to accept defeat.

"There were times when some would want to surrender, but that was always out of the question for me," he said. "I just thought of the shame it would cause my family."

He was on a scouting mission one night in France when shots sounded near his squad. He hit the muddy ground instantly and crawled as low as he could, petrified.

"I just knew I had to stay low," he said. "There was a guy next to me that got his elbow shot away just because he raised his arm." He was about to throw a grenade when he finally saw his first glimpse of the enemy, as a soldier in front of him launched a grenade at him instead.

"It didn't hurt at first. My only thoughts were, 'Damn, they got me.' It wasn't until it got quiet and cold that I realized I had a problem," he said.

He had been hit in the right thigh, but his squad succeeded in capturing the four remaining soldiers hidden in a machine gun nest. Pelaez was sent to a hospital in France. When he recovered, he joined the 3d Infantry Division in Dachau, Germany. The Germans had recently retreated from the area and abandoned a concentration camp to the Allied forces. "I could smell the burnt flesh, and I saw the furnaces and the ashes and little bits of bone. It was unbelievable," he said. "I couldn't believe what I was told, that people were capable of such things."

He was stationed in France for six months after the war. Upon his discharge, Pelaez—who was drafted after high school graduation—studied chiropractric medicine. He married Consuelo Gutierrez and the couple had two children: Belinda and Javier III.

Jesús "Jesse" G.
Reyes

Date of Birth
11 JANUARY 1923
Houston, TX

Interviewed by
Paul R. Zepeda
and Ernest Eguía
23 DECEMBER 2002
Houston, TX

WWII Military Unit
Company C,
8th Infantry
Regiment,
4th Infantry
Division

REYES, JESÚS "JESSE" G. For Jesús "Jesse" G. Reyes, WWII was an experience that gave him his first opportunity to leave Houston, Texas, and taught him perseverance as he fought for his life.

"I still remember hearing President Roosevelt declare war on Japan," he said. "It was so moving, I rushed down to sign up for the military." Reyes' mother, María Gonzales Reyes, would not sign the paperwork for his enlistment, so Jesse waited a year, until he was drafted on July 19, 1943.

He was first assigned to shoe repair in a quartermaster's unit in the Air Corps, but wanted to fight. He had aspirations to be a pilot and tried to become a B-17 gunner. He was finally granted a transfer to an infantry unit going overseas. He joined the 4th Division in France in January 1945.

When Reyes arrived, shortly after the Battle of the Bulge, his company was scattered. He was assigned to help search for troops. He and others in Company C tied themselves together with rope as they searched the hills of Ardennes, staying 15 feet apart to make them difficult targets. The reassembled unit was sent to Germany, where Reyes remembered seeing acres of tanks and dead soldiers. He helped capture small cities and liberated concentration camps outside of Munich.

"We broke down the fence and saw the people running—no they could not run; they were walking," he explained. "They were walking corpses trying to get through the snow."

In March, Reyes was traveling to Frankfurt on a convoy of tanks when the commander of the tank in front of him was shot, spewing blood onto his jacket. In that moment of horror, he prayed that God would allow him to return home so he could find a wife and have a family.

Reyes got his wish later that year and returned to Houston. He worked in shoe repair, and later got a job as an orthopedic technician at Shriners Hospital Medical Center. He married Frances Rodriguez on July 30, 1949, and they had two sons, Jesse "Junior" and Edward.

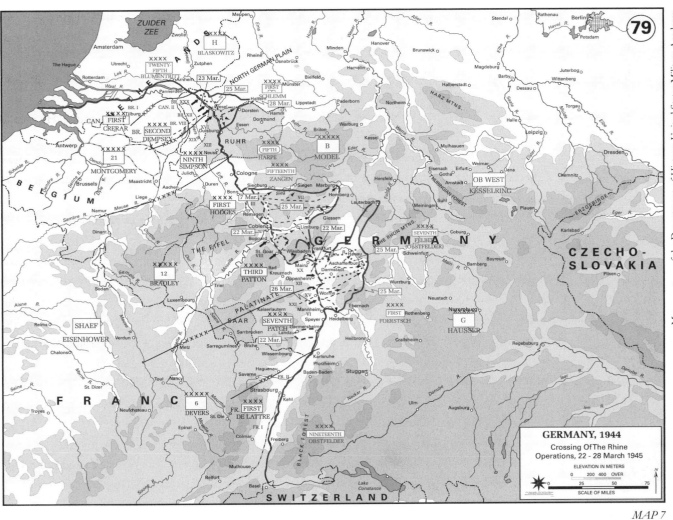

GERMANY, 1944
Crossing Of The Rhine
Operations, 22 - 28 March 1945

ELEVATION IN METERS
0   200 400 OVER

0   25   50   75
SCALE OF MILES

MAP 7

FIGHTING INTO GERMANY

By the end of the Battle of the Bulge in January 1945, U.S. forces had been fighting for four years and the war had been going on for over six. The German effort to break through Allied lines in Battle of the Bulge was their last unsuccessful attempt to gain significant ground against their enemies. To make things worse for the Germans, the Soviets launched an offensive on Poland and East Prussia on Jan. 12, requiring Hitler to concentrate his forces there.

Yet even as the Allied forces drove the Germans out of the Ardennes, there were still months of fighting ahead for the U.S. forces and their allies before the war in Europe could be concluded. The end did not seem so close at hand to those fighting.

"In war, you see all this suffering on both sides," said Calixto Rangel Ramirez of the 9th Infantry Division, a native of Falfurias, Texas. "You're hurt and you hurt others. ... You're wondering if you [are] going to make it to the next day. And then you get to a point where you don't care anymore. The people who are really suffering the most are your relatives."

The Beginning of the End

With the German momentum lost, Gen. Dwight D. Eisenhower began coordinating the advance into the country itself. The goal was to meet the Soviets in the middle of Germany as they invaded from the east.

The Allies had to first break through what remained of the West Wall, the 392-mile line of defenses that included concrete barriers to stop tanks and pillboxes to protect German gunners. Hitler decided to concentrate most of his last western defense there, leading to another devastating loss when the Allies finally breached the West Wall and proceeded to the Rhine River.

Augustine Martinez, a native of Mexico who had grown up in the Midwest and was serving with the 65th Infantry Division, was part of the forces that held to the Saarlautern Bridge along the Western Wall and captured the town of Cologne on the Rhine River. The city in flames, Martinez and his company searched houses for German soldiers. Later, along the shore of the Rhine River, he recalled the most intense fighting as the division then pushed eastward. "You hustle; you're hungry," said Martinez, who would settle in St. Paul, Minn., after the war. "They gave us only 15 minutes to rest. I [was] tired all the time."

Though the Germans had tried to destroy all bridges on the Rhine in a last attempt to keep the Allies out, the Remagen Railroad Bridge was left standing. Joseph Rodriguez, of Santa Fe, N.M., serving with the 78th Infantry Division, was among those to cross the bridge and be among the first forces to cross into Germany.

"They told us to count to ten and follow the guy before us into the bridge tunnel," said Rodriguez. "I went in there with my heart in my hands."

Bombs and shells fell all around him, but he made it across uninjured.

Overrunning Germany

By the end of March, Germany's defenses had fallen and Allied Forces poured into the country. The task now was to subdue the enemy forces in their own territory. Latinos took up the role with boldness and valor.

Lazaro Lupian, a native of San Diego, Calif., was on a reconnaissance mission along the Rhine River with a fellow soldier on March 30. In a small town, they discovered two German officers, who had been in hiding. The Germans opened fire but in the ensuing fray, Lupian forced their surrender. The small town he saved was temporarily named Lupianville in honor of its captor.

On April 8, 1945, José Jesús "Chuy" Urias and his company was assigned to eliminate snipers in a castle on the Rhine River. Armed with grenades, Urias took the position of scout and, with heroism that would earn him a Silver Star for the effort, shouted "Cover me!" and ran to encounter the enemy where they were hiding.

Fighting pockets of resistance from town to town and house to house, the Western Allies eventually met up with Soviets on April 25 in the town of Torgau, 80 miles south of Berlin.

The Allies were assisted by the Soviet Army. After Germany invaded the Soviet Union on June 22, 1941, in Operation Barbarossa, the Soviets had proven they were not to be trifled with. Leon Eguía, a Houston soldier serving with the 82d Airborne Division, recalls meeting up with the Russians on the banks of the Elba River at the end of the war. *(See Leon Eguía's story in Chapter 1, Battle of the Bulge.)*

ALIRES, JUAN RAMÓN. Though Juan Ramón Alires already had two children—María Erlinda and Luis Augustine—when he was called to join the military, he was proud to serve.

When Alires was in sixth grade, his family moved from San Cristobal to East Dale, a southern Colorado farm town. There, his father and three brothers cut down timber from nearby mountains and fashioned them into poles to connect their home to the nearest electrical source, 20 miles away. Alires walked three miles to Jaroso Middle School, until he finished seventh grade. He dropped out to help on the farm, growing cauliflower, and potatoes, and raising pigs, sheep and goats.

He met Marinita Trinidad Santisteran at a dance and they married two years later on Nov. 23, 1940. He was drafted into the Army in 1942, but deferred service on account of his two toddlers. When he entered the service in 1944 and left for basic training in Fort Logan, Colo., Marinita was pregnant with their third child, Irene. She and the children stayed with Alires' family until he returned.

Having specialized in the M1 rifle, Alires joined the 11th Armored Infantry Division. They landed in Normandy on Dec. 16 and by Dec. 30 saw their first combat in Neufchateau, Belgium, defending a highway into Bastogne during the Ardennes Offensive. They fought through northern Luxembourg and into Germany by early March. In the crossing of the Regen River in Germany on April 25, 1945, Alires was wounded when a grenade exploded near his right hand and shoulder. He spent a month in a tent hospital recovering. By the time he was healed, the war had ended in the Pacific.

Upon his discharge on Nov. 28, 1945, from Fort Logan, Colo., he returned home. He and Marinita had two more children: María Barbara and Ricardo Benildo. In 1950, they moved to Pueblo, Colo., where he took a job with Colorado Fuel and Iron Co.'s Pueblo Ordnance Depot. He retired after 22 years.

Juan Ramón Alires

Date of Birth
27 MAY 1919
San Cristobal, NM

Interviewed by
Irene Consuelo
Chávez
11 OCTOBER 2003
Pueblo, CO

WWII Military Unit
11th Armored
Infantry Division

CASTRO, JESÚS. At 30 years old, Jesús Castro was one of the oldest soldiers drafted for duty. He had the chance to ask for a deferment and remain home with his wife, Elvira Hernandez, and their six children. Instead, he chose to go to war.

In Fort Riley, Kan., Castro held his own among the younger troops by joining the organized football team until the end of their 30-day basic training.

"I was an old man in comparison," Castro said. "I impressed them."

From Kansas, he was sent to Fort Meade, Md., and across the Atlantic Ocean on the *Queen Mary* to join the fighting in Europe.

"That was a real luxury," he said, recalling the experience. "Just imagine me, a nobody, on this ship with all those people."

He landed in Scotland and was greeted by a big band playing for the troops. From there, he was sent almost immediately to the front lines in Germany, joining the 4th Cavalry Regiment.

Castro was injured when a .45 caliber submachine gun was accidentally fired into the ground. The sand from the impact flew up into Castro's nose, eyes and ears, incapacitating him. Because of the unit's position near the enemy, he had to stay in a shed for two days. Though some radiomen helped clean the sand out of his eyes and ears, Castro had already lost most of his hearing by the time he was removed to a temporary hospital in Germany.

The war ended during his stay in the hospital. Afterward, he traveled through the Netherlands, Belgium, Germany and France before returning home in 1945.

He continued his work as a self-employed carpenter. After his first wife's death, he married Guadalupe Ornelas in 1973 and had six more children.

Jesús Castro

Date of Birth
26 JULY 1908
Matamoros,
Mexico

Interviewed by
Anthony Sobotik
13 SEPTEMBER 2003
Brownsville, TX

WWII Military Unit
24th Cavalry
Reconnaissance
Squadron
(Mechanized),
4th Cavalry Group,
(Mechanized)

Benigno
Nevarez Diaz

Date of Birth
6 SEPTEMBER 1925
Los Angeles, CA

Interviewed by
Cheryl Brownstein-
Santiago
23 FEBRUARY 2002
Los Angeles, CA

WWII Military Unit
Company E,
2d Battalion,
261 Regiment,
65th Infantry
Division

DIAZ, BENIGNO NEVAREZ. Lying to recruiters about his age, Benigno Diaz left his Los Angeles home just before his 18th birthday and enlisted with 10 other Latinos into the 65th Infantry Division. He was trained as a scout at Camp Shelby, Miss., before he was shipped to Camp Lucky Strike in France. There, Gen. George C. Patton delivered a startling message that Diaz never forgot.

"Do not get killed before you kill at least one of them," he said.

As he traveled through Germany, scouting ahead of his unit, Diaz learned the cruel realities of war. In mid-April 1945 in Neumarkt, a grenade narrowly missed him, as Diaz ducked behind a fence and shot the hiding soldier. Later that day, he threw a grenade through a window at two German soldiers. He discovered later that he had killed a member of the Hitler Youth.

"That made me feel bad, killing a boy," he said. "I sat down and started crying."

Later, near the town of Dillingen, he watched as a fellow scout and sergeant stepped on a tank bomb and blew themselves up.

"Things like that you don't forget," he said. "I was only 19. To me, it was too much."

On April 26, 1945, he was wounded by a bullet to his shoulder, as his company crossed a dike over the Danube River. Through his dizziness and pain, he heard a comrade's cry for help and pulled him out of the water. The man died in Diaz's arms, too far gone to be helped.

Diaz was sent home after his recovery in England and was discharged on Oct. 27, 1945. His injury left him unable to box as he had before the war. After a brief stint as a mail clerk, he secured a job as an upholsterer. He was married for 10 years before the union ended in divorce. After traveling through many cities, he returned to Los Angeles, where he met and married Mary Candelaria on July 28, 1962. The couple had three children: Kimberly, Lisa and Benigno.

Teodoro Garcia

Date of Birth
9 NOVEMBER 1923
Clovis, NM

Interviewed by
Ray Atencio
2 NOVEMBER 2002
Albuquerque, NM

WWII Military Unit
NOT AVAILABLE

GARCIA, TEODORO. To relieve the family's burden during the Depression, Teodoro Garcia left home in Clovis, N.M. to live with his grandmother in Presidio, Texas. He left school in fifth grade to earn a living. This allowed his brothers and sisters to finish their schooling.

"Life was tough and I had to help," he said.

He does not have many memories of his parents, Alejandro and María Aguilar Garcia, but knows that his father was a veteran of the Mexican Revolution.

At the time, Garcia remembered, Presidio was considered *"pura raza,"* meaning almost everyone was Mexican. And everyone was poor. "Sometimes you would eat and sometimes you would not. That's how it was," he said. Garcia went to a non-segregated school and said everyone got along, for the most part. He describes life back then as being the same as it is now for Latinos, except that they were poorer.

At age 20, Garcia was drafted and sent to Fort Bliss, Texas, for training. He was stationed there when the war began. From El Paso, Texas, he was sent to Wichita Falls, Texas, and then to England. He arrived in Germany on Feb. 8, 1944.

"It was cold, snowy, wet in Germany. That was the hardest," he said. Thinking about the war, Garcia grew quiet in contemplation and declined to discuss it in any further detail.

After the war, Garcia said there was more of a racial divide between whites and Latinos.

"There are places I still can't go [in Texas]," he said.

Garcia worked on the railroad and in the oil fields before moving back to Clovis. He married Esther Jimenez in 1946. They had five children: José, Linda, Juan, María and Steve. His family remained very important in his life and he taught his children from his own experiences.

GONZALEZ, CARMEN R. As Carmen Gonzalez came out of the movie theater with his brother on Dec. 7, 1941, newspaper boys in the streets announced the bombing of Pearl Harbor.

"Oh my God," he thought. "We're gonna get drafted."

He was right. Just weeks later, Gonzalez was sent to Camp Chaffee, Ark., for basic training. There, he learned that he could gain the respect of many white soldiers by teaching them Spanish. In Camp Butner, N.C., he learned to use the 81-mm mortar and was asked to train 100 men on the weapon. He earned the rank of sergeant and was even asked to train as a sniper, but declined.

Gonzalez and the 78th Infantry Division landed in France in November 1944 and were sent to the front lines in Germany almost immediately. He remembers the first time he lost one of his men. "I thought I would be next," he said. "But I was never wounded."

In all, Gonzalez was in Europe for 18 months. During that time, he took a short trip with his men to Belgium, renting a house for the whole squad. Although Latinos were banned from some restaurants and forced to sit in the "non-white" section of the theater back home in Newton, Kan., Gonzalez said racial lines were almost nonexistent in the Army.

After the war ended, Gonzalez went to Berlin to train troops. He remained in Europe for six more months before returning to the States and was discharged as a tech sergeant in January 1946.

He met Norma Maldonado at a club in Chicago and the two later married. Gonzalez got a job with the railroad in Newton, and the couple had seven children: Carmen, Yolanda, José, Norma, Hermenio, Laura and Debra. They divorced after 17 years when Norma returned to her native Puerto Rico, leaving her ex-husband to raise the children. Gonzalez lived in Newton after the divorce and was an active member of the American Legion.

Carmen R.
Gonzalez

Date of Birth
16 JULY 1920
Newton, KS

Interviewed by
Nicole Cruz
1 AUGUST 2003
Newton, KS

WWII Military Unit
Company H,
2d Battalion,
311th Regiment,
78th Infantry
Division

JAIME, JOE. After growing up facing discrimination in a small Kansas City community, Joe Jaime—who emigrated with his family from Mexico when he was 4 years old—thought volunteering in the U.S. military would finally earn his American citizenship.

His dream of becoming a fighter pilot was dashed when he was prevented from joining the Air Corps due to his lack of citizenship. He discovered he also couldn't enlist in the Navy, where he had hoped his welding skills would help him get a job building beach-landing craft.

He was drafted by the Army in Sept. 18, 1942, landing in France two years later. The 692d Field Artillery Battalion was equipped with 12 105-mm Howitzers towed behind 6x6 trucks and supported with infantry. Jaime arrived equipped with a prayer book given to him by a priest from his hometown in Argentine, Kan. It gave him strength when he endured a ship of food-poisoned soldiers, ducked German "Buzz Bombs," and saw the U.S. casualties laid out on the streets of Aachen, Germany.

On Dec. 16, 1946—almost a year after his discharge—the decorated veteran was finally granted his citizenship. The accomplishment proved bittersweet and too long delayed.

"If I was good enough to wear their uniform, I should have been good enough to get American [citizenship] without question," he said.

Back home in Kansas, Jaime realized that the situation of prejudice had not changed. A former chemistry teacher told Jaime, years after the war: "Your people will never make it."

Looking back over his own life, which included more than 50 years of marriage to Mary Morales, three children—Richard, Robert and Patty—and postwar jobs in accounting, sales and management, Jaime believes the Mexican-American community has come a long way.

"The chemistry teacher was wrong," he said. "We made it."

Joe Jaime

Date of Birth
18 MARCH 1922
Aguascalientes,
Mexico

Interviewed by
Mary Sanchez
2 AUGUST 2003
Kansas City, MO

WWII Military Unit
Service Battery,
692d Field Artillery
Battalion (105-mm
Howitzer)

Lazaro Lupian

Date of Birth
27 MARCH 1922
Culiacán, Mexico

Interviewed by
René Zambrano
3 DECEMBER 2000
San Diego, CA

WWII Military Unit
385th Infantry
Regiment,
76th Infantry
Division

LUPIAN, LAZARO. Driving on Pacific Coast Highway 101, Lazaro Lupian was on his way to visit his girlfriend when the crackling car radio announced that the United States was going to war. At the time, Lupian wasn't a U.S. citizen, so he didn't think the news would immediately affect him.

"You can imagine our surprise when we were the first ones to go," he said, explaining how he and his Latino friends were systematically recruited. "We weren't even true citizens."

Some of his friends dodged the draft and even his father, José Serrano Lupian, encouraged him to enroll at the Colegio Militar in Mexico to avoid it. He decided instead that serving this country was something he needed to do. He would come back a hero in everyone's eyes but his own.

Lupian arrived in Southampton, England, in November 1944 and joined the 76th Infantry Division. He first saw combat in Luxembourg in late January 1945. The division's assignment, as they crossed the Saar River in early February, was to break through the Siegfried line.

"Look out for yourself was the first thing I learned," he said. It was a lesson he learned the hard way. On Feb. 20, Lupian took shrapnel to the arm while trying to capture a pillbox. His first reaction was relief, but the wound was minor and he returned to the battle a few weeks later.

On March 30, he and another soldier were on a reconnaissance mission along the Rhine River. In a small town, they discovered two German officers who had been in hiding. Lupian opened fire. When the enemy surrendered, the town was temporarily named Lupianville in honor of its captor. Lupian, wounded in the brief battle, was sent to a hospital in Paris.

When he was discharged, Lupian returned to his job as a butcher at the U.S. Grand Hotel in San Diego. He married Grace Elvira Gastelum in June 1947 and they had six children: Lazaro, José Dario, John Michael, Grace Marie, Helen Marie and Martín Gastelum.

Augustine Martinez

Date of Birth
28 AUGUST 1919
Zaragosa, Mexico

Interviewed by
Angela Macias
12 AUGUST 2002
St. Paul, MN

WWII Military Unit
261st Infantry
Regiment,
65th Infantry
Division

MARTINEZ, AUGUSTINE.   When Augustine Martinez landed in Le Havre, France on Jan. 21, 1945, he knew very little about being a soldier. Even after a month of training as a rifleman, he wasn't prepared for the intense battle he and the 65th Infantry Division entered in March 1945.

"Two, three days—you learn," he said. He was soon helping to hold the Saarlautern Bridge in Germany, freezing each time flares—meant to illuminate American soldiers—burst in the air. As they progressed into Cologne, Germany, Martinez witnessed the city in flames and watched people looting department stores as he and his company searched houses.

Intense fighting, backed by orders to keep pushing forward, gave the soldiers little time to think about what was going on around them. Martinez saw a horrific number of casualties on the shore of the Rhine River. As they reached a hill past the river, he asked a man next to him if the area was infested with mosquitoes. The sound he heard was actually bullets whizzing past his head.

"Up the hill, they were shooting at us. ... We were just scared," he said, remembering that it was at the river where more severe fighting occurred, as the 65th Division pushed toward Berlin. "You hustle; you're hungry. ... They gave us only 15 minutes to rest. I [was] tired all the time."

Martinez never reached Berlin. The troops were stopped one day and told that the Germans had surrendered. He returned to France for a couple months, taking three trips to Paris while he waited to be reunited with his wife, Elizabeth Diaz, and two sons, Rudy and Danny.

"I think that was worse than battle, just waiting and waiting," he said.

He returned to Minnesota and his job at American Hoist, where he worked 35 years before retiring. Martinez had two more children, one of whom died as a child, the other a daughter named Rita. He married twice more; he was widowed from all three marriages.

RAMIREZ, CALIXTO RANGEL. Although Calixto Rangel Ramirez fought in the Battle of the Bulge and Germany, his biggest fear while serving in WWII was being separated from his family.

"In war, you see all this suffering on both sides," he said. "You're hurt and you hurt others. After a while, you're wondering if you [are] going to make it to the next day. And then you get to a point where you don't care anymore. The people who are really suffering the most are your relatives."

Ramirez was inducted into the Army Air Corps in October 1924. Around that time, his brother, Ramiro, introduced him to Armandina de la Peña, who worked in the Department of Censorship. When Ramirez was assigned to Lockbourn Air Base in Columbus, Ohio, later that year, Armandina moved there from Laredo, Texas, and they were married.

In 1944, the Army needed more infantrymen and Ramirez was sent to training at Camp Howze, Texas, and assigned to the 9th Infantry Division before being shipped overseas.

"I hated to leave my wife," he said. "She was expecting a baby."

On April 21, 1945, Ramirez was riding atop a tank, leading a convoy in Germany, when they were fired on. In his effort to secure help for his comrades, Ramirez did not realize that he had been struck in the neck by shrapnel. While he was being treated, his wife received a telegram stating he was missing in action. Though the mistake was corrected with another telegram, the Red Cross sent a priest to interview Ramirez so news could be sent to his relatives in Texas.

After the war, Ramirez was promoted to manager. He later owned a drugstore. He and Armandina bought a cattle farm and had two more children: Rolando and Marinela. After Armandina died in 1988, Ramirez married her widowed sister, Bertha de la Peña. Well into his 90s, he prided himself on staying busy: dancing, collecting stamps and coins, and playing golf three times a week.

Calixto Rangel
Ramirez

Date of Birth
14 OCTOBER 1911
Falfurrias, TX

Interviewed by
Karin Brulliard
13 SEPTEMBER 2003
Brownsville, TX

WWII Military Unit
Company L,
47th Infantry
Regiment,
9th Infantry
Division

RODRIGUEZ, JOSEPH. On March 7, 1945, Joseph Rodriguez and the 78th Infantry Division were given orders to cross the Remagen Railroad Bridge—the only bridge left standing over the Rhine River—and be the first to cross deep into enemy territory.

"They told us to count to 10 and follow the guy before us into the bridge tunnel," Rodriguez said. "I went in there with my heart in my hands."

Bombs and shells fell all around him, but the Santa Fe native managed to make it across uninjured. On the east side of the river, he waited for his fellow soldiers. He knew what to expect. The day before entering combat on Germany's border, a commander had given his division a talk.

"I don't know how much battle experience or training you have, but some of you are not going to come back, some of you are going to be wounded," the commander said.

Rodriguez never forgot those words. They would take on new meaning on April 10, 1945, as he woke to the impact of shrapnel hitting his face. In battle later that morning, he suffered a flesh wound on the top of his leg and by afternoon, his foot was almost blown off by a mortar shell. He lay on the battlefield waiting for a medic but later bore no scars.

"I don't call it luck. I call it [being] blessed," he said. "All the people in Santa Fe were praying."

He was shuttled to a hospital in France and later shipped to Van Nuys, Calif. to recover.

After his discharge in May 1945, Rodriguez secured a job with the U.S. Postal Service. He and his wife, Margaret Trujillo, would have eight children: Noah, Patrick, Judith, Simón, Herman, Bernadette, Angelica and Josetta. As he enjoyed his retirement in Santa Fe, N.M., Rodriguez reflected on the horrors he experienced in Europe and agreed that war is hell.

"Freedom isn't free," he said. "Every ounce of blood pays for it."

Joseph Rodriguez

Date of Birth
2 MAY 1926
Gallup, NM

Interviewed by
Ron Pacheco
11 DECEMBER 2001
Santa Fe, NM

WWII Military Unit
Company I,
319th Infantry
Regiment,
78th Infantry
Division

John Rubalcava

Date of Birth
16 MAY 1924
San Diego, CA

Interviewed by
René Zambrano
10 SEPTEMBER 2000
San Diego, CA

WWII Military Unit
95th Infantry
Division

RUBALCAVA, JOHN. Frigid nights out in the snow. Soldiers huddled together for warmth, exposed to the elements and at the mercy of German firepower. Mangled bodies of half-dead soldiers screaming, "Medic!" into the dark.

For over 40 years, these are the memories that have haunted John Rubalcava.

"You feel terrible when you see your friends get killed," he said. "It's something that hits you in the stomach and stays with you."

Born to Mexican immigrants, he felt both national and cultural pride when he was drafted in 1942. "Maybe we were poor and didn't have the money, but everybody wanted to go," he said. "I tried to volunteer, but I had bad eyes, so I got turned down by both the Army and the Navy."

Despite racism at home, Rubalcava recalled the unique brotherhood forged in perils of war. "I was treated real good," he said. "Their lives depend on you, and yours depends on them. You take care of each other." The division was deployed on Sept. 15, 1944. Rubalcava credited the 95th and 90th Divisions' victory at Metz, France, to Gen. Patton's tough leadership. The 95th Division was nicknamed the Victory Division and claimed the citation "the bravest of the brave." Yet grueling defense tactics and surprise attacks by enemy forces took their toll on morale.

"Every day I hoped the war would end," he said. "I didn't want to die at 19 years old."

The pangs for home were strongest when he was alone, craving his mother's cooking and thinking of his young pregnant wife, Hortensia, who later gave birth to his son, John.

Utilizing the GI Bill, he started a career as production controller at the North Island Naval Air Station in San Diego, Calif. He divorced in 1947 and was remarried in 1982 to Emma Cruz. He had one more child, a daughter, Martha.

**Mac Ortega
Salazar**

Date of Birth
28 FEBRUARY 1925
Ellsworth, KS

Interviewed by
Ascensión
Hernandez
2 AUGUST 2003
Kansas City, MO

WWII Military Unit
Battery C,
882d Field
Artillery Battalion
(105-mm Howitzer),
70th Infantry
Division

SALAZAR, MAC ORTEGA. Looking back on his life, Mac Salazar had few regrets. He enjoyed his childhood, served his country, worked a steady job and gave his children more opportunities than he had growing up during the Depression.

"I'm living the American dream," he said. "All I ever wanted was a house and children."

Financial director, fire captain and owner of a construction company are the occupations of three of his nine children. Seven have bachelor's degrees and five have their master's.

"And all I ever did was go to school for nine years and started the 10th [year]," he said with a laugh. "But that's our job."

When he dropped out of school at 16, Salazar worked for the Santa Fe Railway in Kansas City, Mo., cleaning coaches and boiler flues in the railroad house. He was drafted on Aug. 9, 1943.

"They made me grow up too fast," he said. "I still had two or three more years of chasing girls if I'd stayed, but I didn't."

Salazar trained to be an artillery mechanic, making minor repairs and maintaining the weaponry. He joined the 70th Infantry Division in France in mid-January 1945. There, the soldiers slept on the ground and draped their belongings on branches when it rained. Salazar remembered that later the unit stayed in houses while patrolling and conducting combat raids in Germany. The 70th Infantry Division crossed the Saar River and took Saarbrucken and Völklingen, among other German cities.

After the war, Salazar served five months in Texas, before his discharge on Feb. 3, 1946. Salazar returned to his job at Santa Fe Railroad, where he worked until 1985. He married Belia Madrigal on Sept. 28, 1945, and the couple raised nine children: Mac, Mary, Tony, Arthur, Carlos, Robert, Virginia, Irene and Irma.

URIAS, JOSÉ JESÚS "CHUY." During WWII, "Chuy" Urias volunteered for tasks other men were loathe to do: combing the Normandy beaches littered with human remains, detecting mines, going door to door in France in search of German soldiers hiding in private homes and blowing up part of a castle that was a nest of enemy snipers. Yet Urias never felt like a hero: for him, it was just a job.

He was drafted on Feb. 29, 1944. During basic training at Camp Roberts, Calif., Urias noticed racial tension, though he never let names like "wetback" or "Pancho" bother him. Once his company entered combat — arriving in France on Jan. 10, 1945 — the differences disappeared.

To allow the heavy artillery onto the Normandy beach, Urias used his bayonet to scout for mines, marking them for an engineer to deactivate.

Though that task was dangerous, his most heroic feat occurred on April 8, 1945. His assignment was to eliminate the snipers in a castle on the Rhine River. "I was like a Christmas tree with grenades all over me," he said. "I would say, 'Cover me,' and then I would run."

For having "assumed the position of scout in spite of the personal dangers incurred" Urias' commanding officer, Capt. Herbert S. Lowe, awarded him the Silver Star three months later.

Urias, promoted to a sergeant, was preparing his men for the day when the war ended.

"I just lay down in the street," he said. "I just wanted to sleep."

He worked as a drill sergeant in an Austrian POW camp until his discharge a year later.

Back in the States, Urias was able to take welding classes under the GI Bill and worked as an auto-body repairman. He had five children — David, Diane, Daniel, Denise and Derek — with his first wife, Julia Soqui, and one child, David Jesús, with his second wife, Lucy Chávez. He now lives in Scottsdale, Ariz., with his third wife, Emilia.

José Jesús "Chuy" Urias

Date of Birth
26 DECEMBER 1925
Scottsdale, AZ

Interviewed by
Ismael Martinez
4 JANUARY 2003
Phoenix, AZ

WWII Military Unit
**Company E,
355th Infantry
Regiment,
89th Infantry
Division**

VALADES, SALVADOR. When it came to his safety, Salvador Valades knew he could always rely on his mother's prayers. He was the youngest of five and the last of three sons to be drafted into the war in Aug. 1944. During combat on March 13, 1945, Salvador felt sure her prayers saved his life.

That morning the 94th Infantry Division captured a concrete fortification at the top of a hill. They had been charged with clearing the way for the last push to the Rhine River, and the fighting that day marked Germany's last stand before retreating.

Valades' platoon attacked uphill under heavy fire. In a burst of gunfire, Valades took a single bullet to the chest. He was knocked on his back as the bullet hit the bandoleer of ammunition he wore over his chest and cut the crucifix from a rosary hung around his neck. The rosary deflected the bullet from his heart and lodged it in his liver instead. His lieutenant called for a medic, took the radio Valades carried and continued up the hill.

"All I could think of was that the Germans might make an attack," he said. "I grabbed my M1 rifle, took it off safety and prepared to defend myself as best I could."

Eventually, a medic came to dress his wound and help him down the hill where stretcher bearers waited. The bullet was removed in a field hospital in Germany. Valades was being treated for the wound in a hospital in England when the war ended.

When he had recovered, he served at Fort Logan, Colo., typing discharge papers and supervising German prisoners of war who repaired typewriters.

Valades graduated from the National School of Business in Rapid City, S.D. He worked as a clerk typist at the VA Hospital in Fort Mead, S.D., for 36 years. He married Darlene J. Houdek in 1951 and with her had three children: Vincent, Tina and Vance.

Salvador Valades

Date of Birth
7 MARCH 1926
Edgemont, SD

Interviewed by
Rea Ann Trotter

WWII Military Unit
**94th Infantry
Division**

Francisco Venegas

Date of Birth
8 JANUARY 1920
Kingsville, TX

Interviewed by
Erika Rodriguez
18 NOVEMBER 2000
Austin, TX

WWII Military Unit
273d Infantry
Regiment,
69th Infantry
Division

VENEGAS, FRANCISCO. While fighting in Germany, Francisco Venegas fought to stay alive, but did not expect to survive the battlefront. He was tired, hungry, cold and most of all, scared.

"I never thought that I was going to get away from there so I could come home. I lost all faith," he said. "I was scared all the time."

Venegas was the oldest of three children and grew up in Kingsville, Texas. He attended school until he was 17 and his father died. With the family in need of a steady income, he left school to find a job.

Venegas enlisted in the Army in 1942 and was shipped out immediately to the Aleutian Islands. There, he would spend two years enduring some of the worst weather he had ever known.

In June 1944, he returned to the States and was sent out again in November of the same year, landing in England to await assignment.

He eventually joined the 69th Infantry Division. They landed in France in Jan. 24, 1945, and traveled to relieve the 99th Infantry Division in Belgium, holding defensive positions along the Siegfried Line.

Starting on Feb. 27, Venegas fought across Germany. His division would capture Schmidtheim and Dahlem on March 7 and cross the Rhine River into the fortress of Ehrenbreitstein on March 27. On April 5, they relieved the 80th Infantry Division in Kassel and took Munden, Weissenfels, Leipzig and Eilenburg.

As the war was ending, Venegas received orders to be shipped home. He was discharged and returned home to Brownsville, Texas, where he worked as a carpenter for the next 30 years. He married María Soto in 1946 and the couple had five children: Irene, Charles, Lydia, Alfred and Edward.

Raul Cantú
Villarreal

Date of Birth
16 NOVEMBER 1919
Brownsville, TX

Interviewed by
Xochitl Salazár
20 OCTOBER 2003
Brownsville, TX

WWII Military Unit
Company C,
407th Infantry
Regiment,
102d Infantry
Division

VILLARREAL, RAUL CANTÚ. When Raul Villarreal came home to Brownsville, Texas in 1949, he had adjustments to make, as he had lost his right leg from stepping on a land mine in Germany.

"I thanked God I made it back," he said. "Not in one piece, but still I'm ticking."

After working in the fields as a boy, Villarreal spent three years with the Civilian Conservation Corps, building roads and fighting forest fires at Camp Rand, Ore. When he was discharged in 1939, he returned to Brownsville and married Delfina Martinez in November. Their first child, Raul Luis, was born in 1940. He settled to a quieter life, driving city buses and dump trucks.

He was drafted in November 1944. During basic training, he was given the rank of "unofficial sergeant" because he was the only one who could speak both Spanish and English. "There were a lot of guys who didn't know any English at all," he said. "So they'd give orders to break down a rifle or do this or that, and I'd have to explain it to the other guys in Spanish." The unofficial promotion didn't mean anything officially, but did exclude Villarreal from KP duty.

He arrived in Cherbourg France in Sept. 23, 1944, with the 102d Infantry Division and first saw combat near Waurichen and Geilenkirchen, Germany. In December 1944, they were left to guard the 8-mile stretch along the Roer River while most troops left to fight in the Battle of the Bulge.

On February 26, 1945, Villarreal stepped on a land mine in Cologne, Germany. His left leg was fractured in two places and his right leg later had to be amputated. He was sent to hospitals back in the U.S. to recover and was eventually discharged from Battle Creek, Mich. on Feb. 17, 1949.

Villarreal's disability didn't slow him down. He still hunted and fished, and he and his brother remodeled the brake, clutch and gas pedals on a Model "A" car so he could use hand controls instead. He and Delfina had four more children: Alda, Leo, Joe, Noe.

MAP 8

GERMANY SURRENDERS

After wading through the icy waters at Normandy, France, surviving the brutal winter during the Battle of the Bulge, and fighting toward the interior of Germany, Allied forces clinched victory in Europe.

Hitler's loss signaled not only a military defeat but also an ideological one in the minds of many, with the triumph of good over evil. Peace finally returned to Europe on May 8, 1945, or V-E Day. That was not, however, before the continent had been dragged through one of the most violent conflicts in history. The European Allies, spe-

cifically France and Great Britain, were financially and physically decimated by the war. The United States had lost more than 100,000 men and would ultimately lose thousands more as the military's attention shifted to the Pacific Theater.

The Fall of Mussolini

Germany's defeat, which began slowly years earlier in 1941 with a failed attempt to invade the Soviet Union during a punishing winter, continued when Hilter's most powerful ally on the continent, Italian fascist dictator Benito Mussolini, was defeated in 1943.

Joe V. Lopez, a Los Angeles native and a member of the 91st Infantry Division, had been ordered to go after Mussolini.

"We were in contact with the OSS [U.S. Office of Strategic Services], but when we got there, Mussolini was hanging," Lopez said.

Mussolini had been executed and hanged at a public square in downtown Milan, next to his mistress, Claretta Petacci. It appeared that the Axis powers were on the decline.

The Final Offensives and Surrender

Normandy and the Battle of the Bulge weakened the German military and as the push toward Berlin intensified, Allied victory was imminent.

President Franklin D. Roosevelt died of a cerebral hemorrhage on April 12, 1945, before he could see Germany's surrender. Harry S. Truman became commander-in-chief.

With the defeat rapidly closing in, Hitler and his new wife, Eva Braun, swallowed cyanide capsules together in the Führerbunker on April 30, 1945, and the Third Reich surrendered May 7, with official ratification of the surrender signed in Berlin on May 8.

As Gabriel Valades, of South Dakota who served with the 38th Anti-Aircraft Artillery Group, traveled into Germany at the end of the war, a sadness pervaded the scene.

"My memories of the trip were of sadness and devastation," he said. People begged for food and cigarettes; elderly people and young children roamed the streets, their homes and towns devastated. Many cried out: *"Alles kaput,"* all is over with.

"The American and German bombers sure did a complete job in bombing Deutschland," Valades said.

Valades recalled packed trains of people traveling, but with so much devastation, it was difficult to comprehend where their destinations might be.

With Germany's surrender came the release of those who survived the hellish incarceration in Nazi concentration camps. As gaunt, lifeless prisoners flowed out of the camps during the liberation of Germany, many American soldiers saw a concrete result of their service.

Occupation and the Marshall Plan

As per the Yalta conference in early 1945, where Churchill, Stalin and Roosevelt had made plans for Europe following the Allied victory, occupation began immediately. Britain, France, the Soviet Union and America kept troops in the country. Germany was sliced into four sections, with the Soviet Union occupying the eastern portion; France, England and the U.S. in the western half.

U.S. Secretary of State George Marshall designed the plan that bears his name in hopes of helping to reconstruct the war-ravaged continent. The Marshall Plan poured billions of dollars into European economies in hope of aiding Europe's post-war recovery. Britain and France received the most aid.

Raul Rios Rodriguez, of New York City, had joined in the closing days of the war—he celebrated V-J (Victory over Japan) Day while still in basic training. Rios was among those who would be involved in the rebuilding of Europe. He was shipped to Le Havre, France, assigned to guard bridges and supply depots in France and Germany with the 18th Infantry Regiment, 1st Infantry Division.

Rios said he was amazed at how much devastation the war had caused.

"I saw Frankfurt when she was all *kaput*; now I see her and, wow, she's like New York," he said. After two years in Europe, he was discharged and returned home.

ALBELO, HIGINIO. A dense fog enveloped the Navy ship loaded with ammunition destined for Normandy, the site of the beginning of the end of World War II. The ship, on its way to help with the liberation of France, was stuck on uncharted rocks, and Higinio Albelo remembered that he and his mates thought they were facing death. "It was very dark, and the weather was terrible," he said. "We were loaded with ammunition, and we were so scared, and we didn't know when it was all going to explode." Thanks to the tide, the ship was freed and made it to Scotland, where it was unloaded. "The rest of the munitions were sent to Normandy," he said. His ship was sent back to New York for repairs. "We were dry-docked, and then the war ended," he said.

Born Jan. 11, 1918, on a small farm near Aguadilla, P.R., Albelo dreamed of seeing the world. He moved to New York City in 1939, but jobs were scarce, so he enlisted in the Civilian Conservation Corps and trained to be a baker. After working 18 months in the CCC, Albelo returned to New York and found work in hotels, making $10 a week. He met Carmen Irizarry during this time, and after three months of courting, they married.

In 1943, while working for a plant that made airplanes for the war, Albelo joined the Navy. He was primarily stationed on the SS *Alexander Ramsey*, a merchant supply ship. The *Ramsey* was spared from combat, although there were several scares from German U-boats and icebergs hidden beneath the water. Despite the danger, Albelo enjoyed his time at sea.

"Overseas, the service was great," he said. "If I didn't have my wife and son at the time, I would've stayed. I loved it."

After his return from the war, Albelo worked at Howard Johnson Restaurant. He had two children, Higinio "Gene" Jr. and Mary Carmen.

Higinio Albelo

Date of Birth
11 JANUARY 1918
Aguadilla, PR

Interviewed by
Adrian Baschuk
14 SEPTEMBER 2002
Miami, FL

WWII Military Unit
SS *Alexander Ramsey*

DE LA ROSA, TEODORO. While he arrived in Europe after the end of combat, Teodoro De La Rosa found that dangerous situations still abounded. At an Austrian hotel, military police asked the GIs if anyone of their group was missing. A soldier had been killed the previous night, and his body was thrown on the train tracks. Fortunately, De La Rosa discovered the body was not that of his roommate, who had slept somewhere else for the night. One of the men responsible for the death was a farmer nicknamed "Red" who accepted cigarettes and candy from the GIs. De La Rosa later heard Red was a Nazi who would conspire with other men to kill GIs traveling alone.

One of De La Rosa's earliest duties was to patrol the border between Austria and Russia. His company was known as the Circle C Cowboys because of the insignia on their helmets. Each day they would catch Russian soldiers who had gone absent without leave. These deserters were often severely beaten when they were returned to their Russian commanders.

While he wished he had experienced combat, De La Rosa enjoyed his time in the Army. He believed it was a great chance to learn and offered him opportunities he might never have had otherwise. "I got to see a lot of places," he said. These European travels took him far from his birthplace of Pharr, Texas, and his parents—Beatriz and Gregorio. De La Rosa first attempted to enlist when he was 17, but had to wait another year.

Decades after the war, proud of his veteran status, he volunteered at military funerals as part of the honor guard, saying he owed his fellow veterans at least that much.

He married Belia Palacios in March 1947 and the two had four children: Juan, Juanita, Rolando and Roberto.

Teodoro De La Rosa

Date of Birth
16 MARCH 1927
Pharr, TX

Interviewed by
Joe Myers Vasquez
6 APRIL 2002
McAllen, TX

WWII Military Unit
Company D,
22d Replacement Battalion,
6th Regiment

Agapito Casarez
Gonzalez

Date of Birth
6 DECEMBER 1910
Kyle, TX

Interviewed by
Mary L. Nieves
6 APRIL 2002
San Antonio, TX

WWII Military Unit
Company F,
115th Cavalry
Reconnaissance
Squadron
(Mechanized)

GONZALEZ, AGAPITO CASAREZ. When Agapito Casarez Gonzalez was drafted by the Army on June 2, 1942, he never imagined the horrors and devastation his eyes would see, including the bodies of fallen Italian leader Benito Mussolini and his mistress hanging in the square in Milan, Italy.

"I saw them hanging ... him and the lady, in Milan. Like you would see anything," Gonzalez said. "We knew who they were because they told us, and Mussolini was a heavy and big man, and so was the lady."

Decades later, images of hundreds of mangled and mutilated bodies remained etched in his memory as well.

"An awful thing we saw was the dead bodies of the Italian people," Gonzalez said with tears on his face as he remembered. "But it was and it is too much for me."

While he was in Europe, Gonzalez served as a machine gunner and a tank crewman.

He was born in Kyle, a small town 22 miles south of Austin, Texas, on Dec. 6, 1910. He was raised in another small town Moore, Texas, about 120 miles southwest of Austin.

He worked in the fields with his father, José María Gonzalez, while his mother, Tomasita Casarez Gonzalez, stayed home caring for her 10 children.

When he was older, he moved to San Antonio, Texas, where he met Hermila Estevez. They married in 1938 and had six children: Pedro, Raul, Luis, Elva, Tomasita and Hermelinda. Since Gonzalez only studied through the second grade when he was in school, he made sure his own children received a better education than he did.

In the military, Gonzalez earned a Marksmanship Pin and a Rifle Range Sharpshooter Pin. After the war he worked as a laborer, making parts for the Southern Prison Co., until retirement.

Luis Leyva

Date of Birth
11 OCTOBER 1920
Monterrey, Mexico

Interviewed by
Mary Alice Carnes
23 NOVEMBER 2001
San Antonio, TX

WWII Military Unit
Company A,
526th Armored
Infantry Battalion

LEYVA, LUIS. Though not a U.S. citizen, Luis Leyva served his adopted homeland during the war. His dedication eventually led him to stand guard for Gen. Dwight D. Eisenhower.

"I stood guard for Eisenhower in the sleeping quarters at night or in the daytime," he said. "Those places were top secret. You had to have passes to go into each room."

Born to Mexican parents, Guadalupe and Josefina Ramirez, Leyva was raised in Laredo, Texas, by his adoptive parents, José Ángel and Frances Leyva. He enlisted in 1942. In basic training at Fort Knox, Ky., he learned to drive and repair tanks. He and his crew were shipped to a deserted camp at an unknown location and were told that all information they learned was classified. "We were 350 men surrounded by guards," he said. Because their training involved stealth maneuvering, some of the soldiers snuck out of the camp to find out that they were near Virginia Beach.

The soldiers were trained on loading tanks, using landing craft and reacting to enemy fire. "They called us the demonstration regiment," Leyva said. Finally the 526th Armored Infantry Battalion would head to Europe, but not before undergoing amphibious training in Fort Story, Va. Among other skills, he learned to blind the enemy with special lights that were mounted on the tops of the tanks in place of guns. "You could see for miles with that light," he recalled.

When the war ended, Leyva and the other soldiers were greeted with confetti and music when they returned to New York Harbor. "Every minute after I stepped into the United States was like a dream," he said. He returned to Laredo and married Trinidad Medina on Jan. 6, 1946. The couple had six children—José Luis, Mary Alice, Linda Lee, Rose Anne, Frances Trini and Jessica Lucille. Despite assurances of U.S. citizenship for his dedication, Levya never officially was given that designation.

LOPEZ, JOE V. While Joe V. Lopez played his childhood gunfight games, he never imagined that he would find himself in Italy, engaged in a life-and-death firefight against German troops that would eventually earn him a Bronze Star for his heroism on the battlefield. "Me and my brothers used to play cowboys and Indians, but we never thought about the military," he said.

Lopez and two other soldiers earned medals for an encounter they had when away from their company and fought a company of Germans. "They started firing at us, and we had to get in a ditch," he recounted. As the fighting broke out, the three GIs were joined by Italians, in an Italian Army unit, who took up the fight alongside the Americans. "When they [the Germans] stated firing at us, these Italians ... helped us out," he said. "We started charging them, and we captured the whole company of Germans."

Lopez and his company may have fought alongside friendly citizens, but not all Italians were allies. His unit received orders from the U.S. Office of Strategic Services to track down Italian Prime Minister Benito Mussolini. "We had orders to get to Mussolini before [he was] killed," Lopez said. "We were in contact with the OSS, but when we got there, Mussolini was hanging."

During the war, Lopez participated in campaigns in Europe, Africa and the Middle East. In retrospect, he looked on his military exploits with pride.

"I don't regret it because I think I learned a lot from it," he said. "I'm sorry for the guys who didn't come back ... I lost a lot of friends."

After his discharge in September 1945, Lopez worked as an electric plater, and then as a truck driver for 25 years until his retirement in 1980. He and his wife, Dolores, had two children, Joseph and Diana.

Joe V. Lopez

Date of Birth
3 MAY 1921
Los Angeles, CA

Interviewed by
Steven Rosales
13 MAY 2003
Whittier, CA

WWII Military Unit
362d Infantry
Regiment,
91st Infantry
Division

RIOS RODRIGUEZ, RAUL. While some draftees were so scared of combat they feigned mental imbalance so they would be sent home, the war offered Raul Rios Rodriguez the chance to escape the hardened streets of New York City.

Born June 6, 1927, in Puerto Rico, Rios grew up in Spanish Harlem. "As kids we'd fight with the blacks, fight with the Italians," he said. "Some were friends ... but it didn't matter when you go to different areas. It was about territories and cliques."

Rios had a scar hidden under the hair on the back of his head from the time one rival gang member whacked him with a vacuum cleaner pipe.

His brothers joined the Marines one by one and came back with stories of blood and gore. Rios was not dissuaded. "Hey, you gotta defend your country. You gotta go, gotta go," he said.

Rios enlisted in the Army with two friends in September 1945. He was sent to Fort Devens, Mass., for basic training, leaving his sisters and girlfriend behind in New York. At Fort Bragg, N.C., he encountered a strict drill instructor who was particularly harsh on the Hispanic and black soldiers in his unit.

"We were all soldiers; we were all risking our lives for the United States," Rios recalled. "That should never have been done. Never."

But Rios served on. He was shipped to La Havre, France, assigned to guard bridges and supply depots in France and Germany with the 18th Infantry Regiment, 1st Infantry Division. After serving two years, he was sent home.

Following the war Rios opened a beauty parlor with his wife Irma. They had two children together, Raul Jr. and Millazos, before divorcing. He married Magnolia in 1980 and they had a son, Raul III.

Raul Rios
Rodriguez

Date of Birth
6 JUNE 1927
Arecibo, PR

Interviewed by
Paul Harrigan
14 SEPTEMBER 2002
Miami, FL

WWII Military Unit
Company K,
18th Infantry
Regiment,
1st Infantry Division

Gabriel Valades

Date of Birth
24 MARCH 1924
Edgemont, SD

Interviewed by
Rea Ann Trotter

WWII Military Unit
Headquarters,
38th Anti-Aircraft
Artillery Group

VALADES, GABRIEL. Traveling into Germany following the end of the war, Gabriel Valades witnessed the sadness and ruin that can follow battle. "My memories of this trip were of sadness and devastation," he said. The people begged for food and cigarettes, elderly people and young children roamed the streets, their homes and towns virtually destroyed.

When his unit crossed the border into Germany, people appeared to be better fed than the French and seemed pleased at the arrival of the American soldiers, but their homes and cities were also in ruins. "The American and British bombers sure did a complete job in bombing Deutschland," he said. He remembered people crying out, *"Alles kaput,"* meaning "everything is destroyed."

Moving on to Stuttgart, Germany, Valades and his fellow troops guarded railroad yards and passing trains. "The trains were full of people going nowhere," he said. In the war-torn country, Germans and people of other nationalities no longer had homes to return to. Valades said he believes World War II was a necessary fight, but because of the millions upon millions of wasted lives, as well as money, he thinks "nobody won anything."

Valades was on duty when bodies from concentration camps near Munich passed through. "It was a horrible sight, and the stench was beyond words," he recalled. Even decades after the war he still wondered how it was possible for any human being to treat another in such a despicable manner.

Valades served from March 1943 to April 1946. When he returned to the United States, he enrolled in the Chadron State Teachers' College in Chadron, Neb. He taught in Wyoming for three years, attended school in Colorado for graduate studies and worked as a rehabilitation therapist for 29 years in Fort Meade, Md. He and his wife, Helen Cordova, had eight children: Gabe Jr., Rita, Catherine, Andrea, Joseph, Anita, John and David.

Domingo Zatarian

Date of Birth
18 AUGUST 1918
San Diego, CA

Interviewed by
René Zambrano
13 APRIL 2001
San Diego, CA

WWII Military Unit
69th Infantry
Division

ZATARIAN, DOMINGO. When Domingo Zatarian arrived in Europe for the Battle of the Bulge, the fighting had already ended. So he picked up a map and set out to find his brother's division. He found Marty in a ditch, singing "Swinging on a Star." "He was singing 'Would you rather be a mule?' or some such thing," Zatarian said recalling the implausible event with a thin smile on his lips.

Zatarian was one of four brothers from a San Diego family who served in the U.S. Armed Forces during World War II. George, the eldest, was in the European theater; Jerry served four years as a foot soldier in the Pacific; and Marty fought in five major campaigns and the Battle of the Bulge before his brother found him singing in that trench.

Growing up in San Diego to Mexican-born parents, Zatarian enjoyed playing basketball for his team, the Toltecs. While he was not eager to go to war, he never entertained the thought of fleeing to Mexico.

Zatarian first trained in the Mojave Anti-Aircraft Range and was to take a test to enter the U.S. Army Air Corps. However, before he began flight training he was sent to England and later to Germany with the infantry. Zatarian did not see combat during the war and only saw one dead German soldier.

After the conflict ended in Germany, Zatarian was sent to Oahu, Hawaii. His typical day on the base consisted of digging trenches, driving trucks and keeping the camp secure. He received several medals for his efforts and was discharged with the rank of technical sergeant in September 1945.

When he returned home, Zatarian resumed his occupation as a displayer at a local California business, Harry & Frank. Zatarian married twice and had five children: William, Jeanne, Samuel, Marc and Socorro.

Seaman 1st Class Manuel J. Aguirre (top row, left) and crew members aboard the USS *Ozark* in Guam, March 6, 1945.

The Pacific Theater

On the same day as the attack on Pearl Harbor, the Japanese had also successfully attacked Wake Island and the Philippines by air, and also Guam, Hong Kong and Malaya. The first six months after those attacks, the war in the Pacific went almost entirely in favor of the Japanese. Evacuated from Corregidor to Australia on March 12, 1942, a month before the fall of the Bataan Peninsula, Commanding General Douglas MacArthur, had vowed: "I will return!"

It would take some time, but MacArthur would, indeed, be back.

On the main Philippine island of Luzon after the attack on Pearl Harbor, U.S. soldiers knew that the Japanese were headed toward them. It became apparent to U.S. officers, both in the Philippines and in Washington, that the U.S. position on Luzon was untenable: there weren't enough U.S. ships nearby to fight back the Japanese, after the attack on Pearl Harbor. As the Japanese consolidated their hold on Luzon, U.S. soldiers retreated onto the Bataan peninsula, unreachable by ship or air; they could get neither reinforcements nor food and supplies, nor could they leave, except a few to the island of Corregidor in Manila Bay.

As supplies diminished and men weakened from lack of food and medical supplies on Bataan, Ralph Rodriguez, of El Paso, Texas, serving with the 200th Coast (AA) Artillery, was compelled to ask a priest about their fate. "I hated myself for asking," he said later. The priest answered that they would surrender and be taken prisoners by the Japanese. After that surrender, Rodriguez and the other men on the Bataan Peninsula, fatigued from disease and malnutrition, would walk 65 miles to a staging area where they then took a train to a Japanese labor camp. The journey became known as the Bataan Death March.

Elsewhere in the Pacific, fighting continued under arduous conditions: there were disease-bearing mosquitoes, jungle rot and monsoons.

The Japanese were relentless and fearsome. However, their resources, in terms of manpower, equipment and supplies, were finite and were scattered among many islands. Also, they made strategic mistakes at the Battle of Midway, as the war momentum began favoring the Allies.

Joe Medina, of Lamar, Colo., and part of the Support Forces for the 7th Army, served in New Guinea, preparing for the invasion of Leyte. Once Leyte was secured, he helped build airstrips on the island, battled monsoons that often kept supply trucks away from the workers.

One of the units fighting in the Philippines was the Mexican *Escuadron 201*, made up of 42 officers and 249 support members, the Squadron flew 96 combat missions (including 37 training missions) over Luzon, New Guinea, and some in Formosa. Back home, they would be greeted as heroes: Mexico had contributed.

Joe Medina went from Leyte to Manila and then to Okinawa. One morning, shots rang out from Navy ships, the United States had taken the island; the battle was over.

"That day we received our first ration of beer," he recalled.

The battle of Okinawa exacted a heavy toll on the Americans—from April 1, to June 18, 1945, more than 7,600 Americans had been killed or were missing in action. Japanese losses were tenfold the Americans. And more than 100,000 Okinawa civilians were also killed. The heavy losses at Okinawa would signal to the U.S. that any land invasion of Japan would result in similar bloodbath for Americans. An alternative to a land invasion was raised: the still unproven atomic bomb.

THE SECOND WORLD WAR
THE PACIFIC THEATER,
1941 - 1945

N

SCALE OF MILES

0   300   600   900

Cartographic Cell of Excellence
Department of History, United States Military Academy

FIRST PHASE
From 7 December 1941, until June 1942, the Japanese s[...]
the Pacific Fleet's base at Pearl Harbor, took Wake Islan[...]
and conquered the Philippines, Hong Kong, Malaya, an[...]
base of Singapore. They conquered Burma thereby cutt[...]
overland routes to the western allies, and seized the Ne[...]
and British Borneo, thereby securing a much-needed so[...]
Japanese advance came to a halt with the American vic[...]
Coral Sea (May 1942) and the Battle of Midway (June 1[...]

SOVIET UNION

MONGOLIA

MANCUKUO
(MANCHURIA)

Khabarovsk

Harbin

SAKHALIN ISLAND

KURIL ISLANDS

Vladivostok

Sapporo

HOKKAIDO

Mukden

Port Arthur

SEA OF JAPAN

HONSHU

SECOND PHASE
The second phase in the Pacific War was one of relative
stalemate. From June 1942 until late-1943, neither side
could muster the land, sea or air power required to take
the offensive and seize the initiative from the other. The
Battle of Guadalcanal was an example of this stalemate.

Seoul

KOREA

Pusan

Hiroshima Kobe
Nagasaki   Osaka
        SHIKOKU
        KYUSHU

Tokyo
    Yokohama

JAPAN

CHINA

Nanking

Shanghai

Chungking

Changshao

Wenchow

YELLOW
SEA

EAST
CHINA
SEA

Foochow

Amoy

Swatow   Canton

RYUKYU ISLANDS

FORMOSA

Okinawa, 1945

SPRUANCE (Spring)

BONIN ISLANDS

VOLCANO ISLANDS

Iwo Jima, 1945

PACI[...]

Hanoi

HAINAN

Hong Kong, 1941

PHILIPPINE SEA

MARIANA ISLANDS

THAILAND

Bangkok

FRENCH
INDOCHINA

SOUTH
CHINA
SEA

Luzon

Bataan-Corregidor, 1942

Philippine Sea, 1944

Saipan, 1944
Tinian, 1944
Guam, 1944

Saigon

MINDORO

PHILIPPINES (U.S.)

SAMAR

LEYTE

PALAWAN

Leyte Gulf, 1944

SPRUANCE (Spring-Summer 1944)

HALSEY (Summer 1944)

Yap   Ulithi

Eniwetok, 1944

CAROLINE ISLANDS

Kwajalein,

MINDANAO
Davao

SULU SEA

PALAU ISLANDS

Peleliu, 1944

TRUK ISLANDS

SPRUANC[...]

MALAYA
(BR.)

BRIT. N. BORNEO
BRUNEI
(BR.)
SARAWAK
(BR.)

CELEBES SEA

Singapore, 1942

DUTCH
BORNEO

SUMATRA

MAKASSAR STRAIT

Menado

HALAMERA

Sansaporo

MORATAI

MacARTHUR (Spring-Summer)

ADMIRALTY ISLANDS

Kavieng, 1943

NEW IRELAND

HALSEY (Under MacA[...]

CELEBES

Biak, 1944

N.E. NEW
GUINEA
(AUST.)

Rabul, 1943

Bouganville, 1943

Empress Augusta

NETHERLANDS EAST INDIES

JAVA

Java Sea, 1942

BANDA SEA

NETH. NEW GUINEA

Lae

NEW
BRITAIN

SOLOMON ISL[...]

Kolombangara

Flores

Timor

ARAFURA SEA

Port
Moresby

Coral Sea 1942

Guadal C[...]

TIMOR SEA

Darwin

CORAL SEA

GI[...]

Japanese Permiter (July 1942)

SOUTHWEST PACIFIC Area
(MacARTHUR)

Cairns

SOUTHWEST PACIFIC Area
(MacARTHUR)

PA[...]

SOUTHEAST ASIA
(MOUNTBATTEN)
This area was under
British strategic direction.

AUSTRALIA

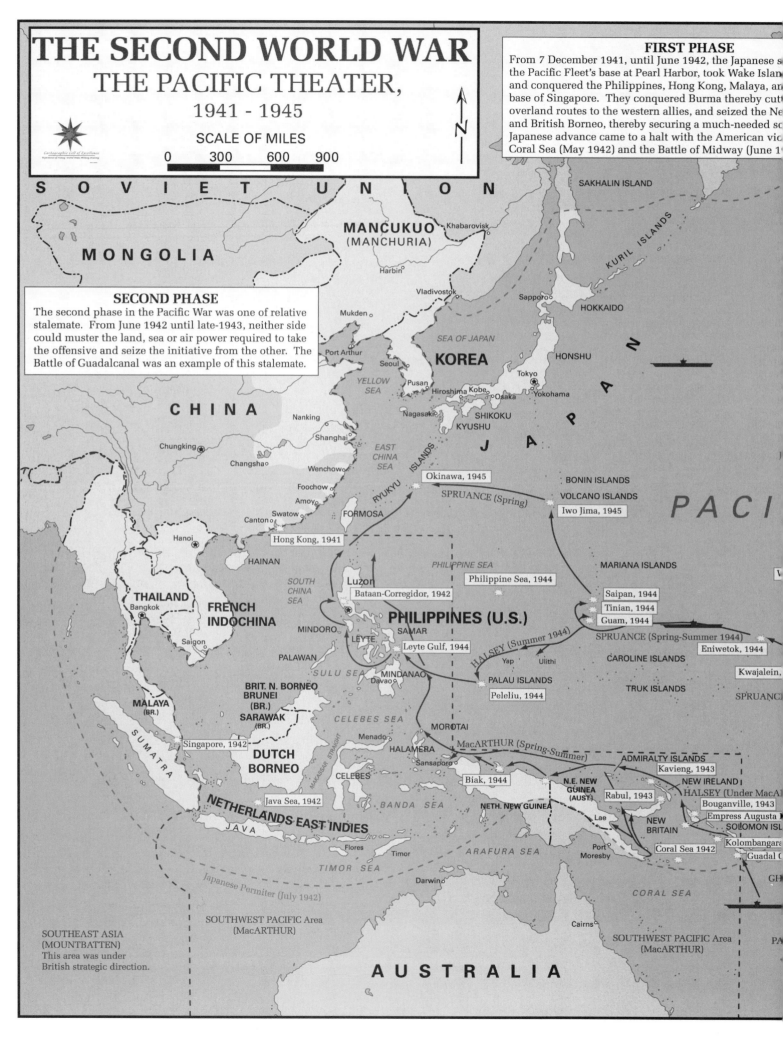

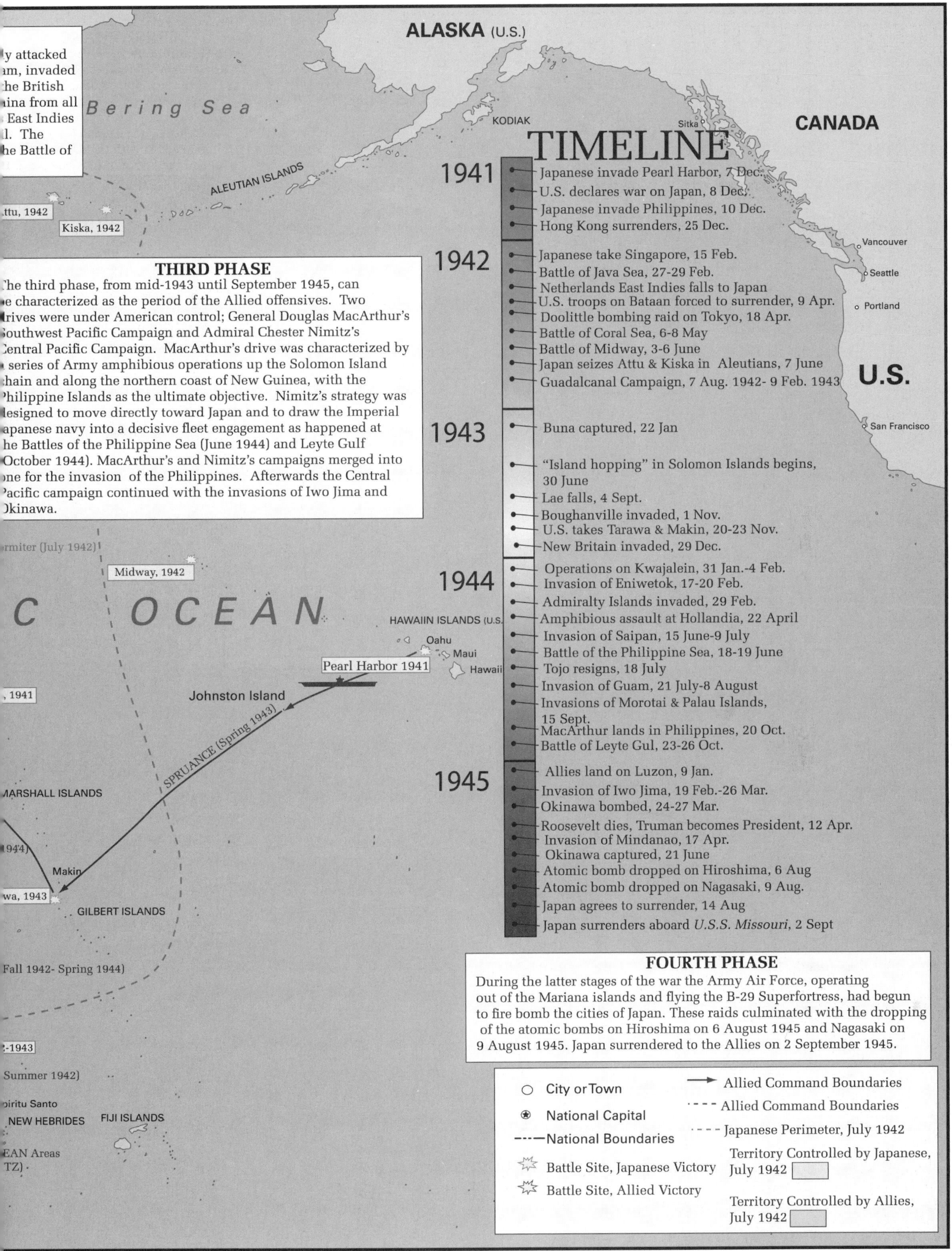
ALASKA (U.S.)
CANADA
U.S.
Bering Sea
KODIAK
Sitka
Vancouver
Seattle
Portland
San Francisco
ALEUTIAN ISLANDS
ttu, 1942
Kiska, 1942
y attacked
m, invaded
he British
ina from all
East Indies
l. The
he Battle of
THIRD PHASE
he third phase, from mid-1943 until September 1945, can
e characterized as the period of the Allied offensives. Two
rives were under American control; General Douglas MacArthur's
outhwest Pacific Campaign and Admiral Chester Nimitz's
entral Pacific Campaign. MacArthur's drive was characterized by
series of Army amphibious operations up the Solomon Island
hain and along the northern coast of New Guinea, with the
hilippine Islands as the ultimate objective. Nimitz's strategy was
esigned to move directly toward Japan and to draw the Imperial
apanese navy into a decisive fleet engagement as happened at
he Battles of the Philippine Sea (June 1944) and Leyte Gulf
October 1944). MacArthur's and Nimitz's campaigns merged into
ne for the invasion of the Philippines. Afterwards the Central
acific campaign continued with the invasions of Iwo Jima and
kinawa.
TIMELINE
1941
Japanese invade Pearl Harbor, 7 Dec.
U.S. declares war on Japan, 8 Dec.
Japanese invade Philippines, 10 Dec.
Hong Kong surrenders, 25 Dec.
1942
Japanese take Singapore, 15 Feb.
Battle of Java Sea, 27-29 Feb.
Netherlands East Indies falls to Japan
U.S. troops on Bataan forced to surrender, 9 Apr.
Doolittle bombing raid on Tokyo, 18 Apr.
Battle of Coral Sea, 6-8 May
Battle of Midway, 3-6 June
Japan seizes Attu & Kiska in Aleutians, 7 June
Guadalcanal Campaign, 7 Aug. 1942- 9 Feb. 1943
1943
Buna captured, 22 Jan
"Island hopping" in Solomon Islands begins, 30 June
Lae falls, 4 Sept.
Boughanville invaded, 1 Nov.
U.S. takes Tarawa & Makin, 20-23 Nov.
New Britain invaded, 29 Dec.
1944
Operations on Kwajalein, 31 Jan.-4 Feb.
Invasion of Eniwetok, 17-20 Feb.
Admiralty Islands invaded, 29 Feb.
Amphibious assault at Hollandia, 22 April
Invasion of Saipan, 15 June-9 July
Battle of the Philippine Sea, 18-19 June
Tojo resigns, 18 July
Invasion of Guam, 21 July-8 August
Invasions of Morotai & Palau Islands, 15 Sept.
MacArthur lands in Philippines, 20 Oct.
Battle of Leyte Gul, 23-26 Oct.
1945
Allies land on Luzon, 9 Jan.
Invasion of Iwo Jima, 19 Feb.-26 Mar.
Okinawa bombed, 24-27 Mar.
Roosevelt dies, Truman becomes President, 12 Apr.
Invasion of Mindanao, 17 Apr.
Okinawa captured, 21 June
Atomic bomb dropped on Hiroshima, 6 Aug
Atomic bomb dropped on Nagasaki, 9 Aug.
Japan agrees to surrender, 14 Aug
Japan surrenders aboard *U.S.S. Missouri*, 2 Sept
rmiter (July 1942)
Midway, 1942
C OCEAN
HAWAIIN ISLANDS (U.S.
Oahu
Maui
Hawaii
Pearl Harbor 1941
Johnston Island
SPRUANCE (Spring 1943)
, 1941
MARSHALL ISLANDS
944)
Makin
wa, 1943
GILBERT ISLANDS
Fall 1942- Spring 1944)
-1943
Summer 1942)
piritu Santo
NEW HEBRIDES
FIJI ISLANDS
EAN Areas
TZ)
FOURTH PHASE
During the latter stages of the war the Army Air Force, operating
out of the Mariana islands and flying the B-29 Superfortress, had begun
to fire bomb the cities of Japan. These raids culminated with the dropping
of the atomic bombs on Hiroshima on 6 August 1945 and Nagasaki on
9 August 1945. Japan surrendered to the Allies on 2 September 1945.
City or Town
National Capital
National Boundaries
Battle Site, Japanese Victory
Battle Site, Allied Victory
Allied Command Boundaries
Allied Command Boundaries
Japanese Perimeter, July 1942
Territory Controlled by Japanese, July 1942
Territory Controlled by Allies, July 1942

Map courtesy of the Department of History, United States Military Academy

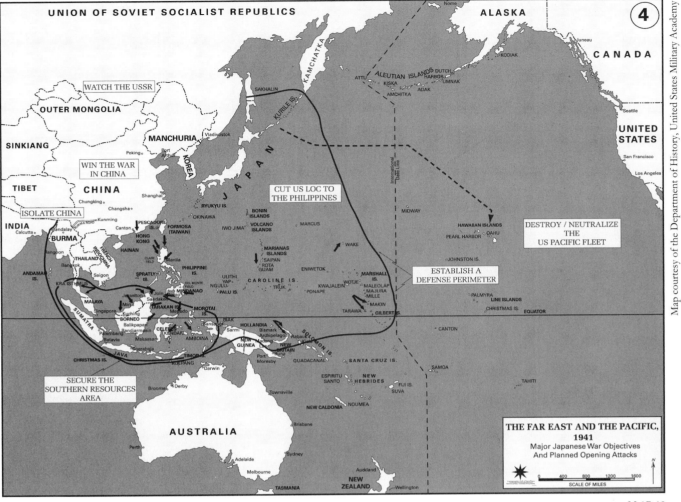

Map courtesy of the Department of History, United States Military Academy

Within the map:

UNION OF SOVIET SOCIALIST REPUBLICS

ALASKA

4

CANADA

WATCH THE USSR

OUTER MONGOLIA

SINKIANG

MANCHURIA

UNITED STATES

WIN THE WAR IN CHINA

TIBET   CHINA

ISOLATE CHINA

INDIA

BURMA

CUT US LOC TO THE PHILIPPINES

DESTROY / NEUTRALIZE THE US PACIFIC FLEET

ESTABLISH A DEFENSE PERIMETER

SECURE THE SOUTHERN RESOURCES AREA

AUSTRALIA

NEW ZEALAND

THE FAR EAST AND THE PACIFIC, 1941
Major Japanese War Objectives
And Planned Opening Attacks

SCALE OF MILES

MAP 10

THE U.S. ENTERS THE WAR

The American public was insistent on an international policy of isolationism and staying out of the war, even as Germany attacked Poland in 1939 and Japan invaded Chinese-occupied Manchuria in 1931, signaling its designs on its Asian neighbors. By late summer 1937, Japan had attacked Shanghai, China, and the war between Japan and China had begun. Still, the United States was committed to remaining uninvolved.

The Draft

In an effort to prepare the nation should a strong military be needed, President Roosevelt signed the Selective Training and Service Act, which in 1940 began the first peacetime draft. One month after it was passed, more than 16 million men between ages 21 and 35 had registered for the draft. This draft had severe restrictions, however: draftees would be limited to 12 months of duty and they could not be stationed outside of the Western Hemisphere. Also, in 1940 and the following year, the entire U.S. National Guard was called up to active duty, reorganized and began training for the war.

In 1941, as the Nazis had invaded the Soviet Union's western borders, after they were gaining momentum in the Mediterranean, the draft needed to be extended. In August 1941, it was extended. After the attack on Pearl Harbor, the Selective Service Act would be revised, to take men from 18 to 65. By late 1942, there would be 42 million men registered. In reality, only younger men would actually be called up. Another change after the attack was that the service period would be for the "duration of the war."

Other American boys had already begun enlisting, before being drafted. Encarnación Armando Gonzales, of Los Angeles, Calif., was inducted on Jan. 22, 1941, and served in the 7th Infantry Division. "I wanted to be part of something that was happening and for job opportunities," he said. "It was doing something for survival and, at the same time, doing something for my country."

Gonzales kept the news of his joining a secret from his family until right before he left for basic training. After he learned they would have approved of his decision, he felt guilty for keeping the news from them.

Pearl Harbor

Frank Arellano, from Arroyo, N.M., and part of the 24th Infantry Division, was stationed in Oahu, Hawaii. Early that Sunday morning, Dec. 7, 1941, Arellano had just gone to breakfast at Schofield Barracks, a 4,695-acre Army post in the center of Oahu, when he heard machine guns firing.

His company scattered and broke into an ammunition locker to retrieve their weapons and fire back at the Japanese, but by that time, the planes had moved on to Pearl Harbor, 17 miles south.

The men at Pearl Harbor responded as quickly as they could to the unexpected attack. Arthur Tenorio, of Las Vegas, N.M., was at Pearl Harbor, manning an anti-aircraft gun aboard the *New Orleans*, throwing the hot castings in the water after the gun was fired.

"I was the hot shell man," Tenorio said. "I had to throw the red-hot shell casings into the water, but I couldn't find my asbestos gloves, so I picked up the first three or four with my bare hands. I didn't have time to digest: I had to react. Finally someone wrapped my hands in old rags." At one point, Tenorio looked up and clearly saw a Japanese plane directly above him.

"I saw the cockpit open. I knew a bomb was going to hit my head," he recalled. "Luckily it angled off and hit the side of the ship."

During the attack on Pearl Harbor, there were 3,435 casualties, five battleships were sunk, three light cruisers and three destroyers hit and 188 planes destroyed. On the *Arizona* alone, 1,177 men died when it sank.

News that the Japanese had attacked Hawaii traveled quickly back to the mainland. It was clearly a blow to the United States, for much of the Pacific Fleet was moored there. The following day, President Franklin D. Roosevelt, in an address to Congress and the nation over the radio waves, called Dec. 7, 1941, a "date which will live in infamy." The Senate declared war at the request of President Roosevelt; there was only one "no" vote. Later that day, the President signed the formal declaration of war.

Pearl Harbor was not the only Japanese target in their initial blow of the day. They attacked Burma, Malaya, Singapore and the Dutch East Indies and destroyed most of the air force in the Philippines in preparation of an eventual takeover of the islands in the following months.

But the attack also set in motion other events in Europe. On Dec. 11, both Germany and Italy, which had a pact with Japan, declared war on the United States. Japan's attack on Hawaii, and Germany and Italy's subsequent declaration of war, dissolved U.S. neutrality and indifference. In its place was a fierce determination to defend the nation and defeat the Axis powers.

GONZALES, ENCARNACIÓN ARMANDO. Lying in a cold stream with a bullet wound to his chest, Armando Gonzales felt his body getting weaker and thought his life was over. Surrounded by the enemy in the Aleutian Islands, he had been shot by a sniper. He dropped his rifle and rolled down a hill into a gully. He knew the sniper was still near, but he could not give up the fight.

With all the strength he had left, Gonzales forced himself to his feet and sprinted back up the hill, where he collapsed. His fellow soldiers quickly came to his aid, firing at the enemy while dragging him to safety.

Gonzales, was one of more than 25 men from his street in East Los Angeles who fought in the war. Inducted in January 1941, Gonzales was stationed in California when the Japanese bombed Pearl Harbor. In June 1943, lying in the medic's tent after he was shot, his first thoughts were to send a personal message to his wife, Soledad Seanez, so she would not be scared by a telegraph she might receive from the government.

Gonzales was sent stateside to recover. He eventually was sent to Europe, where most of his days consisted of taking villages, sleeping in foxholes and braving the cold weather. "It was survival," he said. "You get used to misery inside and drink more when the day is over."

Gonzales was discharged Oct. 11, 1945, but he continued to fight the alcoholism that began during the war. "It was great to be home, and a lot of tears, and a lot of adjustment and a lot of drinking. A lot of horrible drinking," he recalled. "Nowadays people get a lot of help after traumatic situations, but we didn't have that back then." He credited his wife with his recovery. The couple had two children: Armando and Michael. He is active in the VFW and a bust of his likeness has been in a display honoring the WWII generation at Mount St. Mary's College in Los Angeles, Calif.

Encarnación
Armando Gonzales

Date of Birth
13 NOVEMBER 1919
Los Angeles, CA

Interviewed by
Jennifer Sinco
Kelleher
23 MARCH 2001
Los Angeles, CA

WWII Military Unit
Company M,
17th Infantry
Regiment,
7th Infantry
Division

Transferred to
44th Infantry
Division

HERNANDEZ, CANDELARIO. While visiting his family during his weekend leave from Fort Sam Houston, Texas, Candelario Hernandez heard a radio news bulletin recalling all servicemen to duty—immediately. "It was scary," he said, "because you didn't know what was happening."

Hernandez enlisted in the Army just a month before the bombing of Pearl Harbor. In 1942 the Austin native and the 32d Infantry Division were shipped to Australia. Their first battle—in Buna, New Guinea—began on Nov. 27, 1942. "I lost a lot of buddies there," he said of the battle, which proved important for U.S. success in the South Pacific seas. The soldiers contended with mosquitoes and leeches and used machetes to chop a path through the thick jungle vegetation. "The jungles were something," he said. "You don't even see the sun in the daytime."

After the first encounter in New Guinea, most of the men in the division—including Hernandez—came down with malaria. He found himself in battle with a 103-degree fever, but he did not realize he was sick. He was puzzled that he kept falling down when he ran. "I was wondering, 'Why am I falling down?' I am not that weak," he said. The sick men were treated in isolation in Australia. "They took us to a place up there that was near the ocean," he recounted. "That was part of the therapy to cure you from the malaria. All we did was swim and take sun baths."

Hernandez was then recalled to action in Aitape, New Guinea, this time as a staff sergeant leading 12 men. His division's mission was to hold the Drinumor River line as long as possible in the event of an attack. They proved successful: the Japanese never got through.

For three years following his return to the States, Hernandez continued to suffer bouts of malaria. After two years of searching, he found a manufacturing job at Hall Levels in Austin. He married María Macias and had two daughters: María and Claire Susan.

Candelario
Hernandez

Date of Birth
2 FEBRUARY 1920
Seguin, TX

Interviewed by
Lucinda Guinn
15 MARCH 2001
Austin, TX

WWII Military Unit
Company L,
127th Infantry
Regiment,
32d Infantry
Division

Carlos Carrillo
Quintana

Date of Birth
5 MARCH 1920
El Paso, TX

Interviewed by
René Zambrano
29 SEPTEMBER 2000
San Diego, CA

WWII Military Unit
Company L,
165th Infantry
Regiment,
27th Infantry
Division

QUINTANA, CARLOS CARRILLO. During a Japanese mortar attack following a battle in Saipan, mortar fragments pierced Carlos Carrillo Quintana's tongue and severed a major artery in his mouth. He was unable to speak for six years.

Quintana had been called into service on Sept. 21, 1941, and was trained as a member of the elite U.S. Army Ranger forces, a group that began in World War II as scouts. As part of his training he learned hand-to-hand combat and navigational techniques. When war broke out, he joined Company L of the 165th Infantry Regiment and protected the Hawaiian Islands in the aftermath of Pearl Harbor. He was involved in three major battles in the Pacific—at the Gilbert Islands, Marshall Islands and Saipan. Fought in June 1944, Saipan secured the Aslito Airfield, a strategic launch point for future attacks.

After he was injured, Quintana spent the rest of the war in hospitals in Hawaii and elsewhere. During his recuperation, he felt confused and "disgusted with the whole thing [war]." He came back after the war and saw people continuing as usual—making money and dancing—while he had nightmares of his friends and a sergeant who had been killed. "People have no idea what a fighting man goes through," he said.

Quintana was in an Army hospital at Fort Bliss in El Paso, Texas, when the war ended. While he had been unable to eat or speak and weighed 89 pounds, he remained optimistic because of his belief in God, and he began Spanish linguistic exercises to regain his strength. He married Nora Gomez in 1945. She died in 1963 and he married Esperanza Juarez in 1965. They had three children: Martha, María Elena and Carlos. He devoted himself to educating and supporting the young, "the future of our country and the security of our freedom."

Alfonso Rodriguez

Date of Birth
24 AUGUST 1922
Santa Fe, NM

Interviewed by
Andrés Romero
3 NOVEMBER 2002
Santa Fe, NM

WWII Military Unit
2d Cavalry Brigade,
1st Cavalry Division

RODRIGUEZ, ALFONSO. While he enlisted in the Army on Dec. 31, 1940, during peacetime, Alfonso Rodriguez soon found himself in the midst of a war. Following the attack on Pearl Harbor, he trained at Fort Bliss, Texas, and was shipped to Brisbane, Australia, in July 1943. He saw his first action when he was transferred to New Guinea and fought in the invasion of Los Negros Island on March 15, 1944.

He suffered his first injury on Manus Island. "They shot the heel of my foot," he said. After a two month hospital stay, he returned to battle. Another time, he was on patrol when he encountered Japanese soldiers in a village on Manus Island. He was struck by fragments from an exploding grenade, injuring his right leg. All of his toenails had to be surgically removed so tiny shards of shrapnel could be removed.

However, his physical injuries did not wound as sharply as the racial slurs slung his way. Rodriguez was born Aug. 22, 1922, in Santa Fe, N.M. With friends of a variety of backgrounds, he didn't experience racial discrimination until he joined the Army. For example, he and fellow Mexican-American soldiers were confronted by a white soldier demanding they speak English "like Americans." Rodriguez and the white soldier fought. The white soldier, who was the bigger of the two, slapped him around and stormed off. Several weeks later, after a friend taught him some boxing moves, Rodriguez confronted the white soldier and returned the favor with his newfound fighting skills. "I was angry," Rodriguez said. "When I hit him, I laid him out on the floor. He took off running and never bothered us anymore."

After his discharge, Rodriguez married Alice Gonzales and raised five children: Charles, Mary Ellen, Dennis, Melinda and Annette.

SANDOVAL, SANTOS. Armed only with a pair of wire cutters, Santos Sandoval crawled on his back to the edge of the Japanese-held bridge, intent on disarming the two 600-pound bombs with detonating wires leading back to the Japanese camp.

"I got to the first bomb, knowing that if it blew, that's it. It was curtains," he said with a tense chuckle.

Santos Sandoval

Date of Birth
31 OCTOBER 1919
La Junta, CO

Interviewed by
Sandra Murillo
23 MARCH 2002
Los Angeles, CA

WWII Military Unit
Company K,
3d Battalion,
185th Infantry
Regiment,
40th Infantry
Division

Santos' company needed to cross the bridge on March 19, 1945, to unite with troops on the other side of Panay Island in the Philippines. Since he had munitions experience, he was charged with disarming the bombs. While he was unfamiliar with the Japanese wiring system, Sandoval would go, alone, and guess.

"I found a big detonator box underneath one of the beams, filled with explosives. I cut it. I found another big box and cut it, undetected," he said. He cut the wires on both bombs. "I was very fortunate. I got a dozen of my men across before we were detected." Sandoval received a Silver Star Medal for gallantry for his accomplishment.

While his heroics earned him measures of pride and recognition, they also brought him pain and suffering, as, even after his discharge on July 4, 1945, he continued to awaken at night in a sweat, reliving the nightmares of war.

"I thought it would go away, but it has never gone away," he said. "I guess I'll die with it."

Following the war, he worked with the Department of the Army for 15 years and then transferred to the Department of Agriculture as the agency's first bilingual employee.

He married Adele Gutierrez and had five children: Linda, Michael, David, Martha and Patricia.

SENA, LUIS. Before he had even finished learning to fire his weapon, Luis Sena found his training at Camp Roberts, Calif., cut short. After the devastating attack on Pearl Harbor, he was sent to Fort Lewis, Wash., where he guarded bridges along the coast until it became apparent the state was not a target. He and the 163d Infantry Regiment went to Australia for more training and then went to the jungles of New Guinea. In a 34-month span he fought alongside the Allied forces in numerous campaigns on the islands of New Guinea and helped drive the enemy out of Buna and Gona during the Papuan campaign.

Luis Sena

Date of Birth
11 AUGUST 1923
Golondrinas, NM

Interviewed by
Violeta Dominguez
3 NOVEMBER 2002
Santa Fe, NM

WWII Military Unit
Company L,
163d Infantry
Regiment,
41st Infantry
Division

In New Guinea, Sena fell victim to malaria and spent 10 days in a hospital, quarantined with a 107-degree temperature. When he recovered he returned to battle and faced his closest call. On July 10, 1944, he was in the middle of a skirmish, kneeling behind a tree, when a Japanese soldier with a bazooka or a rifle grenade fired toward his hiding spot. The shell exploded close by, hurling shrapnel straight toward him. "All of a sudden I felt something hot running down my chest and my hand, so I unbutton my jacket, and, sure enough, I was bleeding from 11 places. I still have a piece of shrapnel in my hand and two pieces in my chest," he said, pointing to his left hand.

The incident landed Sena in a hospital for a month and earned him a Purple Heart. After recovering sufficiently, he returned to fight with his company. Finally, in December 1944, he returned home to New Mexico.

Soon after his return stateside, Sena met Elvira Trujillo at a dance near Las Vegas, N.M. The two married in January 1945 and he was discharged in August. Sena attended a vocational school where he learned to make boots and saddles, while studying carpentry and cabinetry. He had five children: Stella, Christine, Steven, Catherine and Sandy.

Frank Arellano

Date of Birth
15 MAY 1919
Arroyo Hondo, NM

Interviewed by
Rea Ann Trotter
10 SEPTEMBER 2000
Alamoso, CO

WWII Military Unit
Company C,
21st Infantry
Regiment,
24th Infantry
Division

ARELLANO, FRANK. Early on a Sunday morning, 22-year-old Frank Arellano had just gone down for breakfast at Schofield Barracks, on the Hawaiian Island of Oahu, when he heard the sound of machine guns firing. The men of Company C in the 21st Infantry Regiment broke into the ammunition room to shoot at the planes, but by the time they retrieved their weapons, the Japanese fighter planes had moved on from their attack on Pearl Harbor, Oahu.

Arellano was born in 1919 in Arroyo Hondo, N.M., and grew up in Los Mogotes, Colo. He joined the Army and headed to the Hawaiian Islands in 1940. While he was in Hawaii, Arellano mingled with Japanese Americans and Japanese living in Hawaii and worked hard to learn their language. After his division left Hawaii, the men were moved to Australia and then Goodenough Island near New Guinea. The division landed on April 22, 1944, at Tanamerah Bay, New Guinea, to secure the Hollandia Airdrome, a Japanese aerial stronghold with 350 warplanes. Despite the treacherous, swampy terrain, the enemy was confused and disorganized, allowing the Americans to take the airfields with little resistance after only a few days.

Later in the war, when he was moved to a large plantation in New Guinea, Arellano and his fellow soldiers ate spaghetti and meatballs, served into their hands because they had lost their mess kits in the jungle. "It was hot but we didn't dare drop it," he remembered. "You couldn't hold the bread because the hands were so full of spaghetti."

Arellano, who served as a search light operator and later a messenger during the war, was discharged in 1945. He took the GED and studied industrial arts. He built his own house and made a living doing bodywork and running a radiator shop. He had three children with his first wife. He later divorced and then married Betty Blanton.

Arthur "Chavalito" Tenorio

Date of Birth
5 JUNE 1924
Las Vegas, NM

Interviewed by
M. David Gray
3 NOVEMBER 2002
Santa Fe, NM

WWII Military Unit
USS *New Orleans*
(CA-32)

TENORIO, ARTHUR "CHAVALITO." On Dec. 6, 1941, Arthur "Chavalito" Tenorio spent the night playing craps in a Honolulu hotel with a fellow sailor. He went to bed aboard the USS *New Orleans*, marooned at Pearl Harbor for engine repairs, never guessing that it would be attacked in a matter of hours.

When bombing began at Pearl Harbor, Tenorio ran to his assigned area, a 5-inch, .38-caliber gun that took nine men to operate. "I was the hot shell man," he said. "I had to throw the red-hot shell casings into the water, but I couldn't find my asbestos gloves, so I picked up the first three or four with my bare hands. I didn't have time to digest. I had to react. Finally someone wrapped my hands in old rags." At one point in the raid, Tenorio fell to his knees to laugh in hysteria and helplessness. Another time, he saw a plane directly overhead. "I saw the cockpit open. I knew a bomb was going to hit my head," he remembered. "Luckily it angled off and hit the side of the ship."

According to a letter from J.G. Atkins, the commanding officer, the directors in charge of gun use were on shore that morning and more than 40 percent of the crew on board had little or no training with machine guns or heavy guns. Despite this, Tenorio estimated they shot down a couple dozen planes, and the crew's efforts have been immortalized in song. "The song 'Praise the Lord and Pass the Ammunition' was written about a chaplain on our ship," he said. "And those words were true." Even though they lost all but auxiliary power and lighting, Tenorio suffered only minor burns to his hands and some hearing loss.

Tenorio was discharged in 1945. He married and divorced twice, becoming a single parent to two: Georgia and Arturo. He earned a master's degree in psychology in 1950 and taught in rural areas until he retired in 1980 as the superintendent of the Las Vegas, N.M. school district.

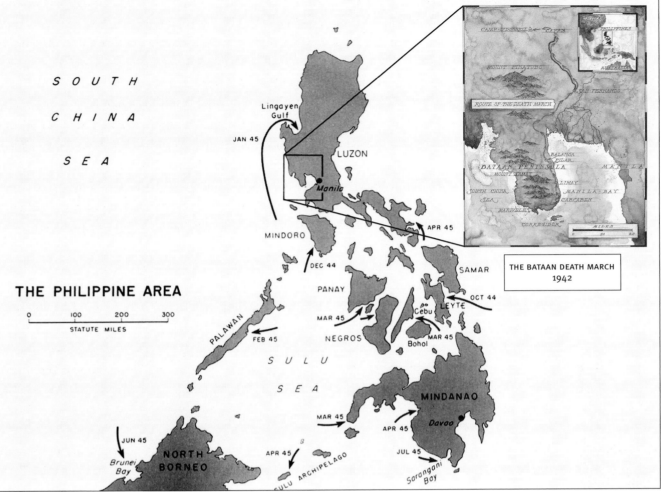

Base map courtesy of Perry-Castañeda Library Map Collections, Map revisions courtesy of Mike Reagan. Map revisions by Melissa DiPiero-D'Sa.

Route of the Death March illustration courtesy of Melissa DiPiero-D'Sa.

MAP 11

THE BATAAN DEATH MARCH

Within hours after the attack on Pearl Harbor on Dec. 7, 1941, Japanese forces had also mounted air raids on Wake Island and the Philippines, as well as Hong Kong, Guam and Malaya.

General Douglas MacArthur led troops in the Philippines — 19,000 Americans and 12,000 Filipinos who served as part of the Army. There was also a Philippine Army of 102,000 men. Civilians would also become involved in the fighting. The island of Luzon, the main island of the Philippines, would fall quickly. The ensuing taking of prisoners on a 65-mile march to

a prison camp would be marked by cruelty and become known as The Bataan Death March, so called because of the many prisoners who died along the way.

Abel Ortega, of the 192d Light Tank Battalion, a native of El Paso, Texas, arrived in Manila in March 1941, eight months before Pearl Harbor was attacked. He and the other men learned about the bombing of Pearl Harbor soon after it happened and, he recalled, they did what they could to prepare: hiding tanks and half-tracks (armored personnel carriers with tracks on the rear end) in the jungles around Clark Field, next to Fort Stotsenberg. Ten hours later, the attack on Luzon began.

"I heard a humming noise. ... I looked up into the sky ... we could see ... bombers ... and as they were coming over we heard hissing sounds," he said. "[There were] hundreds of ... bombers," Ortega said. "To our surprise, these ... were not American ... these were Japanese bombers."

The bombers were accompanied by Japanese fighter planes that strafed Luzon. Ortega began firing his .50 caliber machine gun from his half-track, without waiting for orders.

"It was complete chaos," he said.

On December 22, 1941, Japanese forces landed at Lingayen Gulf, 150 miles north of Manila, and made their way to Manila. Americans had already evacuated to the Bataan Peninsula. Plans for defending the peninsula had relied on the U.S. Navy providing reinforcements and supplies. However, with the loss of Naval power after the attack on Pearl Harbor, Bataan was on its own. In fact, the plight of the Americans and Filipinos, boxed in at Bataan, was well-known to U.S. military officials in Washington, but saving the troops appeared logistically impossible, as the Japanese controlled both the seas around and the skies above the Philippines. It became clear that although there were promises of relief, help was neither on its way, nor forthcoming. The soldiers at Bataan had been abandoned.

War correspondent Frank Hewlett, who covered the fall of Bataan for United Press before escaping first to Corregidor and later to Australia, would write:

> We're the battling bastards of Bataan;
> No mama, no papa, no Uncle Sam;
> No aunts, no uncles, no cousins, no nieces;
> No pills, no planes, no artillery pieces.
> ... And nobody gives a damn.

The Americans on Bataan, 15,000 military personnel, were far outnumbered and poorly equipped and supplied. Japanese forces intercepted medical supplies, and Americans began to succumb to malaria, dysentery and other tropical diseases, as well as to combat fatigue. American troops decreased food to half-rations.

Despite the monumental difficulties, the Americans and Filipinos on Bataan fought off Japanese landings until surrendering in April 1942. After their surrender to Japanese forces, American and Filipino troops would be moved to other camps. During the march, the men were denied food and water for much of the trip. Guards often bayoneted or shot any captives who attempted to rest during the journey, others were decapitated. Between 600 and 1,600 Americans died en route, as did between 5,000 to 10,000 Filipinos.

It would take more than three weeks for the men to walk the 65 miles from Mariveles, to San Fernando, where the prisoners boarded a train to Camp O'Donnell, a former Philippine Army camp that was converted into a labor camp. When Camp O'Donnell became overcrowded, the prisoners were moved again 60 miles east to another camp at Cabanutuan, where the men of Bataan encountered the prisoners from Corregidor. Conditions were again harsh and now the men were forced into 14-hour days of labor. Many were transported to Japan, to yet other labor camps. Conditions were bleak.

"I never gave up hope," said Agapito Silva, a native of San Marcial, N.M., and a member of the New Mexico 200th Coast Artillery. "Guys that gave up hope never made it."

One month after the fall of Bataan, Corregidor, the fortress island known as The Rock in Manila Bay, also surrendered.

BANEGAS, LORENZO. A New Mexico native, Lorenzo Banegas' home state suffered the most casualties during the infamous Bataan Death March. Nearly 1,700 members of the New Mexico National Guard were taken prisoner, and more than 900 paid the ultimate price.

Banegas was fortunate enough to survive the hellish march through the Philippine jungle in spring 1942. He credits the encouragement of one of his fellow soldiers, Adolfo Rivera.

"He picked me up. Rivera said, 'No, Banegas! Come on, let's go out and put some water on you,'" Banegas said. "He took me up there and threw some water on me. I said, 'Oh gosh, I feel a lot better now.'"

During the trek prisoners were denied food and water and were forced to sit in the scorching sun without the shade of even their helmets. Temperatures regularly exceeded 100 degrees during the trip that lasted over 60 miles, but any soldier who was too weak to continue was bayoneted or shot by the Japanese.

Once the prisoners reached Camp O'Donnell, they were put to work, still without proper amounts of food and water. Banegas had a morbid duty at the camp.

"Every morning we had to go out and pick up the fellows who died that night," Banegas said. "We picked up 20 to 80 every day."

After he returned to the States, he married in 1949. He and wife Nina had seven children.

Banegas worked at a hardware store following the war. He later took a job in civil service as a driving instructor until his retirement in 1978.

Banegas later composed a 16-verse song about the Death March, and his lyrics are now in the archives of the Smithsonian Institution.

Lorenzo Banegas

Date of Birth
22 MAY 1919
New Mexico

Interviewed by
Robert C. Moore
27 MARCH 1992
(Story first printed in the El Paso Times)

WWII Military Unit
200th Coast
Artillery (AA)
Regiment

MARTINEZ, JOSÉ FULJENCIO. After surviving the Bataan Death March, José Martinez spent nearly four years as a POW in Japan. Martinez remembered every bead of sweat and each tear 60 years later. "I could feel the tears coming down. They would burn. And then a drop of sweat would run down," he said. "It would be so cold and all of the sudden it would burn like fire! Like you got a lit match and put it against your skin." During the march soldiers were denied food and water as they trudged over 60 miles through the Philippine countryside. Soldiers who succumbed to the blistering heat and tried to rest were killed.

Martinez reached Camp O'Donnell and was later imprisoned at Cabanatuan before he was taken to a labor camp at Hiro-Hata. There he was forced to clean and fill furnaces; the degradation was compounded by random beatings and whippings from Japanese soldiers. Even with the inhumane treatment, Martinez and his fellow prisoners tried to find some humor, joking they were eating steaks and pork chops instead of their meager rations of rice and wheat soup.

The camp was liberated when the Japanese surrendered, and Martinez was discharged on March 4, 1946. He stayed in a Camp Carson, Colo., hospital for nearly two months to "fatten up."

Martinez also needed time to recover from the psychological strain of war. He decided to focus on his work as a cartographer for the U.S. Geological Survey to occupy his mind in the years following the war. He later married Lorraine Vigíl—whom he called an "angel"—in 1953. The couple had five children: Ken, Marvin, Sandy, Rita and Jeffrey.

Despite his harrowing experience during the war, Martinez said he found happiness.

"How come I made it? I don't know. Only God knows how or why ..." he said. "I'm happy now. I am rich: I have my God, I have my wife, I have my family, friends, neighbors and relatives."

José Fuljencio
Martinez

Date of Birth
20 AUGUST 1919
Mosquero, NM

Interviewed by
Rea Ann Trotter
SEPTEMBER 2002
Fort Garland, CO

WWII Military Unit
200th Coast
Artillery (AA)
Regiment

Abel Ortega

Date of Birth
22 AUGUST 1919
El Paso, TX

Interviewed by
Joanne R. Sanchez
29 MARCH 2001
San Antonio, TX

WWII Military Unit
192d Light
Tank Battalion,
Provisional
Tank Group

ORTEGA, ABEL. A life of survival began for Abel Ortega even before his birth. His parents fled the violence after the Mexican Revolution of 1910 a few months before he was born. The strength and resolve he inherited from them served him well during his time as a prisoner of war and helped him survive the Bataan Death March.

Ortega was drafted in March 1941 and arrived in Manila, Philippines, on Thanksgiving Day of the same year, two weeks before the bombing at Pearl Harbor. While he listened to the reports of what was occurring in Hawaii, Ortega and his unit braced for the attack that was soon to come on the Bataan Peninsula where he was stationed.

The attacks were steady and continued from late 1941 until April 1942, when American troops were forced to surrender and become prisoners of war. When ordered to destroy his weapon so the Japanese did not seize it, Ortega remembered falling to his knees and praying: " 'I am too young to die ... but if you let me live ... give me the fortitude to help my fellow man.' Then I cried," Ortega said. "After I had cried, I was ready to accept whatever was expected of us."

After the grueling Bataan Death March to Camp O'Donnell, Ortega continued through the Philippines to Camp Cabanatuan. He then boarded a ship for Japan, where he found the camp had slightly more livable conditions. He remained there for nearly a year. When the camp was liberated, a special flag-raising ceremony was held, and Ortega made flags for each nation who had prisoners in the camp. It was one of his proudest moments in the service.

He returned to the States and married Naomi Rodriguez in 1946. The couple had seven children: Deborah, Daniel, Ruth, Susanna, Priscilla, Abel and Diane. Ortega served in the Korean War and then used the GI Bill to learn the dry cleaning business.

Ralph Rodriguez

Date of Birth
25 OCTOBER 1917
El Paso, TX

Interviewed by
Brian Lucero
17 JANUARY 2002
Albuquerque, NM

WWII Military Unit
200th Coast
(AA) Artillery,
515th Coast
(AA) Artillery

RODRIGUEZ, RALPH. Born during his parents' journey to the United States from Mexico, his dual heritage has always played a major role in Ralph Rodriguez's life.

Drafted during his college search, Rodriguez was placed in an anti-aircraft regiment in 1941. Because he was bilingual, he began his service as a translator. Later, he requested a transfer to the medical corps. After initial reluctance because of his invaluable skills as a translator, his request was granted and he trained as a corpsman to serve as caretaker of the sick and wounded.

He was sent to islands in the Philippines, eventually stationed on the Bataan Peninsula. There, amid the chaos of fighting the overpowering Japanese forces, Rodriguez asked a priest what their fate would likely be. "I hated myself for asking," he said later. The priest's prediction became true: the Americans surrendered and became prisoners.

They were forced to embark on the later infamous Bataan Death March. Without food, shade or water, the soldiers trekked in the intolerable jungle heat, eventually arriving at Camp O'Donnell, a Japanese prison camp. The soldiers were subject to forced labor, meager rations and regular beatings. Rodriguez never abandoned notions of hope, reading a Bible he found at the camp and planting a papaya tree. "You don't give up," he said. "You just give up thinking about the future."

In December 1944, Japanese guards fled their posts as American planes converged on the camp. In January, the 6th Ranger Battalion rescued Rodriguez and the other POWs in a surprise raid.

Rodriguez was discharged in August 1945 and returned to New Mexico. He married Betty Cabaldon, his first wife, and the couple had three children: Ralph, Mona Lisa and Charles Victor. He was offered a job at the New Mexico Timber Co. After graduating from a local college, he earned the position of manager, eventually leading a team of 300 employees.

SILVA, AGAPITO. An unshakable resolve and, above all, the ability to fiercely cling to the hope that he would eventually return to the States allowed Agapito Silva to survive 3 1/2 years as a prisoner of war in Japanese prison camps.

Agapito Silva

Date of Birth
21 OCTOBER 1919
San Marcial, NM

Interviewed by
Brian Lucero
14 NOVEMBER 2001
Albuquerque, NM

WWII Military Unit
200th Coast (AA)
Artillery Regiment

"I never gave up hope," he said. "Guys that gave up hope never made it."

Silva enlisted in the Army in 1941 and left for the Philippines in August of that year. He began fighting on the Bataan Peninsula as part of his anti-aircraft unit. However, Silva said that many times their weapons were useless, and he was unable to shoot down planes. The Japanese also used tanks against the U.S. troops, which Silva said was a huge advantage.

He also remembered food shortages and the prevalence of disease in the Philippine jungle. After almost three-fourths of the American force surrendered at the fall of Bataan, Silva and several other officers retreated to the island of Corregidor in Manila Bay. The island was eventually surrendered to the Japanese on May 6, 1942, and Silva became a POW.

Though he did not have to endure the grueling march, Silva worked 10 to 12 hour days in the Japanese coal mines. The work was so physically taxing some men resorted to breaking their own arms and legs to avoid the work. Silva never resorted to self-inflicted injuries, but instead he suffered broken ribs, a fractured pelvis and a crushed vertebra when the ceiling of a mine caved in.

After the bombing of Hiroshima and Nagasaki, Silva was released and returned to the United States. He was discharged in December 1946, having earned a distinguished unit badge and various other decorations.

He married Socorro Vigil in 1946, and the couple raised their seven children—Frederick, Michael, Patricia, Agapito Jr., Mauricio, Jerome and Erlinda—in Silva's home state of New Mexico.

SMITH, ARTHUR. A wedding dress has significance no matter what the design. But when Arthur Smith married his high school sweetheart Bessie Pacheco in November 1945, her gown held special meaning. The fabric was that of a white parachute that had dropped food and medicine to her husband while he was in a prison camp in Japan.

Arthur Smith

Date of Birth
14 JUNE 1919
Santa Fe, NM

Interviewed by
Karleen Boggio-
Montgomery
21 JULY 2001
Santa Fe, NM

WWII Military Unit
200th Coast
(AA) Artillery

After joining the military in 1940, Smith left for the Philippines in 1941. When the Japanese bombed Clark Field, American troops were unprepared for the attack. The bombing destroyed some 100 planes and left the troops with little supplies to defend themselves. They were forced to surrender to the Japanese and taken prisoner.

After his capture, Smith took part in the Bataan Death March, trekking over 60 miles in relentless heat, without food or water. Smith survived the march, only to be shipped to a work camp in Hanawa, Japan. There he found innovative ways to aid his survival. He would take a small stone with him during his work detail. When he perspired, he wiped the sweat with the stone. When the sweat dried, he would scrape the salt from the stone and add it to his small portion of rice.

Never abandoning their patriotic duty, Smith and his comrades did their best to sabotage anything they could while imprisoned. They loosened the caps on oil drums and bent the fins of bombs to try to make them stray from their course.

After the Japanese surrender, Smith was rescued. He spent several months in a hospital recuperating, and he eventually returned to New Mexico, where he married and found a job at Sears & Roebuck, Inc. He worked as a manager for nearly 30 years before his retirement in 1980. He and his wife, Bessie, had two sons: Carlos and David. He spent his retirement with his family and pursued a hobby carving traditional Native American Kachina dolls. One of his dolls sold for $21,000.

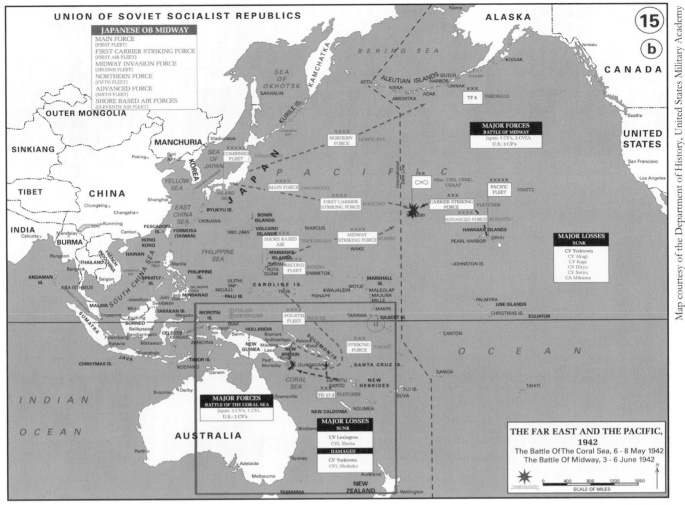

Map courtesy of the Department of History, United States Military Academy

MAP 12

BATTLES IN THE SOUTH AND CENTRAL PACIFIC

The War on the Seas

In the war against Germany, U.S. forces used tanks, infantry, planes, paratroopers and gliders. But in the Pacific, the fighting required different equipment and strategies: island-hopping across the Pacific, with the essential support of battleships, destroyers and air power taking off from aircraft carriers. Island-hopping entailed controlling small islands, or even parts of islands, and then moving to another island—seeking to confound the Japanese about where the next attack might come.

The Japanese enemy was formidable: American forces paid dearly for every inch, on every tiny island they managed to gain.

Miguel Piñeda, of Austin, Texas, and a member of the of the 32d Infantry Division, recalled that after he arrived in Brisbane, Gen. Douglas MacArthur had exhorted to the troops: "You kill him or he'll kill you!"

Island Hopping

In the Central Pacific, Admiral Chester Nimitz began a process of "island-hopping," taking chains of islands methodically, starting with the Marshalls, then the Carolines and then the Marianas.

In the Southwest Pacific, the battles were for the Solomons and New Guinea.

Piñeda would fight in the Battle of Buna, in November 1942. Buna, in northern Papua, New Guinea, had been invaded by the Japanese in July 1941; it was recaptured by American and Australian troops in December 1943.

It was common for men to fight in multiple battles. Thomas Lopez Casso, a native of Chicago, was assigned to the 182d Infantry Regiment and fought at Bougainville, Solomon Islands, as well as at Leyte, Samar and Cebu, in the Philippines.

Philip James Benavides, a French horn player with the 9th Marine Regiment, from Austin, Texas, became a medic in the summer of 1942, during the Battle of Guadalcanal.

"We did first-aid duty to the best of our knowledge. Sometimes it wasn't good enough," he said. "We weren't trained in it ... we did anything we could to stop the bleeding, ease the pain."

Jungle Diseases

In the jungles of the islands, the soldiers battled sicknesses, such as malaria, and many contracted "jungle rot," ulcers caused by fungus in the extreme moisture. Dennis Baca, of Belen, N.M., and part of the 132d Infantry Regiment, fought at New Caledonia, Guadalcanal, and then Bougainville, Solomon Islands. In January 1945, he and his division attacked the Japanese in Leyte and then Cebu, in the Philippines, in March 1945. Baca would develop jungle rot and malaria from the constant hot and wet conditions.

"They gave us machetes to cut through the jungle. It was all jungle, seems like it rained every day," Baca said. "Jungle, swamps and mosquitoes. ... A lot of nights we had to make foxholes and that's where we'd sleep. The mosquitoes — they were bad. They gave us mosquito nets to put over our heads and over our beds. There's where

I got malaria. That's where I got jungle rot, all over my body."

When the hard-earned victories in Papua, New Guinea, and Guadalcanal were secured at the beginning of 1943, MacArthur set his sights on regaining the Philippines through a year-long progression toward the northern New Guinean coast.

A second force was led by Admiral Chester Nimitz through the Central Pacific. Among the islands necessary to capture were Tarawa and Makin Atoll, the Marshall Islands and Guam and Saipan in the Mariana Islands.

Ignacio Servín, fighting in Peleliu, in the Central Pacific, and another man volunteered for a dangerous mission: crawling inside a cave to destroy Japanese ammunition.

The Battle of the Coral Sea, on May 7 and 8, 1942, was later considered to be without a clear-cut victor. In this battle, Japan was steaming toward an invasion of Port Moresby, on the southeastern part of Papau, New Guinea, when Allied forces fought back. Both sides suffered significant damages to planes and ships, but the Allies were heartened when two of the Japanese heavy carriers were so badly damaged that they were out of commission, pending repairs. The American attack on the Japanese fleet caused the Japanese to turn around and never reach Port Moresby.

The United States had a great advantage in cracking Japanese Naval code in early 1942. This enabled the U.S. to learn well beforehand of Japanese plans to attack the Central Pacific island of Midway and to try to divert attention by attacking in the Aleutian Islands, off the coast of Alaska. So when the Japanese attacked Midway on June 4, 1942, U.S. forces were prepared and rebuffed the attack, destroying four Japanese heavy aircraft carriers and 253 planes.

Midway would start to turn the Pacific war in the Allies' favor. But it would take three more years to achieve that victory.

ALCOSER, JOSEPH. With Japanese *Kamikazes* screeching overhead, Joseph Alcoser kept watch on the deck of the USS *Maryland* with a single pair of binoculars, on the lookout for enemy planes and alerting his crewmates of impending attacks.

Enlisting at age 18, Alcoser joined the military immediately after graduating from high school, motivated by his father and by a desire to leave his small hometown of Melvin, Texas. "I volunteered because I felt it was the only way out," Alcoser said. "My dad always said that men had an obligation to defend their country."

Following training in San Diego, Calif., Alcoser was sent to New Caledonia, a French colony north of Australia. There he boarded the *Maryland*, one of three battleships to survive the attack on Pearl Harbor unscathed. During his dangerous mission on the *Maryland*, Alcoser wrote home to his mother only once and seldom thought about life after the war, devoting his energy to the treacherous task at hand. "The scariest battle for me was the midnight Battle of Surigao Strait," he said. "It was dark and we could only see shells flashing by the ship. The unknown was what caused the greatest fear." The constant fear and uncertainty took its toll on many sailors, and Alcoser remembered witnessing the mental breakdown of some of his crewmen.

Alcoser's ship was docked for repairs when he heard of the war's end. He was discharged on March 3, 1946, and returned to Melvin for six months before moving to Lubbock, Texas. He married Beatrice Quiroz in 1947 and the couple had eight children: Ben, Josephine, Katherine, Joseph Paul, Maria Fidelia, Lina, Colleen and Adrian. During the Korean War, Alcoser was assigned to the Japan-Korea headquarters in Yokosuka, Japan. He was stationed there for two years. He then returned to the States and moved his family to California.

Joseph Alcoser

Date of Birth
28 MARCH 1925
Melvin, TX

Interviewed by
René Zambrano
21 OCTOBER 2000
San Diego, CA

WWII Military Unit
USS *Maryland*
(BB-46)

BACA, DENNIS. Though Dennis Baca would contract malaria and jungle rot, for him the hardest part of war was losing so many good friends. In one particular battle, an American patrol followed the Japanese into a ravine, where there were a lot of caves. The group was ambushed.

"By the time we got there, it was getting dark and we couldn't go in," he said. "We had to wait all night until we could go in and get them out. We could hear them all moaning—my friends."
"I know I killed a lot of them," he said, finally able to talk of the war. "I hate to say that, but it was our job. I don't know how we made it. I guess God was with us. That's one thing I believe in."

It was not the first time Baca had mourned the loss of his friends. After a few months in New Caledonia, Baca and the 132d Infantry Regiment joined combat on Guadalcanal, Solomon Islands, on Dec. 8, 1942. They fought there until Feb. 9, 1943, moving to Fiji to regroup. They attacked Bougainville, Solomon Islands, on Jan. 12, 1944. They arrived in Leyte on Jan. 26, 1945, and assaulted Cebu Island on March 26, 1945. Armed with machetes to cut through the overgrowth, Baca contracted malaria and jungle rot all over his body from the prolonged exposure to moisture.

Though wounded on the left shoulder blade by shrapnel, Baca never received a Purple Heart or a promotion above the rank of private. Baca was discharged on Dec. 3, 1945, saved from further combat in Japan when the atomic bombs were dropped. He returned to Albuquerque, N.M.

"A lot of things changed in three years. It was hard to get a job. ... My folks didn't recognize me because I was yellow from malaria. It took me years and years to get over it," he said. Beyond the physical difficulties, Baca struggled with bouts of depression and anxiety, as he worked for many years as a nursing assistant at the VA hospital. He married Margaret Baca and they had three children, Consuelo, Carlos, and Lila.

Dennis Baca

Date of Birth
22 SEPTEMBER 1924
Belen, NM

Interviewed by
Violeta Dominguez
2 NOVEMBER 2002
Albuquerque, NM

WWII Military Unit
Anti-Tank Platoon,
132d Infantry
Regiment,
Americal Division

Philip James
Benavides

Date of Birth
1 MAY 1921
Austin, TX

Interviewed by
Robert Rivas
7 JULY 2003
El Paso, TX

WWII Military Unit
9th Marine
Regiment,
3d Marine Division
Headquarters,
1st Marine Division

BENAVIDES, PHILIP JAMES. A talented French horn player, Philip James Benavides joined the U.S. Marine Corps as a musician. Three and a half years of war would end his musical career.

During his childhood in Austin, Texas, his mother, Guadalupe Estrada Benavides, arranged for Philip to take music lessons from Joseph Koenigseder in exchange for laundry services. In June 1941, Koenigseder took him to Houston, Texas, for an audition with the Marines. Benavides was assigned to the band at the Marine Corps base in San Diego, Calif. He served aboard the USS *Essex* and was sent to Auckland, New Zealand, in June 1942.

In the summer of 1942, his obligations as a French horn player became secondary when the band was called upon to administer first aid, replenish supplies on the front lines and retrieve the dead and wounded during the Battle of Guadalcanal. Benavides was sent to battles in New Georgia, New Solomon Islands, where he contracted malaria in the spring of 1943, and Bougainville, where he lost sight in his left eye when a mortar exploded on Nov. 1, 1943. He recovered and returned to combat in December 1943 for the Battle of New Britain. There, he and 11 other men were taken prisoner by the Japanese and he suffered abuse for three months. In March 1944, aware the Allied forces were on their way, the Japanese began executing their prisoners. An officer put a pistol to Benavides's head and pulled the trigger four times. Nothing happened. "God's on my side; I wonder why," he thought, as Australian soldiers rescued him and the four other surviving prisoners of war.

He came home in December 1944, though his injuries left him unable to play the French horn. He married Isabél Dominguez in 1946 and raised six children: Emma, Isabel, Philip, Guadalupe, Norma and José. After the marriage ended in divorce, he married María Uranga in 1961 and had four children: María, Mary, Hilda and Armando.

Thomas Lopez
Casso

Date of Birth
3 AUGUST 1924
Chicago, IL

Interviewed by
Steven Rosales
2 JULY 2004
Fountain Valley, CA

WWII Military Unit
182d Infantry
Regiment,
Americal Division

CASSO, THOMAS LOPEZ. On Bougainville, Solomon Islands, Thomas Casso took off through the jungle after lighting a smoke signal that would tell the U.S. troops where to target the enemy trailing his company. It was only after he was a couple hundred yards away that he realized he had left his rifle behind and would have to go back. He wondered what would happen if he were captured by the Japanese.

"That was our greatest fear," he said. "They'd butcher you up."

Casso survived his first experience in Bougainville, thanks, he said, to his mother's diligent prayers at home. However, 2 1/2 years in the Pacific gave him malaria and jungle rot on his hands and feet. Decades later, Casso still choked up as he recalled being forced to leave behind fellow scouts who had been killed.

As a member of the 182d Infantry Regiment, Casso fought in the Philippines: in Leyte and Samar. While he was in Cebu, Philippines, the Japanese surrendered to his regiment.

After two months in Japan, Casso was sent home. He later was recalled to serve 10 months in the Korean War.

Casso used the GI Bill to earn his bachelor's degree in history from Texas Western University—now the University of Texas at El Paso. He later earned a master's in public administration from Pepperdine University and a law degree from Texas College of Law. He became a district patrol officer in El Paso, Texas, and personnel director for the city. He retired as a teacher and administrator of public schools in California in 1990. Casso volunteered to work for the Democratic Party and ran for city councilman in El Paso and Fountain Valley, Calif.

In 1948, he married Lillian Palafox; the couple had two children: Adele and Thomas.

CUELLAR, JOSÉ "JOE." At age 18, José "Joe" Cuellar knew he wanted to be a leader. On the island of Bougainville with the Americal Division, he volunteered with a soldier from Waco, Texas, nicknamed "Tex," to become a scout. "A scout is a leader in any operation," Cuellar later explained.

Together, he and Tex tracked Japanese movements and reported back to their commanding officers. On their first scouting mission, the two friends came upon a Japanese scout and froze. Luckily, the Japanese soldier was equally shocked and no fire was exchanged, but Tex decided scouting was not for him. Cuellar, however, was excited and motivated.

He discovered that he liked finding his way through dark nights and had a good sense of direction. One night, he and his fellow scouts followed some Japanese officers back to their camp and killed the men after watching them eat their breakfast in the morning. With the Americal Division, Cuellar said he saw men die in battle almost every day and helped carry many out of combat areas. As an orphan who had to fend for himself during childhood, Cuellar said his strong work ethic helped him survive the harsh conditions in the South Pacific.

He was discharged with the rank of staff sergeant and returned to the States feeling confident and proud. "After I went into the service nothing bothered me because I knew I could do almost anything anybody else could," he said.

In Los Angeles, he met up with Ella Mora, whom he had met before the war. They were married on March 8, 1946, and began a new life in Albuquerque, N.M. Cuellar worked two and sometimes three jobs to provide for his new wife and eventually five children: Joe Jr., Larry, Shirley, Donald and Chris. Cuellar owned a construction company before retiring in Corrales, N.M. After Ella died of lung cancer in 1989, he married his second wife, Delfina Josepha Lujan.

José "Joe" Cuellar

Date of Birth
19 MARCH 1924
Ranchos de
Albuquerque, NM

Interviewed by
Jennifer Sanchez
2 NOVEMBER 2002
Albuquerque, NM

WWII Military Unit
164th Infantry
Regiment,
Americal Division

FUENTES, TOBY. For more than five decades, Toby Fuentes was tormented by the sound of flying bullets and torpedo explosions.

His ship, the USS *Chicago*, was sailing with a convoy of cruisers and destroyers when it was attacked near a contested Rennell Island by Japanese bombers on Jan. 29, 1943. The ensuing battle, known as the Battle of Rennell Island, would be the *Chicago's* last. Two burning Japanese planes lit the sky behind the heavy cruiser, creating a silhouette that was an easy target for torpedoes. It was hit twice, and the ship flooded and lost power. The *Chicago* survived the initial barrage, and was towed out of the area by a fellow cruiser till morning. The Japanese attacked again that afternoon, hitting the crippled cruiser with four more torpedoes, finally sinking it.

"I thought the war was coming to an end in the water," Fuentes said. Six officers and 56 enlisted men were killed. Nearby destroyers collected the 1,049 survivors, including Fuentes.

In 1942, serving in the war had seemed like a good idea when Fuentes enlisted in the Navy at age 19, without his parents' blessing. Though Toby was their only child, his parents could not stand in their son's way. During basic training at the U.S. Naval Training Station, San Diego, Calif., Toby felt sure that he made the right decision in joining the military.

"I wanted to go to war and I wanted to go out there and fight," he said. Before reporting to San Francisco to board the *Chicago*, Fuentes was allowed to return to his hometown of Austin, Texas, for a few days. There he met Sandy Acosta and, within days, the two were married. The war separated them for the next three years, but Toby wrote at least once every two weeks. When the war ended, the couple had four children: Martha, Joanna, Rolando and Cheryl. Fuentes is proud that he provided them with good educations, working as an auto body repairman until his retirement.

Toby Fuentes

Date of Birth
28 NOVEMBER 1923
Austin, TX

Interviewed by
Nora Ramírez
16 SEPTEMBER 2000
Austin, TX

WWII Military Unit
USS *Chicago*
(CA-29)

Guy Gabaldon

Date of Birth
22 MARCH 1926
Los Angeles, CA

Interviewed by
Maggie Rivas-Rodriguez
7 JUNE 2000
Washington, D.C.

WWII Military Unit
Intelligence Section
Headquarters,
2d Marine Regiment,
2d Marine Division

GABALDON, GUY. Though Guy Gabaldon stopped counting how many prisoners he was capturing in Saipan, Mariana Islands, his fellow Marines—during a 1957 episode of "This is Your Life"—credited him with single-handedly capturing more than 1,500 Japanese soldiers and civilians.

Raised in Boyle Heights, an East Los Angeles neighborhood, by age 10 Gabaldon was free to roam the city and learned street smarts that would be useful later in the war. He was 12 when he met Japanese-American brothers Lyle and Lane Nakano. Fascinated by their culture, he moved in with their family and learned their language. Barring a few months spent on his grandfather's ranch in N.M., Gabaldon stayed with the Nakanos for almost seven years—until the family was sent to an internment camp after the bombing of Pearl Harbor. He tried to follow the two into the service but at 16 was too young to enlist. He joined the Marine Corps a year later and became a scout observer.

On the night of June 6, 1944, Gabaldon crept behind the lines near Saipan's northern cliffs. Before daybreak, he realized that enemy troops were gathering around him for one of the largest suicide charges of the war. Cut off from retreat, Gabaldon captured two guards and persuaded them to return to the caves below. Soon a Japanese officer and some of his men were the first of many to surrender to Gabaldon en masse within an hour. Decades later, stories of how the "Pied Piper of Saipan" used fluent street Japanese and shots from his carbine rifle to gather his prisoners continue to be told within the Marine Corps, though many consider them only legends.

After leaving the Marines, Gabaldon married Dunkya Tsidunoff. He began several business ventures, including importing shellfish from Mexico and a truck and farm equipment business. He moved to Saipan with his second wife, Ohana Suzuki, a Mexican native of Japanese ancestry. Together they had five children: Tony, Ray, Hanako, Yoshio and Aiko.

Arnif G. Nerio

Date of Birth
28 SEPTEMBER 1922
Baxter, TX

Interviewed by
Jeffery K. Watanabe
19 OCTOBER 2002
Saginaw, MI

WWII Military Unit
20th Infantry
Regiment,
6th Infantry
Division

NERIO, ARNIF G. In the fall of 1942, 20-year-old Arnif Nerio felt his life was coming together. While many were out of work, he had just landed a job at General Motors in Saginaw, Mich. He was three months married to Trinidad Ayala and the newlyweds were expecting a child. Everything changed when he was drafted into the Army on Dec. 4, 1942. Nerio pleaded with the officials to let him wait until his daughter was born, but they assured him that his new family would be taken care of and shipped him to Camp Robinson in Little Rock, Ark., for training.

On July 30, 1944, Nerio arrived in New Guinea with the 6th Infantry Division. That June, they invaded Papua, New Guinea, and, for the first time, people Nerio knew died before his eyes, shot by snipers and killed amid cries of "banzai" from the Japanese. With so many casualties, men in his unit began to look to him for direction. At one point, Nerio told his sergeant that he thought it was too dangerous and wanted to pull back. "I didn't have any men; I was just a private. The guys wanted me to take charge," he said. "I was too young to realize how much that should scare me." Nerio led the men back just in time to avoid a direct hit that knocked them all off their feet.

After the 6th Infantry Division secured the island, Nerio was shipped back to the States to treat damage in his ears. He was granted a 30-day furlough to visit his wife and daughter for Christmas 1944. Later that winter, he was sent to Camp Wolters, Texas, where he trained soldiers in judo, bayonet usage and first aid. He was transferred to Seattle with the Coast Guard until the end of the war.

Upon his discharge, Nerio reunited with his family, but soon was confronted again with racism that he had not experienced as a soldier. "One time when I was eating in uniform, the mailman came in and paid for my meal," he said. "Then other places wouldn't even let me in."

He was relieved to learn he could resume his job at GM, where he worked for 30 years.

OCHOA, JESÚS. Like many events in his life, Jesús Ochoa will remember the day the Japanese bombed Pearl Harbor in the context of baseball. On Dec. 7, 1941, he was playing a baseball game for a local group against the Navy Team. Without warning, a Navy truck came and took all the Navy ball players away. "I wondered what the heck happened. We were in the middle of the game," he said. Though most people at the ballpark didn't know where Pearl Harbor was, Ochoa recalled that a friend's father had described it as an impregnable fortress.

Ochoa enlisted in the Marine Corps on Nov. 10, 1942. He had heard about a new special mission force called the Raiders, created specifically for the guerrilla-like warfare that was thought to be the best tactic for fighting the Japanese. Ochoa wanted to be a part of it. During an interview to qualify him, he was asked if he would have any qualms about killing Japanese soldiers. He said he would not. Ochoa became a member of the 4th Marine Raider Battalion.

On the battlefields of Guadalcanal and the Solomon Islands, Ochoa shot many enemy soldiers, but was struck hardest by one in particular. "He looked so darn young ... I said, 'My God, he's just about my brother's age,'" he recalled. His brother, Lalo, had recently joined the Marines.

The Raider battalions were disbanded in February 1944 and re-formed into the 4th Marine Regiment, 3d Marine Division with whom Ochoa served until stationed at U.S. Marine Corps Logistics Base, Barstow, Calif. on Sept. 16, 1945.

He was discharged on Nov. 9, 1945, and got a job in the Civil Service, through an apprentice program that trained him as an aircraft electrician. Ochoa married Henrietta Romero on Aug. 5, 1945, and had three children: Irene, Henrietta and Jesús. "Every day is a beautiful day," Ochoa said, treasuring his time since the war. "I thank God I am here."

Jesús Ochoa

Date of Birth
26 SEPTEMBER 1921
Redondo Beach, CA

Interviewed by
René Zambrano
6 APRIL 2001
San Diego, CA

WWII Military Unit
4th Marine Raider Battalion,
1st Marine Raider Regiment

PIÑEDA, MIGUEL. Upon his arrival in Brisbane, Australia, Miguel Piñeda recalled that Gen. Douglas MacArthur gave a speech to inspire the inexperienced soldiers. "You kill him or he'll kill you!" the general shouted. It was then that the reality and hardship of war hit home for Piñeda.

Piñeda was inducted into the Army on Nov. 14, 1941, at Fort Sam Houston, Texas, with the 36th Infantry Division. However, he suffered an appendicitis attack and had to have surgery while the division shipped out. He was eventually sent to basic training in Camp Roberts, Calif.; from there he joined the 128th Infantry Regiment, 32d Division. In Brisbane, the men underwent more training to acclimate themselves to the new environment. In the jungles, they were constantly susceptible to malaria, which Piñeda contracted during the training.

His division was first sent into combat for the Battle of Buna. To protect Port Moresby, Papua New Guinea, they were ordered to occupy pillboxes, machine gun nests in the ground, but then suddenly pulled back. The Japanese moved into the pillboxes and ambushed the American troops when they returned in a flurry of bullets. One bullet ricocheted off a palm tree and hit Piñeda in the calf, making his leg feel the size of a telephone pole. Natives of the island made a stretcher to carry him out of the jungle. Piñeda recovered in hospitals in Australia. When he had relearned to walk, Piñeda worked on Australian bases, unloading cargo, driving trucks and refueling vehicles.

He was sent to Leyte, Philippines, 30 days after the U.S. invasion, where he contracted malaria for the second time. He was sent to Brooks Army Hospital in Texas for treatment. Piñeda was discharged on July 1, 1945. Back in his hometown of Austin, Texas, he resumed his job at the Calcasieu Lumber Co. He married Pauline Reyes in 1951 and the couple had 11 children: Richard, Rachel, Joe, Josie, Fred, Amy, Mary Hope, Mary Catherine "Cathy", Miguel Jr., Sylvia and Michaela.

Miguel Piñeda

Date of Birth
20 MAY 1920
Austin, TX

Interviewed by
Sandra Ibarra
9 MARCH 2001
Austin, TX

WWII Military Unit
Company F,
128th Infantry Regiment,
32d Infantry Division

Manuel Provencio

Date of Birth
2 JUNE 1925
El Paso, TX

Interviewed by
Robert Rivas
2 AUGUST 2002
El Paso, TX

WWII Military Unit
77th Quarter-
master Company,
77th Infantry
Division

PROVENCIO, MANUEL. During his time in the Pacific Theater, Manuel Provencio battled dengue fever and contracted jungle rot, which continued to affect him even 50 years later. Called into service in 1943. Provencio weighed 175 pounds. He returned weighing 115 pounds, having had limited food options, including cereal infested with maggots or bugs. "I went and served my time and forgot about it. Some people live in the past and that's not good. Those memories will kill you," he said. "What's gone is gone. Like they say, '*Vamos.*'"

At age 18, Provencio was sent to Army Service Forces School at Camp Lee, Va., for three months. He was shipped to New Caledonia and joined the 77th Quartermaster Company in Guam on July 21, 1944, fighting 25 days in heavy combat until mid-August. Provencio was still mopping up the scattered Japanese resistance when his division departed for Leyte, Philippines, where they stayed from Nov. 23, 1944, to March 1945. He worked as a goods distributor and, although he spent more time doing manual labor than on the battlefield, bullets and bloodshed remained hauntingly near.

Provencio fought in the Okinawa campaign from March 26 until July 1945. The division rested in Cebu, Philippines. After the war, his unit was sent to Hokkaido, Japan, as an occupational force for five months and to Yokohama, Japan, for one more. He was the only Mexican American in his company. Despite being nicknamed 'Spic,' he faced little discrimination, except from one man who later wrote a letter to apologize for his ignorance.

After his discharge on March 1, 1946, Provencio returned to El Paso, Texas, and went back to work for the Rio Grande Lumber Co. He eventually became a grocer in El Paso. He had five children — Cecilia, Manuel, Arturo, Eddie and Alfredo — with his first wife, Luz Sepulveda. He married Aurora Eguarte on Oct. 18, 1978.

Francisco "Frank"
Rodriguez Resendez

Date of Birth
29 JANUARY 1920
Bluff Springs, TX

Interviewed by
Katherine Hearty
28 MARCH 2001
Austin, TX

WWII Military Unit
318th Engineer
Battalion,
93d Infantry
Division

RESENDEZ, FRANCISCO "FRANK" RODRIGUEZ. Though he was born in Texas, Frank Resendez was sent to live with his uncle, Santiago Rodriguez, on a farm in Aramberri, Mexico, after his mother died when he was 9 months old.

In September 1938, Resendez returned to his family in Austin, Texas, where he first encountered discriminatory practices in movie theaters and in the plant in Freeport, Texas, where he worked.

He was drafted on Nov. 20, 1942, to Camp Wolters, Texas. After training in Florida, Virginia and Maine, Resendez was shipped to New Guinea. There, he was assigned to kitchen police in the 318th Engineer Battalion, which constructed landing strips on the island. Kangaroo was the main meat he served because normal commodities were rationed. It was a smell "you can recognize" anywhere, Resendez mused. Most soldiers declined the meat, much to the delight of the natives who gladly accepted the discarded provisions. Coffee was served in large trash cans and never tasted as good as coffee from home, Resendez remembered.

He worked every other day, spending his off days exploring the jungles. Once, he approached another serviceman to inquire where the front line was. "You're on it!" they told him. A native Spanish-speaker, Resendez learned English during his time in New Guinea. The language barrier sometimes caused confusion, but he was able to understand when phrases were repeated.

After three years in the service, Resendez returned home to discover that two brothers, Ignacio and Edward, had returned from overseas. But a third brother, Rudolph, was killed in the war.

He married Mary Carmona on Jan. 3, 1949. They had three children: Rodolpho, Mary Frances and Gerardo. Resendez held odd jobs after the war, often working in construction or as a welder from 1949 to 1969. He and Mary became lifetime members of the Catholic War Veterans.

RIOJAS, MORRIS. In campaigns from the Solomon Islands to the Philippines, Morris Riojas witnessed countless deaths, of both Japanese and Allied soldiers, and was himself wounded three times. "I don't know how I got through it," he said. "You just lived from day to day and prayed a lot."

Years later, Riojas remembered the bombings, the first time he killed a Japanese soldier, sleeping on the beach night after night and waking with the ocean water up to his chest.

When he was drafted, his wife, Beatriz, was pregnant with their first child in Austin, Texas. Riojas left to train at Camp Roberts, Calif., and was allowed leave to visit his son, Morris Jr., and wife for a couple of days before being shipped overseas. On May 11, 1942, he joined 6,000 other men crowded onto the USS *Harris* to make their way in the Pacific.

Riojas served with the 37th Infantry Division and saw his first combat on Guadalcanal, Solomon Islands. The Japanese rained tracer bullets on the arriving ships. "It was kind of scary," said Riojas, who had never been outside of Texas until he was drafted. "I thought, 'This must be the end.'"

The 37th Infantry Division continued through the Solomon Islands to Bougainville. Riojas was wounded for the first time when a piece of shrapnel slammed into his forehead. The injury did not get him out of the hardships he and the division faced. Once, 250 men went up the hill and only 14 came down unharmed. At times, there was no water to drink so they chewed grass for the juice. Riojas landed at Lingayen Gulf on Jan 9, 1945, and ran for his life onto the Filipino beach. His division fought into the city of Manila and helped liberate the Philippines.

He was discharged after three years and three days overseas. "It never bothered me," he said of his war experience. "I came back and just started to work." Riojas soon found good-paying jobs with a spring company and as a mechanic. He and Beatrice had two more sons.

Morris Riojas

Date of Birth
1922
Manor, TX

Interviewed by
Frank Trejo
12 APRIL 2000
Austin, TX

WWII Military Unit
37th Infantry
Division

SALMERON, GEORGE. Though George Salmeron's father was forced into the Mexican Revolution, his son was willing to enlist in the U.S. Army the day after the bombing of Pearl Harbor.

"In our neighborhood, it wasn't 'Are you going or not?'" he said.

While he stood in line, a retired officer told Salmeron to finish high school and come back. He did just that and was inducted into the Navy on Aug. 3, 1942.

After training, Salmeron was stationed aboard the USS *President Hayes*, a troop transport ship. On Feb. 17, 1943, a Japanese heavy bomber flew ahead, taking pictures. Later that night the Japanese dropped flares to count the American ships. Salmeron was given the duty of pointing out aircraft coming in. A group of 20 or 30 fighter aircraft flew in from the dark horizon.

"Everyone was firing at once," Salmeron recalled. A second wave descended on the fleet from another direction. "That was the beginning of the worst night we ever had," he said.

Salmeron's tour with the Navy was cut short due to a lack of calcium that made his bones brittle. His brother, Alfonso—stationed aboard the USS *Copperhee*—saw his broken wrist and told him to take care of it immediately. "You took it this far; I'll take it to Japan for you," Alfonso assured him. Salmeron spent the next 10 months recovering in hospitals. His brother held true to the promise, and was present in Tokyo Bay for the signing of the peace treaty.

After the war, Salmeron earned a degree from the University of Houston in industrial management, but encountered a tough job market that was only complicated by his ethnicity. Once, a job locator wrote M-E-X on the top of his application.

Salmeron set up his own remodeling construction business. He married Ofelia Gonzales on Feb. 24, 1946, and the couple had two daughters: Flora Marie and Betty Jane.

George Salmeron

Date of Birth
17 JANUARY 1924
Houston, TX

Interviewed by
Ernest Eguía and
Paul R. Zepeda
2 APRIL 2003
Houston, TX

WWII Military Unit
USS *President
Hayes* (APA-20)

Ignacio Servín

Date of Birth
4 MARCH 1922
Miami, AZ

Interviewed by
Brenda Sendejo
29 JUNE 2004
Phoenix, AZ

WWII Military Unit
Company A,
154th Engineer
Combat Battalion

SERVÍN, IGNACIO. Though he was not recognized for his bravery until much later, Ignacio Servín was a WWII hero. On the island of Peleliu in the Central Pacific, he volunteered for a dangerous mission that only one other man was willing to attempt. "I just kept thinking, 'If I die, it will be for a great country,'" Servín said. When other efforts to destroy an arsenal of Japanese ammunition failed, Servín and a comrade crawled inside a tunnel-like cave to destroy the supplies themselves.

Their success was overlooked at the time. It wasn't until 1999, at the encouragement of his daughter, Belen, that Servín and his family began to look for other veterans of Peleliu to validate his story. In 2002, Servín remembered a key name. Frank Vela had given him his Browning Automatic Rifle as Servín embarked on his mission. Over Christmas that year, Vela gave him a list of commanding officers in Company A that he had kept since his discharge in 1946. This enabled Servín to finally get in touch with Russell Schauer, a first lieutenant who served as their commanding officer.

"The danger and difficulty of this mission is indicated by the fact that only two men volunteered, Ignacio Servín and Charles Samario. Their heroism and courage no doubt saved the lives of hundreds of our comrades," Schauer wrote in a letter advocating recognition of Servín's success. On Oct. 27, 2003, Arizona Sen. John McCain contacted the Servíns to tell them that Ignacio would be honored with a Silver Star.

Servín married María Magdalena Menchaca three months after returning from the war. The couple had three children: Johnny, Belen and Joseph. Though he worked in the fields as a boy and only went as far as the fourth grade in school, Servín's children all graduated high school and two finished college with advanced degrees.

Oscar Villarreal

Date of Birth
1 MARCH 1927
Laredo, TX

Interviewed by
Juan de la Cruz
28 SEPTEMBER 2002
Laredo, TX

WWII Military Unit
USS *Cleveland*
(CL-55)

VILLARREAL, OSCAR. Before his discharge on Feb. 6, 1946, Oscar Villarreal was involved in nine campaigns aboard the USS *Cleveland* and spent 29 months overseas. He also served as Honor Guard for Gen. Douglas MacArthur in June 1945. "We were ordered from Okinawa [Buckner Bay] to take Gen. MacArthur from Manila, Philippines, to Borneo," Villarreal explained.

At age 15, Villarreal tricked his mother into signing the papers that allowed him to enlist in the Navy. In order to pass his physical exam, he ate 10 bananas to add weight to his 106-pound frame. After training, he left for Pearl Harbor on July 3, 1943. He boarded the USS *Cleveland* in early August.

On Oct. 31, 1943, he saw his first action in the war, giving fire support to the landings of Marines on Georgia Island and Bougainville and taking Baka Island. "We bombarded all night," Villarreal said. The *Cleveland*—part of the Cruiser Division 12—was attacked by four Japanese cruisers but sank the Japanese *Sendai*. By 7 the next morning, the Japanese torpedo and zero planes attacked. The fleet was saved by P-38 and P-51 fighters. But the *Cleveland* had expended a lot of anti-aircraft ammo and couldn't assist in the campaign in the Marshall Islands. It received more ammunition on Christmas 1943 and embarked on the bombardment of Saipan.

"They had told the natives there that we were animals, and a lot of families jumped off the Suicide Cliff, which we later named," he said. "Full families with babies and children." The *Cleveland* survived a typhoon in the China Sea and days before Japan's surrender, a torpedo narrowly missed it, hitting aft on the USS *Pennsylvania* instead.

After the war, Villarreal worked at a post office in Laredo, Texas, from 1951 until his retirement in 1976. He married Amparo Segura on April 23, 1950, and the couple eventually had 10 children: Hector, Javier, Laura, Oscar Jr., Jorge, Rosa, Anita, María, Ricardo and Graciela.

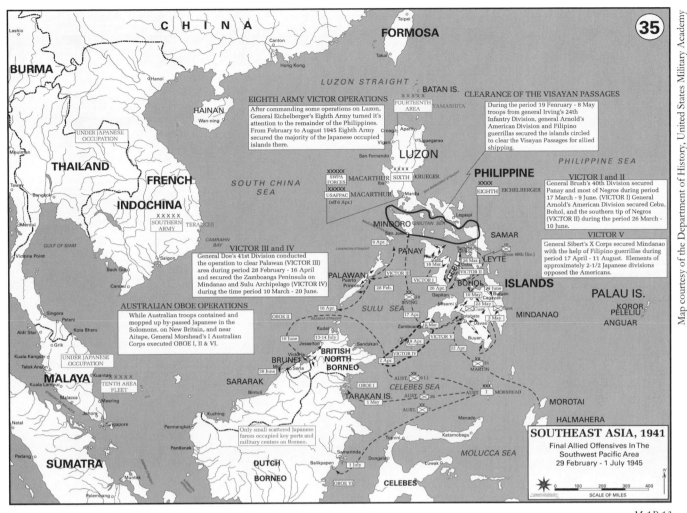

Map courtesy of the Department of History, United States Military Academy

The following text appears within the map:

CHINA

FORMOSA

BURMA

LUZON STRAIGHT

BATAN IS.

EIGHTH ARMY VICTOR OPERATIONS
After commanding some operations on Luzon, General Eichelberger's Eighth Army turned it's attention to the remainder of the Philippines. From February to August 1945 Eighth Army secured the majority of the Japanese occupied islands there.

CLEARANCE OF THE VISAYAN PASSAGES
During the period 19 Fenruary - 8 May troops from general Irving's 24th Infantry Division, general Arnold's American Division and Filipino guerrillas secured the islands circled to clear the Visayan Passages for allied shipping.

HAINAN
Wan-ning

THAILAND

FRENCH

INDOCHINA

LUZON

PHILIPPINE

PHILIPPINE SEA

SOUTH CHINA SEA

MACARTHUR

SIXTH KRUEGER

EIGHTH EICHELBERGER

VICTOR I and II
General Brush's 40th Division secured Panay and most of Negros during period 17 March - 9 June. (VICTOR I) General Arnold's American Division secured Cebu, Bohol, and the southern tip of Negros (VICTOR II) during the period 26 March - 10 June.

SOUTHERN ARMY TERAUCHI

MINDORO

PANAY

SAMAR

LEYTE

VICTOR III and IV
General Doe's 41st Division conducted the operation to clear Palawan (VICTOR III) area during period 28 February - 16 April and secured the Zamboanga Peninsula on Mindanao and Sulu Archipelago (VICTOR IV) during the time period 10 March - 20 June.

PALAWAN

VICTOR III

VICTOR I

BOHOL

VICTOR II

ISLANDS

PALAU IS.

KOROR PELELIU ANGUAR

VICTOR V
General Sibert's X Corps secured Mindanao with the help of Filipino guerrillas during period 17 April - 11 August. Elements of approximately 2-1/2 Japanese divisions opposed the Americans.

AUSTRALIAN OBOE OPERATIONS
While Australian troops contained and mopped up by-passed Japanese in the Solomons, on New Britain, and near Aitape, General Morshead's I Australian Corps executed OBOE I, II & VI.

SULU SEA

MINDANAO

VICTOR V

BRITISH NORTH BORNEO

BRUNEI

SARARAK

Only small scattered Japanese forces occupied key ports and military centers on Borneo.

MALAYA

TARAKAN IS.

CELEBES SEA

MOROTAI

HALMAHERA

SUMATRA

DUTCH BORNEO

CELEBES

MOLUCCA SEA

SOUTHEAST ASIA, 1941
Final Allied Offensives In The Southwest Pacific Area
29 February - 1 July 1945

SCALE OF MILES

MAP 13

LIBERATING THE PHILIPPINES

Japan was quickly losing the Pacific war by the end of the summer of 1944. Allied forces sought to consolidate their power and finally conquer Japan. The big question: which way to go?

There were two strong possibilities:

1. Either going the route of the Central Pacific, which would involve attacking Formosa (now Taiwan) or the Ryukyus Islands, a scant 350 miles from the Japanese home islands; or

2. Going the Southwest Pacific Route, which would involve retaking the Philippines.

Admiral Chester Nimitz, commander of the U.S. Pacific fleet, had control of the Central Pacific. Gen. Douglas MacArthur was in control of the Southwest Pacific. In the end, it was decided to liberate the Philippines first, an accommodation of MacArthur, who was adamant about the retaking of what had been so brutally lost in the spring of 1941. The liberation of the Philippines would begin after the decision was made in September 1944. Allied plans began to launch an invasion spearheaded by attacks on the two largest, most populated islands in the Philippines, Leyte and Luzon. While soldiers took to the beaches, naval battles raged offshore.

Joseph Alcoser, of the small town of Melvin, Texas, was a sailor on the USS *Maryland*.

"The scariest battle for me was the midnight Battle of Surigao Strait," Alcoser said, referring to a battle in the Leyte Gulf that lasted from Oct. 23 to Oct. 26, 1944. "It was dark and we could only see shells flashing by the ship. The unknown was what caused the greatest fear." *(See Alcoser's story in Chapter 2, Battles in the South and Central Pacific.)*

Ernest Montoya, a native of Crawley, Colo., and part of the 42d Rainbow Division, on their way to the Pacific, said he and his fellow soldiers would listen to Tokyo Rose, a woman who broadcast Japanese propaganda to American troops in the South Pacific.

"We'd go to the mess hall and they'd be playing music and she'd be on the radio," Montoya said. "She knew the divisions and some of the officers' names. ... She was the one who told us where we were going to the Philippines, but I didn't think she knew what island."

That island turned out to be Leyte. After landing there in October 1944, Montoya recalled one incident that left a particularly vivid memory.

"One day they called my name to report to some office or some officer. From there they put us on a Jeep ... that's when I started getting nervous," Montoya said. "Just as we arrived, we saw some barges coming in. They had dead soldiers in them, and wounded guys."

Montoya watched the unloading of the corpses and wondered if he would meet the same fate. He would soon confront his own mortality.

"My first day in combat I saw this man ... I didn't even know his name," Montoya said. "We were just there for a few minutes and he got killed. I was one of the guys assigned to carry him out. I remember thinking how that could have been me."

Montoya's unit left Leyte after chasing the Japanese to the west coast of the island. His next destination was Luzon, the largest island in the Philippines. He was wounded in March 1945.

David Loredo, from Sinton, Texas, who served with the 43d Infantry Division, arrived in the Philippines in January 1945. When they first landed, there was little resistance because the Japanese forces had retreated inland, he said.

"We regrouped and headed for the hills," Loredo recounted. "The enemy, they were in the caves and trenches. They could move all over the place without being seen because they were dug in."

On Jan. 9, 1945, MacArthur waded ashore; one month later, he entered Manila, although sporadic fighting would take place until the Japanese surrender.

The liberation of the Philippines was officially declared on July 5, 1945, and American occupation began in the war-torn country. Felix López-Santos, a native of Cidia, P.R., and a sailor aboard the USS *Grant* (AP-29), was one of the Allies who would participate in the takeover of the Philippines. When he arrived on Luzon, Lopez-Santos saw the devastation and the suffering of the Filipino people. He remembered seeing a little girl crying because her family was dead.

"People in the United States and here in Puerto Rico don't know what a war is," López-Santos said. "[People] just don't know what it involves."

CASAREZ, EUGENE. Roughly three months into his basic training, the Army recognized Eugene Casarez's talent in the kitchen. Honing his skills since age 11, Casarez was a veteran baker when he was drafted in February 1944.

Eugene Casarez

Date of Birth
13 JANUARY 1923
Austin, TX

During the 17-day journey across the Pacific while his ship "zigzagged on account of enemy submarines," Casarez began baking for the troops supporting the 35th General Hospital. He soon arrived in New Guinea, pitched a tent and continued baking, using portable outdoor ovens.

Four months later, Casarez and his fellow bakers were thrilled to move to Leyte, where they were given a full kitchen and began filling huge sheet pans with cookies, pastries, donuts and pies. The bakers often made 700 slices of pie each a day. Their homemade goods were a popular comfort for the troops, a reminder of what awaited them at home following their tour of duty.

Interviewed by
Joanne R. Sanchez
27 SEPTEMBER 2000
Austin, TX

Baking from 6 p.m. to 6 a.m., Casarez spent his days sleeping—to prepare for the 12-hour shift ahead. He remembered the camaraderie of the bakers, who affectionately called him "Mex," and how they would often spend their free time together, playing pool.

WWII Military Unit
35th General
Hospital

On his 23rd birthday, Casarez left the Pacific to return to the States. He arrived in Austin, Texas, in February 1946, the first of the three Casarez brothers to return home safely from the war.

Following his service, Casarez returned to his previous job as an optician and lens grinder with Globe Optical, where he worked until age 77.

On January 3, 1953, Casarez married Eladia Cermeño, whom he had known since elementary school. The couple had five children: Margaret, Joseph, María, Mary and Martin.

At home in Austin, Casarez became active in his church, serving as an usher and frequently helping in the kitchen at church functions.

ESPARZA, ANDREW. As he held back Japanese forces in the jungles of the Philippines, Andrew Esparza was one of four brothers who served in the military during the war and returned home unharmed, with memories of the war. "War is hell," he said. "Whoever said that was right."

Andrew Esparza

Date of Birth
9 NOVEMBER 1924
San Diego, CA

Esparza remembered the commotion in the streets when he was leaving a movie theater the day Pearl Harbor was bombed. He dropped out of school shortly after the beginning of U.S. involvement in the war, working at a shipyard to assist in the war effort. His two older brothers served in North Africa and New Guinea and his younger brother joined the Navy. Esparza was drafted in April 1943, and soon left for Fiji to begin his tour of duty in the Pacific.

Interviewed by
René Zambrano
14 OCTOBER 2000
San Diego, CA

His assignment would take him to New Caledonia, Bougainville and eventually the Philippines. Along the way, he was almost constantly in combat. He remembered the first time he saw a fellow soldier fall to enemy fire and the fear that haunted him every moment after.

"I was scared ... always scared that I would lose control," Esparza said. "If a guy [there] wasn't scared, he was a damn fool or a liar."

WWII Military Unit
336th Ordnance
Depot Company

As his unit supported the Army Air Corps, allowing them to move into the Philippines, Esparza's health deteriorated. Eventually, illness forced him to leave the front lines. He rejoined his unit in Japan after the war ended.

He was discharged in December 1945 and returned to San Diego, Calif., on Christmas Eve. All four of the Esparza boys returned home from the war unharmed, and Esparza remembered his parents' emotional reaction. His mother cried for days even after her sons were safe at home.

Esparza married Clementa Peña in 1946. The couple had four children: Andrew, Rita, Rosanna and Adam. Esparza used the GI Bill to attend carpentry classes.

Rafael Fierro

Date of Birth
3 JANUARY 1920
Sanderson, TX

Interviewed by
Elizabeth Flores
23 OCTOBER 2003
El Paso, TX

WWII Military Unit
Troop C,
5th Cavalry
Regiment,
1st Cavalry Division

FIERRO, RAFAEL. Talented on the basketball court, Rafael Fierro's most fervent wish was to attend a small Texas college on an athletic scholarship.

But as WWII loomed, Fierro enlisted in February 1941 and found his niche playing on an Army sports team as he completed his training at Fort Bliss, Texas.

In 1943, Fierro set sail for the Southwest Pacific, arriving in Australia in June for six additional months of training. He continued on to New Guinea, and eventually to the Philippines, where he helped liberate American prisoners in Manila and engaged in house-to-house fighting. He remembered the carnage and horror of land mines and machine guns. Often, he could do little more than pray.

After Manila, his unit moved to Lucena, Philippine Islands, where he readied to invade the Japanese mainland. As the troops began preparations, their officers gave them the dire prediction that nearly 40 percent of the soldiers who took part in the invasion would become casualties.

"We all just tried to survive," he said. "Death had no prejudice."

Shortly before he was scheduled to return to combat, Fierro was informed he had accumulated enough points to return to the States. He promptly turned in his equipment and boarded the ship that would return him to the friends, family and life he had left behind.

Fierro lost his only brother, Bernardo, during fighting in the Pacific, a mere four months before the war's end.

Earning a Bronze Star, Fierro was discharged on August 20, 1945. He returned home to his wife, Mary De La Rosa. The couple had six children: Rafael Jr., Wally, David, Irene, Rebecca and Sally. All three sons served in Vietnam.

Moises Flores

Date of Birth
15 FEBRUARY 1925
Los Angeles, CA

Interviewed by
Joe Myers Vasquez
2 FEBRUARY 2002
El Paso, TX

WWII Military Unit
81st Infantry
Division

Transferred to
11th Airborne
Division

FLORES, MOISES. Born in the United States but raised on a farm in Chihuahua, Mexico, Moises Flores left home at 17, moving to El Paso, Texas, to volunteer for the Army. He was initially turned away because he was underage, so Flores bided his time until his draft notice came.

He was inducted into the Army on July 20, 1943, at Fort Bliss, Texas. After more training in Oregon, California and Hawaii, Flores began a 43-day journey to the Pacific theater with the 81st Infantry Division. "My goodness, I was anxious to get off that boat," he said. "But then again we didn't want to get off because we were going into combat."

Despite the stress of war, Flores made a point to remain positive, and he had a reputation for being a prankster in his unit. During one entertainment assembly, he yelled "fire in the hole!"—the warning of an attack—just to clear the crowd so he could meet a dancer he found attractive. "I called myself during those instances a 'morale builder'," he said. "[They] would say 'Ah, there's that crazy guy.' They would laugh. Laughter is the best medicine there is."

On Anguar Island in Palau, Flores was wounded in the back and spent four months in the hospital. He returned to his job as messenger with his unit in the Philippines. When he finished his service, he re-enlisted for another year, becoming part of the 11th Airborne Division.

He eventually received a promotion to acting platoon sergeant. However, since he only recorded his time in English-speaking schools on his application, the Army mistakenly assumed he had only a fourth-grade education, so he was never given the official title of sergeant.

Discharged in November 1946, Flores returned to the States. Two years later, he married Alicia Paez and the couple had five children: Frances, Moises Jr., Antonio, Oscar and David. Flores remained in El Paso, and became a plumber.

FLORES, RAMÓN C. At the start of the Persian Gulf War, Ramón Flores had already celebrated his 64th birthday. Still confident in his combat skills and unable to contain his patriotism, he marched to his local recruitment office and tried to re-enlist.

He was turned away because of his age, but the incident is a testament to his unwavering devotion to his country, a devotion that began with his service in WWII. Flores was drafted in July 1944, and trained at Fort Bliss, Texas, and Camp Roberts, Calif. He left for the Philippines from California, first landing in New Guinea and, after a brief three-day stay, traveled to Manila.

The humid, rainy Philippines were a striking contrast to the dry heat of El Paso, Texas.

"Water would be pouring all over the food and there was nothing you could do about it," he said. "Our daily ration of little yellow AtabrineTM tablets for malaria would have to be swallowed as soon as they were passed out, because they would melt in the rainwater in our hand."

As a rifleman, Flores patrolled the shores of the island and narrowly escaped an ambush because of his position. He was chosen to stand guard while the rest of his squad was shipped to a different island; those who had been sent off were all ambushed and killed.

He survived the rest of his tour of duty without injury and was discharged on August 12, 1946. He returned to his young wife, Olga Delgado, and their first son.

He began working as a baker at a local hospital, and he eventually served his delicacies to then-Commander-in-Chief Lyndon B. Johnson.

"When President Johnson came to El Paso, I made the cake for him," Flores said. "It was a pyramid and I was on television."

He and his wife had six children: Ramón Jr., Elena, Ruth, Elvia, Sandra and David.

Ramón C. Flores

Date of Birth
22 APRIL 1926
El Paso, TX

Interviewed by
Andrea Williams
2 FEBRUARY 2002
El Paso, TX

WWII Military Unit
Company C,
136th Infantry
Regiment,
33d Infantry
Division

FRANCO, TEODORO. Despite back problems he said should have prevented the Army from drafting him, Teodoro Franco left for the Pacific theater without argument or protest in 1942.

"That's part of growing up. You're supposed to do what the country tells you to do," Franco said.

During his childhood, Franco was proud of his Latino heritage. He often defended his classmates when teachers tried to punish them for speaking Spanish in the classroom.

He trained at Camp Wolters, Texas, before he set sail for New Guinea. After 29 days, he made landfall and began fighting. His only true combat experience was in New Guinea, though it was "just enough to scare the hell out of you."

Franco also fought in four small skirmishes in the Philippines but was able to escape injury throughout his tour of duty. He looked back on his experience with mixed feelings of pride and sadness.

"Battles are not won. Nobody wins anything," he said. "I saw a lot of things. You don't know what to expect."

Discharged in 1946, Franco returned to El Paso, Texas. He worked for Lone Star Motors in sales. During his 28 years with the company, he said he was the first person in the El Paso-New Mexico region to offer automobile financing services across the border in Mexico.

Franco had three children with his first wife: Ted Jr., Judith Ann and Michael David. That marriage ended in divorce. He met the woman who would become his second wife, Monserath Gutierrez, a Mexican-born U.S. citizen, when she was shopping for a car.

"When they brought her into the office, it was love at first sight," Franco said.

Teodoro Franco

Date of Birth
14 AUGUST 1921
El Paso, TX

Interviewed by
Andrea Shearer
2 FEBRUARY 2002
El Paso, TX

WWII Location
Stationed in the
South Pacific

Elías "Jesse"
Guajardo

Date of Birth
25 SEPTEMBER 1925
Pflugerville, TX

Interviewed by
Kristen Henry
9 MARCH 2001
Austin, TX

WWII Military Unit
USS *Lexington*
(CV-16)

GUAJARDO, ELÍAS "JESSE."   Using beautiful, poetic language, Elías "Jesse" Guajardo vividly recounted the scenery in the Pacific Theater during WWII. Guajardo described the colors of the coral and ocean as rich jewel tones and, despite the death and destruction of war, looks back on his experiences in the Navy with a certain fondness and profound appreciation.

He recalls the day he was inducted into the Navy: November 11, 1943. He remembers it more quickly than the birthdays of his siblings. Guajardo was 18 when he left for San Diego to master anti-aircraft artillery.

He went to New Guinea and Leyte where he was transferred as a petty officer to the aircraft carrier the USS *Lexington*. It was aboard the *Lexington* that Guajardo first experienced combat. In Manila Harbor, a 30-minute raid of 30 Japanese planes and tracers tested Guajardo and his crew of eight.

He remembered the war's end; he had an excellent view of the surrender in Tokyo Bay from a ship docked in Sabu, Philippines. "We were anchored in the bay," he said. "And you could just see thousands and thousands of Japanese coming down the mountains with flags, surrendered."

After a warm welcome in San Francisco, Guajardo was sent to New Orleans, La., where he was discharged on December 15, 1945. He then returned to Austin, Texas, where he met and married María Rios on July 31, 1949. The couple had two children: Hector and Robert.

Guajardo worked for H-E-B grocery stores upon his return to civilian life and was one of the first Latino store directors in the Austin area. He later worked for the University of Texas at Austin as a food buyer. His passion for the sea life that began in the Navy still remains, and he sails in California each year with his family.

Felix López-Santos

Date of Birth
18 OCTOBER 1920
Cidia, PR

Interviewed by
Doralís Pérez-Soto
20 DECEMBER 2002
San Juan, PR

WWII Military Unit
USS *Grant* (AP-29)

LÓPEZ-SANTOS, FELIX.   Amid the disease and devastation of war, Felix López-Santos found humor, which helped to keep him grounded during his tour of duty in the Pacific.

"[A kangaroo] came running, and it seems that he crashed on me," López-Santos said, recalling an incident in Australia, his first stop during his service.

Born in Puerto Rico, he moved to Connecticut at age 15, learning English at school where he was the only Latino. He was drafted in 1942, and began training at Fort Dix, N.J., He completed his basic training at Camp Davis, Calif. From California, he left for Australia. Aboard the USS *Grant*, he recalled being fired upon by an enemy submarine, but a small destroyer accompanying the ship was able to sink the sub before any major damage was done.

From Australia, López-Santos began working in the communications department in New Guinea. Between preparations for the invasion of Luzon, López-Santos and his crewmates found time to fish and relieve some of the stress of war. But as his ship departed for the Lingayen Gulf, he was quickly reminded of his purpose in the Pacific.

Suicide bombers exploded near his ship and his ship was bombarded as it approached the shores of the Philippines. During the intense months of combat, López-Santos rarely wrote home, leading his family to assume the worst. He also remembered the heavy government censorship of letters.

"I wanted to write nice things about the small island," he said. "And describe this place, but everything was cut short and censored."

López-Santos arrived home to the States in 1945 and soon married Emerita Negrón, another Puerto Rico native. The couple had three daughters: Elsa, Lissette and Gloria. The family lived in Brooklyn, N.Y., until 1954, when they returned to Puerto Rico.

LOREDO, DAVID. When David Loredo was shot in the stomach in the hills of the Philippines, his first thought was that he would never see his mother again.

David Loredo

Date of Birth
20 MARCH 1925
Sinton, TX

"I remember standing there in a daze," he said. "I felt like I had gotten hit with a huge rock. I was scared I was going to die." It was March 17, 1945, and Loredo had been leading his squad on a reconnaissance mission in the hills when he and one of his scouts were shot.

Decades later Loredo, remained convinced his faith helped pull him through the near-fatal wound. As a child he attended a Pentecostal Church. During the war, his family regularly went to their church, which stayed open 24 hours a day while the U.S. fought overseas.

"The prayers of my mother and sisters helped a lot," he said.

Loredo — who first saw combat action in the invasion of the Philippines on Jan. 9, 1945 — would later be awarded a Silver Star for heroism. When he recovered, the war had almost ended. His company trained for the invasion of Japan, but the Japanese surrendered following the atomic bombings. Following the Japanese surrender, he and the rest of the 169th Infantry Regiment, 43d Infantry Division were sent to Yokohama, Japan, in September 1945 to assist in the occupation. They went from house to house to disarm the Japanese.

Interviewed by
Ernest Eguía and
Paul R. Zepeda
5 MAY 2003
Houston, TX

WWII Military Unit
Company L,
169th Infantry
Regiment,
43d Infantry
Division

On Dec. 18, 1945, he was discharged and returned to his hometown. After "partying" with buddies who'd been in the war, he eventually used the GI Bill to attend watch repair school. "I wanted a job where I'd be clean," he said. He began to work as a watch repairman in Houston, Texas.

Loredo first married Teresa Hernandez. When they divorced, he married Martha Ortiz Calderon on Dec. 3, 1963. In all, Loredo had eight children: Irene, David, Patricia, Javier, Antonio, Joe, Margarita and Martha.

MONTOYA, ERNEST J. Determined to arrive at his Army induction on time, but having no car, Ernest Montoya hitchhiked to Fort Logan, Colo. The nearly 125-mile journey was just the beginning of the long, rough road that lay ahead.

Ernest J. Montoya

Date of Birth
28 MARCH 1925
Crawley, CO

Montoya was assigned to 42d Infantry Division and began training at Camp Gruber, Okla., where he earned the rank of sergeant at age 19.

It was during more advanced training at Camp Ord, Calif., that Montoya realized the gravity of his duties. He was transferred to the 127th Infantry Regiment, 32d Infantry Division and left for Oro Bay in New Guinea, where he received additional training.

Interviewed by
Rea Ann Trotter
21 SEPTEMBER 2000
Avondale, CO

As he was shown Japanese weapons and learned their battle tactics, he prepared himself for the invasion of the Philippines and the terrifying possibilities that came with combat. Montoya and his unit landed on the island of Leyte on November 14, 1944.

"My first day in combat I saw this man ... I didn't even know his name," Montoya said. "We were just there for a few minutes and he got killed. I was one of the guys assigned to carry him out. I remember thinking how that could have been me."

WWII Military Unit
Company C,
127th Infantry
Regiment,
32d Infantry
Division

Montoya then moved on to Luzon, storming the beaches of the island on January 27, 1945. He continued to the north of the island, pursuing Japanese forces until March 11. When enemy forces infiltrated their position and took the lives of two squad leaders, Montoya took charge of the men in his company as they supported Company A of their same regiment. Moments later, he was shot three times, twice in the elbow and once in the foot.

Montoya was discharged in October 1945. He returned to the States and married Natividad "Tivi" Autobee. They had two sons, Robert A. and Gerald G.

Jesse Nava

Date of Birth
30 JUNE 1925
Los Angeles, CA

Interviewed by
Oscar Garza
23 MARCH 2002
Los Angeles, CA

WWII Military Unit
Company C,
21st Regiment,
24th Infantry
Division

NAVA, JESSE. After switching divisions to stay in the infantry, Jesse Nava traveled to the South Pacific, serving in New Guinea and the Philippines.

Drafted shortly after his 18th birthday in 1943, Nava trained at Fort McArthur, Calif., before he went to basic training at Camp Roberts, Calif. There he was transferred from the infantry to a heavy weapons company, an assignment he found less than appealing.

Dissatisfied with the prospect of carrying mortar rounds and huge base plates, he snuck into the infantry's barracks late one evening. He attended roll call for the infantry regiment the next morning, telling his superiors he was new, and that his paperwork was inadvertently transferred to the heavy weapons company. The ruse complete, Nava became part of the 24th Infantry Division.

He arrived in New Guinea in May 1944, and he began patrolling the forests, a job full of uncertainty that kept him constantly on edge. "You never know who's there, who's looking," Nava said. "The trees were so tall, the bushes were so dense ... a night was like a year."

Following combat in New Guinea, Nava traveled to the Philippines, where he was separated from his unit and captured briefly by the Japanese, who beat and bayoneted Nava. When a Japanese officer ordered the men to stop, the soldiers left Nava by the roadside, where his unit later discovered him.

Now a sergeant, Nava continued through the Philippines. He was wounded again when shrapnel struck him while he was dragging two soldiers to safety. He recovered and was preparing to invade Japan when the war ended. Nava was discharged Jan. 11, 1946. He returned to his hometown and married Margaret Mauro. The couple had six children: Daniel, Frances, Barbara, Patricia, Michael and Joey.

Carlos Peña

Date of Birth
4 AUGUST 1925
San Benito, TX

Interviewed by
Rick Leál
14 MARCH 2004
San Benito, TX

WWII Military Unit
Company H,
21st Infantry
Regiment,
24th Infantry
Division

PEÑA, CARLOS. With broad shoulders perfect for football, Carlos Peña was a star on his high school team. When the draft came, he left his football helmet and took up one of an infantryman.

On Dec. 7, 1943, Peña entered the Army. He began training at Camp Shelby, Miss., specializing in 81-mm mortars. After jungle training in California, Peña boarded a ship for New Guinea with 5,000 other soldiers. It was there that Peña said he learned about other cultures and was exposed to different religions.

The 24th Infantry Division landed on the island of Leyte on October 20, 1944. Once there, Peña was assigned to guard and shoot a 105-mm howitzer. From Leyte, he moved to island of Midori in late December 1944. There, troops quickly constructed an air base that was later used in the bombing of Japan.

When Peña contracted malaria, he was sent to recover on a ship. As he boarded, he recognized a hometown friend, Santiago de la Fuente nicknamed "Pino," who worked in the ship's kitchen. Peña discovered his connection afforded him special treatment during his recovery.

"He would bring sirloin and potatoes to me in bed while the other men had to eat wieners and kraut," he said. "They'd complain and ask 'Why's he get that and we get this?' Pino would just say, 'Doctor's orders.' He even brought me Neapolitan ice cream."

Peña then returned to the battlefield on the island of Mindanao, where he saw men fall to friendly fire in the confusion of combat. He then traveled to Japan, confiscating weapons from civilians.

Peña was discharged on March 22, 1946. He married Ofelia Rodriguez on Aug. 5, 1951. The couple had one son, John. Peña worked at LT Boswell Ford as an auto parts manager, and prided himself on his dedication to the job, never missing a day of work.

RAMÓN, ROBERT. Even with the strenuous physical and emotional demands of war, Robert Ramón still looked back on his service in the Pacific fondly. He remembered taking photos in the streets of Tokyo, trying to learn Japanese and visiting Mt. Fujiyama. But before he enjoyed the sights, Ramón served as part of the "mop up" crew on the Philippine Islands of Leyte and Luzon.

Robert Ramón

Date of Birth
1 MAY 1923
Smithville, TX

Interviewed by
Antonio Gilb
2 MARCH 2002
Houston, TX

WWII Military Unit
8th Regiment,
1st Cavalry Division

Patrolling for enemy soldiers in the Philippines, he fought in two battles, but often wondered about the slain Japanese soldiers' families.

Receiving his draft notice in September 1944, Ramón trained in Kansas and California before leaving for New Guinea. He later moved into the Philippines and then into Yokohama and Tokyo. As he moved from island to island, he was constantly aware of the ever-present threat of an attack. He also recalled the harsh conditions, such as a period of 72 hours without water.

"We were so thirsty we were spitting cotton," Ramón said. He remembered that when his unit found a small pond, they disregarded their training and ravenously gulped the unpurified water.

Ramón then spent two years as part of the military police in occupied Japan. It was during this time he had some of his best experiences during his tour of duty, embracing life in Tokyo and courting the daughter of a Mexican diplomat.

He returned to the States in February 1947. Despite a friend's suggestion that he join the police force in El Paso, Texas, he began working as a truck driver.

"By that time, I didn't want to carry a .45 no more," Ramón said. "I told him, 'No, no.' I'd take my chances with a truck."

He married Concepción Ramirez in 1948. The two played in their own band, the Ramón Marimba Combo, from 1961 to 1973. They had four children: Carmen, Elvira, Robert and Armando.

REDE, ALBERTO. High above Australia, Alberto Rede heard the bullets rip through his plane and the engine begin to sputter. His pilot was able to safely land the plane, but once on the ground, Rede noticed a bullet hole a mere 6 inches from where he sat.

Alberto Rede

Date of Birth
30 MARCH 1921
Marfa, TX

Interviewed by
Robert Rivas
12 OCTOBER 2004
El Paso, TX

WWII Military Unit
57th Troop
Carrier Squadron,
375th Troop
Carrier Group,
5th Air Force

Rede was drafted in 1942, after two years at college. He trained in Boca Raton, Fla., Chicago, Missouri and Kentucky before eventually leaving for the Pacific from San Francisco. He worked as a radio operator, and provided supplies in a C-47 cargo plane.

With 2,500 hours of flying previous to leaving for war, Rede stayed on cargo planes and flew on supply missions. Rede said he was never engaged in front lines combat, and despite his brushes with bullets, considers himself lucky. On Sept. 5, 1943, the 375th Troop Carrier Group took part in their first airborne paratroop assault at Nadzab, New Guinea. Rede and the crew also provided transportation in Biak, Indonesia, and in the Philippines: on Mindoro and Luzon.

Rede contracted malaria and was in a hospital recovering when he was discharged on Sept. 6, 1945. He had earned the rank of staff sergeant and a Distinguished Flying Cross.

On Christmas Day, 1946, he married his childhood sweetheart, Esperanza Flores, a teacher who served in the Coast Guard. The couple had two children, Martín and Marta.

Rede knew the immense value of education and used the GI Bill to earn a master's degree in Spanish from Columbia University. He later taught for 42 years.

"Education's my life," he said. "Get all the education you can."

He passed on his two passions—service to his country and education—on to his children. Martín served in the Coast Guard and became a teacher. Marta served in Naval Reserve for 12 years and is also a teacher.

Estanislado Reyna

Date of Birth
5 JULY 1925
Valentine, TX

Interviewed by
Nicole Muñoz
29 JANUARY 2002
El Paso, TX

WWII Military Unit
Company M,
148th Infantry
Regiment,
37th Infantry
Division

REYNA, ESTANISLADO. Dodging enemy fire, Estanislado "Stanley" Reyna ran across a battlefield in the Philippines to retrieve his sergeant, who had been shot. He signaled to medics and helped place his superior on a gurney.

Drafted in 1943, Reyna trained at Camp Fannin, Texas. From there he left for New Guinea in October 1944, then went directly to the Solomon Islands in November. Preparations then began for the invasion of the Philippines at Luzon.

Reyna continued through the Philippines to Manila. It was in Manila that Reyna was wounded for the first time, when shrapnel lodged in his arm on February 8, 1945. He recovered and four months later was sent back to combat in Northern Luzon.

He was injured again in June 1945 when his unit was ambushed, and he credits his gun for saving his hand.

"If I hadn't been holding my rifle, it might have cut my hand off," he said. "The gun absorbed some or the shock."

Even after that injury, Reyna returned to the battlefield after three weeks of recovery. He continued in combat until his discharge on January 26, 1946, awarded a Bronze Star for his service.

He returned to his hometown of Valentine, in far West Texas and began working as a laborer and carpenter's helper with Southern Pacific Railroad. He later worked as a painter and in the supply room of White Sands Missile Range in New Mexico. He eventually settled in El Paso, Texas, working at Fort Bliss.

After moving to El Paso, Reyna married Eva Ortiz on January 21, 1951. The couple had three children: Dolores, Diane and Sonia.

Esequiel Zamudio

Date of Birth
20 AUGUST 1921
San Antonio, TX

Interviewed by
Desirée Mata
23 OCTOBER 2003
San Antonio, TX

WWII Military Unit
Company K,
123d Infantry
Regiment,
33d Infantry
Division

ZAMUDIO, ESEQUIEL. Skittish nerves and a constant sense of fear were what Esequiel Zamudio remembered about war. But despite the need to be alert and on edge at all times, he said that after his service, he felt he had truly become a man.

On Feb. 10, 1945, Zamudio and the 33d Infantry Division invaded the island of Luzon after spending time in New Guinea, where U.S. forces were "mopping up" and destroying Japanese planes and ammunition. While his service was during the final battles of the war, that did not diminish the feeling of uncertainty and danger.

"You couldn't get out of your foxhole at night," he remembered. "Cause anything that moved we would shoot at. At night, you don't know who's friend and who's enemy until the next morning."

Zamudio was drafted in October 1942 and spent time training in the Mojave Desert before traveling to Hawaii to stand guard against the threat of another Japanese attack. From there he left for the Pacific, landing in New Guinea at the end of 1942. He stayed in the Pacific until the end of the war.

His unit was in amphibious training to prepare for an invasion of Japan when the atomic bombs were dropped on Nagasaki and Hiroshima. In September 1945, Zamudio arrived on the Japanese island of Honshu, where he spent four months confiscating and destroying Japanese weapons.

Zamudio was discharged in January 1946. Upon returning to the States, he had trouble finding a job because he was disabled due to injuries he sustained during the war. Eventually, he found work as an airplane engine mechanic at Kelly Field, Texas, where he worked until his retirement.

Zamudio married Susana Longoria and the couple had two sons: Thomas and David. Both of the couple's sons served in the Air Force.

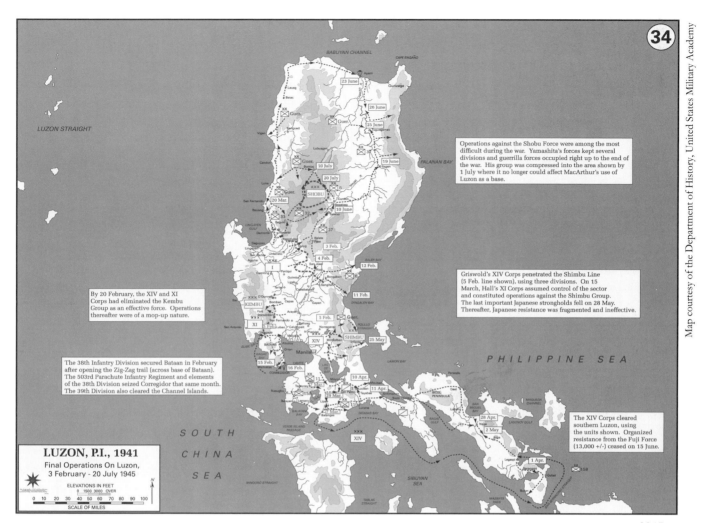

Map courtesy of the Department of History, United States Military Academy

Operations against the Shobu Force were among the most difficult during the war. Yamashita's forces kept several divisions and guerrilla forces occupied right up to the end of the war. His group was compressed into the area shown by 1 July where it no longer could affect MacArthur's use of Luzon as a base.

Griswold's XIV Corps penetrated the Shimbu Line (5 Feb. line shown), using three divisions. On 15 March, Hall's XI Corps assumed control of the sector and constituted operations against the Shimbu Group. The last important Japanese strongholds fell on 28 May. Thereafter, Japanese resistance was fragmented and ineffective.

By 20 February, the XIV and XI Corps had eliminated the Kembu Group as an effective force. Operations thereafter were of a mop-up nature.

The 38th Infantry Division secured Bataan in February after opening the Zig-Zag trail (across base of Bataan). The 503rd Parachute Infantry Regiment and elements of the 38th Division seized Corregidor that same month. The 39th Division also cleared the Channel Islands.

The XIV Corps cleared southern Luzon, using the units shown. Organized resistance from the Fuji Force (13,000 +/-) ceased on 15 June.

LUZON, P.I., 1941
Final Operations On Luzon,
3 February - 20 July 1945

ELEVATIONS IN FEET
0   1500 3000 OVER

0 10 20 30 40 50 60 70 80 90 100
SCALE OF MILES

MAP 14

MEXICAN SQUADRON 201

It was July, 1944. The Allies, on two fronts, were beginning to roll east and west toward Berlin, assured that their momentum and their almost inexhaustible supply of men and material would end in total victory in Europe by the next spring. That year, Mexico, in a show of support for the Allied war effort, unveiled its plan to deploy an all-Mexican fighter-plane unit to the Pacific.

The proud country to the south showed an independent streak on trade and diplomatic relations at the start of the war, openly trading with Axis powers. The history between the United States and Mexico had been generally disadvantageous to Mexico: the U.S. had won the U.S.-Mexico war handily and then, in 1848, under terms of the Treaty of Guadalupe Hidalgo, forced Mexico to cede what is now California, New Mexico, Nevada, and parts of Colorado, Arizona and Utah—for $15 million. More recently, during the Depression, the U.S. "repatriated" thousands of Mexicans *and* Mexican Americans to Mexico.

But 1942 became a turning point for Mexico's approach to the war. In May of that year,

Germany bombed and sank two of Mexico's oil tankers, the *Potrero del Llano* (Colt of the Plains) and *Faja de Oro* (Golden Belt). Mexico declared war on the Axis powers on May 22 and then made it official on May 30, 1942. There was no turning back. Mexico's ships had been attacked on the high seas. Its honor had been tread upon and it became apparent that the Axis presented a menace not only to Europe and Asia but to the rest of the world, Mexico included. The nation was now preparing its resources and manpower and going to war in conjunction with the United States.

At first Mexico embarked on a plan to provide troops for the war effort. However, she found her resources at the time could not support such a venture and, in the end, decided that Mexico and the U.S. could and should create an aerial attack force to help, even in a limited way. Thus, the creation of the famed but short-lived *Escuadron 201* (Squadron 201), or *Las Aguilas Aztecas*, the pride of Mexico. More a symbolic contribution to the war effort at first, Squadron 201 became a lethal and respected part of the Allied effort in the Pacific by the war's end.

The raw numbers tell of a small group of fighter pilots and ground support: The *Fuerza Aerea Expedicionaria Mexicana* would total 42 officers and 249 enlisted men under the command of Antonio Cardenas Rodriguez. Most would be English-speaking. Thirty-eight of them would be pilots, flying P-47D fighters provided by the United States.

Squadron members arrived in Laredo, Texas; made stops in San Antonio, Brownsville and Greenville, Texas; Alabama; Idaho; and, finally, Topeka, Kan.

After ceremoniously receiving the Mexican flag on Feb. 22, 1945, the *Fuerza Aerea Expedicionaria Mexicana* was ready for overseas duty: Mexico now had its wartime aviators. Its flag with the tricolors and the eagle clutching a snake atop the cactus would be represented in the Pacific. As the war wound down, the *pilotos* of the squadron would show courage under fire and turn in a credible, if short, tour of duty.

At war's end, *Escuadron 201* had flown 96 combat missions (including 37 training missions), mostly in Luzon and New Guinea, but in Formosa as well.

Numbers aside, there are a number of vignettes about the *Escuadron 201*, mostly of valor but sometimes showing the exuberance of youth.

While training in Greenville, Texas, in 1945, Reynaldo Perez Gallardo of the *Escuadron* took a "joyride" and "buzzed" the city. Needless to say, he was disciplined for "buzzing" Greenville. But perhaps the joyride by the young pilot was an affirmation of Mexican pride that its best and brightest sons of Mexico were in the U.S. to train before taking the fight to the Japanese.

Mexico contributed in another major way to the war effort, although perhaps nothing to parallel the glamour of the *Escuadron 201*. Its other contribution was a U.S.-sanctioned force of thousands of "soldiers of the furrows," *braceros*, who worked the agricultural fields in the U.S. to keep the food supply flowing. Perhaps one of those agricultural workers might have seen Gallardo's whimsical joyride over Greenville that day in 1945.

In the furrows and in the clouds. Mexico's contributions to a war effort.

— *Guillermo Torres*
Copy Editor,
San Antonio Express-News

GALLARDO, REYNALDO PEREZ. A son of a Mexican Army general and an aficionado of airplanes since childhood, Reynaldo Perez Gallardo was a perfect candidate to become one of 38 fighter pilots in the 201st Fighter Squadron, the only Mexican combat unit to actively participate in WWII.

Born and raised in San Luis Postosí, where his father, Reynaldo Gallardo, was a governor in the 1940s, he would go to an aviation camp in the city instead of school. In exchange for cleaning the planes, Gallardo would get a plane ride around the airport. He joined the Mexican military at age 16 and trained at the Military College of Mexico and the Military Aviation School in Guadalajara. He was an aviation instructor there when a call for a squadron to participate in the war went out.

"As it was expected, I was one of the first ones to volunteer," he said.

After a year of training in the United States, Gallardo and *Escuadron 201* left for the Philippines on March 27, 1945 to join the Allies in bombing Luzon and Formosa.

Gallardo recalled feelings of distrust from the rest of the 58th Fighter Group, sentiments that were dispelled when the men of the 201st Squadron began to successfully complete missions.

They would participate in 59 combat missions before the end of the war. A celebration awaited the squadron when they returned on Nov. 18, 1945. "All of Mexico City ... was standing along the streets. They were excited and anxious to see us," Gallardo said. "We felt very proud."

After the war, Gallardo was responsible for choosing and training new aviators. He married Angelina Gonzalez in 1969 and the couple had two children: Francisco and Carla. He became an aviator for the government of Michoacan, Mexico, and served as director of the security department of the Mexican Social Security offices and as a civil aeronautics inspector in 1975. In 1984, Gallardo moved to Austin, Texas, where he owned a freight-hauling business.

Reynaldo Perez
Gallardo

Date of Birth
10 AUGUST 1923
San Luis Potosí,
Mexico

Interviewed by
Lucy Guevara
9 MARCH 2000
Austin, TX

WWII Military Unit
201st Mexican
Fighter Squadron,
58th Fighter Group,
5th Air Force

ZENIZO, JAIME. As a pilot in the Mexican 201st Squadron serving in the Philippines, Jaime Zenizo had to write home to quash rumors that his plane had crashed.

A newspaper called La Noche had incorrectly reported him killed in action. Zenizo sent a letter home to assure his parents that he was well, but it took 15 days for it to get to the United States and then 15 more to arrive in Mexico.

Zenizo was a pilot in the squadron of more than 300 Mexicans who flew in 59 combat missions from Porac and Clark Fields on the island of Luzon. He flew mainly ground attack missions in support of the infantry. At one point, the engine on his P-47 Thunderbird caught fire and Zenizo made an emergency landing and jumped from the plane.

He remembered that his only rest during the war was the 15 days he was hospitalized for minor injuries after that landing. "I didn't cry because I didn't have time to cry," he said. "I believe that my parents cried enough."

Upon the return of the 201st Squadron to Mexico on Nov. 18, 1945, President Ávila Camacho and a proud nation gave squad members a grand welcome. But the only thing important to the young Zenizo was to see his family and girlfriend again.

"I think that we are a group of pilots who had a mission and we completed it," he said. "But we are not heroes."

Though he acknowledged that people will forget what he and members of this squadron did for the Allies and for their country, Zenizo appreciated most the respect he received from his military friends, most of whom became generals.

"I'm a lieutenant," he said. "But they all call me Commander."

Jaime Zenizo

Date of Birth
6 APRIL 1921
Pueblo, Puebla,
Mexico

Interviewed by
Dana Calvo
25 JUNE 2003
Mexico City, Mexico

WWII Military Unit
201st Mexican
Fighter Squadron,
58th Fighter Group,
5th Air Force

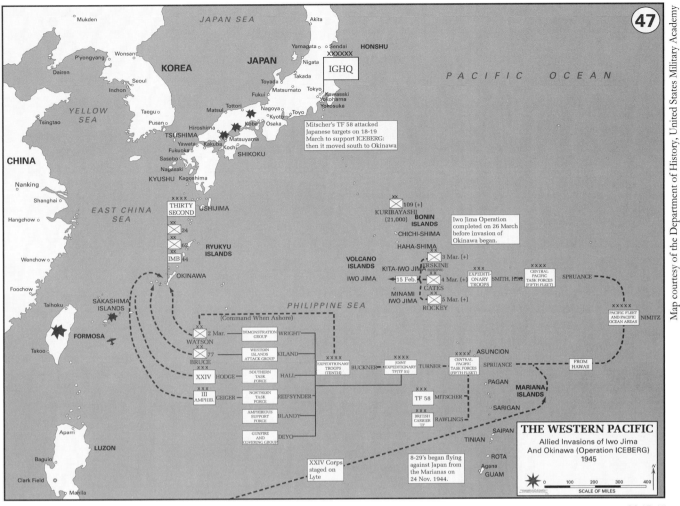

Map courtesy of the Department of History, United States Military Academy

Mitscher's TF 58 attacked Japanese targets on 18-19 March to support ICEBERG; then it moved south to Okinawa

Iwo Jima Operation completed on 26 March before invasion of Okinawa began.

8-29's began flying against Japan from the Marianas on 24 Nov. 1944.

XXIV Corps staged on Lyte

THE WESTERN PACIFIC
Allied Invasions of Iwo Jima And Okinawa (Operation ICEBERG) 1945

SCALE OF MILES
0   100   200   300   400

MAP 15

INVADING IWO JIMA AND OKINAWA

Even before the U.S. had taken back the Philippines, the U.S. Navy was working on gaining a foothold closer to the Japanese coast. Battles at Iwo Jima and Okinawa established an unquestionable point: the Japanese would relinquish nothing without a complete rout.

Charles Samarron, a native of San Antonio, Texas, who served with the 3d Marine Division, 3d Amphibious Tractor Battalion, would voice the conclusion reached by American military experts, as well as the public: "The Japanese were fanatics, they were never gonna give up. So

just how many lives were we going to lose trying to land on Japan and capture it?" *(See Samarron's story in Chapter 9.)*

Iwo Jima, which means "sulfur island" in Japanese, is some 660 miles from the Japanese coast. When Antonio F. Moreno, of Gulf, Texas, stormed Iwo Jima as a U.S. Marine medical corpsman with the 5 Marine Regiment, he instantly recognized the odor.

"It smelled like rotten eggs; that's why it reminded me of home," Moreno said.

Home for Moreno was a company mining

town, run by a sulfur company. The sulfur was used for medicine, explosives and ammunition.

While geographically small—not more than three miles wide at its widest and only five miles long—the island of Iwo Jima presented a huge strategic asset for Allied forces. With two large airfields, the island served as the perfect location for the Japanese to intercept Allied planes headed for mainland Japan. But under Allied control, the island could be used for emergency landings or refueling.

The Japanese had constructed dozens of concrete "pillboxes" in the hills of the volcanic island. From those fortresses, as well as many caves and tunnels, the Japanese stood their ground from Feb. 19, 1945, when the first U.S. Marines landed on Iwo Jima until the end of March. Four days into the battle at Iwo Jima, Marines raised a flag on Mount Suribachi and Associated Press photographer Joe Rosenthal documented the event with a picture that would be published around the world. Edward Romero, of Winkelman, Ariz., of the 4th Marine Division witnessed it firsthand and recalled the emotion it evoked.

"I saw the raising of our flag. God bless America!" he said.

It would be another month of grinding battle before the Japanese were vanquished there, but the flag-raising boosted morale.

Remembered as the final battle of WWII, Okinawa was by no means the fastest or cleanest. With nearly 130,000 civilian casualties alone, it was a bloody campaign that stretched over three months. Japanese forces initially retreated from the beaches, creating a war of attrition, but also used *Kamikaze* (which means "heavenly wind") suicide attacks by Japanese planes.

Jesús Herrera, of San Antonio, and part of the 1st Marine Division, reached the Okinawa beaches on April 1, hitting the ground running and not stopping for days. His duties included tending to wounded soldiers and pulling them to safety. He witnessed horrible injuries.

"In that situation you just go forward," Herrera said. "You're not looking. I just prayed and prayed and prayed."

When the battle was over, out of 255 men in Herrera's company, only 16 were still in fighting shape; the rest were either dead or wounded. Herrera was the only corpsman left of the original seven.

Fighting in Okinawa lasted until June 21, 1945. Okinawa was later the staging point that allowed America to successfully bomb Japan. On March 9, 1945, U.S. forces began dropping incendiary bombs over Japan—more would follow. Those incendiary bombs were to lead to the eventual dropping of the atomic bomb on Hiroshima on Aug. 6 and Nagasaki three days later on Aug. 9.

CHAVEZ, ROBERT JOHN. Brushes with death, the loss of friends and the overall emotional strain of war remained fresh in Robert Chavez's memory long after the war ended. He avoided discussing his valiant service and was haunted by nightmares of war.

"It was terrible," he said of his time in Okinawa.

Chavez was drafted in September 1944 and began training at Fort Bliss, Texas. He continued his training in California before he finished with jungle training in Hawaii. Chavez remembered learning different species of plants to avoid touching or eating the ones that were poisonous.

The invasion of Okinawa began Easter Sunday 1945. It was a lengthy, bloody campaign meant to serve as a preview of the invasion of the main islands of Japan.

Throughout the campaign, tension and uncertainty mounted, and Chavez said soldiers were afraid to even speak to each other for fear it would draw the attention of the enemy. Officers and soldiers were not allowed to wear their ranks on their uniforms, as the Japanese would aim to eliminate soldiers with more authority first.

Following the campaign at Okinawa, Chavez was transferred to the Philippines, where he trained as a paramedic and assisted doctors during surgery. Eventually, he said, he was unable to continue working as a medic, because the blood and gore were simply overwhelming.

He was discharged in November 1946. His division received the Presidential Unit Citation.

Chavez returned to his hometown of Albuquerque, N.M., and began working in a sawmill. Later he would work for a news agency and as a service coordinator at a laboratory.

Chavez married María Sanchez on February 28, 1948. The couple had seven children: Robert, Rudy, Carol, Roland, Rita, Anita and Michelle.

Robert John Chavez

Date of Birth
14 APRIL 1926
Albuquerque, NM

Interviewed by
Erika Martinez
2 NOVEMBER 2002
Albuquerque, NM

WWII Military Unit
Company B,
381st Infantry
Regiment,
96th Infantry
Division

DELEON, JAMES ARTHUR. With his older brother, John, already in the Army in Europe, James DeLeon was determined to serve his country. "My parents were against me joining, but I thought I should do my part," he said. When Carlos and Charlotta DeLeon finally gave him the permission he needed, James joined the Marines. "They were the best," he said of the Marines—a point argued for decades with, his four brothers, who each served in a different branch: Army, Navy, Marines and Air Force.

DeLeon trained at Moffit Field, Calif. He entered battle in August 1942, one of the 6,000 Marines sent to seize the beginnings of a Japanese airfield on Guadalcanal, Solomon Islands. Outnumbered, the Japanese were unable to recover from the Allied success, and as reinforcements landed on the island, the 1st Marine Division was sent to Australia for rest and relaxation. DeLeon was not so lucky and went to New Caledonia to recover from malaria.

He was reassigned to the 6th Marine Division and returned to combat in New Georgia, Solomon Islands, where U.S. troops took control in October 1943. Landing under fire in Okinawa, he dug trenches to escape snipers' bullets. DeLeon operated his platoon's Browning Automatic Rifle, which weighed 20 pounds. The division moved from battle to battle in Okinawa until the end of the war. It was one of the few divisions largely unhurt during combat.

DeLeon returned to his parents who had moved to the city while he was away. He planned to attend college, but returned to Texas to visit his girlfriend, Susie Marie Elizondo, to whom he had written during the war. A month later they married. DeLeon eventually got a job as a carpenter at a local Texaco plant where Susie worked, and he stayed for nearly 40 years. The couple had seven children: Gerald, Robert, Deborah, Theresa, Anna, James and Judy.

James Arthur
DeLeon

Date of Birth
3 OCTOBER 1919
Goliad, TX

Interviewed by
Theresa DeLeon
Weeks
8 DECEMBER 2000
Port Arthur, TX

WWII Military Unit
Company B,
5th Marine
Regiment,
1st Marine Division

Transferred to
6th Marine Division

Manuel Espinoza

Date of Birth
7 NOVEMBER 1925
Pueblo, CO

Interviewed by
Xochitl Salazár
25 OCTOBER 2003
San Antonio, TX

WWII Military Unit
USS *Sarasota*
(APA-204)

ESPINOZA, MANUEL. Struggling through the Great Depression and dropping out of school to help support his widowed mother, Manuel Espinoza was determined to provide a better life for his own family someday. His service in the Navy during WWII was the first step to making it a reality.

Espinoza enlisted in November 1943 and trained in San Diego and San Luis Obisbo, Calif., before boarding the USS *Sarasota*, an amphibious troop ship, for the Pacific.

His first invasion was on the Philippine Island of Leyte. However, when the ship arrived, the Army had already secured the island. They then traveled to San Antonio, Philippines, where they were welcomed by grateful Filipinos. "Thousands and thousands of people came out of the mountains to greet us," Espinoza said.

The ship docked on the island of Luzon on January 9, 1945, and began preparations for the invasion of Japan at Okinawa.

During the landings at Ie Shima during the Battle of Okinawa, Espinoza was wounded by shrapnel, with metal slicing the center of his forehead. His tour of combat over, he spent six months in a hospital recuperating.

He then went to Camp Wallace, Texas, to supervise German prisoners of war. Espinoza next spent time near Nashville, Tenn., helping civilians during a flood before his discharge on April 18, 1946.

Espinoza returned to San Antonio, Texas and he began working as a radar repairman and at the local brewery in the evenings. In 1950, he married Theresa Prado. The couple had six children. Espinoza made a point to provide his children with educational opportunities he never had, sending them to private schools. Three of his children went on to earn master's degrees.

Esteban R. García

Date of Birth
28 NOVEMBER 1925
Mission, TX

Interviewed by
Liza Moreno
6 APRIL 2002
McAllen, TX

WWII Military Unit
USS *Kilty* (APD-15)

GARCÍA, ESTEBAN R. As he sailed through the Pacific en route to battles in the Philippines and later the assault on Okinawa, Steve García relied on memories of his mother to persevere. "The love of a mother is a true love. If you don't love your mom, you don't love anyone," he said. "Even when I was overseas, my mother was with me. I imagine that's what kept me alive."

He was one of six García brothers to don a uniform during WWII. One of his brothers, Daniel García of the U.S. Marines, died in the first wave of troops going into Iwo Jima on March 2, 1945. Another brother, Agustín R. García, twice received the Purple Heart for injuries. Three other brothers served stateside.

García enlisted in the Navy on Dec. 18, 1941, and set sail for Alaska for training that month. From there he left for the Pacific Theater. As a gunner's mate 2d class on the USS *Kilty*, he was involved in nearly 30 actions. García reinforced Marines at Guadalcanal, in the Solomon Islands and in New Guinea. In October of 1944 the ship transported rangers to Leyte in preparation for the invasion of the Philippines.

In April 1945, the *Kilty* served as an escort to several ships transporting soldiers to the beaches of Okinawa. The ship made another voyage to Okinawa and on May 4, 1945, rescued soldiers of the USS *Luce*, which was sunk by a *Kamikaze*. The ship returned to San Diego, Calif., in June, and García was discharged on Oct. 25, 1945.

He returned to Texas. After trade school, he owned and managed his own carpentry shop until his retirement. He had six children by his second wife: José Edward, José Edian, José Eli, Heriberto, Estéban Jr. and Elda. He had three stepchildren from his third marriage: Armando, Roberto and Alma. And two stepchildren from his fourth marriage: Sergio and Jorge.

HERRERA, JESÚS. As a corpsman in the U.S. Marines, Jesús Herrera dodged a hail of bullets as he rushed through the battlefields on Okinawa tending to the wounded.

He was so eager to join the Armed Forces that he lied about his age to enlist in 1943 at age 16. Piling himself and two friends onto a bike, the three pedaled to the recruitment office to begin their military careers. Despite being a quarter of a pound under the military's minimum weight requirement, he passed the military's health exam. Herrera said doctors pushed him through the exam because he appeared so eager to begin serving his country.

After scoring well on an entrance exam, Herrera was assigned to the naval hospital corps school and, after training, began working at the naval hospital in San Diego, Calif. He completed boot camp with the Marines and then went to field medical school.

He became part of the 10th Army, which invaded the island of Okinawa in April 1945. Herrera remembered the turbulent trip to shore and the constant barrage of enemy fire.

"Airplanes were bombing," he said. "Battleships were shooting; *Kamikazes* were terrible."

His company suffered massive casualties during the invasion. Only 16 of the 255 men in his company were still able to fight. Herrera was the only corpsman to survive.

He was wounded in June 1945 when a shell knocked him unconscious, but he returned to battle just 10 days later. Later, he served in China and in the occupation of Japan.

Herrera was discharged on May 6, 1946. He returned to San Antonio, Texas.

He worked as a carpenter while taking night classes in San Antonio at St. Mary's University, and graduated in 1962. He went on to teach English, work as a proofreader at Kelly Air Force Base and manage apartments.

Jesús Herrera

Date of Birth
21 JULY 1926
San Antonio, TX

Interviewed by
Jane O'Brien
25 OCTOBER 2003
San Antonio, TX

WWII Military Unit
Company F,
7th Marine
Regiment,
1st Marine Division

LOPEZ, CRESENCIO. Raised on a ranch in western New Mexico, Cresencio Lopez loved his work breaking horses and raising cattle. The draft interrupted life on the range in September 1944.

Already a married father of two, Lopez was forced to leave his young wife, Trinidad, and their daughters, Pearline and Freida, when he began basic training at Camp Roberts, Calif. Lopez's amphibious training was completed at Fort Ord, Calif., before he boarded a ship at Fort Lawton, Wash. He had jungle training on the Hawaiian island of Oahu and headed to Saipan, where he prepared for the invasion of Okinawa.

Lopez spent four months fighting in Okinawa, landing in early April 1945. The horrors of battle at Okinawa scarred Lopez. He remembered watching as his friends were struck by enemy fire. The day he carried a wounded 9-year-old Japanese girl 13 miles to a military hospital also remained etched in his memory. "I don't like to talk about it," he said. "But we all got used to it back then. In the front lines, you're not afraid of anything."

At the height of the fighting, Lopez remained in his foxhole for days, forced to bail out chest-high rainwater with his helmet.

Lopez contracted malaria while in Okinawa. He received medical treatment but placed his duties on the battlefield above his own health. "I was sick all the time," he said. "But you couldn't say you were sick, because they needed you."

At the war's end, Lopez flew to Tokyo and boarded a ship for the States. Lopez was discharged in February 1946. He returned to ranching in New Mexico, and he and his wife welcomed their third daughter, Gloria, in 1948. Lopez sold most of his cattle during a drought in the 1950s and became an electrician in the uranium mines of New Mexico.

Cresencio Lopez

Date of Birth
22 FEBRUARY 1923
Moquino, NM

Interviewed by
Brian Lucero
2 NOVEMBER 2002
Albuquerque, NM

WWII Military Unit
27th Infantry
Division

Jess Medina

Date of Birth
5 AUGUST 1921
Ray, AZ

Interviewed by
Ernesto Portillo
5 JANUARY 2003
Tucson, AZ

WWII Military Unit
USS *Tennessee*
(BB-43)

MEDINA, JESS. Aboard the USS *Tennessee*, Jess Medina remembered the sheer force as the gun batteries on the deck of the ship fired. The powerful naval guns shook the ship with each shot, as a fierce boom echoed over the waters of the Pacific.

"It was a heck of a noise," Medina said. "It was a big boom. It could knock you down if you weren't holding on to something."

Medina enlisted in the Navy two months after the attack at Pearl Harbor. He completed boot camp and boarded the *Tennessee*. He lived aboard the ship for three years and nine months. He learned how to use the ship's radar equipment, but sometimes wondered if his ethnicity kept him from advancing, having never earned a rank higher than radarman third class.

In the Pacific, the *Tennessee* regularly fended off attacks from *Kamikazes*. In one assault on April 12, 1945, during the battle of Okinawa, the gunners were able to shoot down a *Kamikaze*, but the plane still crashed through the deck. The bomb aboard the plane detonated, killing 22 men on the *Tennessee*, and injuring 107. Medina was below the deck during the explosion and after it was safe to leave his post, he immediately volunteered to gather the fallen soldiers and arrange for a proper burial at sea for his comrades. Medina said that the only time he ever felt afraid during his tour of duty was the night he helped gather the remains of his fellow soldiers who had been killed.

"That evening, I got sick to my stomach and threw up," Medina said.

Medina was discharged on Nov. 24, 1945. He began working at Douglas Aircraft in Santa Monica, Calif. He married Emma Torres in 1947. The couple had two children—Michael and Patsy—before divorcing. Medina moved to Arizona in 1955 and found work as a radio technician at Davis-Monthan Air Force Base. He married Betty Muñoz in 1956.

Joe Medina

Date of Birth
24 AUGUST 1924
Lamar, CO

Interviewed by
Steven Rosales
21 JANUARY 2003
Palos Verdes
Estates, CA

WWII Military Unit
Support Forces,
7th Army

MEDINA, JOE. In 1943, Joe Medina marched to the local recruiting office and enlisted.

He trained in Denver and Utah and took classes in the officer training school in North Dakota, where Medina put in 13-hour days studying. His hard work earned him the rank of second lieutenant. He was transferred to Angel Island, Calif., where he served with the military police. From there he set sail for New Guinea, and 28 days later, he landed in Nadzab. His time in New Guinea was spent preparing for the invasion at Leyte and the soldiers were constantly on high alert, diving into trenches at the first sound of gunfire.

After U.S. troops secured Leyte, Medina began building airstrips on the island. He remembered the difficult conditions during monsoon season, when often supply trucks could not reach the men with food and other necessities.

Medina was sent to Manila and then Okinawa to aid in the end of the fighting there.

"One night we were bombed all night long and we couldn't sleep," he said. He remembered the following morning, when he heard shots from navy ships, signaling the war's end.

"That day we received our first ration of beer," Medina said.

After fighting ended, Medina was sent to Tokyo and began working for the Far Eastern Air Force Intelligence Group. The group studied blueprints of Japanese jets and sent the information to intelligence teams at Wright Field, Ohio.

Medina was discharged in December 1945. He attended Pacific Coast University School of Law and then Southwestern University School of Law, earning his doctorate in law. He practiced administrative government law throughout the Los Angeles area until his retirement in 1988.

MENDOZA, ALVINO. A comment from his girlfriend and future wife, Rebecca Vasquez, motivated Alvino Mendoza to join the Navy when he was drafted in 1944. He initially felt indifferent about his assignment, but his sweetheart thought the Navy might be safer than the Army.

"I don't care where I go, it's not my choice," he told his recruiter. "And that's when I remembered her, when she asked me [to choose the Navy]. So I said, 'I'll take the Navy.'"

He began his amphibious training at Galveston, Texas, and set sail for the Pacific Theater in October 1944. He then began preparations for the Okinawa campaign, the largest amphibious assault on the Japanese during WWII. Mendoza said that from the beginning of fighting in March 1945, the attacks were unrelenting.

"Immediately, when we arrived, we were constantly under attack," Mendoza said.

Mendoza's ship, the USS *George*, was full of ammunition and explosives. It was struck by a *Kamikaze* plane and was sent to Guam for repairs. While in Guam, Mendoza and his fellow sailors learned of Japan's surrender and the war's end. He then was sent to Nagasaki.

Upon his discharge, he returned to Austin, Texas, and married Rebecca. The couple had seven children: Alvin, Rebecca, Esperanza, Samuel, Benjamin, Caleb and Seth. Each of the couple's sons served in the Armed Forces, either in the Navy or Air Force.

Mendoza said that war gave him a new outlook on race relations, and even himself.

"I did come back with a little more self-confidence," he said. "Because I had mingled with nothing but Anglo troops, and I couldn't see how they could be better than me. I knew I could do anything just as good as anyone else."

Alvino Mendoza

Date of Birth
1 MARCH 1926
Round Rock, TX

Interviewed by
Haldun Morgan
20 OCTOBER 1999
Austin, TX

WWII Military Unit
USS *George*
(DE-697)

MORENO, ANTONIO F. With a 75-pound supply pack on his back, Antonio Moreno dodged enemy fire as he darted across the battlefield of Iwo Jima to tend to the wounded.

The eldest son of Mexican immigrants, Moreno was drafted on March 10, 1943. He initially joined the Navy but was later assigned to the Marines. He completed his basic training at Camp Pendleton, Calif. After additional training at Camp Tarawa in the Hawaiian Islands, Moreno set sail for the South Pacific.

He spent 16 months as a medic in the Pacific and was witness to the atrocities of war daily, losing friends and watching as bombs destroyed everything in their paths.

But Moreno also witnessed troops raising the American flag at Iwo Jima, a sign, he said, that the United States was about to win the war—and one of his proudest moments in the service.

Moreno and his fellow Marines were preparing for the invasion of mainland Japan when the war ended. He was discharged on Feb. 21, 1946.

He returned to Texas, where he said that life for Latinos improved by "leaps and bounds" following the war.

Utilizing the GI Bill, Moreno earned an associate's degree from Wharton Junior College in 1988. He was the produce manager at a local supermarket before he began working for the U.S. Postal Service, where he stayed until his retirement.

Moreno married Gloria Gutierrez, a teacher, in 1950. The couple had two children.

He stayed active in his church and with the Scottish Rite Masonic Society. Moreno advised Latinos to participate in their community and get an education.

"Stay in school and educate yourself to enter the fabric of life," he said.

Antonio F. Moreno

Date of Birth
22 APRIL 1924
Gulf, TX

Interviewed by
Erika Martinez
4 DECEMBER 2001
Austin, TX

WWII Military Unit
2d Platoon,
E Company,
27th Marine
Regiment,
5th Marine Division

Emilio Rodriguez

Date of Birth
11 MARCH 1920
Vergel, TX

Interviewed by
Joe Myers Vasquez
6 APRIL 2002
McAllen, TX

WWII Military Unit
184th Regiment,
7th Infantry
Division

RODRIGUEZ, EMILIO. Traveling through the Pacific with the 184th Infantry Regiment, 7th Infantry Division, Emilio Rodriguez survived some of the bloodiest, most treacherous battles of WWII. From Leyte to Okinawa, Rodriguez and his unit stormed the shores of the Philippines and Okinawa during the second half of the war.

Rodriguez was drafted in May 1942 and began his training at Fort Lewis, Wash., and Fort Ord, Calif. He was then shipped to the Japanese-occupied Aleutian Islands, where U.S. forces invaded Attu on May 11, 1943. The battle on Attu lasted until June.

Rodriguez and his division continued to the eastern Philippines, helping to secure Leyte. They then prepared for the campaign at Okinawa. Rodriguez was in the first wave of troops who made their way ashore with ease—but that was only the beginning of the battle.

One evening, when he was stationed in his foxhole, a mortar shell exploded above Rodriguez. The shell caused a landslide and buried the men in the foxhole. Rodriguez was rushed to a field hospital and was later told that his fellow soldiers had to dig him out of the mud to save his life.

The injuries he sustained during the landslide ended his time in combat. After he was transferred to a hospital in Guam, Rodriguez was sent back to the States.

On November 18, 1945, he was honorably discharged and moved to McAllen, Texas. There he began working as a poultry deliveryman. In 1966, he founded his own food-distribution company, Rodriguez and Sons. Rodriguez later retired, and his sons took over running the daily operations of the business, now called Valley Pride Food Distribution.

He met María Olivia Escobar and the two married on January 9, 1949. The couple had four sons: Emilio, Edward, Homer and Mario. All pursued degrees after high school.

Edward Romero

Date of Birth
2 JANUARY 1926
Winkelman, AZ

Interviewed by
Joe Olague
5 JANUARY 2003
Tucson, AZ

WWII Military Unit
Company F,
2d Battalion,
23d Regiment,
4th Marine Division

ROMERO, EDWARD. When he left for Marine Corps training in San Diego, Calif., Edward Romero's entire hometown of Mammoth, Ariz., lined the main street to wish him well.

Romero enlisted at age 17, obtaining parental consent to enter the Marines early. "The whole town of Mammoth came to wish me Godspeed and goodbye ... Mom cried very, very much," he said. Romero completed his training at Camp Pendleton, Calif., with amphibious maneuvers. He then left for his first mission, to secure the islands of Roi and Namur in the Marshall Islands. It was there that Romero first met enemy fire on the battlefield.

"As they started shooting at us, I threw myself on the ground," he said.

Crawling along the ground and diving into ditches for cover, Romero continued fighting until the Marines secured the islands. From there, he received more training in Hawaii. His unit then traveled to Saipan, which was full of constant danger and close calls, in June 1944.

"By the grace of God, I am still alive," he said.

Following combat at Saipan, Romero continued through the Pacific to Tinian.

"After taking the island of Tinian we sailed back to Maui [Hawaii] where we started training for the battle of Iwo Jima," he said. "I saw the raising of our flag. God bless America!"

At Iwo Jima, Romero was struck by a shell. He was treated and quickly returned to battle. He then suffered a concussion and returned to the States, completing his service on guard duty.

He was discharged in November 1945 and returned to Arizona, where he began working in carpentry. Romero married Isabel Herrera in 1951. They had six children: Percilla, Carmen, Benjamin, Robert, Larry and Steven.

SOTO, TRINO J. The brotherhood that developed in the close quarters of the USS *Haggard* is something that Trino Soto continued to cherish decades after WWII ended. Soto lined the halls of his home with vintage photographs of himself and his fellow sailors. Nearly half a decade later, he remembered the *Haggard* going full steam as flagship in front of eight other destroyers during practice maneuvers as "the most beautiful sight I ever saw."

Trino J. Soto

Date of Birth
16 AUGUST 1924
Fresno, CA

Interviewed by
Cindy Cárcamo
4 MAY 2001
Fresno, CA

WWII Military Unit
USS *Haggard*
(DD-555)

Soto eagerly enlisted shortly after Pearl Harbor and spent three months training in Seattle, Wash., while the *Haggard* was being built. After two months of additional squadron training in Hawaii, the ship and its crew were prepared for combat in the Pacific. From there, he set sail for the Marshall Islands. The destroyer fought in 13 battles throughout the Pacific, including the battle of Leyte Gulf and the Luzon campaign in the Philippines.

The *Haggard* would then participate in the largest battle of the Pacific Campaign, the invasion at Okinawa. It was there that Soto experienced his most intense combat, and *Kamikaze* attacks nearly sank the *Haggard*. On the deck with his 40-mm, Soto fired furiously at the planes overhead, but he could not halt the attack. "I couldn't fire on that sucker. But I was watching him," he said. "And just before he hit the ship, he stood up on the cockpit. And then he rammed the ship. He hit her right on mid-ship." The ship was rescued and kept afloat when the Navy brought a patch to repair the hole from the *Kamikaze* attacks.

When Soto returned home he found increased opportunities for Mexican Americans. He said the war created new avenues for advancement in the lives of Latinos: for example, they were no longer forced to work as laborers, and they could buy their own homes. Soto was able to own a business and build a house for his family. Soto had two children: Richard and Leslie.

TODD, WILLIAM HENRY. His military service evolved into a tour of the globe, taking William Todd from Mexico to Panama to the Pacific Theater. Born in Mexico, Todd did not learn English until his mother moved the family to the United States when Todd was 12. Nonetheless, he enlisted in the Arizona National Guard on Feb. 28, 1940, at age 16.

William Henry Todd

Date of Birth
3 AUGUST 1923
Colima, Mexico

Interviewed by
William R. Todd-
Mancillas
11 SEPTEMBER 2001
Phoenix, AZ

WWII Military Unit
158th Regimental
Combat Team

Shortly after the bombing of Pearl Harbor, Todd was shipped to Panama, where he went on missions into the jungle for days, surviving on only raisins and peanuts.

In January 1943, Todd was shipped to the Pacific, landing in Brisbane, Australia, where he completed more training. From there, he traveled to New Guinea, where the 158th Regimental Combat Team was re-forming. The team was nicknamed the "Bushmasters."

His first battle was in a cornfield, and Todd remembered "all hell broke loose."

"I was very scared," Todd said. "But nothing was going to make me weaken. I was very determined."

He survived the battle and next went on to fight throughout New Guinea. At the Battle of Slaughter Hill, his team took several prisoners, including one named Ogata, who would eventually save Todd's life. Ogata persuaded a Japanese solider not to throw a grenade at Todd by pouncing on him and then reasoning with him.

The team then moved into Luzon on the Philippines, and Todd was regularly engaged in heavy combat on the island until his discharge on May 25, 1945. He then returned to Arizona after 40 months overseas and enrolled in Arizona State University, earning a degree in engineering. Todd married Helen Mancillas in 1947 and the couple had four children: Carlos, Guillermo, Ana and William. The couple divorced in 1965 and Todd married Ana Lavin, but they divorced in 1985.

Antonio Trujillo

Date of Birth
15 MAY 1926
Albuquerque, NM

Interviewed by
Iliana Limón
2 NOVEMBER 2002
Albuquerque, NM

WWII Military Unit
Company F,
2d Battalion,
4th Marine Division

TRUJILLO, ANTONIO. Volunteering for some of the most dangerous missions of the Pacific campaign, Antonio Trujillo defied the advice his fellow Marines, who urged him to stop offering to serve in these risky assignments.

"I remembered that the other Marine had told me not to volunteer," he said. "I had more pride in myself, so I did volunteer."

His dangerous tasks ranged from transporting ammunition to the front lines to using a flame-thrower to drive Japanese soldiers out of their strongholds in caves.

Trujillo enlisted in the Marine Corps on April 8, 1944, at age 17. After training at Parris Island, S.C., he studied weaponry at Cherry Point, N.C. From there he was deployed to Guam for reconnaissance training. Trujillo's next stop was Okinawa, but he wasn't aware of his destination as he boarded the vessel.

"They put us in the ship, and we didn't know where we were going," he said. "We were about two weeks at sea when one morning I heard 18-inch guns. Then they cut off all the power on the deck. ... We started sweating and suffocating because they had all the power on the guns."

In April 1945, Trujillo landed on the beaches of Okinawa. He engaged in unrelenting combat with Japanese suicide bombers, *Kamikazes*, and eventually U.S. troops secured the island. Trujillo then volunteered to be part of a security force in Guam and eventually returned to Japan in 1946 as part of the U.S. security force.

He was discharged in August 1946 and returned to New Mexico. He married Stella Quinones and had three children: Janet, Anthony Rey and Stella. Following his first wife's passing, Trujillo married María Cisernos on June 26, 1957, and they had three children: Anthony, Joseph and Cecilia.

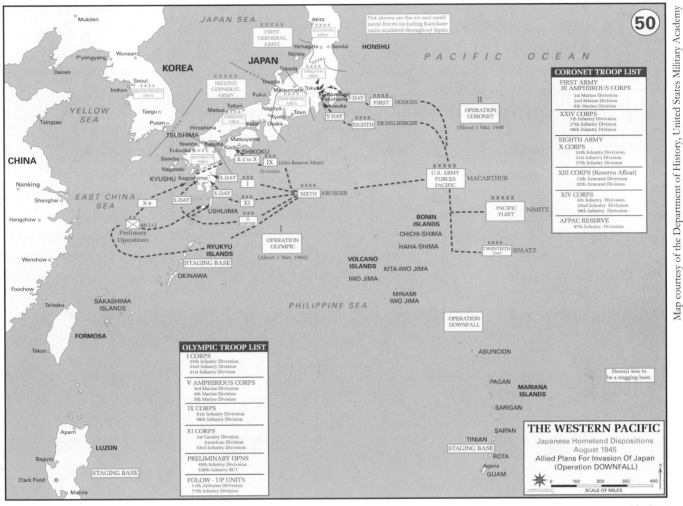

Map courtesy of the Department of History, United States Military Academy

MAP 16

ENDING THE WAR

Americans celebrated V-J Day, Victory over Japan, on Aug. 15, 1945. It was the day that Japanese Emperor Hirohito made a speech broadcast over Japanese airwaves exhorting his people to "accept the unacceptable and endure the unendurable." Japan was surrendering.

Hirohito's pronouncement came as his country had suffered numerous incendiary bomb attacks and two atomic bomb attacks on Hiroshima and Nagasaki days earlier.

The formal surrender was accepted by Gen. Douglas MacArthur from Foreign Minister Manoru Shigemitsu, aboard Admiral Chester Nimitz' flagship, the USS *Missouri* on Sept. 2, 1945, in Tokyo Bay. Rodolfo Saenz Sr., of Tracy, Texas, was standing nearby on the deck of the USS *Havre* (PCE-877), when it happened.

"One of my proudest moments was standing on my ship, looking over on the *Missouri* and seeing the Japanese surrender," Saenz said. "I was so happy the war was over."

For thousands of Americans in the military, poised to attack Japan, the surrender signaled a reprieve. Richard Dominguez, a native of

Los Angeles, serving with the 11th Airborne Division, had just arrived in the Pacific but a month before the bombing of Japan. Instead of fighting, he was selected as part of MacArthur's honor guard for the surrender and would later be part of the occupation force in Japan.

"They picked the tallest, ugliest, most vicious-looking guys because they wanted to impress the Japanese," Dominguez said.

Instead of combat, the military forces still in the Pacific were used to occupy Japan or to help clean up after the war in the Philippines and elsewhere. Amid the devastation that the atomic bombs had caused in Japan, soldiers patrolled the streets and disarmed the Japanese.

Herman Saiz, of Anton Chico, N.M., serving with the 24th Infantry Division, recuperated from shrapnel wounds sustained in the Philippines but was then shipped to Hiroshima to rejoin his regiment in October 1945, two months after the bombing.

"We had no special suits [for protection against radiation]," Saiz would observe. Perhaps, he reasoned later, that contributed to his prostate cancer in the 1980s.

After the war, Eliséo Lopez, of Ganado, Texas, served in the 81st Infantry Division in the military police. Many of the men had accumulated enough points for time served to be sent back home, but Lopez found himself in Tokyo among the ruins left behind by U.S. bombers.

"You could just see nothing but concrete and steel rods sticking out of the ground," he said. "There wasn't much left of Tokyo."

Although the war was over, the danger was not, and the GIs traveled in groups. It was difficult to be among people he had been fighting the whole time.

"Lots of guys got ambushed and killed, even after the war," Lopez said.

In fact, the suspicion between the Japanese and the American occupying force made Lopez apprehensive about the food served in restau-rants, worrying about the possibility of poison. But the chopsticks were also a problem.

"They give you those little sticks to eat with, I almost starved," he said. "I could never get it right. Those things, they'd slip one way and another," he said. "I said, 'Oh forget it, give me a fork!' "

José Ramirez Jr., a native of Peñitas, Texas, was stationed in Japan six months after the atomic bombs were dropped.

"You hardly could see anything standing," he recalled.

Three of the 11 drivers Ramirez served with were Latinos. Their job: to transport American troops from their docking sites to various strategic positions throughout Japan.

In the Philippines, Latinos would find people who could speak Spanish and whose skin was brown, like theirs. Rudolph Tovar, of Los Angeles, serving with the 86th Infantry Division, was sent to Manila in 1945. His job was to operate tractors and cranes and help his unit clear roads and clean up after the war.

Tovar felt an affinity with the local population, but he felt that the white soldiers often treated the Filipinos poorly.

"Most of us Latino soldiers got along fine with the Filipinos," said Tovar. "... We could relate to them more because of our skin color, our history and because we could communicate with them in Spanish."

Another soldier, Norberto Gonzalez, a native of Puerto Padre, Cuba, serving with the 1315th Engineer Construction Battalion (Colored), was impressed by the hardship suffered by the Filipinos. He remembered many Filipinos waiting for the scraps from the soldiers' meals.

"I thought, 'How was it possible for us to have too much when these people had nothing?' " he said.

DOMINGUEZ, RICHARD. When he was selected by General Douglas A. MacArthur as a member of the Honor Guard during the occupation of Japan, Richard Dominguez counted it as one of his most memorable experiences of the war. "They picked the tallest, ugliest, most vicious-looking guys because they wanted to impress the Japanese, I guess," he said. As part of the Honor Guard, he escorted MacArthur to the battleship USS *Missouri* to sign the peace treaty on Sept. 9, 1945.

Dominguez grew up in the tight-knit community of Boyle Heights, a multicultural neighborhood in East Los Angeles, Calif. Both of his parents appeared in Hollywood films. The neighborhood families, mostly immigrants, were close. "I was in my final year of high school when the war started and those of Japanese ancestry were taken away to detention camps," he said. "Included were classmates and it was my first close-up experience with racial discrimination, although at the time I guess I didn't recognize it as such since it didn't happen to me."

While Dominguez did not travel overseas until right before the atomic bombs were dropped, he did witness the aftermath in Japan. He was discharged in March 1946, even though he'd been offered a promotion and a bonus to stay. Part of this decision stemmed from the death of his brother, Eugene, who was killed by a sniper in Saipan toward the end of the war. "Quite a few fellows I knew and grew up with were killed in the war, including my older brother," he said.

Dominguez married Norma Romera on June 19, 1949. He joined the National Guard in 1950 and then fought in the Korean War, but he returned Stateside to care for his mother in 1952. After his return, Dominguez used the GI Bill for his studies and later got a job as a police officer.

He and his wife had eight children: Theresa, Richard, Loretta, David, Michael, Mariella, Phillip and Lawrence.

Richard
Dominguez

Date of Birth
27 JUNE 1924
Los Angeles, CA

Interviewed by
Steven Rosales
26 MARCH 2003
Whittier, CA

WWII Military Unit
11th Airborne
Division

GONZALEZ, NORBERTO. Despite the poverty and hardships of his youth in Cuba, Norberto Gonzalez was shocked and horrified by the desperation of Filipinos during his tour of duty in the Pacific. Each day, he watched as starving people waited for the scraps from soldiers' meals.

"That affected me greatly," he said. "I thought, 'How was it possible for us to have so much when these people had nothing?'"

Gonzalez left Cuba in 1944, arriving in New York City on August 2. He then enlisted in the Army, hoping to send his salary home to his mother and wife, Lucila, who remained in Cuba.

He learned English during basic training and his first assignment was in an all-white unit. He said he experienced some discrimination, and this prompted Gonzalez to request a transfer to a black battalion. It was there he said he finally felt at home.

"My relationship with the soldiers in my battalion was good; they were down-to-earth people," Gonzalez said. "I felt good. I felt like I could progress with them."

His battalion was sent to Manila in 1945, after the war had ended, where he said he saw only destruction. His time in the Philippines was spent building roads and guarding prisoners.

Gonzalez was discharged on November 18, 1946. After the death of his first wife, Gonzalez married two more times. He had five children from his second and third marriages: Jenny, Gloria, Norberto, Eduardo and Juan.

Gonzalez credits his immigration to the States with providing him opportunities and allowing him to reach many of his goals.

"This country changed my life," he said. "By coming here, I have grown and made a better life for myself. This country can help many others."

Norberto Gonzalez

Date of Birth
4 SEPTEMBER 1919
Puerto Padre, Cuba

Interviewed by
Erika Martinez
14 SEPTEMBER 2002
Miami, FL

WWII Military Unit
1315th Engineer
Construction
Battalion (Colored)

Eliséo Lopez

Date of Birth
13 SEPTEMBER 1925
Ganado, TX

Interviewed by
Kimberly Tilley
5 FEBRUARY 2001
Austin, TX

WWII Military Unit
Company 1,
305th Infantry
Regiment,
77th Infantry
Division

Transferred to
American Division

Transferred to
81st Division

LOPEZ, ELISÉO. After the war ended, Eliséo Lopez was one of the few members of his division to be sent to Japan. He was transferred from his American Division to the 81st Infantry Division to serve in the military police. Although the war was over, the danger was not; the GIs had to go everywhere in groups. "Lots of guys got ambushed, even after the war," he said.

Lopez had been first sent to Guadalcanal to fight in the South Pacific jungle. "I never heard of Guadalcanal, I never heard of New Caledonia," he said. "I never heard of none of those places." As a mortar crewman, Lopez was part of a division that landed at Guadalcanal shortly after the initial invasion in late 1943. From there, they headed to various other battle fronts in the South Pacific, encountering the heaviest resistance in Cube City and Bougainville.

"I slept about halfway scared all the time," he said. "I was always homesick. It's a real experience and I was just lucky to make it home."

When Lopez was drafted into the U.S. Army in 1943, his family had to lease their farm. Raised in Ganado, Texas, Lopez was 15 when his father died of a brain tumor, so the teen quit school to run the farm with his older brother.

"When they draft you, you don't go 'cause you want to," he said. "You go because they take you. And so, there went the farm."

While Lopez was overseas, his family relocated to Austin, Texas. Upon his return, he started vocational school under the GI Bill, studying for 18 months to be a radio technician.

He met Vera Moncada and the two married. "I guess you might say it was love at first sight," he said. "When we married in 1947, she was 17. Everybody thought I'd robbed the cradle!" They had three children: Rosa, Linda and Robert.

José Ángel Ramirez

Date of Birth
24 APRIL 1921
Alice, TX

Interviewed by
Kevin and
Sharon Bales
10 MARCH 2001
Rockville, MD

WWII Military Unit
141st Ordnance
Base Artillery
Battalion

RAMIREZ, JOSÉ ÁNGEL. As he attempted to grapple with the horrifying potential for nearly 600,000 U.S. casualties, José Ramirez and his unit prepared to invade Japan in the summer of 1945. Atomic bombs on Nagasaki and Hiroshima pre-empted the invasion however, and allowed Ramirez to return home to his young wife, Marian Joyce Aiken, unharmed.

Ramirez's passion for serving his country began early. He joined the National Youth Administration in Texas after high school, training as a sheet metal apprentice. Soon after, he moved to Washington in search of more opportunities.

Ramirez was working for the Office of Dependency Benefits, allotting funds to the families of soldiers serving overseas, when he was drafted on April 14, 1943. He completed his basic training in Mississippi and was then shipped to Pomona, Calif., for POM—Preparation for Overseas Movement. After additional classes at General School of Advanced Administration in Fort Washington, Md., Ramirez left for New Guinea on Easter Sunday, 1944.

Setting up camp at Finchhaven, Ramirez's unit began their mission to repair and overhaul automotive and ordnance equipment. His unit then inched closer to invading Japan when they established a camp, in the Philippines, in May 1945. However, the war ended before Ramirez, who had earned the rank of sergeant, saw combat.

After his discharge, Ramirez returned to the States. He and wife Marian had two children: Richard and Cynthia. He continued working for the Army, doing administrative work as a civilian. Upon his retirement in 1976, he was the highest ranking Hispanic civilian employee in the Department of the Army. Ramirez was also active in the American Legion, the VFW and LULAC.

RAMIREZ, JOSÉ JR. If it weren't daunting enough for an 18-year-old to be drafted into the Army in 1945 after years of reading newspaper reports on the battles raging overseas, couple that with a personal account from a 16-year-old brother.

José Ramirez, Jr.

Date of Birth
9 JULY 1927
Peñitas, TX

Interviewed by
Monica Jean Alaníz
16 OCTOBER 1999
Peñitas, TX

WWII Military Unit
24th Air Engineer
Squadron,
5th Air Force

While José Ramirez Jr. never saw combat in the war—he was stationed in Japan about six months after the atomic bombs were dropped—the tales from his siblings were enough to shell-shock anyone. His two older brothers fought in the war, and they were his heroes.

His second eldest brother, Leonel, spent some time in a VA hospital after he was wounded overseas. Ramirez's eldest brother, Leobardo, entered the war at the age of 16, after forging his parents' signatures. Leobardo came home suffering from shell-shock. Memories of the war plagued him until his death in 1952. With obvious emotion Ramirez recounted his brother's experience. He remembered seeing this brother cry as his father made him board a bus in 1941. Some of Leobardo's friends had tried to persuade him that he could go AWOL and avoid going into combat. His father would not allow this.

"He was crying when he went to the bus—Hell, he was only 16," Ramirez said. This incident left Ramirez with mixed emotions. "I feel proud of my dad; I feel sorry for my brother," he said.

While he was in Japan, Ramirez saw the ruins at both Hiroshima and Nagasaki. "You hardly could see anything standing," he remembered. "Hiroshima and Nagasaki was bad."

When he returned from his overseas service, Ramirez followed in his father's footsteps as a rancher, receiving $40 a month under the GI Bill to study agriculture. In 1949, two years after his discharge, Ramirez married Maria Zamora. The two had 10 children: Irma Nelda, Efraín, José III, Fernando, Servando, Geraldo, Jaime, Lisa Ann, Anyssa Roxanna and Cesar.

SAENZ, RODOLFO "RUDOLPH" SR. On board his ship floating in Tokyo Bay on Sept. 2. 1945, Rodolfo "Rudolph" Saenz Sr. watched the official end of World War II. "One of my proudest moments was standing on my ship looking over on the USS *Missouri* and seeing the Japanese surrender," he remembered. "I was so happy the war was over."

Rodolfo "Rudolph" Saenz Sr.

Date of Birth
15 DECEMBER 1912
Tracy, TX

Interviewed by
Alfred Saenz
25 MARCH 2003
Taylor, TX

WWII Military Unit
USS *Havre*
(PCE-877)

Along with his family, Saenz worked as a sharecropper growing up and only attended school through the third grade. He met María Luisa Ortiz at the post office one day and the two married in August 1941. Saenz joined the Navy in 1943, leaving his wife and two young children, Rudy Jr. and Emma. He served as a gunner's mate onboard the USS *Havre*, a Patrol Craft Escort. He traveled to Pearl Harbor and then went to support the Marines and Army troops in the invasions of Iwo Jima and Okinawa.

After Saenz returned, he had five more children: Velia, Alyce, Gilbert, Enrique, and Alfred. He returned to his job at Taylor Bedding Company in Taylor, Texas, and was also offered a full-time job at Kerr-Ban Manufacturing Co. He accepted—but kept his first job, working from 8 a.m. to 5 p.m. at Taylor Bedding and then at Kerr-Ban from 5:30 p.m. to 2:30 a.m. When he retired, he bought the 20 acres of land he had helped his family sharecrop so many years ago.

Saenz remembered how, later, he and his wife were rejected by a local bank for an educational loan so their eldest son, Rudy Jr., could attend the University of Texas at Austin. The banker told them they "didn't do that" and ordered them to "get out." "The way he said it hurt me more than anything else," Saenz recalled. Rudy Jr. obtained a loan from the university and earned his degree in mathematics. Saenz and his wife later started a scholarship in honor of their daughter, Emma, who died in 1990 of breast cancer. The scholarships help families who need a "little hand."

Herman Saiz

Date of Birth
10 AUGUST 1924
Anton Chico, NM

Interviewed by
M. David Gray
3 NOVEMBER 2002
Santa Fe, NM

WWII Military Unit
Company G,
2d Battalion,
34th Infantry
Regiment,
24th Infantry
Division

SAIZ, HERMAN. As he came over the hill and saw Japanese with guns drawn, first scout Herman Saiz hit the ground. But when the second scout emerged, Saiz remembered, the enemy "just let him have it." Saiz sat with his fallen friend for a few minutes. "He just asked me to do him a favor: 'Write a letter to my mom and dad. Don't tell them what happened; just tell them I am dead.'"

Saiz was 7 when his father died in a railroad accident. Only one of his 14 siblings lived to adulthood. In June 1944, Saiz was inducted into the Army. He and the 24th Infantry Division were soon sent to cross the beachhead at Leyte in the Philippines.

After a couple of months in Leyte, his battalion was sent to Luzon, where the fighting was so fierce that he likened the multitude of mortar shells to falling rain. "As the shells came down, the man on the left of me and the man on the right of me were hit and killed," he recalled. By the end of the day only 50 of the 250 men in his company escaped unharmed.

After Luzon, they moved to Mindanao. During the battle of Davao, Saiz saved his unit by spotting a Japanese machine gun position across the river and warning his patrol. His good fortune finally ran out, however, when he was hospitalized for shrapnel wounds. He later was shipped to Hiroshima to rejoin his regiment in October of 1945, two months after the atomic bomb had been dropped.

"We had no special suits [for the radiation]," he said. He later wondered if his prostate cancer diagnosis in the 1980s was a result of the radiation exposure.

He was discharged on May 17, 1946, and received numerous medals, including a Purple Heart, a Bronze Star and an Expert Marksmanship Badge with pendants for multiple weapons. Saiz married Lucy Fresquez on July 8, 1946, and the couple had three children. Herman Jr., John and Patsy.

Rudolph Tovar

Date of Birth
NOVEMBER 1922
Juarez, Mexico

Interviewed by
Henry Mendoza
26 SEPTEMBER 2003
Los Angeles, CA

WWII Military Unit
342d Infantry
Regiment,
86th Infantry
Division

TOVAR, RUDOLPH. The day after Pearl Harbor, Rudolph Tovar hurried to his local recruitment office and tried to enlist in the U.S. Marines, but he was turned away because he was born in Mexico and thus was not a U.S. citizen. Later, he was drafted into the U.S. Army in 1943. This allowed Tovar to serve his country while earning his citizenship.

He was thrilled with the opportunity and returned to Mexico so he could make a legal entry into the States. His only regret was his decision to legally change his name from Rodolfo to Rudolph. He then began training at Fort Lewis, Wash., and then Camp Roberts, Calif., where he joined the 342d Infantry Regiment, 86th Infantry Division.

The regiment then fought in Europe before returning to the States to prepare to enter the Pacific Theater. Tovar arrived in the Philippines in 1945. He became part of the clean-up crew, operating tractors and cranes and clearing roads. Though he spent little time in the Philippines, its impact on him was huge.

"I was not a world traveler; I was brought up in the barrio," Tovar said. "But it opened my eyes to a lot of things."

After his discharge on Dec. 27, 1946, Tovar returned to California and earned his bachelor of arts from Cal State–Los Angeles. He worked as a youth counselor at the California State Youth and Adult Corrections Agency and as a rehab counselor with the California State Department of Rehabilitation.

Tovar married Esther Cosio in April 1949 and the couple had five children: Rudy, Michael, Edmund, Randolph and Adela. The couple divorced and Tovar married Rosemary Pingarron in 1974. The two divorced and Tovar married Nancy Jean Von Lauderback in 1995.

Working in a top secret control room. Raymond J. Flores (left) with a coworker. Oakland, Calif., in 1945. (Tech Service Command)

Beyond the Main Fronts

The Second World War was a truly global conflict. American soldiers traveled to virtually every corner of the earth serving the Allied cause. Although the largest theaters in Europe and the Pacific required the most manpower, troops were also sent to Latin America and central Asia. Others were sent to more remote locations in the Pacific and Europe, away from the main front, stocking ammunition, building facilities, or working administrative jobs. Still others served stateside, training and preparing the troops for their overseas assignments.

Soldiers would not need to be fighting in the most violent battles to sustain injuries: simply getting to an assignment overseas to provide needed support was fraught with danger. There were other dangers in training exercises and some men would be injured before leaving their country.

In the Pacific, there were assignments like the frigid and bleak Aleutian Islands, off the coast of Alaska. The Japanese would attack the Aleutians in May 1943 and occupy two islands in the chain, Attu and Kiska, in a strategy to divert attention from the real objective of their efforts: Midway. Six hundred Americans were killed in the retaking of Kiska in May 1943. By the time Canadian and American forces arrived on Attu to retake it in August, the Japanese had already quietly evacuated.

Ramón Rivas, of Charlotte, Texas, served with the 3d Replacement Battalion, in Dutch Harbor, the Aleutian Island closest to the coast of Alaska in the North Pacific. By day, Rivas and the other men constructed heavily fortified bunkers, trenches and concrete fortifications. But they also made sure to be on their guard constantly. He would be stationed there for almost the duration of the war. Also in the Pacific, soldiers

helped guard U.S. bases and territories, refuel and repair ships and planes as well as build temporary structures for troops. Salvador Aguilar, a San Antonio, Texas, native and a member of the Navy Seabees, recalled that on the voyage across the Pacific, the men were admonished to keep still, for fear of detection by a Japanese submarine or ship.

Those moments were tense.

"You're just waiting there," Aguilar said. "You're praying, wondering. 'If a torpedo hits the ship, which side will it hit?'"

After the Allies captured Iwo Jima, Aguilar's battalion was responsible for constructing temporary cities: hospitals, officers' quarters and landing strips.

Others were stationed in the Panama Canal Zone, maintaining the security of that important passageway. Panama, sometimes overlooked in WWII history, was the site of major espionage missions and training. The Canal Zone was an important U.S. holding, and its safety was paramount. Ángel Velázquez, of Yabucoa, P.R., was a guard in Panama who later taught troops stationed in the Canal Zone how to prepare for a chemical attack and also helped them with English. As part of the 470th Counterintelligence Corp Detachment, José Moreno, a native of Brownsville, Texas, helped the government cultivate informants and eventually worked with the Panamanian police.

Campaigns in the China-Burma-India Theater, or the CBI, were crucial to ensuring the safety of the continent. American soldiers built roadways, flew planes and carried out a host of other duties. The devastation of the area and the poverty of many of the countries had a profound effect on the soldiers. José Sena, who operated construction equipment used for building roads in India, remembered the children of Calcutta begging for scraps from the troops.

Tomás Z. Cantú remembered "Flying the Hump," weaving through the Himalayas as his plane flew the "aluminum trail," which earned its nickname from the many fallen planes laying in the crevices of the mountains that rose to 20,000 feet.

One Cuban-American soldier, Evelio Grillo, of Ybor City, Fla., served in the CBI, as part of the 823d Engineer Aviation Battalion (Colored). It would take the men two years to construct the Ledo Road from India into Burma, connecting with the Burma Road at Myitkyina, Burma, in the northeastern part of the country.

"By the time we had achieved our objective, the war was over," Grillo said.

Twice, the men were bombed by Japanese planes, but both times the Japanese were downed by Allied planes. The greater concern for the unit commanders was keeping the men's spirits up as they worked under difficult conditions in India, with heat and monsoons. Grillo, who was popular among the other men, was appointed "recreation and morale sergeant" and organized several activities, including a volunteer jazz band, movies, building a basketball court and a baseball diamond, and publishing a newspaper, The Hairy Ears Herald, a daily newspaper named for the nickname they gave engineers. The Hairy Ears Herald's stories came via radio broadcasts: a group of men took notes from the broadcasts and then wrote news summaries. The Herald was mimeographed and widely distributed. *(See Grillo's story in Chapter 11.)*

England and other countries in Europe were also the sites of important Allied missions. Many soldiers, though not part of the invasions or major battles, readied the supplies that would sustain the troops entering combat. They repaired artillery, organized weaponry and ensured that every soldier had the proper equipment to defend himself during battle. Richard Savala, of Dallas,

Texas, served with the 1450th Ordnance Supply and Maintenance Company, preparing ammunition and taking care of the bombs before D-Day. His main skill was in carpentry, but he would do what needed to be done in England: mostly getting supplies ready for the front-line soldiers.

"Not only was I never in combat, I never even saw combat," Savala said. "I am one of the lucky few."

Though some soldiers never left American soil, their contributions were equally important in sustaining the troops overseas, as well as morale at home. Many helped train troops or served as translators. Raymond J. Flores, of Miami, Ariz., was stationed in Oakland, Calif., and used his bilingualism to help Spanish-speaking recruits, teaching them what he called "Army English," which included commands and other common words heard around the base. Pablo Segura, of El Paso, Texas, would do the same.

"We trained a lot of recruits from Texas that didn't speak English," Segura said. "We were the only 100 percent Mexican American company in World War II. We made a name for ourselves."

WWII sent American soldiers to destinations throughout the world, allowing them the chance to serve their own country and see the world. From counterespionage in Panama, to delivering supplies by truck to the troops who fought at Normandy, to the stateside training of soldiers headed for combat, Latinos and Latinas in the United States Armed Forces contributed substantially to the war effort across the globe.

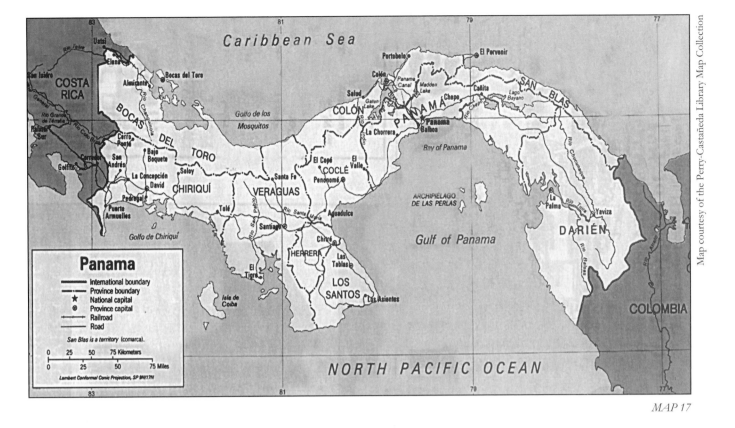

MAP 17

PANAMA

With the Canal Zone and its strategically crucial location, Panama needed Allied defense to ensure its safety. In 1903, the U.S. had begun administering control over the Canal Zone, allowing for a direct trade route that averted the long voyage around the tip of South America.

With the States' stake in the Canal's tolls, it was already a lucrative partnership between the Panamanian government and the U.S. government. But as WWII loomed, Fort Clayton, a U.S. military base in Panama, became an increasingly important holding. A rush of soldiers was sent to Fort Clayton at the beginning of the war, including Ángel Velázquez, of Yabucoa, P.R., serving with the 346th Anti-Aircraft Artillery Searchlight Battalion, who was assigned to Fort

Clayton and later taught troops about chemical warfare. Velázquez also taught English to other Puerto Rican soldiers. The colonel who assigned him to teach English attended his classes and participated in the language exercises.

Intelligence and espionage was also vital in the U.S. troops in Panama, and undercover agent José Moreno worked in the Canal Zone, cultivating informants and performing background checks.

Fort Clayton's 2,180 acres were the headquarters of the U.S. Army-South from World War II until December 1999, when the facility was closed and handed over to the Panamanian government as part of the Panama Canal Treaty and Neutrality Treaty of 1977.

José Moreno

Date of Birth
3 NOVEMBER 1917
Brownsville, TX

Interviewed by
Celina Moreno
20 APRIL 2002
San Antonio, TX

WWII Military Unit
470th Counter
Intelligence Corp
Detachment

MORENO, JOSÉ. Working in counter-intelligence operations during WWII, José Moreno did not have the traditional military experience. One of his assignments in Panama involved befriending cabaret girls, who were often used as couriers for spies.

"I was making friends with the cabaret girls, cultivating them as informants," Moreno said. "Buying them drinks, sitting with them ... whatever was necessary."

Moreno was a pharmacy student at the University of Texas at Austin when WWII began. He was under deferment because of his rigorous academic program, but on February 2, 1942, he enlisted.

He began training at Fort Sam Houston, Texas, and was stationed at Camp Barkeley, Texas. He was working in the payroll department when he was promoted to sergeant. Moreno was bilingual and had completed years of higher education, so he was a desirable candidate for the Army's intelligence school. He trained in Chicago, Ill., and initially helped police with the city's local gangsters.

Moreno was then transferred to Panama. Working as a secret agent, he protected the Panama Canal Zone through counterespionage. He cultivated sources and conducted background checks.

After a German U-Boat sank an Allied ship between Colombia and Panama, Moreno began his nightly trips to the cabaret to interview informants.

As the war drew to a close, Moreno was transferred to David, Panama, to work with local police. It was in David that Moreno met Brigida Falcón, a Panamanian nurse. The two married on Christmas Day, 1943. The couple had four sons: José, Nicholas, Luis and Carlos.

Moreno was discharged on October 23, 1945 and returned to Austin to complete his pharmacy degree. He went on to teach at the University of Texas, and was active in the G.I. Forum, League of United Latin American Citizens (LULAC) and the Anti-Defamation League.

Ángel Antonio
Velázquez

Date of Birth
1 OCTOBER 1917
Yabucoa, PR

Interviewed by
Doralís Pérez-Soto
5 DECEMBER 2002
San Juan, PR

WWII Military Unit
Battery B,
346th Anti-Aircraft
Artillery Search-
light Battalion

VELÁZQUEZ, ÁNGEL ANTONIO. As a junior-high English teacher in Puerto Rico, Ángel Antonio Velázquez developed skills that would serve him well during his tour of duty in WWII. His educational abilities were crucial during his time in Panama.

Drafted in 1942, Velázquez trained at Camp Tortuguero in Puerto Rico. His training was cut short as the demand for soldiers increased.

"It was very short training," he said. "They needed more people to cover at Fort Clayton." Velázquez was a fast learner and advanced quickly. His training focused on chemical warfare protection techniques.

His ship left for Panama and stopped in Cuba. "They told us we were going to Guantánamo, to Cuba for the big parties," he said. "The truth was that we were trying to avoid submarine attacks."

Velázquez and his unit finally arrived in the Panama Canal Zone at Fort Clayton, and he began his duties as a guard. But when officers discovered his knowledge of chemical warfare, he began teaching his fellow soldiers how to prepare for an attack. He also taught English to soldiers, which earned him the respect of his colonel, as well as passes to Panama City.

He continued his service in Panama and served in a host of other positions, including monitoring the radar for approaching planes and guarding the jungle and beaches from an observation tower.

"It was a very tall tower," he said. "When I would climb the stairs I would grab on to the climbing tubes so tight that I thought I would break them and fall."

After his discharge, Velázquez returned to Puerto Rico and continued teaching. He later earned a degree from the University of Puerto Rico and worked for the Puerto Rican government for 33 years.

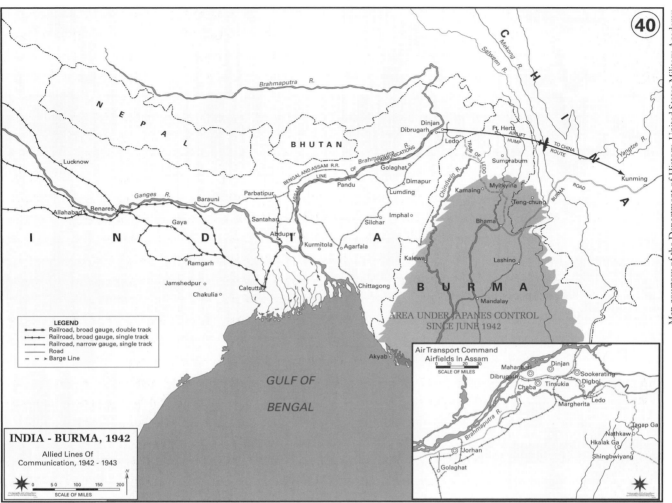

Map courtesy of the Department of History, United States Military Academy

MAP 18

THE CHINA-BURMA-INDIA THEATER

As the war in the Pacific Theater raged on, Allied forces sought to ensure the war would not expand further into mainland Asia.

After the Japanese forces invaded the Chinese territory of Manchuria in 1937, the larger country had been closed off from supplies, except for two overland supply routes, one of which was the Burma Road, through the British colony of Burma, to China. By February 1942, the Japanese had taken over Burma and Singapore. Allied soldiers helped to supply China in two ways: by the building of the Ledo Road, through India, and by flying supplies missions over a treacherous route through the Himalayas, a route known as "the Hump." The route through the Himalayas was only 500 miles, but it reached altitudes of up to 20,000 feet, which required oxygen, and the cargo planes were beset by icing, a significant problem early on when the planes had no de-icing equipment. They also contended with severe thunderstorms. Over 1,000 men and 600 planes were lost over "the hump" before the Burma road was re-opened and the flight plan discontinued.

Tomás Z. Cantú

Date of Birth
2 FEBRUARY 1923
Robstown, TX

Interviewed by
Bettina Luis
23 MARCH 2001
Corpus Christi, TX

WWII Military Unit
555th Army Air Forces Base Unit

CANTÚ, TOMÁS Z. Weaving through the Himalayas, Tomás Cantú flew through the infamous mountain range to elude the Japanese. He weathered snow, ice and winds of nearly 115 mph as he flew the "aluminum trail." The route earned its nickname because the fallen planes glistened against the snow, forming a silvery path in the mountains. The terror on the trail was palpable.

"It was scary. I've seen the pilot, many a time, sweat," Cantú said. "I mean sweat cold. Being scared. Because many times they didn't think they were going to make it."

Cantú left high school at 17 to participate in a program funded by the Defense Department to train youth to assist with the war effort. On Nov. 12, 1942, Cantú enlisted in the Army Air Corps. He began basic training in Mississippi and then studied to become an aerial engineer. He was stationed in Reno, Nev., but after eight months, Cantú volunteered for an overseas tour of duty. He boarded a plane in Florida and made stops in Puerto Rico, Brazil and South Africa before finally landing at his station in the China-Burma-India Theater. He immediately began working on supply missions, "pre-flighting" plane engines, maintaining instruments onboard and keeping track of the fuel.

After surviving dangerous missions high above the Himalayas, Cantú earned the necessary points to return home to Corpus Christi, Texas. He was discharged on Nov. 24, 1945, with the rank of corporal. Cantú worked at his father's meat-packing company while taking business and psychology courses at Del Mar College with the aid of the GI Bill. He eventually bought the meatpacking company from his father. He later sold the business and went into car sales, first as a manager at Lew Williams Chevrolet, and later as the owner of Tom Cantú Motors Inc.

Cantú married Claudia Ramirez in 1947. The couple had four children: Cynthia, Catherine, Christine and Thomas.

Julius Casarez

Date of Birth
9 MAY 1920
Austin, TX

Interviewed by
Rasha Madkour
21 NOVEMBER 2002
Austin, TX

WWII Military Unit
Battery B HDSF

CASAREZ, JULIUS. After serving nearly four years in the Army, Julius Casarez had earned the necessary points to return to the States, but the road home would prove difficult. Casarez hitchhiked through China to reach his plane. Once aboard, more problems arose.

"I almost died three times. First, in India, we lost a tire when we hit the runway," Casarez said. "Second, when we were flying over Africa in a two-engine plane, we lost one of the engines. And lastly, when we were near Puerto Rico, we had to fly through a tropical storm."

Casarez enlisted just days before the bombing at Pearl Harbor and began boot camp in California. He found the days at camp too monotonous and was eager to volunteer for "real duty."

"They didn't tell you where you were going," he said. "But I was tired of it [boot camp], so I just volunteered."

Casarez trained with machine guns in New Mexico and then left for Africa in June 1942. From there he went to India, where he served as a machine gunner before beginning to cross the Himalayas. Casarez guarded bridges in Burma, and his unit shot down Japanese planes that attempted to bomb the bridges.

After his tumultuous journey home, Casarez finally landed in Florida in late 1945, and said he "kissed the ground" upon arrival. He was discharged in November 1945, with the rank of sergeant. He returned to his hometown of Austin, Texas, and married Trinity Castruita. The couple moved to several different cities but finally returned to Austin. They had six children: Albert, María, Anthony, Lawrence, Yvonne and George.

Casarez completed courses at an electronics school for former GIs and worked in the electronic organ business for 35 years before retiring.

ORTEGA, GUADALUPE. A sports star in his youth, Guadalupe Ortega excelled as a boxer and baseball player. He planned to attend high school, but his father's death put education on hold.

He entered the work force, holding several different jobs until he was inducted into the Army on May 12, 1943. He trained at Fort Riley, Kan., and was assigned to the Cavalry Training Replacement center. Ortega was excellent with the horses and often earned passes for leave because of his expertise. He was also a skilled marksman.

"At a gallop, everybody that makes expert gets a three-day pass," he remembered. "So at a gallop, I hit 42 out of 43 silhouette targets."

Following training, he was transferred to Fort Brown, Texas. He eventually became a gunner and served in the 5332 Brigade, Provisional. He was informed by his superiors that his brigade would only have one assignment, but that provided little relief for the soldiers.

"We were told that we would have one mission only," Ortega said. "And everyone thought, 'That's great' ... but one particular mission meant that we had to fight our way up the Burma Road and then circle behind enemy lines to cut them off at southern China."

The mission was perilous, with the soldiers' only water supply coming from bamboo stalks and swamps. The brigade marched nearly 300 miles, with many men falling to dysentery and malaria.

After his discharge, he returned to Michigan. He used the GI Bill to attend barber college and then opened Lupe's Barber Shop, which he ran for 25 years. While he ran the barbershop, he attended electrician class at night and eventually earned his master contractor's license. He owned Ortega's Electrical Contracting, Inc.

He married Carlota Ayala in 1942.

Guadalupe Ortega

Date of Birth
10 MARCH 1921
Asherton, TX

Interviewed by
Gloria Monita
19 OCTOBER 2002
Saginaw, MI

WWII Military Unit
5332 Brigade
(Provisional)

SENA, JOSÉ VALENTINE. During his tour of duty in China, India and Burma, José Sena saw poverty in the faces of malnourished children begging in the streets of Calcutta. Sadness washed over Sena's face as he remembered giving away his rations to the starving children.

"If it was up to me, I'd take a piece of bread out of my mouth and give it to them," he said. "There's nothing that breaks my heart and brings so many memories than those poor kids."

In contrast with the heart-wrenching events he witnessed later, Sena's military career began with a joke. He and his twin brother were chatting with a friend about how dapper soldiers looked in their uniforms, and made a pact to enlist the next day. Sena was the only one who followed through on Jan. 3, 1942, calling his brother and friend "all talk."

He began training at Fort Bliss, Texas. From there he was transferred to the 359th Fighter Squadron of the Army Air Corps and trained in Tucson, Ariz. He then was assigned to the 1880th Aviation Engineering Battalion and left for Asia, and where he operated dirt movers to clear paths for Allied supply routes and convoys. Often working at night and deep in the jungle, Sena had his share of scares. He remembered when a tiger leaped onto the front of the machine he was operating. He dove into a toolbox and slammed the metal door to keep the animal away.

While working on the China-Burma road, Sena was wounded by a land mine. A piece of metal was embedded in his head near his right ear. He recovered and was discharged on Dec. 18, 1945.

Sena returned to the States with a newfound appreciation for his country. He married Victoria Otero on Sept. 28, 1946. The couple had eleven children: Manuel, Rosemary, Leroy, Antonia, Virginia, José, Richard, George, Joseph, Laura and Loretta. He worked as an equipment operator for the New Mexico highway department.

José Valentine Sena

Date of Birth
14 FEBRUARY 1925
Las Vegas, NM

Interviewed by
Brian Daugherty
4 NOVEMBER 2002
San Antonio, TX

WWII Military Unit
Company C,
1880th Engineer
Aviation Battalion

Henry Sillik

Date of Birth
31 MAY 1926
Phoenix, AZ

Interviewed by
Violeta Dominguez
5 JANUARY 2003
Tucson, AZ

WWII Military Unit
USS *John Deere*,
SS *Alcoa Pegasus*,
SS *John B. Floyd*,
Navy Army Guard

SILLIK, HENRY. Despite the racial divisions he saw at home in Arizona, Henry Sillik said that when he entered the Navy, sailors united to accomplish their common goals and left racism behind.

Sillik's father, Lafal, served in World War I, and inspired his son to enlist in the Navy on July 1, 1943, at age 17. He left high school to serve but said that the Navy afforded him opportunities he would not have had otherwise.

"The first time I saw the ocean was when I got to the training station in San Diego," Sillik said.

After training in San Diego, Calif., Sillik trained at the San Francisco Armed Guard Center on Treasure Island. There he was assigned to the USS *John Deere*.

Sillik was stationed in the China-Burma-India Theater on the *Deere*, and served as a naval gunner for 10 months. He remembered the weapons on the Deere were outdated and "almost antique." The bombings at Pearl Harbor had destroyed many of the more modern ships in the U.S. fleet.

Sometimes called "the forgotten theater," China-Burma-India assignments were crucial in stopping Japanese forces from invading the region.

Sillik also served on the SS *Alcoa Pegasus* and the SS *John B. Floyd*, a troop transport ship. He helped transport soldiers and prisoners of war from Japanese camps.

After his discharge on May 1, 1946, Sillik re-enlisted and trained as a "frogman," or underwater demolition specialist. He served with Underwater Demolition Team in Coronado Beach, Calif., until his discharge on Feb. 27, 1948.

Sillik married María Antonieta Carrasco on Aug. 13, 1955. The couple had four children: Francisco Xavier, Guadalupe, Henry and María Dolores. He worked as a hard-rock miner in Arizona for the Magna Copper Co.

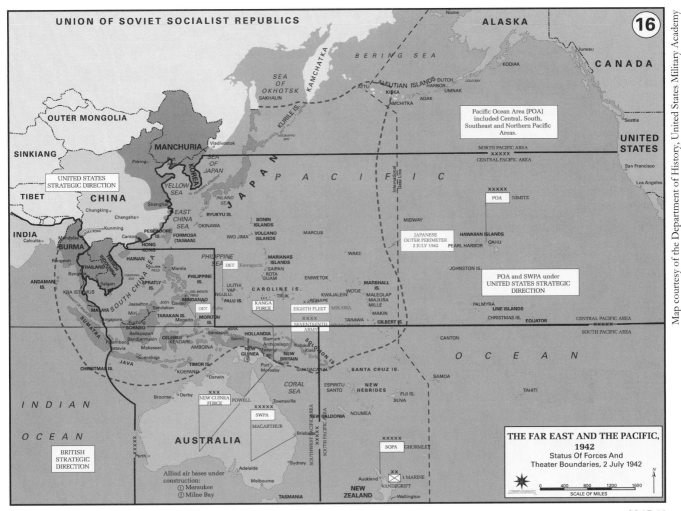

MAP 19

IN THE PACIFIC

With the Pacific Theater serving as one of the sites of the most intense combat during WWII, American military forces were scattered throughout the region. Places that had been unknown to most Americans before 1941—with names like Manila, Iwo Jima, Okinawa—now became the subjects of newspaper stories.

But elsewhere in the Pacific, other important duties, sometimes support work, were ongoing.

From the repair and refueling of ships and planes, to firefighting, to building makeshift hospitals, to hurricane watching, soldiers who were not on the front lines performed essential services. The contributions of the soldiers serving on the lesser-known islands of the Pacific served as the backbone upon which many of the campaigns in the region rested.

And there was no such thing as a "safe" assignment in the Pacific—danger was a constant for all sailors, marines, soldiers and airmen. Navy Seabee Salvador Aguilar, of San Antonio, Texas, built roads, airstrips, warehouses and hospitals on islands throughout the Pacific, including Iwo Jima. He recalled the nights he spent on a ship in the middle of the Pacific as he awaited his next assignment. Beneath the silent surface, Japanese submarines trolled the waters, aiming to sink ships like Aguilar's.

"Everything was pitch black. No radio, no nothing," he said. "Everything had to be silent. Submarines could pick up any kind of sound."

Ramón Rivas, of Charlotte, Texas, served with the 3d Replacement Battalion, in Dutch Harbor, on the Aleutian Island closest to the coast of Alaska in the North Pacific. Rivas and the other men spent their days building elaborate systems of bunkers, trenches and concrete fortifications. At night, they took turns standing guard, looking for Japanese planes, in hopes of fending off the diversionary attacks the Japanese launched on the U.S. territory.

The Japanese did indeed attack Dutch Harbor and occupied Attu and Kiska, two other islands in the Aleutian chain farther west. The Japanese strategy was to take the islands, and attack Dutch Harbor during the Battle of Midway, hoping to divert and pin down U.S. forces. The occupation of Attu and Kiska would represent the only foreign occupation of U.S. land in the 20th Century. U.S. forces fought back. And on May 11, 1943, troops landed on Attu, fighting a tough battle that would last until May 30 and result in 600 U.S. deaths and the deaths of 2,350 Japanese. In August, 34,000 U.S. and Canadian troops landed on Kiska, but found that the Japanese had already left, hidden from view by fog.

Dutch Harbor had also been strafed by Japanese Zeros and bombed and Rivas recalls the terror of the men.

"Anybody who says 'I didn't cry' or things like that, I say they had to be crazy, something wrong with their *cabezas* [heads]," he said. "When you see bombs coming down like that, you cry and pray for your life."

Peter Salcedo serving on the USS *Lindenwald* (LSD-6), and the USS *John Land* (AP-167), first served on the island of Maui in 1943, repairing military ships for 18 months. Then he moved to Oahu, Hawaii, for four months as Master of Arms, 2d Class. His job was to make sure everyone entering the canteen was dressed properly. In Oahu, he became aware of the danger—even at a canteen.

"They handed me a rifle and gun ... Said there was a submarine close by ...," Salcedo said. "I didn't even know how to load the damn thing."

Domingo Treviño, who grew up in Houston, Texas, would be a hurricane hunter in the Pacific. Treviño was the assistant engineer, charged with checking the gas on the plane and switching the plane from auxiliary to regular power after it took off.

The crew was assigned to Guam as the first members of the 55th Weather Reconnaissance Squadron.

"We were the first, last and only hurricane hunters in the Pacific. We were called the 'Hurricane hunters of the Pacific,'" he said.

Treviño and his crew "flew weather" all over the Pacific. During one flight through a particularly rough storm, the pilot and co-pilot were drenched in sweat controlling the aircraft and later many would say they were surprised that the men had survived. The plane was so badly damaged after that trip that it would take weeks worth of repairs before it could fly again. For their performance, the members of the Weather Squadron were awarded Distinguished Flying Crosses.

Treviño flew 37 combat missions as assistant flight engineer and lower ball target gunner.

ACEDO, HECTOR. In the Indian Ocean — just after leaving Cape Town, South Africa — the SS *Harvey Scott* and seven other ships were torpedoed by German submarines. Hector Acedo was one of the 64 survivors. The sailors drifted along in two lifeboats until they saw land.

Hector Acedo

Date of Birth
11 JULY 1923
Douglas, AZ

Interviewed by
Claudia I.
Provencio
4 JANUARY 2003
Phoenix, AZ

WWII Military Unit
SS *Harvey Scott*

Back on shore, they were fed and clothed by a Dutch-English family and then took a train to Durban, South Africa, where they found a camp for survivors of torpedoed ships.

"We didn't know what to do; we didn't have any leaders," Acedo said.

The South African Army gave the sailors uniforms, which they wore until they arrived in San Francisco, Calif., after waiting a month for a new ship assignment. The sailors were given a seven-day leave, during which Acedo visited his wife, Celsa Ybarra, and his 3-month-old daughter.

He was then sent to Okinawa and would travel to Australia, Guam, Saipan and New Guinea before he was discharged on Jan. 7, 1946.

Acedo had first said goodbye to his wife on July 28, 1942, though he said he enjoyed "every second" of his time in the Navy. His first destination was Seattle, Wash., where the crew took on a load of lumber to transport to Panama. Traveling through the Panama Canal, their crew brought sugar from Cuba to New York. When it crossed the equator, the vessel developed structural problems and docked at Port Arenas, Chile. As the only one on the ship who spoke Spanish, Acedo played an integral role as interpreter. It would be two months before the ship received the materials required for repairs and would be able to shove off again.

From Chile, the *Harvey Scott* left for Cape Town, shortly before it was sunk.

Acedo and Celsa Ybarra had six children: Mary Anne, Frances, Martha, Susan, Jimmy and John. He worked in the mines and later returned to Phoenix, Ariz., to work in real estate and remodeling.

AGUILAR, SALVADOR. Desperate to help his widowed mother support the family, Salvador Aguilar changed the date on his birth certificate so he could enlist in the Navy at age 15. He was eager to be surrounded by older sailors and officers, hoping to learn the respect his late father would have taught him.

Salvador Aguilar

Date of Birth
1 JUNE 1928
San Antonio, TX

Interviewed by
Joel Weickgenant
25 OCTOBER 2003
San Antonio, TX

WWII Military Unit
Navy Seabees

"Everybody was older than me, and I just listened," he said. "Military life was just that: listen and do what you're told."

Aguilar began basic training at Camp Paul Jones, Calif., and began his service with the Navy Seabees. The Seabees was a combat and construction battalion. They built airstrips, bridges, roads and makeshift hospitals and warehouses throughout the Pacific during WWII.

Aguilar remembered setting up temporary cities on islands that the United States occupied, including Iwo Jima, where he helped build officers' quarters. When not building on land, Aguilar was aboard his cargo ship. Nights spent floating in the middle of the Pacific were often terrifying for the sailors, who were forced to lie in silence so the ship could not be detected by the Japanese submarines that stalked the waters.

"Everything was pitch black. No radio, no nothing," he said. "Everything had to be silent. Submarines could pick up any kind of sound."

Discharged on March 23, 1946, Aguilar returned to his hometown of San Antonio, Texas, and began working as a warehouse specialist.

He married his first wife, Herminia, in 1946 and the couple had two daughters: Mary Louise and Gloria. They later divorced and Aguilar married Sylvia in 1953. The couple had three sons: Salvador Jr., Roland and David.

**Manuel Joseph
Aguirre**

Date of Birth
3 JUNE 1925
Mason City, IA

Interviewed by
Angela Macias
12 AUGUST 2002
St. Paul, MN

WWII Military Unit
USS *Ozark* (LSV-2)

AGUIRRE, MANUEL JOSEPH. Though his small stature prevented Manuel Aguirre from joining the Marines, it made him an ideal coxswain during special amphibious training in the Navy.

"They lined us up according to height," he said. The shortest were picked to steer the boat. "Being short, your head didn't stick up high going into the beach in landings and invasions."

After practicing for two months and learning to maintain his boat, Aguirre left for Pearl Harbor in December 1944 to serve aboard the USS *Ozark*. They were soon rescuing 800 sailors whose ships had been sunk in the Lingayen Gulf, near Luzon, Philippines. During the rescue mission, the *Ozark* started leaving before Aguirre's rescue boat returned, and he and another sailor barely caught up with them in time. In February 1945, they evacuated wounded Marines as Allied forces tried to secure Iwo Jima, and the *Ozark* served as a hospital ship to about 1,000 soldiers. It arrived at Okinawa on April 1, 1945, and transported wounded Americans and Japanese prisoners of war to Guam.

Aguirre rarely left the ship and sent extra money home as often as possible. His correspondence would be the last he would have with his mother, who died before he came home.

On Aug. 27, 1945, the USS *Ozark* was the first ship to anchor in Tokyo Bay, where it stayed until the Japanese formal surrender on Sept. 2, 1945. During the surrender ceremony, Aguirre watched the signing of the treaty on the USS *Missouri*, anchored next to the *Ozark*.

Ozark crew members were greeted with cheers as they pulled under the Golden Gate Bridge on October 2, bringing home American and Canadian soldiers who had been prisoners of war.

Aguirre was discharged on Jan. 19, 1946. Back home in Minnesota, he married Dorthy L. Hansen. The couple had three sons, Theodore, Edward and Adrian, and a daughter who died at birth. Aguirre returned to his job as a butcher in a meatpacking house, until the plant closed in 1979.

Henry A. Bebón

Date of Birth
20 DECEMBER 1925
Brownsville, TX

Interviewed by
Lynn Maguire
13 AUGUST 2003
Brownsville, TX

WWII Military Unit
US Naval Support
Unit in the Marshall
Islands

BEBÓN, HENRY A. Not everyone in World War II worked on the front lines or manned the battleships. Some served behind the lines, providing basic services and support that often could be taken for granted. Henry A. Bebón served in such a capacity, following orders and carrying out his assignments alongside his fellow countrymen.

Bebón was stationed in the Marshall Islands in the South Pacific, assigned to work in the officers' club, until the end of the war in 1945. His jobs varied: "You know, odd jobs and whatever there was to do. But I was never on a ship or anything," he said.

He remembered standing guard in the middle of the night on the islands. Other times he assisted in replenishing ships with munitions and food supplies.

Bebón came from a military family. His father, Frank Bebón, served in the Army for 30 years and fought in World War I. His grandfather, Jacob Bebón, was a soldier in the Spanish-American War.

After his release from the Navy in 1946, Bebón returned home and met his future wife, María Lesbia Ramirez. In 1947 he enlisted in the Army so he could save money to get married. He proposed before he was sent to Tokyo, Japan, and they married three years later, when he returned. "It was still peace time in those three years before the Korean War broke out," he said.

After his service, Bebón got a job as a clerk at the U.S. Post Office in Brownsville, Texas, where he worked for 37 years and retired in 1988.

He also joined the Veterans Honor Guard. "We give services to veterans," he said. "You know, someone has to do it." Much of his time was spent helping disabled veterans of WWII who were unable to physically care for themselves.

Bebón and his wife had four children: Cynthia, Henry, Sandra and Norman.

CASTRUITA, GEORGE.   Though most of his childhood was without segregation or racism, George Castruita remembered the Zoot Suit Riots that took place just minutes away from the area of East Los Angeles where he grew up. During the riots, sailors and GIs beat up Mexican youths.

"The sorry thing is the majority of those fellows who got beat up later went into the military to defend the rights and liberties of the country," he said. "Amen."

Castruita was going through basic training in San Diego, Calif., when the riots occurred. Though he was restricted to the military installation, the homesick Castruita disobeyed orders and hitchhiked home. Just four blocks away from his home, he was spotted by young Mexicans in a 1934 Ford sedan. The youths took one look at his sailor uniform and began to chase him. They never caught up with him, as he ran through back alleys and streets he knew well.

Castruita served as radio operator aboard the SS *Morgan Robertson* and the SS *Cyrus H. McCormick*. Both armed merchant ships carried troops, Seabee sailors, Marines, munitions and other cargo. He settled into a routine of cleaning the guns and restrooms along with his radio work.

"When you're out at sea, especially if you are in a war zone, you are in God's hands. In some time and some date, you may have been there in harm's war continuously, but it didn't affect me nor did it affect too many of my comrades," he said.

While he experienced no discrimination aboard his ship, he was disheartened by apartheid in Cape Town, South Africa, where non-whites had to leave town at sundown and return at sunup.

Castruita was discharged in April 1946. Despite some postwar nightmares, he said he had many great experiences in the Navy and fondly reflected on his years in the service.

George Castruita

Date of Birth
24 FEBRUARY 1925
Los Angeles, CA

Interviewed by
Steven Rosales
1 MAY 2003
Los Angeles, CA

WWII Military Unit
SS *Morgan Robertson* and SS *Cyrus H. McCormick*

CHAVARRÍA, RALPH.   Drafted in February 1943 at age 27, Ralph Chavarría was older than most recruits. Already married with a young son, he was initially reluctant to leave his family, especially after he returned on leave and his son did not recognize him. The confusion cleared, and his son would soon proudly declare that his father was "overseas."

Chavarría trained in Missouri, Georgia and Alabama before he left for Asia. He trained as a firefighter in the Army Air Corps and he arrived in Guam before traveling to Tinian in the Northern Mariana Islands. He saw little combat action on the island but was regularly called upon when planes crashed and burst into flames.

"When there's an emergency, you see the ambulance, you see the fire truck coming down," he said. "That was my job."

Chavarría was present for the takeoff of the planes carrying atomic bombs to Nagasaki and Hiroshima in August 1945. He remembered the mystery surrounding the planes, and troops did not know which one had the atomic bomb on board, a fact that made many soldiers nervous.

Chavarría was discharged in January 1946 and returned to Arizona. He attended Arizona State Vocational School with the help of the GI Bill. He later worked as an auto mechanic. He was perhaps best known in his local community in Phoenix for his musical talents. He played violin in his father's group, the "Chapito" Chavarría Orchesta, at age 9. He continued playing even during his time in the service, playing the upright bass in the Air Force dance orchestra.

Chavarría had married Consuelo Huerta on July 27, 1941. Their first son, Ernest, was born before the war. Three other children—Barbara, Ralph and Michael—were born after Chavarría returned from the service.

Ralph Chavarría

Date of Birth
7 APRIL 1914
Solomonville, AZ

Interviewed by
George Diaz
4 JANUARY 2003
Phoenix, AZ

WWII Military Unit
Stationed in Tinian Islands, Air Force

Raúl Chavez

Date of Birth
14 FEBRUARY 1926
Chihuahua, Mexico

Interviewed by
Paul R. Zepeda
28 AUGUST 2001
Houston, TX

WWII Military Unit
Naval Patrol
Bombing
Squadron 205,
VPB 205

CHAVEZ, RAÚL. At 18-years-and-a-day, Raúl Chavez enlisted in the Navy on Feb. 15, 1944. Without U.S. citizenship, he could not serve sooner nor could he later qualify as an officer.

After training at gunnery school, Chavez headed to Florida for operational practice. His first trip was an overnight, navigational flight to Guantanamo Bay, Cuba. He described the plane—a large seaplane called a PBM—as "a flying whale with [huge] wings that go on forever." PBMs only landed on water, and they could carry about 4,000 pounds of bombs. The mission of the aircraft was to search out enemy subs, locate lost American fliers and haul goods such as milk and mail. Chavez was a flight engineer and gunner, in charge of the preflight procedures.

The crew left for Hawaii in March 1945 for training and finally—after weeks of firing machine guns, shooting at aerial targets and surprise mayday runs—went off to battle. They stopped at several islands, including Kwajalein and Eniwetok—where Chavez said "not a single palm tree was left after the invasion." They landed in Saipan, Northern Mariana Islands, after the U.S. victory there, and patrolled for Japanese submarines. He remembered the B-29 bombers: "Fleets of 400 to 500 planes just burning up the whole Japanese empire." He was grateful that he never faced combat.

After the war Chavez became a registered actor and had roles in many Spanish-language films and commercials and did voice-overs for the likes of Cap'n Crunch and Ross Perot. He married Doris Fields, whom he had met at a USO club in San Diego, Calif., after returning from the war. He also returned to a childhood hobby: "I was a member of the Boy Scouts for four years as a kid, never dreaming that someday I would get a monthly paycheck from the Boy Scouts of America as a full-time executive," Chavez said. His work with the organization lasted 17 years and included helping launch the first outreach to Hispanic children for the Scouts.

Peter De Leon

Date of Birth
29 APRIL 1917
San Antonio, TX

Interviewed by
Antonio Gilb
13 NOVEMBER 2001
San Antonio, TX

WWII Military Unit
USS *Manlove*
(DE-36)

DE LEON, PETER. From August 1943 to June 1945, Peter De Leon served as a fireman on the USS *Manlove*, an escort destroyer, in the Marshall Islands, the Philippines, Guam and Okinawa. He considered himself lucky to return home to Chicago alive. Many of his friends never came back. His experiences in war allowed him to meet people of different backgrounds and gave him an appreciation of life. "Everybody had their own ideas," he said.

As a fireman, his primary responsibilities were to work in the engine rooms and stand watch for incoming attacks. As an engineer, he worked on maintenance, diesel engines and controls.

Off Okinawa, a plummeting *Kamikaze* plane grazed the *Manlove*. The pilot was aiming for a larger ship but was gunned down at the last minute.

De Leon had been head of his household since he was 16 when his father was killed by in a hit-and-run accident while stepping off the bus. De Leon considered dropping out of school to support his family, but he decided against it and became the first one in his family to graduate from high school in 1937. He began to work in a lamp factory and avoided the draft during the first years of the war because he was supporting his mother, younger brother and two sisters.

In August 1943, the draft board informed De Leon that he was eligible for the draft. Instead of waiting, De Leon volunteered and was trained at the Naval Training Center, Ill.

Following the war, De Leon returned to his job at the lamp factory, where he did electrical wiring. He joined a veterans group, where he met Henry Yarbrough and his sister Theresa Bonita Yarbrough. He and Theresa were married in 1953 and moved to Los Angeles the next year. In June 1982, De Leon retired from the electrical business. That same year, his mother and wife died. De Leon traveled for a year and eventually married Zulema Blanca Estrada in 1984.

GARCIA, GILBERT. During the long stretches at sea, sailors entertained themselves with movie nights, games and dishes of ice cream. Gilbert Garcia relished poker. He boasted of being the best poker player on the USS *Hammondsport*, winning hands even when his fellow sailors shared cards to try to beat him.

Gilbert Garcia

Date of Birth
11 MARCH 1924
Mercedes, TX

Interviewed by
Ernest Eguía and
Paul R. Zepeda
6 MAY 2003
Houston, TX

WWII Military Unit
USS *Hammond-sport* (AKV-2)

Drafted in 1943, Garcia had originally planned to enlist with his friend, Homer Hernandez, but overslept. Hernandez joined the Army without him and was killed two days after Pearl Harbor. Two years later, Garcia told the recruiting officer that he would prefer to be in the Navy but was told that they had met their quota. An eavesdropping Navy recruiter pulled him aside. "See that Navy car over there?" he asked. "Run over and jump in!"

In San Diego, Calif., he completed basic training. He tested into torpedo training school and for three months pledged to "do the best I could do with it." Having only finished eighth grade, he was at a disadvantage compared to those who had been to college. He decided to apply to go to sea.

His jobs aboard the *Hammondsport* ranged from painting and scrubbing the deck to loading the 20-mm guns, though the only target he shot at was an out-of-range plane. The carrier ship transported trains, replacement aircraft and troops from the Fleet and Industrial Supply Center in Oakland, Calif., to Hawaii, Fiji, the Gilbert Islands and Guam, among other islands. Oakland was Garcia's favorite port because from there the sailors could spend time in San Francisco. The ship was never under attack, but Garcia always feared it would be because of its important cargo.

After the war, Garcia returned home to Houston, Texas, and reunited with an old friend, Minerva Herrera, whom he married in 1947. He went to photography and barber schools but settled on working for a car dealership. He and Minerva had two children, Gilbert Jr. and Robert.

GONZALES, NORMAN. Despite blindness in his right eye, Norman Gonzales served in clean-up efforts throughout the Pacific during WWII. He did not discover his disability until he tried to enlist in the Marines and doctors discovered it during his physical. Though the Marines denied him, the Army welcomed Gonzales, drafting him in 1942.

Norman Gonzales

Date of Birth
6 JUNE 1919
Lufkin, TX

Interviewed by
Ernest Eguía and
Paul R. Zepeda
20 FEBRUARY 2003
Houston, TX

WWII Military Unit
766th Military
Police Battalion

Transferred to
1565th Engineer
Depot Company

Though he was never in combat, his duties in the Army took him around the globe. He worked as a company clerk in Arkansas, Louisiana and Germany, organizing records for his company, such as immunization documents.

In 1945, he was assigned to the 1565th Engineer Depot Company, ordering parts for tanks and trucks. Gonzales then delivered supplies to troops stationed in the Philippines. It was there he heard of the bombings at Nagasaki and Hiroshima. He witnessed the destruction of those cities firsthand when he traveled through the country en route to Sapporo, Japan.

"That place was really devastated," he remembered. "You could see nothing."

Gonzales was discharged in February 1946 and moved to Texas. He used the GI Bill to attend business school, and after holding a host of different jobs, Gonzales began working as a distribution and accounting clerk for the postal service in 1961, where he worked until his retirement in 1988.

In 1965, Gonzales married Estéfana Hernandez. He became active in his church in Houston, Iglesia Luterana San Pedro, serving as treasurer for 50 years.

Gonzales stressed the importance of education to young Latinos today, and said that goals and passion will help propel them forward in a world with more opportunities.

"You can be governor, you can be lieutenant, you can be a general now. You couldn't do that back then," he said. "But you can't do it just because you're here. You have to know something."

Rafael Guerra

Date of Birth
30 NOVEMBER 1915
La Reforma Ranch,
Starr County, TX

Interviewed by
Nicole Muñoz
6 APRIL 2002
McAllen, TX

WWII Military Unit
134th Anti-Tank
Company

GUERRA, RAFAEL. With his optimistic view on life, Rafael Guerra took his war service in stride—even though it meant serving three years longer than his original commitment. He joked: "For 3 1/2 years I never left the States, and then when I tried to get out, they sent me overseas."

Born in 1915, Guerra grew up on his family's ranch in Starr County, Texas. He was inducted into the U.S. Army at Fort Sam Houston, Texas, the day before Pearl Harbor. As a member of the 134th Anti-Tank Company, Guerra helped guard the California coastline, walking the beach overnight for three months until he was sent to Alabama for additional training.

He then received Italian language training and was assigned to guard Italian prisoners of war transported to the United States. "I couldn't read it [Italian], but I knew enough to get by in a conversation because it is very similar to Spanish," he said. After transporting German prisoners of war and serving out an assignment in mail duty in New York City, he was sent to train for a tour of the South Pacific.

En route to Saipan, Guerra learned of Germany's surrender. He then was stationed in Okinawa building structures to house bombs and ammunition. Ironically, while the nation celebrated the near-end of the war following the atomic bombing in Japan, Guerra first encountered the ugly aftermath of war: In Okinawa, he picked up an abandoned Japanese boot from the ground, only to discover a human shinbone still attached.

"I didn't see much action," he said. "They only time I almost got shot was by a nervous GI; we didn't halt and so he took a crack at our truck, but he missed because I am still here."

After he returned to the States, Guerra married Carmen Chapa and returned to the family business. He and Carmen had six children.

Guadalupe "Lupe" Hernandez Jr.

Date of Birth
22 JULY 1921
Reynosa, Mexico

Interviewed by
Nicole Muñoz
6 APRIL 2002
McAllen, TX

WWII Military Unit
3449th Ordnance
Medium Automotive
Maintenance
Company

HERNANDEZ, GUADALUPE "LUPE" JR. When he arrived at the local Army recruitment office, eager and ready to enlist, Guadalupe Hernandez Jr. was one pound too light. Doctors encouraged him to go back to town and eat a pound of bananas, drink plenty of water and come back. Hernandez instead decided to discuss his decision to enlist with his parents, who were unaware of his plans.

He was eventually drafted in November 1942 and trained at Camp Barkeley, Texas, and Camp Shelby, Miss. He was teased for being Latino while training and after he was shipped to a combat zone in New Guinea. "It made me mad. One guy ... and asked me if Mexicans really live with chickens. Incidents like that happened a lot and it really aggravated me." Also feeling the strain of war, Hernandez often had his stripes taken away for misconduct, but told a superior he didn't care if he were court-martialed, as then he would be able to escape the bad treatment he endured from his fellow soldiers. He was eventually sent to a hospital in Van Nuys, Calif., for treatment for a nervous condition, which was diagnosed as 100 percent service related. He was discharged in June 1946 and earned his U.S. citizenship for his service.

Hernandez began working at Roper's appliance shop as a technician. He also worked as a technician in a hotel at a Baptist church. He eventually owned his own repair shop.

After a divorce with his first wife, Pauline, Hernandez married Emma Villareal. Hernandez had six children: Sherry, Debbie, Richard, Bobby, Mark and Michael.

Despite the hardships of the war, Hernandez has remained active in military organizations, serving in the Honor Guard and helping prepare ceremonial funerals for veterans. "We are the only Honor Guard in the area and we are very proud to do it," he said. "I regretted being in the military at the time, because of the treatment I got. But everything I know, I owe to the service."

HERNANDEZ, TOMÁS A. Though he dropped out of school after fifth grade and never went back after the war as he had planned, Tomás A. Hernandez said he received an education from other venues, especially during WWII. "[War] was my schooling in life. I was 100 percent a different person when I got out than when I went in."

After begging his parents to let him enlist for a year after Pearl Harbor, Hernandez joined the Navy at age 17. He was sent to San Diego, Calif., for basic training and began amphibious training. Being away from his family was hard. "I used to cry every night," he said. "But I felt a little better because I was not the only one crying. Everyone was crying."

Hernandez became an instructor at the amphibious base in Coronado, Calif., for a year before he was sent overseas. He served on three different tank landing ships: *LST-882*, *LST-660* and *LST-666*. Tank-landing ships were designed to carry a significant quantity of vehicles, cargo and troops directly onto a beachhead. Hernandez's missions included transporting American troops from Iwo Jima, after the island was conquered, to Okinawa, to begin the invasion there. His ship was preparing for the invasion of Japan when the war ended. Hernandez was discharged in February 1946.

"When I came back I was more alert to things of life. ... Things were more important," he said. "It was like someone opened a door to the world."

Hernandez also discovered that most of his siblings had moved out of Texas and gotten married. Though he attended vocational school for farm machinery, Hernandez ended up driving a taxicab in his father's business. He stayed in McAllen, Texas, to take care of his mother and youngest siblings when his father died. Hernandez had two sons — Agapito and Reymundo — from two marriages that ended in divorce. He later had two daughters: Anna and Vanessa.

Tomás A.
Hernandez

Date of Birth
29 DECEMBER 1925
Temple, TX

Interviewed by
Andrea Shearer
6 APRIL 2002
McAllen, TX

WWII Military Unit
USS *LST-882*,
USS *LST-660*,
USS *LST-666*

ORNELAS, GILBERTO. In war, life or death can rest on seemingly innocuous decisions. For Gilberto Ornelas life rested in his assignment to drive a forklift.

He grew up in Globe, Ariz., where his father worked for a local mining company. He was drafted and joined the Navy on May 10, 1944. He traveled to the South Pacific in September on the USS *Volans*, where survival was contingent upon keeping alert; he slept an average of only four hours each night, as the crew had to be ready to protect itself from unexpected attacks. He traveled to various islands already captured by American troops — including New Caledonia, where ships and submarines stocked up on supplies and ammunition.

Ornelas later drove a forklift and carried supplies on board to visiting ships and submarines. It was then that his inland assignment saved his life. His original ship, the *Volans*, was attacked near Manila Bay. "The ship was attacked and destroyed, and killed all of my friends," he said.

Assigned to the USS *Amsterdam*, Ornelas worked with a determination that moved him up the ranks from Seamen 2d Class to 1st Class to Fireman 1st Class in 1946. During important missions, the crew put biases aside. "Everyone respected one another," he said. Even the captain of the ship became his friend after they talked during Ornelas' watch duty.

The bomb was detonated on the morning of Aug. 6, 1945, over Hiroshima and Aug. 9, over Nagasaki. Ornelas, as part of the crew of the USS *Bottineau*, was ordered to test the bombs' effects. But Ornelas became ill from an infected appendix and was unable to participate in the testing. After his discharge in 1947, he returned to El Paso, Texas, and worked for the railroad company.

He married Lucy A. Avila when he was 28 years old. The couple had four children: Gilberto, Richard, Irene and Gloria.

Gilberto Ornelas

Date of Birth
18 OCTOBER 1925
Globe, AZ

Interviewed by
Liliana Velazquez
2 FEBRUARY 2002
El Paso, TX

WWII Military Unit
USS *Volans* (AKS-9),
USS *Amsterdam*
(CL-59),
USS *Bottineau*
(APA-235)

Pedro "Pete"
Prado

Date of Birth
29 JUNE 1921
San Antonio, TX

Interviewed by
Gabriel Manzano
24 FEBRUARY 2000
San Antonio, TX

WWII Military Unit
86th Engineering
Aviation Battalion

PRADO, PEDRO "PETE." Though Pete Prado said that the lives of Mexican Americans have improved dramatically since WWII, he also acknowledged the brutality and inhumanity of war.

"I hope ... that younger generations realize that war is terrible," he said. "When I was in the Philippines, I saw people picking up what you'd throw away as trash. ... That's how bad war is."

Prado's parents died when he was 14 and Pete, the youngest of four children, sold San Antonio Light newspapers at a nickel a piece. At 19, he went to live with his sister, Bessie, in Houston, Texas, and worked in a pool hall. He was living in San Antonio, Texas, again, and visiting with a friend at his corn tortilla shop, when he heard about the attack on Pearl Harbor. "They're going to get you," his friend told him. "I'm ready," Prado replied. "And I'll go wherever they send me."

He was drafted into the Army Air Corps and served in the 86th Engineer Aviation Battalion. They embarked on a 19-day voyage to Australia, during which a *Kamikaze* plane nearly missed hitting the deck of the ship. From Australia, the battalion island hopped. On Owi Island, Indonesia, two men digging a well and a lieutenant were killed by a pocket of deadly natural gases. In the Philippines, the battalion learned how to concoct "jungle juice" out of fermented apricots, potatoes and sugar to help relieve stress. On Biac Island, East Dutch Indies, the natives taught them to make "tooba," from the resin of palm trees, and fry field rats, though Prado couldn't stomach the meat.

After he was discharged in 1946, Prado used the GI Bill to go to electronic wiring school. His new skill got him a job at Kelly Air Force Base, Texas, where he worked until he retired in 1978. In the course of his career, he noticed how his lack of education inhibited his promotion.

He married Bertha Gonzalez on May 3, 1947. Prado is proud that his three daughters—Cecilia, Diana and Bessie—his daughters all got educations and became professionals.

Ramón Martín Rivas

Date of Birth
19 FEBRUARY 1921
Charlotte, TX

Interviewed by
Maggie Rivas-
Rodriguez
21 JUNE 1999
San Antonio, TX

WWII Military Unit
Battery A,
436th Field Artillery
Battalion,
Special Troops,
3d Company
Replacement
Battalion

RIVAS, RAMÓN MARTÍN. Stationed in Alaska's Aleutian Island during WWII, Ramón Rivas cherished the moments in the middle of the night when he could pick up the faint radio waves that brought Spanish-language broadcasts from Texas. "Since I was the only Mexican American in my outfit. ... I used to keep myself speaking Spanish so I could speak to people when I came home," he said.

Rivas was raised in rural Texas, the youngest of 10 children. His parents died within a month of each other when Rivas was 4, and his 19-year-old brother Carlos became head of the household. The younger children went to a school for Mexican Americans—students had to complete fourth grade before attending an integrated school, though most children never made it that far.

Rivas joined the Work Progress Administration at 18 and in 1941 he enlisted in the Army to support his family. After basic training, he shipped out to Dutch Harbor, Alaska, where he spent nearly three years building elaborate systems of bunkers and trenches. Two other Aleutian islands, Attu and Kiska, were occupied by the Japanese, and Rivas recalls terrifying moments. Japanese planes flew overhead, dropping bombs and strafing Dutch Harbor.

"Anybody who says 'I didn't cry' or things like that, I say they had to be crazy, something wrong with their *cabeza*," he said. "When you see bombs coming down like that, you cry and pray for your life."

After his discharge, Rivas attended barber school, courtesy of the GI Bill, and opened his own barbershop in Devine, Texas, 30 miles south of San Antonio.

Rivas married Henrietta Lopez in 1945, and the couple had seven children: Robert, Irma, Henrietta, Carmen, Maggie, Connie and Guadalupe.

SALCEDO, PETER. Though the first to admit that during childhood he sometimes shirked responsibilities at school, Peter Salcedo credits his time in the military for giving him the direction he needed to succeed later in life.

Drafted in September 1943, Salcedo's father offered him a chance to return to Mexico, where both his father and mother were born, if he chose not to serve. Salcedo declined his father's offer and decided to join the Navy. He eventually was stationed in Hawaii on the islands of Maui and Oahu.

His first assignment in Maui involved repairing military landing craft boats. The assignment lasted 18 months until he was transferred to Oahu. There, Salcedo served as Master of Arms, 2d Class, for four months. It was his responsibility to ensure that all those entering the canteen were properly attired.

Despite the prejudices he experienced within the ranks, Salcedo is extremely proud of his service. He said that WWII brought international attention to the U.S.' military prowess, one positive aspect of war.

After he was discharged in January 1946, Salcedo returned to San Diego, Calif., and resumed his job painting aircraft. Salcedo also worked as a production-control specialist as a civil servant for the Navy.

Active in VFW, he lobbied for the rights of his fellow veterans. He also returned to school, earning his high school diploma in 1969.

Salcedo married María Navarro in 1949. The couple had three children: Betty Jean, Peter Jr. and Mariano.

Peter Salcedo

Date of Birth
5 JUNE 1920
Sespe, CA

Interviewed by
René Zambrano
10 DECEMBER 2000
National City, CA

WWII Military Unit
USS *Lindenwald*
(LSD-6),
USS *John Land*
(AP-167)

TREVIÑO, DOMINGO. Hard work and determination made Domingo Treviño a success. "Being poor, it gave me a motivation to do something," he said. When Treviño and his brothers decided to leave Mexico and return to Houston, Texas, where they had picked cotton as children, they nearly starved. At one point Treviño told his brother, "You know what? The heck with this. I ain't gonna be hungry. I'm gonna work. I'm going to get myself out of this hole."

Treviño would do just that. In Houston, he found a job at a motel and in 1937 began to work at Nagel's Coat Hanger Co. He married Isabel Flores on Aug. 23, 1941.

Treviño was drafted and sent to San Antonio, Texas. In Wichita Falls, Texas, an officer told him to separate from the group and go with the rest of "the Mexicans." Treviño refused. "I'm just as American as the rest of them," he said. He went on to airplane mechanic school and gunnery school and was assigned to Oklahoma for long-range photo reconnaissance. Treviño and a crew took pictures of dropped practice bombs and then pieced them together in mosaic pictures for study.

After a storm caused extensive damage in the Pacific, the crew was assigned to long-range weather reconnaissance. In Guam, Treviño, now assistant engineer, and his crew became the 55th Weather Reconnaissance Squadron.

"We were the first, last and only hurricane hunters in the Pacific," he said. The squadron recorded the weather, flying into Okinawa and Iwo Jima and Guam, where Treviño was able to translate from Spanish. In all, Treviño flew 37 missions. For flying through a storm that no one expected them to survive, he and the Weather Squadron earned a Distinguished Flying Cross.

Treviño returned to Houston and his job at Nagel's Coat Hanger Co. after the war. He and Isabel had four children: Gloria, Irene, Lydia and Elizabeth Ann.

Domingo Treviño

Date of Birth
4 AUGUST 1921
Hempstead, TX

Interviewed by
Paul R. Zepeda
30 MARCH 2000
Houston, TX

WWII Military Unit
55th Weather
Reconnaissance
Squadron

Manuel Castro Vara

Date of Birth
1 JANUARY 1925
San Antonio, TX

Interviewed by
Martha Treviño
15 NOVEMBER 2001
San Antonio, TX

WWII Military Unit
340th Engineer
Combat Regiment

VARA, MANUEL CASTRO. When he heard about the bombing of Pearl Harbor, high school senior Manuel Vara was eager to serve. A month after the announcement, Vara turned 18 and volunteered to fight with the U.S. Army. He had been in ROTC for three years while in high school, "so it was a big thrill to sign up" for the "real" Army, he said.

All six of the Vara brothers joined the military to fight in WWII, and all returned safely. "We all thought it would be a great adventure, but we learned different. [War] takes a lot out of you as an individual, but at the same time it makes you wiser to the realities of life," he said.

He participated as a tech sergeant in a number of Pacific battles, including the capture of a number of New Guinea islands and the liberation of the Philippines, but he was never in the direct line of combat. He served as part of the post-war occupation force in Japan. "The Japanese were just glad it was over, I guess," Vara said.

He said he returned to the United States a wiser, more mature man. "Prior to [shipping out] I didn't know what I was capable of achieving, of what it is that we wanted to get out of life," he said. "When we came back, we, the Mexicans, had much more confidence in ourselves and we realized that we deserved to get a better education, just to see how far we could go."

He attended St. Mary's University in San Antonio, but did not graduate. He made a career working for the U.S. Postal Service, where he experienced some discrimination when he tried to rise within the ranks but eventually rose to the position of postmaster.

"I was refused the opportunity for promotion once," Vara said. "The reason they said was that the public was not ready to have a Mexican selling stamps at the [post office] window. I kept after it until I got the job. That tells me that it is only a difficulty if you make it so."

José R. Zaragoza

Date of Birth
21 OCTOBER 1920
Los Angeles, CA

Interviewed by
Anica Butler
23 MARCH 2002
Los Angeles, CA

WWII Location
Coast Guard
LORAN Station,
Ulithi Atoll

ZARAGOZA, JOSÉ R. Six months after the Japanese bombed Pearl Harbor, José Zaragoza volunteered for the U.S. Coast Guard. "Everyone was ready to go," he said. "Everyone was patriotic."

In the Coast Guard, he patrolled the Pacific coast, defending against sabotage and Japanese invasion. When the imminent threat of invasion waned, Zaragoza requested to go to radar school. During his training, he received instruction on the emerging and secretive field of LORAN technology, or Long Range Navigation. Zaragoza was sent to the Ulithi atoll., Carolina Islands, where the Coast Guard and Navy tracked movement in the Pacific. LORAN was a system in which signals were sent out by two pairs of radio stations and then used to determine the geographical position of a ship or airplane.

"I saw ... different islands, got to mingle with the natives, things that I would have never dreamed of seeing if I hadn't went there and the war hadn't come along," said Zaragoza, who eventually achieved the rank of Radarman 3d Class, "I wouldn't trade it for anything."

The Allied forces used the Ulithi atoll for an airfield and naval port when the Japanese determined the islands too small and rugged to use. There were 25 men on the small island assigned for navigation. "It was like isolated duty," he said. "Gets kind of tiresome being there over a year."

Zaragoza was discharged in March 1946 and returned to a Los Angeles that offered Latinos more opportunities. He worked in his brother's grocery store, where he met his first wife, Blasa Fernandez, with whom he had four children: María, Victor, Martha and Henry.

Zaragoza worked as an electrician at a local community college until his retirement in 1982. In 1976, he married María Teresa Santiago, who had four children from a previous marriage and one daughter with Zaragoza, Joanna.

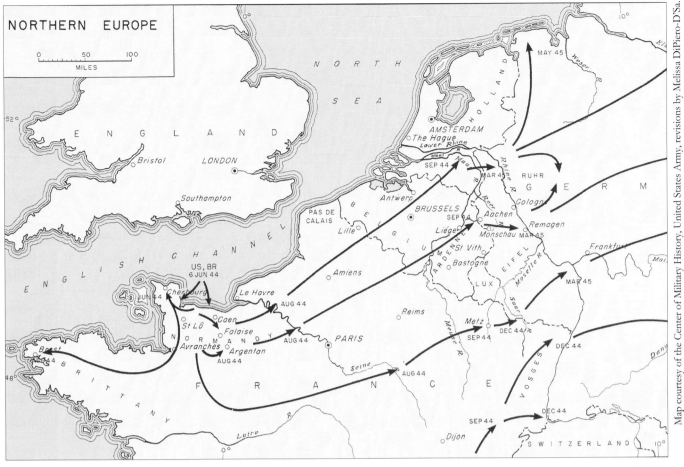

Map courtesy of the Center of Military History, United States Army, revisions by Melissa DiPiero-D'Sa.

MAP 20

IN EUROPE

The European Theater was the site of countless battles during WWII, which required the preparation and logistical support of noncombat troops. Diligent troops worked feverishly away from the front lines throughout Europe, ensuring that those entering combat from the sea and sky had what they needed and that it was in working order. And it wasn't only the official military branches that pitched in: the Merchant Marines also performed valuable support.

Their jobs were varied: readying ammunition and supplies for the troops storming the beaches of northern France, processing shells and packaging munitions, guarding the supplies, escorting ships, driving trucks. They operated teletype machines, relaying coded messages. They navigated ships and drove trucks throughout Europe to keep the flow of materials constant.

As was true elsewhere, WWII would insist that the soldiers remain flexible—the overwhelming demands of the war effort were such that one day, there was a need for a carpenter, the next, that carpenter would need to drive a truck. Several would be trained in one area, and then—when a need was found in something completely different—there was an abrupt about-face and the man would be required to take on a duty he knew little about.

Sam Casarez, of Austin, Texas, was aboard the Merchant Marine's SS *Minot Victory*, which ferried 128 train-car loads of ammunition across the Atlantic. As the war in Europe intensified, Casarez' ship joined a 68-ship naval convoy, constantly working to avoid German submarines. He prided himself on the successful delivery of the supplies.

The Merchant Marines during WWII traveled from ship to cargo boats, to tankers. They served in virtually every theater of war.

"Without the Merchant Marines, they [the Army] wouldn't have a damn thing to fight with," he said.

While Alejandro De Los Santos, of Laredo, Texas, who served with the 66th Chemical Base Depot Company, called his everyday work "routine," others might disagree. His unit's mission was to operate in the rear area: receiving, maintaining and issuing to front line troops the chemical warfare weapons and equipment—smoke and flame, war gases and decontamination equipment—needed. In World War II, lethal gases were not used by mutual aversion and restraint, but were available for retaliation if chemical warfare broke out. The 66th Chemical Base Depot Company was never involved in combat; they were always behind the lines.

Others worked as Teletype operators or interpreters, ensuring that communication among the Allied forces flowed, while keeping clandestine information out of the hands of the Axis.

Richard Savala, from Dallas, Texas, served with the 1450th Ordnance Supply and Maintenance Company, preparing ammunition and taking care of the bombs before D-Day. If there was any carpentry work to be done, he did it, but most of the time his job was preparing the supplies and protecting the bombs and ammunition.

"Not only was I never in combat, I never even saw combat," Savala said. "I am one of the lucky few."

Savala was one soldier whose skills and experience were put aside in favor of a more pressing need. First, in the military he spent nearly a year as a carpenter at McCord Air Force Base in Tacoma, Wash. After Tacoma, Savala was assigned to Drew Air Force Base in Tampa Bay, Fla., where he learned to plot the speed and flight of airplanes. He also spent a few weeks in Orlando learning the metric system. That training would help him prepare supplies in England.

Savala said his most challenging days in the Army were those just before and after D-Day, June 6, 1944, when more than 5,000 ships, 11,000 airplanes and 150,000 service men invaded Normandy in France, turning the tide of war against Germany.

"We loaded bombs and then waited for another shipment," Savala said. "I did not sleep much for several days. We would rest for two hours and then a new shipment would come in which we had to get ready."

In England, Pablo Cavazos, a native of Corpus Christi, Texas, was a trained and experienced carpenter, having worked as a carpenter's assistant at the Corpus Christi Naval Air Station. During the war, he received carpentry training in California and then was sent to England, as a truck driver. After his discharge in April, 1946, Cavazos would say that his experience was "pretty good": his fellow soldiers, his work—even English food, were all "pretty good."

Whatever their task while abroad, the soldiers who served away from the front lines in Europe provided a solid network of support for the troops charging into combat throughout the continent.

MARTINEZ, JUAN. From the concentration camps of Germany to the jungles of the Philippines, Juan Martinez's military service took him around the globe. The exotic backdrops and his passion for the military made his time away from his family bearable.

Eager to join the ranks, Martinez tried to enlist at age 16 but was turned away for being too young. In 1940 at age 18, he was finally old enough to enlist and start his military career. He began basic training in Brownsville, Texas, and continued in Rio Grande City, Texas.

He met and married Marta Estena at a dance hall in Mission, Texas, during a brief leave from training in 1942, shortly before Martinez was sent overseas.

His first assignments were in Europe, where he was an invaluable asset to his unit. Fluent in Italian, Martinez was able to act as an interpreter for his squad. "We went to demonstrations in Italy," Martinez remembered. "I got the best soldier of the year [award] while I was there." The distinction earned him a furlough in Austria, with all expenses paid.

His unit then moved into Germany, where he witnessed the horror of the concentration camps. From there he continued on to aquatic training, where he saved a fellow soldier from drowning.

Martinez eventually was promoted and reassigned to the second squadron as the commander's assistant. He again came to the rescue when harsh conditions in the waters off the Philippines threatened to sweep his colonel away. Martinez was able to steady himself; in the current and save the colonel's life. In the Pacific, Martinez was shot twice, once in the leg, later a bullet hit his helmet.

He returned to Texas in 1950, and he and Marta had six children. Martinez served as pastor of an Apostolic church for more than 30 years and also worked as a supervisor at a janitorial company.

Juan Martinez

Date of Birth
30 AUGUST 1923
Grulla, TX

Interviewed by
Celina Moreno
2 FEBRUARY 2002
El Paso, TX

WWII Military Unit
1st Cavalry Division

ANGEL, ALBERT. After being drafted in 1943, Albert Angel was working stateside when he began to worry he might never see service outside of the States. He decided to sit down with his supervisor and ask for an overseas assignment.

"You're wasting your time and mine too," Angel told his superior. "I want to go overseas."

Angel had been waiting for his turn to serve his country since hearing about the bombing of Pearl Harbor. His wish was granted, and he served in Europe for nearly two years.

After he received basic training in Amarillo, Texas, he spent time at Sheppard Field, Texas, training as an airplane mechanic. He learned to type and how to transmit coded messages at Camp Kearns, Utah, a skill that he would use during his tour of duty in Europe.

In late 1943 Angel boarded the *Queen Mary* and set sail for England. He was greeted by a group of kilted regiments and ate mutton pie while he learned more about British culture.

In England, he worked as a teletype operator, spending his days sending and receiving coded messages. He was never told what the messages said.

Angel was back in the States awaiting reassignment to the Pacific Theater when the war ended. He was discharged on Oct. 23, 1945.

He began working for the U.S. Bureau of Reclamation as an engineering aide. Later he worked as a security inspector for Sandia Research Laboratories in Albuquerque, N.M. He stayed with Sandia for 36 years.

While on a brief leave from the service in 1943, Angel met and married Ana Baca. The couple had three children: Catherine, Albert and Robert. After Ana's death in 1988, Angel married Patricia Esquibel Plent.

Albert Angel

Date of Birth
14 MARCH 1923
Glenrio, NM

Interviewed by
Norman L. Martinez
2 DECEMBER 2003
Albuquerque, NM

WWII Military Unit
784th Bomb Squad,
466th Bomb Group,
8th Air Force

Sam Casarez

Date of Birth
7 MAY 1923
Austin, TX

Interviewed by
Porteskcia Kelley
21 AUGUST 2001
Austin, TX

WWII Military Unit
Minot Victory,
Merchant Marine

CASAREZ, SAM. Patrolling the Atlantic as part of the Merchant Marine, Sam Casarez weathered rough waters, Nazi U-Boats and storms that pummeled his ship. Casarez's service took him from Cuba to the Northern Atlantic.

After passing an advertisement for the Merchant Marine on the street in August 1943, Casarez enlisted. He trained in St. Petersburg, Fla., and learned how to operate machinery in the engine rooms of naval vessels. His first assignment was to operate a tugboat transporting sugar and other goods from Miami to Cuba. The mission allowed him to use his Spanish skills regularly.

As WWII intensified, the Merchant Marine was called upon and Casarez was assigned to a ship delivering ammunition to troops in Europe. The ship carried 128 train-car loads of ammunition across the Atlantic. It sailed from New Orleans, La., to New York and joined a 68-ship naval convoy. En route to Europe, the ships fended off Nazi submarines and arrived on the shores of England with all the ammunition intact. He prided himself on the successful delivery. "Without the Merchant Marines, they [the Army] wouldn't have a damn thing to fight with," he said.

Casarez's missions were treacherous, and one in 26 merchant marines died during combat in WWII. The life of a merchant mariner was nomadic during the war, traveling from cargo ships to tankers and serving in the Middle East, Asia and Africa.

Casarez was discharged in November 1947 and returned to Austin, Texas. In December he began working with Capital Linen Service as a truck driver. He worked his way through the ranks at the company, eventually becoming plant manager. He left to work for other linen companies and also owned a furniture store.

He married Mary Candelas on June 12, 1948. The couple had two sons: Jesse and Sam Jr.

Pablo Cavazos

Date of Birth
25 JANUARY 1924
Corpus Christi, TX

Interviewed by
William Luna
20 JULY 2002
Corpus Christi, TX

WWII Location
Stationed in
England as a
truck driver

CAVAZOS, PABLO. Some 50 years after he served as a truck driver in England during WWII, Pablo Cavazos was still an advocate of the military, and he encouraged young people to get their start in the armed forces.

"If they go into the military, they'll learn a lot of things there," he said.

One of three military sons in his family, Cavazos was drafted on Jan. 14, 1943. He began training in California as a military carpenter, a job he excelled in because of his experience as a carpenter's assistant at the Corpus Christi Naval Air Station. He trained in Missouri and then traveled to Boston, Mass., to await his overseas assignment.

In 1944, Cavazos boarded a ship for England, arriving after a nine-day journey. Once there, he served as a truck driver, earning $66 per month. Cavazos said that everything about his service was "pretty good," from the treatment he received from fellow soldiers to the ship he took to England. He even enjoyed the food.

Cavazos was discharged on April 8, 1946, after three years in the service. Though he saw no combat, he gained experience that he would use throughout his life.

He began working in Chicago, Ill., where he met his wife, Gloria Luna. The two married on June 3, 1950, and moved back to Cavazos' hometown of Corpus Christi, Texas. The couple had one daughter, Esther.

Cavazos worked as a truck driver, and then went into welding with Southwest Welding Works. He later worked for the Lone Star Liquor Distributing Co. for 17 years.

Cavazos looked back fondly on his time in the service and enjoyed getting together with his military friends regularly at the *Taqueria Mexico* in Corpus Christi.

DE LOS SANTOS, ALEJANDRO. During his nearly 40 months overseas, Alejandro De Los Santos supplied and processed weaponry for front line troops during some of the most crucial battles of WWII.

Alejandro
De Los Santos

Date of Birth
26 NOVEMBER 1922
Laredo, TX

Interviewed by
Denise Chávarri
13 OCTOBER 2001
San Antonio, TX

WWII Military Unit
66th Chemical
Base Depot
Company

As part of the 66th Chemical Base Depot Company, De Los Santos was never directly involved in combat, but he still remembered the storms of gunfire and the constant whir of enemy planes overhead. He also recalled the destruction in historic cities throughout Europe.

Despite where he has been and what he has seen, De Los Santos remained humble.

"For me, as I said, it was just another job," he said. "I don't regret joining the military and I don't think my life has changed a lot after the war."

Raised on a farm in Laredo, Texas, De Los Santos enlisted at age 18, and began a military career that would earn him three medals and a chance to see Belgium, England, France and Iceland.

He spent most of this time in Europe doing what he called "routine" work—keeping equipment, including war gases and decontamination supplies, clean and organized. Some 50 years later, there are still some aspects of his service he was unable to discuss. Because of his role in the preparation of weaponry, not combat, his company was lucky enough to not lose a single soldier during their time in Europe.

Following the war, De Los Santos returned to Laredo for one year, then moved to San Antonio, Texas, in search of a more promising job. He worked in civil service and became a mechanic before retiring at age 61. He also intermittently studied business and English at San Antonio College. He married Carmen De Leon in 1949 and the couple had three children: David, Daniel and Diana.

SAVALA, RICHARD. June 6, 1944, more commonly known as D-Day, was a true test of Richard Savala's endurance. Though not directly involved with combat, he had little rest in the days preceding D-Day. As he frantically loaded bombs and prepared ammunition for the Allied invasion of Normandy, sleep was not a priority. His tireless work led to several distinctions, including the Good Conduct Medal and the rank of Technician 5th Class.

Richard Savala

Date of Birth
1 APRIL 1920
Dallas, TX

Interviewed by
Anabelle Garay
27 JUNE 2002
Cumming, GA

WWII Military Unit
145oth Ordnance
Supply and
Maintenance

Born in Dallas, Texas, to Mexican parents, Savala began to learn English around age 14 and largely taught himself by reading bilingual books. He later attended a technical high school, where he excelled in history and English students regularly asked to copy his homework.

After graduation, Savala worked in carpentry, primarily building cabinets. Around his 21st birthday, Savala received a draft notice, and he soon left for training. He was a company carpenter at the McCord Air Force base in Tacoma, Wash., and plotted the speed of planes at Drew Air Force Base in Florida before leaving for Europe.

Overseas, he prepared supplies and protected bombs and ammunition at North Pickenham Airfield, England.

"Not only was I never in combat, I never saw combat," Savala said. "I am one of the lucky few."

While abroad, Savala met Violet Rosina Land, an Englishwoman, whom he married June 7, 1945. Savala was discharged on Nov. 11, 1945, and returned to Texas. Violet remained in England until she moved to the States in 1946. The couple eventually settled in Michigan. They had one son, Robert.

Savala found work with Great Lakes Steel, sometimes working 15-hour days to support his family and to help finance the education of his son, who later became an industrial engineer.

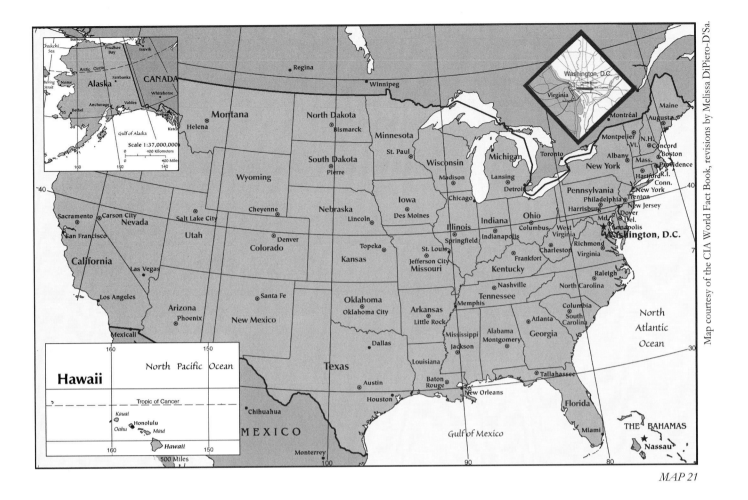

Map courtesy of the CIA World Fact Book, revisions by Melissa DiPiero-D'Sa.

MAP 21

STATESIDE

Soldiers in WWII did not need to leave American soil to contribute to the military effort throughout the war. Thousands remained stateside, training other soldiers and ensuring that bases were running smoothly for the new recruits.

Those men who were drafted and stayed in the continental U.S. often worked repairing tanks and planes.

Some men remained stateside after suffering injuries in training, assigned to duties that would not tax them, but were crucial nonetheless.

And Latino military personnel who were bilingual were valuable as translators and interpreters for soldiers who spoke no English. Those non-English-speaking soldiers came from throughout the Southwest and Puerto Rico. Even those bilingual men not assigned to translate often spent their spare time teaching other men enough English to get by.

Pablo Segura, of El Paso, Texas, was one of those bilingual soldiers. Segura's troop, Company E, was composed entirely of Latino men. All of the non-commissioned officers were fluent in English and Spanish.

"We trained a lot of recruits from Texas that didn't speak English," Segura said. "We were the only 100 percent Mexican-American company in World War II. We made a name for ourselves."

Another willing translator was Raymond J. Flores, of Miami, Ariz. He helped the non-English-speaking soldiers from Texas learn "Army English." He would spend two hours every morning, teaching the soldiers the words they needed to follow basic commands and avoid punishment.

Pablo Segura had been part of a Texas National Guard unit that was mobilized in 1940, but he applied for and was accepted into the Army Air Corps. In the Army Air Corps, Segura trained as a navigator. Of 200 cadets in his class, he was the only Latino. He received his "wings" as a navigator and was commissioned a second lieutenant on May 1, 1943 and was stationed at Biggs Air Field in El Paso, Texas.

However, Segura was one who would change plans because of an injury.

"I was teaching a new navigator how to fire [aircraft weaponry] when my eardrums got busted," Segura said. "I kept flying and damaged my nerves more. When one pilot reported me, I had to go to the flight surgeon. He grounded me, and I was sent to Randolph Air Force Base [San Antonio, Texas]."

Segura's hearing recovered somewhat, but he was no longer qualified to fly. Instead, he went on to teach emergency procedures and survival tactics to other men training as pilots.

Another man whose injury would prevent him from carrying out the assignment he was trained for was Alfred Dimas of Las Vegas, N.M., Dimas enlisted in 1942 and his first job was to break horses for the cavalry. Before long, he was transferred to Fort Benning, Ga., to train as a paratrooper. During a practice jump, Dimas injured his leg and the break was bad enough to end his training and put him on limited duty. Among his jobs was driving for a colonel and a sergeant.

Many soldiers traveled throughout the United States with their assignments. But August R. Segura, a San Antonio, Texas, native, didn't have far to go. He would serve at Laredo Army Air Field, 160 miles from his hometown.

Segura started out working as an aircraft mechanic, was sent to Tennessee to train on boats and tank mechanics, and then returned to the Laredo base, resuming his work as an aircraft mechanic.

"I never went overseas because they told me that I was too essential down here," he said.

Raymond J. Flores, of Arizona, had a problem with one leg that prevented him from entering combat. But Flores, who was fascinated by languages, still wished to be assigned to Germany and develop his German. He would submit 10 signed waivers to support his request, but was denied; he was needed elsewhere. Because of his knowledge and experience with construction, Flores, who was not assigned to a unit, was made a draftsman and helped design buildings and other facilities for four air bases in California. His first assignment was at the San Bernardino Technical Service Command (Engineering Office). Eventually, he was transferred to Oakland and helped investigate suspected sabotage at the San Bernardino base after 13 planes crashed mysteriously. Later, he would work in intelligence.

The stateside soldiers who would have preferred to go overseas, made the best of their lot. Others, like Segura, the San Antonio soldier, did not resent his stateside assignment.

"You couldn't go anywhere when I was growing up," he said. "But the war gave me the chance to travel our own country."

DIMAS, ALFRED. Searching for work as he traveled throughout the country, Alfred Dimas developed an insatiable appetite for adventure. He decided that the Army was a way to find steady employment while also satisfying his love of travel.

Dimas enlisted in 1942 and began basic training at Fort Bliss, Texas. He began in the cavalry, and was assigned to break horses, something he truly enjoyed.

"At that time I was trying to train horses, whatever was an excitement to me," he said. "I used to love the formations when you would see thousands and thousands of horses doing the same thing. It was really something. I loved it."

Dimas was one of three siblings to serve during WWII, with brothers Dan and Pete also answering the call. Dan was also in the cavalry, and the two would sometimes run into each other during their training. Dan was later killed in action when he was sent overseas.

After Fort Bliss, Dimas began to train as a paratrooper at Fort Benning, Ga. He injured his leg during a practice jump, and the injury was serious enough to end his training. He was transferred to Fort Meade, Md., to recover. There he was placed on limited duty and worked several jobs, including a stint as a driver for the colonel and sergeant.

He was discharged in 1945 as a staff sergeant, and returned to Phoenix, Ariz., and his young wife, Beatrice Escudero.

After his discharge, Dimas attended Apache Leather School with the help of the GI Bill. He made saddles and purses, but eventually, his sense of adventure led him to a slightly more dangerous profession. He went into the tiling business, often working on high-rise buildings that were more than 20 stories.

Alfred Dimas

Date of Birth
25 APRIL 1917
Las Vegas, NM

Interviewed by
Maggie Rivas-
Rodriguez
4 JANUARY 2003
Phoenix, AZ

WWII Military Unit
8th Cavalry
Regiment,
1st Cavalry Division

Transferred to
82d Airborne
Division

FLORES, RAYMOND J. Fighting discrimination since his youth, Raymond Flores' passion for education was fueled by the obstacles constantly set before him. He survived military service and racism to become a role model for young Latinos everywhere.

Flores grew up in the small Arizona mining town of Miami, where most young men immediately began working. Because of his obligations to his father's mining company, Flores attended school only once a week, to hand in assignments and take tests. Upon graduation in 1941, he left Miami to attend Arizona State Teachers College. He was the first from his neighborhood to do so.

In 1942, Flores enlisted in the Army and trained on various bases throughout California. Despite his strong desire to be stationed overseas, a problem with one of his legs kept him from crossing the Atlantic. He wanted to serve in Germany to learn the language and satisfy a linguistic curiosity that led him to teach Apache children to write their names in English when he was a boy.

Stationed in Oakland, Calif., Flores began to work for counterintelligence; in one assignment he attempted to determine the cause of the crash of 13 airplanes near the San Bernardino base. During his time on the base, he also helped other Latinos learn what he called "Army English," so they could understand orders and avoid punishment. He was discharged on Jan. 31, 1946.

Flores completed his degree at the University of Arizona at Tempe, though initially he continued working in military intelligence after he married Leota May Resler in 1951. As a teacher, he created ANYTOWN, Arizona—a weekly program to open dialogue between high school students of diverse backgrounds—which is now a national nonprofit organization. Flores received an award for his work in civil rights from state Attorney General Robert Corbin.

He and Leota had six children: Deborah, Rebecca, Raymond, Roderick, Kathryn and Greg.

Raymond J. Flores

Date of Birth
11 MARCH 1922
Miami, AZ

Interviewed by
Violeta Dominguez
4 JANUARY 2003
Phoenix, AZ

WWII Location
Stationed in
Oakland, CA,
Naval Security
Group

August R. Segura

Date of Birth
11 FEBRUARY 1922
San Antonio, TX

Interviewed by
Unity Peterson
12 APRIL 2002
San Antonio, TX

WWII Location
Stationed at Laredo
Army Air Field, TX

SEGURA, AUGUST R. With the attack on Pearl Harbor still fresh in his mind, August Segura went to the local recruitment office and joined the Army Air Corps on Nov. 2, 1942.

He began his basic training at Fort Sam Houston, Texas. There, he slept in a small tent with four men, and he remembered his sergeant's tactics for rousing them for their early-morning wake-up.

"The sergeant would have a weeping willow branch and hit that thing [the tent]," he said. "It sounded like bullets and that would get us up in the mornings."

After training, Segura was sent to Laredo Army Air Field, Texas, and began working as an airplane mechanic. Eager to learn more, he told his superiors he was interested in hydraulics and that he hoped to someday become an auto mechanic. He was sent to Tennessee for additional training and began working on tanks.

He eventually returned to the base in Laredo and continued repairing planes until his discharge on Feb. 3, 1946. "I never went overseas because they told me that I was too essential down here [in Laredo]," he said.

However, Segura viewed his travel in the States positively. "Sure, the war made a better man out of me," he said. "You couldn't go anywhere when I was growing up, but the war gave me the chance to travel our own country."

During his service, Segura met Margarita Cárdenas on the plaza in downtown Laredo. The two married on April 14, 1945, and they had three sons: August, José and Roberto. Segura began working at Martin Linen and Supply Co. in Laredo following his discharge. He played semi-professional baseball on the weekends. The family moved back to Segura's hometown of San Antonio, Texas, in 1958, where Segura began working as an auto mechanic and later worked for a brewery.

Pablo Segura

Date of Birth
31 MAY 1917
El Paso, TX

Interviewed by
Ernest Eguía and
Paul R. Zepeda
9 SEPTEMBER 2002
Houston, TX

WWII Military Unit
Company E,
141st Infantry
Regiment,
36th Infantry
Division

Transferred to
Army Air Corps,
Biggs Air Field, TX

SEGURA, PABLO. Despite discrimination in the Army and in civilian life, Pablo Segura met challenges and completed college and a demanding service in the Army Air Corps. Even with the unfair treatment he received because of his ethnicity, he remains proud of his heritage.

"You don't have to lose your roots to be a proud American," he said.

Segura grew up in a poor barrio in El Paso, Texas, and as a child, he dreamed of using education as his ticket to get away. With the help of his thrifty mother, he was able to finance two years of college at the Texas College of Mines and Metallurgy, now the University of Texas at El Paso. When his money was exhausted, he joined the Texas National Guard to pay for his remaining years of school. Segura's guard unit was mobilized on Nov. 25, 1940, and became part of the Army.

He began training at Camp Bowie, Texas, where his company was composed completely of Mexican Americans. Segura was transferred to Camp Blanding, Fla., where he passed the exam to enter the Army Air Corps and trained as a navigator. He was the only Latino in his class of 200 cadets and earned his wings in May 1943, with the rank of second lieutenant.

Segura was working at Biggs Air Field, Texas, when an accident cost him his hearing. "I was teaching a new navigator how to fire [aircraft weaponry] when my eardrums got busted," he said.
He tried to continue flying, but was grounded. Hearing aids allowed him to regain some of his hearing, and he went on to teach emergency procedures and survival tactics to air crews, as well as serve as a translator. He was separated from the Air Corps in January 1946.

Segura returned to college, earning his engineering degree in 1949, and then worked as a metallurgist until 1980. He became active in LULAC, serving as his chapter's president in 1974. He married Juanita Roque in 1941 and they had four children: Ricardo, Oscar, Edward and Estér.

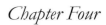

Rafaela M. Esquivel, back row, third from left, at the doorsteps of the Town Hall in Bruxelles, Belgium.
June 23, 1945.

Latinas in the Military

The Navy Nurse Corps had been established by Congress in 1908 and was greatly expanded to meet the nation's needs in WWII. But during the war, another branch of the military, the Army, also established women's units, allowing women to serve in capacities other than nurses for the first time. While initially assigned traditional roles such as typists and file clerks, the Army soon found an increasing variety of roles for women. It presented opportunities women had not often encountered and Latina women were among those who would join. During the war, an estimated 350,000 women served in all branches of the military.

Congresswoman Edith Nourse Rogers of Massachusetts introduced a bill to create the Women's Army Auxiliary Corps, giving women much of the benefits of their male counterparts for their participation in the coming war effort. The bill was passed and President Roosevelt signed it into law in May 1941. Two years later, the WAAC was transformed from an auxiliary role to that of the regular Army (WAC), giving women benefits men received, in the event of an overseas tour, and realigning the ranking to match and equal the Army's system.

The WAACs first director was Oveta Culp Hobby, a graduate of the University of Texas Law School and an executive with the Houston Post-Dispatch (later the Houston Post). Her husband, William P. Hobby, was a former governor of Texas and publisher of the Houston Post-Dispatch.

Oveta Culp Hobby had the challenge of promoting WAAC to a public skeptical of the necessity and decency of women in the military. The goal, Major Hobby clarified, was for the women to fill jobs in support of the Army, freeing up men for combat.

Women like Anna Torres Vazquez, of Indiana, would join, becoming the only female from her neighborhood in the military.

Fort Des Moines, Iowa, was the first training center for the WAAC and over 35,000 applications for the officer training program poured in. Their first classes started on July 20, 1942. The equivalent of enlisted applicants were first trained on Aug. 17. Most of the newly trained officers began training more women auxiliaries and the numbers of women in the Army gradually expanded.

Women in the Navy

Females had long served as nurses in the Navy. Arizona's Beatrice Amado Kissinger, in nursing school in Tucson, Ariz., was impressed when she saw nurses who had graduated from her school, returning in a Navy uniform to recruit.

"And the hype with patriotism was so high that you wanted to be a part of the service," she said.

Kissinger served stateside in Long Beach, Calif., at the U.S. Naval Hospital, and then in San Francisco.

Carmen Romero Phillips, of Silverbell, Ariz., who befriended Kissinger when they were both in the Navy, was stationed in Santa Ana Army Air Base, Calif., treating men returning from battle in the Pacific.

"When they got to the States, we had to do the final repair, especially if they had fractures with casts. In those days, those were hard casts. Some of them smelled bad, some of them not so bad," she said. "You take that cast off, and you would see a lot of maggots. ... Those maggots had cleaned the wound because they ate all the blood and pus."

Phillips would also find herself thrust into

leadership positions as a nurse.

"For some reason I was always in charge of whatever I was doing, and it was usually an operating room," she said. "I got to train a lot of the new nurses and help them. If we wanted them to do a good job, I had to teach them."

WACs

Elsie Schaffer Martinez, a native of San Antonio, Texas, would join the WACs and be sent to a high-security post in Colorado, where she would develop photos taken by Allied reconnaissance and make maps from those photographs. Among Martinez' memories are the 5 a.m. wake-up calls and having to wear long, olive-colored GI underwear, along with olive stockings and brassieres. Her aunt, who owned a department store in Abilene, sent her nylon stockings and comfortable underwear to wear underneath.

The first women the Army sent overseas were part of the campaign in North Africa and Italy. Carman Contreras Bozak, a native of Cayey, P.R., was among the women in the 149th Post Headquarters Company, the first WAAC unit to be sent overseas.

"I was only out of basic training not two months and I was going overseas already," she said. "I was so happy that I did join."

In Algiers, Bozak worked as a teletype operator, transmitting encoded messages to the battlefield.

Rafaela Muñiz Esquivel, of San Antonio, Texas, served in the 242d General Hospital, in Sissonne, France. She and other women were forced to burn curtains in their quarters to keep warm. Later, she was transferred to the 101st Evacuation Hospital in Luxembourg. An evacuation hospital is where wounded men are sent after receiving first aid and treatment at a field hospital. It was the evacuation hospitals where the decision would be made as to whether to send the patient to surgery, or to hospitals in England or even to the United States.

"... They used to bring them [the wounded] by the loads. [We were] always on the go. ... Most of the time we were dressed. We didn't have time. There was no way that we could really get undressed [to sleep]," said Esquivel.

Supporting the Troops

Some women had already been introduced, in a way, to military matters. Concepción Alvarado Escobedo had worked as an air raid warden in San Antonio, making sure shades were drawn during night-time military air-raid practice. Uniforms and the discipline of the military fascinated her. Inspired after attending a rally promoting women in the military, Escobedo enlisted.

"I felt if I could play some small part in the war effort, I would want to do it." She recalled. She would work as a file clerk, and then as a baker at Randolph Field, Texas.

WACs were assigned to the Pacific Theater, where they would contend with the miseries of the jungle. Still, the experience was invaluable to many.

María Sally Salazar, of Laredo, Texas, served with the WAC, in New Guinea and the Philippines with the Surgeon General's office. Later she would say she was "stuck in the jungle" for a year and a half. She contracted malaria, hepatitis and suffered from dysentery.

With the success of the Women's Army Corps in WWII, the Army embraced the use of women within its ranks. It became a permanent and separate corps of the Army on June 12, 1948. The WAC remained until 1978, when the separation of the corps was abolished and women were allowed in every non-combat part of the Army.

BOZAK, CARMEN CONTRERAS. Looking back on her war experiences, Carmen Contreras Bozak remembered that as many women sought cover, she headed to the roof of the hotel where she worked the night shift to watch the artillery fire.

During her 18 months in Algiers, Algeria, she witnessed four air raids and the dropping of a bomb near one of the residences, as Algiers was not far from the battlefield action.

In January 1943, she was one of 196 members of the 149th WAAC Post Headquarters Company, the first WAAC unit to go overseas. "I was only out of basic training not two months and I was going overseas already," she said, "I was so happy that I did join."

In Algiers she worked as a teletype operator, transmitting encoded messages to the battlefield. She had been chosen for the job because of her ability to speak more than one language. After a short period in Italy, her time overseas ended. Back in the States, she was sent to a hospital in Valley Forge, Pa., for treatment of an eye infection she had contracted in Algiers. At the hospital she met her husband-to-be, Theodore J. Bozak.

Carmen Contreras grew up in Puerto Rico, and later moved to New York City. After graduating from high school, she worked for the National Youth Administration and later as a payroll clerk in the War Department in Washington, where she first picked up the patriotism that drove her to enlist in the WAAC.

Following the war, Bozak started a chapter of the WAC (previously WAAC) Vets in Fort Lauderdale, Fla., in 1989 and a chapter of the Society of Military Widows in 1998. She also volunteers her time at the Oakland Park VA Outpatient Clinic, attends VFW meetings and travels. She and her husband had three children: Brian, Robert and Carmen.

Carmen Contreras Bozak

Date of Birth
31 DECEMBER 1919
Cayey, PR

Interviewed by
Vivian Torre
14 SEPTEMBER 2002
Miami, FL

WWII Military Unit
149th WAAC Post Headquarters Company

Transferred to
2625th Signal Company

ESCOBEDO, CONCEPCIÓN ALVARADO. War service did not always bring Concepción Alvarado gratitude and appreciation. After the war she found it took some time for her to win the approval of people in Harlingen, Texas. "Several of the women in the Army had a wild reputation, so people didn't think well of women in the service," she recalled. "I kind of had to prove that I was a good person, that I was not a wild person."

Born Concepción Alvarado on Dec. 8, 1923, while in school she met young ROTC officers and was fascinated with their uniforms and the idea of drills and organization. Her interest in the military continued when she volunteered as an air-raid warden in San Antonio, Texas, where she checked to make sure lights were turned off during military air-raid practices.

She joined the Armed Forces after attending a military rally that promoted women in the service; she enlisted in April 1944 in Recruiting Station, San Antonio. "I felt if I could play some small part in the war, I would want to do it," she said.

After basic training at Fort Oglethorpe, Ga., she was transferred to the Women's Army Corps at Randolph Field in San Antonio. Working there seemed "just like a regular job," as she served as a file clerk and later as a baker for the WAC unit. She met her husband, Carlos Escobedo, during a night of celebration after Germany surrendered. Six months later the couple married—on Armistice Day.

The two moved to Harlingen but she gave up her military job reluctantly. "I would have liked to stay in longer," she said. "I enjoyed my time in the Army." She had five children: Robert, Gerard, Arnold, Deborah and Asella. While struggling to raise her children, Escobedo still found the time to make use of the GI Bill and attended beauty school and business college. She later worked as a bookkeeper and business clerk, and stayed involved in several veterans' organizations.

Concepción Alvarado Escobedo

Date of Birth
8 DECEMBER 1923
Southton, TX

Interviewed by
Sandra Freyberg
13 SEPTEMBER 2003
Brownsville, TX

WWII Military Unit
2532d Army Air Force Base Unit, Women's Army Corp

**Rafaela Muñiz
Esquivel**

Date of Birth
5 MAY 1920
San Antonio, TX

Interviewed by
Joanne R. Sanchez
12 APRIL 2001
San Antonio, TX

WWII Military Unit
242d General
Hospital

Transferred to
101st Evacuation
Hospital,
Army Nurse Corps

ESQUIVEL, RAFAELA MUÑIZ. Caregiving was a way of life for Rafaela Muñiz Esquivel from an early age, as she was the second oldest child, with 14 siblings. Rafaela Muñiz grew up in San Antonio, Texas, and graduated from nursing school in May 1942 with four other Mexican-American classmates. She joined the Army Nurse Corps. Commissioned as a second lieutenant in the Army Reserve, she reported for duty in 1942 trained and served stateside for two years.

On Dec. 9, 1944, she sailed to Europe on the *Queen Mary*, arriving in Scotland and traveling to the 242d General Hospital in Sissonne, France.

The nurses were quartered in an old cavalry post and had to "make their own heat," so she burned her roommate's hand-made, burlap curtains and shelf cover. She was later moved to the 101st Evacuation Hospital in Luxembourg, on the site of Duchess' summer palace. "It could have been beautiful before all those casualties," she said.

In the winter of 1945, she moved to a hospital, in a German town near Coblenz, in a monastery about five miles from Patton's 3d Army Headquarters. Although the hospital was never hit, they heard exploding bombs in the distance. "It seemed like [the injured] were coming in droves," she remembered. They also treated civilians.

She reached the rank of 1st Lieutenant before the end of the war, and was discharged Jan. 16, 1946. She married Efraín "Frank" Esquivel, who had been an Air Force sergeant and radio operator based in the South Pacific, in 1950; two years later she quit nursing, frustrated with unprepared employees. In 1954 she and Efraín adopted Mary Margaret, who had learning disabilities. A charter member of Women in the Military in Washington, Esquivel also was the only woman in VFW Post 4700 — a life member and former post chaplain.

**Felicitas Cerda
Flores**

Date of Birth
18 MAY 1921
Houston, TX

Interviewed by
Paul R. Zepeda
2 FEBRUARY 2002
Houston, TX

WWII Military Unit
Auxiliary 1st Class,
WAAC Detachment

FLORES, FELICITAS CERDA. With a firm belief that education is the door to opportunity, Felicitas Cerda Flores pursued it throughout her life. She left high school to work full time, but she later earned her GED. In the work force, she became a skilled typist, an ability she used upon enlisting in the Army. She received basic training in Ruston, La., at the site of a future German POW camp. She then was sent to Maryland to perform clerical work, the only Latina in the 1,000 Women's Army Corps members assigned there.

Born Felicitas Cerda, she lived in the barracks for seven months, from February to August 1943, and then was discharged. She excelled in the Army and, near the end of her service, was chosen as one of four women who traveled to Washington, D.C., to visit with congressmen. Visiting museums and sightseeing provided exciting opportunities to expand her knowledge of the nation.

She rose to the rank of corporal before the end of her service. She used her experiences in the Army to explore other cities across the nation, and her interaction with fellow corps members provided a lesson in cultural comparisons.

After her discharge, she returned to her hometown of Houston, Texas, and married Jorge G. Flores. The couple had three children: Mario, María and Daniel. Throughout her employment and volunteer work, Flores focused on education — of her own children and others'. Her testimony of her life as a first-generation American was recorded by the Evangelical Church as part of an educational mission and was sent to Mexico, to inspire Mexican youth and encourage their dreams.

After earning her GED, Flores eventually studied child psychology at night, while working during the day. She continues to stress the importance of education to students: "If I went to college at the age of 52, you can too."

HERNANDEZ, EMMA VILLAREAL.   One needn't look further than her own family—well-known in their community of Pharr, Texas, for their humanitarian efforts—to understand why Emma Villareal Hernandez has devoted her life to civic service.

Her aunt—who, along with her uncle, served as a surrogate parent after Hernandez' mother died when the girl was 4—demonstrated to young Emma Villareal the importance of serving others, as her aunt assisted others by raising monetary donations and collecting clothing.

She learned from this example and joined the U.S. Navy in 1943. She was assigned to Rodd Field, in Corpus Christi, Texas, for two years, during which time her main responsibility was to log pilots' training hours.

"The most important thing that I learned I have kept with me, and I will have it with me until I die: discipline," Hernandez said.

As was customary, she was honorably discharged when she became pregnant with her first son. Since her husband, Guadalupe "Lupe" Hernandez Jr., was stationed in and out of the country, Hernandez and her children moved into Georgia Hall in Washington, D.C., where many soldiers' families lived. After her husband's service ended, the family moved to McAllen, Texas.

The couple regularly attended funeral services of veterans and Hernandez was very active in veterans' activities: as treasurer of the VFM Auxiliary, member of the Disabled American Veterans Association, and as one of six D.A.V.A. "Sunshine Ladies" who visit VA nursing homes at least twice a year—usually on Veterans' Day or Memorial Day. Hernandez raised six children: Robert, Richard, Debbie, Cherrie, Mark and Michael. One son was a member of the Air Force Band, another served in the Air Force and yet another in the Navy.

Emma Villareal Hernandez

Date of Birth
16 APRIL 1923
Petronila, TX

Interviewed by
Gary Villereal
1 JULY 2002
McAllen, TX

WWII Location
Stationed at Rodd Field, TX

KISSINGER, BEATRICE AMADO. The war gave Beatrice Amado a ticket out of small-town life in southern Arizona as a nursing student at a strict Catholic school.

"I wanted to get ... out of the control of the nuns," Beatrice Amado Kissinger said. "The nurses that left would come back with these beautiful uniforms, and the hype with patriotism was so high that you wanted to be a part of the service."

She enlisted in 1943 and was eventually sent to the U.S. Naval Hospital in Long Beach, Calif., for six months. Her initial orders for the Pacific were reversed and she served in San Francisco instead. "I was doing the good work there, and they didn't need me overseas; otherwise they would have sent me," Kissinger said. "Personally I didn't want to go."

She enjoyed her years in the Navy. She recalled dating many of her patients and spent a great deal of time dancing to big band music. She got along well with her fellow nurses, although they came from varied backgrounds. "The nurses came from every state of the Union, and here we were thrown together," she said. "It was a beautiful experience."

After the war she served at the Great Lakes Naval Hospital, just north of Chicago, Ill. In 1946 she met Jim Kissinger, a Marine who was ill with scarlet fever. It was not love at first sight.

"He was a recalcitrant Marine that didn't obey my routine," she said.

At the end of his hospital stay, his Navy chief bet him that he couldn't get the nurse to go out with him. After two rejections, she agreed and the two discovered they had much in common.

"He was a guy who didn't put on airs," she said. "I met so many that were putting on airs."

The two married in 1946 after a seven-month engagement. They had six children: Jim, Beverly, Janet, Dorothy, John and Elizabeth.

Beatrice Amado Kissinger

Date of Birth
19 NOVEMBER 1922
Tucson, AZ

Interviewed by
Ernesto Portillo
26 MARCH 2003
Tucson, AZ

WWII Location
Stationed in U.S. Naval Hospital in Long Beach, CA, Navy Nurse Corps U.S. Naval Receiving Hospital in San Francisco, CA

Elsie Schaffer
Martinez

Date of Birth
11 FEBRUARY 1922
San Antonio, TX

Interviewed by
Raquel C. Garza
28 SEPTEMBER 2002
Laredo, TX

WWII Military Unit
Stationed in
Pueblo, CO,
Army Air Force,
WAAC

MARTINEZ, ELSIE SCHAFFER. Developing aerial photographs taken by Army photographers taught Elsie Schaffer Martinez a multitude of new skills, including shooting photos herself. However, the images themselves she would try to forget.

"The things we saw, and the people that came back, it was horrible," she said.

Born Elsie Schaffer in 1922, she enlisted in the Army Air Corps when she was 21 and joined the Women's Army Corps. After a three-month training period in Arkansas, she graduated and was sent to a high-security base in Pueblo, Colo., where she worked with three other women and eight men as they developed the photographs taken by Army reconnaissance and constructed maps from the photos. She was sworn to secrecy regarding the pictures.

In November 1945, after three years in the Army, she was discharged as a corporal. After traveling for four weeks in Washington, D.C., and spending a few months in Georgia, she returned to Laredo, Texas, which she had moved to in 1941 from her birthplace of San Antonio, and worked for a year.

Then she moved to Mexico City and stayed with an aunt while attending El Colegio de México, paid for by the GI Bill. She studied Spanish for three years, with the intention of becoming an interpreter in Mexico.

Occasionally she went with her aunt to a local meat superstore in Mexico City, where she met her future husband, the owner of the store, Pablo Martinez. They married on March 26, 1952, and Martinez decided to be a full-time wife and mother. The couple had three children: Ignacio, Jaime and Selma.

She logged more than 1,500 hours of volunteer work at the Veterans Clinic in Laredo, where she received an award for her service.

Carmen Romero
Phillips

Date of Birth
19 JANUARY 1921
Silverbell, AZ

Interviewed by
Delia Esparza
5 JANUARY 2003
Tucson, AZ

WWII Military Unit
Squadron F,
591st Army Air
Force Base Unit

PHILLIPS, CARMEN ROMERO. Even after removing maggot-infested casts from men returning from the battlefronts in WWII, Carmen Romero Phillips was eager to serve again. After Sept. 11, 2001, she volunteered her abilities to the Red Cross but was turned down on account of her age.

In December 1943, the former Red Cross nurse entered the Army and was assigned to Santa Ana Army Air Base, Calif. An orthopedic doctor from Tucson, Ariz., where Carmen Romero had attended nursing school, had already reported to duty in Santa Ana.

"So he asked our charge nurse, 'Will you please send Carmen Romero to the operating room the first day she gets here?' So here I go to the operating room," Phillips recounted. At the base, she mostly tended to men wounded in the Pacific.

"When they got back to the States, we had to do the final repair, especially if they had fractures with casts. In those days, those were hard casts. Some of them smelled bad, some of them not so bad. You take that cast off, and you would see a lot of maggots," Phillips said. "But those wounds—those maggots had cleaned the wound because they ate all the blood and pus."

In August 1944, she transferred to Stockton Air Field, Calif. A brief marriage in 1945 lasted less than a year. She left the military on Nov. 1 that year with the rank of first lieutenant and went to work at St. Mary's Hospital in Tucson. In 1946, one of her flight surgeons asked her to work at a clinic and hospital in Corpus Christi, so she moved to Texas and worked for him for one year and then accepted a job at Memorial Hospital.

She married Charles Alexander Phillips—who had been a bombardier aboard B-24 bombers in the Pacific—in January of 1947. The two had four children: Charles, Christina, Camille and Constance. Phillips continued to work as an operating nurse until her retirement in 1986.

SALAZAR, MARÍA SALLY. At 19, María Sally Salazar was two years shy of the age required for women to enlist without parental consent. So Salazar snuck off—150 miles from Laredo, Texas, to San Antonio—with her older sister's birth certificate, under the guise of visiting her sister.

She managed to keep her enlistment a secret until her parents intercepted her acceptance letter. Her mother, fearing the legal repercussions of assuming another's identity, dissuaded her father from reporting Salazar. She went by her sister's name, Amelia, during the war. When she left the service she had to hire a lawyer to correct the discharges so she could have her own name and age.

With the Women's Army Corps, Salazar was sent to New Guinea and then the Philippines, to help with the invasion in October 1944. She was assigned to work specifically for the Surgeon General's office. "Anywhere they needed us we worked, but mostly in the medical field," she said.

Under high stress and with fewer nutrients in her diet, Salazar fell ill but worked on. By the end of the war, Salazar was hospitalized in Manila, Philippines, with several illnesses, including malaria, hepatitis and diarrhea. She would continue to suffer from five service-related illnesses, including chronic hepatitis and amoebic dysentery, even decades after the war. She received a medical discharge but re-entered the service to pay her medical bills. After the war, she finished high school and attended a junior college. She married in 1974 and put her three step-children through college on her benefits. She later divorced.

Although the war brought her continued physical and mental ailments, Salazar does not regret her service.

"To me it was an experience I would not change for anything in the world, because not just anybody can have that," she said. "And my nightmares are with me, and my dreams are with me."

María Sally Salazar

Date of Birth
23 SEPTEMBER 1923
Laredo, TX

Interviewed by
Nicole Muñoz
28 SEPTEMBER 2002
Laredo, TX

WWII Military Unit
Stationed in
New Guinea and
the Philippines,
Women's Army
Corps

VAZQUEZ, ANNA TORRES. Side-by-side with her husband, Anna Torres Vazquez found a life-long duty in service to her country and to her heritage. Through war and discrimination, the Vazquezes pioneered the path for Latin Americans' opportunities in the United States.

While Anna Torres was born in Mexico, she was raised in Indiana, and was the only Hispanic female from her neighborhood to join the WWII effort. She began in the WAC and later became part of the 3d Air Force; she was sent to Florida to train Allied pilots in the Mexican Squadron 201 to fight in the Pacific. Family members had a scare at one point, when her plane made a forced landing during a training mission and was reported missing in action. It was feared they'd had an accident, but she and her fellow crew members landed safely.

She met Roberto Vazquez after the war, in East Chicago, Ind., where they married—she had been married once before—and continued to reside. The couple had three sons: David, Arturo and Richard. They became involved in LULAC, fighting for equality for Latinos by organizing both men's and women's councils in East Chicago, Ind.

With a veterans' discount and the help of Vazquez's mother, who Roberto said landlords "took for granted she was European" because of her light skin color, the couple was able to rent an apartment. "We were the first Hispanic family [in that neighborhood]," Roberto said.

Vazquez served in a variety of leadership positions for veterans' and Latinos' organizations, including president of her local VFW post, president of the Latin-American Veterans Auxiliary and first woman to become president of LULAC in Indiana, to name a few. The couple also worked to honor a family friend who fought in the Vietnam War by naming the Harold Gomez Post Office for him. "It's the only Midwest post office named for a Hispanic," Roberto said—as far as he knew.

Anna Torres
Vazquez

Date of Birth
17 MARCH 1918
Le Piedad, Mexico

Interviewed by
William Luna
20 JUNE 2002
East Chicago, IN

WWII Military Unit
WAC Squadron
W 902 AAFBU

From left to right, Trinidad, Joe, their mother Genoveva, Antonio, Frank, and Tomás Jasso in 1946.

Brothers in Arms

Small banners with blue stars hung in millions of American homes during WWII, signifying that a member of that family was serving in the military. When one of those men or women was killed, the blue star was replaced by a gold one. Mothers who had a son or daughter killed while serving would be known as "Gold Star Mothers," a designation that continues in 2006.

Latino families hung many of those banners. In fact, in some cases, there was more than one banner in a home's window. Some families had two, three, four, five, and even more sons serving.

There are numerous stories of how brothers emulated their elder's example in joining the service, how some lost and found each other overseas, how they returned with a new appreciation for family life. This chapter is a sampling of stories of brothers who simultaneously served their country in war.

Salvador "Sal" and Manuel "Manny" Rivas, twins from El Paso, Texas, served in the same Marine unit, 1st Regiment, in the Central Pacific. Their father had been opposed to the two of them serving in the same unit; he feared losing them both. But their mother responded: "They were born together. They've been to school together. They've had their fights together. Let them be together."

Serving in Peleliu, Caroline Islands, the Rivas brothers fought in different platoons during the day, but often shared a foxhole for sleeping. At one point, Sal went out on patrol with four other men and went missing for three days. Their lieutenant concluded that the men were dead. But Manny, keying in with his "twin instinct," knew his brother was alive.

"I took two guys with me and we found them," Manny Rivas said. "They were behind enemy lines and we got 'em out. My instinct, like a homing pigeon's, brought me to my brother."

In San Antonio, Texas, the five Jasso brothers would serve, two with the Army Air Corps, two more with the Army, and the youngest, in the Navy. Their older brother, Jesús "Jesse," who was in his mid-30s at the start of the war and had five children, was devastated that he couldn't join as well. Their father passed away while his sons were overseas.

For the Zepeda family of Baytown, outside of Houston, Texas, there would be four sons serving, two of them would be taken prisoner by the Germans. Their younger brother, Paul, would recall when his parents received word that Elías was missing in action.

"Two weeks later, they received another telegram notifying them that Isaac was also missing in action," Paul Zepeda said. "My mother cried and cried and cried and my father would try to console her."

"We have always been a family grounded in faith and that, I believe, is the only thing that pulled them through those hard, trying days."

Five León brothers served their country. The two older León brothers were born in Parral, Mexico, the third in El Paso, Texas, a fourth in Arizona and the youngest, Salvador, in California.

"None of us even earned a medal," said Salvador León. "There was really nothing outstanding about our service.

"The only thing I think is outstanding, and I'm very proud of this part, is that all five of us were in the service at the same time and overseas at the same time."

THE ANTUNA BROTHERS

Ralph and Philip Antuna were interviewed by William Luna February 21, 2002 in Hegewisch, Ill.

Ralph and Philip Antuna both survived the atrocities of the Battle of the Bulge. The brothers, assigned to different divisions, fought in different areas in Europe until that battle. But when the fighting began in Ardennes, they searched for signs of the other. "I would stop every truck or man [from Philip's unit] and ask about Philip," Ralph said. "But I could never find him."

Ralph and Philip, who had four other brothers and three sisters, both were drafted into the Army. Older brother Ralph had been rejected from the Navy in 1941 because he was too short. The following year, he was drafted on his 21st birthday: Oct. 17, 1942.

Ralph trained at Camp Carlson, Colo., with the 277th Field Artillery Battalion. He was sent to Scotland aboard the *Queen Elizabeth*, which departed from New York City on Sept. 27, 1942. During the voyage, the ship zigzagged a lot to avoid German submarines. They were nonetheless fired upon but were able to outmaneuver the torpedoes.

The 277th Field Artillery Battalion eventually landed in Reims, France, where they entered combat and were constantly in pursuit of the Germany army. In a battle in Metz, France, Ralph Antuna's back was permanently injured when the battalion was shelled by German artillery.

"We lost a lot of men there," he said. Ralph was in a field hospital for more than a month and unable to get up or move. He was treated with painkillers and heat treatments but was never transferred to a real hospital.

Because of his injury, Ralph was taken off his frontline position as an artillery gunner and placed on light duty as a driver, assigned to a communications unit that was in charge of stringing communication wire for the field telephone on the battlefield. "We were always on the go,"

he said. "It kept me busy. [General George C.] Patton wanted to know everything: where the enemies ate, how far behind they were, how close we were to them."

Philip Antuna was drafted and sent to Fort Bliss, Texas, for basic training. He was one of two Mexican Americans in the 113th Anti-Aircraft Artillery Battalion. The battalion was sent overseas, landing in Oran, Algeria, on Sept. 2, 1943, and continuing on to Algiers. From North Africa, they were sent to the invasion of southern France. "We tracked German planes, fired on them and chased them away," Philip said.

In December 1944, both brothers went into combat at the Battle of the Bulge. Taking place during one of the coldest winters in 20 years, Ralph searched through knapsacks of dead German soldiers to find food. "We had to eat it or we'd starve to death," Ralph said. "All through the war it was hard for us to get something to eat." Patton's priorities were not on food. Ralph laughingly recalled what he would say to the troops, "I know it's hard for you guys. You don't get enough sleep. You don't get enough to eat. But just think of them goddamn Germans. ... They don't get nothing either. We want to catch them."

After the Battle of the Bulge, the brothers were finally united in Marseilles, France. By Christmas 1945, they both had been discharged and returned home. After the war, both returned to U.S. Steel Corp, working there for more than 42 years.

The injury Ralph suffered in Metz still bothered him. He was a member of the Disabled American Veterans and used a wheelchair. Ralph married Dolores Hernandez on April 27, 1948. They had six children: Constance, Ralph, Paul, Maria Glena, Donna and John.

Philip married Lois Triplett and the couple had three sons: Glen, Edward and Arthur.

THE CASILLAS BROTHERS

The Casillas family of Chula Vista, Calif., had four of its seven sons serve in WWII. They were: Joseph, Ruben, Nicolás, and Joe David. Joe David Casillas was interviewed by René Zambrano on September 23, 2000, in Chula Vista, Calif. Ruben Casillas was interviewed by René Zambrano on July 13, 2000 in Chula Vista, Calif.

Felix Ledesma Casillas first came from Mexico in 1914 to work in the copper mines in Arizona. The working conditions, however, were terrible so he decided to move to California, buy some land and eventually build a house in Chula Vista where his nine children — seven sons and two daughters, Rebecca and Mary — would grow up.

All seven of his sons served their father's adopted country in the military. Unfortunately, Felix died in 1943, leaving his wife, Urbana Anton Casillas, to worry about her four oldest sons: Joseph, Ruben, Nicolás, and Joe David, coming home safely from WWII.

Her eldest, Joseph, was serving in Europe, specifically France, Belgium and Germany, with the 78th Infantry Division. Near Schmidt, Germany, Joseph saved 11 men from German machine guns. He and his squad had been left behind during the night and discovered they had to cross a road heavily guarded by the Germans. Joseph was the last one to cross and in the process was hit in the head. He was captured by the Germans for one day and a German doctor saved his life.

"Can you imagine? My mother was widowed ... when she got the really bad news that my brother had been hurt over in Germany," said younger brother, Joe David, who was still at home when the news came.

Joseph later received a Silver Star for his bravery. He earned a degree in animal husbandry from the University of California at Davis. He and his wife, Julieta, had two children, Sylvia and George. Joseph became a businessman, producing and selling furniture. A school in Chula Vista, Calif., was named after him.

While worrying over Joseph, the Casillas family waited to hear news from Ruben. "We didn't know what was going on with him but he made it," Joe David said.

Drafted into the Army in August 1944, Ruben was forced to leave his first wife, Zoa St. Clair, and his son Ruben Jr., when he began training at Camp Roberts, Calif.

His division landed in New Guinea and continued through the Pacific, engaging in combat throughout the region. The division also built bridges, roads and docks on several islands. Ruben and his unit eventually landed in the Philippines to help in the liberation of the islands.

While those around him began to crumble under the pressure of war, Ruben focused on the family he left behind to carry him through his tour of duty in the Pacific.

Ruben and his platoon were still in the Philippines preparing to invade Japan when they were informed of the war's end. He said that if the Japanese had not surrendered, he would not be alive to tell about his experiences. "If we had gone to Japan, it would have been a massacre," he said.

As his ship sailed into the California harbor on his return voyage to the United States, his elation was almost uncontrollable. "It is a feeling I'll never forget. The ship was going under the Golden Gate Bridge on my birthday," Ruben said. "Coming home: if you live to be a hundred you'll never forget stuff like that."

When he returned to the States, Ruben utilized the GI Bill, finishing high school and taking college courses. He married his second wife, Rosalie Silva, in 1949. The couple had four children: Christine, Ralph, Loretta and Paul.

The third Casillas son, Nicolás, enlisted into the Army Air Corps. He served as a mechanic and trained pilots at Chanute Field, Illinois and Yuma Air Field, Arizona. He eventually became a bomber crew chief until his discharge.

Nicolás married Paula Silva in 1946 and they had three daughters: Gloria, Mary Helen and Alice. He worked for the Registrar of Voters in San Diego County and served on the county's Grand Jury. He became very involved in the Knights of Columbus, becoming a state-wide officer.

The youngest of his brothers to enter in WWII, Joe David joined the military toward the end of the war and only weeks after the shooting part was over. "The military was in chaos," he said, recalling how everyone was trying to get out and back home.

Joe David left high school in his senior year and in October 1945 enlisted in the Army Air Corps. He trained in Sheppard Field, Texas, where he said half of the new recruits were Mexican Americans. He became a radio operator and served in a control tower for the Army Air Corps.

"It was a good experience but it was a waste of time—I could have gone to college," he said.

In 1948, Joe David started to work for the Navy as a civilian. "I started out as the lowest paid person in the department and in about four years, I became an engineering technician," he said. He attended college, mostly night school, and graduated in 1962 from California Western University—now the United States International University—with a bachelor of science degree in management and engineering.

He helped design the facility to manufacture guided missiles. "I was one of 13 engineers working to design the first factory in the world to manufacture rockets, it was one of our rockets that got the first guy on the moon," he said, adding that he was no longer with the company when that rocket was built. Joe David enrolled in law school and attended for two years at California Western but left and worked as a regional director of the Office of Economic Opportunity in the executive office of President Lyndon B. Johnson and Richard Nixon. He also worked for the Mayor of San Diego, as director of the Office of Manpower Development.

Joe David became active in the fight against discrimination, in working with the American G.I. Forum, the Mexican-American Political Association (MAPA), the Chicano Federation and the Salvation Army. He also served on the Civil Service Commission for seven years and achieved a 7.5 percent wage differential for people who were bilingual. As a member of the Planning Commission, he fought for the streets in Chula Vista to be named after WWII veterans. Joe David also founded his own organization, the North Island Hispanic Association, to fight discrimination and promote equal opportunity and job advancement.

In 1949, he married Gloria Castillo, and they had two children. His son, David Felix, is a physician, and Carol Ann is a lawyer.

The three youngest Casillas brothers also served. Armando, Ysidro and Charles served in the Korean War. Felix served in the Strategic Air Command after the conflict ended.

"All of us became solid citizens and we never got in trouble," Joe David said, proud of the way his parents educated him and his siblings. Nonetheless, he sympathizes with his mother, who bore the brunt of the family worry by herself. "It's the kind of thing that probably shortens people's lives," he said. His mother died of a heart condition in 1961, at the age of 68.

For Ruben, the war had a tremendous impact in the effort to eliminate discrimination in the lives of Latinos. "It had to change," he said. "I think it's too bad that it has taken so long for this country—the government—to realize the efforts that were put in by Latinos during World War II."

THE FALCÓN BROTHERS

Four sons of the Falcón family of Palito Blanco, Texas, served in the war: Raúl, Lorenzo, José and Alejandro. Lorenzo Falcón was interviewed by Raul Tamez, June 2, 2003, in San Diego, Calif. Supplying additional information was Emma Falcón Tamez, interviewed by her son, Raul Tamez, November 2, 2002, in Premont, Texas.

The sons of Pedro and Francisca Falcón, Raúl, Lorenzo, José and Alejandro grew up with their sisters—Amelia, Adelfa and Emma on Blue Ribbon Ranch in Palito Blanco, Texas.

Raúl was the oldest and the first to enlist in the military before the United State's entry into WWII. He joined the cavalry, stationed Ft. McIntosh, Texas. Later he was transferred to Ft. Bliss, Texas, and became part of the military police there. When the war started, Raúl joined the Army Air Corps. He served as a technical sergeant in the Pacific.

The second of the brothers, Lorenzo, was assigned to the Air Transport Command, which supported the Army Air Corps in the transportation of troops and supplies. He was stationed at Gander, Newfoundland, which—positioned on the east of Canada—served as a stop-off point for all aircraft on their way to England and Europe.

Though trained as an airplane mechanic, Lorenzo was assigned to search and rescue missions.

"There were never people to rescue. When a plane crashed, there were never survivors," he said. "We were equipped only with gloves, coveralls, boots, and when we did find bodies, we used mattress covers as body bags.

He remembered that the Hispanics in the Army had creative ways of informing their loved ones where they were stationed. For example, they might spell out the syllables of the location within a sentence in Spanish. Embedded in, *"No mando retratos porque a las cameras les falta film,"* is *"a las ca ..."* or Alaska.

Lorenzo was injured during his tour and was told that he could go home since he already had three brothers serving, but decided to stay. It was a difficult decision as he had started a family before enlisting.

José Falcón was nicknamed "Dr. F" while stationed in Pearl Harbor. In the Navy, he was a Pharmacist Mate, First Class. On Dec. 6, 1941, he was on a ship headed for San Diego, Calif. The bombing of Pearl Harbor that took place the following day altered their itinerary. The ship was carrying medical supplies to the continental U.S. But because the supplies and medics were suddenly needed back in Hawaii, they turned around to bring them back. José, though his training as a medic was minimal, returned to help the victims.

After the war, José graduated from Baylor University in Waco, Texas. The scarcity of jobs in Texas took him to Chicago, Ill., with his mother and sister, Amelia. There, he taught in public school until retirement. He died in 2000.

Alejandro was the only brother to serve in the European Theater. He was a jeep driver for the 84th Infantry Division, which entered combat in Geilenkirchen, Germany in November 1944, and he fought in the Battle of the Bulge.

In 1945, the *Corpus Christi Caller-Times* ran a story about Francisca Falcón and her four sons.

The family's tradition of military service continued to the next generation. During the Vietnam War, Raúl's oldest son, Raúl Barrera Jr. died on Nov. 24, 1969 en Binh Hoa, South Vietnam. He was 22 years old.

José's youngest son, Arthur Curtis Falcón, served in Iraq with the 4th Infantry Division, which participated in the capture of Saddam Hussein.

Alejandro's son, Alex, also served his country as a member of the United States Marine Corps. He served as a pilot from 1971 through 1976 and later served in the Marine Forces Reserve from 1987 to 2002, when he retired as a lieutenant colonel.

THE GIL BROTHERS

Four of five sons of the Austin, Texas, Gil family served: Paul, Narciso, Otis, and Simón. On Oct. 20, 1999, Andrea Valdéz conducted an interview with Paul, Narciso, Otis and younger brother, Pete.

The Gil family story is one of overcoming the Depression, discrimination and the war, which would call their sons to arms. Paul, Simón, Narciso and Otis answered the call to defend their country, leaving their home, their mother and sisters — Ruth, Julia and Sally.

"I think the suffering was here. I think that's what took my old man," said Paul Gil, the oldest of the brothers, explaining that they had all been recently married when they were drafted. "He took that pretty hard. I know because I got to see him when I got back."

After his induction into the Army at Fort Sill, Okla., Paul kept volunteering for different units in hopes of going overseas. On his way to Europe, his ship zigzagged across the Atlantic to avoid German submarines. Three days into the invasion of Normandy, the big steel door of a landing craft opened to let Paul and his fellow soldiers onto the shore of France. "You are so scared that you just don't care anymore. You're so tired, so disgusted, so everything," Paul said. "All you could hear was 'Boom!' " While doing reconnaissance through a town, an enemy machine gun let loose and Paul was wounded by pieces of a brick wall that shielded him. He was hospitalized for three days before returning to battle through France and into Germany.

He returned to wife, Lucy Ortiz. They had three children: Paul Jr., Gloria and Joe.

Simón served in the European Theater as well, leaving behind his wife, Elogia Sanchez. He had three children: Theresa, Robert and Rudolph.

Narciso had two young sons, John and Jesse, and a wife, Eugenia Aleman, at home when he boarded a ship bound for the Pacific. Shortly after the bombing of Pearl Harbor, the ship couldn't stop to unload in Hawaii and spent 35 days on the seas, before landing to train the men.

Eventually Narciso and his fellow soldiers invaded a beachhead in the Philippines, under fire. "They were unloading both sides of the boat ... we all hit land and started running," Narciso said. Behind them, the boat that brought them to shore was sunk. "So we just carried on and we got inland to where we could establish ourselves." Narciso repeated the drill twice more in the Philippines.

Narciso served as a demolition expert, disarming mines ahead of the troops with his squadron. Later, he helped in the liberation of labor camps in the Bataan Peninsula.

Otis Gil became an engineer in the Air Corps. "They do all the dirty work," he explained. "Once they would land, their job was through. Ours was just beginning." Otis also manned a machine gun mounted on a truck. He received a medal for shooting down a German plane, but remembered being so scared, he shot it with his eyes closed.

Pete Gil was only 15 by the time his brothers all left and too young to enter the service, "All I knew is that they were gone. They were gone and the families had been left behind," he said. All the Gil brothers agreed that society has changed and discrimination lessened from their school days, when they had to drink from a cup labeled "Mexican."

Pete married Frances Rocha and had three children: Vickie, Michael and Elizabeth.

After the war, Narciso became active in LULAC, the G.I. Forum and the Catholic War Veterans and added many positive changes in the way Mexican Americans were treated. He and Paul were regular members of the Grand Jury.

Otis — married to Olivia Rios — had nine children: Arturo, Alice, Otis Jr., Amelia, Daniel, David, Richard, Sylvia and Cynthia.

The Jasso family of San Antonio, Texas, saw five of their sons go off to war: Joe, Frank, Trinidad, Tomás and Antonio. Joe Jasso was interviewed in San Antonio, Texas, by his daughter, Evelyn Jasso Garcia, on July 1, 2001. Additional information on the other Jasso brothers was provided by Evelyn Jasso Garcia.

Antonio and Genoveva Jasso immigrated from Zacatecas, Mexico to work in the cotton fields of El Campo, Texas. The couple eventually moved to San Antonio, where Antonio found work as a carpenter and Genoveva ran portions of their rented home as a boarding house. They had 11 children, though two sons and a daughter died in childhood.

Antonio took all five to the train station when they were called to duty, accompanied by his eldest son, Jesús "Jesse" Jasso. At age 35, Jesse had been rejected by the military on account of five of his own children. He was anguished that he was unable to join his brothers.

Antonio did not live to see if his sons made it back from the war. He died of pneumonia in 1943 at age 56.

"It would not surprise me if my grandfather, in his conversations with God, had asked Him to bring all his sons home safely from the war ... and take him instead," said Evelyn Jasso Garcia, daughter of Joe Jasso.

If such was the prayer, Antonio Sr. got his wish and all five sons returned home after the war, reunited with their mother, older brother and sisters, Lydia and Isabel.

Frank Jasso was studious, lured to the field of journalism at an early age. He began at the bottom of the industry, selling the local paper at the St. Mary's and Travis streets intersection in downtown San Antonio. At 13, he joined La Prensa mailroom and later became editor of Lanier High School's El Nopal newspaper. He attended Trinity University.

He was drafted into the Army Air Corps in May 1942, primarily stationed stateside at Brooks Field, Texas and wrote for the Air Force magazine, The Observer.

By now the writer of the family, he helped compose "mourning notices" for family and friends for his father's funeral. The task of alerting his brothers—one in Africa, another in Missouri for basic training—fell on him.

"¡Ya acabó Papá!" he wrote them. (Father is gone.)

He later was shipped to England, where he worked in communications for the 8th Air Force.

After the war, Frank became Credit Manager at Penner's Clothing Store in San Antonio. The League of United Latin American Citizens (LULAC) twice named Frank "Man of the Year" for helping to found its *La Feria de las Flores*, an annual scholarship fund-raiser in San Antonio. He married Anita Bonillas. They had three children: Alfonso, Aida and Jaime.

Trinidad Jasso was the first to volunteer in the military. He joined the Army Air Corps on March 26, 1941. In Ellington Field, Texas, he repaired aircraft carburetors.

After the war he would return to Kelly Air Force Base and repair carburetors for 30 years. A supervisor, he was often sent to Langley Field, Va. to learn the latest technology repair work for C-47 aircraft.

His legacy would be his dancing.

"I've never seen anyone dance better to 'In the Mood,' his sister-in-law Dorothy Seevers Jasso said, recalling that Trinidad danced best when partnered with Mary Loera, the wife of one of his cousins. "They were terrific."

Trinidad married Alicia Cardenas and they had four children: Patricia, Robert, Carla and Jerome.

Tomás Jasso worked as a stock clerk at Penner's Clothing Store before the Army drafted him in January 1943. He was still in basic training in New Mexico when his father died and he was unable to attend the funeral.

Tomás served in the engineering corps as a demolition specialist in the China-Burma-India Theater. He helped to build the 500-mile Ledo Road from India to Burma, which connected with the refurbished Burma Road in attempts to wrest control of China from the Japanese.

He came home a changed man. He took his war experiences hard and was reluctant to discuss them with anyone. He worked as a bicycle courier and as a janitor at a school district. Tomás is remembered as having lived *un dia a la vez*—one day at a time—until his death at age 56.

Antonio Jasso Jr. dropped out of high school to help his mother after his father died. In 1944, he volunteered for the Navy and trained in San Diego, Calif. In the Philippines, he transported U.S. troops to shore on landing craft carriers. He was discharged on July 1, 1946.

After the war, Antonio earned his GED through the GI Bill. At age 19, he married Elodia Gomez in Seguin, Texas. The couple, though together only briefly, had two children: Linda and Eddie.

Antonio worked as a surveyor with the Texas Department of Transportation and then in Pasadena, Calif. There he met Dorothy Seevers, who would become his second wife. They had two children: Tony and Elena. He later returned to San Antonio, Texas, with his family. He was the family BBQ expert and his *chicharron* tacos were consumed with fervor at family gatherings.

When Joe Jasso—known as *el cabezudo*, or hard-headed one—was drafted into the Army, he called to tell his father with the news. *"¿Ay, m'ijo, que hiciste mal ahora?"* Antonio asked before his son could say anything. ("What have you done wrong now?") Joe told him why he had called, and the proud father later gave him his blessing, an embrace and $2 before saying goodbye.

Once in the service, Joe passed exams to be trained as a medic and then a surgical technician. At William Beaumont General Hospital, Texas, he treated the injured from the Bataan Peninsula and Corregidor Island, Philippines—many of them malnourished and dehydrated. When he graduated as surgical technician, Joe sent home the program for his family to frame in place of a diploma.

He later served in an operating room of a convent hospital in Leopoldville, Congo, and a surgeon in Port Lyautey, Morocco, and in Marseilles and Epinal, France. In post-war France and Germany, he helped control communicable disease in evacuation efforts.

Upon his discharge, Joe returned to San Antonio and worked at Brooke Army Medical Center as an operating room technician until 1952. He then returned to Kelly Air Force Base—where he had worked before the war—and eventually became a supply inspector.

In 1956, he joined the Texas Air National Guard 182d Fighter Squadron as a medic. When the unit moved to Kelly Air Force Base, he became an aero-medical technician with the 149th Tactical Unit, from which he retired at Technical Sergeant after 20 years of service.

He served as union steward and vice president to the American Federation of Government Employees and as a board member of the Legal Aid Association and the Barrio Betterment Development Corp., the latter of which he served as president.

Joe married Mary Ynman on Dec. 28, 1947. The couple had five children: Evelyn, Joycelyn, Marilyn, Joaquin and José.

THE LEÓN BROTHERS

Four brothers of the family of León family, of Arizona, served in the military during the war: George, Edward, Victor and Severino. Salvador León was interviewed by Ismael Martinez, January 4, 2003, in Phoenix, Ariz.

Immediately after the Japanese attacked Pearl Harbor, the two oldest of the León brothers were drafted. George chose to join the Navy and Edward entered the Army. Shortly thereafter, the third and fourth sons entered the military. Victor became an aviation radioman in the Navy and Severino entered the Air Corps, specializing in communication.

The youngest, Salvador, had the option of taking automatic deferment as the family's last son not in the military or serve his country. He decided to go anyway.

"My mom said, 'This country has been good to us, so you do what you think is right,'" Salvador said. "She never had any doubts that we would all come back. She had that much faith. Everybody came back. Nobody got even a scratch."

The five León brothers and their older sister, Ruth, were born to Gumesindo and Soledád León. After Salvador was born, the family moved from Hanford, Calif., to Arizona, where three more siblings: Esperansa, Josefine, María were added to the family. In 1931, Gumesindo died, leaving Soledád to care for her nine children alone. The five oldest brothers worked to help out, picking cotton, strawberries or whatever was in season.

"Just about any kind of work that came around, we did it," Salvador said. "We had a lot of mouths to feed." The boys would hunt and fish for fun, but would bring the results of their expeditions home for the family to eat.

Despite the hardships, Soledad instilled the importance of education in her children.

"My mother wanted to make sure we graduated," Salvador said. "She had hard times in Mexico and thought we could do better. Six of her children graduated high school.

Salvador was a senior at Phoenix Union High School in Phoenix, Ariz., when the United States entered WWII. The day after graduating, with his mother's blessing, the 18-year-old was on a train to San Diego, Calif., to join in the Navy. He enlisted on June 15, 1943 and was sent to Camp Elliot, Calif., for boot camp.

Toward the end of summer of that year, Salvador was shipped out into the Pacific from Bremerton, Wash., aboard the USS *Sangamon*, an escort aircraft carrier.

On Oct. 20, 1943, the ship arrived in the Gilbert Islands to support the assault on Tarawa Island, New Guinea. The crew would later participate in the Battle of Leyte Gulf, and received a Presidential Unit Citation for their efforts there and in many other battles in the Pacific.

Salvador was discharged on Sept. 22, 1945, with the rank of third-class machinist's mate, and returned to his home in Phoenix. He attended Lamson Business College for a year and, after working a series of jobs in the carpentry, began working for the city of Phoenix as a building inspector.

Salvador and his wife, Estela—whom he married on March 9, 1947—had four children: Philip, Alexander, Patrick and Patricia.

Salvador passed his mother's value of education to his children and eventually to his grandchildren, to whom he has given $5 for every A they earn in school.

Looking back over his life, Salvador is most proud of he and his brothers' service in the war.

"None of us even earned a medal. There was really nothing outstanding about our service," Salvador said. "The only thing I think is outstanding, and I'm very proud about his part, is that all five of us were in the service at the same time and overseas at the same time."

THE RIVAS BROTHERS

Manuel "Manny" Rivas was interviewed by Christopher Nay February 2, 2002, in El Paso, Texas.

Salvador "Sal" and Manuel "Manny" Rivas were born in El Paso, Texas, to Salvador and Lydia Miranda in 1925. The twins were the second oldest of their siblings, which included Julio, Yolanda and Pelicano. They attended Burleson Grammar School, where Manny often got in trouble. Since the teachers couldn't tell them apart, they were both punished with whacks across their behinds.

"I was a little fighter, always getting into fights with everybody," Manuel said.

The brothers worked after school cleaning bathrooms, wiping chalkboards and sweeping floors to earn extra money—$15 per month—as part of the federal National Youth Administration program, designed to give low-income high school and college students part-time jobs to keep them in school.

"We were like peas in a pod. We were together all the time, everywhere. We even joined the Marines together," Manuel said. They registered on their 17th birthday in El Paso and soon headed off to San Diego, Calif., for boot camp. The days began at 5 a.m. and the men were taught to "Kill! Kill! Kill for our country," Manuel said. They were eventually shipped to New Caledonia where they were placed in the 39th Replacement Battalion of the 1st Marine Division. After fighting in New Guinea and New Britain Island, the Marines went to the Solomon Islands to rest.

On Sept. 15, 1944, Manny and Sal Rivas were among the second wave of Marines to hit the beach of Peleliu, Caroline Islands, for an invasion that would last three months. The brothers fought in different platoons during the day, but sometimes shared a foxhole. Any time Manuel would come across someone who knew his twin he would ask, "Where's my brother?"

One evening, Sal was went on patrol with four men and did not return for three days. The lieutenant surmised that they were most likely dead. But Manny somehow knew this was not true and went out searching for his brother, accompanied by other Marines. "With my 'twin instinct,' I took two guys with me and we found them," Manuel said. "They were behind enemy lines and we got 'em out. My instinct, like a homing pigeon's, brought me to my brother."

After Peleliu, the 1st Marines Division headed for Okinawa, where they fought from April 1 to June 22, 1945. Manuel recalled the massive bloodshed on both sides. "We had to walk over bodies, we had to sleep with bodies. They were stinking; and there were maggots."

When the war ended in August, 1945, the brothers were stationed in China. In May 1946, they returned to San Diego and made their way back to El Paso.

Manuel used the GI Bill to earn a degree in accounting from the International Business College in El Paso, Texas. He worked for country schools for a few years before taking a job as a counselor for the U.S. Department of Veterans Affairs for the next 30 years. He married Laura Garcia in 1949 and together they had a son, Adrian. Manuel stayed active in the VFW, serving as State Commander and the National Council Administration

Salvador began working in the optical business and later opened his own company. He married Bertha Gonzales had three children: Teresa, Salvador Jr. and Eduardo.

The war shaped the twins lives forever and fortified a bond between them. Salvador remembered how their father had not wanted them to join the same branch during the war for fear of losing them both. He remembered his mother's response: "They were born together. They've been to school together. They've had their fights together. Let them be together."

THE ZEPEDA BROTHERS

Roberto, Elías, Isaac and Daniel Zepeda served in WWII. Roberto, Elías and Isaac were interviewed by Paul R. Zepeda (their youngest brother), March 17, 2000.

Four stars hung in the front window of the house of 1608 Ave. L in Bay City, Texas during WWII. Each represented a son of Guadalupe Zepeda, who fled from San Luis Potosí, Mexico because he didn't want to take part in the Mexican Revolution, and Lina Rodriguez, who grew up in the area of San Marcos, Texas.

The couple settled in Bay City, Texas, where Guadalupe worked for the Santa Fe Railroad and his wife helped raise vegetables, milk cows and tended to 40 chickens. They had 11 children: Roberto, Daniel, Rebecca, Elías, Isaac, Ester, Ruth, Sara, Marta, James and Paul. It was a close-knit family, faithful to their Presbyterian Church and hard workers. With so many mouths to feed, it was soon necessary for the older children to drop out of school to work.

Roberto got to finish sixth grade. Then, one day his father asked his eldest son if he wanted to continue school or help the family. "I said, 'I will help you, Daddy,'" Roberto later recalled. He began work as a grave digger, earning $4 a grave. In 1940, he joined the Civilian Conservation Corps, and was stationed in Arizona.

He was drafted into the Army and served with the 506th Engineer Company. The company was stationed in New Guinea and Luzon, Philippines.

Roberto said that while men, mostly from South and North Carolina, didn't harbor prejudice against Mexican Americans, there was a deep-seated hostility toward black soldiers. In Luzon, there was a black unit stationed close to his. A few of the men in unit were said to have gone "hunting colored people ... shoot[ing] them like snipers," Roberto recalled. The culprits were transferred out of the area before military officials came to investigate.

When Roberto returned home, he suffered bouts of malaria for ten years and used quinine to stabilize his health. Discrimination abounded back home, but he said, "It's in the way they [prejudiced people] grow up; it's what you have been taught by your parents."

Roberto worked for the Bay City Gas and Water Department for 29 years, installing and reading meters. He and his first wife, Paula Delgado, had two sons, Guadalupe Jr. and Robert Jr., before divorcing. He and his second wife, Tomasilla Villareal, had one son, Issais.

Both Isaac and Elías were German prisoners of war. The youngest Zepeda, Paul, recalled the day his parents received a telegram that told them that Elías was missing in action.

"Two weeks later, they received another telegram notifying them that Isaac was also missing in action," Paul explained. "My mother cried and cried and my father would try to console her ... We have always been a family grounded in faith and that, I believe, is the only thing that pulled them through those hard, trying days."

Elías had participated in the invasion of Normandy. Later in the Battle of the Bulge he and three other men found themselves hiding in a hole from the Germans when they realized that they needed to surrender. The lieutenant, who was in charge out of the four, balked at the idea, but a sergeant stood up to his superior: "I can't let them kill my men without them having any defense," he said.

Unfortunately, they had nothing with which to announce their surrender.

"All our clothes were green, we didn't have anything white," Elías said. The sergeant remembered the first aid kit, wrapped the white strips of gauze around his hand and lifted his hand out of the hole to announce their surrender.

"The Germans took our gloves and our overcoats because the snow was above our knees and they didn't have any," Elías said. "And we continued forward."

At the POW camp, the Zepeda son was surprised to learn that on the third day of not eating, he wasn't hungry anymore. Once, there were green worms floating in their soup.

After the war, Elías was set free. When he finally reached the American forces, he had his first shower in six months. "We had fleas in our clothes and everything," he said. "We took a bath and used soap and then got clean clothes." Elías and Isaac met up in Camp Lucky Strike, France, and returned home one day apart.

After his return, Elías worked as a laborer in the Bay City area. He and his first wife, Lupe DeLeon, adopted two children before getting divorced. He married Minerva Medina in 1975.

Isaac was first sent to Camp Butner, N.C., in 1942 for basic training, and trained without rifles. "We were very proud when we got real rifles and steel helmets. Now we were real soldiers."

He took part in the Normandy Invasion and fought in the Battle of the Bulge. While he was on patrol behind enemy lines, Isaac was taken prisoner.

"I felt like I was in a dream. I didn't have fear or pain or anything," he said. A German officer pointed a gun directly at Isaac's head and he stood up taller, "so he wouldn't miss." Later, another soldier said that it was Isaac's bravery that had saved him. "If that officer had killed you in front of his men, he would have lost respect of his men," he was told.

He was sent to interrogation camps and asked questions that an infantry soldier would never be privy to. From then on, he acted like "just a simple soldier," one time even responding in Spanish: *"Señor, no entiendo ni una solo palabra"* (Sir, I don't understand a single word).

The German interrogator almost fell off his chair. "How do you know how to speak Spanish?" he asked in well-spoken Spanish. "My father is Mexican," Isaac told him. "You mean to tell me that Mexico has Mexican troops here in Normandy?" the German questioned.

"And then I didn't say anything," Isaac said. "They said if you are taken prisoner, don't lie, instead don't say anything."

As a prisoner, Isaac saw German refugees from bombings arrive in the city. Half of them died of exposure to the bitter winter on the trains upon arrival and the prisoners would remove the bodies from the railroad cars.

For the living, there was no place to go. "There were ladies with babies standing all night. [The town] was just full of people," he said.

Eventually, U.S. and British planes bombed the area and the prisoners were freed and came upon Russian soldiers, who thought that the presence of American troops meant the Allies had met from opposite fronts. "They even danced with us and jumped and danced like children. They showed us their tanks and trucks ... All we wanted was food," Isaac recalled. The newly-freed Americans made their way through Germany, and eventually found the U.S. lines. Isaac was flown to France, where he found his brother.

Isaac returned to Bay City after the war and found work as a laborer for a building contractor, then in the shipping yards in Galveston, Texas, in a hardware store and finally in a rice drying company. He married Dolores Arias and with her had four children: Mary, Gloria, Yolanda and Isaac Jr.

Daniel was stationed in Bermuda during World War II.

LATINOS AND LATINAS ON THE HOME FRONT

Josephine Ledesma teaches a soldier how to repair the fuselage of an airplane at Randolph Field, San Antonio, in January 1942.

Latina Civilians who Served

World War II provided many new experiences for women on the home front. With many of the men needed on the front lines of combat overseas, the military services and bases in the United States began hiring women to fill much needed positions. There were also jobs with defense manufacturers, as the United States had embarked on a campaign to help the Allied powers arm themselves for war. President Franklin D. Roosevelt, in late 1940, called on American workers and industry to concentrate on production "Guns, planes ships and many other things have to be built in the factories and the arsenals of America ..." to supply the Allied powers in Europe.

"We must be the great arsenal of democracy. For us this is an emergency as serious as war itself," Roosevelt said. "We must apply ourselves to our task with the same resolution, the same sense of urgency, the same spirit of patriotism and sacrifice as we would show were we at war."

After the war began, production went into overdrive and, to entice women to the workplace, the U.S. government produced posters and other literature that would show that a woman could contribute to the war effort by working in factories. Rosie the Riveter became a popular figure. By the end of the war, 35 percent of the American work force would be comprised of women.

In some cities, the attention was ship and airplane building. In San Antonio, Texas, at Kelly Field, jobs were abundant.

Two sisters, Delfina Cooremans Baladez and Wilhelmina Cooremans Vasquez got jobs at Kelly Field balancing propellers on air planes. Delfina noted that the job was crucial: improperly balanced propellers would vibrate and could cause an airplane to go off course, or even crash.

At first, Wilhelmina said, the men in the shop resisted women taking what had previously been men's jobs.

The Cooremans sisters were recruited by Boeing to work in Seattle, Wash., in 1945 and they went together.

"By the time we got to Boeing, they [men] were more used to it, the war was really going. They gave us work that was too delicate for their hands," Wilhelmina noted. "It was more grown-up work."

The jobs also involved repairing equipment. Josephine Ledesma Walker, of Kyle, Texas, signed up for a six-month training class at Randolph Air Force Base, near San Antonio. Her husband had been drafted and, while she was in training, the couple's son, Alfred Jr., stayed in Austin, Texas, with her mother and her sister in-law. She would work at Bergstrom and Big Spring Army Air Fields from 1942 to 1944.

"In Bergstrom Field our duty was 'to keep them flying,'" she said. "We were taking care of all transit aircraft that came and needed repairs. You had people working on the electric part, on the hydraulic part, on the engine. I happened to work on the fuselage, the body of the plane."

Henrietta Lopez Rivas of San Antonio, Texas, got a job with the Civil Defense Department, translating for Spanish-speaking residents — advising them to keep their shades drawn at night and other measures. Later, she would also work at Duncan Field. Spanish, what had once been a liability in school now became an asset. The Civil Service Department was in need of Spanish-speaking interpreters — Rivas' income rose from $1.50 a week she made cleaning houses to $90 a month.

Not only were these Latinas in an environment where few or no other women worked, but dealt with the added factor that they were often the only Hispanic present as well. Such was the case for Ester Arredondo Perez, of Needville, Texas, who had already become the first Hispanic to graduate from her high school. At Kelly Field, she repaired airplane engines. "I was the first female engine repair [mechanic]," she said. The assignment later allowed her the opportunity to travel to Sacramento, Calif., where she underwent additional training in engine installation. In November 1944, Perez and 39 other women were shipped to Hawaii to work on aircraft that would be used in battle.

There were many clerical jobs opening up as well. And Latinas were able to enjoy those new opportunities. Betty Muñoz Medina, of Tucson, Ariz., applied for a job with Civil Service and was sent a job offer by telegram—to start working for the War Department in Washington, D.C. With the reluctant approval of her parents, she took a train there and began her job. Her first duty was alphabetizing index cards with the name and rank of a commissioned officer. Later, she would file requests for active-duty officers from different base camps.

New Perspectives

Latina women, like Medina and the Cooremans sisters, who traveled away from home, would expand their world view beyond their hometowns. There was a new sense of self-sufficiency from that experience.

"When we got back, we didn't expect anything from our parents," said Delfina Cooremans Baladez. "I mean, *we* helped our parents—not expected *them* to help us." [author's emphases]

Simply obtaining good-paying, steady employment—and feeling that they were making a contribution to the war effort—was remarkably satisfying. Josephine Ledesma Walker later would become effusive when describing her wartime work: "Oh, I loved it. I thought I was just doing a real big thing."

For women like Henrietta Rivas, who were stung by the everyday inequality that faced Mexican Americans, proving her worth alongside non Hispanics was an affirmation.

"It made me feel equal, more intelligent because what I did, very few Anglos could do," she said.

Rivas also pointed out that she was promoted in her workplace because of her ability, not because of favoritism: she was good at her job.

At the close of the war, hundreds of thousands of women were "pink slipped," as their services were no longer needed. Millions of American veterans were returning home and would take those high-paying jobs that still existed.

"They expected women to go back to their rightful place: go back to the kitchen, go back to whatever," recalled Wilhelmina Cooremans Vasquez.

The wartime experiences would transform Latinas; hundreds returned to school, many after raising their children. Women like Aurora Gonzalez Castro, a San Antonio native, who rose to a supervisory position at Kelly Air Force Base, sometimes found it difficult, as a Hispanic woman, to be treated with respect.

"But now, women are great in their professions," she said.

AGUILLON, JULIA RODRIGUEZ. She first knew tragedy when she was 10 years old, when her father passed away due to cirrhosis of the liver. As an adult Julia Aguillon would feel a deeper sorrow, when her baby was stillborn and, much later, when a daughter and a granddaughter died.

Julia Rodriguez grew up in Laredo, Texas. In 1937 she graduated high school. "I would have liked to go to college," she said, but she lacked the means. Instead, she began to work at Kress, a 5 and dime, as a sales clerk the following year. In 1942, with a wartime shortage of men, she was promoted to receiving clerk, a post she kept for the next five years. Her responsibilities included receiving merchandise and checking invoices. She also joined the Civil Defense, teaching the skills that would be necessary in the event of an enemy attack. She represented the Civil Defense in Laredo's traditional George Washington Celebration Parade in February 1943.

Her involvement in social events, friendships and work kept her busy. On one of her visits to San Antonio, Texas, 150 miles northeast of Laredo, she met her future husband. Through her childhood friend, Socorro Garcia, she met Luciano Aguillon, who had been discharged from the Army in 1945 after serving in the Philippines and Okinawa. The two married Sept. 2, 1951, and began married life in San Antonio. A year later, she gave birth to their first son, who was stillborn. Her critical condition cost all her husband's savings when they hired a nurse to care for her 24 hours a day during her week of hospitalization. The two later adopted two children: Luciano William and Laurie Ann. Laurie Ann and her daughter Pamela Ann later died in a car crash. This, the Aguillon couple's "greatest tragedy," led them to attend church every day for a whole year.

"To me, the loss of a child is the most hard ... but God will never give you anything more than you can bear," she said. "So I had faith, and we pulled through."

Julia Rodriguez Aguillon

Date of Birth
17 FEBRUARY 1917
Laredo, TX

Interviewed by
Yolanda Urrabazo
25 OCTOBER 2003
San Antonio, TX

WWII Military Unit
Civil Defense

BALADEZ, DELFINA COOREMANS. Throughout her life Delfina Cooremans Baladez did nearly everything with her sister Wilhelmina Cooremans Vasquez — including joining the work force during World War II.

Baladez and her sister took jobs at Kelly Field in San Antonio. Baladez's job consisted of balancing propellers. This was an important job, she said, because if the propellers were not balanced, the vibration could throw an airplane off course or even cause it to crash. In 1945, Baladez was recruited by Boeing to work at its Seattle plant and her sister followed.

The sisters left San Antonio, Texas, for three reasons: Boeing paid better, they felt it was their patriotic duty and, for two young women who had been "cloistered" their whole lives, it was an adventure. They rented a room in the home of a married couple and continued to live according to the values their parents had instilled.

The experience "made me more independent," Baladez said. "When we got back, we didn't expect anything from our parents," she said. "We helped our parents, not expected them to help us."

The sisters said they drew much of their strength from the strong example their mother set when they were growing up. Their parents were both immigrants — their father, Johannes Cooremans, was Dutch and their mother, Ofilia Cruz Cooremans, was Mexican.

Left for a time in McAllen, Texas, with her five children, Ofilia Cooremans got a job for the first time and struggled through new circumstances — including living in a rough neighborhood.

"We were not prepared for what we had to go through, but my mother was bound and determined to hang in there until Daddy got back," Baladez said.

She married Albert E. Baladez and had two sons: Albert N. and Daniel John.

Delfina Cooremans Baladez

Date of Birth
23 MARCH 1924
Álamo, Veracruz, Mexico

Interviewed by
Brenda Sendejo
9 JULY 2005
San Antonio, TX

WWII Location
Kelly Air Field and Boeing Aircraft in Seattle, WA

Aurora Gonzalez
Castro

Date of Birth
31 AUGUST 1925
San Antonio, TX

Interviewed by
Anna Zukowski
25 OCTOBER 2004
San Antonio, TX

WWII Location
San Antonio, TX

CASTRO, AURORA GONZALEZ. While a student at San Antonio Vocational and Technical High School, she was a clarinetist in the school band; ever since, Aurora Gonzalez Castro's life has been linked to music and musicians.

She met her first husband in the high school band, where he played brass instruments. Caesar Castro and Aurora Gonzalez married in 1945, after they graduated. Shortly after, Caesar enlisted in the U.S. Army, where he served as a member of a military band.

Castro was a secretary for the State Department of Public Welfare at Kelly Field in San Antonio, Texas, during the war, and she said the war allowed Hispanic women to be more independent, because they could earn higher salaries than before.

Castro eventually rose to supervisor, overseeing military service records. In her 39 years in the Civil Service, Castro said she sometimes had difficulties as a woman in a leadership position.

"But now, women are great in their profession," she said.

Castro and her two sons joined Caesar in Tripoli, Libya, in 1954. "We had a chance to travel, like to Istanbul, Turkey, but I was afraid to travel by myself with my two boys," she said. "It seems like I was always afraid of traveling alone with my boys without my husband. I was afraid to get lost."

After the Army, Caesar was a freelance musician until his death in 1966. "I would like people to remember him as a very, very intelligent person ... with great musical ability," Castro said.

Following the death of her oldest son, Caesar Charles, in 1968, Castro grew close to her late husband's half-brother, Alfred Castro, also a musician who served in a military band in World War II. The two married in 1968, and Alfred worked as a highly acclaimed musician. He died in 2003. Castro is the proud mother of Jacqueline, Alfred, Mark and Caesar, all of whom went to college.

Elena "Helen"
Pimentel Guerra

Date of Birth
16 SEPTEMBER 1917
San Antonio, TX

Interviewed by
Markel Riojas
6 NOVEMBER 2004
San Antonio, TX

WWII Location
San Antonio, TX

GUERRA, ELENA "HELEN" PIMENTEL. Censorship was a crucial part of American strategy during WWII, in order to keep enemy forces from intercepting information that could supply information about the location of troops and the next planned attack. Elena "Helen" Pimentel Guerra was responsible for much of that censorship, and spent a good part of WWII blacking out letters and intercepting correspondence from Spain and Mexico.

Born Elena Pimentel, she was the child of Mexican immigrants who made education a priority for their children. Her parents stressed the importance of proper manners, and taught their children perfect Spanish diction and grammar. She learned English in school, a huge challenge that she eventually met. She graduated valedictorian of her high school and was teaching at the Catholic Ursuline Academy when WWII began.

After her sweetheart, Juventino Guerra, left to serve overseas, she began working with Naval Intelligence. She monitored Spanish international telegrams and long-distance phone calls, translating much of what came from Spain and Mexico. She enjoyed her work as she diligently blacked out all words that were deemed too sensitive by the military.

Following the war, Juventino returned and the two were married. The Guerras had four children: Cristina, Juventino, Olga and Victor. Much like her own parents, Guerra encouraged her children to pursue their education, and all four earned degrees.

Guerra became active in local civic and religious organizations, working with the Altar Society, Parent Teacher Club and Maternity Guild. She also worked to increase voter turnout, going door to door to encourage citizens to register to vote, and was active with the Democratic Party.

LEDESMA WALKER, JOSEPHINE KELLY. With the United States producing more than 250,000 airplanes from 1939 to 1945, air craft played a major role in the war, and Josephine Ledesma helped keep them ready for battle. "In Bergstrom Field our duty was 'to keep them flying,'" she said. "We were taking care of all transit aircraft that came that needed repairs."

She volunteered to work as an airplane mechanic after her husband, Alfred Ledesma, was drafted. While his duty later was waived when officials learned of the couple's 5-year-old son, Ledesma had already signed up for her six-month training class. At training at Randolph Field, she was the only Mexican-American woman. After training, women were less scarce—two Anglo women worked at Bergstrom—but at Big Spring Army Air Field in Big Spring, Texas, she remained the only woman working in the hangar.

One typical approach to the work was having several people working on one plane. "You had people working on the electric part, on the hydraulic part, on the engine," she said. "I happened to work on the fuselage, the body of the plane." Ledesma, who was 24 when the war broke out, worked as a mechanic between 1942 and 1944. "Oh, I loved it," she said. "I thought I was just doing a real big thing." After the war she returned to work as a sales clerk and homemaker and later, among other jobs, as a nurse for 14 years.

The daughter of John Kelly and Josephine Barrera, Ledesma grew up in a country house in Kyle, Texas, with her parents and her grandparents. One grandmother on her mother's side was said to be a distant relative of José Antonio Navarro and a great-grandfather on her father's side was a full-blooded Sioux. Ledesma and her husband had four children: Alfred, John, Dolores and Linda. After husband Alfred died, she married Elco Walker.

Josephine Kelly Ledesma Walker

Date of Birth
25 FEBRUARY 1918
Kyle, TX

Interviewed by
Mónica Rivera
17 FEBRUARY 2001
Austin, TX

WWII Location
Bergstrom Air Field Base, TX, Big Spring Army Air Field, Big Springs, TX

MEDINA, BETTY MUÑOZ. During WWII, commissioned military officers received deployment orders by telegram, often believing that they had been called up for duty by their senator. Little did they know the assignments were actually issued by people such as Betty Medina.

Medina got an entry-level job at the War Department in Washington, D.C., when she was 20, alphabetizing 3x5-inch cards with the name and rank of a commissioned officer. She was then promoted to filing lists of requests for active-duty officers from different base camps.

She would randomly match a request with one of the index cards. "We didn't even look at the names; we just looked at the ranks and handed them to the supervisor," she explained.

One day Medina arrived at work to find several high-ranking officers in the office. Her supervisor confronted her and asked if she ever read the race listings on the forms. Frightened for her job, she replied that she hadn't. "From now on, be sure to do that," the supervisor said. Medina had assigned a black officer to a white unit—something she had never thought's of as an issue. "I didn't know anything about discrimination," she said. "This was the first time I had heard the word."

Meanwhile, Medina's brother Paul was in the South Pacific in the Army Medical Corps. She corresponded with Paul regularly, but all soldiers' letters were censored. "Lots of times [the letters] were cut off and you wondered, 'What did he want to say?'" she said. Medina and her brother circumvented this by developing a code. In her letters, she designated a certain salutation ("Dear Betty," etc.) for each area that he could be stationed, and he used the salutation that corresponded to his current location. "I'd always know where he was by following that code," she said.

Medina eventually returned to Tucson, Ariz., and continued to work as a state employee. She married Jess Medina and raised two step-children: Michael and Patsy.

Betty Muñoz Medina

Date of Birth
19 JULY 1921
Tucson, AZ

Interviewed by
Olga Briseño
5 JANUARY 2003
Tucson, AZ

WWII Location
Washington, D.C.

Ester Arredondo
Perez

Date of Birth
25 APRIL 1920
Needville, TX

Interviewed by
Erika Martinez
23 MAY 2002
San Antonio, TX

WWII Location
Stationed at Kelly
Air Field, TX

Transferred to
Honolulu, HI

PEREZ, ESTER ARREDONDO. San Antonio resident Ester Arredondo Perez always worked hard to accomplish her goals either at work or play, whether traveling the world or becoming the first Latino high school graduate in Fort Bend County, Texas.

Ester Arredondo graduated from high school in 1939. Her father sent her to San Antonio, Texas, after her graduation, where he believed she would have more opportunity to use her education on the job. She lived with an uncle and worked for Steve Sash and Door Co. where she helped make cabinets. During the war, her duties were reassigned to making lockers.

In January 1942, she went to work for Kelly Air Field, Texas. At that time, the military was hiring women to replace the men going into battle.

"I got a job at Kelly Field and there again, I was the first female engine repair [mechanic] at Kelly Field," she said excitedly, noting that she was the only Latina there, too.

To satisfy her wanderlust, she volunteered for overseas duty but told her family she was being forced to go. Her mother was not fooled. Despite their objections, she traveled to Sacramento, Calif., to master engine installation. After her training, in November 1944, she moved to Hawaii, to begin work as an engine mechanic. She was among 40 other women shipped to Hawaii to work on aircraft intended to fly into battle.

In 1946 she returned to San Antonio to fulfill her dream and attend nursing school. After graduation she worked at Robert B. Green Hospital (now University Hospital) from 11 p.m. to sunup in the men's ward.

She met Edward Perez, who also worked at Kelly Field, at her nursing school roommate's wedding. They married in 1950 and had three children: Edward, Ernest and Denis.

Henrietta Lopez
Rivas

Date of Birth
14 FEBRUARY 1924
San Antonio, TX

Interviewed by
Veronica Flores
6 JUNE 1999
San Antonio, TX

WWII Location
Civil Service
Department and
later Civil Service
at Duncan Field,
San Antonio, TX

RIVAS, HENRIETTA LOPEZ. Growing up on the South Side of San Antonio, Texas, Henrietta Lopez Rivas encountered obstacles because of her Mexican heritage; however, as an adult this same heritage brought her success and fulfillment.

Her mother, a native of Monterrey, Mexico, took pride in her children's education. By the time she started school Henrietta Lopez already knew her multiplication tables and could read — in Spanish. But the education system was unsympathetic to the needs of its Spanish-speaking students, and she failed the first grade because she did not know English. At the age of 14, Rivas began to work as a migrant farm worker. Then she returned to San Antonio and worked cleaning houses.

In 1942, though, the war changed the economy. What had once been a liability in school (speaking Spanish) now became an asset. The Civil Defense needed interpreters to help inform Spanish speakers of Civil Defense responsibilities. She went from making $1.50 a week to making $90 a month — and she found a sense of equality. She was valuable because of her heritage. "It made me feel equal, more intelligent because what I did, very few Anglos could do," Rivas said.

At this time she also met Ramón Martín Rivas, who was home on leave from his assignment in Dutch Harbor, the Aleutian Islands.

She then took a series of tests to secure a job repairing airplane instruments in the employ of the Civil Service at Duncan Field. Her exceptional ability paid off in a promotion to assistant supervisor of her department. Ramón returned after the war and the couple married on Feb. 11, 1945. They had seven children: Robert, Irma, Henrietta, Carmen Aida, Maggie, Concepción and Guadalupe. Her experiences during the war gave Rivas a strong sense of independence and self-reliance, which she tried to instill in her children.

THOMAS, MARÍA ISABEL SOLIS. Looking back, Isabel Thomas remembered her little-girl dreams of becoming a teacher or a nurse, but money and the war altered her dreams. María Isabel Solis and her sister, Elvia, moved from Brownsville, Texas, to Richmond, Calif., to become "Rosie the Riveter" welders, welding pipes and repairing cargo ships. "It [the war] was in full force," Thomas said. "They needed us to go and help them to build these ships to get them out because they needed the ammunition, they needed the food and they needed to transport these boys where they had to go." Recruiters wanted small, short and thin women for crawling into dangerous places in the ships. Thomas worked nine-hour days, six days a week, striking and sealing steel rods with precision and purpose. "I was proud because, man, I did it just exactly the way they wanted [me] to," she said. "And here I come out, and they said, 'Hi, shorty. You did pretty good.'"

While working in the shipyards, she loved the Navy, the work she did and the camaraderie. She remembered trading clothes and sharing soap. "We shared as if it were one big, happy family," she said. She did, however, learn not to make assumptions when she met Italian-American and Portuguese-American women. Her sister chastised her for assuming the women were Mexican and speaking Spanish, to them just because of their facial features.

She married James A. Thomas, who fought in the South Pacific. Her husband, an Anglo, shocked her parents when he asked for her hand in marriage. They had not realized the couple had been dating; previously their daughter dated only Mexican Americans. Eventually the two received her parents' blessing and they married in 1944. Thomas later lived with her in-laws after she was no longer needed at the shipyard, while her husband was still in the South Pacific. The couple's son James A. Thomas Jr. later served in the Air Force during the Vietnam War.

María Isabel
Solis Thomas

Date of Birth
10 MARCH 1923
Veracruz, Mexico

Interviewed by
Anna Zukowski
13 OCTOBER 2003
Brownsville, TX

WWII Location
Richmond, CA

VASQUEZ, WILHELMINA COOREMANS. Eager to follow in her older sister's footsteps, Wilhelmina Vasquez—15 when the war started in 1941—joined sister Delfina Baladez in the WWII work force in early 1942. Vazquez, then Wilhelmina Cooremans, had relatives in Holland, as her Dutch father had immigrated to Mexico, where he met her mother, in 1903. The daughters were not allowed to join the civil service in Washington, D.C. Instead, they took jobs at Kelly Field (now Kelly Air Force Base) in their hometown of San Antonio.

When the sisters began working, the men viewed the new women in the workplace as a nuisance. "The men were more resistant because it was something so new it'd never happened before," Vasquez said.

When her sister was recruited by Boeing to work at its Seattle, Wash., plant in 1945, Vasquez was not allowed to go because her mother thought she was too young. But she cried until her mother let her move to Seattle, too. There, the workplace seemed more welcoming, the men less hostile.

"By the time we got to Boeing, they [men] were more used to it, the war was really going. They gave us work that was too delicate for their hands," Vasquez said. "It was more grown-up work."

When the sisters returned to San Antonio after the war, however, some attitudes had not changed. "They expected women to go back to their rightful place: go back to the kitchen, go back to whatever," Vasquez said.

On Jan. 17, 1946, she married Refugio Miguel "Mike" Vasquez, a native of Laredo, Texas. Mike had served in the Civilian Conservation Corps for 18 months and then served for two tours of duty—nearly four years—with the 756th Tank Battalion in Italy, Northern Africa and Central Europe. The two had two sons, Michael and René.

Wilhelmina
Cooremans
Vasquez

Date of Birth
11 NOVEMBER 1926
McAllen, TX

Interviewed by
Brenda Sendejo
9 JULY 2005
San Antonio, TX

WWII Location
Kelly Air Field
and Boeing Aircraft
in Seattle, WA

Chapter Seven

EVERYDAY LIVES OF LATINOS AND LATINAS DURING WWII

Carmen I. Albelo and her son, Gene Albelo in Manhattan, New York in 1948.

Everyday Lives of Latinos and Latinas during WWII

Life at home changed drastically during WWII. The struggle for survival during the poverty of the Depression flowed into survival during the war. After the Japanese attack on Pearl Harbor and the declaration of war by the Axis Powers, the U.S. had a unifying goal: defending the country. Those who stayed Stateside were performing many activities that supported the troops' efforts overseas, they were often said to be in a different campaign: that of the Home Front.

Younger siblings watched as their older brothers marched to war and helped their families as they could: conserving gasoline, recycling rubber and metals, buying war bonds, planting Victory Gardens, knitting sweaters for soldiers far away. New jobs opened up as the demand for supplies and equipment in the war effort grew and millions of men were drafted, thus workers were needed to take the place of those men.

U.S. Latinos and Latinas were part of those efforts; they, too, were caught up in the spirit of sacrifice to a larger cause. At home, they stayed busy and productive, while waiting for the war to end, waiting for their loved ones to return.

Living Without a Husband

Many of the men called to arms were recently married and left young wives, sometimes pregnant, or with small children, at home while they trained at bases across the United States, before going overseas. These young wives were expected to keep the fires burning and wait for their men, hoping and praying that their husbands would return home safely. They anxiously listened to the radio for news from the fronts of war and feared telegrams that would inform them that their beloved was injured, missing or killed in action.

Lina Martinez Cordova had two children with her husband, Alfredo, before he was drafted and fought in France, Germany and Austria. She wrote to him two or three times a week.

"Every night I would pray, 'Please God, bring him home,'" she recalled. "I didn't care how he [came] home—without an arm or a leg—as long as he came home to me and the kids."

Cordova recalls that telegrams, delivering bad news, brought at night were delivered by bicycles with small headlights. One night, she watched an approaching bicycle light and froze, afraid it was headed for her home. But it passed and she breathed a sigh of relief.

In some cases, couples married just before the men shipped out.

"He told me he wanted someone to come home to," Ventura Terrones Campa, of Newton, Kan., said of her husband. She married Diego Campa in September 1942—they were high school sweethearts—and was pregnant before he shipped out. Two of her brothers, Eugene and Alfred, also enlisted, Eugene in the Navy and Alfred in the Army.

"All I did was worry," Campa said. "I didn't want them to be killed."

When Diego Campa returned, he was greeted by his wife, and a new daughter.

Sandy Acosta Fuentes met sailor Toby Fuentes in 1944 and married him three days later. He proposed to her the night they met, but she told him she wanted a traditional wedding. Remarkably, a very motivated Toby Fuentes was able to arrange everything in three days: the church, the rings, the wedding dress.

On June 6, 1944, Lillian Hollingsworth Ramirez was baking gingerbread cookies for a neighbor's birthday party at her home in Biloxi, Miss. Her husband, Oswaldo Ramirez, was half a world away and, unknown to her, storming the beaches at Normandy. Every time she walked into a room, either her brother-in-law, Rafael, or friends would switch off the radio—wishing to keep news of the invasion from her. She didn't think too much about it, but later that afternoon, when she went to deliver the cookies to her neighbor, it all made sense. Her neighbor asked: "Well, what do you think about the invasion in Europe?" Lilian H. Ramirez ran home and learned that her husband's unit, the 16th Infantry of the 1st Infantry Division, was at Normandy. The following day, listening to her radio, she heard her husband's name.

"He was alive, and he had been on the beach and he had rescued some of the wounded out of the water," she said. "I suppose he had been nearby where the correspondent had been talking. That's how I knew he was alive: I heard it on the radio after D-Day."

The Ramirezes had been married in March 1943, after two and a half years of letter-writing and only seven face-to-face meetings. She wanted to marry him before he went overseas so he would fight hard to come home to her. She gave birth to their first child in April 1944.

In essence, many wives became single mothers trying to raise a family. While some were able to live off their husbands' military pay, others took jobs. Carmen Irizarry Albelo, a native of Puerto Rico who lived in New York during the war, worked briefly as a seamstress. But when she learned her nanny was leaving her infant son alone, she hastily left her job and took care of him full time, working odd jobs to scrape by until her husband, Gene Albelo, returned from the Navy.

Communication

Mothers, wives, girlfriends and sisters could only keep in contact with their loved ones through letters. "He used to write me and send me money … he used to say he missed me," said Trinidad Nerio of her husband, Arnif Nerio.

The correspondence was often censored, because the military wanted to keep the whereabouts of the troops secret from the enemy. "It made them awfully hard to read," remarked Eva Maria Rains Archuleta, of Las Tusas, N.M., often frustrated by the letters she received from her husband. "I didn't keep any of those letters."

Many developed their own private codes to circumvent military censors.

Many soldiers, like Austin's Martha Ortega Vidaurri's brothers, were able to let their family know where they were through codes, inside jokes, familial references or nonsense phrases in Spanish. One of her brothers wrote, "tell the boys to save me some Mexican beer." Vidaurri went through all the beers and figured out it was Carta-Blanca, so her brother must be stationed in Casablanca.

The codes were used throughout the war, tricks that developed during desperate times.

Siblings

Many younger siblings were left home, some barely aware of why their brothers were overseas. Herminia Guerrero Cadena, of Central Texas, for instance, worked in the fields as a young girl, she and her family pretended weeds were Nazi or Japanese soldiers.

"I didn't recognize the importance [of the war] until my brother went in," she said. When she was 9 years old, though, her brother enlisted in the Marines and was sent to Guadalcanal. Later, after his return, she invited him to her school, to her sixth-grade class, to show him off.

Older siblings watched as young men entered the war, and found them changed when they returned. Davie Elizardo, in San Diego, Texas, was the oldest of 12 siblings. She took care of the family, including her brother, Cipriano, who was drafted into the Army.

"His mind was different when he came back," she said.

Job Opportunities

Manuel Cavazos Cadena, of Luling, Texas, was too young to serve, although he would later, his two older brothers helped build the San Marcos Army Air Field in Central Texas. After the base was completed, one brother worked in maintenance and the other worked as a bus boy.

Women also got unprecedented opportunities to work while the U.S. work force had gone overseas to fight. Noting that for the first time it was socially acceptable for women to work outside of the war, Aurora Estrada Orozco made buttons from seashells and sewed them to soldiers' uniforms.

Carmen Esqueda Abalos worked at the carpentry shop — sorting nails, moving lumber and cleaning walls — at a Santa Rita, N.M., mine while her husband was in the Navy.

"[The soldiers] were doing a job over there," Abalos said. "So they had to have a replacement over here. [We were] just looking forward to seeing them coming home."

In the small New Mexico mining town of Santa Rita, most of the male mine workers were drafted or enlisted. Dora Gutierrez Madero got a job in the mines, and worked her way up. Her first job was greasing switches on trains, so they could descend into the open pit mine and transport the ore.

"I had a bucket of grease and a little brush," Madero said. The job took all day, walking back and forth ensuring that the train could safely pass and pick up the copper.

She had a couple of other jobs at the mines, before she was able to work in an office, out of the elements.

Such were the activities on the home front, as Latinos and Latinas did what they could to support the war effort.

Women on the Home Front

Support of the troops took many forms. Teresa Herrera Casarez, of Austin, Texas, joined a group of college students who performed for soldiers at USO clubs and at Camp Swift, Texas.

"We did the typical dances, the jarabe tapatio, the zandunga ... just about any dance that was typical at the time," she said. "For every different dance we did, we had a different costume."

Herlinda Buitron Estrada, of Bastrop, Texas, baby-sat for soldier's families at Camp Swift, Texas, and remembers conserving scrap metal and buying savings stamps that went toward war bonds.

Cooking meals on rations was sometimes difficult. Zoila "Sallie" Castillo Castro remembered the strict rationing of food and goods that were needed for the war effort. "When [the stamp books] were gone, you couldn't purchase any more, even if you had the money," Castro said. "We managed. [My mother] had learned when we lived in the country."

Castro was in high school and had four sisters; there were no brothers to be drafted.

"I was young when the war broke out," said Castro. "I was taken care of and well-fed."

She and some friends got together often to write letters to the servicemen. They called their club "Blue Horizon." They would exchange names of friends and family that they knew overseas, just to keep their spirits up.

Carmen B. Salaiz
Esqueda Abalos

Date of Birth
16 MAY 1920
Morenci, AZ

Interviewed by
Brenda Sendejo
15 JULY 2004
Hurley, NM

WWII Location
Santa Rita, NM

ABALOS, CARMEN B. SALAIZ ESQUEDA. During World War II, Carmen Abalos helped the war effort by taking a job that once belonged to men—working in a mine.

"[The soldiers] were doing a job over there," Abalos said. "So they had to have a replacement over here. [We were] just looking forward to seeing them coming home."

While her husband Mike Abalos was serving in the Navy, she helped at the Kennecott mine in Santa Rita, N.M. She worked at the carpentry shop, sorting nails, moving lumber and cleaning walls. "It didn't matter who worked, women or men, as long as the work got done," she said.

When she was just 5 months old, her father abandoned the family. When her mother remarried, she was adopted by her stepfather, and she changed her name from her father's surname, Salaiz, to her stepfather's, Esqueda. The Esqueda family moved to Colorado for a time, and she helped her stepfather stack hay. They moved back to New Mexico, where she was able to enjoy her youth.

She married Mike Abalos in August 1941. They had a son, Mike Jr., before Mike Sr. left for duty in the Navy. The couple would have four more children: Rodolfo, Richard, Pat and Arlena.

During the war years, she said, Mexican Americans were treated poorly—they had to enter the mine through a different entrance than Anglos, and they lived in different parts of town, separated by railroad tracks. She told a teacher at her children's school: "You are no better than I am, and I am no better than you are! These men are going overseas and they don't care what color you are."

She volunteered with VFW and Disabled American Veterans. She held various officer positions in both organizations. Of her work, she said: "We are still right behind them ... working to support our veterans."

Josephine Trujillo
Aguilera

Date of Birth
21 OCTOBER 1921
Deming, NM

Interviewed by
Maggie Rivas-
Rodriguez
15 JULY 2004
Hurley, NM

WWII Location
Deming, NM

AGUILERA, JOSEPHINE TRUJILLO. When she compares her life to that of her daughters, Josephine Aguilera sees how far women have come: she dropped out of school in the eighth grade, but her daughters not only graduated from high school, they even went to college.

"They knew more than I did," she said.

When she did not understand some aspects of the hysterectomy she was about to undergo, her daughters were able to explain it to her. "It's hard when you don't know how to explain yourself," Aguilera said.

Born Josephine Trujillo, she grew up in Deming, N.M., during the Depression. Times were tough, but, she said, "We just got used to it."

She worked in housekeeping and took care of other people's children after she quit school.

"I couldn't ask for anything more because I wasn't educated," Aguilera said.

She was 16 years old when she married Manuel Aguilera, who was 19. They had two sons before Manuel left to fight in World War II. She remembers that her sons, who did not remember their father, were scared of him based on the photograph they had hanging in their home and the stories she would tell about him and his deep voice.

When Manuel returned, they had a daughter. Aguilera remembers her husband saying, "I'm gonna take care of this baby all the time."

But when the baby cried, he didn't wake up, and she had to tend to the child, she said, laughing.

They moved to Hurley, N.M., in the 1950s. They had four children: Gilbert, Manuel, Yolanda and Thelma. Aguilera and her husband worked in a mine until they retired. When he retired, Manuel renovated their house and built several additional rooms.

ALANÍZ, GLORIA ARAGUZ. The third of eight children, Gloria Araguz Alaníz was just 15 when her dying mother asked her to take care of her siblings.

Gloria Araguz
Alaníz

Date of Birth
16 APRIL 1927
McAllen, TX

Interviewed by
Yvonne Lim
18 OCTOBER 2000
Austin, TX

WWII Location
McAllen, TX

Her mother asked her specifically to be sure her sickly 5-month-old brother, Arturo, was baptized. The whole family prayed for Arturo for several days but he passed away shortly after his baptism. Alaníz helped raise the rest of her siblings until she had a family of her own. She helped her brothers recover from illnesses ranging from measles to lockjaw.

When 6-year-old Alfred came down with the measles, she used a salve of baking soda and shortening to ease the itch.

"He got well. Those home remedies that were used a long time ago, now you find them at H-E-B [grocery store]," she said. "Praise the Lord."

She was working at the jewelry counter of the C.R. Anthony department store when she met Sgt. Rodolfo "Rudy" Alaníz in 1951. The couple married on Jan. 21, 1952. Rudy Alaníz caught pneumonia on their honeymoon and Gloria Alaníz fell ill shortly after. She later joined her husband in Fort Bliss, Texas.

They had four children and moved around the world, following Rudy's military assignments. Alaníz said the family was able to live comfortably on a military salary in Germany, but struggled at times in the United States.

"But we were happy," she said.

Alaníz settled in Austin, Texas, with her husband, where she became an active member of St. Ignatius Catholic Church.

"At my age, I want to see my Jesus face-to-face," she said, "when it is His will."

ALBELO, CARMEN IRIZARRY. Decades later, Carmen Albelo remembered her expectations for a land of opportunity when she left Puerto Rico for the United States in 1939. The challenges she found there surprised her. "When I came here I thought I was going to have a better life," Albelo said. "But it wasn't like that."

Carmen Irizarry
Albelo

Date of Birth
1 OCTOBER 1925
Sabana Grande, PR

Interviewed by
Helen Aguirre Ferré
14 SEPTEMBER 2002
Miami, FL

WWII Location
New York, NY

Carmen Irizarry was born in Sabana Grande, P.R., in 1925. Her mother moved to the United States in 1933, seeking work, and sent for her and her brother in 1939. From the start, Albelo said she could tell that her stepfather did not want her around.

"So I told my mother, 'I'm going to get married,'" Albelo said. "I didn't want my mother, because of me, having problems."

She was engaged to her neighbor, Higinio Albelo, within two years of moving to the United States, and she was ready to move out of her stepfather's house.

The couple married Nov. 19, 1941, and Albelo gave birth to Higinio "Gene" Albelo Jr. in 1943, after three days of intense labor. Her husband was visiting his parents in Puerto Rico before being sent to fight with the Navy in World War II, and missed the birth of his son.

Albelo tried to work as a seamstress while her husband was away but quit after she discovered that the nanny was leaving Gene alone for hours at a time. Higinio did odd jobs for extra money, and the family scraped by. Higinio surprised the family with a visit at Christmas one year.

"That was so nice, because my baby was happy, I was happy, and he was happy," Albelo said.

When Higinio returned after three years at war, the couple had a second child, Mary Carmen. Both of the Albelo children graduated from college. In the end, Albelo said, she achieved all she set out to do when she came to the United States in 1939.

Eva Maria Rains
Archuleta

Date of Birth
20 OCTOBER 1926
Las Tusas, NM

Interviewed by
Adrianna Lujan
3 NOVEMBER 2002
Santa Fe, NM

WWII Location
Las Vegas, NM

ARCHULETA, EVA MARIA RAINS. Growing up in the small town of Las Tusas, N.M., the family of Eva Maria Rains Archuleta was not wealthy. The simplest trips to neighboring towns were a treat, and she and her three sisters would have to share a single gift at Christmas.

Unlike many families she remembered from her youth, her parents encouraged their seven children to go to school. "My father always told us that he wanted us to have an education," she said. "He told us it didn't matter if other kids teased us about our old clothes or that we wore the same dresses every day. He told us to pay no attention to them."

She was teased by white students at school, especially if she spoke Spanish, and white students were given preferential treatment by teachers.

Rains met her future husband, Bennie Archuleta, when she was a 16-year-old at Highlands Training School. Bennie left to fight with the Army in 1943, and she worked while he was gone.

"Sometimes I would get his letters in the mail and parts would be cut out," Archuleta said. "We never knew why the Army was doing that, but it made them awfully hard to read. I didn't keep any of those letters."

The couple married in June 1946 and had four sons: Tony, Bennie, Ruben and Anthony. Archuleta returned to high school at 36 and graduated with one of her sons, Bennie, in 1967. "It was the first time in the history of West Las Vegas [New Mexico] that a parent had graduated with their child," Archuleta said.

Society is more accepting of Hispanics today than it was when she was young, Archuleta said. She said young Hispanics should not be afraid to stand up for themselves. "Don't let people tell you that you can't do something, because you can," she said.

Imogene "Jean"
Davis Avalos

Date of Birth
12 JULY 1920
Hico, TX

Interviewed by
Karin Brulliard
18 OCTOBER 2003
San Antonio, TX

WWII Location
Mineral Wells, TX

AVALOS, IMOGENE "JEAN" DAVIS. On her first day as a clerk at Eckmark photography studios at Camp Walters Army Base in Mineral Wells, Texas, Imogene "Jean" Davis noticed handsome photographer Alfred Avalos, who went by "Pat" because he was born on St. Patrick's Day. "Well, you don't know the town very well," Pat told her. "We'd better go on a date."

Three weeks after their first date at a barbecue restaurant, the two married. Sept. 28, 1942, marked the beginning of a long, loving marriage. It also introduced Jean Avalos, an Anglo, to the discrimination her Mexican-American husband had known for years, when she set out to find an apartment.

"That's when I found out there was a difference" in the way many people treated Latinos and Anglos, she said. "He was Hispanic and I wasn't, so I could get an apartment and he couldn't," Avalos said. "It was such a shock to me. ... I wasn't taught that there was two different kinds."

She spent most of her childhood in Crystal Falls, Texas, a close-knit rural community where she and her four younger siblings played and attended school with the Mexican and Mexican-American children who lived nearby and learned some Spanish.

Following her marriage, Avalos ignored the disapproving stares and raised eyebrows at the couple. Her family adored Pat, and his family treated her "like a queen." Just two months after their marriage, Pat was drafted into the Army and left for Europe with the 112th Infantry Regiment, 28th Infantry Division. Avalos, pregnant with their first child, rushed to the mailbox each day; Pat often sent love letters and photos of himself in front of French cottages and Belgian bridges. After the war, Pat stayed as a photographer of war crimes, such as concentration camps. Not until he returned did Avalos learn Pat had been wounded during the Battle of the Bulge. The couple had three children: Jeannie, Michael and Kathy. Pat had one daughter, Amalia, from a previous marriage.

BARRERA, PLACIDA PEÑA. When Placida Peña met her future husband, she said he was "too quiet." But Raymundo Barrera pursued her over the years, writing letters to her while he was stationed in Delaware during World War II, and the couple married in 1950.

Throughout Raymundo's years in the Air Force, the couple moved every few years, including a three-year stint in Tokyo, Japan, and bases in Vermont, Kansas and Maine.

"Maine was very primitive," Barrera said. "We had no gas ... and we were without a refrigerator."

Barrera was born in Guerra, Texas, the eldest of three children, and she remembers life during the Depression as tough but manageable.

"The county commissioner would hold back relief goods because it wasn't profitable for the stores in town," Barrera said. "We really didn't get too much help from anyone or anything."

She enrolled in Texas A&M University-Kingsville after graduating from high school in Mission, Texas, but her family's financial situation meant that she could not complete her degree.

When she married Raymundo, she kept busy traveling and raising six children. After Raymundo's retirement from the Air Force, the couple relocated to Laredo, Texas, where they pursued further education.

Barrera earned a degree in political science and Spanish from Texas A&M International University in Laredo at age 52. Her husband earned a degree in political science and law enforcement, and they taught for the United Independent School District in Laredo until their retirement.

She said that she is "very happy with the way [her] life has turned around." She is the proud parent of Nora, Raymundo, Cynthia, Sandra, Carlos and Judith, and has 22 grandchildren and nine great-grandchildren.

Placida Peña
Barrera

Date of Birth
13 JULY 1926
Guerra, TX

Interviewed by
Virgilio Roel
28 SEPTEMBER 2002
Laredo, TX

WWII Location
Guerra, TX

CADENA, HERMINIA GUERRERO. The war was a time when her sister worked in a firearms plant, her father left the fields to work in a foundry, and Herminia Guerrero Cadena and her 13 siblings ate carefully rationed food. She and her family worked in the fields, and they pretended that the weeds were Nazis or Japanese soldiers.

When Herminia Guerrero was 9 years old, her brother left to fight in WWII. Though she knew about the war before, his absence made the fighting real to her.

"I didn't recognize the importance [of the war] until my brother went in," Cadena said.

She brought her Marine brother to school for show-and-tell in sixth grade, but she said he rarely talked about his time at war, where he fought in Guadalcanal and searched for Japanese soldiers hiding in caves.

Her family moved from the Hill Country, southwest of San Antonio, Texas, to Saginaw, Mich., while she was still in school. She said the teacher at her mostly Anglo school had trouble pronouncing Herminia and called her "Minnie" instead, a name that she hated, but one that stuck with her through school. She was the first member of her family to get a high school diploma.

She married Manuel Cadena, whom she met at a baseball game, when she was 21 years old. The couple eventually had six children.

In the first years of her marriage, she was active in the Chicano civil rights movement. She participated in letter-writing campaigns, fasted on Thanksgiving, and brought her children along to march in civil rights protests. She said Latinos' status has improved since she was a girl. "We went from living in houses with dirt floors, no indoor facilities of any kind, to our children having $250,000 homes; from my parents never going to school to [our children] having college degrees."

Herminia Guerrero
Cadena

Date of Birth
29 NOVEMBER 1932
Fall City, TX

Interviewed by
Ismael Martinez
4 JANUARY 2004
Saginaw, MI

WWII Location
San Antonio, TX

Manuel Cavazos
Cadena

Date of Birth
18 OCTOBER 1932
Luling, TX

Interviewed by
Antonio Cantú
25 JUNE 2002
Austin, TX

WWII Location
Lockhart, TX

CADENA, MANUEL CAVAZOS. As a boy during World War II, Manuel Cavazos Cadena remembered his grandmother praying every day to a statue of the Virgen de Guadalupe—which she kept in a corner of her room—for the safe return of his uncle, Eluterio "Ted" Estrada, then a prisoner of war in Germany.

Cadena was born in 1932, in Luling, Texas, the sixth of 10 children of immigrants from Nueva Rosita, Coahuila, Mexico. He worked in the cotton fields from a young age, and his father was a sharecropper and cotton picker for Martindale, then the world's largest cotton mill. "I can't remember at what age I started. It's like swimming—it just happens early," Cadena said. "We would get a pillowcase, fill it and then put it in our dad's sack."

Their family worked at the whim of the landowners; sometimes they were paid to burn crops. "In one year, you would move three times, but that was because you were poor," he said. "That's what happened to a lot of people, especially during World War II. When us guys talk about it, we laugh, because Dad never paid the rent. There was no money."

Cadena studied in a three-room elementary school in Martindale and was later bused to school in Lockhart, Texas. "There was a junior high school, we called it *'la escuela de los güeros'* [the Anglo school]," Cadena said. Two of his brothers got jobs at San Marcos Army Air Field, seven miles west of Martindale, because of the war. When the base was built, one brother was a maintenance worker and another was a bus boy in the mess hall.

His family moved to Saginaw, Mich., in 1947 because his father found work opportunities there. He married Herminia Guerrero in Saginaw, and the couple had six children. He worked as a welder at the Grey Iron Foundry for 28 years.

Ventura Terrones
Campa

Date of Birth
14 JULY 1921
Newton, KS

Interviewed by
Delia J. Lujan
1 AUGUST 2003
Newton, KS

WWII Location
Newton, KS

CAMPA, VENTURA TERRONES. Expecting that her high school sweetheart would be sent to war, Ventura Terrones married Diego Campa 3 months before he enlisted.

"He told me he wanted someone to come home to," Campa said. When Diego Campa returned, two people would be waiting—Campa and their new daughter, Gloria.

The couple married in September 1942 and Diego left soon after, as did Campa's brother Eugene, who enlisted in the Navy, and her brother Alfred, who enlisted in the Army.

"All I did was worry," Campa said. "I didn't want them to be killed."

She worried that the Germans might invade the United States, but life in Kansas, went on quietly.

Campa, born Veronica Terrones, lived at home with her parents, immigrants from Guanajuato, Mexico, while her husband was overseas. The family had what they needed to survive, she said.

"We never had food trouble," Campa said. "We always had food, even during the Depression. I used to take the wagon down to Dillon's [grocery store] and fill it up with cantaloupes, oranges and apples for 50 cents."

She saved the money she made working at an egg-packing plant, sorting eggs and plucking chicken feathers, hoping to make a down payment on a house and save for her children's college education.

Her husband and her brothers returned safely from the war.

The couple took their children—Gloria, Patricia, Becky, Carol, Roger Edward and Tomás—on trips to the Rocky Mountains because they reminded him of the mountains in Germany, Campa said. Her husband insisted that the children speak only English, but they learned about Mexican traditions, including food and holidays.

CÁSAREZ, TERESA HERRERA. Growing up in Austin, Texas, Teresa Herrera Cásarez loved to sing, dance and recite poetry. During World War II, she put those skills to work as an entertainer at USO clubs and Camp Swift in Bastrop, Texas.

"[For] *Cinco de Mayo* (5th of May) and *Diez y seis de Septiembre* (16th of September) *fiestas* ... my mother helped me to learn *poesias* (poems)," Casarez said. "She ... made sure I learned a different one for every year. ... People had no other form of entertainment. ... We looked forward to putting on the big show."

At age 16, she joined a dance troupe that performed at Zaragosa Park throughout the war. She was the only person in her family to graduate from high school, and one of only three Hispanics to graduate from her high school in 1945. She also joined a group of University of Texas students who performed for soldiers from 1944-46.

"We did the typical dances, the *jarabe tapatio*, the *zandunga* ... just about any dance that was typical at the time," she said. "For every different dance we did, we had a different costume."

Her brothers, Raul and Abdon Herrera, served in the war and she kept in touch with a soldier she met before the war, Pete Cásarez, who was stationed in Guam. The two married in 1948.

As a young woman, Cásarez was active in the League of United Latin American Citizens (LULAC), and participated in its activities.

She worked as an accountant for the IRS, from which she retired in 1988 after 20 years, arranging her schedule so that she could be at home for her children, Pete Jr., Carlos, Herlinda and Veronica.

"In order to get ahead, you need to get educated, and you need to be a responsible person," she said. "You need to know that as a citizen ... you have an obligation to cast your vote."

Teresa Herrera Cásarez

Date of Birth
21 APRIL 1926
Bertram, TX

Interviewed by
Joanne R. Sanchez
11 OCTOBER 2000
Austin, TX

WWII Location
Austin, TX

CASTRO, ZOILA "SALLIE" ANTONIA CASTILLO. When the United States entered the war, none of Sallie Castro's immediate family had to serve—they were all female. Today, she is the proud wife, mother and grandmother of veterans.

She was in high school when the war started, and formed a club called "Blue Horizon" to write letters to soldiers. Members would exchange names of family and friends who were overseas.

She remembers the strict rationing of food and goods that were needed for the war effort. "When [the stamp books] were gone, you couldn't purchase any more, even if you had the money," Castro said. "We managed. [My mother] had learned when we lived in the country."

Castro was born in San Marcos, Texas, in 1927, and her father died just a month after her birth. Her mother raised her and her four sisters alone until she remarried and moved the family to Austin, Texas, when Castro was 12. She lived with an aunt and uncle in Toledo, Ohio, toward the end of the war and remembers the celebration there on D-Day. "It was a riot," she said. "People were hugging and kissing. It scared me half to death. I was still pretty much a country girl."

After the war, Castro was involved in the League of United Latin American Citizens (LULAC), where she met her husband, World War II veteran Ladislao Castro. The couple married Aug. 21, 1948, and Ladislao later fought in Korea. Their son Jimmy fought in Vietnam and their grandson James fought in the Gulf War. She credits these wars with helping improve life for Hispanics.

"I guess the war did it because of all the connection the boys had," Castro said. "I mean if you need to jump into a foxhole, I imagine you didn't question who was in it or what color they were. They basically learned to deal with it, and then through them, we did."

Zoila "Sallie" Antonia Castillo Castro

Date of Birth
13 JUNE 1927
San Marcos, TX

Interviewed by
Nicole Griffith
1 MARCH 2001
Austin, TX

WWII Location
Austin, TX;
Toledo, OH

Lina Martinez Cordova

Date of Birth
8 MAY 1921
Pena Blanca, NM

Interviewed by
Maggie Rivas-
Rodriguez
2 NOVEMBER 2002
Albuquerque, NM

WWII Location
Albuquerque, NM

CORDOVA, LINA MARTINEZ. While her husband was fighting in France, Germany and Austria, Lina Cordova was living with his parents in Albuquerque, N. M. She wrote letters to Alfredo Cordova two or three times a week, and prayed continually for his safe return.

"Every night I would pray, 'Please God, bring him home,' " Cordova said. "I didn't care how he [came] home — without an arm or a leg — as long as he came home to me and the kids."

Lina Martinez met her future husband when she was 15, and they married when she was a senior in high school. The couple lived with her husband's parents while Alfredo worked at an ice cream parlor for 15 cents an hour. They moved to San Diego, Calif., in 1943. Shortly afterward, Alfredo was drafted, and they bought a Plymouth for $150 and went back to Albuquerque.

Cordova said that during the war, as she sat on the porch writing letters, she would sometimes see the tiny lights of a bicycle messenger. She knew these riders delivered bad news, and would pray that they would not stop at her house. "One night they gave me a scare," she said. "[The messenger] was looking for an address. My heart sank. Luckily, it was not for me."

During the war, Cordova and her two children, Naida and Alfredo Jr., abided by her in-laws rules. Her father-in-law was very protective, and he put her and her husband's car on blocks, because he didn't believe she needed to be out while her husband was away.

"When I was young, every decision was made by my husband," she said, adding that today she and her husband are equals. "I guess he has figured sometimes my ideas were better than his."

Two years after Alfredo left, Cordova spotted his name in a list of men returning from war, published in a local paper. A third child, Dorothy, was born after Alfredo returned.

"God was good to me," Cordova said.

Ascencíon Ambros Cortez

Date of Birth
12 MAY 1926
Laredo, TX

Interviewed by
Desirée Mata
25 OCTOBER 2003
San Antonio, TX

WWII Location
Laredo, TX

CORTEZ, ASCENCÍON AMBROS. The sacrifices the men in her life made for their country brought Ascencíon Cortez to tears. Her husband Hernán, lost his right hand, while her brother, Enrique Ambros, lost his life. She remembered that both served their country with enthusiasm.

Enrique had become head of the household of seven children after Cortez's father died, so the loss of her brother was especially devastating. She said it was like losing another father.

Through all of the trials she faced, Cortez remained a devoted wife and mother, often reading the Bible and relying on her Christian faith to carry her through.

Cortez married her husband when she was 15, and when he left for the war, she was already pregnant with their first child.

Hernán served as a medic in the Pacific during the war, and Cortez remembered receiving letters from Hawaii. Her husband even sent her a Bible he received an Evangelical meeting while he served, and Cortez began reading it regularly.

Cortez was 17 years old when Hernan returned to the States, missing his right hand. "One day a grenade hit the foxhole where he was tending to an injured man," she said. "He picked up the grenade to throw it back and it exploded in his hand."

Anguished by the pain of losing his hand, Hernan entertained thoughts of suicide, but ruled it out. At a hospital in Temple, Texas, he learned how to write, eat and tie his shoes with only his left hand. He went on to become a police officer for the Laredo Police Department, private detective, notary public and a debt collector. He was even able to play the organ at their church.

Cortez and her husband had 11 children: Irma, Hernan, Ruth, Herlinda, Juan, David, Diana, Noemi, Rosa Hilda, Rosa Elda and Martha.

CUELLAR, DELFINA JOSEPHA LUJAN. When Delfina Lujan Cuellar was growing up, girls were not expected to finish school. They were supposed to marry and have children.

Delfina Josepha
Lujan Cuellar

Date of Birth
8 MAY 1925
Albuquerque, NM

Interviewed by
Maggie Rivas-
Rodriguez
20 NOVEMBER 2002
Albuquerque, NM

WWII Location
Albuquerque, NM

"We were very deprived of getting more education," said Cuellar, who completed eighth grade. "They thought that we would be too free and have babies before marriage and things like that, and so I didn't go to high school."

She said their family did not have the hardships some experienced during the Depression. "There are some people who had a very hard time," she said.

Even though her family had very little, her mother was always ready to share what little they did have.

"Once in a while people would come and ask Mother for a cup of this and a cup of that. My mom would help people that needed food and whatever."

The war affected many families in her neighborhood. "We would hear about so many people that we knew," Cuellar said. "Their sons were killed. There was a lot of grief."

At the end of the war, "there were flowers and flags when the world was at peace, she said. "It was beautiful when the war was over. Everyone was praying on the streets, singing."

Six years later, she married Louis A. Metzgar, who had been stationed at Pearl Harbor. The couple had two daughters, Yolanda and Lois, before divorcing in 1963, much to the disappointment of Cuellar's Catholic mother. Cuellar married her second husband, WWII veteran Joe Cuellar, in 1975, who she considers a great hero.

She is glad her daughters got an education. "Now they [Latinas] are free to talk, to be whatever they want," she said. "Like my girls — they got educated, and they're doing good."

DIMAS, BEATRICE ESCUDERO. Growing up on the outskirts of El Paso, Texas, Beatrice Dimas rarely was allowed to go out. But on Valentine's Day 1942, her father made a rare exception, allowing her to go to a fiesta at the San Antonio Church in El Paso.

Beatrice Escudero
Dimas

Date of Birth
23 NOVEMBER 1923
El Paso, TX

Interviewed by
Maggie Rivas-
Rodriguez
4 JANUARY 2003
Phoenix, AZ

WWII Location
Fort Meade, MD;
Phoenix, AZ

That night, Alfred Dimas, a soldier, spotted her from across the room. "He said, 'See that girl in the pink dress? I'm going to marry her,'" she recalled. "And he did."

The couple dated for a few months, in spite of warnings from her parents, and on July 22, 1942, they got married. "My mother said it wasn't going to work out because he was in the service," Dimas said. "But here I am, married 61 years to the man!"

Shortly after they married, Alfred was sent to Fort Benning, Ga., then to Fort Meade, Md. There he sent for his wife, who had been living with Alfred's parents. They soon found out they were expecting a child.

Alfred was injured while parachuting out of an airplane and, permanently disabled, he never fought in World War II. After a stay in a military hospital, the couple moved to Phoenix, Ariz., where Alfred had a hard time finding a job. "Luckily for us, [Alfred] was highly intelligent and got a job," Dimas said.

Dimas, who had not graduated from school, was determined to get an education. She earned her GED in 1973 and her associate's degree in Spanish in 1985. Her husband went to school for leather-crafting and supported their family. "I have never fallen out of love with that fellow," she said.

They had four children: Alfred, Rudolf, Daniel and Caroline.

"It's been a good life," Dimas said. "We've had our ups and downs like everybody else, but we've been able to overcome them."

Davie Elizardo

Date of Birth
29 DECEMBER 1919
San Diego, TX

Interviewed by
Israel Saenz
29 NOVEMBER 2003
Alice, TX

WWII Location
San Diego, TX

ELIZARDO, DAVIE. She never attended a day of school; instead Davie Elizardo worked hard her entire life. She said that the thing she cares about most is her family.

"I just want that my grandchildren find good work and not have to struggle." Elizardo said. "They have very good opportunities."

When Elizardo was young, she worked in the fields. The oldest of 12 children, it was her responsibility to help her family by working in the fields near her home of San Diego, Texas.

"They didn't pay us much," she said. She remembers earning around $5 per week at that time. She did, however, enjoy working with the animals, including goats, pigs and sheep.

During World War II, her brother Cipriano was drafted, and he served in the U.S. Army. "His mind was different when he came back," Elizardo said.

Elizardo enjoyed horseback riding, going to the movies and sewing when she was growing up. "I would sit on the bed, sew by hand and make my own dresses," she said.

After the war, she worked at Rancho Colorado, near Alfred, Texas, about 50 miles west of Corpus Christi. The Orange Grove Naval Auxiliary Landing Field was near the ranch, and she remembered that the ranch owner threatened to sue because the noise from the planes was disturbing.

She had a daughter, Diana Elizardo, in 1961, when she was 42 and working at Rancho Colorado. Her family, especially her sister Rosa, helped her raise Diana.

Her two grandchildren both have bachelor's degrees, and she said she is very optimistic for their future. "We had more opportunities for education [after WWII]," Elizardo said. "And today we can have even more."

Gregoria Acosta
Esquivel

Date of Birth
12 MARCH 1931
Lockhart, TX

Interviewed by
Laura Herrera
11 NOVEMBER 2002
Austin, TX

WWII Location
Austin, TX

ESQUIVEL, GREGORIA ACOSTA. When Gregoria Esquivel was young, her uncles served in World War II, and their involvement and heroism affected Esquivel her whole life. She remembers visiting one uncle in the hospital after he was wounded in Luxembourg.

"I always feel a lot of respect for the military people when there's a war, because I think it just stayed with me," Esquivel said. "I wanted to do something to participate and help, so I went into nursing."

Gregoria Acosta was raised by her grandparents in Lockhart, Texas. She recognized the importance of learning at an early age. "My grandfather used to say, 'If you're going to go anywhere, you need to go to school and you need to get your education,'" she said.

Even as her family lived off food purchased with WWII-era food stamps, Esquivel attended school. She translated for her grandparents when she was as young as 6 years old.

She remembered experiencing discrimination during the war. "At that time, [segregation] didn't bother me," Esquivel said. "I felt like that's the way it was supposed to be."

Moving to Austin, Texas, helped her realize that there was an alternative to segregation, and she said the end of WWII brought positive changes for Latinos. "I did notice that when the soldiers came back from World War II, there was a lot of education in the families, like they were inspired while they were in the military," she said.

She married Harry Esquivel in 1952, and they had five children: Debbie, Edward, Jeanette, Tamara and Patricia. She became a licensed vocational nurse in 1955. In 1986 she earned the "Best of Brackenridge" award at Brackenridge Hospital in Austin for her exemplary patient care and excellence in teaching new nurses. "I think I have met all my goals that I had in life," she said.

ESTRADA, HERLINDA MENDOZA BUITRON. As the war took the men in her life around the world, Herlinda Estrada stayed on the home front, caring for the children of soldiers serving abroad and working in the Texas cotton fields.

Herlinda Mendoza
Buitron Estrada

Date of Birth
17 JUNE 1930
Bastrop, TX

Interviewed by
Gloria Monita
19 OCTOBER 2002
Saginaw, MI

WWII Location
Bastrop, TX

While her brother served in the Pacific theater, and her future husband, Johnnie, worked as an engineer in Europe, Estrada, born Herlinda Mendoza Buitron, made regular trips to Camp Swift, Texas, to baby-sit at the base. She remembered conserving scrap metal and buying saving stamps, which went toward war bonds. Despite the tough times, Estrada said her youth was a happy one.

"We didn't realize we were poor or anything," she said. "Because everyone was in the same condition. We had a good life."

Estrada studied hard, with her older sister teaching her English and mathematics before she entered elementary school. She became so proficient that she eventually began keeping records of her family's work hours and the pounds of cotton they picked during the summers when they traveled and worked in the fields. Her meticulous recordkeeping ensured that the family received the maximum payment for their labor.

Following the war, Estrada's family left Texas for Michigan. It was there that she met her husband. He knocked on her door one day, asking for help to complete a WWII scrapbook he was compiling. The two married on Nov. 1, 1947.

Johnnie worked for General Motors, while Estrada remained at home, raising the couple's five children.

After her children were grown, Estrada returned to school to earn her high school diploma then worked in a bakery until her retirement.

FUENTES, SANTOS "SANDY" ACOSTA. At the age of 28, Santos "Sandy" Acosta had given up hope of marriage. However in 1944, she was swept off her feet by a sailor, whom she married just three days later.

Santos "Sandy"
Acosta Fuentes

Date of Birth
21 APRIL 1916
Buda, TX

Interviewed by
Karla E. González
13 OCTOBER 2000
Austin, TX

WWII Location
Austin, TX

Toby Fuentes proposed to her the night they met, but she insisted on a traditional church wedding. He told her, "We'll go to church tomorrow and we'll do everything we need to do."

"And he did," Fuentes said. "He bought my wedding dress, and he bought my rings, and then in three days we got married."

The newlyweds headed west to Vallejo, Calif., where they stayed until Toby was shipped overseas. They had not been there long when Fuentes remembered her husband telling her it was time to go.

"He just told me, 'Well, I've got to send you home, 'cause they just told us the ship is ready and we're gonna go out to sea,'" Fuentes said.

Time passed slowly while Toby was gone. Fuentes remembers writing and receiving letters about how much they loved each other. She said Toby was very romantic, writing in code to get around the censors and tell her where he was stationed.

In 1945, the letters stopped coming. Fuentes did not know if her husband was alive. One day, however, Fuentes was out having coffee with a friend when she spotted her husband.

"I couldn't believe that he was home," she said.

Fuentes was already working as a cosmetologist. Eventually, she owned two hair salons in Austin. Her son followed in her footsteps, opening his own salon. The couple raised four children: Rolando, Martha, Cheryl and Joanna, all of whom graduated from Del Valle High School.

Elizabeth
Ruiz Garcia

Date of Birth
2 JULY 1924
Austin, TX

Interviewed by
Hannah McIntyre
2 FEBRUARY 2000
Austin, TX

WWII Location
Austin, TX

GARCIA, ELIZABETH RUIZ. The horrors of war took their toll on her husband Willie, but Elizabeth Garcia became the force that helped him rebuild his life after the war.

Garcia, born Elizabeth Ruiz, was the daughter of immigrants from Monterrey, Mexico, and she grew up with seven siblings. The family embraced their heritage, and Spanish was spoken at home, with her parents constantly correcting the children's grammar to ensure their speech was perfect. She learned English at Our Lady of Guadalupe Catholic School in East Austin, Texas.

In 1944, a friend introduced her to Willie Garcia, who was stationed at Camp Swift, Texas. The two dated for three months, and two days before he left for his tour of duty overseas, they married.

Willie served in North Africa and Italy, transporting ammunition by train each night. He returned from the war 100 percent disabled, having suffered the effects of post-traumatic stress disorder, or "shell shock," as it was more commonly known.

"The stress was so bad he couldn't eat, he couldn't walk," she said. Willie stayed in the hospital for nearly a year before he could come home.

She was warned by doctors he might become violent, but he never laid a hand on his attentive wife and they later moved in to a home they built together.

They later adopted two children, Ann Marie and Elizabeth. Garcia worked tirelessly to give them a life full of opportunities she did not have growing up. She bought each daughter a car during her senior year of high school and never burdened the girls with cooking and cleaning.

Garcia and her husband were active in their church, attending Mass six days a week and helping distribute communion. The couple, eager to help others, worked with elderly individuals in their community, taking them to appointments and helping them with everyday chores.

Victoria Partida
Guerrero

Date of Birth
28 SEPTEMBER 1924
La Feria, TX

Interviewed by
Elizabeth Aguirre
19 OCTOBER 2002
Saginaw, MI

WWII Location
Saginaw, MI

GUERRERO, VICTORIA PARTIDA. With her fiancé in the South Pacific, Victoria Partida nervously awaited his return. A phone call in May of 1946 set her mind at ease. Her future husband, Luis Guerrero, had been discharged from the Marine Corps and was preparing to reunite with his love.

Raised in the Rio Grande Valley of South Texas, Guerrero enjoyed school, and her teachers worked hard to ensure that Latino children and Anglo children related to each other; she did not feel any discrimination.

The couple met in 1941, with Luis instantly declaring that he would marry Victoria Partida. After he obtained permission from her father, the two began dating. Their outings were always chaperoned by her younger brother, Pedro. Luis Guerrero enlisted in 1943, and the couple's wedding plans were put on hold when he left for the Pacific. He spent time in Guam and China, sending letters to his bride-to-be from each exotic location.

"We wrote back and forth all the time," Guerrero said. "The fear [that he could be killed or wounded] was within you constantly."

She and her family prayed for peace and stayed close to the radio, waiting to hear the names of those soldiers who had been killed in battle. Guerrero lost two cousins in the war.

As she and her family conserved sugar, clothing, coffee and meat, Guerrero worked in the fields to help feed the nation and the troops abroad. She worked side-by-side with German POWs, and was often scared they might escape.

Once Luis returned, the two married on June 23, 1946. They lived in Raymondville, Texas, until the birth of their first daughter, Ester. The family then moved to Michigan, and lived with Luis' family. The couple had three more children: Diane, Patricia Ann and Catherine Gloria.

LÓPEZ, ELVIRA ORTA PARDO. The memories of her brothers' valiant service are what stood out most in Elvira López's mind when she reflected on the WWII era. One cousin, Rogelio, was killed in Europe during the war.

"He never came home," López said.

López' parents were originally from San Luis Potosí, Mexico, and had settled in Goliad where they raised three sons and three daughters. All the children helped in the harvesting of cotton, corn and beans.

Apolonio, or "Polo" as he was affectionately called by family and friends, was 21 years old when he was called to serve. López admired her brother's devotion to family. He had quit school in fifth grade so he could work on the family farm to help support his siblings.

She remembered his service in Europe and North Africa, and his injuries, for which he earned a Purple Heart.

While her brother was at war, López stayed at home, helping her family, doing chores and cooking for the household. Pardo's mother died of pneumonia in 1940 so the housekeeping fell on her.

When the war ended, López remembered that there was no celebration at her home, just anxiety about Polo's return.

He did return on March 30, 1947. He married and moved to Detroit to make a better life for his new wife Romana Layton and their five children: María, Delma, Rene, Nelda and Paul Mark. Unfortunately, he was murdered in 1960, in a case of mistaken identity.

More opportunities are available to Hispanics today because of veterans like her brother and the sacrifices they made for their country, she said.

Elvira Orta
Pardo López

Date of Birth
6 SEPTEMBER 1925
Goliad, TX

Interviewed by
Wilfredo Pardo
López
20 JUNE 2003
Edinburg, TX

WWII Location
Goliad, TX; Elsa, TX

LUJANO, LORENZA TERRONES. The daughter of Mexican immigrants from Guanajuato, Lorenza Lujano devoted herself to providing a better life for her family and giving them opportunities she did not have growing up. With perseverance and an unshakable work ethic, she was able to make that dream a reality.

During her childhood in Kansas, she worked diligently on her musical skills, learning to play the violin. She was largely self-taught, because her family could not afford lessons.

At school, she felt the sting of racial prejudice, as Mexican Americans were in the minority and had little power. Finally, tired of the discrimination, she left school in the 10th grade.

She began working for Hurst Poultry and Egg Co., plucking feathers from dead chickens and sorting through eggs. She worked alongside German POWs during the war years. The prisoners lifted heavy crates and filled other jobs left vacant by soldiers serving overseas.

In her spare time, Lujano played on Newton's female basketball squad. The team was a mix of ethnic groups, and Lujano counts a victory against a team from Witchita on Independence Day as one of the fondest memories of her youth.

While Lujano worked at the poultry company to support her family, her two brothers served in the Army and Navy. Her brother Gene introduced her to one of his fellow sailors, Ángel Lujano, during the Christmas holidays, 1946. The two married on April 17, 1948.

Lujano stayed at home to raise her four children—Dilly, Alice, Anna and Ernesto—until they reached college age. To help finance her children's college educations, she started working as a housekeeper and her husband worked three jobs. It paid off: four earned their degrees.

Lorenza Terrones
Lujano

Date of Birth
5 SEPTEMBER 1927
Newton, KS

Interviewed by
Patricia Aguirre
1 AUGUST 2003
Newton, KS

WWII Location
Newton, KS

Dora Gutierrez
Madero

Date of Birth
11 JULY 1926
Silver City, NM

Interviewed by
Robert Rivas
7 JULY 2004
Arenas Valley, NM

WWII Location
Santa Rita, NM

MADERO, DORA GUTIERREZ. Despite a foreman's prediction that women would fold within months of taking jobs in the mines of Santa Rita, N.M., Dora Madero was determined to prove him wrong and demonstrate women's strength.

When most of the men in her hometown volunteered or were drafted during the beginning of the war, she was eager to fill the vacancies left by the soldiers. Born Dora Gutierrez, she began her workdays at 8 a.m., and she put in 40 hours every week. She remembered that women and Native American men stepped up to fill the void when local men were drafted.

Madero began at the bottom and worked her way through the ranks, constantly being given more responsibilities and more challenging jobs. She began by greasing switches so trains could easily come in and out of the mine to pick up ore. She then worked as a water girl, navigating the underground tunnels while she carried large bags of water to groups of women working in the mines.

Madero then was put in charge of ensuring that the rail lines that went in and out of the mines functioned properly. She and another woman monitored the lines from a motorized cart, which they rode through the mine.

After her labor in the harsh weather outside and in the mines, Madero was finally given one of the most prized promotions—a chance to work in the mine's office.

Despite her hard work, Madero remained modest, and said she had it easy compared to many.

"I didn't do anything compared to the others," she said. She worked in the mines for over two years, until the war ended.

Madero had a son and a daughter, Robert and Virginia Sandoval, from her first marriage. She married Robert Madero, a WWII veteran who served in England and Germany, in 1961.

Juanita Tapia
Montoya

Date of Birth
15 MARCH 1926
Santa Fe, NM

Interviewed by
Adrianna Lujan
3 NOVEMBER 2002
Santa Fe, NM

WWII Location
Santa Fe, NM

MONTOYA, JUANITA TAPIA. While soldiers took to the battlefield overseas, people at home, including Juanita Montoya, worked to ensure the country's resources were preserved. Born Juanita Tapia, she was ever mindful of the sacrifices being made abroad, but rarely stopped to think of the sacrifices she made on the home front every day.

"In those times, we didn't care if we didn't have a turkey on the table at Thanksgiving," she said. "Everyone was poor then because of the war ... in those days, we didn't have the good things; we just made do with what we had."

The youngest of 14 children, she lived with her grandparents after her father died when she was 18. She stayed with them until she married Maclovio Montoya on Sept. 18, 1946. Her husband was a WWII veteran and later served in Korea. She remembered the pain of separation during his service.

"I went through the mail three times a day," she said. "And when I didn't get mail for months, I felt real bad."

Montoya remained strong in the face of the challenge of caring for her family alone, hauling water to the house for drinking and cleaning. She chopped wood to warm her home, all while caring for her two children during her husband's service.

"It was hard," she said. "My son used to go pray to San José, so that he would come back. I give thanks to God that he is alive and complete. We had a wonderful life when he came back."

Montoya and her husband had five children: Gertrude, Santos, Elizabeth, Maclovio and Susan. She said that once her husband returned, the two shared responsibilities and built an adobe-style home.

NERIO, TRINIDAD AYALA. Beginning a life with her husband, Trinidad Nerio was settling into a brand-new home and pregnant with the couple's first child when the war began. The draft interrupted the newlywed's bliss and her husband, Arnif, entered the Army in 1942.

Born Trinidad Ayala, she lived in Mexico until age 6, when her family moved to Texas. She eloped at age 16 with her first husband and had two children, Jack and Gloria. The two divorced, and she began working in a restaurant.

During one evening out with her sister and friends, she met Arnif Nerio. Trinidad was three years older than Arnif when they married, something family and friends enjoyed teasing her about.

"Oh that little boy you married!" she remembered friends saying.

When Arnif left for the war, Nerio returned to work to support her family. With her wages from the restaurant where she worked, coupled with the money Arnif sent home, she was able to make a comfortable life for her children, and she stayed strong despite the painful separation from her husband.

"He used to write me and send me money ... he used to say he missed me," she said of her husband of nearly 60 years. "Those were good letters. He's been a good man."

After he was discharged, her husband was home for a mere two weeks before he was called to serve again.

Nerio stopped working to focus on her children, after her husband returned a second time. Armida, Menlinda and Arnif Jr. were from her marriage to Arnif, but she said he always treated Jack and Gloria as his own.

"They call him 'Dad' and they're all married now. We've had a good life," she said.

Trinidad Ayala
Nerio

Date of Birth
22 JULY 1918
Piedras Negras,
Mexico

Interviewed by
Elizabeth Aguirre
19 OCTOBER 2002
Saginaw, MI

WWII Location
Saginaw, MI

OROZCO, AURORA ESTRADA. When the work force shrank as the draft took many men from the jobs, Aurora Estrada Orozco later recalled how she quickly stepped in to fill the void.

Born Aurora Estrada in Serralvo, Nuevo Leon, Mexico, she left the country with her family when she was about 5 years old and moved to Mercedes, Texas.

While she was excited to move to the States, the transition was still trying for her. "In Mexico, we were living better," she said. "But then we came to the U.S., and we had to start all over, and we didn't know how to speak English."

A child of the Depression, she began working at age 10, picking cotton with her father. Despite their financial trouble, the family regularly gave food to those who had even less.

When the war began, she watched as her male relatives were called to serve. As the young men of Mercedes left for the war, the town changed, its mood darkened and its streets were often emptier.

"We didn't have fiestas anymore," Orozco said. The townspeople cried often and the Christmas holidays were sad.

She watched as the town had its first military funeral and huddled by the radio to listen to President Franklin D. Roosevelt address the nation. The town also strictly rationed, and she often went to Mexico to buy things like leather shoes and sugar.

She entered the work force during the war. She made buttons from seashells and sewed uniforms for soldiers. She remembered this as the first time it was socially acceptable for women to work outside the home. After the war, she met her husband, Primitivo Orozco, an immigrant from Guadalajara, Mexico, at a Mexican fiesta in town. The couple married and had six children. All six earned college degrees.

Aurora Estrada
Orozco

Date of Birth
8 MAY 1918
Seralgo, Mexico

Interviewed by
Desirée Mata
17 OCTOBER 2003
Austin, TX

WWII Location
Mercedes, TX

Bernarda Lazcano
Quintana

Date of Birth
21 AUGUST 1927
Ciudad Juárez,
Chihuahua, Mexico

Interviewed by
Yazmin Lazcano
6 FEBRUARY 2005
Austin, TX

WWII Location
Ciudad Juárez,
Chihuahua, Mexico

QUINTANA, BERNARDA LAZCANO.   As a young girl, Bernarda Quintana and her brothers and sister carried heavy buckets of water to their father, who mixed straw and adobe to create their home in Ciudad Juárez. When Quintana was 12, her father was shot to death after publicly opposing the 1940 presidential winner. Quintana quit school to help support her family, first by doing odd jobs, then by making uniforms for soldiers.

Days filled with bicycle riding, softball and school at the Escuela Revolución were replaced by hours amid the hum of sewing machines at Don Medina's factory when she was just 14. She soon began earning more money to help the family than the aunt who had made the job possible.

In 1942, while working at the factory, Quintana was reunited with former sweetheart Roberto Perea, and they soon married. Their son Manuel was born in 1943. She said her husband's infidelity prompted her to seek a divorce in 1944 and, not long after, she learned Perea had died in a hunting accident. She was devastated and swore never to marry again.

In 1945, Quintana took a job as kitchen assistant at Casa Hogar, a government-funded kindergarten in Ciudad Juárez. She excelled in the post until the director promoted her to teacher. Despite loving her job, she chose to resign after a few years rather than continue to bear the hostility of a jealous co-worker.

At this time, she met Fortino S. Quintana, a former Air Force staff sergeant, who was working at the El Paso International Airport as a mechanic. In 1954, after a year of courtship, they married in Las Cruces, N.M. They had three daughters, Carolina Bitar, Edna Amador, and Rosa María Cardoza. Quintana's goal has always been to provide a loving home with the same dignity as her father.

"It was a lot of work," she said of her childhood home. "A lot of effort, a lot of love, primarily."

Lillian
Hollingsworth
Ramirez

Date of Birth
12 JULY 1922
Bessemen, AL

Interviewed by
Raquel C. Garza
9 SEPTEMBER 2001
Austin, TX

WWII Location
Biloxi, MS

RAMIREZ, LILLIAN HOLLINGSWORTH.   While Lillian Hollingsworth Ramirez's husband stormed the shores of Normandy on D-Day, her friends and family switched off the radio to shield her from the reports coming out of France. The next day she heard her husband's name on the radio: a radio correspondent was describing how Ramirez had rescued several soldiers in the icy waters.

Lillian Hollingsworth grew up traveling the country, following her father's assignments as part of the Civil Aeronautics Administration. During the Pan-American Student's Conference in Biloxi, Miss., she met the man who would become her husband, Oswaldo. Their first exchange, however, wasn't terribly friendly.

"Dr. Sparkman [sponsor of the Pan-American Student Forum] introduced us and said, 'And she's the state president of the Pan-American Forum,'" Ramirez remembered. "And my husband looked down and said, 'You can't be, you're just a baby,' and I was infuriated!'"

Despite the bumpy start, when the couple met again at a dance the same evening, the situation was very different, and she recalled the entire town witnessing her fall in love on the dance floor that night. After 2 1/2 years of writing letters and occasional meetings, the two became engaged and were married in March 1943.

During the war, Ramirez stayed at home, raising her quickly growing family. The couple eventually had seven children: John, Catherine, Paul, James, Mary, Barbara and Margaret.

Because of her husband's job as a labor-relations attorney, the Ramirez family traveled throughout Latin America, and Lillian taught English, literature and a host of other subjects while in Peru. Ramirez loved being exposed to more Latin cultures.

"I enjoyed it. Wherever we went, I made a home," she said.

RAMIREZ, VIRGINIA TELLEZ. With two siblings in the military, the realities of war hit close to home for Virginia Ramirez. She was plagued by the uncertainty of a brother declared missing in action. An unexpected phone call surprised her initially, but then eased her mind.

"I was at work downtown, and my brother called me at the phone over at the store," she said. "And I couldn't believe it. It was like talking to somebody from the dead."

Her supervisor allowed her to leave work early that day and Ramirez remembered the exuberant welcome her brother Henry received when he finally returned to the States. A band played in the living room as neighbors and relatives danced.

Born Virginia Tellez, Ramirez saw the effect of WWII in her hometown in Tucson, Ariz. She remembered the rationing of meat, tires and shoes, as well as the embargoes on iron and steel scrap and the freezing of Japanese assets in the U.S. She also recalled how many stores cleared their shelves of Japanese goods.

"When they had the Pearl Harbor strike, I remember they had us take everything off the counters that came from Japan," she said. "So that left the counters almost bare because everything at that time before the holidays was from Japan."

Besides working, Ramirez had the responsibility of helping care for her brother's young daughters while he served overseas. She also helped with household duties, learning how to provide for a family and to make her mother's famous homemade flour tortillas.

Following the war, Ramirez met her husband Guadalupe, a WWII veteran. The two were introduced at a club in August 1952 and were married Oct. 11 of that year. The couple adopted two children, Henry and Joseph.

Virginia Tellez Ramirez

Date of Birth
21 DECEMBER 1922
Tucson, AZ

Interviewed by
Violeta Dominguez
5 JANUARY 2003
Tucson, AZ

WWII Location
Tucson, AZ

RESENDEZ, MARY COLUNGA CARMONA. Leaving high school at age 16 to begin working to support her younger siblings, Mary Resendez spent her life helping and caring for others. Constantly putting others' needs before her own, she balanced career and family all her life, relying on her strong Catholic faith to carry her through trying times.

Resendez spent most of her life in Austin, Texas, but during the war she lived in Big Spring, Texas, where her father owned a barbershop. She remembered the strain war placed on the nation, but she was eager to assist in the war effort. She participated in recycling programs at her church, collecting tin cans and other scrap metal for the manufacture of weaponry.

After the war, she began working at Austin Laundry, pressing and drying clothes. She stayed with the company for 10 years. She attended church regularly with her family. It was during a wedding at the parish that she met her future husband Frank, a veteran who had built airfields during the war.

"[Frank] was outside and I saw him, and he saw me, and he invited me to dance with him," Resendez said.

They married in 1949 and had three children: Rudolfo, Mary Frances and Gerardo.

As she took care of her children, Resendez continued to work at Capitol Laundry and later at Anthony's Laundry, where she used her sewing talents at the company for 31 years. She retired in 1989, and she and her husband became active in the Catholic War Veterans of the U.S.A.; both are lifetime members.

While planning a trip to the organization's convention in 1992, her husband suffered a stroke, and Resendez devoted her days to caring for him.

Mary Colunga Carmona Resendez

Date of Birth
9 APRIL 1927
Austin, TX

Interviewed by
Cliff Despres
29 MARCH 2000
Austin, TX

WWII Location
Big Spring, TX;
Austin, TX

Elvira Trujillo Sena

Date of Birth
4 NOVEMBER 1925
Las Vegas, NM

Interviewed by
Adrianna Lujan
3 NOVEMBER 2002
Santa Fe, NM

WWII Location
Las Vegas, NM

SENA, ELVIRA TRUJILLO. Education was always at the top of Elvira Sena's priorities. Determined to reach her goal of becoming a nurse, she resisted the urge to neglect her education when obstacles stood in her path.

Elvira Trujillo was born the daughter of farmers, and she said that their livestock and crops kept the family afloat during the Depression. She remembered her father's sacrifices to ensure she could attend school and was not forced to work. Life on the family's New Mexico farm was hard, with no electricity or running water. Because her mother was often ill, Sena, the oldest girl in the family, was also forced to balance her studies and the responsibilities of acting as a "second mother" to her younger siblings.

When WWII began, Sena desperately wanted to enlist and serve as a nurse. Her father was unsure whether the military was right for his daughter, and Sena remained a civilian.

She met her husband, Luis, on a blind date in December 1944. Luis was a veteran who had recently returned from his tour of duty in the Pacific. By January 1945, the two were married.

She left school after marrying Luis, but returned to school after giving birth to the couple's first child. She earned her diploma and completed college courses at New Mexico Highlands University.

She then began working at the New Mexico State Hospital, now Las Vegas Medical Center, eventually becoming a licensed practical nurse. Though she never completed college to obtain certification as an LPN, Sena challenged the state board and eventually passed all the necessary tests to earn her status as an LPN. She later worked at a doctor's office.

Sena and her husband had five children: Stella, Christina, Steven, Catherine and Sandy.

Juana Mani Sierra

Date of Birth
6 MAY 1925
Fierro, NM

Interviewed by
Brenda Sendejo
15 JULY 2004
Hanover, NM

WWII Location
Fierro, NM

SIERRA, JUANA MANI. Growing up surrounded by the mines of New Mexico, Juana Mani Sierra, throughout her life, was constantly supportive of the male members of her family who worked in the hazardous mining industry. She lost two brothers to the mines and was willing to picket to save other family member's jobs.

Born Juana Mani to Mexican immigrants from Zacatecas, she has always been proud of her dual heritage. "God gave me my mom and dad and their Spanish," Sierra said. "It is so beautiful to talk real Spanish."

Though her father was fiercely protective of his daughters and hoped they would never be forced to work, WWII made it necessary for her to help support her family and fill jobs left by men fighting abroad.

She began working at a local gas station, filling miner's tanks as they traveled to work each day. She often blessed family members and friends as they passed by the station every morning.

When mining companies attempted to withhold important health benefits from miners, she and other women took to the picket lines, facing police resistance and tear gas. The strike inspired the 1954 film "Salt of the Earth."

Sierra met her husband at a dance. He was unable to serve during WWII because he was blind in one eye. He left to work in California, but eventually returned to his love and the two married.

The couple had three children. One of Sierra's sons entered the Marines Corps, a frightening scenario for Sierra.

"I cried, but it is their choice," she said. "My son wanted to go places, and he did not fight in a war."

SILVA, BETTY CHAVEZ. With two brothers overseas during the war, Betty Silva's house was uncomfortably empty, one brother, Serefino Chavez, did not survive his tour of duty. The loss devastated her family, who had eagerly awaited his letters that described his plans to return home and marry his sweetheart.

Born Betty Chavez, she grew up in a small adobe home in New Mexico, and despite the financial difficulties of the Depression, she considered herself very fortunate.

"We always had something to eat," she said. "So we were OK during the Depression."

Her parents stressed the importance of education, and all the Chavez children graduated from high school. Her two brothers began college, but their academic careers were interrupted when Pearl Harbor was bombed.

She stayed at home, finishing high school. She listened attentively to the radio with her father, waiting for news, and she prayed alongside her mother, hoping that her brothers would return safely. Henry returned from the war in 1947. It was then he could finally share his experiences with his sister and family, since his letters were heavily censored during the war, leaving the family confused.

On Nov. 8 1948, she married Mike Silva, whom she had known since elementary school. They moved from Polvadera to Albuquerque, N.M., in 1954. There they raised their four children: Michael, William, Philip and Melissa.

Today, Silva is proud of the progress Latinos have made, and attributes the success to education and determination. Her advice to younger generations is similar to what her parents told her some 60 years ago. "Get an education. It is very important," she said. "The most important thing in life is education."

Betty Chavez Silva

Date of Birth
4 AUGUST 1924
Polvadera, NM

Interviewed by
Jennifer Sanchez
2 NOVEMBER 2002
Albuquerque, NM

WWII Location
Polvadera, NM

TAFOYA, ELENA ESCOBAR. Music was always a refuge for Elena Escobar Tafoya, and she worked diligently to hone her talents. From purchasing a piano on her own as a young woman to praying to the Virgin of Guadalupe to bestow talent on her, she made music a priority. It gave her solace in trying times, and she shared her gift with her community, playing the organ at her church.

Elena Escobar grew up in the mining towns of New Mexico. Her mother withdrew her from school in the 10th grade, and she helped around the house and with her siblings. Times were difficult, but perseverance and teamwork helped the family survive.

"I don't know how my mother did it, but we did it," she said.

Just before the beginning of WWII, she met her future husband, Raymundo Tafoya. Her mother did not approve of him, but that did not deter the young man. He once arranged to have musicians serenade her, playing beneath the window of her bedroom, with the gentle melodies wafting through the air.

The two eloped in 1941 and moved into a home on the property of the Empire Zinc Co., the company that Raymundo worked for. His dangerous work in the mines worried his young wife. After the U.S. entered WWII, Raymundo volunteered, but failed the entrance exams so he was passed over for military service. During the war, Tafoya was too young to work in the mines. Instead, she stayed at home and worked in the community.

After the war, discrimination was rampant in the mines, and Tafoya remembered supporting her husband while the workers picketed during a strike.

She and her husband had five children: Catalina, Alvino, Rosalina, Raymundo Jr. and José.

Elena Escobar Tafoya

Date of Birth
18 AUGUST 1916
Santa Rita, NM

Interviewed by
Brian Lucero
15 JULY 2004
Hanover, NM

WWII Location
Santa Rita, NM

Martha Ortega
Vidaurri

Date of Birth
8 AUGUST 1921
Austin, TX

Interviewed by
Tammi Grais
12 SEPTEMBER 2001
Austin, TX

WWII Location
Austin, TX

VIDAURRI, MARTHA ORTEGA. Using riddles and wordplay, Martha Vidaurri's brothers were able to communicate their locations throughout the war and avoid having their messages censored. Inside the letters were veiled references and inside jokes that communicated details about the war, and gave Vidaurri the challenge of deciphering the writings.

She remembered when one brother wrote, "Tell the boys to save me some Mexican beer." Vidaurri deduced that he was referring to Carta-Blanca brand, and reasoned he was stationed in Casablanca, Morocco.

Another time, another brother wrote, "Tell Dr. Garcia's youngest daughter I say hello." The doctor's youngest was named Virginia, and Vidaurri was able to figure out he was currently in Virginia.

Martha Ortega was one of eight children, with five brothers serving during WWII throughout Europe, North Africa and the Philippines.

After graduating from high school, she dreamed of becoming a nurse, but when the war began, she was desperately needed at home to help her mother manage the household.

Her husband, Edelmiro Vidaurri, also served during the war. She remembered that he rushed home on every free weekend to spend time with her before he left for Iceland, where he was stationed during WWII. The couple married in 1942 before Edelmiro went overseas.

With her husband gone, Vidaurri worked hard to support the war effort on the home front, helping collect scrap metal. She also wrote letters to all the soldiers from her church.

Following her husband's return from the war, they began their own family. The couple had six children: Abel, David, Anna, Edward, Robert and Stephen.

Chapter Eight

MEXICAN CIVILIANS WHO WORKED IN THE U.S. DURING WWII

Photo courtesy of UT Institute of Texan Cultures at San Antonio, No. 96-1184, Courtesy of Rev. Mak and Alice Mae Williams.

Day laborers standing in a truck parked in cotton field near Tivoli, Texas, circa 1949.

Mexican Civilians who Worked in the U.S. during WWII

With much of its manpower fighting overseas, the United States relied on men from outside its borders to keep the country going. Nearly 300,000 Mexican workers were hired under a guest worker program while many more with specific skills were given special visas to work in the United States.

Skilled Workers

By 1935, Abraham Moreno repaired and maintained old airplanes in southeast Mexico on a salary that barely paid for room, board, and a few living expenses. Moreno made temporary repairs on airplanes that crashed in jungles or mountains and flew them back to their bases.

The Mexican company he worked for bought parts from Mauldin Aircraft, based in Brownsville, Texas. Moreno got to know people at the company, and in 1941, they recruited him to work as a chief mechanic. Moreno jumped at the chance: he had plans to earn his Aircraft Engine Mechanic's License upon arrival in Brownsville in August 1941. Exempt from the draft due to a childhood leg injury, Moreno stayed busy with his work and studying both English and mechanical textbooks.

By late June, 1944, Moreno had passed a 600-question test to earn his mechanic certification. He made his home in the U.S., marrying and later having six children there.

Braceros

Other Mexican workers worked in the railroad and agriculture industries. On July 23, 1942, the government signed an agreement with Mexico that allowed the U.S. to temporarily employ Mexican workers to man the agriculture and railroad industries.

The first workers to be hired for the "Mexico-United States Borrowed Workmanship Program," better known as "The Labor Worker Program," arrived in Stockton, Calif., on Sept. 29, 1942. Seizing the opportunity to explore a new country, help the war effort, and be paid in U.S. dollars, thousands of Mexicans—mostly youths—traveled to recruitment centers to sign up.

Many had rarely ventured outside of their hometowns. José Miramontes, of Zacatecas, Mexico, had never even traveled to the capital of his state before he was sent to work as a laborer in Wisconsin.

The laborers often encountered rumors that they would be drafted in the U.S. and sent to the battlefield, causing some to return home before crossing the border. Nonetheless, many still ventured into a country they knew little about.

Once there, their conditions varied. Generally, the laborers worked eight to ten hours a day and had weekends off. Some lived in apartments or small houses near the worksites, while others lived in the barracks or camps that were poorly adapted to accommodate them.

California, Montana, Washington, Colorado, Michigan and Arizona hired a large number of workers. The Mexican government prohibited the employment of laborers in Texas because of prevalent discrimination.

However, Mexican workers were not exempted from racism. Mariano Chores of Santa Clara Coatitla was thrown out of a bar in Minnesota because he was Mexican. To the laborers, the unwelcoming attitudes disregarded the vital roles the Mexicans were playing.

"We were working for those who were sent off," said Genaro Cortes.

—*Violeta Dominguez*
Researcher, Tucson, Arizona

Marcelino Ramirez Bautista

Date of Birth
2 JUNE 1906
Zacatecas, Mexico

Tribute Provided by
Mercy Bautista-
Olvera (Daughter)

WWII Location
Ohio; Missouri;
Kansas

BAUTISTA, MARCELINO RAMIREZ.   One of the first to be hired for the "Labor Worker Program," Marcelino Ramirez Bautista had already lived once in the United States.

Shortly after Marcelino's mother, Petra Ramirez Bautista died, his father found a job in New Mexico. Tiburcio Bautista took young Marcelino, the youngest of his sons, with him while the others stayed in the city of Zacatecas. Marcelino attended school in New Mexico until his father lost his job and decided to return to Mexico.

Bautista fell in love with Anastacia Nunez Robles, whom he married on June 7, 1930. He worked in the mines and had six children — Victoria, Enrique, Andrea Petra, Modesta, Maria Guadalupe and Esther — before hearing about the opportunity to work in the United States.

He was hired to work for the railroad and traveled around the States, among them: Ohio, Missouri and Kansas. Bautista sent home pictures to his wife of himself posing with his co-workers in overalls on the side of a train. He also visited his family still living in Mexico during vacations. He and Anastacia had three more children — Carlos, Jess and Mercy — during the war despite Marcelino's frequent travel.

He returned to Mexico as U.S. soldiers came back from overseas. Having experienced the opportunities in the States, Marcelino emigrated back as soon as he could, taking a job at Sully Miller Construction Company until he retired. With the help of his sister, María, he eventually brought his family — including two daughters who already had families of their own — to the United States.

"He was such an inspiration in my life," said his daughter, Mercy Bautista-Olvera. "My dad was a man that wanted a better life for his children and grandchildren. He was generous, kind, positive, funny, and above all he loved his family."

Máximo Pérez Butanda

Date of Birth
11 MAY 1913
Sarabia,
Guanajuato,
Mexico

Interviewed by
Violeta Dominguez
29 MARCH 2001
Iztapalapa,
D.F., Mexico

WWII Location
Pomona, CA

BUTANDA, MÁXIMO PÉREZ. Despite an injury to his hand, Máximo Butanda remembered the time he spent in the United States fondly.

In 1943, he was living in Mexico City when he decided to go to the laborers recruiting center. A shoemaker by trade, he received a contract that allowed him to work in California.

Butanda ended up in a town called Pomona, where he harvested beets and worked in a nut-packaging plant for the California Walnut Growers Association.

He and some of his co-workers met and befriended a man of Mexican descent who lived in the area. During their time off, he would drive them to see the sights of Los Angeles. Returning from one of these excursions, they were in an automobile accident and Butanda fractured his hand. He was rushed in an ambulance to the hospital and underwent an operation. The mishap kept Butanda in the hospital for nearly three months.

He later returned to his work at the plant and in the fields. A usual work day lasted from 7 a.m. to 5 p.m. Butanda was proud to have fulfilled a vital role during the war.

"We were hired as laborers," he said. "But our title was soldier."

Butanda said that he and his co-workers were always treated kindly and were never subject to discrimination.

After spending nine months in California, Butanda had completed his contract. He left for Mexico to seek a second operation on his hand, which had not healed correctly and continued to ail him. Butanda returned to his wife, María Granadas Veloz, whom he had married in January 1934. In Celaya, Mexico, he resumed work as a shoemaker.

He and María had a daughter, María Louisa. Butanda later had a son, Antonio.

CHORES, MARIANO OLIVERA. At 24, married, and with two children, Mariano Chores decided to come to the United States to work as a laborer. His adventurous spirit led him to want to know more about the country where he lived and worked.

Chores entered the United States at El Paso, Texas, and immediately traveled north to Minnesota to begin a series of farming jobs.

In 1943, he arrived at a ranch in Oslo, Minn., where he worked picking beets. Upon completion of the job, he renewed his contract in 1944. Chores then worked in Eloy, Ariz., where he harvested asparagus, broccoli, potatoes and carrots for packaging.

During that time, he subscribed to La Opinion, a newspaper that kept him abreast of the latest developments in the war. He also relied on his RCA Victor Radio to stay on top of world events.

Chores regrets that all too often, discrimination prevented many North Americans from recognizing the crucial role laborers played during WWII.

"We were soldiers of agriculture and of the railroads," he said. "But we were never recognized as such."

Discouraged by the discrimination he encountered and with a strong desire to be reunited with his family, he returned to Mexico in 1946.

Once he arrived home in Mexico, he opened Imprenta Chores, a printing business he owned and operated.

Chores and his wife, Esperanza Gonzalez Martínez, raised 14 children: Juana, Angel, Porfirio, Mariano, Felipe, Sebastian, María de Jesús, María del Refugio, Ana, Julia, Magdalena, Guadalupe, Virginia and Laura.

Mariano Olivera
Chores

Date of Birth
4 JULY 1919
Santa Clara
Coatitla,
D.F., Mexico

Interviewed by
Violeta Dominguez
19 MARCH 2001
Santa Clara
Coatitla,
D.F., Mexico

WWII Location
Oslo, MN; Eloy, AZ

CORTES, GENARO GARCIA. It wasn't the hard work he would have to endure as a laborer that scared Genaro Cortes as he considered his decision to travel to the United States to work during WWII. At 24, he was most worried about the possibility of being drafted.

A mason by trade, Cortes remembered that rumors were rampant that recruitment for labor work was simply a guise. The workers were scared that the program was actually a way to "draft people and send them to the Pacific to fight."

However, the need to support his family was greater than his fears, and in 1944 he decided to travel to the recruitment office where he was to be given a contract to work for Santa Fe, Topeka & Atchinson Railroad in the towns of Richmond, Madera and Bakersfield, Calif.

Cortes left behind three children and a pregnant wife when he entered the States, but knew the benefits of employment in the States would help his new family.

His employment at the railroad went without a hitch. Thanks to his previous work experience, he was skilled with the tools he employed on the railroad: the shovel and the pickaxe.

He completed two contracts of six months each. He remembered his time working in the United States with pride.

"Although we didn't go to the war, we were there to work for those who were sent off," he said.

He then returned to Mexico in December 1945. Cortes eventually returned to the States in 1974, working in Chicago at a factory.

Cortes had married Consuelo Rangel Moreno in 1938. Their children included: Antonio, Gloria, Jorge, Dolores, Juan, Jaime, Sergio, Roberto, José, María Guadalupe, María del Carmen, and Alicia.

Genaro Garcia
Cortes

Date of Birth
10 JULY 1918
Mexico City,
D.F., Mexico

Interviewed by
Violeta Dominguez
4 APRIL 2001
Iztapalapa,
D.F., Mexico

WWII Location
Richmond, CA;
Madera, CA;
Bakersfield, CA

Alfonso Lara

Date of Birth
14 OCTOBER 1914
Acámbaro,
Guanajuato,
Mexico

Interviewed by
Violeta Dominguez
23 MARCH 2001
D.F., Mexico

WWII Location
Hinkley, CA;
Hodge, CA

LARA, ALFONSO. In 1944, Alfonso Lara was living in Mexico City with his wife and two children, when he and his brother-in-law decided to work as laborers.

Earning a salary in U.S. dollars was just one of the reasons the men chose to go to the recruitment office. They also were interested in visiting the United States and learning more about their Northern neighbors.

Born in 1914 in Acámbaro, Guanajuato, Lara eventually moved to Mexico City, where he was working as a bus driver when he made the decision to venture north for work during the Second World War.

The 30-year old Lara became a railroad worker for Atchinson, Topeka and Santa Fe Railroad near the towns of Hinkley and Hodge, Calif.

He and countless other laborers were aware of the importance of their work during the war efforts.

"We were the soldiers of production," he said. "We were there to replace those who had been sent to the war."

After having worked six months and the end of his contract, he chose to return to Mexico to care for his ailing son.

Despite a strong desire to return to the United States, Lara remembered not having the means to do so, and remained in Mexico. He returned to his job as a driver with the Penitenciaria-Niño Perdido Bus Line.

Lara had married Teresa González Suárez in June 1940, prior to his trip to the United States. The couple raised four children: Rubén, Alfonso, María and José.

José Pablo
Miramontes

Date of Birth
15 JANUARY 1924
Momax,
Zacatecas, Mexico

Interviewed by
Violeta Dominguez

WWII Location
Wisconsin

MIRAMONTES, JOSÉ PABLO. For José Pablo Miramontes his train ride to Wisconsin in 1944 was a great adventure. "I had never left the small town," he explained. Based on the comments he heard from others, he imagined the United States as being "a large city without any fields."

He remembered that others in his small town weren't as excited at the notion of becoming a laborer. "They [labor contractors] practically begged because people didn't want to leave," he said.

Miramontes wasn't afraid. He signed up to work for 11 months as an apprentice on the railroad for Chicago, Milwaukee and Pacific Company.

During that time, he had the opportunity to visit Chicago with some of his co-workers and remembers his surprise when first seeing the metropolis, as well as the trains full of soldiers that he would continuously see go by.

At the end of the war, Miramontes finalized his contract and returned to Momax, Mexico, where he eventually married.

MORENO, ABRAHAM ELEUTERIO. Recruited by Mauldin Aircraft, Abraham Moreno arrived in Brownsville, Texas, on Aug. 7, 1941, to work as chief mechanic. His previous job in Mexico sent him to repair planes crashed in the mountains and jungles, but Moreno was eager to be immersed in the latest aviation technology.

Abraham Eleuterio
Moreno

Date of Birth
20 FEBRUARY 1912
Monterrey, Nuevo
León, Mexico

Interviewed by
Yolanda Urrabazo
13 SEPTEMBER 2003
Brownsville, TX

WWII Location
Brownsville, TX

"Even though I had a very good job over there, [I] couldn't get any higher," he said. "And my wish was to work on American airplanes."

Moreno attended night school to learn English while studying mechanics for his Aircraft Engine license and his Mechanical Certificate, which he earned on June 21, 1944.

During the war, Mauldin Aircraft bought and sold aircraft parts. The Mauldin Civilian Pilot Training School trained pilots to expand the Army Air Corps. "We used to have a lot of guys that went to work for us as an apprenticeship and then they went to the Air Corps," Moreno said.

In 1944, Moreno married Julia Resendez and the couple had their first child, Marie, in 1946. That same year, Moreno left Mauldin and began working in an emergency crew for Pan American Airways. He repaired C-46 cargo aircraft and traveled as far as the jungles of Santa Cruz, Bolivia, to get planes up and running again. In 1948, Pan American sent him to wok from Miami, Fla., where he would earn his citizenship on April 12, 1951. From there, he worked at Intercontinental Engine Services, where he retired in 1974.

Moreno's six children, Abraham, Maria, Sylvia, Sandra, Sonia and Michael, spoke Spanish and learned English from their neighborhood friends. Moreno himself was never able to attend school past fifth grade due to his father's untimely death. However, his children all earned college degrees, drawing inspiration from their father's belief that "education is key."

MOSSO, GUERRERO NAHÚM CALLEJA. First contracted to work in the United States when he was 23, Guerrero Nahúm Mosso remembered the subsequent months he spent as a laborer as a happy time in his life.

Guerrero Nahúm
Calleja Mosso

Date of Birth
24 FEBRUARY 1921
Tlapa, Guerrero,
Mexico

Interviewed by
Violeta Dominguez
22 MARCH 2001
Iztapalapa,
D.F., Mexico

WWII Location
Portland, ME

Mosso was working for the Secretary of Foreign Affairs, when he decided that he wanted to travel to the United States. His employer helped him with the necessary documentation for Mosso to obtain a contract as a laborer.

He left from Querétaro by train. As they traveled through the States, , the train dropped others off at different work sites in Laredo and San Antonio, Texas; San Louis, Mo., and Boston, Mass., among others. His was the last stop in Portland, Maine. They arrived on Christmas in 1943 and he and the other workers were greeted with festivities.

Mosso worked on the railroad. He recalled the living quarters being stocked with all the necessities and never enduring any form of discrimination. He was reminded of the friendships he forged with some of the North Americans who lived near the work camps.

He remembered his experiences in the States as "an adventure." For that, he said he thoroughly enjoyed his time as a laborer. Mosso decided twice to renew his contract and worked for the United States 18 months until the end of the war. "It was a beautiful thing when the war ended," he said, recalling the celebration that took place when the news came. Though he wanted to stay in the U.S. and continue working, Mosso returned to Mexico at the end of his third contract.

He married Guadalupe Arellano Martinez on September 21, 1932. The couple had nine children together: Aurora, Irene, Raul, Altredo, Victor, Joaquín, Marco, Nahúm Jr. and Guadalupe.

Andrés Chávez
Rodríguez

Date of Birth
18 MAY 1921
Nuevo León,
Mexico

Interviewed by
Yolanda Chavez
Padilla
26 JULY 2000
McAllen, TX

WWII Location
Houston, TX

RODRÍGUEZ, ANDRÉS CHÁVEZ. After working seven years at his uncle's hotel, Marvillas de Monterrey, Andrés Chávez Rodríguez decided that he could help his family best if he left Monterrey, Mexico, and traveled to the United States to find work.

He was deterred at his first attempt but obtained a local passport in Reynosa, Mexico, and entered the U.S. legally. He met up with is brother, Guadalupe Chávez Rodríguez in Houston, Texas, where he found a job on an assembly line making parts for the war.

"World War II was at its apogee; a lot of beautiful and sad things were seen. Many mothers would cry when they would say good-bye to their sons who were going to the battlefields," he said.

Chávez continued working in Houston after the war ended, until he was reported to immigration. He was deported to Mexico on Feb. 25, 1949.

Within days, he secured a job in Matamoros as a policeman. While unsatisfied with his position, it allowed him to earn a green card to work in the United States and meet Ernestina Treviño García, with whom he fell in love. On his third time into the U.S., he decided to settle in Adrian, Mich., finding a job making parts for Tecumseh Products Co. He saved his money in order to marry Ernestina on Jan. 29, 1956, just across the border in Mexico.

Their first child, Yolanda, was born in Michigan while Araceli, Andrés Jr. and Esmeralda were born after the family moved to Texas. Chávez's three daughters were all able to attend college and his son ran his own business.

Chávez retired from his job as a janitor in Brownsville public schools. He then bought a house to be close to his daughters in McAllen, Texas, where he volunteered at the Senor Citizens Center.

Juan Bravo
Saldaña

Date of Birth
12 AUGUST 1925
Coyoacán,
D.F., Mexico

Interviewed by
Violeta Dominguez
22 MARCH 2001
Iztapalapa,
D.F., Mexico

WWII Location
Pittsburg, PA

SALDAÑA, JUAN BRAVO. After hearing others talk about working in the United States, and about the profits gained by those who chose to "go north," Juan Saldaña decided that the best way to financially support his family would be to obtain a contract as a laborer. Intent on saving enough money to allow him to better his life and the lives of his mother and siblings, Saldaña went to the recruitment office where he landed a contract working for Pennsylvania Railroad.

On the train to the United States, he and the other laborers couldn't help to think of the risk of being drafted and having to be sent to participate in the war. "Many of them wanted to go back," he said. "I was never scared."

For Saldaña, it was clear that being a laborer meant being a soldier, not on the battlefield, rather, on the home front. "We weren't workers; we were practically soldiers, because we were replacing the soldiers," he said. "We were aware that there was an obligation for us to go there [to the United States] and work."

Saldaña arrived in Pittsburg, Pa., and went to work at the East Liberty Camp, which was in the east part of the city. He and his co-workers worked from 6 a.m. to 3 p.m. On their time off, they would travel to Pittsburg, but were aware that many places, like the movie theater, did not welcome Mexicans.

In total, he spent seven months in the United States. He recalled missing his family the most. After fulfilling his contract, Saldaña was happy to return to them in Mexico.

Waiting for his return was Saldaña's girlfriend, Benita Gómez Arredondo. On Feb. 2, 1946, he and Benita were married in Mexico City. The couple would have eight children together: Graciela, María Estela, Juan José, Ricardo, María Soledad, Susana, Sergio Javier and René.

TORRES, ANTONIO AURELIO MARTÍNEZ. In spite of his young age, 21-year-old Aurelio Torres left Pénjamo where he had been born and raised and had helped his farther run a ranch. The elder Julio Torres had died at age 40, having worked hard his whole life, and his son wished to help his mother and seven siblings financially. So Aurelio secured a contract to work in the United States and left, sending his earnings back home to Mexico.

Crossing the border through Juárez, Torres traveled by train directly to Sydney, Mont. There, he worked on a ranch that harvested beets. On Sundays, he was taken into town, to see movies and buy supplies, a task which forced Torres to pick up a few vital English words.

He was transferred to Minnesota where he harvested corn and peas for packaging and later had a stint in Colorado and Iowa as well.

After six months in the U.S., Torres returned to Mexico in 1943. There, he accepted a railroad apprenticeship for Southern Pacific. The job sent him to the towns of Caliente, Bealville and Tahachapi, Calif. His performance over the next two years eventually led to a promotion to a steward's assistant.

He fondly remembered the time he spent as a laborer, except for one unfortunate incident in Colorado when a friend of his was subjected to racist treatment at a restaurant where he was denied service. He recalls being angered over the injustice.

"We were soldiers of the war in agriculture," he said.

Torres returned to Mexico at the end of the war, motivated by a strong desire to be with his family. He married Udelia León Roldán in 1955. The couple had three children: María Cristina, Rosalinda Guadelia and Marco.

Antonio Aurelio
Martínez Torres

Date of Birth
12 NOVEMBER 1921
Pénjamo,
Guanajuato,
Mexico

Interviewed by
Violeta Dominguez
24 MARCH 2001
D.F., Mexico

WWII Location
Montana,
Minnesota,
Colorado, Iowa,
California

TREJO, JUAN CONCEPCIÓN DOMINGUEZ. In 1943, Juan Concepción Dominguez Trejo — a native of the capital city of Querétaro — was living in Mexico City and working as a driver for Penitenciara-Alamos Bus Line. In April, he decided to go to a recruitment office, where he was given a contract to work in the United States.

He and his family had moved to Fort Worth, Texas, when Trejo was 8 years old, but moved back to Mexico in 1937 as rumors of war in Europe began to circulate in the United States.

Trejo's second trip to the U.S. was a whole new experience. As a railroad apprentice for the South Pacific Railroad, he was stationed in Lovelock, Nev. Aside from working on the railroad, Trejo also worked Sundays at a nearby potato packing plant.

At the end of his contract, he returned to Mexico, which led him to another job with the South Pacific in California, close to the cities of Eureka and Oakland. Unfortunately in California, he suffered an accident on the job. The injury left Trejo hospitalized for three months.

Nonetheless, Trejo renewed his contract in 1945. This time, he was assigned to work for the Atchinson, Topeka and Santa Fe Railroad in Nelson, Ariz.

It was in Arizona that he participated in the celebration and festivities at the conclusion of WWII before returning to Mexico.

In the end, Trejo recalled his work as a laborer with pride. "We signified a great thing for the United States, because in some way we helped reach victory," he said.

Trejo retuned to Mexico's Federal District and, in January 1945, married Carmen Márquez García. The couple had eight children together: Francisco, Javier, Juan, Concepción, Miguel, Leticia, Obdulia and Evelia.

Juan Concepción
Dominguez Trejo

Date of Birth
8 DECEMBER 1922
Querétaro, Mexico

Interviewed by
Violeta Dominguez
20 MARCH 2001
Coyoacán,
D.F., Mexico

WWII Location
Lovelock, NV;
Eureka, CA;
Oakland, CA;
Nelson, AZ

Part Three

POST-WAR OPPORTUNITIES AND CONTRIBUTIONS

Homero Alvarado (right) at a protest for better housing for Hispanics in Chicago, 1981. At center is Brenda Gaines, Commissioner, Chicago Dept. of Housing.

In many ways, World War II was the beginning of the Latino struggle for civil rights. Returning veterans had a new perspective: they had clearly defended their nation, and thus felt entitled to equal rights. Also, they had worked alongside non-Hispanics and had proven to themselves, if not to everyone else, they were as capable as the next man or woman.

"We had had a taste of equality," said Tempe, Ariz., native Pete Moraga. There was no turning back.

Significantly, the GI Bill provided the tool, education, that would give them the wherewithal to accomplish their goals. Individually and collectively, Latinos and Latinas asserted their rights, creating opportunities not only for themselves, but also for their children and later generations.

Although efforts were underway, now the efforts were re-invigorated and bold.

"I was not afraid," said Laredo, Texas, native Ed Idar, Jr. "I had been in the service and had dealt with generals, colonels, and this and that and the other."

Segregation

Discrimination against Latinos across the Southwest was pervasive: in many areas Hispanic children attended segregated schools.

In some rural areas, the "Mexican school" did not include schooling beyond elementary grades. Nicanor Aguilár, from a rural West Texas town, recalls that only through the insistence of a determined teacher, an Anglo woman, was his younger sister able to attend high school, over the objections of the school principal. At school, Hispanic children were usually punished for speaking Spanish.

Schools often argued that they did not discriminate against Hispanic children because of their ethnicity, but rather because of their language limitations—many spoke little English.

In Baytown, Texas, near Houston, activists found a solution. Antonio Campos, a teacher, began formulating a pre-school program for non-English speakers: he and others developed a list of 400 English words to be used in the first grade. After introducing these 400 words, teachers noticed a marked improvement in Hispanic children's academic performance.

The "Little Schools of the 400" were the model of what later became Head Start.

For some Latino activists, desegregation carried significant personal costs. In the far West Texas town of Alpine, Pete A. Gallego and his wife, Elena Peña Gallego, also became enmeshed in the battle to desegregate schools. Pete Gallego was elected to the seven-member school board, the only Latino, in 1959. It would take a decade, and the need for a new school building, to finally force the issue.

State officials finally told the Alpine schools that segregated schools were illegal. "They were very angry that they had to do it," Gallego said.

But for their troubles, the Gallegos were besieged by angry phone calls, letters, and visits from people unhappy with the changes taking place. Their restaurant lost customers and they were forced to relocate.

Other Types of Segregation

The discrimination also applied to employment: many jobs, including those as police officers and firefighters were off-limits. Dual-wage systems were common.

New organizations were created to help. One of them was the American G.I. Forum, founded in 1948 in Corpus Christi, Texas, spearheaded by veteran Dr. Hector P. Garcia. Another was the Mexican American Legal Defense and Educational Fund (MALDEF), begun in 1968 in San Antonio, Texas. Both organizations, as well as existing organizations, such as the League of United Latin American Citizens (LULAC), applied pressure to institutions and public officials to eliminate unfair practices.

Pete Tijerina, originally of Laredo, Texas, had become a lawyer and was frustrated with the injustice in the courts. Repeatedly, there were no Hispanic jurors called. With a grant from the Ford Foundation, MALDEF was created. Now the work would begin to systematically dismantle a system of institutionalized racism through the courts, to train lawyers to do so, and to give scholarships to Hispanic law students.

Individuals made inroads as well. In rural West Texas, Nicanor Aguilár led other Mexican Americans to demand better treatment, enlisting the intercession of LULAC.

"We would investigate. For example ... I would see [signs that read] 'No Mexicans, whites only.' There was only one [restaurant] that would serve us," he said. "We would write reports so they could give us the reasons. Some would answer us well; others, not so well. I brought those reports to El Paso [Texas] and gave them to a LULAC associate. I don't know what he did with them after that. Once, a more powerful LULAC associate came to see me from San Antonio [Texas] and congratulated me."

City by city, civil service jobs were opened up to Latinos. In El Paso, attorney Albert Armendariz was appointed to the civil service commission and put an end to the automatic rejection of minority applicants to jobs with the police and fire departments.

Gilbert Castorena of San Diego, Calif., worked in the newly formed Equal Employment Opportunity Committee.

Political Advancement

There was much to address: a "poll tax" in some states required voters to pay before they could cast a vote, at-large elections made it difficult for any Latino to be elected, and elected officials often did not consider Hispanics their constituents, much less their equals.

In Texas, the poll tax was $1.75 per person. "For two people in a marriage, a husband and a wife, it was quite a bit of money," said Ed Idar. "It was a big hindrance, no question about it."

Idar, who had moved to San Antonio, was active in the Viva Kennedy Clubs, campaigning for John F. Kennedy. In 1961, an umbrella group was organized: the Political Association of Spanish Speaking People Organizations, or PASSO. Oftentimes, during his political work, Idar's wife and children traveled with him by car, the children sleeping on blankets in the back seat.

Idar would work with the American G.I. Forum to foment the change necessary for Hispanic advancement.

Also in San Antonio, Ruben Mungia, who owned a print shop, became involved in promoting Hispanic candidates. Among the campaigns he worked on were those of Henry B. Gonzalez, also of the WWII generation, who was elected to the city council, then Texas Senate and finally served in the U.S. Congress from 1961 to 1998. Gonzalez would be the national co-chair of the Viva Kennedy Club, along with New Mexico Sen. Dennis Chavez.

In California, activists created the Mexican-American Political Association, or MAPA.

"The main thing we did was to make the life of the Mexican American better than what it was at that time," Ruperto Soto Juarez of MAPA explained.

In the end, the generation accomplished much. "We owed it to our children," said Mary Murillo, of Austin, Texas, "They have more opportunities and I think they want to do better."

AGUILÁR, NICANOR. Following his service in the infantry during the war, Nicanor Aguilár returned to his West Texas hometown and found that prejudices had not disappeared.

Growing up on a farm in the small town of Grand Falls, Texas, Aguilár and other Hispanic classmates were denied promotion from grade to grade on numerous occasions, and Aguilár eventually left high school without graduating.

He enlisted in the Army in the hopes of finding his younger brother Isavino, who had already enlisted and was stationed in Germany. Aguilár then shipped out to Italy and fought with the 36th Infantry Division on the European front.

After the war, conditions had not improved back home. "There was the same discrimination in Grand Falls, if not worse," he recalled. "First, we'd work for a dollar a day. After the war, they raised it to $2 [for] 10 hours. And the whites would get $18 [a day] in the petroleum [field.]"

Virtually none of the town's petroleum jobs were available to Latinos. Aguilár managed to hold down such a job for one year with a small company, but only through a friend's assistance. "It wasn't right," he said. "I started calling other veterans and I told them, 'We have to do something good.'"

Toward that end, they secured assistance from LULAC. "We would investigate," he said, explaining how they would pressure restaurants with "No Mexicans" signs. "We would write reports so they could give us the reasons," he said. "Some would answer us well; others, not so well. I brought those reports to El Paso [Texas] and gave them to a LULAC associate."

Gradually, the oppressive signs came down from diner windows. In 1948 Aguilár moved to El Paso and continued his work for LULAC as a member at large. He married Mercedes Borunda and the couple had four sons: Nick Jr., Pete, Paul and Joe.

Nicanor Aguilár

Date of Birth
10 JANUARY 1917
Grand Falls, TX

Interviewed by
Maggie Rivas-Rodriguez
29 DECEMBER 2001
El Paso, TX

WWII Military Unit
36th Infantry
Division

ALVARADO, HOMERO. Throughout his life, Homero Alvarado has been an advocate of civil rights. He has promoted Chicago-area political campaigns and supported the rights of minorities.

Alvarado grew up in Laredo, Texas, and attended school until he was 10 years old. He remembered being frustrated in school because the poor and non-white students were placed in the back of the classroom. He was expelled from school because he fought with other students frequently. "They kicked me out of school because I was always defending people," Alvarado said. His mother home-schooled him until he was 17 years old. His father was a cattle rancher from Veracruz, Mexico, and his mother was from Italy. He grew up speaking Spanish and Italian fluently.

A group of friends decided to enlist when Alvarado was 17. "We were young and we wanted to be somebody," he said. Two of his brothers were already serving, and 14,000 of Laredo's 40,000 residents eventually joined the armed forces.

He trained as a paratrooper in Fort Benning, Ga. "Training was very rough because you're Mexican, and you have to be strong because you think you're better than everybody," he said. He was assigned to the 17th Airborne Division and participated in Battle of the Bulge. In one landing, his parachute dragged him an entire block, and he felt paralyzed. He was sent to New York, where hospital staff thought he might be a spy, because his coloring resembled that of Germans and he spoke Italian well. He was discharged from the Army because of his injuries.

He married Hortencia Sanchez, and they had one son. Homero Jr. Alvarado went to college for five years to be a welder and had his own construction company in Laredo and San Antonio, Texas. He moved to Chicago, Ill., and continued in the construction business, becoming well-known for finding good jobs for Mexicans without legal status.

Homero Alvarado

Date of Birth
12 MARCH 1925
Veracruz, Mexico

Interviewed by
William Luna
22 AUGUST 2002
Chicago, IL

WWII Military Unit
17th Airborne
Division

Albert Armendariz

Date of Birth
11 AUGUST 1919
El Paso, TX

Interviewed by
Maggie Rivas-Rodriguez
16 MARCH 2001
El Paso, TX

WWII Military Unit
1852d Service Unit
Fort Bliss, TX

ARMENDARIZ, ALBERT. With more than 50 years as a practicing attorney and judge, Albert Armendariz continued his work well into his 80s, driving to rural West Texas towns on weekends to help immigrants adrift in the legal system. Over 80 years old, Armendariz needed hearing aids—earphones and an amplifier—but refused to retire, even when one judge suggested he step down.

"I'll retire when I want to retire," he said.

The determination and self-sufficiency was something he learned from his parents, who left Mexico for El Paso, Texas, to provide a better life for their family. When he entered elementary school, Armendariz spoke no English, but he was a fast learner and quickly caught on.

His father, who urged him to support his country in the war effort, instilled a strong sense of patriotism in Armendariz. He served as sergeant, and oversaw Italian prisoners at Fort Bliss, Texas.

Following his discharge, Armendariz used the GI Bill to attend the University of Texas at El Paso and the University of Southern California Law School. He was the only Latino in his law school class. He experienced some discrimination, but with the support of his loving wife, Mary Lou [Regalado], he persevered. He graduated and moved back to El Paso, where he began practicing law. He was also active in his community with LULAC and served as national president in 1954. Armendariz was also a founder of the Mexican American Legal Defense and Educational Fund.

Armendariz served as an administrative judge for the Immigration and Naturalization Service from 1976 through 1985 and was a judge on the Texas Court of Appeals for the 8th Circuit in 1985.

Armendariz had six children with Mary Lou: Albert Jr., Cesar, María Leticia, John David, Mary Lou and Michael Lawrence. After Mary Lou's death in 1993, Armendariz married María de Jesús Jauregui, who became his driver on weekend trips to see clients.

Antonio Campos

Date of Birth
21 AUGUST 1923
Baytown, TX

Interviewed by
Veronica Garza
2 MARCH 2002
Houston, TX

WWII Military Unit
46oth Parachute
Field Artillery
Battalion,
517th Parachute
Regimental
Combat Team

CAMPOS, ANTONIO. Dedicated to advancing equality for Latinos, Antonio Campos began his campaign at an early age. After he was denied entry into the Boy Scouts, Campos formed a Hispanic troop. "We showed them that we were able to produce and be the leaders of the community," he said. Eventually, he was one of the first Hispanics in Baytown to earn the designation of Eagle Scout.

Campos graduated from high school and joined the U.S. Army, serving as a paratrooper. His first jump was across enemy lines in southern France on Aug. 15, 1944. After his discharge, Campos used the GI Bill to attend Baylor University and law school. During college, he married his high school sweetheart, Alicia Torres. They had four children: Sylvia, Michael, Aida and Marc.

He then worked for the U.S. Department of Labor, verifying that farmers who contracted laborers from Mexico were meeting the requirements for pay and medical and housing benefits.

Campos later formulated a preschool program for non-English speakers. As of result, the Texas State Legislature mandated preschool programs for non-English-speaking children. The bill eventually became the Head Start Program.

Politically, Campos worked to establish single-member election districts in Baytown, as it was difficult for a Hispanic to win the popular vote in an at-large district. "One day we went over to the city council to explain [what we wanted], and one councilman said, 'If you don't like it, why don't you go back to Mexico?'" Campos said. "I got up and said, 'Hey! I was born here in Texas. I went overseas and put my life on the line so you people can make decisions like that?'" The struggle eventually reached the U.S. Supreme Court, which upheld an appellate court decision ruling the at-large system in violation of the Voting Rights Act.

Campos takes pride in having fought two wars—one a global conflict, another a social one.

CASTORENA, GILBERT. When his high school principal asked Gilbert Castorena what he planned to do, he said he would join the Navy. "He said that the Navy wouldn't take just anybody and asked me what I would do about that," Castorena said. Undeterred, he joined as a hospital corpsman in 1940 and was sent to a naval training station in San Diego, where he treated wounded patients for over a year. He traveled to Iceland, New Zealand and Guadalcanal, Solomon Islands, during the war.

In Guadalcanal, Castorena served as part of the International Red Cross team established by the Geneva Convention in 1919 to protect wounded soldiers and develop humanitarian policies. In 1943 he contracted malaria, recuperated at Fort Worth Medical Center in Texas and returned home.

He worked briefly at the San Diego Post Office then took a job at the North Island Air Station where his father had worked. He worked as a metalsmith, preparing helicopters and airplanes for the war. In addition, he served at the station as chair of the Equal Employment Opportunity Committee—a product of the civil rights movement—helping to open doors to higher employment positions and wages. "In different instances, if they were discriminated against, we could find jobs with higher pay," he said. "A painter could go to a foreman and no higher, but we opened the door and helped him reach superintendent."

He also dedicated his life to service, serving, among other positions, as president of the Balboa Optimist Club of San Diego and chairman of the G.I. Forum. As chairman of the Veterans of Foreign Wars of Mexican Ancestry he helped distribute $500 scholarships to 15 Mexican-American high school seniors, so they could pursue a higher education. "I think one of the things that concerns me a lot is for [students to get] more schooling and to get the highest education they can," he said. "The better educated they are, the more it will help them."

Gilbert Castorena

Date of Birth
20 DECEMBER 1920
San Diego, CA

Interviewed by
René Zambrano
8 NOVEMBER 2000
San Diego, CA

WWII Military Unit
Company C,
1st Battalion,
6th Marine
Regiment,
2d Marine Division

CHAPA, JUANA ESTELA GONZALEZ. Despite her husband's military service for the country in WWII, Estela Chapa and her husband Roberto faced discrimination when they sought housing at Southwest Texas State University. The leasing agent was going to rent the apartment to light-skinned Roberto until his brother came to sign the lease. The agent told them, "I'm sorry, but we don't rent to Mexicans," Chapa said. Angered, Roberto Chapa complained to a sympathetic university administrator. He provided modest accommodations for the Chapas in a room where the football players had stayed. Their beds were cots and their showers were in a community bathroom that consisted of 16 showerheads. "We only used one," she said. "I wasn't going to clean that many showers!"

During the war, Chapa, born Juana Estela Gonzalez, worked on projects in her high school classes in Rio Grande City, Texas: her Glee Club visited nearby Fort Ringgold to sing to soldiers; in her English class she wrote letters to faraway soldiers; and in her homemaking class, they knitted sweaters together to send overseas. "I was so tired of that Army green," she said.

Chapa's family and community mourned their losses during the war. "I recall a lot of people crying," she said. Three of her brothers—in a family of 11 children—served in the war. One served in England and saw no combat, another was badly injured and the third died at Normandy.

She graduated from high school in the top 10 in 1945, and then studied at Pan American Junior College, which became a four-year university, and she earned her bachelor's degree and certifications in both elementary and secondary education. Shortly before she graduated she met Roberto at a small party. Within six months, they married. At Southwest Texas State, Roberto obtained his administrative certificate and Chapa took an English course. The couple had two boys: Roberto Tomás Jr. and Ricardo José. Chapa became a full-time mother but later taught school for 30 years.

Juana Estela
Gonzalez Chapa

Date of Birth
24 JUNE 1928
Rio Grande City, TX

Interviewed by
Misty Roberts
16 MARCH 2000
Austin, TX

WWII Location
Rio Grande City, TX

Ernest Eguía

Date of Birth
7 NOVEMBER 1919
Lockhart, TX

Interviewed by
Claudia García
3 FEBRUARY 2001
Houston, TX

WWII Military Unit
981st Field
Artillery Battalion

EGUÍA, ERNEST. Going from the forefront of the Allied Invasion of Normandy to the front lines of the civil rights movement, Ernest Eguía pioneered the movement for Hispanic integration in the Houston area after the war. After serving as coastal defense on the California shore, facing brutal fighting in France and promoting the restoration of German society during the occupation, Eguía returned home to disappointingly familiar race relations: "I thought that coming back to Texas, things would have changed," he said.

Determined to put an end to some of the anti-Hispanic racism in Texas, Eguía joined LULAC, prompted by the story of Macario Garcia, who received a Medal of Honor but was denied service at a hamburger restaurant because he was Mexican-American.

Eguía held several posts in the Houston chapter, one of the nation's most prominent. He was involved with LULAC projects to integrate Hispanics into various levels of Houston city government. For instance, at a meeting of LULAC members and city officials, the officials first argued a height minimum for police officers.

"And we were prepared," Eguía said. "We had about a dozen young men that were Hispanic that were 6 feet tall or higher than that." When officials countered with education requirements, six of the men had completed college.

"So they couldn't back down and it was the start of when the police officers got into the police force," Eguia said.

Eguía married Maria Ortensia Martinez Nov. 11, 1948, and the couple had four children: Diane, Rebecca, David and Mark. He continued his participation in LULAC events and remained active in the VFW and the American Legion.

Elena Peña Gallego

Date of Birth
18 AUGUST 1928
Ft. Stockton, TX

Interviewed by
Maggie Rivas-
Rodriguez
9 MARCH 2002
El Paso, TX

WWII Location
Fort Stockton, TX

GALLEGO, ELENA PEÑA. As discrimination prevailed in her hometown, Elena Peña Gallego began a crusade to overcome adversity and continue her education, something that would remain constant in her life. With separate seating movie theaters, and segregation in public places such as restaurants and swimming pools, many were discouraged, but she stayed motivated, graduating from high school and beginning college.

Born Elena Peña, she fought battles for civil rights in her hometown in Fort Stockton, Texas. She refused to take tests in school that she knew were different than the tests given to Anglo students. She left college when she married Pete Gallego in 1947, but she still remained passionate about the importance of education, insisting that Pete attend college.

"I'll marry you if you get an education," she told him.

Gallego continued her civil rights work with her husband and children. She pushed for integration, and her husband served on the school board in hope of realizing those goals.

Gallego and her husband also ran a credit union for the disenfranchised out of their home for 12 years. Initially, the Gallegos worked as volunteers for Our Lady of Peace Credit Union, working other jobs to support their family. Gallego worked in a bank, where she experienced discrimination and unfair treatment, but she kept the job to pay for college educations for her three children: Imelda, Pete and Rebecca. Imelda and Pete became lawyers, and Rebecca became a physician.

Later, Gallego began working with the Texas Department of Health and Human Services, working in Child Protective Services and geriatric services and distributing food stamps.

After a long, varied career, Gallego was proud of the advancement of women. "They [women] are not worried about making it on their own," she said. "Because I think they realize they can."

GALLEGO, PETE A. With his fellow soldiers in WWII, Pete A. Gallego finally experienced an integrated community but returned to the same segregation that he had known growing up in Alpine, Texas. Gallego, who served with the 1886th Aviation Engineer Battalion in Hawaii, Guam and Okinawa, returned to the States in 1946. He earned a business degree from Sul Ross State College, one of only four Latinos in a class of 100. "My career was actually trying to see more [Latino] people get involved in politics and do better than what we had accomplished in the past," he said.

During his first year of college, Gallego met Elena Peña of Fort Stockton, Texas, and married her the next year. The two took over operation of his mother's restaurant and started a family in 1952. They had four children: Imelda, Rebecca, Pete and Robert.

At the request of community members, Gallego ran for a school board seat. "We wanted to try to get the system equalized for our students," he said. Gallego was elected as the only Latino on a seven-member school board in 1959 and immediately began pushing for school reform and desegregation. When bonds were set to finance construction on a new school, Latinos galvanized for desegregated schools and a caravan of concerned citizens traveled to the capital in Austin.

Back in Alpine, the harassment began with phone calls, letters and visits targeting Gallego's family. His wife said the bank manager dropped by their diner to tell Gallego he wouldn't have anything but the shirt on his back if he continued his cause.

"Pete started unbuttoning his shirt then," Elena said. "He said, 'Would you like to have it now?'" The restaurant was forced to move from lack of business but found patronage in supportive college students. In 1970, the bond-financed schools were built and community members monitored for integration.

Pete A. Gallego

Date of Birth
17 FEBRUARY 1925
Alpine, TX

Interviewed by
Maggie Rivas-Rodriguez
9 MARCH 2002
El Paso, TX

WWII Military Unit
1886th Aviation Engineer Battalion

GARCIA, SARAGOSA. From recess to the shipyard, as a child and as an adult, Saragosa Garcia faced discrimination, but through his love of music and his faith Garcia remained strong.

In school in Rosenberg, Texas, Garcia's teacher banned him from playing the drums or saxophone with the ethnic "Bohemians"—what he termed the "white folks." In his segregated school he was denied promotion to fourth grade more than once. During recess, Hispanic children learned to dig holes outside rather than play. Garcia's father protested: "My children didn't come here to learn how to dig holes," he told the teacher. The family moved to Houston, Texas, where Garcia's experience with his teacher was more positive: a teacher named Mrs. Smith gave him a Bible. "I still have that Bible today," he said.

In 1942 Garcia was drafted into the Army. Garcia was in the second wave of American soldiers to land in Normandy. "A sniper shot at me from a hill and just barely missed," he recalled. "And I was laying down and praying for some guy to make a road so we could get by."

After the war, Garcia, who came from a family of musicians, played for his church and also in a country-western band. "We used to play all over the place," he said. His band played at parks, parties, weddings and hotels. "I even played with a symphony," he added. In 1952 he married Ophelia Turnini. The couple had three children: Daniel, Sarah and Robert.

He began to work at a shipyard, where he again faced discrimination. His supervisor assigned him to "Mexican labor" and gave the white workers the good jobs, Garcia said. He sued the shipyard for discrimination and won. His action changed the way the company treated minorities, and the shipyard was forced to grant everyone equal facilities.

He later worked for the U.S. Postal Service for 28 years and continued to play in his band.

Saragosa Garcia

Date of Birth
22 OCTOBER 1922
Corpus Christi, TX

Interviewed by
Ernest Eguía
18 NOVEMBER 2002
Houston, TX

WWII Military Unit
Battery B, 197th Anti-Aircraft Artillery Automatic Weapons Battalion, Company E, 393d Infantry Regiment, 99th Infantry Division

Jack Greenberg

Date of Birth
22 DECEMBER 1924
New York, NY

Interviewed by
Maggie Rivas-
Rodriguez
26 APRIL 2004
New York, NY

WWII Military Unit
LST 715

GREENBERG, JACK. When he saw a continued need for lawyers fighting for civil rights for Hispanics in the United States, Jack Greenberg, then an official with the NAACP Legal Defense Fund, contacted Pete Tijerina, a leader of LULAC in San Antonio, Texas. Thus began what would become a concerted effort by Greenberg, Tijerina and others, including the Ford Foundation, to provide legal representation for civil rights cases involving Hispanics. "There were a lot of issues and nobody was addressing them," Greenberg said. "A lot of people were in oppressive situations."

Greenberg had been working with the NAACP Legal Defense Fund for 17 years in 1966, when he received repeated requests for assistance from Mexican Americans and Native Americans.

"We had a great deal of success with civil rights cases, and people who we ordinarily didn't represent came to us asking us to represent them," said Greenberg, who was named director-counsel of the defense fund in 1961.

With both Tijerina and Greenberg convinced of the necessity of a Hispanic legal defense fund, Greenberg arranged a meeting with Ford Foundation officials.

"People like to feel that they are in charge of their destinies ... not manipulated from the outside," Greenberg said, explaining why it was crucial that the Hispanic attorneys form their own organization.

In 1968, the Ford Foundation granted the new Mexican American Legal Defense and Educational Fund two times more than its organizers originally had requested—$2.2 million over five years, with the stipulation that $250,000 of the grant was for scholarships for Mexican-American law students. Decades later, MALDEF has addressed issues including school segregation, police brutality and the denial of due process to individuals active in the Chicano movement.

Alfred J. Hernandez

Date of Birth
23 AUGUST 1917
Mexico City, Mexico

Interviewed by
Ernest Eguía
24 OCTOBER 2002
Houston, TX

WWII Military Unit
2615th Technical
Supervision
Regiment

HERNANDEZ, ALFRED J. After serving his time in the Army and tasting equality in Virginia, New York, North Africa and Europe, Alfred Hernandez liked being treated as an American.

Back home in Houston, Texas, with its deep racial divisions even after the war, he was, again subjected to different treatment because of his ethnicity. He told his wife, Herminia Casas, he wanted to move up north or back to Mexico.

"After discussing the way I felt with my wife, she soon convinced me we should stay in Houston and get involved and make an effort to fix the problems here," he said. Hernandez earned his law degree, which provided him the tools he needed to change hiring practices in Houston. He also became a national president of LULAC in 1965 and, later, Houston's first Hispanic judge. "I wish I could have done more," he said. "I didn't open doors. I was just part of the movement."

Hernandez had served in North Africa during the war. "I have a propensity for languages," he said. "And I picked up French and Italian easily." After Hernandez conversed with a French general at a party one day, his commander heard his Italian skills, and Hernandez became an interpreter for the Army. Prior to being transferred to France, Hernandez received his U.S. citizenship on a cold, icy morning in Italy.

He later watched over POWs from Italy and Germany. "I got along with the POWs very well, and by the time the war was almost over I got a chance to take them [the Italians] back to their countries," Hernandez said.

Back in Houston after the war, Hernandez helped get jobs for Hispanics by protesting to civil service agencies. He helped with the hiring of the first two Hispanic police officers in Houston. He and his wife were married in April 1942 and had two children, Alfred Jr. and Anna Marie.

IDAR, ED JR. Returning from WWII at age 25, Ed Idar Jr. was young, passionate and bold. He soon tackled issues of Mexican-American rights and equality. "I was not afraid," Idar said. "I had been in the service and had dealt with generals, colonels and this and that and the other."

Using the GI Bill, Idar earned his degree in journalism from the University of Texas at Austin. As a member of the university's Laredo Club, he wrote a resolution criticizing Attorney General Price Daniel for an opinion Idar said "opened the door" to segregation of Mexican-American students.

While in Austin, he worked as the executive secretary for the American Council of Spanish Speaking People, conducting research about Mexican-American issues. Three years later he was awarded a fellowship to finish law school, and in 1956 he moved to McAllen, Texas, to practice law.

In 1950 he joined the G.I. Forum, a veterans' organization that sought to end discrimination against Hispanics, and became state chairman in 1951. When Idar served as executive secretary of the Forum, he compiled newsletters to raise money for court expenses for the Hernandez case in 1954—the first case argued by Mexican-American lawyers before the Supreme Court. The case established Hispanics as a "special class" with protection under the 14th Amendment. "Our people were dedicated," he said. "They believed in what they were doing. They weren't expecting a salary."

Idar was influential in a multitude of other civic groups, including the Viva Kennedy Club, which helped galvanize Mexican-American voters during the presidential election in 1960; PASSO—the Political Association of Spanish Speaking Organizations; and MALDEF—the Mexican American Legal Defense and Educational Fund. He also served as assistant attorney general in Austin. Idar married Joan Stringer, an Englishwoman, and had two children: Rebecca and Edward. Joan died in 1985. In 1994, Idar married María Meza Rodriguez.

Ed Idar, Jr.

Date of Birth
28 DECEMBER 1920
Laredo, TX

Interviewed by
Maggie Rivas-Rodriguez
2 DECEMBER 2000
San Antonio, TX

WWII Location
Stationed in Kachrapara, India

JUAREZ, RUPERTO SOTO. Orphaned as an adolescent, Ruperto Soto Juarez fibbed about his age to join the Navy and serve his country in WWII. He later became a political activist, fighting for a fairer world; and stayed by his wife's bedside when she was terminally ill.

To get overseas during WWII, Juarez reported his age as 18 when he was only 16. Then, with his departure postponed, he found out that if he went AWOL he would be shipped overseas immediately. "I thought that was my chance," he said. "One day I jumped over the fence and got my little briefcase and I went hitchhiking to El Paso." He joined the Army and was court-martialed by the Navy. After a 35-day confinement he was shipped to Guam—mission accomplished.

After WWII, Juarez married Guadalupe Martinez; the couple had eight children: Margarita, Ruperto, Lorenzo, Rita, Armando, Virginia, Martha and Benito.

He served during the Korean war. When he returned, he joined the Mexican-American Political Association. "The main thing we did was to make the life of the Mexican American better than what it was at that time," he said. MAPA worked to pressure California ranchers to stop calling immigration officials when payday came to avoid paying Mexican immigrants.

As a member of MAPA, Juarez also worked hard to improve the political landscape for Mexican Americans. "The only way we can do that is by helping to get Mexican Americans into office," he said. "As long as their aims were for the betterment of Mexican Americans, we would back them up even if they weren't Mexican." In April 1994, at age 66, Juarez decided to run for city council in Norwalk, Calif. "This was quite an experience for me," he said. "Even though I had always been involved in politics and helping people in one way or another." Juarez collected 1 percent of the vote but was happy with the overall outcome, which "ousted" the incumbents.

Ruperto Soto Juarez

Date of Birth
24 MARCH 1928
El Paso, TX

Interviewed by
Valerie Talavera-Bustillos
25 JANUARY 2001
Norwalk, CA

WWII Location
Stationed in Guam

Agustín Lucio Jr.

Date of Birth
27 NOVEMBER 1922
San Marcos, TX

Interviewed by
Denise Chavarri
10 FEBRUARY 2003
San Marcos, TX

WWII Military Unit
Company L,
3d Battalion,
23d Infantry
Regiment,
2d Infantry
Division

LUCIO, AGUSTÍN JR. With elite Ranger training, as well as airborne and ski training, Agustín Lucio was sent to Europe and eventually fought in the D-Day invasion. After months without a station, Lucio said one day he and his platoon were asked to sit around a sand table—a representation of Normandy—to discuss tactics for the following day's invasion.

"I remember General Eisenhower saying, 'You have been chosen to make this invasion, a great crusade, something that some of you will remember: Good luck,' " Lucio said.

A bullet hit Lucio's platoon sergeant after the first day of combat, and Lucio took his place, leading the 45 men through the Cerisy Forest. Lucio was wounded in the leg when his division took the Port of Brest in Southern France. "It was not something serious," he said. "The next day I got back to combat." After eight months of combat, Lucio was able to return home for 30 days. He visited his girlfriend, Delia Saldivar, every day. She asked him to marry her before he returned to the war front, and they wed on April 15, 1945.

After the war Lucio returned to the San Marcos, Texas, area, where he grew up, and began work at Austin's Bergstrom Air Force Base. He studied business administration at Southwest Texas State University but discontinued his studies when he was promoted at Bergstrom. His final position was as chief of quality control, and he worked for Bergstrom for 35 years.

Active in his community, Lucio served on the San Marcos school board as president, vice president, secretary and treasurer. In total, he served 19 years. On May 5, 1972, Lucio led a boycott of all the schools in the district to protest unequal treatment of the growing Hispanic community. There were not enough Hispanic teachers, he said. The school district named a library after Lucio.

He and his wife had four children: Rosemary, José, Robert and Carol.

Ernesto Pedregón
Martinez

Date of Birth
26 FEBRUARY 1926
El Paso, TX

Interviewed by
Jeffrey Lee Johnson
28 JUNE 2001
El Paso, TX

WWII Military Unit
104th Infantry
Division

MARTINEZ, ERNESTO PEDREGÓN. Before he reached the age of 22, Ernesto Pedregón Martinez had already worked as a bullfighting poster painter, helped liberate a Nazi concentration camp and returned home to start a new life—including becoming a nationally-known artist.

During his high school years in El Paso, Texas, Martinez found a passion for painting and drawing. He enjoyed attending bullfights in Juarez, Mexico, and created bullfight promotion posters at age 17. He graduated in 1944, eager to join the military. "They call it the innocence of youth because you don't realize what you're asking for," he said. "It's no picnic."

In 1945, when he and his fellow soldiers first heard gunfire, they didn't recognize it. "We were so innocent at the time, we thought it was a rainstorm," he said. When they saw bodies lying outside a church in Belgium, the soldiers assumed a lack of space forced people to sleep outside. "It did not register that they were already dead," he said. Martinez and his unit later discovered the Mittelbau-Dora Concentration Camp in Nordhausen, Germany, with thousands of people who looked like skeletons. "Some of them must have weighed 80 pounds," he said.

Back in El Paso, he attended International Business College, where he met Mary Trejo. The couple married in 1949 and had five children: Irma, Ernie, George, Lorraine and Ralphael. When he was 48, the Movimiento Estudiantíl Chicano de Aztlán, a student group involved in Chicano issues, gave him the opportunity to put on his first art exhibit, launching his artistic career. His paintings rose in value from $10 to $300.

Martinez did work for many activists in the Chicano Movement, including Cesar Chavez, Corky Gonzales and Reies Tijerina. He received numerous accolades, including 1998 Texas State Artist of the Year and Artist of the Year by LULAC chapter No. 9 in 1974 and No. 664 in 1975.

MORENO, LEOPOLD RODRÍGUEZ. Fear of failure never kept Leopold Rodríguez Moreno from seeking his goals — from surviving WWII, to marrying the woman of his dreams, to overcoming racial adversity at work.

Leopold Rodríguez
Moreno

Date of Birth
8 AUGUST 1923
Houston, TX

Interviewed by
Paul R. Zepeda
8 AUGUST 2003
Houston, TX

WWII Military Unit
Company A,
169th Infantry
Regiment,
43d Infantry
Division

"If I don't make it, at least I tried," Moreno said of his philosophy.

During the Battle of Luzon in January 1945, Moreno was shot in the back, by what he surmised was a ricochet wound that only penetrated his body slightly. Many high-ranking soldiers died and Moreno was promoted to sergeant. He recovered at a prison converted into a hospital in Manila, Philippines, and returned to his unit. Most of his friends had been killed.

Later that year, in September, Moreno married Rosa Villagomez while he was on a 30-day leave. He had met Rosa at a party in 1939, when he was 16 and she was 15. The couple eventually had nine children: Dolores, Charles, Stella, Ruth, Teresa, Oscar, Norma, Caroline and John.

One of Moreno's proudest moments was the day he helped open a door for minorities while he was employed at Southern Pacific Railroad Co. At the time, no blacks or Mexican Americans were allowed to be sent to other states to conduct freight-car inspections. After climbing the employment ladder from apprentice to journeyman and then to inspector, Moreno went to his union representative requesting that something be done about the practice.

He was soon sent to West Virginia to inspect cars, along with another employee — the first black man sent. The two formed a pact. "We got to set an example for other guys," Moreno told his friend. The two helped other workers gain overtime.

Their manager praised them, sending a letter to upper management commending them on their superb work and ability to catch every flaw on the line.

MUNGUIA, RUBEN. Running the print shop at Air Force headquarters at Randolph Field in San Antonio, Texas, Ruben Munguia "had it made" during the war. First rejected from service because of a minor eye problem, Munguia tried again and was assigned to his hometown.

Ruben Munguia

Date of Birth
30 SEPTEMBER 1919
Mexico City, Mexico

Interviewed by
Martha Treviño
11 NOVEMBER 2001
San Antonio, TX

WWII Location
HQ, Randolph
Airfield,
San Antonio, TX

Munguia, who rose to the rank of corporal during his two years of service, said with a grin, "I had a furlough and went home every night, so yes, [military service] was ideal for me."

His father was a journalist and his mother, whom he described as "the first women's libber," hosted a daily, hour-long radio program on Mexican culture and history. Munguia was influenced by his parents and inherited the family print shop, as well as a no-nonsense demeanor and a willingness to take on injustices.

Munguia believed discrimination is based more on social and economic issues rather than on race. But he nonetheless recalled the one time he felt his ethnicity was used against him. In post-war San Antonio, he and his wife, Martha Isabel (Lopez), whom he married in 1945 after he left the service, were looking to buy land for a house. The deal was accepted until the next day when the sales person asked about the origin of Munguia's unfamiliar name.

"I said, proudly, 'I'm Mexican.' All of a sudden the guy said there was a slight problem with the paperwork and could he call me back? I said, 'No, you so-and-so — I know what you are doing, not selling to me cause I am Mexican. To hell with you.' And I called off the deal."

That incident prompted Munguia to join such groups as LULAC and the G.I. Forum. He later backed legendary Texas politicians, such as Henry B. Gonzalez, as well as his own nephew, Henry Cisneros, to promote the next generation of Mexican-American politicians.

Munguia and his wife had three children: Martha, Ruben Jr. and Mary Margaret.

Mary Martinez
Olvera Murillo

Date of Birth
8 JULY 1924
Austin, TX

Interviewed by
Ana Cristina Acosta
15 OCTOBER 1999
Austin, TX

WWII location
Austin, TX

MURILLO, MARY MARTINEZ OLVERA. It took a war and a courageous fight on the home front to change a society of discrimination. Mary Murillo was on the front line of this fight.

While Murillo, born Mary M. Olvera, was growing up in Austin, Texas, Mexican Americans were kept from the white part of town, kicked out of many stores, and excluded from privileges such as free lunch in school. "They started giving us lunch after a few years, but we had to wait until the white children would finish," Murillo said. " ... Only then we could go inside the cafeteria."

It was the war, Murillo said, that propelled change. When the scores of men in her community — including Murillo's four brothers and several cousins — returned home from overseas, they questioned society's standards and began to demand more rights. After all, they had not been treated as inferior in the military and had fought for their country the same as Anglo men.

"There was more talk about the boys wanting to educate themselves, and you know, thinking about going to the university, going to college," she said.

Murillo and other Mexican Americans in South Austin began improving their neighborhood. They would travel from house to house, encouraging people to vote, to get a good education and to influence change. Eventually, the community organized a night school where Murillo earned her GED at 50 years old. Her relatives joined LULAC and other Latino civil rights organizations.

Though the struggle is not over, Murillo believes discrimination has lessened over the years.

"We owed it to our children," she said. "They have more opportunities and I think they want to do better."

She married Leo Murillo on Oct. 13, 1946, and they had three children: Thomas, Michael and Edward.

Manuela Maymie
Garcia Ontiveros

Date of Birth
22 DECEMBER 1921
Lockhart, TX

Interviewed by
Raul García Jr.
19 OCTOBER 2002
Saginaw, MI

WWII Location
Saginaw, MI

ONTIVEROS, MANUELA MAYMIE GARCIA. Though she had never traveled to Mexico, Manuela Ontiveros dedicated her life to her family and community and preserving her treasured Mexican heritage. "You instill in your children and grandchildren pride," Ontiveros said. "Even through my grandchildren are half-white, they know how to cook enchiladas and tamales. I try to pass on the traditions of the Mexican people, traditions that they have nothing to be ashamed of."

After her mother and sister died of spinal meningitis when she was 9, Manuela Garcia was raised by her grandmother, who taught her to value her Mexican culture.

She married Jesús Quiroz Ontiveros in 1941 after she graduated from high school. The couple had five children: Jesús, Robert, Raquel, Daniel and Celia. Twenty years her senior, Jesús served as president of the Mexican Civic Union. The couple both worked through the union to fight discrimination. "Men were coming back from the war, and even though they served, they were discriminated against," Ontiveros said.

Civic union members would go to public schools and perform original Mexican cultural dances. Their goal was to build a meeting hall for the Mexicans in Saginaw, Mich., like other groups had. "We had our dances in any hall we could get," she said. "The Italian and Polish had their halls, so the Mexicans decided to build a hall."

Ontiveros' community activities included the Young Women's Christian Association and the Bridge of Racial Harmony. "We have different people come and talk about their experiences [with racism]," she said. She spent nine years mentoring children who were behind in reading. Also active in politics, she was a member of the League of Women Voters, helped start the Saginaw chapter of LULAC, served as an election inspector and helped register voters.

RICO, ANTONIO. Stationed in Guam in 1945, Antonio Rico remembered the long hours pulling guard duty on the island. Fortunately, however, he found some solace in ice cream.

"Ice cream saved my life," he said. "It was a lonely time, but the best past was that we could have all the ice cream we wanted." They also had concerts in the mess hall.

Rico enlisted in the Navy in December 1941. He was sent to Camp Perry, Va., for basic training, where he remembered his instructors being hard on him. Assigned to the Seabees, Rico transferred to Newfoundland, where he provided service and support for ships coming in from Europe for fresh water supplies. He later transferred to Guam where he earned a stripe when he was placed in charge of a guard team as "corporal of the guard." While with the Seabees, he was trained in building pontoon bridges and laying down airfield strips, living quarters and other types of buildings.

When the Japanese surrendered, Rico and the other troops in Guam celebrated like it was the Fourth of July. He remembered the sound of ships blowing their horns and shooting flares; soldiers ripped off their uniforms because the war had ended.

After the war he returned to his former job at a warehouse facility in Houston, Texas. The day he returned, he met Ernestine Del Toro; the couple married 2 1/2 years later and had two sons: Alfred and Robert.

While he was not very political, Rico said, he worked for LULAC because the organization opened doors for Latinos in many walks of life. He served as secretary of the Houston chapter and eventually became president of the chapter in 1963.

He recalled one dedication ceremony attended by President John F. Kennedy and his wife. "I was thrilled to hear Jacqueline Kennedy speak to us in Spanish," Rico said.

RODRÍGUEZ, MARÍA ELISA REYES. Never shy about speaking her mind when something's not right, Elisa Rodríguez formed solid opinions about her country, discrimination and the relationship between the two.

"We're in America, and everybody has to be treated equally," she said. "But if you don't have the guts to speak out for yourself, nobody's gonna do it for you."

Her first civil service job was in 1943 at Blackland Army Airfield in Waco, Texas. Only hours before she landed her job at Blackland, she was turned down from a job as a stenographer with a defense company in nearby McGregor — because she was Mexican-American.

"I says, 'Sir, are you just denying me a position because of my nationality?' He grinned and said, 'Yes, if I hire you, the other secretaries will quit. We just have white secretaries,'" Rodriguez recalled.

In 1952, she was transferred to Bergstrom Air Force Base in Austin, Texas, where she worked as a secretary and equal employment opportunity coordinator. She worked at various jobs in civil service, including in adjudication within the Veterans Administration.

A group of minority veterans at the base called her because they were about to get laid off. "They go to war, they fight for you, and they get nothing but a reduction in force?" she asked the personnel director. She complained that several non-veteran Anglos should be laid off instead. "If you don't do this, I'm gonna do something about it. I'm gonna go to the paper, the Green Berets — tell the whole world what you're doing to these vets," she said. The veterans were retained.

A first marriage to Rudy Cisneros ended in divorce after she had two children, Rudy and Julie Cisneros. She later married Benito Rodríguez.

Antonio Rico

Date of Birth
7 SEPTEMBER 1924
Mexia, TX

Interviewed by
Ernest Eguía and
Paul R. Zepeda
7 JULY 2003
Houston, TX

WWII Military Unit
128th Naval
Construction
Battalion
(Seabees)

María Elisa Reyes
Rodríguez

Date of Birth
24 FEBRUARY 1922
Waco, TX

Interviewed by
Ryan Bauer
10 MAY 1999
Austin, TX

WWII Location
Blackland Army
Airfield, Waco, TX

Virgilio G. Roel

Date of Birth
2 JUNE 1922
Laredo, TX

Interviewed by
Alicia Rascon and
Stacy Nelson
1999 AND 2000
Austin, TX

WWII Military Unit
Headquarters,
517th Parachute
Infantry Regiment,
13th Airborne
Division

ROEL, VIRGILIO G. Post-WWII brought what Virgilio G. Roel termed "The Golden Era" for Mexican Americans. With the GI Bill, "for the first time in the history of our country, and our ethnic experience, they had the opportunity to attend colleges and universities all over the United States," he said. Roel had served with the Army, first training with the 84th Infantry Division. He was selected for the Army Specialized Training Program and went to Ohio State University to study geopolitics and languages. After five months he was assigned to a communications unit in Missouri then joined the paratroopers and traveled to England, France and Germany.

Under the GI Bill he attended the University of Texas, and in 2 1/2 years graduated magna cum laude with a degree in international relations. At the university, he helped organize the Laredo Club, which was active in civic affairs, challenging Attorney General Price Daniel to reverse an opinion he issued that condoned segregation of schoolchildren based on language.

Roel received his law degree from Georgetown University, passed the bar exam in D.C. and Texas, and worked in various volunteer and official capacities advancing the role of Mexican Americans, including serving as associate justice of the High Court of American Samoa and co-founding the first national Hispanic lobbying group, which eventually became El Congreso. He traveled with a delegation to petition for a Mexican-American appointee as U.S. federal district judge. When a resolution seemed unclear, Roel, who along with the others had campaigned for John F. Kennedy for president through "Viva Kennedy" clubs, pushed for an immediate answer from U.S. Attorney General Robert F. Kennedy. Fewer than two months later, Reynaldo Garza was appointed. Roel and Emilia Salinas married June 1, 1957. The couple had four children: Laura, Virgilio, Diana and Aida.

Tizoc Romero

Date of Birth
7 SEPTEMBER 1924
San Diego, CA

Interviewed by
René Zambrano
4 SEPTEMBER 2000
San Diego, CA

WWII Military Unit
USS *Admiral W. L.
Capps* (AP-121)

ROMERO, TIZOC. Although he faced criticism from some minorities for fighting in the war, Tizoc Romero's involvement in WWII opened the doors to a lifetime of achievement. Romero was in high school during the attack on Pearl Harbor, but after he became the first in his family to finish high school, he enlisted in the Navy, serving as port security in San Diego, Calif., aboard the Coast Guard vessel the USS *Admiral W. L. Capps.*

"For me it really changed my perspective on Mexican Americans and how we were as patriotic and vulnerable as the next person," Romero said.

After the war, Romero joined the Merchant Marines for a short while but left for health reasons. Back in San Diego, he became a barber. While in his early 30s, Romero attended San Diego State University and earned a degree in education. "I suppose I wanted to make a difference," he said. "Being a barber was OK, but I guess I needed a challenge."

Romero then began teaching at Memorial Junior High, his alma mater, and it was there that he became active in the Chicano Movement of the 1960s and '70s. He was involved in several demonstrations involving minority civil rights and other organizations such as the American G.I. Forum, a Latino veterans' group and the Mexican American Educators Organization. "Politically we supported Cesar Chavez," Romero said. "We were not militant, but we did try to influence people of the cause, which was to establish more rights for minorities."

After teaching for 26 years, Romero retired. "Education is the basic thing to work for," he said. "Educate yourself in a broader sense and have goals, because without goals you're kind of lost."

A first marriage to Margaret Ramirez ended in divorce, but he helped raise her two children, Patrick and Kim, as his own; the couple also had a son, Eric. He married Barbara Alexander in 1982.

SAENZ, ENRIQUE LEON. When he arrived at Texas A&I University, Enrique Saenz had just 25 cents to his name. He was 26 years old the first time he went to college, and he had to rely on his brother to pay for his classes. Saenz had to wait until his brother got paid before he could buy his books or pay for classes. He failed in his second semester, took a summer off, and went back again the next semester. "But I just couldn't settle down, so I quit," he said.

He took the entrance exam for the Air Corps and missed the cutoff by just one point. A few days later, however, he received a draft notice from the Army. He was stationed in Casablanca, Morocco, and Sicily, Italy, during World War II. When he returned home, he said, little was the same. "Things got better after the war," Saenz said. "There in McAllen [Texas] before the war ... we couldn't get coffee there on Main Street. We couldn't eat in the restaurants. When I came back everyone would say 'Let's go there,' and it surprised me." He would later move to Austin.

He married Elmerida Herrera at this time, and they had five children: Alejandra Isidra, Enrique José, Pedro Antonio, María Elena and Tomás Adrian. He worked at ButterKrust, a local bread producer, until 1967. He returned to college in 1951, at the age of 32, hoping to get a degree in education. After a year, with a new child on the way, he decided that he could not balance family, work and school. He worked at the Internal Revenue Service after leaving ButterKrust, and stayed there until his retirement. Though he was successful without earning a college degree, he recommends that others make college education a priority.

"But I'd say to our people ... that they can succeed, but it requires hard work and dedication," he said. "Go to school. Stick with the job. And stay off gangs and drugs, because that's what's giving us the black eye."

Enrique Leon
Saenz

Date of Birth
19 APRIL 1920
Moore, TX

Interviewed by
Jamie Stockwell
and Leslie Ann
Garza
11 MAY 1999
Austin, TX

WWII Military Unit
65th Armored Field
Artillery Battalion

SAMARRON, CARLOS "CHARLES" GUERRA. Three weeks after Japan bombed Pearl Harbor, Charles Samarron joined the fight and enlisted in the Marine Corps, where he would gain a fresh perspective. "You know you're mortal and you can die anytime," he said. "I feel more kinship with my fellow man than I did before."

In November 1943, Samarron departed for New Caledonia. On July 21, 1944, Samarron took part in the beach assault on Guam. When he arrived via armored vehicle, Samarron feverishly dug a trench while mortars exploded all around him in his first combat experience. Above him, U.S. fighter planes dropped flares to highlight the locations of Japanese troops for U.S. ships to barrage with 16-inch shells. Samarron would survive this battle and also the Battle of Iwo Jima a year later. He was sent to Hawaii to train for an invasion of Japan that never came.

"The Japanese were fanatics; they were never going to give up," he said. "We were elated when Japan got bombed." He was discharged in January 1946 and returned to San Diego, Calif., with boosted confidence. "As a veteran you have equal rights like everybody else, so it gave Mexican Americans new opportunities," he said. "It gave us a feeling of being equal."

Samarron worked for the next 30 years in the Civil Service, serving as a deputy equal employment officer for the Navy. In addition to hearing and resolving complaints, he was in charge of examining each unit and exploring why there were few Hispanics enlisted. He also was involved in the G.I. Forum and worked to find jobs for Mexican-American veterans.

"There's always going to be a need for Hispanics to have a voice," said Samarron. "The best thing to do is get educated and try to do something with your life that's beneficial not only to you and your family, but also the community."

Carlos "Charles"
Guerra Samarron

Date of Birth
16 JULY 1922
San Antonio, TX

Interviewed by
René Zambrano
28 OCTOBER 2000
San Diego, CA

WWII Military Unit
3d Amphibious
Tractor Battalion,
3d Marine Division

Pedro "Pete"
Tijerina Jr.

Date of Birth
4 AUGUST 1922
Laredo, TX

Interviewed by
Maggie Rivas-
Rodriguez and
Maro Robbins
2 DECEMBER 2000
San Antonio, TX

WWII Military Unit
322d Air Engineer-
ing Group

TIJERINA, PEDRO "PETE" JR. Legal advocacy efforts by Pete Tijerina were built on ideals he learned during the war. "It taught me that I was a first-class citizen, that I was an American," he said. During his time at the Citizens' Military Training Corps at Camp Bullis part of Fort Sam Houston, Texas, Tijerina already stood for equality. When Mexican Americans—only—were instructed to get an unpopular crew cut, Tijerina was chosen spokesman to protest for the 75 Mexican Americans at the camp. He was discharged and returned to school. He later joined the Army Air Corps in 1941 and was stationed for a period in Guam.

After the war, Tijerina attended law school, courtesy of the GI Bill, and passed the State Bar. Before long he was involved in the struggle for equal treatment for Mexican Americans. He worked through LULAC, but without money, the group could do little more than file resolutions and write letters of protest, hoping for change.

In 1966, one case convinced Tijerina more had to be done. Tijerina was forced into an out-of-court settlement for a client, a Hispanic woman who had lost her leg in an automobile accident. Without Mexican-American jurors, his client would gain little. "The [non-Hispanic] jurors were not the peers of my clients, who were poor people from the West Side [of San Antonio]," he said.

Tijerina spearheaded the creation of the Mexican American Legal Defense and Educational Fund (MALDEF), with advice from the NAACP Legal Defense Fund and financial backing from the Ford Foundation. "It was important to the Movement, and to the Cause, and to the Mexican-American community that we have our own lawyers fight our own cases," he said.

Tijerina retired in 1992 but continued to do some legal work. Tijerina married Grace Gonzalez Feb. 13, 1954, and the couple had three children: Lynn, Peter III and Christina.

Roberto Vazquez

Date of Birth
1 AUGUST 1922
Laredo, TX

Interviewed by
William Luna
20 JUNE 2002
East Chicago, IN

WWII Military Unit
12th Field
Artillery Battalion,
2d Infantry
Division

VAZQUEZ, ROBERTO. Raised in Laredo, Texas, on the U.S.-Mexico border, Roberto Vazquez was among the 7,000 Mexican Americans who made up nearly half his WWII division. He went to Fort Sam Houston in San Antonio, Texas, for basic training and then to Wisconsin for ski training. His division was sent to Normandy, France; Germany; and Czechoslovakia.

One of his most vivid memories was storming the beaches of Normandy during D-Day-plus-one in 1944. "In Normandy, we *wanted* to get off the boat because we were afraid that they would sink our boat," he said. "We *wanted* to get on that beach. We started praying and felt lots better on the beach than we did in the water."

Throughout the war, Vazquez said his relationship with his fellow soldiers eased the trauma and distress. "We acted like brothers," he said. "Once we got into battle, we had no differences; we just protected each other." A number of Hispanic officers also made him feel emboldened as a Latino soldier. And then he returned to the States. "We came out of the service, and they used to seat us in a separate colored section in the theaters," he said. "Here we were out of the war with a bunch of medals, and we had to sit on the side. So we got involved in politics and changed a lot of things."

In 1948, Vazquez and his wife, Anna Torres, who had served in the Women's Army Air Corps, joined LULAC, an organization that embodied their philosophy that the will of a people can overcome inequalities of discrimination and injustice. The two organized men's and women's councils in East Chicago, Ind., and attended a total of 39 national conventions.

Vazquez was a pioneer president of the East Chicago council and later became 2nd national vice president. Anna was 1st state president in the Midwest. The couple had three sons: David, Arturo and Richard.

Virgilio G. Roel at his graduation from Georgetown University Law School, Washington D.C. February 1952.

The Value of Education

Returning to civilian life following WWII, there was a greater appreciation for education. It had been apparent that those with more schooling were eligible for promotions and higher pay. Many would later exhort their children to "get an education: it's the one thing nobody can take away from you."

Most important, the returning veterans were handed a "golden ticket": the GI Bill.

Austin radio personality Lalo Campos called the GI Bill "one of the greatest things the government could have done for all its citizens, but certainly for the Hispanics who went to war and found out that there were better things out there than just what you had at home."

Many used the government benefit to become teachers, lawyers and a host of other professions. Once they got a taste of higher education, many wouldn't stop until they received a terminal degree in their field. Gonzalo Garza, who had grown up as a migrant farmer, had vowed to himself to earn an education. He became a teacher and eventually earned a doctorate; today, there is a high school in Austin, Texas, named in his honor.

Juan Lujan, of West Texas, had already attended college for two years when he entered the military. He would also earn a doctorate and work as a school principal.

Gilberto Delgado went on to a distinguished career in deaf education, becoming the first Latino in the state of New Mexico to serve as a superintendent at a school for the deaf.

Frank Bonilla, became a leader in Puerto Rican Studies, receiving his doctorate from Harvard University in sociology. Bonilla was a professor at Stanford University and later at the City University of New York, where he was the director of the Center for Puerto Rican Studies.

As women's roles evolved after the war, women who had dropped out of school before the war went on to get a general equivalency diploma (GED) and attended college, despite the lack of government benefits. Felicitas Cerda Flores, of Houston, got her GED after retiring from a civil service job and went on to college.

"If I went to college at the age of 52, you can too," Flores often told young people. *(See Felicitas Cerda Flores' story in Chapter 4.)*

Many took on leadership roles in their community and workplace. Elena Tamez De Peña of Corpus Christi, Texas, earned a master's degree and worked in public health. She credits her own education with helping better the lives of her children. De Peña also remembered the influx of Latino professionals in the workplace following the war.

The government was another entity where Latinos made a difference. Representing the Hispanic population of the United States, they were able to bring the problems they faced to the forefront and work for change. Armando Rodriguez of San Diego, Calif., used his education to serve as an adviser to two presidential administrations, focusing intently on education reform and Latino issues. He was appointed the first director of the Mexican-American Affairs Office in the Department of Health, Education and Welfare by President Johnson and later worked under President Nixon as a regional education commissioner.

The GI Bill, coupled with the drive of the WWII-era Latinos and Latinas, created a generation of leaders who made huge contributions by educating themselves and their communities. And in a clear-cut demonstration of the multiplier effect, their children often attained college degrees as well.

Frank Bonilla

Date of Birth
3 FEBRUARY 1925
New York City, NY

Interviewed by
Mario Barrera
5 SEPTEMBER 2001
La Jolla, CA

WWII Military Unit
290th Infantry
Regiment,
75th Infantry
Division

Transferred to
65th Infantry
Regiment

BONILLA, FRANK. Just two weeks after his high school graduation, Frank Bonilla was drafted into the Army. He had been planning to go to college, but he put his plans on hold to serve his country. He served in the 290th Infantry Regiment, 75th Infantry Division, as a mortar gunner. After he was wounded on the front lines in the Battle of the Bulge, he was transferred to the Puerto Rican National Guard unit, the 65th Infantry Regiment, where he served as a company clerk.

"The soldiers in the regiment, although proud to be U.S. citizens, felt that they were a Puerto Rican army, not the U.S. Army," Bonilla said.

When Bonilla returned from the war, he used the GI Bill to fund his education. He graduated cum laude with a bachelor's degree from the City University of New York in 1949, with a master's degree in sociology from New York University in 1954, and with a doctorate in sociology from Harvard University in 1959.

Bonilla helped to found the Puerto Rican Hispanic Leadership Forum, later Aspira, to address the needs of Puerto Ricans in New York. He was a member of the American Universities Field Staff, conducting research surveys in Argentina, Chile, Mexico and Brazil in 1960.

He was on the faculty at the Massachusetts Institute of Technology as an associate professor, and later as a full professor. He researched Venezuelan politics there and served as a visiting professor at the Universidad Federal de Minais Gerais in Brazil from 1968 to 1970.

He was a professor at Stanford University from 1969 to 1972 and a senior associate in the Institute of Political Studies. He joined the faculty of the City University of New York in 1973, where he served as director of the Center for Puerto Rican Studies. He stepped down in 1993, but continued to work with the Inter-University Program for Latino Research until his retirement in 1995.

José María Burruel

Date of Birth
28 FEBRUARY 1925
Phoenix, AZ

Interviewed by
Delia Esparza
4 JANUARY 2003
Phoenix, AZ

WWII Location
Stationed in
San Francisco, CA

BURRUEL, JOSÉ MARÍA. During the Depression, José María Burruel's family was poor, but Burruel was determined to succeed. He went from working in the fields and shooting wild game for food as a boy to the highest levels of academia.

A turning point in his life was his service in the Navy, starting in 1943. He went through training at the Naval Training Center and the Electronics Technician School in San Diego, Calif., and the Gyrocompass School in San Francisco. He was discharged after six months because he was injured.

He worked in a machine shop, rebuilding machines for the war effort, but decided he wanted to change his life for the better. "I said to myself, 'Hey, I don't wanna be doing this for the rest of my life, and I sure as heck don't wanna go back and work in the fields like I did before,' " he said.

Burruel studied at Northern Arizona University and earned his bachelor's degree from Arizona State University. He taught and became principal of an elementary school in Arizona, then became the first Mexican-American teacher in Santa Monica, Calif. He returned to Arizona State University for his doctorate, where he simultaneously served as assistant dean of students and an assistant professor of education. He was the first University ombudsman, at a time of political unrest. He urged Hispanic students "not to let the long-haired, marijuana-smoking kids steal their thunder."

He also worked as director of the Teacher Corps at California State College, helping graduates find jobs. He served as director of supplementary programs for Santa Ana Unified School District in California and superintendent of multiple districts. He returned to ASU to teach English for a time.

In 1978, Burruel married Frances Ann Barnard. Both retired and devoted their time to promoting education and human rights. Burruel remained humble about his success and multiple awards. "Love, friendship, trust and respect for anyone," he said. "There are no greater honors than these."

CALDERON, ERNESTO. A trip to a drive-in movie theater with his friends changed Ernesto Calderon's life. They were driving to see a movie when his friend Eldon Adams, said he had joined the 11th Airborne Division and asked Calderon to do the same. "Just like that, I said 'sure' and I agreed to do it," he said.

He had second thoughts, but he ultimately decided that the military might be better than the migrant farm work available to Mexican Americans in Waco, where he lived.

"The military was our way out," Calderon said.

He tried to enter the 11th Airborne in 1946, about eight months after the end of WWII. He was 7 pounds under the 11th Airborne's weight requirement, but he and Adams decided to still join the Army Air Corps.

He spent 20 years in the military. He was stationed in the Philippines and later trained Air Force pilots in Waco. There he re-met Ruby Treviño—the two had known each other when they were younger—and they married June 28, 1953. He was stationed, with his family, in Spain from 1959 to 1962, and he retired from the military in 1967.

He and his wife both earned their GEDs because they had not completed high school. Calderon went to Tarleton State University for his bachelor's degree and earned his master's degree in 1976 from Juarez-Lincoln University, a Mexican-American university open from 1971 to 1979 in Austin. After his retirement from the military he worked as an office manager for a brewery, a computer operations manager, an editor of publications and a financial aid officer at Juarez-Lincoln University.

He and Ruby, who had a bachelor's degree in education, had three children: T. Reynaldo "T-Rey," Ruby and Diana.

Ernesto Calderon

Date of Birth
31 DECEMBER 1928
Waco, TX

Interviewed by
Miguel Castro
10 NOVEMBER 2000
Austin, TX

WWII Military Unit
13th Air Force,
25th Liaison
Squadron,
6200 Troop
Carrier Squadron

CAMPOS, LALO. Enlisting in the Navy at the age of 17 was a move that shaped the rest of Lalo Campos' life. He was born in San Diego, Texas, in 1924, and after living in the countryside for a brief period, the family moved back into town. Campos remembers that his father said, "Son, we're moving to town so that you can all go to school, because in this country only with an education will you be able to get ahead."

Campos traveled around the world with the Navy aboard the SS *Alexander Graham Bell* during World War II, starting in San Francisco and stopping in such places as Australia, New Zealand, Egypt, South Africa and South America and going through the Panama Canal before docking in New York. He visited home for a short time before heading out on another global mission. As a signalman, he said he was privy to information that only captains knew otherwise.

Campos and his wife, Eloise Garcia, moved to Corpus Christi when he returned. Campos enrolled in the University of Texas at Austin under the GI Bill and earned his bachelor's degree. His three brothers all also earned degrees under the GI Bill. "The GI Bill was one of the greatest things the government could have done for all its citizens, but certainly for the Hispanics who went to war and found out that there were better things out there than just what you had at home," he said.

Campos worked as a disc jockey for 45 years with KVET radio in Austin. He hosted one program, "Noche de Fiesta" that played Mexican music and included commercials in Spanish and English. He left the airwaves in 1972 and entered sales.

Eloise took care of their three children: René, Belinda and Yvonne, while Campos worked, often taking them by bus to their various lessons because the family had only one car. "I don't know how she did it," he said. "I was busy all the time. I had three jobs going on simultaneously."

Lalo Campos

Date of Birth
8 NOVEMBER 1924
San Diego, TX

Interviewed by
Sofia Mena
21 OCTOBER 1999
Austin, TX

WWII Military Unit
SS *Alexander*
Graham Bell

Hilario Cavazos Jr.

Date of Birth
12 JULY 1925
Laredo, TX

Interviewed by
Virgil Hines Jr.
28 SEPTEMBER 2002
Laredo, TX

WWII Military Unit
290th Infantry
Regiment,
75th Infantry
Division

CAVAZOS, HILARIO JR. The war interrupted Hilario Cavazos Jr.'s education. He was drafted during his senior year at Laredo's Martin High School and applied for an extension, to no avail.

Cavazos was the second member of his family to join. His brother was already in the 9th Armored Division when he was assigned to the 290th Regiment, 75th Infantry Division. "I think I was trained very well and learned how to defend myself and how to fight," Cavazos said. "It was very tough, but it's something we had to do to defend our country."

He served as a messenger in the Battle of the Bulge, going back and forth along the front lines. "I did everything I was told, and I never backed down," Cavazos said. "If I was scared, I don't remember, because I had so many things [to do]. I was always kept busy." He kept in touch with his family regularly, sending and receiving letters. "I tried to write every night," he remembered.

He was discharged in March 1946, seven months after the end of the war, and he returned to Laredo, Texas. He finished his high school education and went to Laredo Junior College for two years. He took time off to start a mail-order business, and then went to the University of Texas, where he graduated with a bachelor's degree in accounting. He earned a master's degree in business administration from A&I University-Kingsville and was a professor of business and accounting at Laredo Community College for 30 years.

He now owns a small business, selling Mexican products, and is active in many community activities, and veteran and church groups. He married Thelma in 1959 and they had two children.

"I think with determination and desire you can accomplish about anything you want to. ... You can do it whether you're a Mexican, black, Indian—whatever you are, whatever you may be—it's a matter of [if] you decide to do it," Cavazos said.

Roberto Chapa

Date of Birth
25 NOVEMBER 1922
Salineo, TX

Interviewed by
Joshua Leighton
19 OCTOBER 1999
Austin, TX

WWII Military Unit
415th Infantry
Regiment,
104th Infantry
Division

CHAPA, ROBERTO. He became accustomed to hard work at an early age, helping his father raise cattle and grow cotton and other crops, but Roberto Chapa's involvement in the U.S. Army is what gave him the opportunities that shaped his life. Under the GI Bill, Chapa was able to attend college at St. Mary's University in San Antonio, Texas.

Shortly after graduating from Roma High School in Roma, Texas, Chapa joined the Civilian Conservation Corps and was sent to Colorado for training in soil conservation. He enlisted in the Army Dec. 2, 1942, and was sent to Camp Adair, Ore., for basic training.

He saw action in Belgium, France, Germany and Holland, participating primarily in night attacks intended to cut off supply lines. He stayed in Europe until 1945. "War is about being able to survive," he said.

After the war he was glad to take advantage of the GI Bill. "I knew that I had to go to school and get a degree and better myself," Chapa said. He was a teacher in San Marcos, Texas, and moved to Austin in 1967.

He served as a member of the board of MexicArte, a Mexican-American cultural museum in Austin and was a member of the Lions Club. In 2004, the Mental Health Mental Rehabilitation Center dedicated the Robert T. Chapa Building in Austin, for his 10 years of service as chairman of the board. He also was an active volunteer with the Boy Scouts and the Hispanic Council on Scouting. He served with the Army Reserves for 22 years.

"There has to be a means where every child in this country has a chance at an education or a chance to prove themselves—then there's some good in everybody," he said.

He and his wife, Estela Gonzalez Chapa, had two sons: Roberto Tomás Jr. and Ricardo José.

DELGADO, GILBERTO. When he was growing up in Santa Fe, N.M., Gilberto Delgado had a friend who used sign language with her deaf grandmother. Later in his life, he took a leading role in deaf education, becoming the first Hispanic superintendent of a state school for the deaf.

He worked with the U.S. Department of Education, developing devices to aid the deaf including television closed-captioning and TTY text-based telephones. He edited four books on deafness and helped translate a book on American Sign Language to Spanish. He helped develop versions of sign language in Costa Rica, Colombia, Mexico and Puerto Rico. "We don't get a lot of Hispanics in the field," he said of deaf education. "Why? I'm not sure."

When Delgado graduated from high school in 1946, he enlisted in the Marine Corps and was stationed in Okinawa, Japan, for a month before moving to Saipan, Mariana Islands.

After completing his service, he signed up for three years in the Army Reserves. He had trouble adjusting to his life as a postal worker while attending the College of Santa Fe.

"You don't quite fit into the routine that you left," he said. "You've changed, you're more mature, and you have a different perspective."

He earned a bachelor's degree from the College of Santa Fe, a master's degree from Gallaudet University in Washington, D.C., and a doctorate from Catholic University of America.

He taught at the California School for the Deaf in Riverside, Calif.; was principal of a school for the deaf in Berkeley, Calif.; served as superintendent of the New Mexico School for the Deaf; and retired in 1994. He still serves on the boards of various schools.

He married Cecilia Ortiz on Jan. 31, 1949. The couple had six children: John, Jacqueline, Elizabeth, Elena, Carmen and Celeste.

Gilberto Delgado

Date of Birth
3 SEPTEMBER 1928
Santa Fe, NM

Interviewed by
Andrés Romero
3 NOVEMBER 2002
Santa Fe, NM

WWII Location
Stationed in
Okinawa, Japan

Transferred to
Saipan, Mariana
Islands

DE PEÑA, ELENA TAMEZ. When Elena De Peña was growing up, her parents emphasized the importance of a good education. Her father was a mechanic and her mother ran a grocery store in San Benito, Texas; De Peña said they set a good example for her and her siblings.

Born Elena Tamez, she and her sister Rosa wanted to be nurses after they graduated from high school, and their mother insisted that they follow their dreams.

They attended George Peabody University in Tennessee, where they received training in public health. "We were the first Spanish-speaking students in nurses' training. We had to prove ourselves," De Peña said.

She transferred to Incarnate Word College and earned a degree in public health nursing. She married Hector De Peña in 1942. During World War II, she entered Corpus Christi's school of nursing, where she became a registered nurse. She worked for the State Health Department in Corpus Christi. De Peña earned her master's degree from Sam Houston State University in Huntsville, Texas.

After the war she said she noticed more Spanish-speaking teachers and professionals. "They were just as American as any other American here. We might have been a little darker, but that didn't make any difference. What mattered was what we had to offer."

She said children of post-war families with two professional, bilingual parents had opportunities her peers did not.

"They had advantages growing up that we didn't have. We [as parents] were able to give them an education ... and they can achieve all their goals," she said.

Her children have gone on to success: Hector Jr. is a county judge, Carla has her master's degree in counseling and psychology, and Charles is a neuroradiologist.

Elena Tamez
De Peña

Date of Birth
19 FEBRUARY 1916
San Benito, TX

Interviewed by
Erika Martinez
18 AUGUST 2001
Corpus Christi, TX

WWII Location
Corpus Christi, TX

Gonzalo Garza

Date of Birth
10 JANUARY 1927
New Braunfels, TX

Interviewed by
Juan Campos
17 MARCH 2001
Georgetown, TX

WWII Military Unit
Company E,
7th Marine
Regiment,
2d Marine Division

GARZA, GONZALO. Inspired by a pamphlet outlining the institutional pillars of the Marines that listed education as the chief principle, "central to all Marines, not just a select few," Gonzalo Garza was determined to pursue his education post-war.

He entered the Marines at age 17 with a ninth-grade education, having dropped out of school to help support his family. "I promised myself, if I ever get back, I would graduate from high school, number one goal, and think about furthering my education and going on to college," Garza said.

Garza served with Company E, 7th Marine Regiment, 2d Marine Division in Saipan, Mariana Islands, where he studied Japanese; he also served in Okinawa.

He returned to the States in the last days of the war and resumed his education, earning his GED and taking classes at Del Mar, a two-year college in Corpus Christi, Texas. He transferred to St. Mary's University in San Antonio, Texas, to become a teacher under the GI Bill. In 1950, just two semesters short of graduation, Garza was called to serve in the Korean War. After he was wounded in Korea, he received the Purple Heart, among many other awards. He was sent home in late 1951.

He earned degrees in Spanish and history and went on to receive his doctorate; he also became a sixth-grade teacher, and worked in administration with the Austin Independent School District. He said that the Latino tradition of respect was at least partly the reason that Mexican-American servicemen were successful. "We did our duty with honor and glory, I would say, and we were ... obedient to charges, to orders, to things that we were told, because that's the way we were taught."

He married Dolores Scott, also a teacher. They had five children: Charles, Louis, Patricia, Lawrence and David.

Gonzalo Garza Independence High School in Austin is named for him.

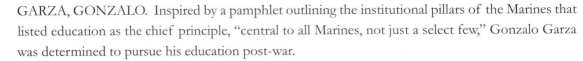

Julian L. Gonzalez

Date of Birth
29 NOVEMBER 1924
San Antonio, TX

Interviewed by
Raquel C. Garza
and Veronica
Franco
13 OCTOBER 2001
San Antonio, TX

WWII Military Unit
Civil Affairs Division,
in the Philippines

GONZALEZ, JULIAN L. When the class of 1944 walked across the stage at Thomas A. Edison High School in San Antonio, Texas, Julian L. Gonzalez was not among the students with whom he had spent his school years. His father, however, walked in his place. "It was announced that I wasn't there, that [my father] was receiving [my diploma] because I was in the service," Gonzalez said. "They told me that he got the biggest applause of anybody there."

Gonzalez had completed his high school education a semester early to enter the Armed Services. He was stationed in the United States for eight months, where he was hospitalized after catching poison oak, and sent to stack tomato crates at a Del Monte packing plant.

He then served in two cities in New Guinea and then in the Philippines, where he was in charge of water purification. In the Philippines he sustained another non-combat injury, a bite by a large centipede.

While stationed on Mindanao Island, he made friends with the Spanish-speaking commanding officer of a Philippine constabulary, who helped to protect Gonzalez's regiment. After the war, he was stationed in Taejon, South Korea, for six months before he was eligible to return home. He retired as a technical corporal and earned various medals.

He was discharged April 13, 1946, and returned to his father's home in San Antonio, Texas. He attended St. Mary's University in San Antonio under the GI Bill and earned a bachelor's degree in sociology. He began working at Alamo Cement Co. in 1947 and worked as a timekeeper and in the accounts receivable office as an office manager. He later worked as an officer manager for Midwestern Limestone Co., a subsidiary of Alamo.

He and Florence Gonzales, a childhood friend, married in Dec. 1953. They had three children.

GONZALEZ, ROBERTO. While he was in high school in Harlingen, Texas, Roberto Gonzalez and his father, Catarino, listened to the radio together every Sunday for news about WWII. Soon after he graduated in 1943, he was drafted, and his love of radio translated to his service as a radio and Morse code operator in the Air Force.

Roberto Gonzalez

Date of Birth
13 APRIL 1924
Mercedes, TX

Interviewed by
Kevin and
Sharon Bales
17 JUNE 2000
Richardson, TX

WWII Military Unit
501st Bomb Group,
315th Bomb Wing,
15th Air Force

When he entered the force, a test determined his skills. "I was given an IQ test and an aptitude test for languages and math," he said. "I scored pretty high."

He trained in advanced air-to-ground radio communication and worked with a B-29 bombardment wing stationed primarily in Guam. He helped build runways that were later used to launch attacks on Japan. He was in Guam for the majority of his service. He said that there was less discrimination in the Air Force than in his hometown "because we were all fighting for the same cause."

After the war he returned home to Harlingen but soon left again to take advantage of the GI Bill by attending school at the University of Texas at Austin. He earned his bachelor's of business administration in accounting in 1952.

He graduated with a master's degree in public administration from the University of North Texas in 1974.

Gonzalez worked as a federal auditor for the U.S. Department of Health, Education and Welfare for 12 years. He served as the deputy director of the Office for Civil Rights in the U.S. Department of Education in Dallas, Texas, until his retirement. He continued to learn throughout his life, taking classes in French and history in 2000.

He met Eloisa Mojica at a Presbyterian church camp. They married in 1949 and had five children: Norma, Catherine, Ruth, Lisa and Robert.

GUERRA, FRANCISCO. Though he was not even a U.S. citizen when Pearl Harbor was bombed, Francisco Guerra was eager to serve his adopted country. He had moved to Laredo, Texas, from his birthplace of Nuevo Laredo, Mexico, at age 3, but it was not until 1942 when he tried to enlist in the Army—and was denied because of his Mexican citizenship—that he became a U.S. citizen. He was one of about 300 people who took the oath of citizenship that day in Tacoma, Wash.

Francisco Guerra

Date of Birth
5 DECEMBER 1918
Nuevo Laredo,
Tamaulipas, Mexico

Interviewed by
Raquel C. Garza
28 SEPTEMBER 2002
Laredo, TX

WWII Military Unit
74th Ordnance
Battalion

The policy was changed later. "When the war got tough, then they drafted anyone who was a resident in the United States," including his brother Luis, who was killed in action in the Southwest Pacific.

Guerra participated in the D-Day invasion and helped clean up the beach afterward. Fifty years later he was awarded the Jubilee Liberty Medal, among other awards, in honor of his service.

After the war, he studied at Trinity University and St. Mary's University in San Antonio, where he received his bachelor's degree in 1949.

Soon after graduating, he began a career with the Internal Revenue Service. He was a deputy collector with the IRS, an agent in the audit division from 1950 to 1976 and, ultimately, a senior agent, a position he held for 18 years. "My advice to all veterans and others is [get an] education. That's why I had a good job," Guerra said. "Work hard, go to school, get your degree."

The Army helped him succeed in life. "For being in the Army, I [got the chance] at continuing my education under the GI Bill ... and earning a university degree, which otherwise I would not have been able to do," Guerra said.

He married Carmen Garza in 1948. They had six children: Lucia, Francisco, Luis, Graciela, Ricardo and Cecilia. Luis served in the Navy and Francisco served in the Army in the Vietnam War.

Antonia Medina
Guerrero

Date of Birth
17 JANUARY 1930
Seguin, TX

Interviewed by
Juan Martinez
19 OCTOBER 2002
Saginaw, MI

WWII Location
Lockhart, TX

GUERRERO, ANTONIA MEDINA. Though she was able to complete her high school education later in life, Antonia Guerrero remembered the discrimination she faced growing up. She quit school when she was young because the long walk to her segregated school, like the walk many other Mexican Americans had to make every day, was too difficult.

"We lived on a farm and we had to walk four miles, rain or shine," Guerrero said. "There was a bus for white kids and they would tease us as they drove by. We had only one teacher who taught kindergarten through 12th grade. She would teach the 11th and 12th grades first, and then they would help with the younger kids."

Born Antonia Medina, she helped her family out on the farm after she quit school.

She met veteran Ignacio Guerrero in 1948, while he was working at a dry cleaners in Lockhart, Texas, and they started dating. They attended movies and dances sponsored by the local Mexican community.

After the couple married on Aug. 6, 1949, they moved to Saginaw, Mich. They had five children: Irene, Ester, Edward, Raymond, and Pauline. Guerrero was responsible for raising their children, but when they were old enough, she decided to go back to school.

She had dropped out in the eighth grade, and despite school authorities' efforts to persuade her to get her GED, as her husband had done when he sought a higher paying position with General Motors, she decided to finish all the years of school she had left to complete. She earned a high school diploma by graduating from every grade.

"I always say, 'Study hard,' [to her children and grandchildren] because I didn't get to go to school," she said.

Ignacio Guerrero

Date of Birth
23 JUNE 1926
Lockhart, TX

Interviewed by
Juan Martinez
19 OCTOBER 2002
Saginaw, MI

WWII Military Unit
USS *Sperry* (AS-12)

GUERRERO, IGNACIO. He went on to become a successful electrician, but Ignacio Guerrero remembered the discrimination he faced as a young man growing up outside Lockhart, Texas. He quit school when he was young because he could not handle the long walk to and from his segregated school each day.

"I had to quit because I had to walk four miles. They didn't pick Mexicans up on the bus," Guerrero said. "Everybody else rode the bus except us."

He helped his family at home until he joined the Navy in 1944. He served from January 1944 to March 1946 on the USS *Sperry*, a fleet Submarine Tender, which carried 250 seamen and a load of torpedoes. He was stationed at Honolulu, Guam and Saipan during his tour of duty, and he was discharged as a seaman second class.

After the war, he went back to his job as a caddy at a local golf course. He played golf every day, hoping to learn the ins and outs of the sport, but he decided he was not good enough to become a professional.

He met Antonia Medina in 1948, and they started dating. He remembered facing some discrimination after the war, but significantly less than before. "There was a change: People were a little better. They spoke to you—especially if you came in your uniform. They gave you a lot of respect."

After the couple married in 1949, they moved to Saginaw, Mich., where Guerrero earned his GED and was employed by General Motors, where he worked for 35 years—18 as an electrician. They had five children: Irene, Ester, Edward, Raymond, and Pauline.

"We had a bad life. We made it good," he said. "I said to myself, 'I can't remain poor.' All you gotta do is try, try, try."

LONG, TERESA LOZANO. Growing up on her parent's dairy farm taught Teresa Lozano Long life-long lessons on the importance of education and philanthropy early in life—lessons she remembered as an adult. Her parents were dedicated not only to their own family's education, but also to those of their employees on the farm. "If my parents saw one of the employees' children outside playing during the day, they would ask why the child wasn't in school," she said.

Teresa Lozano Long

Date of Birth
20 JULY 1928
Premont, TX

Interviewed by
Brenda Sendejo
7 DECEMBER 2004
Austin, TX

WWII Location
Premont, TX

Her parents' influence echoed throughout her life. Born Teresa Lozano, she was her high school valedictorian. She attended the University of Texas at Austin, where she earned her degree in physical education. She went on to earn her master's degree and a doctorate.

She took a job teaching physical education in Alice, Texas, after completing her master's, and was one of the first Mexican-American teachers in a department other than Spanish. She spent seven years in Alice, where she met fellow teacher and future husband, Joseph Long, before returning to the University of Texas for her doctoral work. Joseph also moved to Austin, earned his law degree and later worked for the state attorney general. The two married in 1958.

Volunteer work and philanthropy became a focal point for both Long and her husband. She volunteered at St. Austin's Church, Seton Hospital and the Pan American Recreation Center. She was devoted to the promotion of education and the arts. Because of her philanthropic contributions and work with the Latino community, the Teresa Lozano Long Institute for Latin American Studies at the University of Texas is named for her. Long is proud of her dual heritage, and loves the term "Mexican-American," because it indicates her Latino roots while indicating she is an American and Texan as well. "That's the reason I use Lozano," she said. "Because if something just reads 'Teresa Long,' it doesn't mean as much to people."

LUJAN, JUAN. If his father had not died when Juan Lujan was in sixth grade, he probably would have followed in his footsteps as a cotton farmer in the small, all-Hispanic town of Redford, Texas, where there was only a primary school. Instead, his mother moved the family 75 miles away to Marfa, Texas, the closest town with secondary schools. Lujan attended a segregated "Mexican" school in Marfa, where the teachers were forced to do their best on limited resources. He quit school at 16 to pick beets in California for 35 cents an hour. "I came home [that winter], and, according to my mother, I cried all night, and she said, 'You're going to school,' " he said. "So I did."

Juan Lujan

Date of Birth
16 MAY 1922
Redford, TX

Interviewed by
Joel Weickgenant
18 OCTOBER 2003
Austin, TX

WWII Military Unit
62d Troop
Carrier Group,
51st Wing,
12th Air Force

After graduating from high school, Lujan attended New Mexico A&M University and worked for the Civilian Conservation Corps. He was in his second year of college when he was drafted. His aptitude was recognized quickly, and he was sent to train at the Army Air Corps' radio school, where he remembers studying for long hours.

Lujan worked with the 62d Troop Carrier Group, in North Africa, helping glider pilots learn to be towed by C-47s. His most dangerous assignment involved training glider pilots to land their planes. He was discharged from the Army with the rank of staff sergeant.

After the war, he returned to Texas, and completed his college education, eventually earning a doctorate from the University of Texas at Austin. He spent his life in education, first as a teacher and later as a school principal in Harlingen, Texas, and later worked for the Austin-based non-profit Southwest Educational Laboratory. He also held teaching positions at various universities before retiring in 1968. He and his wife remained active, taking classes at UT after retirement.

Lujan married Socorro Esparza in 1948 and had five children: Hector, Denis, Nolan, Annie and Don.

Eladio Martinez

Date of Birth
10 FEBRUARY 1921
Eagle Ford, TX

Tribute Provided by
The Martinez
family

WWII Military Unit
Company G,
123d Infantry
Regiment,
33d Infantry
Division

MARTINEZ, ELADIO. When Eladio Martinez grew up in West Dallas, Texas, education was a priority. His father was a laborer and inspired his children to learn. Like his three younger siblings, he graduated from Dallas Technical High School. Growing up, the Martinez children enjoyed outdoor activities such as fishing and hunting—an area in which Eladio excelled.

He was in the ROTC program and involved in sports in high school. He aspired to be a chemist and took correspondence courses during high school. Eladio had the only bike in the family, so the others could not participate in after-school activities because they could not walk all the way home.

His brother, Enrique, remembered the day Eladio left for the Army. "We were always together. I missed him greatly when he went off to war," Enrique said. "I remember getting up early that morning to gather his personal belongings. We were greatly saddened by this."

Eladio was drafted into the Army and sent to fight in the Pacific Theater. His younger brother Filiberto, who often followed in his brother's footsteps, enlisted in the Army Air Corps and was sent to the Pacific with the 13th Air Force, where he helped build an airstrip in New Guinea. After 18 months overseas, Filiberto found his older brother, and they had a short-lived but happy reunion in the midst of war. Filiberto stayed with Eladio's unit for three months, but Eladio encouraged him to return to his unit, so that in case something happened, they would not both die. They would meet whenever they could and tried to get around the censors. Filiberto was the last member of the family to see Eladio alive. Eladio was killed by a sniper while in the Philippines.

His family, especially his surviving brothers, Filiberto and Enrique, were grieved by the loss of Eladio. Since Eladio's own educational aspirations were cut short, his brothers honored him in 1990 with the opening of a new school—The Eladio Martinez Learning Center—in West Dallas.

Eliséo Navarro

Date of Birth
5 MARCH 1925
Asherton, TX

Interviewed by
Francisco Venegas
13 OCTOBER 2001
San Antonio, TX

WWII Military Unit
97th Infantry
Division

NAVARRO, ELISÉO. In Asherton, Texas, Mexican Americans and Anglos were segregated in many ways. Eliséo Navarro attended an integrated school for the first time in seventh grade. "There, we were only allowed to speak in English. When my friends and I would go outside and play, we would speak Spanish. If we were heard, we would get in trouble by the teachers," Navarro said.

After graduation, he entered basic training. He entered pilot training, but the Army cut off training more pilots before he finished. Navarro was sent to France with the 97th Infantry Division and fought throughout Belgium and Czechoslovakia. His unit was sent to Yokohama, Japan, after the dropping of the atomic bombs. Among soldiers from other states, he experienced less discrimination than he had at any other point in his life.

"This was the best learning education I could have gotten," he said. "I was thankful I was able to be alive and learn to understand the different cultures."

Navarro attended the University of Texas at Austin and earned a degree in social work. He later earned his master's degree and doctorate. Additionally, he worked as a probation officer in Bexar County, Texas, for 10 years while working on his master's degree, and in Chicago, worked training the staff of the Cook County Family Court and supervising social work students from Loyola University. He taught courses in social work at the University of Texas and the University of Michigan.

After retiring from teaching college in 1978, he worked on a major social worker training project funded by the National Institute of Social Work. He taught elementary school for a few years; then he developed his skills in real estate, and owned several rental properties that kept him busy into retirement.

He married Dora Elia Jimenez in 1954 and they had four children who all attended college.

ORTEGA, CARLOTA AYALA. Take it from Carlota Ortega, a woman who spent her life in education: Teaching graduate students who were eager to learn was not that hard. "It wasn't a challenge," Ortega said of her time as a professor. "Now teaching kids to read—that was the challenge."

Ortega was a junior high school teacher and later taught courses in curriculum and instruction to master's students at Saginaw Valley State University.

She was honored in 1990 as the Michigan Outstanding Hispanic Educator of the Year for her efforts to improve education of disadvantaged children. Her program was nationally recognized.

Ortega wrote, developed, implemented and supervised various programs for migrant children throughout her career, including bilingual programming for three school districts.

She earned her bachelor's degree from Saginaw Valley State University, her master's degree from Central Michigan University and a doctorate from Wayne State University in 1981.

Born Carlota Ayala in Mexico, she and her family moved to Texas when she was 3 years old. Though she was young at the time of the move, she remembers being sad leaving her native country. "I cried and cried," she said. "I just missed my grandparents so much."

Her family moved to Saginaw, Mich., when she was young, and she has fond memories of growing up there. It was there that she met her husband, Guadalupe Ortega. They married in 1942 and their daughter, Yvonne, was born shortly before Guadalupe left to fight in WWII. When he returned from war, they had two more children, David and Joseph. Ortega was the president of American Legion Post 500 Auxiliary in 1949 and was offered positions at the state and national levels. She refused in order to spend time taking care of her children—her main priority.

Carlota Ayala Ortega

Date of Birth
26 JUNE 1923
Piedras Negras,
Coahuila, Mexico

Interviewed by
Gloria Monita
19 OCTOBER 2002
Saginaw, MI

WWII Location
Saginaw, MI

PENICHE, EDUARDO "ED." He earned the Purple Heart, two Bronze Stars and other medals for his heroism in World War II. "I received those in the midst of destruction and hate and despair," Ed Peniche said. The base of a monument to soldiers in Longchamp, Belgium, bears his name because of the valor he showed in defending that city.

But amid all the acclaim Peniche has enjoyed, his most prized possession is a framed citation recognizing his 22 years as a teacher at Central Virginia Community College. The paper names him as a professor emeritus, calling him an inspirational influence to generations of students.

"Once you have the education, that opens the doors everywhere," Peniche said.

Born in Mexico to self-educated parents, Peniche came to America in 1942 at age 17 to go to school. But it was evident when he moved to Paducah, Ky., where his aunt Pilar and her husband Eduardo Menedez lived, that he was not entirely prepared for school in the United States. He attended junior high and high school simultaneously until he was drafted in 1943.

He fought in D-Day, the Battle of the Bulge and in other battles across Europe as part of the 101st Airborne Division. He was wounded in Longchamp, and the city later named the base of their WWII monument Stele Peniche in his honor. After the war he worked in Mexico, helping the country reorganize its airborne units. He re-entered the U.S. Army in 1952. He married Dean Baggett in 1953, and the couple lived in Taiwan for two years. When they returned to the States, Peniche worked at the InterAmerican Defense College, where he earned a degree. He also earned a degree in history from the University of Nebraska, and a master's degree from Murray State University in just 18 months. He went on to teach at Central Virginia Community College until he retired, and continued to teach on a limited basis after retirement.

Eduardo "Ed" Peniche

Date of Birth
28 JUNE 1925
Progreso, Yucatán,
Mexico

Interviewed by
Fernando Dovalina
17 MAY 2000
Kingswood, TX

WWII Military Unit
81st Airborne Anti-
Aircraft Battalion,
101st Airborne
Division

José Ramirez

Date of Birth
1 FEBRUARY 1923
San Diego, CA

Interviewed by
René Zambrano
14 JULY 2000
San Diego, CA

WWII Military Unit
15th Air Force

RAMIREZ, JOSÉ. After walking two miles home at the end of his first day of work, José Ramirez was proud to show his parents the three cents he had earned, selling newspapers in downtown San Diego, Calif. He was 8 years old.

By the time he was 12, he was paying for most of his personal expenses to ease the burden on his parents, who had 11 children. His father was a laborer and his mother worked at a fish cannery.

He worked through high school, setting pins at a local bowling alley, and he saved enough money to buy a suit for his graduation from San Diego High School. He said that he did not experience outright harassment at his high school, but the teachers did tell the Hispanic students, "Don't bother going to college. You can't cut it there."

Ramirez enlisted in the Army Air Corps in 1943, because "it was a matter of that or being drafted." He missed most major action in WWII, as he received his assignment after the Battle of Normandy. He flew 33 missions as a fighter pilot in the 15th Air Force, mostly in Italy.

He went back to school on the GI Bill when he returned, earning a degree from San Diego State University. "We came back and we thought we were all entitled to a piece of the pie," he said. "We were not going to be satisfied living in the barrio. We felt we could get ahead. We felt we had earned it."

He credits the war with changing the lives of Latinos. "We were dealing with a new kind of citizen," he said. "It was a turning point in the barrio."

For 36 years, Ramirez worked as an auditor and office manager for the California Employment Development Department. He married Estreberta "Rachel" Gastelum and they had two children, Joseph A. and Lorraine.

Armando Miguel Rodriguez

Date of Birth
30 SEPTEMBER 1921
Gomez Palacio, Durango, Mexico

Interviewed by
René Zambrano
2 August 2000
San Diego, CA

WWII Military Unit
837th Signal Corps

RODRIGUEZ, ARMANDO MIGUEL. A lifetime of service to his adopted country began when Armando Rodriguez joined the U.S. Army in December 1942. His military training encouraged him to pursue educational opportunities he had not thought available to him before, as the Mexican child of uneducated immigrants and an employee of a fish cannery.

"I was put in a program where I had to compete with the university people, and I found out that I could compete with them," he said. "If I could compete with them in the service, I could compete with them in the streets and in the schools. At that point I said, 'I gotta find a way to go to school.'"

As part of the 837th Signal Corps, Rodriguez went to cryptography classes, where he learned to manipulate code. He was stationed in Brazil during the war and relayed messages to help planes navigate. He was given a medical discharge because he had asthma after a bout with malaria.

He helped found an American Legion post in San Diego, Calif. He attended San Diego State University under the GI Bill for his master's and bachelor's degrees. He played football for the school and coached the wrestling team, which made it to the 1948 Olympic trials. He is a member of the national Wrestling Hall of Fame. Rodriguez taught junior high in San Diego for several years. He was given honorary doctorates from the National Hispanic University and John F. Kennedy College.

He lost a bid for a seat in the California State Assembly in 1962. He was appointed the first director of the Mexican-American Affairs Office in the Department of Health, Education and Welfare by President Lyndon Johnson. President Richard Nixon named him a regional education commissioner. In 1973 he became the first Hispanic president of East Los Angeles College. He was chair of the national Equal Opportunity Employment Commission from 1978 to 1983.

He and wife Beatriz Serrano Rodriguez have two children: Ruth and Roderick.

Vincente Ximenes and President Lyndon B. Johnson at the White House in 1965.

Community Notables

When the American troops returned to their communities at the end of the war, they had new ideas. These veterans had enjoyed invaluable life experiences, were imbued with a strong patriotism and optimism and had a desire for a better life. Latinos who served their country during World War II went on to become leaders in business, education, and law serving their communities in innumerable ways.

The GI Bill helped many veterans afford educational opportunities that were once out of reach. The GI Bill financed college and trade school for those who served, allowing many ambitious men and women to improve their station. Journalist Pete Moraga graduated from the University of Arizona and would later make sure a Latino perspective was included in general news stories; Randel Fernandez studied design and tailoring with the help of the GI Bill, allowing him to later open his own shop in Los Angeles, Calif.

Some veterans worked with local organizations to honor other veterans. With groups like the Catholic War Veterans, the Veterans of Foreign Wars (VFW) and local chapters of the American Legion, veterans gave proper funerals for other servicemen and helped to ensure their valor was honored. Pete Casarez established a post of the Catholic War Veterans at his home parish in Austin, Texas.

Others became prominent leaders in business. Joseph Unanue, of New Jersey, helped make Goya Foods a major player in the market. Ramón Galindo opened a tailoring business in downtown Austin, and tailored suits for President Lyndon B. Johnson. His brothers took their family's small tortilla factory in Austin and made it a regional business.

The veterans' contributions to the arts were also substantial. Musician Johnnie Martinez bought a nightclub in Houston, and it became the famous Palladium, where renowned artists such as Elvis Presley appeared. San Antonio Musician Alfredo "Alfred" Castro and his band, Al Castro's Marimba Sounds, were popular throughout Texas, even playing for President George Bush, Sr.

Still others worked to foster unity and advancement for the Latino community—years after the war's end. Daniel Muñoz, founded La Prensa, a Latino advocacy newspaper in San Diego in the 1970s. Robert Soltero, of Kansas City, Mo., sat on the board of Guadalupe Inc., one of the area's first social agencies for Latinos, and also acted as a sponsor for the group's culinary arts program. Apolonia Muñoz Abarca, wife of a WWII soldier, worked diligently to obtain grants for health care at Corpus Christi, Texas, hospitals where she volunteered, and taught English and nursing at a settlement home.

Following the war, Latinos founded the American G.I. Forum, an organization spearheaded by Dr. Hector P. Garcia, to address issues that faced Latino veterans. Chapters sprang up across the country. Alejandra Rojas Zuniga, of Saginaw, Mich., worked with a women's chapter, starting a program called Adopt-a-School through the Forum.

Fighting for their rights at their workplace was also important to many Latinos; several worked with union boards and other organizations to obtain better working conditions. Latinos in postwar America were determined to contribute to their communities. Whether they were helping other veterans, educating their community or instituting programs for future generations, their work ethic and a strong sense of heritage allowed them to make a difference.

Apolonia Muñoz
Abarca

Date of Birth
5 SEPTEMBER 1920
Mission, TX

Interviewed by
Erika Martinez
18 AUGUST 2001
Corpus Christi, TX

WWII Military Unit
Memorial Hospital
in Corpus Christi, TX

ABARCA, APOLONIA MUÑOZ. A lifetime of dedication to the health of her community began for Apolonia when she was still a young nursing student during WWII. Her brother and her fiancé, Antonio Abarca, were sent to Europe. As money became scarce on the home front for her family, she considered joining the Cadet Corps as a nurse. In correspondence with her brother and future husband—Apolonia Muñoz would marry Antonio after the war ended—both men begged her to stay at home. "I think they talked me out of it," she said. "I was up there ready to help anybody."

Volunteering was her passion since age 15, when she began helping nurses take handicapped children to the hospital. She was able to finish nursing school when her brother sent money home. In 1944, she graduated as a registered nurse. She began working at Memorial Hospital in Corpus Christi, Texas, setting up operating and emergency rooms, and soon becoming supervisor of the outpatient clinic.

Eager to serve others, she worked at the U.S. Public Service Hospital in Corpus Christi and volunteered with the Red Cross. She worked at a settlement home, where she helped teach home nursing in both Spanish and English.

After the war, Abarca balanced family—she and her husband had one son, David—and her service to her community, working with the City-County Health Department. In 1964, Abarca helped win the first grant for family planning, supporting birth control because she said many children she saw in her hospitals were neglected and undernourished. In 1965 she was hired as the executive director of her local Planned Parenthood center. She then worked as the director of nursing at a school for mentally retarded children, until she retired in 1974. Abarca has spent her retirement years volunteering with her church.

Valentín Aguilar

Date of Birth
14 FEBRUARY 1922
Laredo, TX

Interviewed by
Peter Mendoza
7 OCTOBER 2000
Laredo, TX

WWII Military Unit
Company F,
339th Regiment,
85th Division

AGUILAR, VALENTÍN. After his service in Europe, Valentín Aguilar devoted his spare time to honoring his fellow veterans and celebrating the many honors his fellow Latino soldiers received.

Raised in Laredo, Texas, Aguilar was drafted in 1942 and, after being inducted on Nov. 25, began training in Texas, and then at Camp Clarborne, La.

Aguilar was deployed to Italy and moved to the Gothic Line, a region of mountains and a strong defensive line for the Germans. It was the site of front line combat with German troops. The offensive began on July 30, 1944, and Aguilar remembered the harsh conditions.

"The Gothic Line is composed of a bunch of hills," he said. "So it's very, very high and the level is very steep."

During a battle in Quinzano, Italy, Aguilar was wounded when shrapnel pierced his lung. He was sent to Rome to recuperate.

Once he recovered, he began guarding German prisoners, not a glamorous assignment, but one that brought him a measure of respect. In the U.S. Army, he was required to salute officers first. But it was different with the German POWs.

"Every time they have a German detail, the [German] colonel is supposed to salute me first, and then I had to return the salute," he said, adding that "I felt very good about that."

Aguilar married Olivia Medrano in 1951 and the couple had five children: Diana, Rosalinda, Valentín Jr., María Raquel and David.

Aguilar worked with the G.I. Forum as the organization's vice commander and also served as the senior vice commander of the Laredo Veteran's Hall of Fame. He was the chairman of the Laredo Veterans' Commission and worked to raise funds for a monument to honor Latino war veterans.

BORJA, JOSÉ. After serving as a Merchant Marine in WWII, José Borja devoted his life to fighting for equal rights for veterans of the Merchant Marines. Many who served were undocumented immigrants, and were told they would never receive the same benefits as other veterans for their service.

José Borja

Date of Birth
3 APRIL 1927
Quito, Ecuador

Interviewed by
Maggie Rivas-Rodriguez
24 APRIL 2004
Bronx, NY

WWII Military Unit
SS *Athos II*

Borja was born in Ecuador and later lived in Colombia before stowing away on a French ship bound for New York harbor. The French sailors put Borja to work, and he drained a huge cask of wine into bottles. Each French sailor was allotted two bottles each day.

"The French, if they don't drink wine, they can't eat," Borja joked. "The food won't go down."

When the ship docked in New York Harbor in 1944, Borja joined the Merchant Marines almost immediately. He traveled throughout the world on several different ships.

In 1946, Borja met a Puerto Rican girl who worked in a New York factory. He married Stella Carattini and the couple had three children: Ronald, George and Rosita. After his service, he held a host of different jobs, including a waiter at the famous New York restaurant Tavern on the Green. He also self-published several fiction novels.

His true focus, however, was his work for the Merchant Marines. He founded an organization called the Association of Merchant Marine Veterans and wrote letters to public officials. He has spoken to interest groups and journalists and written newspaper columns addressing the unfair treatment Merchant Marines have received.

Though the Merchant Marines were finally awarded most of the benefits of other veterans in 1988, the triumph was "too little, too late" for Borja.

"You can be certain that we're not going to find a Merchant Marine lawyer," Borja said. "In those times, you had to have money to study. How is the GI Bill going to help me?"

CANTÚ, DOMINGO. The military has played a prominent role in the life of Domingo Cantú since he was drafted in 1943. From that point on, serving his country shaped his life, and its impact never lessened.

Domingo Cantú

Date of Birth
1 JANUARY 1922
Nuevo Laredo,
Mexico

Interviewed by
Antonio Cantú
13 OCTOBER 2001
San Antonio, TX

WWII Military Unit
101st Airborne
Division

Cantú initially trained as a medic, but when paratroopers stopped by his camp to recruit, he was intrigued and joined.

He landed in Europe in October 1943. He participated in the invasion of Normandy, where he took a bullet in his leg. He recovered and continued on to campaigns in Rhineland, Holland and Germany, as well as Battle of the Bulge. During fighting in Belgium he was wounded again. The war had ended before he recovered, and he was later discharged from Camp Fannin, Texas. He earned two Purple Hearts, a Bronze Star and Airborne Wings with combat jump star.

He returned to Texas and married Rose Flaus, with whom he corresponded during his service in Europe. The couple had two daughters: Julia Rose and Sylvia.

He worked as a painter and later as a bus driver for the San Antonio Public Transportation Co.

Long after his discharge, Cantú remained active in his support of the armed forces. He worked extensively with San Antonio's chapter of VFW. He was also a part of Alamo Silver Wings Airborne Association, a group of veterans from all branches of the military. Cantú visited veterans' hospitals with the Military Order of the Purple Heart.

Cantú's devotion to his fellow veterans was recognized by the Texas Legislature on June 8, 2001. Texas Rep. Carlos Uresti recognized his achievements and Cantú was awarded certificates for his service with his VFW post and for his volunteer hours at Fort Sam Houston National Cemetery.

Felipe Cantú

Date of Birth
23 AUGUST 1919
Nuevo Leon,
Mexico

Tribute Provided by
Antonio Cantú
(Son)

WWII Military Unit
Company A,
16th Signal
Battalion

CANTÚ, FELIPE. With an ability to depict war with words and with his paintbrush, Felipe Cantú brought his experiences during WWII to the public.

He spread his message through his column in La Prensa, a newspaper that covered Latino issues, and his striking watercolor paintings.

Cantú enlisted in the Army and was inducted on Sept. 23, 1942. He was sent to the South Pacific, where he served as a Teletype operator.

He later followed tanks as they ventured into enemy territory and was a rifleman, earning several decorations and helping liberate the Philippines.

After his discharge, Cantú returned to his job at La Prensa, writing pieces that detailed many battles in the war in his series of columns titled "From Reporter to Soldier." He also illustrated his stories with detailed pencil sketches of his recollections of life in the Philippines. His columns were often given entire pages with photographs and provided a firsthand account of the war.

He continued his journalism career in San Antonio, Texas, at the Spanish-language radio station KCOR-AM. Cantú eventually went into public relations and advertising, becoming a pioneer in marketing to the Latino market.

Cantú headed the Spanish-language marketing and advertising for HemisFair in San Antonio in 1968, as part of the commemoration of the 250th anniversary of San Antonio's founding. He created a Spanish-language division at Bloom Advertising Agency in Dallas, Texas, and ended his career as a freelance copywriter, helping with campaigns for the Boy Scouts of America and Libby's Nectars.

After the war, Cantú married and had two children before divorcing. He later married Celia Palacios, whom he met during a business trip to Mexico, and the couple had six children.

Peter "Pete"
Casarez

Date of Birth
9 SEPTEMBER 1924
Port Huron, MI

Interviewed by
Joanne R. Sanchez
13 OCTOBER 2000
Austin, TX

WWII Location
Stationed in Guam,
Navy Seabees

CASAREZ, PETER "PETE." As part of the Seabees, the Navy's construction unit, Peter Casarez built a home for the commander of the U.S. fleet and helped construct a Naval base on the island of Guam. After his service, he devoted countless hours to the Catholic War Veterans.

The son of Mexican immigrants, Casarez said that his parents provided a good life for him and his siblings during the Depression and that he was lucky to live much better than some of those around him. They owned a 1924 Buick, and Casarez's favorite hobby was popping the hood and tinkering with the car. The Navy would later capitalize on his abilities as a mechanic and handyman.

Casarez enlisted in the Navy and began training at Camp Wallace, Texas, and then went to San Diego, Calif. From there he was shipped to Guam and began building a base and residences for officers. He enjoyed the job, especially after meeting Admiral Chester Nimitz.

"When we were working ... he'd say 'Hi there. How are you all doing?'" he said. "He looked like a down-to-earth person. We built him a nice two-story home ... with a tennis court. He was there up until the end of the war."

After he was discharged, Casarez returned to Austin, Texas, and began working for an optometrist as a lens grinder. He also fit glasses for some of Austin's most prominent residents.

"I had a lot of good patients," he said. "I serviced and fitted glasses for lawyers, representatives, governor—one time I even adjusted glasses for Lyndon Johnson."

Casarez made a point to honor veterans with the Catholic War Veterans. He helped to establish the post of the CWV at his home church. He also volunteered with the American Legion.

Casarez married Theresa Herrera in 1948. The couple had four children: Pete Jr., Carlos, Herlinda and Veronica.

CASTRO, ALFREDO "ALFRED." A musical prodigy, Alfred Castro used his talents in bands in his youth and later as part of the Army's band. Castro hailed from a long line of musicians, and his father had played with San Antonio's symphony.

In his youth, Castro played shows all over San Antonio, and was proficient with a marimba, violin, vibraphone, snare drums and the glockenspiel. Castro was playing a show in San Antonio when he met his first wife, Aida Garcia, who died of tuberculosis in 1937. They had one daughter, Aida.

Castro was drafted in May 1942 and began training at Camp Livingston, La. While training in Robins Field, Ga., he boarded a bus to tour the town of Macon and was told by the bus driver to sit in the back. When he would not move from his front seat, the driver called the military police. They asked him the name of his outfit and said, "Soldier, you can sit wherever you want."

After basic training, he was assigned to the 132d Engineer Battalion but was soon transferred to the band. When his unit was mobilized to Europe, he was again transferred, this time to a band that had been in the Dakota National Guard and was shipped to Langley Field, Va., with the Eastern Coastal Defense for a year. For six months, Castro was assigned to an anti-aircraft unit in Camp Shelby, Miss. They were headed for Japan, but the war ended before they left the country.

He was then discharged and returned to his wife Ruth Pequignot and their son, Danilo in Indiana. They divorced in 1968. That same year, he married his half-brother's widow, Aurora Gonzalez. The two had one son. Castro moved back to San Antonio and continued pursuing music. He formed a trio, Al Castro's Marimba Sounds. The group was renowned throughout the area and played for President George Bush Sr. and his wife Barbara during a state dinner he held for Latin American presidents and Moroccan Prince Abdallah Alaou.

Alfredo "Alfred" Castro

Date of Birth
11 JUNE 1914
Laredo, TX

Tribute Provided by
Aurora Castro,
(Wife)

WWII Military Unit
Army Bands

CAVAZOS, CARLOS. Some 50 years after he was discharged, Carlos Cavazos still kept his olive green Army uniform perfectly pressed and ready to wear on special occasions. The uniform serves as a testament to his devotion to honoring his fellow veterans.

Cavazos was drafted in 1943, and began training at Fort Hood, Texas. He was preparing to leave for overseas duty when he was pulled from the train by his platoon sergeant and told to await new orders from his colonel.

He was then given the duty of an infantry instructor, training servicemen for nearly two years at Camp Joseph T. Robinson, Ark. He was a strong advocate of a more gentle psychological technique, sometimes crawling alongside nervous privates who were scared of the barbed wire, machine gun fire and other obstacles on infiltration courses.

"You see, psychology goes a long way," he said. "And it's my belief that if you use psychology, you can have people in the palm of your hand."

Cavazos' techniques were so effective that he was recognized for his training methods and given a "superior performance instructor" certificate.

Cavazos was discharged in April 1946. He began working as a map drafter and earned a certification in watch making, jewelry repair and engraving. He later worked at Kelly Air Force Base for more than 40 years as a painter and sheet metal worker.

His work with veterans' organizations was another huge part of his post-war life.

"I'm sure the good Lord will help me to continue honoring veterans. ... The veterans can never be forgotten," Cavazos said.

He married Florence Lopez in 1950 and they had three children: Sonia, Mark and Charles.

Carlos Cavazos

Date of Birth
4 SEPTEMBER 1925
El Paso, TX

Interviewed by
Yvonne Lim
25 OCTOBER 2003
San Antonio, TX

WWII Military Unit
Company B,
177th Battalion,
96th Training
Regiment

Hector De Peña

Date of Birth
22 OCTOBER 1914
Hillsboro, TX

Interviewed by
Karla E. González
18 AUGUST 2001
Corpus Christi, TX

WWII Location
Corpus Christi, TX

DE PEÑA, HECTOR.   When an abdominal hernia prevented Hector De Peña from serving in combat, he served instead as a civilian in the Office of Censorship for the Navy, recording phone calls from Mexico to the United States.

Working in Corpus Christi, Texas, as an attorney before the war, De Peña had encountered discrimination at restaurants, in movie theaters and in other public places. In one restaurant a waitress told him she "didn't serve Spanish-speaking people," he said. His first encounter with segregation had been as a pre-law student at Texas A&I University in Kingsville. "We were only about 10 Hispanic students in the college, and they had a separate bus for us," he said. Once he received a certificate to teach high school, he found he could not get a teaching job in the Kingsville area because he was Latino, so he studied to get his license to practice law.

His brother Fernando helped organize LULAC in Corpus Christi, where De Peña joined and was elected the second president. One of the organization's major accomplishments was challenging a city ordinance that barred Hispanics from swimming at Cole Park.

Working to fight discrimination on the political front, De Peña tried unsuccessfully to run for several offices, including state representative and judge for the Court of Domestic Relations. He even tried, after serving six years as an assistant county attorney, to run for the position of county attorney but this, too, proved fruitless. His break finally came when the judge's position for County Court-at-Law No. 2 became vacant. When an Anglo judge who occupied the position died, De Peña was appointed by Commissioner Solomon Ortiz and served for 16 years.

De Peña married Elena Tamez in 1942 and they had three children: Hector Jr., Carla and Charles. Hector Jr. rook over his father's position on the bench in the same court.

Randel Zepeda
Fernández

Date of Birth
21 MAY 1924
Ciudad Juarez,
Mexico

Interviewed by
Steven Rosales
30 JUNE 2004
Fontana, CA

WWII Military Unit
315th Infantry
Regiment,
79th Infantry
Division

FERNÁNDEZ, RANDEL ZEPEDA.   When his family moved from Ciudad Juarez to El Paso, Texas, and then to Los Angeles, Randel Zepeda Fernández was only a baby. But later, as a young man, his lack of U.S. citizenship hampered him. "I couldn't find a good job because I was an alien," Fernández said. "At the time, joining the Armed Forces was the fastest way to become a citizen."

In March 1943, Fernández enlisted in the Army and trained in Virginia, Massachusetts, and Maryland before he left for Europe. He served throughout the continent, spending time in France, Belgium, Holland, Germany and Czechoslovakia. He fought in the Battle of the Bulge, crossed the Rhine and even helped liberate several concentration camps. "At those camps we gave men our rations we had with us and it was amazing," he said. "These men were crying at my feet like babies."

In December 1945, he was finally naturalized before being discharged in March 1946. Fernández returned to Los Angeles and used the GI Bill to attend a technical school to study design and tailoring. His godfather began teaching him how to sew during a summer he spent with him and Fernández started his own business, Randy's Tailor and Cleaners. He owned the business for 15 years before selling it.

Fernández began using his talents at a new tailoring job, with Charles Malley Tailors, catering to movie stars and other entertainers. He later worked as the head tailor at Zeidler and Zeidler Men's Clothing. Though he retired in 1989, faithful customers still sought him out for alterations.

Serving his fellow veterans also became a priority for Fernández, who found time to volunteer with the VFW, American Legion, the Elks Lodge and Knights of Columbus. "It's important to volunteer your time to organizations that count."

Fernández married Lillian Barella and the couple had two children, Steve and Loretta.

FLORES, ARMANDO. Though he was a member of one of the "first families" of Texas and the grandson of a man who lived in the state before it gained its independence, Armando Flores did not remember being recognized as an American until he served in the U.S. Army.

He was 19 years old and in basic training at Sheppard Field in Texas on a cold winter day, standing in a line of soldiers huddled to avoid the wind, when a lieutenant shouted: "American soldiers stand at attention on a cold day or a hot day, and they never keep their hands in their pockets." The soldiers snapped to attention. "The funny thing about it — and the reason that I remember that — was because nobody had ever called me an American until that time," Flores said. "I had been called a lot of things ... wetback, Spic, and greaser."

Flores was sent home after eight months because of heart problems resulting from rheumatic fever, but he remained active in civic affairs. He was involved in the American G.I. Forum as a charter member. After becoming a scoutmaster for the Boy Scouts in 1951, he continued to attend G.I. Forum meetings, but "didn't raise hell because he had to set an example."

Through his membership in the Disabled American Veterans, Flores got a job at a print shop. He became an employee of Nueces County in 1949 and was in charge of its printing, including warrants, citations and other legal paperwork.

His career with Nueces County spanned 51 years. After a time as the county printer, he was a court interpreter, and he eventually rose to the position of justice of the peace. He still attends meetings and is a dues-paying member of the G.I. Forum.

He met María Louisa Villa while attending Corpus Christi Business College, and they married in September 1947. They had four children, all of whom graduated from college.

Armando Flores

Date of Birth
17 SEPTEMBER 1921
Mission, TX

Interviewed by
Bettina Luis
24 MARCH 2001
Corpus Christi, TX

WWII Location
Stationed at
Sheppard Field, TX

GALINDO, RAMÓN. After the death of Adolf Hitler, Ramón Galindo and his unit had one of the most difficult jobs: to guard Hitler's headquarters, which were filled with portraits of Nazi officials and swastikas. Galindo had to suppress the urge to destroy the paintings and flags that were a painful reminder of the war's purpose.

"I didn't realize I was sitting in a building that was going to be a big part of history," he said.

Galindo volunteered for the Texas State Guard and was trained at Camp Mabry, Texas. After his time in the State Guard, he enlisted in the Army and was trained to shoot down planes. He was somewhat disappointed, because he initially thought he would be flying planes.

Born in Mexico, Galindo earned his U.S. citizenship in 1943 while in the military. He then left for Europe, where he fought in the Battle of the Bulge in 1944 and a battle at the Rhine River in 1945.

He was discharged in February 1946 and returned to Texas to begin working as tailor. In 1948, Galindo took out a loan and opened Galindo the Tailor in downtown Austin, Texas.

His shop was popular and he had several famous clients. For 20 years, he made the uniforms for the University of Texas' cheerleading squad and tailored Lyndon Johnson's suits when Johnson served in Congress.

Galindo retired after 21 successful years in tailoring and began focusing on one of his favorite hobbies: magic. He worked as semi-professional magician, and even appeared on the 1991 cover of International Conjuror's Magazine, a publication for magicians.

In November 1946, Galindo married Pauline Santos. The two had met as children, and reconnected after the war. They had two daughters: Gloria and Josephine.

Ramón Galindo

Date of Birth
29 MAY 1921
San Juan, Nuevo
Leon, Mexico

Interviewed by
Martamaría
McGonagle
27 SEPTEMBER 2000
Austin, TX

WWII Military Unit
571st Anti-Aircraft
Artillery Automatic
Weapons Battalion,
Self-Propelled

Thomas Galindo

Date of Birth
2 NOVEMBER 1922
Goforth, TX

Interviewed by
Antonio Gilb
29 SEPTEMBER 2001
Austin, TX

WWII Military Unit
358th Airdrome
Squadron

GALINDO, THOMAS. The work ethic he developed as a young man growing up in Texas carried Thomas Galindo through a challenging tour of duty in Europe during WWII and later brought him success as he expanded his family's tortilla business.

Galindo enlisted in November 1942, as a radio operator and after his training, was sent to Europe. Despite his dangerous mission, he was still grateful for the opportunity to travel. "It was like a dream, something you read in a book," he said. "I never thought I'd be over there."

While in Europe, Galindo repaired planes. He also gathered intelligence and helped transport men and supplies through the mountains of Southern France. He flew injured soldiers to hospitals in England and even delivered freight to Gen. George Patton, whom he greatly respected.

"Some ... didn't like him," Galindo said. "I thought he was a good pusher, he had to push. He was about the best we had of the generals. I'm pretty sure the Germans didn't like him."

Galindo was discharged in September 1945 with the rank of sergeant and four Bronze Stars.

He began working at the family's tortilla company, El Fenix. He said that when he started, it was a small business, with only about nine customers a week. However, Galindo devoted himself to expanding the business. He eventually changed the name to El Galindo when the company expanded to Dallas, Texas, since El Fenix was already taken in that city.

Soon Galindo was selling millions of tortillas each week, and at the peak of his success, his company employed 70 people. He said his secret was not clever marketing or fancy packaging, but the quality of his tortillas. "You have to work fast and hard, and work a lot of hours," he said. "If you make something good, you don't have to advertise, they'll buy it anyway."

Galindo married Ernestine Guajardo in 1950 and they had two sons, Thomas and Guillermo.

Evelio Grillo

Date of Birth
14 JUNE 1919
Tampa, FL

Interviewed by
Mario Barrera
26 JANUARY 2003
Oakland, CA

WWII Military Unit
823d Engineer
Aviator Battalion
(Colored)

GRILLO, EVELIO. As a black Cuban American, Evelio Grillo was embraced by African Americans: he attended a black high school in Washington, D.C., and later the historically black Xavier University in New Orleans. He was nurtured by successful African American patrons who saw promise in him.

In the military, Grillo was placed in an "all-colored" unit and aboard the USS *Santa Paula*, where there was uneven treatment of black and white troops.

A petition circulated for equal treatment, but nothing changed, although he and his fellow black soldiers felt empowered simply for protesting.

When Grillo arrived in India, his unit was forced to sleep in tents on the muddy ground during monsoon season; white officers slept on elevated bamboo pallets.

"We were just like slaves and slave masters," he said. The officers in charge of black troops were white, he said. Grillo served as a recreation and morale sergeant, creating a volunteer jazz band and publishing a mimeograph newspaper, The Hairy Ear Herald—"hairy ears" was slang for engineers—for the soldiers.

Grillo's worked in community relations in Oakland, Calif., seeking to bring together black and Latino community leaders and later worked for the Oakland city manager. He also worked for the Carter administration from 1977 to 1979 as an executive assistant for the policy development in the Department of Health, Education and Welfare. In all the positions he held, he felt integration was a crucial goal.

He had four children—Elisa, Trina, Evelio Martin, and Antonio—with his first wife, Catherine Elizabeth Patalano. The couple divorced in 1974 and he later married Eleanor Engram. They were also divorced.

HERNANDEZ, AUGUSTÍN LOUIS. His life has been full of service to others, and Augustín Louis Hernandez was able to look back on his life with only one regret: that he never learned how to swim.

Augustín Louis Hernandez

Date of Birth
28 AUGUST 1924
Houston, TX

Interviewed by
**Ernest Eguía and
Paul R. Zepeda
24 FEBRUARY 2003**
Houston, TX

WWII Military Unit
**451st Bomb Group,
49th Bomb Wing,
15th Air Force**

Indicative of the life he led, Hernandez was a goal-oriented man in his youth. He enlisted at age 17, with the consent of his father. He trained at Fort Sam Houston, Texas, before he began training to become an engineer and gunner in Salt Lake City, Utah. Before he left for Europe, he received additional training on a B-24 bomber in Peterson Field, Colo.

Hernandez was assigned to a tour of duty in Foggia, Italy, and he flew on more than 50 missions throughout Yugoslavia, Romania, Bulgaria, Germany and France.

He was discharged with the rank of staff sergeant in October 1945, with five combat stars and a presidential citation.

He opened a watch repair shop when he returned to Houston, but soon was drawn back into a life of public service, as a firefighter at the No. 9 Fire Station, where he was one of the first Latinos to work for the Houston Fire Department.

He enjoyed the work, but retired after 11 years when he was injured on duty. He fell and was hit by one of the trucks, breaking his leg.

Hernandez then began working for the Harris County Sheriff's Department, spending 26 years there. When he retired at 74, he was the first Hispanic to retire from the department with the rank of sergeant.

Hernandez married Canuta "Connie" Muñoz in 1947. The couple had three children: Rebecca, Joseph and Martha.

HOLGUIN, ARTURO. Growing up with three older brothers in the military, Arturo Holguin, though too young to experience the horrors of war firsthand, knew the sting of separation and the constant worry that families of soldiers experience better than most.

Arturo Holguin

Date of Birth
24 APRIL 1930
Santa Clara, NM

Interviewed by
**Maggie Rivas-
Rodriguez
15 JULY 2004**
Arenas Valley, NM

WWII Location
Santa Clara, NM

Holguin's hometown was in the shadow of Fort Bayard, N.M., which housed a tuberculosis clinic. He believed the clinic's proximity to the town contributed to the rampant outbreaks of the disease, which claimed the lives of many of his family members.

When Holguin's father died, he became head of the household, despite being the youngest son, since his brothers were married and had moved away or were serving in the military. His mother was forced to work outside of their home to help support the family. She worked at Fort Bayard.

As the desolation in his hometown reached devastating levels, Holguin saw the need for change, to save what was left of his community. After the town's junior high school was shut down because it lacked proper sewage and water systems, there was talk of shutting down the local elementary school as well. At a town meeting, the city council prepared to vote on abandoning both their efforts to get water and save the schools. "I stood up and said, 'Wait a minute,'" Holguin said.

Those three words launched his activism in his community. He insisted that the city continue to explore other avenues to correct the problems at local schools. He was appointed to the vacant seat on the city council, and he agreed on one condition: he would be put in charge of all the city's water issues. The council agreed, and put him in charge of the local sewage issues as well.

Holguin's career in local politics was successful. He started construction on a 700-ft. well—which the city used for nearly 50 years—and negotiated a deal with Fort Bayard to improve his town's sewer system.

Tony Holguin

Date of Birth
18 OCTOBER 1926
San Antonio, TX

Interviewed by
William Luna
18 OCTOBER 2002
Chicago, IL

WWII Military Unit
76th Infantry
Division

HOLGUIN, TONY. While he valiantly served the country he loved in WWII, Tony Holguin's true love is the game of golf. Few can boast they have defeated legendary golfer Sam Snead, but by age 22, Holguin had earned that right, beating Snead by six shots in a professional tournament.

Before he earned tournament titles, Holguin spent time in Europe during WWII. He was drafted immediately after he graduated from high school in 1944. He trained at Fort Hood, Texas, and later at Fort Meade before setting sail for Glasglow, Scotland. He then crossed the English Channel to join the 76th Infantry Division in France. He was involved in several skirmishes, but escaped injury during his tour of duty.

"I was lucky to never get wounded," he said. "I think of the 11 guys in our squad, there were only four or five that got wounded. Nobody–luckily–got killed, but we were in toward the end of the war."

When he arrived back in the States, he was inspired to continue pursuing his dreams of a career in professional golf. "At that time I won two tournaments and won $2,000," Holguin said.

With the help of a sponsorship from businessman Tom Crawford, he was able to practice six hours a day and quickly became the best golfer in the San Antonio area. He won the Mexico City Open in 1948, less than three years after his discharge from the Army. In 1953, he won the Texas Open.

While he showed obvious promise as a competitive touring professional, he chose to pursue a position as a pro at a country club, eventually landing a position as the head pro at a country club in Midlothian, a Chicago suburb.

In 1951, Holguin married Lena Mayin. The couple had one son, Tony Jr.

Robert Leyva

Date of Birth
10 MAY 1915
Chihuahua, Mexico

Interviewed by
Andrea Williams
2 FEBRUARY 2002
El Paso, TX

WWII Military Unit
254th Field
Artillery Battalion

LEYVA, ROBERT. A star athlete, Robert Leyva had plans to attend college on an athletic scholarship and eventually become a professional basketball player. But WWII began and he received a draft notice soon after his first year at the Texas College of Mines. Leyva put his dreams on hold.

Leyva arrived in the United States at age 5, after his mother moved him, his brother and sister to El Paso, Texas. Raising her children alone was difficult, but Leyva's mother placed a high value on education and worked as a farm laborer while her children attended school. Her dedication to the family helped Levya to excel in school and sports, earning a full scholarship to college.

Drafted in 1944, Leyva trained at Camp Gordon, Ga. From there he was shipped to New York, then to England. He first saw combat in October 1944. He fought in the Battle of the Bulge, the Central European campaign and in the German Rhineland.

Leyva was never seriously injured, but was hurt in a truck accident. Because medical attention was not available for 20 days, his wounds had to heal themselves.

He was discharged in December 1945 with the rank of private first class and with three Bronze Stars. He returned to Texas and finished his degree at the College of the Mines and earned his master's degree there as well.

After the war, he pursued a career in coaching. He taught physical education in the El Paso Independent School District for 45 years. He also spent 50 years working part-time with the city's parks and recreation department.

Leyva's service was recognized with the Conquistador Award, the highest honor in El Paso.

He married Bertha Garcia before his military service began, in 1943. The couple had five children: Yolanda, Martha, Robert Jr., Roy and Patricia.

MARTINEZ, JOHNNIE. A star in the Houston music scene since the 1940s, Johnnie Martinez was constantly in the spotlight. He would eventually use his talent and passion to lead a band, own a nightclub and start his own record label.

Johnnie Martinez

Date of Birth
6 JANUARY 1916
Waco, TX

Interviewed by
Ernest Eguía
12 MARCH 2003
Houston, TX

WWII Military Unit
Texas National Guard

He began his music career early in life under his father's tutelage, and was an excellent trumpeter by the time he completed eighth grade. When he moved from Waco, Texas, to Houston, Texas, with his wife Gloria Sepolio, his career took off.

Martinez played at dances and clubs around town, and even met jazz legend Tommy Dorsey. By the end of the evening, he was sipping cocktails with Dorsey, surrounded by fans asking both musicians for their autographs.

As WWII loomed, Martinez enlisted and was sent to Kelly Field, Texas. There he worked as an interpreter until he was sent overseas. In France, Martinez drove a supply jeep and also ran messages to the front line. Luckily, during his days as a courier, he escaped major injury, completing his duty with little more than a scrape on his forehead.

Martinez was discharged in November 1945, and he returned to Houston and to music. He formed his own band, The Johnnie Martinez Band. He also became the owner of the Palladium in downtown Houston, which hosted Elvis Presley and other famous musicians. Martinez remembered receiving little credit for his many achievements, with the press often focusing on the Anglo members of the band instead of Martinez, who was the leader and conductor.

He later pursued a career outside music, working as a representative for various breweries. It was lucrative and allowed him to provide for his wife and six children: Alice, Irene, Gloria, Mary Louise, Carol and Janette.

MILLAN, ALBERTO. When the final shots of WWII rang out, Alberto Millan was a few weeks from his 15th birthday. Though he was unable to serve his country in the military, he had already begun working in the copper mines for a year to help support his family.

Alberto Millan

Date of Birth
18 AUGUST 1930
San Lorenzo, NM

Interviewed by
Robert Rivas
15 JULY 2004
Arenas Valley, NM

WWII Location
Santa Rita, NM

Millan was the son of a miner; his father died of a heart attack at the Santa Rita mine. His own job in the Santa Rita mines was fraught with problems: dangerous physical conditions and rampant discrimination. Coupled with tense conditions between miners and owners who sought to keep wages low, the environment was difficult, prompting Millan to join the local union, Mine & Smelter Workers, AFL/CIO.

He worked with the union throughout his career, eventually becoming the chairman of the grievance committee. He was a fierce negotiator, often traveling to Washington, D.C., and Chicago, Ill., to represent his fellow miners. His headstrong nature made him an obvious choice to defend the rights of miners, but he often angered the businessmen he worked with.

"One time, this guy got up and said, 'You know what Albert? I don't like you,' " Millan said. "I never stayed quiet. I always answered back, 'What makes you think I love you?' "

His determination and relentless devotion to the cause of miner's rights made him a major threat to many businesses that profited from less than favorable working conditions. He was offered a job at another mine, but refused to abandon his cause.

"That's the only job I ever had," he said. "I gave them all my life."

Millan married Concha Dominguez Gonzales in 1952 and the couple had six children. He moved his family to nearby Silver City, N.M., so his children could attend better schools. "You know, so they could better themselves," he said. "It looks like I raised them right."

Gloria Flores
Moraga

Date of Birth
5 DECEMBER 1930
Phoenix, AZ

Interviewed by
Violeta Dominguez
4 JANUARY 2003
Phoenix, AZ

WWII Location
Phoenix, AZ

MORAGA, GLORIA FLORES. Defying traditional gender roles, Gloria Moraga was a trailblazer; becoming an on-air personality at Arizona's Spanish-language radio station in the late 1940s.

Born Gloria Flores, she dubbed herself a "Depression Baby," she was born a little over a year after the stock market crash. She remembered difficult times, and recalled that an uncle snatched milk off porches in the neighborhood, because her family could not afford milk to feed her.

She was forced to drop out of school a year and a half before graduation, to help her mother care for her siblings. While she understood her important role at home, she missed attending classes and extracurricular activities.

"But I did like high school; I was very active," Moraga said, and she remembered being on the drill team, in the choir and on the Girls Athletic Association. "I used to be so active in everything and at times, I was the only Latina, the only Mexican in these things."

In 1948, she met a WWII veteran, Pete Moraga, who would become her husband, and who helped her secure an exciting job at KIFN radio station.

She remembered that before a date at the movies, Moraga stopped by the station to do a job interview and brought her along. She charmed the interviewer and was soon working as a music librarian and eventually hosted her own show *"La Linda Mujer Mexicana."* She amassed a fan base quickly and was a local celebrity until she moved to California with her family a year later.

Her romance with Pete Moraga continued for nearly six years until the two married in June 1954. The couple had five children: Peter, Monica, Linda, Gloria and Catherine.

Moraga eventually returned to school and earned an associate's degree in theater arts from Santa Monica College.

Pete Moraga

Date of Birth
11 JUNE 1926
Tempe, AZ

Interviewed by
Maggie Rivas-
Rodriguez
4 JANUARY 2003
Mesa, AZ

WWII Military Unit
10th Service
Squadron,
7th Service Group,
IV Air Service
Command,
5th Air Force

MORAGA, PETE. As a young man growing up in segregated Tempe, Ariz., Pete Moraga was sometimes afraid to speak in public. But those fears did not keep him from becoming *"La Voz Mexicana"* or "the Mexican Voice" during his successful career as a broadcast journalist. He credited his military service with helping him gain the confidence to succeed.

Moraga was sworn into the service on D-Day, June 6, 1944. During his tour of duty, he operated the ship-to-ship radio.

After he was discharged, he immediately enrolled in the University of Arizona, earning a degree in advertising in 1949 and becoming the first member of his family to graduate from college.

Moraga then began working in Phoenix, at KIFN, the state's first Spanish-language radio station. He diligently covered news in the Hispanic community for eight years, until he started a career in public relations with the U.S. Information Agency. He stayed with the agency's broadcast component for 12 years, traveling throughout Latin America as a press attaché. He said his job was to "sell American foreign policy," something he found increasingly difficult during the Vietnam War.

Moraga decided to return to journalism. He began working for KNX-CBS radio in Los Angeles. Calif. Later he worked as the news director at KMEX-TV and provided commentary for KCBS-TV, bringing the Latino perspective on the news. He retired in 1992, but stayed active in the Latino community with intergenerational outreach programs at the Mesa Senior Center.

Moraga received a host of awards throughout his distinguished career, and was inducted into the National Association of Hispanic Journalists' Hall of Fame in 2001.

Moraga married Gloria Flores in 1954 and the couple had five children: Peter, Monica, Linda, Gloria and Catherine.

MUÑOZ, DANIEL. Segregation at movie theaters and other public places plagued Daniel Muñoz during his childhood, but it also fueled his passion for social justice and led him to publish a successful newspaper targeting Southern California's Latinos.

Daniel Muñoz

Date of Birth
9 NOVEMBER 1927
San Fernando, CA

Interviewed by
Maggie Rivas-
Rodriguez
25 OCTOBER 2002
San Diego, CA

WWII Military Unit
Headquarters,
Pacific Fleet,
Pearl Harbor, HI

Muñoz grew up in California's San Fernando Valley, where he said that most Mexican Americans were "programmed to go to the fields," and forgo education.

Muñoz enlisted in the Navy in 1945 and became more aware of the disparities between Latinos and Anglos. He could barely stomach the "rich" food he was fed when he joined the military; before his time in the military, he had never eaten steak.

He was eventually taken off his ship to attend Radio Code and Teletype school, where he excelled. While the average soldier could code 16 to 18 words per minute, Muñoz could type 24 to 26. He eventually earned the rank Radioman 3d class. Following his discharge, he returned to California. He served in the Korean War and later in Vietnam as a Chief Warrant Officer. In 1969, Muñoz returned to civilian life. He taught Chicano studies and Mexican culture at Mesa Community College.

During his time as a professor, he chafed at the lack of Latino voices in the local news media and began considering creating a newspaper to give a voice to Latinos in the San Diego area. He eventually developed that idea into La Prensa, a weekly bilingual publication that brought news to over 300,000 Latinos in San Diego. In addition to founding the paper, Muñoz was the publisher and editor. La Prensa's first issue was published in 1976 and it was published continuously. La Prensa concentrated on political and community news, particularly as it affected Latinos.

He married Lydia Hernandez on April 24, 1949. They had six children: Phyllis, Daniel, Ruben, Pricella, Gabriel and Angela.

NEVAREZ, JOE. As the sports editor of Lincoln High School's daily paper, Joe Nevarez began his long career in journalism. But before he could become one of the first Mexican-American reporters at the L.A. Times, he spent time serving his country during WWII.

Joe Nevarez

Date of Birth
6 JANUARY 1912
Tepehuanes,
Durango, Mexico

Interviewed by
Steven Rosales
5 JULY 2004
Monterey Park, CA

WWII Military Unit
419th Technical
Squadron

Born in Mexico, Nevarez immigrated with his parents when he was 3 months old. He started to learn English while attending an integrated grammar school. He began working at the L.A. Times as a copy boy, posting New York Stock Exchange quotations and sometimes helping with the financial section of the paper.

At age 31, Nevarez was drafted into the Army. He eventually reached the rank of lieutenant, but was never sent overseas for combat. He was part of the Air Corps, and spent much of his military career stationed at Sheppard Field, Texas. He continued his newspaper work while in the service, writing a monthly report for the Army Air Base Newspaper.

Later, he was transferred to the Azores, Portuguese islands, in the middle of the Atlantic. During his time on the islands, he developed asthma and was hospitalized. He was sent back to the States a month before his discharge in 1945.

He returned to the L.A. Times as a reporter in the business section. He worked at the Times for 52 years total, and said it was some of the most rewarding work of his life.

"There's nothing better than being a reporter," he said. "There's something new every day."

Nevarez also volunteered with his local post of the American Legion. He later served as the commander of the post.

Navarez married Theresa Juarez in May 1944, and the couple had three children: Margaret, Daniel and Cecilia. All three children completed college.

José "Joe" Solis
Ramirez

Date of Birth
27 MARCH 1918
El Paso, TX

Interviewed by
Andrea Shearer
2 FEBRUARY 2002
El Paso, TX

WWII Military Unit
USS *Gleaves*
(DD-423)

RAMIREZ, JOSÉ "JOE" SOLIS. While patrolling the waters of the Pacific off the coast of the Philippines, José Ramirez helped rally morale by serenading his fellow soldiers, when he wasn't busy scoping out enemy soldiers on the deck of the USS *Gleaves*.

"They'd say: 'Come on, Joe; sing that song again, while some of us go to sleep while you're singing,' " he said.

His parents had moved to the U.S. from Mexico just two weeks before Ramirez was born. He spoke Spanish at home, but quickly learned English when he went to school. He remembered eventually forgetting some of the Spanish of his youth, and when his family moved back to Mexico, he sometimes struggled with the language.

Ramirez was working as an assistant engineer on a road project when the war began. He was already married, to Eleanor Aldaña, with two children—Juanita and Robert—when he entered the service. He enlisted as the war was coming to its end, and he saw little combat. He remained aboard the *Gleaves* for most of his service.

He was discharged in March 1946. He began working on a railroad as foreman, a position that was in demand, and Ramirez remembered winning the promotion over 22 other men.

He tried to get involved in veterans' organizations as well. He found many of his fellow Latino veterans did not feel as welcomed at the Anglo-dominated American Legion, so he founded his own organization for Latino veterans.

Ramirez went on to become the first Latino policeman to become deputy sheriff and commissioner of streets and alleys in Cheyenne, Wyo.

Ramirez divorced in 1966 and married María de Refugia Ayala.

Robert Salcido

Date of Birth
26 MAY 1924
El Paso, TX

Interviewed by
Joe Myers Vasquez
2 FEBRUARY 2002
El Paso, TX

WWII Military Unit
746th Tank
Battalion

SALCIDO, ROBERT. The gruesome images of war are burned into Robert Salcido's memory, as vivid as the day he saw them. But despite the horrors he witnessed, his pride in the military never wavered. He was devoted to providing proper funerals for his fellow veterans.

Salcido's military career began early, when he participated in the ROTC at Bowie High School. After graduation, he was drafted a week later. Because of his ROTC training, he was immediately shipped to Fort Knox, Ky., for armored force and reconnaissance training. He continued on to Fort Meade, Md., where he received armored training. Salcido was then shipped to England, prepared to invade France and then landed on the shores of Normandy.

Because he spoke Spanish, Salcido was then transferred to the G2, the intelligence section of his division. He was given a small unit of soldiers to lead in performing reconnaissance missions behind enemy lines. In May 1945, Salcido was discharged and returned to El Paso, Texas. He attended printer trade school and then took a job at Fort Bliss in the print shop, where he stayed for 31 years.

His retirement was full of community service and helping others. He began Sun City Graffiti Busters, an organization that worked with teens and the police department to help clean up graffiti. Perhaps his most personal crusade is his constant fight to have a bugler supplied to sound "Taps" at veterans' funerals. He believes it is every veteran's right to have a live bugler at his or her funeral. He authored a petition, with over 2,500 signatures to help this cause.

"It's just like putting salt in a reopened wound," he said of the pre-recorded version of "Taps" that families often hear for the funeral.

Salcido married Dolores Quintana in 1946. The couple had three sons: Robert, Manuel David and Pedro Martín. All three sons became police officers.

SANCHEZ, RAYMOND. Throughout his life, Raymond Sanchez served his country and community, while clinging to his Mexican heritage, instilling that same pride in his children.

"I always made it a point ... if they ask you what you are, tell 'em you're Mexican American and don't be ashamed," he said.

Sanchez served aboard the USS *Saranac* during WWII, a tanker that transported fuel, aviation gas and ammunition. The crew supplied other ships, such as aircraft carriers, destroyers and minesweepers. Because of it precious cargo, the ship was often a target of enemy attacks.

"Our ship got hit and we lost quite a few men," Sanchez said. "Two of us got wounded, but we refused to go home, we decided to stay and keep on going."

Following the war, Sanchez returned to Austin, Texas, and opened his own shoe store, Raymond's Workshoes Store, where faithful customers and their families flocked to his shop. Sanchez has been in the shoe business since his childhood, when he shined shoes for extra money in the evenings.

He also devoted his time to serving his local community in Austin. He worked with the Century Club to build the Cantu/Pan American Recreation Center on East Third Street. He also worked to have a fence installed at Zaragosa Park, and worked with high school dropouts under the Distributive Education Program. Sanchez also coached his children's basketball, volleyball and baseball teams.

Sanchez married Jane Guerrero. The couple had three children: Michael, Patti and Janet.

Some of the men he served with became his lifelong friends and he kept in touch with them for over 50 years. He and his wife Jane traveled all over the country to attend military reunions to spend time with his fellow veterans.

Raymond Sanchez

Date of Birth
30 JULY 1926
Austin, TX

Interviewed by
Rhonda Miller
12 OCTOBER 1999
Austin, TX

WWII Military Unit
USS *Saranac*
(AO-74)

SOLTERO, ROBERT. Though war was never easy for Robert Soltero, he willfully enlisted to escape the discrimination that plagued him in his hometown of Kansas City, Mo., where he remembered police officers constantly watching young Latinos.

Soltero joined the service in 1944 at age 17. He said that there was the occasional prejudice in the military, but overall his experience was positive. He became an electrician's mate third class and attended demolition and gunnery school while in the Navy.

He was stationed at Coco Loco NAS in Panama City, Panama. Because of his Spanish-language skills he was assigned to shore patrol. Soon he was working as interpreter in civilian clothes.

Soltero returned to the States and was assigned to the USS *Pecatonica*, a gas tanker that ferried back and forth from Jacksonville, Fla. to Baton Rouge, La.

He was discharged in 1948 but stayed in the reserves for four additional years. He returned to the hotel business, forgoing the GI Bill, because he said that he received his education in the Navy.

"I got to meet all sorts of people," he said. "I got my education that way."

Soltero used much of his free time to volunteer with a host of different organizations in his community. As part of the American Legion, he honored his fellow veterans. He spent 10 years on the board of directors for the Guadalupe Center Inc., one of the country's first social service agencies for Latinos. He acted as the sponsor for the Center's culinary arts school and Alta Vista Charter High School.

He volunteered at a local golf course, working as a start marshal and teaching golf.

Soltero married Carmen Tinoco in January 1950. The couple had three children: Gary, Larry and Jo Aann.

Robert Soltero

Date of Birth
5 NOVEMBER 1927
Kansas City, MO

Interviewed by
Ascensión Hernandez
30 OCTOBER 2003
Kansas City, MO

WWII Military Unit
USS *Pecatonica*
(AOG–57)

Felix Treviño

Date of Birth
14 OCTOBER 1920
San Antonio, TX

Interviewed by
David Zavala
13 OCTOBER 2001
San Antonio, TX

WWII Military Unit
Company E,
274th Infantry
Regiment,
70th Infantry
Division

TREVIÑO, FELIX. In his native San Antonio, Felix Treviño has been a mover and a shaker: a member of the San Antonio City Council in the 1960s, president of the Pan American Optimist Club, and the president of the board of directors of the Tejano Music Awards. He also taught citizenship classes and English to Mexican immigrants. He tried to help the disadvantaged.

"I had always seen many people being mistreated, and my idea was that I want to help those people," he said.

Treviño faced discrimination while growing up; at one point, when he applied for a job as a typesetter he was told that the company "didn't hire Mexicans." Rather than be discouraged, he began his own printing company. But during the war, paper rationing started and he was forced to start working at the print shop at Kelly Field to support his family. But when he quit that job in 1944, Treviño was drafted.

He trained at Camp Fannin, Texas, and was eventually shipped to France. At one point on a battlefield, Treviño tried to show compassion for a young German who had lost his lower leg. But when he offered the man his morphine shot, issued to soldiers in the event they were wounded in battle, the German refused. Treviño offered him a cigarette, and the German spit in Treviño's face.

He was en route to Japan when he received word that the war had ended. He was discharged in February 1946 and returned to San Antonio. He earned a degree from Southwest Texas State University and then reopened his printing business.

He devoted his time on the San Antonio City Council to making improvements to the neglected West Side of San Antonio.

Treviño married Alicia Piña in 1941 and had three children: Margarita, Felix Jr. and Imelda.

Joseph Unanue

Date of Birth
14 MARCH 1925
Brooklyn, NY

Interviewed by
Maggie Rivas-
Rodriguez
11 APRIL 2002
Secaucus, NJ

WWII Military Unit
Company A,
63d Armored
Infantry Battalion,
11th Armored
Division

UNANUE, JOSEPH. He is better known for his role as the former head of Goya Foods, but Joseph Unanue is also a WWII veteran who fought at the Battle of the Bulge.

Unanue's father, a native of Spain, founded Goya Foods, a distribution company. Joseph Unanue grew up packing olives for the plant, and helping his father build his company, despite some discrimination in the early stages of the company.

Even in times of financial trouble, education was crucial to Unanue's parents, and he attended the best Catholic school, despite its high tuition of $5 a month.

Drafted into the Army in July 1943, he attended basic training at Camp Roberts, Calif. He then trained in foreign languages and later with the armored infantry. He went to Europe with the 63d Infantry Battalion and fought in the Battle of the Bulge.

"We had to travel three days in the cold. Some claim it was one of the coldest winters in Europe ever. We joined General [George S.] Patton's 3d Army at the Battle of the Bulge," said Unanue. "We lost half our company in the first 10 days!"

He used the GI Bill to earn a degree in mechanical engineering from Catholic University of America, but then returned to the family business, and spent his life learning the ins and outs of food distribution. In 1976, he became president of Goya Foods and the company became the largest distributor of Latino foods in the U.S., with more than 1,000 products.

He expanded the company with the help of his brothers, and spread the business throughout the hemisphere, from its headquarters in Secaucus, N.J., to Houston, Texas, to the Dominican Republic and beyond.

Unanue married Carmen Ana Casal in 1956, and the couple had six children.

URANGA, CHARLES. His father's unshakable work ethic and conviction that Latinos should enjoy equal rights had a powerful effect on Charles Uranga. He attributes all his successes, including a million-dollar business in the energy industry, to his father's influence. And Uranga's father attributed much of his own success to his wife, who helped him learn to read and write.

Uranga was drafted into the Army in 1942 and trained at Camp Hulen in Palacios, Texas, and then practiced maneuvers in Louisiana. He eventually landed in England, and began preparing for the D-Day invasion. He stormed the shores of Omaha Beach and despite his trepidation, he pushed forward alongside his lieutenant.

"I was shaking, my hands were going this way and so were his," Uranga said. "And he says 'Are you scared?' and I said, 'Yes I am.' And he said 'I'm scared just like you are. But don't let your subordinates know that you're scared because they look at the leaders. And you and I are leaders.'"

Uranga continued through the continent, participating in campaigns in the Ardennes, Central Europe and Germany.

He was discharged in October 1945 with a Bronze Star. He then returned to Texas and began his successful career in business. He began running a grocery store in Alpine, Texas. He later purchased the Eagle Oil Co. He purchased refined products — gasoline, diesel, propane and butane — and then exported them to Latin America. He built the business from the ground up, starting with only "one, beat up truck." Soon he was running a business with 40 trailers and 700 railroad cars traveling all over Central and South America.

A first marriage to Minerva Cuellar resulted in two children: Norma and Yvonne, but ended in divorce. Uranga married Yolanda Mendoza in 1977.

Charles Uranga

Date of Birth
30 APRIL 1921
Alpine, TX

Interviewed by
Antonio Cantú
27 JANUARY 2001
San Antonio, TX

WWII Military Unit
29th Infantry
Division

VALDERAS, HAROLD. Just a few months after the attack on Pearl Harbor, Harold Valderas dropped out of high school to enlist in the U.S. Army Air Corps Cadet Program. But his dropping out was not a predictor of his future: after the war, he became a lawyer and later, a judge.

Valderas was the son of Chilean merchant mariner and an Irish-Polish mother and grew up speaking only English. In the military, Valderas was the only Hispanic training at Hicks Field in Fort Worth, Texas. He taught instrument flying to pilots and cadets at Waco Army Airfield. He also taught instrument flying to B-26 pilots at Dodge City Army Airfield in Kansas. Shortly after D-Day, Valderas was shipped to England where he directed air traffic with the 8th Air Force.

After the war, he returned to Texas and attended Southern Methodist University in Dallas, where he received a bachelor's of business administration in 1950.

Valderas was recalled to active duty during the Korean War. Afterward he returned to Texas to finish his law degree and open a private law practice in Fort Worth in 1955.

Valderas married Marisa Garcia, of Seville, Spain, in 1965 and they had four children: Harold, Elizabeth, Sean, and Cristian. The marriage eventually ended in divorce. In 2002, Valderas married Ruby Gillian.

He began a series of firsts for the Hispanic legal community in 1969, while in the Air Force Reserve at Carswell Air Force Base, when he was the first Hispanic to serve as staff judge advocate for the 301st Tactical Fighter Wing, legal adviser to the commanding general.

He became the first Hispanic judge in the North Texas area when he was appointed municipal judge for the city of Fort Worth in 1971; the first Hispanic in Central Texas to be a state district judge in 1977; and the first Hispanic senior district judge in 1987.

Harold Valderas

Date of Birth
17 DECEMBER 1923
New York, NY

Interviewed by
Violeta Dominguez
18 SEPTEMBER 2003
Austin, TX

WWII Location
United States;
England

Raymond Vega

Date of Birth
22 APRIL 1924
East Chicago, IN

Interviewed by
Violeta Dominguez
12 DECEMBER 2003
Pinellas Park, FL

WWII Military Unit
USS *Long Island*
(CVE-1)

VEGA, RAYMOND. His faith carried him through his service in the Pacific during WWII, and when he returned, he devoted his life to the church, becoming a Roman Catholic priest.

Vega was one of five brothers to serve in the military during WWII. All five returned home, and only one was wounded. By the time Vega had graduated from high school, his older brother was already serving in the Navy. Inspired by his brother's service, Vega enlisted in the Navy in 1942.

Following basic training, Vega went to hospital corps school, boarding a train bound for San Francisco, Calif., to attend classes as a hospital apprentice. Following his schooling, he was assigned to the USS *Long Island*, an escort aircraft carrier. Aboard the *Long Island*, Vega traveled to Pearl Harbor, Samoa and the Marshall Islands, treating wounded and ill soldiers along the way.

"As a hospital corpsman, whenever anybody got sick, they had to come to me," he said. Because of his responsibility, Vega remembered most sailors tried to stay in his good graces.

Vega vividly recalled V-E and V-J Days. "Everyone was dancing; everyone was singing," he said. "Everyone was asking, 'When can I go home?'" But Vega had signed on for six years in the Navy, and he stayed in the service even after the war.

Vega was discharged in 1948. He used the GI Bill to attend traffic management school. However, he soon realized his true calling and in 1955 began studying at the Divine Heart Seminary in Plymouth, Ind. After he became a member of the Priests of the Sacred Heart of Jesus, Vega served as a priest in camps of immigrant laborers. After working with the laborers, he contacted the Indiana Department of Health to ensure the workers were not being abused.

Vega did missionary work in Indonesia for seven years. When he returned to the States, he was a priest in several different cities and was a chaplain at a veterans' hospital.

William "Bill" Raymond Wood

Date of Birth
25 AUGUST 1926
Santa Rita, NM

Interviewed by
Maggie Rivas-Rodriguez
15 JULY 2004
Arenas Valley, NM

WWII Military Unit
Fleet Air Wing 11

WOOD, WILLIAM "BILL" RAYMOND. Growing up in Santa Rita, N.M., was tough for Bill Wood. The town was divided strictly along ethnic lines. The town was slowly devoured by an open pit copper mine, where Wood worked in his teens. There, he witnessed a great deal of discrimination. "I'm glad it was tough," he said. "It made a better person out of me."

He was 15 and under the legal working age, but he added two years to his age to qualify for employment. His boss knew about this but kept silent. Some of his clearest recollections are of the 105-degree heat and the biases of employers. "I remember the discrimination," said Wood who is Hispanic. "No consideration, no respect and no feeling for people."

Wood noticed that Mexicans with seniority and better skills could never advance beyond the lower levels at the mine, while Anglos progressed through the ranks quickly.

"I saw a bunch of dumb Anglos," he said. "The only qualification they had was an Anglo name. You'd see the Anglos on top driving trucks. Hispanics ran the shovels because they weren't 'smart enough!'"

When he entered the Navy to get a better future, he promised that he'd come back to the mine some day and drop feces on it to symbolize his discontent with its policies.

After serving in the Navy in WWII, helping destroy 21 German submarines, he returned to the States with training in electronics that led to positions with Western Electric, American Can Co., American Showcase and Fixture, O'Keefe & Merritt, Hercules Electric Machinery Co., American Electronics and Minneapolis Honeywell. He returned to Santa Rita with a bag filled with dried dog feces and flew a small airplane over the copper pit where he had worked day in and day out as a teenager. He dropped the paper sack down the center of the mine. His promise was fulfilled.

XIMENES, VICENTE. A long road, filled with dangerous military assignments and segregation eventually led Vicente Ximenes to working within two U.S. presidential administrations.

Vicente Ximenes

Date of Birth
5 DECEMBER 1915
Floresville, TX

Interviewed by
Jim Morrison
10 OCTOBER 2001
Albuquerque, NM

WWII Military Unit
97th Bomb Group,
8th Air Force

Raised in Texas, Ximenes saw discrimination. He boycotted his commencement ceremony to send a message to school officials. Two years after graduation, Ximenes enlisted in the Army Air Corps. He was promoted to the rank of 2d lieutenant after bombardier school, and was deployed to North Africa. He served overseas until 1943. After his return to the States, he was a flying instructor at San Angelo Air Base, Texas.

Even after his success in the military, he returned to the States to find little had changed during his tour of duty, with segregation and racism still problems. He was eager to help change the system and saw education as the first step. He moved to Albuquerque to attend the University of New Mexico, eventually earning his master's in economics. He researched at the Bureau of Business Research and discovered more details about the distressing living conditions for many Latinos.

In 1961, the Kennedy administration appointed him to the U.S. Agency for International Development in Quito, Ecuador, and in Panama. Under President Lyndon Johnson, he served as the commissioner of the Equal Employment Opportunity Commission. Johnson also appointed him chairman of the committee on Mexican-American affairs. He was later the vice president of field operations for the National Urban Commission.

Through his work in the government he helped cities with large Latino populations. He felt his work benefited all people because it helped integrate ethnic groups.

Ximenes married María Castillo in 1943. They had four children: Steve, Ricardo, Olivia and Ana María.

ZUNIGA, ALEJANDRA ROJAS. As she watched her brothers go off to war during the 1940s, Alejandra Zuniga was much impressed by the sacrifice they made for their country. Some 60 years later, she worked with the American G.I. Forum to help Hispanic veterans.

Alejandra
Rojas Zuniga

Date of Birth
17 MAY 1923
Gonzalez, TX

Interviewed by
Raul García Jr.
19 OCTOBER 2002
Saginaw, MI

WWII Location
Saginaw, MI

Born Alejandra Rojas, she grew up one of 11 children. Five of her brothers served in the military and she went to work during the war to help support her family.

She worked in a plant in Greenville, Mich. While working, she was able to save a bit of money, and later put herself through cosmetology school. After graduating from the School of Cosmetology in Saginaw, Mich., she opened her own beauty shop in 1948, a year after she married Amado Zuniga.

Inspired by her brothers' service, she became active in military organizations following the war. The G.I. Forum created a women's chapter, and Zuniga was a prominent member in her local chapter. She tackled issues such as employment, housing, civil rights, women's programs and youth activities with the Forum.

"I learned a lot from my own people joining this organization, because it is a national organization," she said.

She focused on the educational aspect of the Forum's volunteer work. After attending a convention in the 1970s, she was inspired to help local students finish high school. She began a program called Adopt-a-School with the Forum.

Zuniga also served on the Women in Community Service National Board. The board recruited young people for job corps throughout the country.

Zuniga and her husband had five children: Thomas, Ruby, Dennis, Elizabeth and Deborah.

Angel Esparza

Date of Birth
11 February 1922
El Paso, Texas

Interviewed by
Robert Rivas
29 OCTOBER 2003
El Paso, Texas

WWII Military Unit
463 AAF BU

ESPARZA, ANGEL. Education was always very important in the Esparza home. Angel Esparza, born in 1922, already expected at an early age that he and his six siblings would graduate from high school and go on to college.

"My mother was pro-education like you won't believe," Esparza said. "We were all going to get all the education possible, so we did."

Shortly after he entered college, the Japanese attacked Pearl Harbor. Soon the United States military called for volunteers. Esparza joined the Army Air Corps.

Over the next three years, Esparza trained at 10 military bases where he fine-tuned his aviation skills so that he would be ready for battle. However, while training at Harlingen Army Air Field in Harlingen, Texas, Esparza learned that Japan had surrendered and that the war had ended. He was discharged in February of 1946. He was awarded a Good Conduct Medal, a Victory Medal, and an American Service Medal.

Esparza returned to his family in El Paso and after a short break returned to school.

"I went back to what I had started and I finished my degree in science with a minor in geology and a major in chemistry," he said.

Armed with a science degree and a teaching certificate, Esparza began teaching science at Jefferson High School, a predominantly Mexican American high school.

After a year of teaching, Esparza decided to find a higher-paying job. He started working at Fort Bliss in El Paso as a draftsman and in 1968 became a computer programmer.

Esparza married Alicia Alvarez, a friend of his sister's in August of 1950. The couple had 12 children, six boys and six girls; however two sets of twins — one set female and one male — were born prematurely and "didn't make it," Esparza said.

Angel and Alicia Esparza emphasized education, as his parents had. All of his eight surviving children attended local public schools and earned at least a bachelor's degree.

Esparza said he and his wife worked outside of the home to finance their children's educations, but he added, his children also worked hard to get their schooling.

"It was quite an effort," he said. "I remember at one time we had five [children] at the University of Texas at Austin. I had two jobs and Alice had two jobs. It was an effort, but we made it."

Chapter Twelve

MILITARY SERVICE BEYOND WWII

Ladislao Castro (center) and his son James (right) and grandson James Jr. (left) in April 2001. James and James Jr. are also veterans: James served in Vietnam, his son James Jr. served in the Gulf War. (Photo by Alan K. Davis.)

At the end of the war, men who were discharged went home, glad to return to civilian life, many using the GI Bill for an education.

Others, including many Latinos, had found their niche in the armed forces and either stayed in, or later returned to serve their country in a second and sometimes a third armed conflict. At the conclusion of WWII, a new tension pervaded: the Cold War, in which the United States and its Allies vied for power and influence with the Communist Soviet Union and China. Civil wars around the globe were cast in an ominous light.

There would be repeated need for military service and Latinos responded. In some cases, Latino veterans were able to gradually rise to the ranks that few minorities held. Many were younger than 18 and would require their parents' signature. Other underage men lied about their age and got away with it.

Many Latino WWII veterans were still in the reserves and answered the second call to arms after the June 25, 1950, North Korean invasion of the Republic of South Korea, which pitted the U.S. against the Chinese in the following months. The fighting would last three years and analysts would later say that U.S. involvement in Korea would pave the way for its involvement in Vietnam, from 1961 to 1973.

Men such as Miguel de la Peña of San Antonio, Texas, simply felt military service was more rewarding. De la Peña had served with the 23d Infantry Regiment, landing in Normandy on D-Day. He married a Canadian nurse who was stationed in Taunton, England, during the war and afterward the two moved to Michigan, where he took a job at a local bank. And he was bored.

"One day I said to [his wife], 'For two cents, I'd go back into the Army,' " he said. "And she

handed me two cents."

De la Peña re-enlisted in 1948 and fought in the Korean and Vietnam wars, retiring as a lieutenant colonel.

Many others were in the National Guard and Reserve units that were activated again.

Belisario Flores of San Antonio was one of those. He served stateside in the Army in early 1945 and was discharged in August 1946. He then attended St. Mary's University in San Antonio, and was in its ROTC program, earning the rank of 2d lieutenant. A year later, he was called into active duty and deployed to Korea for nine months as an artillery forward observer. He would join the Texas Air National Guard in 1954 and would observe that he was only one of three Hispanic officers in the entire Air National Guard. Later, he was appointed comptroller of the 149th Fighter Wing and was given command of the 365-man Combat Support squadron in which he had once served. Flores also served during Vietnam.

When he retired in 1986, Flores had risen to the rank of brigadier general. Texas' governor at the time, Mark White, promoted him to the rank of major general. Looking through photo albums of his successful military career, Flores pointed to several group photographs of officer training programs.

He was acutely aware that he was usually the only Hispanic officer and it rankled him.

"It was discrimination," he concluded.

Even during the Vietnam war, some of the WWII veterans were still young enough to serve their country in various capacities.

Concepción "Chon" Pompa, of Devine, Texas, would serve two tours of duty in Vietnam. His first stint in the military had been in the Navy after WWII, assigned to Pearl Harbor, doing cleanup, even nearly a year after the attack. From there, he was sent to various Pacific islands, preparing airfields.

"When they would take over an island, we had to go there and set up so the rest of personnel would come in and land the aircraft," he said.

Back in the States, he took aviation mechanics and welding classes. By 1950, "when Korea broke open," he remained in the reserves, working in structural repair. In a citation, his expertise—particularly his assistance and suggestions in handling engine modifications related to the 100-series aircraft—was acknowledged.

Again, during the Vietnam War, Pompa was sent to Cam Rahn Bay in 1968, as a welder. That was when he was wounded one early morning as he slept, when a rocket hit his barracks and blew him out of the building. On his second tour of duty in Vietnam, which began on Aug. 23, 1972, he worked as a welder adviser. Pompa retired on Dec. 8, 1983, ending a military career spanning four decades.

Serving in the different conflicts gave the veterans a bird's-eye view of different types of combat. Rafael Hernandez was born in a small town near Corpus Christi, Texas, and grew up in Mexico and the Rio Grande Valley of Texas.

"Vietnam—it was a guerrilla war," he said. "You could get hit from anywhere."

And he was. As he and his unit were securing a space for a helicopter to land and pick up wounded in An Loc, Hernandez was hit on his leg and back. He turned around, and all he saw was smoke. He was the only one who was left standing.

He had seen danger before, but nothing like Vietnam.

During WWII, Hernandez served on the USS *Gherardi* (DMS 30), destroying floating mines in the Pacific Ocean.

Later, when he was 37 years old, Hernandez guided an Army rifle squad as a staff sergeant. And then, in 1964, Hernandez trained soldiers in jungle survival and battle tactics in Panama. Later he moved to Fort Polk, La., and instructed soldiers on infantry tactics. He volunteered twice for Vietnam, first on June 29, 1968, in the operations NCO battalion as sergeant first class, where he created and constructed camps while in the HHC 1st Battalion 2d Brigade 1st Infantry Division, and later as an adviser for the Vietnam Civil Operations Rural Development Support (CORDS), where he stayed with the soldiers in the battalion from April 6, 1971, to March 5, 1972. He retired from the military in 1980, at 53, as a master sergeant.

WWII, he said, gave him the opportunity to live a different life.

"That was the best thing that happened to me: to go ahead and serve my country, fight for something that I believe and, at the same time, better myself," Hernandez said.

One Latino had already served before WWII, in WWI. Joseph V. Julius was born in Monterrey, Mexico, in 1902. In 1917, he lied, adding years to his age of 16, and volunteered at Fort Sam Houston, in San Antonio. Julius served eight months on the front lines as a medic and then worked in the jewelry business, ending up in San Antonio.

When Pearl Harbor was attacked, Julius was 39. He enlisted again, subtracting 10 years from his age this time. He was stationed at Brooks Army Hospital. After the Korean War was underway, Julius called a recruiting office to volunteer. But this time, when he gave his date of birth as 1902, the recruiter hesitated.

"I have good news and bad news. The good news is we could use a guy like you because you have had military service," the recruiter said. Then, he added, jokingly: "The bad news ... you have to get permission from your mother, to join."

Joseph Julius would have to sit that war out.

AGUIRRE, ANDREW. Through his younger years, Andrew Aguirre witnessed atrocities on the battlefields of two wars that would continue to haunt him later in life.

He joined the Marine Corps in May 1944 and was soon sent to Guadalcanal and Russell Island in the Solomon Islands and finally to Okinawa, Japan, on Easter Sunday of 1945. There, he entered his first battle. "Part of you dies with them," he said, mourning the passing of his fellow Marines.

Aguirre was an operator of an AmTrac, an amphibious landing vehicle that delivered supplies and men across beaches. Aguirre's job sometimes meant he had to drive through monsoons to load up dead Marines because trucks couldn't make it through the violent weather. He was in Okinawa until August 1945 and was sent to Tientsen, China, to accept the surrender of Japan military there.

He returned to San Diego, Calif., in May of the following year with a new perspective.

"The Marine Corps had opened my eyes," he said. "I told myself I could find better than field work." Aguirre got a job with General Dynamics as a painter.

In June 1950, Aguirre was again called to serve his country during the Korean War. He was sent to Kobe, Japan, and assigned to be a gunner in a tank. In September, on the way to the Chosin Reservoir in North Korea, the tank malfunctioned and was surrounded by Chinese soldiers. Aguirre and three other men fled and evaded the enemy forces for a while but were eventually captured and sent to a prisoner of war camp. He remained a prisoner until 1953, enduring horrible living conditions and long lectures in Chinese attempts to convert the Americans to communism.

On Sept. 9, 1953, Aguirre returned to San Diego. Bearing the guilt of war, he was diagnosed with post-traumatic stress disorder, but resumed his job at General Dynamics, where he would retire in 1989. He and his wife, Gloria, had two children: Edward and Carol.

Andrew Aguirre
(picture taken two days after release from POW camp)

Date of Birth
4 JANUARY 1925
Vinton, TX

Interviewed by
René Zambrano
22 JANUARY 2001
Chula Vista, CA

WWII Military Unit
Company B,
1st Amphibian
Tractor Battalion,
1st Marine Division

AGUIRRE, MIKE. Through the lens of his cameras, Army photographer Mike Aguirre captured the war on film, from the ground and from the sky.

His early days in the service during WWII ignited a passion for the military that would lead Aguirre to enlist in the Merchant Marines after the war. He enlisted for the first time in 1939 after his high school graduation. He looked to the military for an opportunity to demonstrate his patriotism while experiencing the excitement of Army life.

"We [his generation] could join the service and, you know, at that age, you have no fear," he said. "You don't know what will happen tomorrow and you care less sometimes."

Aguirre spent his time overseas repairing and installing cameras in aircraft, as well as developing photos and even flying with pilots to take aerial shots.

After his first tour of duty, he enlisted, this time in the Merchant Marines. He married Ingeborg Analyssa Elbe, in 1950, a German woman he had met on a blind date during his service in Europe. Their family eventually settled in San Marcos, Texas, because of the local church and more important, the four-year college. Both of Aguirre's children earned degrees.

Following his retirement from the military, Aguirre tried to get a job at the local post office, but was subjected to discriminatory hiring practices. With the help of Sen. Ralph Yarborough and his staff, he fought for equal rights, and eventually became the first minority hired at the San Marcos post office. He also helped changed some racist practices, such as having three separate mail bins for whites, blacks and Latinos.

Through it all, Aguirre held no grudges, looking to his faith to teach him tolerance. "Our Bible says we should forgive people. We love people; we don't hate them," he said.

Mike Aguirre

Date of Birth
19 NOVEMBER 1919
San Antonio, TX

Interviewed by
Aryn Sedler
24 MARCH 2000
San Marcos, TX

WWII Military Unit
9th Photo
Reconnaissance
Squadron

Rodolfo "Rudy"
Alaníz

Date of Birth
21 SEPTEMBER 1928
Mission, TX

Interviewed by
Rajesh Reddy
18 OCTOBER 2003
Austin, TX

WWII Military Unit
Battery A,
13th Field Artillery
Battalion,
24th Division

ALANÍZ, RODOLFO "RUDY." In the spring of 1945, 16-year-old Rudy Alaníz's older brother, Ricardo, a rifleman with the 8th Infantry Division, was killed in Germany. Alaníz traveled to Fort Worth, Texas, to bring his brother's body home. The event would alter the young man's life forever.

"I presented my brother's flag to my mother," he said. "That was the saddest part of my life."

Ricardo's death prompted Alaníz to join the military on Oct. 23, 1946, just after he turned 18. He left his home in Mission, Texas, to begin basic training at Fort Knox, Ky.

In total, Alaníz would serve 11 years in the Army and 10 in the Air Force.

For 13 months following the end of WWII, he served in the occupation of Japan. He remembered the tension between the American soldiers and Japanese civilians during the few opportunities he and his fellow troops had to leave their base. "They would frown on us, with their heads down," he said, recalling the demeanor of the Japanese. "They feared us, but there wasn't much they could do about it because they didn't have anything to defend themselves."

After his time in Japan, Alaníz worked in a drugstore and eventually decided to re-enlist in the Army on October 1948. While stationed at Fort Hood, Texas, he met Gloria Araguz and married her before leaving to fight in Korea. There, he served as a platoon sergeant and at one point was hit on the forehead with shrapnel. He later was stationed in Fort Sill, Okla., and Gissen, Germany.

In 1958, he joined the Air Force, serving as an aircraft mechanic with the Military Air Transport. Selected for his fluency in Spanish, Alaníz toured Central and South America for five years with the *Friendship 7* spacecraft, the vessel John Glenn used to make the first U.S. orbit of the earth.

Alaníz retired in 1967 and settled his wife and two children—Rosemary and Rodolfo II—in Austin, Texas, where he found a job as a postal worker.

Alberto Bosquez

Date of Birth
8 NOVEMBER 1927
San Antonio, TX

Interviewed by
Jane O'Brien
18 OCTOBER 2003
Austin, TX

WWII Military Unit
1st Brigade,
1st Marine Division,
USS *Phaon* (ARB-3)

BOSQUEZ, ALBERTO. Fourteen-year-old Alberto Bosquez grabbed his stack of papers, headed to downtown San Antonio, Texas, and began dealing them out. "Extra, Extra!" he shouted. "Japan bombs Pearl Harbor!" In December 1941 Bosquez didn't think about the implications of the war past the newspapers he could sell. It wasn't until 1943 that he enlisted, dropping out of high school and altering his birth certificate to make him one year older so he could join the Navy.

Bosquez was sent to the Mariana Islands aboard the USS *Phaon*, a repair ship. For 18 months, he washed dishes, repaired rust spots on ships and made supply runs to Saipan. "I hated that ship, and I hated the island," he said. "I volunteered for every duty I could, and they wouldn't send me ... I cried like a baby because I wanted to go to Iwo Jima and they wouldn't let me go."

Bosquez, discharged in 1946, supposed his young age kept him from combat in WWII. He would experience it in the Korean War several years later, after enlisting in the Marines in 1948.

In 1950—after liberating the South Korean capital, Seoul—Bosquez and the 1st Provisional Marine Brigade landed at Pusan, South Korea. It was a confident victory, Bosquez said, "We stopped them, we made them run and I was one of those guys: No prisoners, no mercy." The battle for the Chosin Reservoir, in below-50-degree temperatures and against about 200,000 Chinese soldiers, was not so easily won. As the 1st Marine Division retreated, Bosquez felt pain spread from his feet to his legs and hands. He passed out from the frostbite and was evacuated and discharged in 1951.

Back home, Bosquez struggled with the after-effects of war. He used the GI Bill to study welding at Del Mar College in Corpus Christi, Texas, where he met his future wife, Minne Magallan, with whom he had five children: Albert III, Aurora, Jimmy, Rudy, and Joann. Despite his training, employers still discriminated against his ethnicity. Bosquez eventually took a job in construction.

CASTRO, CAESAR CATALINO. As a young man in San Antonio, Texas, Caesar Castro was already an accomplished pianist. His talent would allow him to be a part of the Air Force band from 1942 to 1960.

His father, Luis Castro, was an accomplished musician who had studied in Mexico and became well-known in Texas, even playing with the San Antonio Symphony Orchestra. He taught all of his children music theory before they could choose an instrument to play. Both Caesar Castro and his half-brother, Alfredo "Alfred," became professional musicians.

The U.S. entered WWII during Castro's senior year of high school. That year, he dropped out and enlisted in the Army Air Corps at Kelly Field, Texas.

With his musical background, Castro served in the Air Force marching and concert band throughout his military career. In addition to piano, he played trombone, baritone, French horn and tuba.

Castro married Aurora Gonzalez on May 25, 1945. The couple had three children: Caesar Charles, Mark Anthony and Jacqueline Adrienne.

The family settled in San Antonio and built a house in 1950.

In 1952, Castro was transferred to Wiesbaden, Germany, and—before his family could join him—was transferred again to North Africa. Aurora and the children made the move finally in 1954 to Wheelus Air Force Base, Libya.

In 1956, Castro made his final transfer to Eglin Air Force Base, Fla., where he and his family remained until his discharge in January 1960. Castro continued to perform and freelance in the music business until his death on Aug. 25, 1966.

Caesar Catalino Castro

Date of Birth
27 OCTOBER 1924
San Antonio, TX

Tribute Provided by
Aurora Gonzalez Castro (Wife)

WWII Military Unit
584th Air Force Band, Eglin Field, FL

DE LA PEÑA, MIGUEL. When Miguel de la Peña suffered a concussion at Normandy, all he got was two days in the infirmary. But after he was wounded by an artillery shell in Bretagne, France, he was talked into a blind date, with a nurse who worked at the hospital in Taunton, England. He was attracted to Ruby White's smile right away and two months later asked her to marry him. Their bliss was interrupted when de la Peña rejoined the 23d Infantry Regiment in Belgium, as they crossed the Rhine River and traveled toward Leipzig, Germany.

De la Peña had tried to enlist into the Army in 1941, but was turned down because of his poor eyesight. He joined the California National Guard until he was drafted in 1942. He and the 23d Infantry Regiment landed at Normandy on D-day. "I can't describe it. You know you're in danger, but you can't be terrified because you're helpless," he said. He was in Czechoslovakia when the war ended and he was granted leave to visit Ruby in Verdun, France, where she worked in the 101st General Hospital. On June 2, 1945, they were married, first by the mayor of Verdun and then by a Catholic chaplain in the Cathedral of Verdun.

The newlyweds returned to the States and settled near Ruby's family, originally Canadian, in Michigan. De la Peña took a job at a local bank but wasn't satisfied with it.

"One day I said to Ruby, 'For 2 cents, I'd go back into the Army,'" he said. "And she handed me 2 cents." De la Peña re-enlisted in December 1948 and stayed on active duty until his retirement on April 1, 1967. During his 19 years in the service, he fought in both the Korean and Vietnam wars. When he retired, he had reached the rank of lieutenant colonel.

"My heritage, my family, I'm proud of 'em," de la Peña said. "But I'm American. Ruby's from Canada. She's an American. I came from Mexico. I'm an American."

Miguel de la Peña

Date of Birth
17 FEBRUARY 1919
San Antonio, TX

Interviewed by
Rajesh Reddy
25 OCTOBER 2003
San Antonio, TX

WWII Military Unit
23d Infantry Regiment, 2d Infantry Division

Belisario J. Flores

Date of Birth
22 JULY 1926
Eagle Pass, TX

Interviewed by
Cheryl Kemp
11 NOVEMBER 2004
San Antonio, TX

WWII Military Unit
Headquarters,
38th Field
Artillery Battalion,
2d Infantry
Division

FLORES, BELISARIO J. As he worked through the military ranks and became an officer, Belisario Flores was very much aware that he was one of the few Hispanics in a position of authority.

"It was discrimination," he said without hesitation, adding that lack of understanding was a factor. Flores served his country for more than 40 years, in three wars, with the Army and the Air Force. When he joined the Texas Air National Guard in 1954, there were only three Hispanic officers out of the entire Air National Guard. Flores vowed to add one more to that number.

He retired in the summer of 1986, having already risen to the rank of Brigadier General. Gov. Mark White decorated him with the rank of major general.

Flores had first enlisted in the Army against his parents' wishes after graduating from San Antonio Vocational. From Jan. 10, 1945, Flores served stateside as a supply clerk and then radio operator until his discharge in August 1946. He then enrolled at St. Mary's University in San Antonio, graduating with honors in 1950 and earning the rank of 2nd lieutenant through the ROTC program.

One year later, he was called to active duty and deployed to Korea for nine months as an artillery forward observer. During the Battle of Triangle Hill on Oct. 17, 1952, Flores earned the Bronze Star though he considered the campaign a waste. "We needed to show the Chinese we were stronger than they thought," said Flores. "We lost 1,600 men for no apparent reason."

As a civilian, Flores was an assistant manager of a department store and an accountant for the City of San Antonio. In the Texas Air National Guard, he became a comptroller of the 149th Fighter Wing and was given command of the 365-man Combat Support squadron where he had once served. In 1954, he married Josephine Guerrero. After her death, he married Adelina N. Greco in 2000 and embraced her two children as his own.

Ernest "Ernie" George Gonzalez

Date of Birth
1 JANUARY 1924
Oatman, AZ

Interviewed by
René Zambrano
18 DECEMBER 2000
San Diego, CA

WWII Military Unit
USS *La Vallete*
(DD-448);
USS *Amycus*
(ARL-2)

GONZALEZ, ERNEST "ERNIE" GEORGE. After the bombing of Pearl Harbor, Ernie Gonzalez vowed to join the Navy as soon as he could. His enlistment started a 30-year military career. Fifteen promotions later, Gonzalez retired from the Navy as lieutenant commander.

The youngest of three brothers, Gonzalez started training in June 1942 as an engineer. Among men mostly from Texas and Oklahoma, he quickly discovered that had to stand up for himself.

"These guys—Mexicans from Texas—were used to getting pushed around, and I wasn't ... I'd clock 'em." After two weeks of constant fighting, the commander called him in. Gonzalez was afraid he would be kicked out of the Navy, but instead he was promoted to Master at Arms. Every morning, he gave the men their details and said "there weren't many complaints."

The training was cut short after 60 days and the men were sent to Vallejo, Calif. Gonzalez was assigned aboard a destroyer, the USS *La Vallete*. The destroyer traveled to Samoa, New Caledonia, New Guinea and New Zealand, among other islands in the Pacific. On Jan. 30, 1943, it was torpedoed, taking the lives of 22 sailors, including 14 of Gonzalez's friends.

"You don't know whether to go hooray for me or cry for you because it could have been me just as easily as anyone else," he said. "The saddest thing about it is you have to get rid of the bodies. You have to put them in bags and throw them overboard."

Gonzalez became a repair officer on the landing craft repair ship, the USS *Amycus*. In 1946, he joined the VFW and later helped form the Brother Rats with the younger VFW members. The group raised money for a plaque to commemorate their fallen comrades.

Gonzalez married Maddy María Perez in Yuma, Ariz. The couple had four children: Linda, Susan, Ernest and Rachel.

GUERRERO, CARLOS "CHARLIE" GUZMAN. At many times in his life, Charlie Guerrero's ability to keep calm under pressure proved valuable. One incident in particular stood out in his mind. He was a part of the Army's 65th Infantry Division, participating in the liberation of a German concentration camp, when his intoxicated platoon sergeant began calling their major, an African American man, derogatory names.

The major threatened to kill the platoon sergeant, but Guerrero was able to talk him down. "I'm not trying to be [disrespectful]," he said to the furious major. "But he's a little bit tipsy, a little bit drunk. I don't think you'll accomplish anything killing him. We're fighting the same war here, for the same cause." He would later say he believed he saved that platoon sergeant's life.

Guerrero returned to the United States after WWII and joined the National Guard. He still experienced discrimination as a Latino and the only minority in his unit. When a restaurant in Round Rock, Texas, refused to serve him, his superior officer, Gen. K. L. Berry, defended him and threatened to shut down the establishment unless they agreed to serve Guerrero. The café backed down. "I wasn't mad — I was disappointed," he said. "Getting mad ain't going to help."

He retired from the civil service in 1977 and from the National Guard in 1982. He and his wife, Bertha, had five sons: Chuck, David, John, Rudy Cruz and Kendrick Stanley. Following his retirement, he followed baseball and rooted for "any team — except the Yankees," he joked. He often wore a WWII cap when visiting Austin bars and people often bought him beer in recognition of his military service.

"I like to make friends or acquaintances with people," he said. "You might see [them] again, because you never know."

Carlos "Charlie" Guzman Guerrero

Date of Birth
4 JUNE 1922
Lockhart, TX

Interviewed by
Antonio Gilb
19 MARCH 1999
Austin, TX

WWII Military Unit
65th Infantry Division

HERNANDEZ, EZEQUIEL R. When the Japanese bombed Pearl Harbor, many Hispanics were drafted. But in 1942, Ezequiel Hernandez enlisted in the armed forces, following in his brothers' footsteps by taking a stand against a foreign power and joining the military as a volunteer.

"When I turned 18, none of my brothers were home, so I joined," he said.

He had grown up helping his father work the fields near his birthplace of Mackay, Texas. He enjoyed playing baseball in his free time. When he left to fight, he had not completed high school, choosing to quit after ninth grade to help his family.

He was sent to Normandy, in 1945 as part of the 14th Armored Division. There, he was involved in guarding German prisoners.

At one point, he took a trip to England. Much to his surprise, he met back up with his brother, Elías, who was stationed in Ipswitch, England. Upon his return to France, he learned that another brother, Joel, was in the barracks there. He remained in France until the end of the war.

He stayed in the Army Reserves after the war, and was put back on active duty for the Korean War, where he served in the 1008th Engineer Service Battalion as a welder.

When he came home from WWII, he graduated from the University of Houston as an auto mechanic. He married Linda Guzman in 1952. They had five children: Richard, Rachel, Veronica, James and Elsa.

Hernandez worked in the upholstery business for many years, mainly upholstering planes and cars. He owned and ran a Texaco gas station for eight years, but the threat of robberies and the long hours persuaded him to try something else. He opened a vehicle inspection service in 1978, which he ran until he retired. His daughter Veronica took over the business.

Ezequiel R. Hernandez

Date of Birth
18 APRIL 1924
Mackay, TX

Interviewed by
Ernest Eguía and Paul R. Zepeda
11 MAY 2004
Houston, TX

WWII Military Unit
14th Armored Division

Rafael Hernandez

Date of Birth
28 AUGUST 1927
Tynan, TX

Interviewed by
Juan de la Cruz
6 APRIL 2002
McAllen, TX

WWII Military Unit
USS *Gheradi*
(DMS-30)

HERNANDEZ, RAFAEL. Though also a veteran of the Korean and Vietnam Wars, Rafael Hernandez said it was WWII that made many new opportunities for Latinos.

"That was the best thing that happened to me: to go ahead and serve my country, fight for something that I believe and, at the same time, better myself," he said. Hernandez enlisted in the Navy on Oct. 10, 1944, on the encouragement of his two older brothers, who were in the Army. He was trained in minesweeping equipment, and with the crew of the USS *Gheradi* he destroyed floating land mines in the Pacific Ocean. The *Gheradi* participated in the Battle of Okinawa during which Hernandez served as a gunner and loader of a 20-mm gun, shooting down enemy aircraft.

After his discharge, Hernandez attended an aircraft and mechanic school in Harlington, Texas. His first marriage gave him a daughter, Cynthia, but ended in divorce. On June 3, 1950, he married his childhood sweetheart, María Gloria Fernandez, and with her raised Juan José and María Lourdes.

Hernandez volunteered to organize the 112th Calvalry Regiment of the Texas Army National Guard in McAllen, Texas. In Korea, he guided an Army rifle squad as a staff sergeant. In 1964, he trained soldiers in jungle survival and battle tactics in Panama and infantry tactics in Fort Polk, La.

Vietnam was very different from WWII. "You could get hit from anywhere," he said. In Ahn Loc, Hernandez and his unit were securing a place for a helicopter to land and pick up wounded, when he was suddenly hit in his leg and back. He turned and saw he was the only one left standing.

Hernandez later served as adviser for the Vietnam Civil Operations Rural Development Support.

In 1980, he retired as master sergeant. He became manager for an alarm company and later as a technician in the reconstruction of Auto Marts. He joined many veterans' organizations: the American Legion, VFW and the Military Order of the Purple Heart.

Julius V. Joseph

Date of Birth
21 MAY 1902
Monterrey, Mexico

Interviewed by
Jacob Collazo
15 SEPTEMBER 2000
San Antonio, TX

WWII Military Unit
133d Infantry
Regiment,
34th Infantry
Division,
Brooke Army
Hospital,
Fort Sam
Houston, TX

JOSEPH, JULIUS V. At the onset of the Korean War in 1952, Julius V. Joseph called his recruiting office to volunteer. While the recruiting officer was pleased to hear that Joseph had prior military experience, he hesitated when Joseph gave his date of birth—Joseph was 50 years old.

He never let his age stop him from entering war before. Inspired by his father's service in the Spanish-American War, Joseph presented himself at Fort Sam Houston, Texas, in 1917 to join the effort in WWI. Before his father could stop him, he lied about his mere 16 years and enlisted. In the end, his father decided to join him. Joseph was shipped to France and the frontlines, serving eight months as a combat medic in the Infantry. Though the war was almost over when he arrived, it still left painful memories. "Things were difficult, and it is something I don't like to talk about," he said.

After WWI, Joseph returned home to the family jewelry trade. The business took him all over the world, buying and trading jewelry and precious stones. In 1933, he landed a temporary position with Zales Jewelry Corp. in Wichita Falls, Kan. There, he met Jewel Belle Gordon, a co-worker. On March 3, 1933, they were married. Joseph moved back to San Antonio, Texas, and managed Gulf Mart Jewelry for the Zales Corp. The couple had two sons: Francis and Julius.

He was at home when he and his wife heard that Pearl Harbor had been bombed. His younger brothers, Adam and Carlos, were already serving as pilots in the Army Air Corps in London. They wrote him: "If the three Joseph brothers were in London, they'd turn this town upside down."

Once again, he lied about his age—this time subtracting 10 years—and enlisted, asking to be sent overseas in hopes of joining his brothers. He was stationed instead at Brooks Army Hospital, where he helped rehabilitate soldiers, mostly black, returning from overseas. He formed a baseball team for his patients, helping to take their minds off the war with exercise.

MONTOYA, MACLOVIO. Though Maclovio Montoya fought in WWII and later in the Korean War, his longest battle was for recognition of the contribution he had already made to his country. It took 37 years for Montoya to obtain the Purple Heart he deserved for being wounded in WWII.

On Nov. 22, 1944, he and the 311th Infantry Regiment landed in France and crossed into Belgium on Nov. 27 and finally into Germany on Dec. 7. "[We were] crossing the Rhine River [and we were] hit terribly from the hill. The huge river ran across an open field. The 88s shook you here," Montoya said, pounding his fist to his chest to emphasis the destructive force of the German 88-mm mortar shells that rained on his regiment. "That's why I'm sick." As a result of that day in 1945, ironically coinciding with his birthday, Montoya suffered hearing loss and chronic headaches.

He felt that discrimination played a factor in the long delay to receive his medal. He was no stranger to it. Once, an Anglo soldier boorishly asked, "If you're Mexican, why are you in the American Army?" It took all his self-restraint to keep from decking the soldier. In fact, Montoya was also three-quarters Native American and felt honored to be nicknamed "Chief" during his time in the service.

After returning to Santa Fe, N.M., after the war, Montoya married Juanita Tapia on Sept. 18, 1946. The couple had four children: Gertrude, Santos, Elizabeth and Maclovio.

Montoya could not let his lack of recognition rest. He contacted several government offices but to no avail. The problem was that a fire at Fort Benjamin Harrison, Ind., had destroyed his personnel file in 1973. He found his platoon squadron, but needed a higher ranking officer.

Finally, he employed the help of a lawyer friend, John Cassell, who procured documents the Army would accept. On Oct. 13, 1982, Montoya was presented with a Purple Heart. "What [the Army] did to me was not right," he said. "But I'm proud to be an American, to fight for the flag."

Maclovio Montoya

Date of Birth
15 MARCH 1926
Sante Fe, NM

Interviewed by
Violeta Dominguez
3 NOVEMBER 2003
Santa Fe, NM

WWII Military Unit
Company A,
311th Infantry
Regiment,
78th Infantry
Division

MORALES, JESÚS HUMBERTO. Enduring 11 months in the jungles of New Guinea unharmed, Jesús Morales left for the Philippines. It was there that shrapnel hit him and his partner as they were reloading a bazooka. His comrade died, but Morales survived, sustaining an injury that required an artificial joint to be implanted in his thumb.

Following a divorce from his first wife, Morales enlisted in the Army in July 1941, starting a military career that would span more than a decade and take him around the world. After training at Fort Leonard Wood, Mo., he left for San Francisco. Morales remembered the dismal odds — 10 to 1 — of survival, and recalled the poignancy of the song, "So Long, It's Been Good to Know You," playing as he left the harbor. "That hit you right in the guts," he said.

Serving as his squad's scout during their tour of duty in the Pacific, Morales was in combat regularly. Following his injury in the Philippines, Morales returned to the States in July 1945.

Back at home, Morales felt the effects of war. His nerves "were shot up" and he was unable to keep his hands from constantly shaking, which prevented him from returning to the watch repair job he held prior to enlisting. Instead, he returned to the military, re-enlisting later in 1945. He served in the Texas State Guard until 1947, when he transferred into the Air Force. With the Air Force, he served 11 months in Korea and was eventually discharged on April 12, 1953, with rank of technical sergeant.

In 1947, he married Mary Becerra. Following his discharge, he worked at Lackland Air Force Base, Texas. Morales had nine children from his two marriages: Dolores, Felix, Jesús, David, Eva, Santa, Blanca, Victor and Humberto.

Jesús Humberto
Morales

Date of Birth
25 OCTOBER 1918
San Antonio, TX

Interviewed by
Maro Robbins
13 FEBRUARY 2000
San Antonio, TX

WWII Military Unit
Company L,
20th Infantry,
6th Division

Concepción "Chon"
Pompa

Date of Birth
8 DECEMBER 1923
Devine, TX

Interviewed by
Maggie Rivas-
Rodriguez
5 JANUARY 2002
Devine, TX

WWII Location
Pearl Harbor, HI

POMPA, CONCEPCIÓN "CHON." News of the bombing of Pearl Harbor reached Concepción "Chon" Pompa on his 17th birthday, one day after the attack, and resulted in the closure of the Civilian Conservation Corps camp in Springdale, Utah, where he was helping develop a national park.

He joined the Navy in October 1942, and was sent to the Navy's Hawaiian base. There, his first duty was to collect bodies that sank with the USS *Oklahoma* and *Arizona* during the attack on Pearl Harbor. Almost a year after the attack, they were still taking bodies out of the water. "They would turn loose from their compartment and come up in the water and float to the side of the harbor," he said.

"The sea was plumb black. You could get your hand like that and pick up all the oil, you know, that would turn loose from the ships," he said with his hand cupped. "It took almost two years before they cleared all the oil out of there."

His next assignment was to prepare airfields on various Pacific islands, a different one each month. He was sent home in 1944.

He remained in the reserves during the Korean War and was awarded the Texas Medal of Merit for his work modifying engines in aircraft. He was stationed in Camp Rahn Bay as a welder during his first tour of duty in the Vietnam War, and in Bien Hoa on his second tour, where he was a welding adviser. He earned a Purple Heart on this tour.

He retired from the military on Dec. 8, 1983, as a technical sergeant, after four decades of dedicated service. He served as vice commander of the VFW post in Devine, Texas, his hometown. A longtime member of St. Joseph Catholic Church Knights of Columbus in Devine, he was recognized by the church for 40 years of dedication as a parishioner.

Fortino S. Quintana

Date of Birth
12 AUGUST 1926
Terlingua, TX

Tribute Provided by
Yazmin Lazcano,
(Granddaughter)

WWII Location
Stationed at
Olmsted Field, PA

QUINTANA, FORTINO S. While his unflappable work ethic on the farm made him an invaluable asset to his employer, Fortino Quintana longed for more. He looked to the Armed Forces and found opportunities and a career that would let him advance for nearly a decade.

Quintana spent his life working on ranches, and he left school after fourth grade. But he soon realized the importance of education, and when he enlisted in the Army, he completed his GED in two short years. He also earned his Aircraft Instrument Specialist certification while stationed in Olmsted Field, Pa.

Quintana was discharged for the first time on March 1, 1949, but re-enlisted on May 28, 1951, at Biggs Air Force Base near El Paso, Texas. Flying had always been Quintana's dream, but an ear problem kept him from leaving the ground. He continued working as an airplane mechanic, and specialized in repairing B-29 planes.

He was promoted to staff sergeant before his second discharge on March 4, 1953. He graduated from El Paso Technical Institute during his time in the service as well, ever mindful of education's importance. Quintana began working for Phelps Dodge Refining Corp. and stayed with the company for 20 years, until a labor strike cost him his job. He chose to be loyal to his coworkers and refused to take back his job at the refinery. He then worked a host of odd jobs, including a maintenance worker and janitor.

During a shift at El Paso International Airport, where he worked as a mechanic, Quintana met Bernarda Lazcano, a kindergarten teacher from Juarez, Mexico. They married in 1954 and raised four children: Carolina, Edna, Rosa and Manuel. Quintana's dedication to his work, no matter the job, provided a full, happy life for his family, and he credited the service for opening many doors.

RAMIREZ, GUADALUPE G. "JOE." With a military career that spanned two decades, Guadalupe "Joe" Ramirez began his service as a member of the Marine Corps in 1944 and remained in the service until September 1964. His career included fighting in World War II and the Korean War, as well as time in Cuba.

Ramirez dropped out of school at 13 and worked as a newspaper delivery person. He was 15 when the Japanese bombed Pearl Harbor and was eager to join the military, but he had to wait until he turned 17 to enlist. When he went to the recruiter, he found that he did not meet the weight requirement, so he ate tortillas, bread and beans until he weighed in at over 110 pounds.

He was sent to the Marshall Islands for communications training, then to Saipan, in the Mariana Islands, for infantry training. "Anywhere you went [in Saipan], you took a rifle with you," Ramirez said. As part of the 2d Combat Engineer Battalion of the 2d Marine Division, he landed in Okinawa in April 1945 with the USS *Hinsdale* (APA-19).

The *Hinsdale* was bombed by a *Kamikaze* during its attack on Okinawa, and 15 men were killed. Ramirez escaped injury. "If they had hit the holds, I wouldn't be here, 'cause we had gasoline, oil and ammunition coming out of our ears," he recalled.

In his time in the service, Ramirez said he encountered little discrimination, though there were few Latinos in his regiment. "We called each other 'men,' " he said.

He served a total of 14 years and seven months overseas during his service, including 23 months in the Pacific during WWII. He maintained many of his military habits when he left the service, including self-rationing of water.

He married Virginia Tellez and they adopted two sons, Henry and Joseph.

Guadalupe G. "Joe" Ramirez

Date of Birth
28 SEPTEMBER 1926
Los Angeles, CA

Interviewed by
Hector Espinoza
and Erika Martinez
5 JANUARY 2003
Tucson, AZ

WWII Military Unit
2d Combat
Engineer Battalion,
2d Marine Division

RAMIREZ, LUIS ÁNGEL. Despite witnessing some of the most devastating aspects of WWII, Luis Ángel Ramirez says his most prominent memory of his military service was the friendships that developed among soldiers.

"Those guys were like my brothers: they worry about me and I worry about them," he said.

Born in Puerto Rico, Ramirez later moved to New York City with his parents and 10 brothers and sisters. Ramirez was working in an eyeglass factory and concentrating on improving his English when he was drafted in April 1941.

He completed his training and left for Europe, arriving in England on Oct. 6, 1942. He remained there until his squadron was assigned to invade Normandy. His platoon did not lose a single man, which was a surprise to even Ramirez himself.

"My best memory was that we all looked out for each other," he said. "Nothing touched [us], thank God. [We] were in the middle of it, but nothing happened. Maybe it was because we were good fighters, I don't know."

His squadron continued through France, to the Battle of Saint-Malo, and then to Czechoslovakia. While traveling, Ramirez saw the gaunt faces and lifeless bodies of those in concentration camps.

"We saw people walking like skeletons," he remembered.

Ramirez continued to serve in the military after WWII ended. He was discharged from the Army on Aug. 30, 1963. He married Abigail Garcia in 1954 and the couple had a son, Robert Bruce.

In 2002, at nearly 90 years of age, Ramirez said he would still serve in the military again.

"If [the military] would call me, I think I would go," he said. "I still have patriotism in me. I am very proud of serving my country."

Luis Ángel Ramirez

Date of Birth
17 SEPTEMBER 1914
Lajas, PR

Interviewed by
Adrian Bashick
14 SEPTEMBER 2002
Miami, FL

WWII Military Unit
120th Cavalry
Reconnaissance
Squadron,
102d Cavalry Group

Benito L. Rodriguez

Date of Birth
16 DECEMBER 1920
Creedmore, TX

Interviewed by
Andria Infante
21 FEBRUARY 2000
Austin, TX

WWII Military Unit
2d Infantry Division

RODRIGUEZ, BENITO L. He started his work with the American government at 16 years old, when he joined the Civilian Conservation Corps (CCC). Benito Rodriguez spent 20 years with the U.S. Army, beginning in 1938.

Rodriguez said he does not regret a second of his time in the military. He earned a Purple Heart during his service in WWII.

He fought in the Ardennes during the Battle of the Bulge in 1944. He was shot in the back during the battle and was sent to a first-aid tent. From there he traveled to France, where he spent four to five months recovering before he was sent back to fight.

He had been working with the CCC in Tulle Lake, Ore., since 1936, chopping down trees for $30 per month, $25 of which he had to send home to his family, when he decided to enlist. At home during the Depression, work was sparse. He dropped out of school in Lockhart, Texas, at age 15 and took any jobs he could find, but his main job was at a dry cleaner.

Rodriguez was one of four brothers who enlisted around this time. Edward was stationed in Okinawa; Pete was in the 101st Airborne Division in Germany; and Gilbert was in the Navy for 23 years, including WWII, the Korean War and Vietnam.

He said that their mother, Trinidád Rodriguez, prayed daily, and that she gave him the strength to carry on. "Sometimes I feel I was away from my family for so long and lost touch, especially [with] my mother," he said. "She would really work hard."

He married Margaret Castillo in 1946 and they had a daughter, Linda. That marriage ended in divorce. He later married María Elisa Reyes in 1972.

Joe M. Ruiz

Date of Birth
28 NOVEMBER 1924
Tempe, AZ

Interviewed by
Delia Esparza
4 JANUARY 2003
Phoenix, AZ

WWII Military Unit
389th Anti-Aircraft
Artillery Battalion

RUIZ, JOE M. As a prisoner of war, Joe M. Ruiz narrowly escaped death at the end of WWII. His experiences in war continued to haunt him throughout his life and during his subsequent service.

He was at a matinee movie with his girlfriend when the bombing of Pearl Harbor was announced. He was scared but enlisted in the Marine Corps two weeks later, switching to join the Army when he found out he could leave two weeks sooner. "I don't know why, but I wanted to go," he said.

Ruiz first encountered danger on the Dutch East Indies, where Ruiz and a friend got lost behind enemy lines. They were lucky to be discovered by the natives, who smuggled them through a Japanese checkpoint and back to the U.S. forces under blankets of their cargo boats.

But later, during a mission with the 389th Coast Artillery Battalion, he was captured and taken to Kobe, Japan, where he endured beatings and starvation. "When the Red Cross got me out, I was more dead than alive. I was 104 pounds," he said. He underwent reconstructive surgery in a hospital in Manila, Philippines, to repair a broken jaw, damaged eye and multiple scars.

After his Army service, he earned his high school diploma and attended Arizona State University. Nine hours short of his degree, he was recruited by Motorola and worked for the company in California. He joined the Marine Corps in 1953 and was stationed for two years overseas, in the Dominican Republic and Lebanon. In 1964, he went on three tours of Vietnam, where he began struggling with long-suppressed memories of his previous time in combat. In Okinawa, awaiting transfer for his final tour, he got in enough trouble in three days to be court-martialed.

Years later, the smallest mention of war caused nightmares for Ruiz, who said he tries to avoid thinking about the details of his time in the service. Ruiz had one child, Richard, with his wife, Martha, whom he married in 1948. After she died, he married Rose Rodriguez in 1983.

SANCHEZ, EDDIE. Using his talents in the kitchen, Eddie Sanchez fed soldiers while he served in Europe. Fifty years later, he was still feeding soldiers, as commander of the Catholic War Vets post in Austin, Texas.

Sanchez was not originally assigned to kitchen duty. He enlisted at age 17 and went to Fort McClellan, Ala., for infantry training and was shipped out to Europe from Camp Kilmer, N.J.

His first duty overseas was a gruesome one, as part of a "clean-up" crew: he was to pick up bodies and retrieve their dog tags.

"You get used to it," he said. "There's nothing you can do. It's a job."

Later he left camp without permission and was technically absent without leave. His punishment was kitchen duty. A mess sergeant eventually offered him a chance to become a dining room orderly and soon he was off to Utine, Italy, to attend cooking school for three months. After cooking school, he attended baking school and eventually he went to mess management school. He earned the rank of corporal, then buck sergeant and was recommended to replace his mentor as tech sergeant. "I owe him quite a bit," Sanchez said. "But I straightened up too, I straightened up fast."

Sanchez stayed abroad for four years, overseeing menus, worksheets and the shift leaders in his kitchen. He became a perfectionist, demanding excellence and ensuring his staff was always up to date on rules and regulations.

Sanchez was discharged but almost immediately re-enlisted. He eventually retired from the military in 1976. As a civilian, Sanchez worked with IBM in its food service department, retiring at age 62. Sanchez and his first wife, Janie Nuñez, had two children, Eddie and Yolanda. He married Manuela Casarez in 1994.

Eddie Sanchez

Date of Birth
20 MARCH 1929
Austin, TX

Interviewed by
Vicki Lamar
9 FEBRUARY 2002
Austin, TX

WWII Military Unit
Company B,
249th Battalion

SOLIZ, FELÍPE. As a first-generation American, Felípe Soliz is proud to have served his country in two wars. His time with the Army and Air Force began as World War II was winding down, in 1945, and continued through the Korean War to 1967, when he retired.

In WWII he was trained as an Air Force wire and radio communication technician, and he served in Germany for 33 months. He also helped guard German POWs. He said that they would help each other learn languages: They would teach him German and he would teach them English, and they would practice with each other.

Soliz's parents died when he was still a child, and he spent years being shuffled from home to home, among family. His two brothers also joined the Army; one was in the Bataan Death March and the other fought at the Battle of the Bulge.

"I found a home in the Army," Soliz said.

When he returned to the United States, he decided to stay in the Air Force. He was stationed at Kearny Air Force Base near Omaha, Neb., for three months, then at Bergstrom Air Force Base in Austin, Texas. He has lived in Texas ever since.

Just six months after marrying Mary, Soliz was sent to Korea, where he did administrative and technical work for a year. He and Mary eventually had 13 children.

Soliz said he wants his children and grandchildren to know the hardships, adventures and joys of his life; he wants them to learn from the mistakes that he made. The most important thing for young people to do is to get an education, he says. Soliz said he didn't take advantage of schooling when he was in the military, but he hopes his grandchildren will get an education.

Felípe Soliz

Date of Birth
23 JANUARY 1927
Harlingen, TX

Interviewed by
Susan Miller
22 OCTOBER 1999
Lockhart, TX

WWII Military Unit
United States Army

Elfren Solomon

Date of Birth
8 FEBRUARY 1921
Glendale, AZ

Interviewed by
René Zambrano
15 JUNE 2000
San Diego, CA

WWII Military Unit
82d Airborne

SOLOMON, ELFREN. In the military, Elfren Solomon said he rarely encountered discrimination and recalled his experiences in the war with pride.

"When you come to face the reality, we were fighting for our lives. We weren't bringing any nationality into factor. ... The main thing is we were fighting for survival. You had to depend on your buddy because he was watching your back," he said. "I am a U.S. citizen. It was my business. I never thought of [prejudice]. I had too many good friends in the service to worry about it."

Having dropped out of high school to work in the Civilian Conservation Corps, Solomon recognized that the benefits of joining the military included an opportunity to learn skills and to get an education. He joined the Army during WWII, serving in North Africa and Italy.

Far removed from the familiar environment of his Mexican-American culture, Solomon matured in war.

"The reality was, you'd get killed or you'd become a POW," he said, marveling at the U.S. victory. "We were not prepared for any war. We had antiquated equipment from World War I, rifles from World War I and tractor-drawn guns from World War I."

When he returned home, after being discharged, Solomon found it difficult to adjust to civilian life: "I was used to someone trying to kill me. You are always looking around to see if you are safe."

In 1950, Solomon joined the Air Force and in all, served in the military for 13 years. Many of his experiences troubled him much later. "When you see a dead cadaver. ... You can visualize yourself lying down like him," he said.

He married Virginia Moreno and had four children with her: Antonio, Richard, William and Nicholas Patrick. After she passed away, he married Olivia de la Rosa in 1979.

Esteban Soto

Date of Birth
2 SEPTEMBER 1925
Royce City, TX

Interviewed by
Rea Ann Trotter
26 JUNE 1995
San Antonio, TX

WWII Location
Stationed in
Pearl Harbor, HI

SOTO, ESTEBAN. Military tradition runs deep in the Soto family. After hearing his father's stories of mustard gas and other atrocities he experienced in World War 1, Esteban Soto served in WWII, the Korean War and the Vietnam War. He said he felt proud when three of his own sons also served their country in Vietnam. "How does a father help sons when they come home? First, by thanking God for a safe return home and talking to them," Soto said. "We did what we had to do."

An uncle, Emilio Salazar, had been a captain in the Mexican Army. Soto's brother and brother-in-law served in the Air Force and Soto had several cousins in the Army. At age 18, Soto joined the military himself. During WWII, he served as a guard at Pearl Harbor. After his discharge in 1946, he joined the Navy Reserve.

A year later, he joined the Army's 41st Armored Infantry Battalion, 2d Armored Division. At the Port of Hungnam, he and his battalion loaded refugees: children, women and old men. The Navy bombed the North Korean harbor on Christmas 1950. "I started praying when I saw the whole harbor go up in flames; it was like the Fourth of July!" In the Chonan area of South Korea, he and Cpl. David Dykes came upon a small Korean girl, covered in debris, near a destroyed village. "I talked to her in Korean, '*Iriwa*' (come here). She was scared and dirty. ... She stayed with us a few days." To this day, he wonders what became of her and he dreams about her and wishes he could hear what ever became of that little girl.

After helping train Cubans in Florida in 1964, Soto volunteered for combat in Vietnam. There, he manned a machine gun and helped refugees escape, under fire.

He married Leonor Cervantes and they had five children: Esteban Jr., Louis, Benjamin, Theresa and Lydia.

TRUJILLO, CHARLES. Inner turmoil plagued Charles Trujillo during his service in WWII. His strong Catholic beliefs often conflicted with the rules of war. "My biggest conflict was with religion," he said. " 'Thou shalt not kill.' How do you deal with something like that?"

But as he continued his tour of duty through the South Pacific, he tried to focus on his own survival. Though he still contemplates his actions—even today—he saw his duty to his country as the paramount responsibility.

Drafted in his senior year of high school, Trujillo was eager to begin his career in the military. He began his training at Fort Ord, Calif. From there he left for Oro Bay, New Guinea. He made landfall in September 1944, and was assigned to the 21st Infantry Regiment, 24th Infantry Division. Trujillo trained and began serving as the lead scout, carrying a Thompson submachine gun instead of the standard rifle. He continued on to the Philippines, fighting in battles on the island of Leyte in October 1944. Reaching Samar, he came under fire by 8-inch shells from Japanese ships. He credits a ditch with helping him survive the constant hail of shrapnel. "There's nothing stronger than earth," he said. "Ships, boats, planes, anything. They're all stopped by Mother Earth."

Cheating death and quick thinking would help Trujillo again. Following his service in WWII, he was again called to serve in the Korean War. When it started in 1950, Trujillo was unsure who was at fault. In the end, he came to feel that there was no defeat, no great ending, just the loss of money, time and people.

Trujillo and his first wife, Esperanza "Hope" Villagrana, had three children: Charles "Chuck" Simon, Rita and Mary Magdalene. The couple divorced. He later married Ellen Runkle, who died in 2000.

Charles Trujillo

Date of Birth
23 APRIL 1925
Walsenburg, CO

Interviewed by
Rea Ann Trotter
14 DECEMBER 2000
Avondale, CO

WWII Military Unit
21st Infantry
Regiment,
24th Infantry
Division

VASQUEZ, EDWARD. The war years for Edward Vasquez represented the ultimate adventure. He begged his parents to let him enlist and threatened to run away with the circus, as he had twice before. When they finally relented, Vasquez joined the Navy at age 15.

He first served on kitchen patrol and then as a mechanic—as his father had taught him—at Suva, Fiji Islands. He entered his combat experience in Guadalcanal, Solomon Islands, where he was injured when another soldier jumped into his foxhole. While fighting in Bougainville, Vasquez earned the right to go home. It was one of the few times in his life he couldn't wait to go home.

On his 17th birthday, the war over, Vasquez enlisted again. "I found a home in the Air Force," he said. He would spend 15 more years in the military.

In 1968, Vasquez was sent to Vietnam as a helicopter mechanic. That year, he met Vietnamese native Anh Ngu, who became his wife. They had their first child, Rosy, in September of that year. In addition to starting a family, Vasquez figuratively struck gold when he opened the first Mexican restaurant in Saigon. Anh did the cooking while he acted as waiter and official food taster to ensure the authenticity of their fare.

The couple left Vietnam in 1975. In San Antonio, Texas, they tried to duplicate their restaurant success. When it failed, Vasquez traveled to Iran to work for Bell helicopter. His family joined him for a time, but social unrest chased them out of the region.

With the money he made in Iran, Vasquez bought a house and land in San Antonio, but in 1980, moved the family to Saudi Arabia for four years. Once in the States for good, finally, Vasquez often "escaped" the house and ran errands for his wife, who had a school of cosmetology.

The couple had two children, Rosie and Van.

Edward Vasquez

Date of Birth
23 MAY 1927
San Antonio, TX

Interviewed by
Andrea Williams
12 APRIL 2002
San Antonio, TX

WWII Military Unit
Carrier Aircraft
Service Unit 5

Edelmiro Treviño Vidaurri

Date of Birth
6 SEPTEMBER 1914
McAllen, TX

Interviewed by
Michael Taylor
9 DECEMBER 2001
Austin, TX

WWII Location
Stationed in
Reykjavik, Iceland

VIDAURRI, EDELMIRO TREVIÑO. In a lifetime of military service, Edelmiro Vidaurri worked on airplanes ranging from the A-T6 to the B-52 to the KC-135. He said he grew to admire airplanes over the 27 years he served.

When he joined the Army in 1937, he was assigned to the 15th Field Artillery Battalion, 2d Infantry Regiment. His mechanical aptitude led to a transfer to the Army Air Corps in 1940. He retired from the Air Force in 1968.

He married Martha Ortega before WWII, and they were stationed in Reykjavik, Iceland, at a fueling and maintenance station.

"As a matter of fact, all the aircraft from the 8th Air Force passed through Iceland from the United States," Vidaurri said. "They'd refuel and from there they'd go to England in case they needed repairs."

They were the only people on the base who spoke Spanish, he said, and their six children primarily spoke English. He said it was common for him to be the only Mexican American in his unit.

He said that the lack of commitment to the war effort was evident among the soldiers during the Vietnam War, and that it was the reason he retired early.

"They were just going into the service to fill in their military obligation," Vidaurri said. "When you're working with sophisticated aircraft, you don't want these kind of people with you because there's no room for mistakes."

He and Martha had six children: Abel, David, Anna, Edward, Robert and Stephen. Three of their sons, Abel, David and Stephen, served in the military.

Epilogue

Coming Home

As Americans of the WWII-era recall what they were doing upon learning of the attack on Pearl Harbor, the end of the war is similarly etched in their memories. Soldiers not assigned to the occupation in Japan, or rebuilding Europe, returned to the States, greeted by a heroes' welcome, complete with parades and salutes.

Wartime experiences had transformed the individuals who lived through it, both in the military and in civilian life. In positive ways, and in other ways, their lives would never be the same. It was what happened after the war, the effects of the war, that would leave a mark.

The baby boom began, with the WWII generation starting families and integrating themselves back into the fabric of American society. The GI Bill afforded new education opportunities, and Latino veterans served as leaders and role models in their home communities. Latinas had ventured far away from home, physically and figuratively—but after the war, many assumed their pre-war roles, for a time. It has been interesting to learn that many of these women carried out their responsibilities to husbands and children, but after the children were grown, got that GED, and sometimes college degrees.

Turning Points

The end of the war signaled many changes for the United States and for the men and women who were part of the war effort.

While much of the results were positive—educational opportunities, a new world perspective—the war also exacted a heavy toll on the United States and on many individuals. There were, of course, the families of the 405,399 Americans who were killed in the war. Their world would never be the same.

Tomás A. Hernandez, of Temple, Texas, says for him, the war was his education.

"When I came back, I was more alert to things of life. ... Things were more important," he said. "It was like someone opened a door to the world."

Charles Samarron, of San Antonio, survived the battle at Iwo Jima and found an acceptance of his mortality, as well as his bond with others.

"You know ... you can die anytime," he said. "I feel more of a kinship with my fellow man than I did before."

Many people interviewed said that, for the first time in their lives, the war provided that opportunity to see just how far they could go, removed, as they were, from the social constraints that relegated Latinos to second-class citizenship.

Manuel Vara, of San Antonio, Texas, served in the Pacific, and later worked for the U.S. postal service, insisting that he be considered for promotions.

"Prior to shipping out, I didn't know what I was capable of achieving, of what it is that we [Mexican Americans] wanted to get out of life," he said. "When we came back, we, the Mexicans, had much more confidence in ourselves and we realized that we deserved to get a better education, just to see how far we could go."

José "Joe" Cuellar, of Albuquerque, N.M., noted that the war gave him some measure of self-confidence: "After I went into the service, nothing bothered me, because I knew I could do almost anything."

For many Latinos and Latinas, working alongside Anglos would rid them of any notion, if they had it before, of any inherent inferiority. Jesse Ortiz, of Fresno, Calif., saw whites in a different way, as fellow soldiers.

"It was a source of education for all of us

in the sense that we could look in the eye of each other," Ortiz said. "That was very, very important to get to know each other. It brought us to an understanding that we are all human beings. That we all need love. That we all need nourishment."

José Ramirez, of San Diego, Calif., put it like this: "We were dealing with a new kind of citizen. Veterans who had seen a lot came back, and were not going to take any crap. It was a turning point in the barrio."

Lasting Effects

Not all the effects were good ones: the war also crushed some dreams: wounds and injuries would prevent returning veterans from resuming their pre-war work. Take the case of Philip Benavides, a French horn player from Austin, Texas, who became a medic in the Philippines. Benavides was subjected to torture as a captive of the Japanese military. When he was released, he no longer had the control over his embouchure, the way his lips position on the mouthpiece of the horn, that is essential.

He also lost much of his hearing.

"It did the job," Benavides said. "I was unable to function again as a musician. ... I could listen to music and I would usually be half a tone behind the rest of them. ... I was getting completely tone-deaf so I just gave [music] up completely."

The war had also exacted a price in other less visible ways. Some men couldn't overcome their "nerves," what today might be called "post traumatic stress disorder." Santos Sandoval of La Junta, Colo., who served in the Pacific, would always suffer from night sweats.

"I thought it would go away, but it never has gone away," Sandoval said. "I guess I'll die with it."

In Laredo, Texas, Francisco Guerra has a recurring dream about Normandy. "... I am driving a 2 1/2-ton Army truck with defective brakes in deep valleys, hills and winding dirt roads," he said. "Suddenly, I wake up just as I am about to crash."

Some veterans would "self-medicate," escaping their memories by taking a drink.

Encarción Armando Gonzales, a native of Los Angeles, Calif., recalls the joy of returning home after serving both in the Aleutian Islands, as well as in Europe.

"It was great to be home, and a lot of tears and a lot of adjustment and a lot of drinking," Gonzales said. "A lot of horrible drinking."

"Nowadays people get a lot of help after traumatic situations, but we didn't have that back then." Gonzales eventually got sober, relapsing briefly after the death of his wife.

Marriages

Some of the wartime marriages did not survive; among the men and women interviewed, divorce is not uncommon. But it is also common to find couples married in the romantic whirlwind of the war years to have celebrated 50th wedding anniversaries and more. Lina Martinez Cordova of Albuquerque, N.M., married her husband, Alfredo, in 1940, before the war. By the time he left for Europe, the couple had two children.

"When I was young, every decision was made by my husband," Cordova said. The two developed more of a partnership and decisions were made jointly.

"I guess he figured sometimes my ideas were better than his,'" she said.

Wives had the sometimes difficult task of caring for their spouses when they came back from the war. They served as a comfort as their husbands fought through memories of war, woke from nightmares of battlegrounds and nevertheless tried to move on with their lives. Sometimes they had to help them through injuries and disabilities incurred during battle.

Geographic Mobility

With new educational opportunities, the men and women interviewed here could move to locations that were more hospitable. People like Anastacio Perez Juarez, whose family worked the cotton fields in Texas, stopped farming. Juarez took a job at Kelly Air Force Base in San Antonio, Texas, working as a mechanic for 10 years and another 20 as an aircraft sheet metal worker.

Alfred J. Hernandez was ready to give up on Texas, and its many race problems, after he returned. He told his wife that life would be more pleasant up north, or perhaps in Mexico, the land of his birth.

"She soon convinced me we should stay in Houston and get involved and make an effort to fix the problems," he said.

He did, working through the League of United Latin American Citizens (LULAC), and becoming Houston's first Hispanic judge.

Richard Savala, of Dallas, Texas, married an English girl, Violet Rosina Land, and brought her back to Dallas. But it was difficult to find an apartment building that would rent to them, a complaint many Latinos and Latinas had about finding rental units in the 1940s.

"So we moved back in with my parents," he said.

His wife didn't want to raise their children in such a difficult environment, so they moved to Detroit, Mich.

"Things were much different in Michigan," he said. "They treated us better, and Violet felt better."

New Identities

Many Latinos and Latinas came to see themselves in a different light during the war. Frank Bonilla was a New York-born American of Puerto Rican descent who served with the 65th Infantry. Serving with the predominantly Puerto Rican 65th Infantry, Bonilla found that the Puerto Rican soldiers considered themselves less part of the U.S. Army, and more part of the 65th. He was also more aware of the divide between New York-born Puerto Ricans and those born on the island. The Puerto Ricans who had emigrated to the mainland were seen as "American Joes." Puerto Ricans from the island considered themselves "pure" Puerto Ricans, Bonilla said.

"We were American GI Joes to them, and not Puerto Ricans," he said. "The military experience helped to consolidate my sense of being Puerto Rican and also a sense of wanting to study and be a scholar."

For Cuban American Evelio Grillo, the war experience would solidify his strong conviction that he was a hybrid—both black and Hispanic. After all, as an Afro-Cuban child in Ybor City, near Tampa, Fla., he had attended segregated black schools, and had graduated from a black high school in Washington, D.C., then gone to college at a historically black, Catholic college in New Orleans, La.

Grillo served with the 823d Engineer Aviation Battalion (Colored).

"I saw myself as a possible bridge between English-speaking and Spanish-speaking people, but especially between English- and Spanish-speaking blacks," Grillo said.

Latinos serving in the U.S. military in WWII felt some ambiguity. Andrew Tamayo, a native of San Antonio, had wanted to enlist immediately after Pearl Harbor. But later, in the thick of battle in Sicily, on July 1943, doubts crept into his head.

"I remembered how they used to treat us [Mexican Americans] over here [in the United States]," he said.

After turning the matter over in his mind, Tamayo began to feel that there was something larger at issue, a principle at stake, that transcended the ugliness of discrimination.

Many of the veterans interviewed who were Mexican citizens were sworn in as U.S. citizens during the war. Randel Zepeda Fernandez, who was born in Ciudad Juarez, across the border from El Paso, Texas, was naturalized in Germany in December 1945, in a simple ceremony with about ten other enlisted men.

"At the time, joining the Armed Forces was the fastest way to become a citizen," he said.

Contributions

Those who have conducted these interviews often comment on the life of service that dominates this group. These are men and women who worked hard to provide for their children, providing guidance to keep them on the right path. They often mention that all of their children graduated from high school, or, how many attended college.

In some cases, they'll note that they took care of an ailing parent for several years.

"My mother lived with us for ten years before she died," said Trinidad Nerio of Saginaw, Mich.

They volunteered for organizations like the VFW, the American Legion, the Disabled Americans Vets, the Catholic War Veterans, the Military Order of the Purple Heart.

And they were also active in civil rights organizations, ensuring that future generations would have fewer obstacles to face.

"Our people were dedicated," said Ed Idar, Jr., who was a leader in both the American G.I. Forum and later with the Mexican American Legal Defense and Educational Fund (MALDEF). "They believed in what they were doing. They weren't expecting a salary."

People like Idar and many others desegregated schools, contributed to greater political participation of Hispanics, and made lasting contributions to their communities and to the nation.

For the men and women interviewed as part of the U.S. Latino & Latina WWII Oral History Project, what they bequeathed to the generations that were to come was a legacy greater than words.

Selected References

Ambrose, Stephen E. *Eisenhower: Soldier and President.* New York: Touchstone, 1990.

Appleman, Roy E., James M. Burns, Russell A. Gugeler, and John Stevens. *Okinawa: The Last Battle: The U.S. Army Campaigns of World War II.* Washington, D.C.: U.S. Army Center of Military History Publication 5-11, 1948.

Armed Forces Information School. *The Army Almanac: A Book of Facts Concerning the Army of the United States.* Washington, D.C.: U.S. Government Printing Office, 1950.

Bailey, Jennifer L. *Philippine Islands: The U.S. Army Campaigns of World War II.* Washington, D.C.: U.S. Army Center of Military History Publication 72-3, 1992.

Baldwin, Hanson W. *Battles Lost & Won: Great Campaigns of World War II.* New York: Konecky & Konecky, 1966.

Bellafaire, Judith A. *Army Nurse Corps: A Commemoration of World War II Service.* Washington, D.C.: U.S. Army Center of Military History Publication 72-14, 1994.

————. *The Women's Army Corps: A Commemoration of World War II Service.* Washington, D.C.: U.S. Army Center of Military History Publication 72-15, 1993.

Buchanan, Russell A. *The United States and World War II.* Vol. 1. New York: Harper & Row, 1964.

Clancey, Patrick W. *HyperWar: A Hypertext History of the Second World War.* Lafayette, Colo.: HyperWar Foundation, 2005. http://www.ibiblio.org/hyperwar/

Cole, Hugh M. *The Ardennes: Battle of the Bulge.* Washington, D.C.: Office of the Chief of Military History, Department of the Army, 1965.

Dzwonchyk, Wayne M. and John Ray Skates. *A Brief History of the U.S. Army in World War II: The U.S. Army Campaigns of World War II.* Washington, D.C.: U.S. Army Center of Military History Publication 72-2, 1992.

Goralski, Robert. *World War II, Almanac: 1931-1945, A Political and Military Record.* New York: Bonanza Books, 1984.

Hammond, William M. *Normandy: The U.S. Army Campaigns of World War II.* Washington, D.C.: U.S. Army Center of Military History Publication 72-18, 1994.

Isserman, Maurice. *America at War: World War II.* New York: 1991.

Keegan, John. *Atlas of the Second World War.* Ann Arbor, Mich.: Borders Press, 1989.

Kennedy, David M. *Freedom From Fear: The American People in Depression and War, 1929-1945.* New York: Oxford University Press, 1999.

Lyons, Michael J. *World War II: A Short History.* 3rd ed. Upper Saddle River, N.J.: Prentice Hall, 1999.

MacGarrigle, George L. *Aleutian Islands: The U.S. Army Campaigns of World War II.* Washington, D.C.: U.S. Army Center of Military History Publication 72-6, 1992.

Maddox, Robert James. *The United States and World War II.* Boulder, Colo.: Westview Press, 1992.

McPherson, Ernest. *The California State Military Museum: Preserving California's Military Heritage.* Sacramento, Calif.: California State Military Department, 2005. http://www.militarymuseum.org/

Newell, Clayton R. *Burma, 1942: The U.S. Army Campaigns of World War II.* Washington, D.C.: U.S. Army Center of Military History Publication 72-21, 1994.

Parker, R.A.C. *The Second World War: A Short History.* New York: Oxford University Press, 1989.

Province, Charles M. *Patton's Third Army: A Chronology of the Third Army Advance, August 1944 to May 1945.* New York: Hippocrene Books, 1992.

Sides, Hampton. *Ghost Soldiers.* New York: Anchor Books, 2002.

Stanton, Shelby L. *Order of Battle: U.S. Army in World War II.* Novato, Calif.: Presidio Press, 1984.

U.S. Congress. Joint Committee on the Investigation of the Pearl Harbor Attack. *Investigation of the Pearl Harbor Attack.* 79th Cong., 1946.

U.S. Naval History Division. *Dictionary of American Naval Fighting Ships.* Washington, D.C.: Navy Historical Center, 1959.

Young, Peter, ed. *The World Almanac Book of World War II.* Englewood Cliffs, N.J.: World Almanac Publications, 1981.

Ziemke, Earl F. *The U.S. Army in the Occupation of Germany 1944-1964.* Washington, D.C.: U.S. Army Center of Military History Publication 30-60, 1990.

Original Interviewers

The goal of the U.S. Latino & Latina WWII Oral History Project is to create an archive of primary source material for future research, so that the perspectives of Latinos are included in writings about their period. The main component of the archive are the 500-plus videotaped interviews.

The Project's methods have been adapted from the Oral History Association's best practices guidelines, which can be found online at *http://omega.dickinson.edu/organizations/oha/codes*.

It has also relied heavily on consultations with Project Advisory Committee member Professor David Gracy, an international authority on archives. The Project's own guidelines for interviewers can be found at *http://utopia.utexas.edu/explore/latino/*.

Interviewers have come from several quarters: many have been students in a class dedicated to the Project; students were required to conduct at least one interview in the semester. But the majority of the interviewers have been volunteers, some have been family members or friends who were insistent that their loved ones interviews be included. All interviewers have been expected to adhere to the Project's standards.

The Project has counted heavily on its partnerships, most notably with the Department of Veterans Affairs Readjustment Counseling Service, as well as with the National Association of Hispanic Journalists (NAHJ) and the California Chicano News Media Association (CCNMA). Those organizations helped organize large-scale interview sessions, in which WWII Latinos and Latinas were videotaped individually. Through those partnerships, as well as other regional ones with universities and Latino cultural centers, the Project was able to extend its reach far beyond Austin and Texas.

Ana Cristina Acosta	*Olga Briseño*	*Terrie Cornell*	*Ruben Alí Flores*
Nancy Acosta	*Cheryl Brownstein-*	*Francisco Cortés*	*Veronica Flores*
Elizabeth Aguirre	*Santiago*	*Nicole Cruz*	*Veronica Franco*
Patricia Aguirre	*Karin Brulliard*	*Cynthia Cueva*	*Sandra Freyberg*
Helen Aguirre Ferré	*Anica Butler*	*Lisa Cummings*	*Milton Carrero Galarza*
Trinidad "Tito" Aguirre	*Dana Calvo*	*Brian Daugherty*	*Norma Gallegoz*
Monica Jean Alaníz	*Juan Campos*	*Alan K. Davis*	*Anabelle Garay*
Carmen Amoros	*Antonio Cantú*	*Juan de la Cruz*	*Claudia García*
Bruce Ashcroft	*Cindy Cárcamo*	*Cliff Despres*	*Evelyn Jasso García*
Ray Atencio	*Mary Alice Carnes*	*George Diaz*	*Humberto García*
Kevin Bales	*Miguel A. Castro*	*Violeta Dominguez*	*Raul García, Jr.*
Sharon Bales	*Denise Chávarri*	*Fernando Dovalina*	*Veronica García*
Mario Barrera	*Irene Consuelo Chávez*	*Ernest Eguía*	*Leslie Ann Garza*
Adrian Bashick	*Roberta Elaine Chávez-*	*Delia Esparza*	*Mariel Garza*
Ryan Bauer	*Morris*	*Hector Espinoza*	*Oscar Garza*
Karleen Boggio-	*Jacob Collaza*	*Gail Fisher*	*Raquel C. Garza*
Montgomery	*Carlos Condé*	*Elizabeth Flores*	*Veronica Garza*

Antonio Gilb
Carla Gonzalez
Karla E. González
M. David Gray
Tammi Grais
Nicole Griffith
Lucy Guevara
Lucinda Guinn
Ann Harbour
Paul Harrigan
Katherine Hearty
Kristen Henry
Ascensión Hernandez
Carlos I. Hernandez
Minette Hernandez
Robert Hernandez
Laura Herrera
Virgil Hines Jr.
Sandra Ibarra
Andria Infante
Jeffrey Lee Johnson
Jennifer Sinco Kelleher
Porteskcia Kelley
Cheryl Kemp
Kevin Klauber
Vicki Lamar
Kelli Lambert
Yazmin Lazcano
Rick Leál
Joshua Leighton
Yvonne Lim
Iliana Limón
Jennifer Lindgren
Laura Loh
Manny López
Wilfredo Pardo López
Brian Lucero
Bettina Luis
Adrianna Lujan
Delia J. Lujan
William Luna
Angela Macias
Rasha Madkour

Lynn Maguire-Walker
Gabriel Manzano
Juan Marinez
Adrian Gerald Marquez
Domingo Marquéz
Erika Martinez
Ismael Martinez
Juan Martinez
Norman L. Martinez
Stella Martinez
Shamiso Masowsue
Desirée Mata
Robert Mayer
Martamaría McGonagle
Hannah McIntyre
Manuel Medrano
Sofia Mena
Henry Mendoza
Peter Mendoza
Rhonda Miller
Susan Miller
Gloria Monita
Robert C. Moore
Antonio Moreno
Celina Moreno
Liza Moreno
Haldon Morgan
Cody Morris
Jim Morrison
Nicole Muñoz
Sandra Murillo
Jesse Nava
Christopher Nay
Stacy Nelson
Mary L. Nieves
Jane O'Brien
Joe Olague
Julio C. Ovando
Ron Pacheco
Yolanda Chavez Padilla
Doralís Pérez-Soto
Christina Perkins
Unity Peterson

Ricardo Pimentél
Ernesto Portillo
Claudia I. Provencio
Chandler Race
Joseph Ramírez
Nora Ramírez
Alicia Rascon
Rajesh Reddy
Pedro Reynoso
Chris Riley
Markel Riojas
Robert Rivas
Maggie Rivas-Rodriguez
Laura Rivera
Mónica Rivera
Maro Robbins
Misty Roberts
Erika Rodriguez
Virgilio Roel
Andrés Romero
Steven Rosales
Lorena Ruley
Alfred Saenz
Israel Saenz
Louis Sahagun
Xochitl Salazár
Marcello Salcido
Vanesa Salínas
Jennifer Sanchez
Joanne R. Sanchez
Mary Sanchez
Aryn Sedler
Brenda Sendejo
Andrea Shearer
Agapito Silva
Cheryl Smith
Anthony Sobotnik
Frank O. Sotomayor
Jack Steingart
Stephen Stetson
Jaime Stockwell
Valerie Talavera-Bustillos
Raul Tamez

Michael Taylor
Kimberly Tilley
William R. Todd-
    Mancillas
Vivian Torre
Luis Torres
Vanessa Torres-Villescas
Matthew Trana
Frank Trejo
Martha Treviño
Rea Ann Trotter
Yolanda Urrabazo
Andrea Valdéz
Yudith Vargas
Joe Myers Vasquez
Liliana Velazquez
Carlos Vélez-Ibañez
Francisco Venegas
Luz Villareal
Gary Villereal
Jeffery K. Watanabe
Theresa DeLeon Weeks
Joel Weickgenant
Andrea Williams
René Zambrano
David Zavala
Paul R. Zepeda
Anna Zukowski

Original Story Writers

The stories included in this volume were derived and summarized from previously written stories. Longer versions of these stories, for the most part, were published in one of eight issues of Narratives: Stories of U.S. Latinos & Latinas and WWII. The Austin American-Statesman and the San Antonio Express-News alternated production of the newspaper.

Most of the original writers were students in J320D, an intermediate reporting class at UT. Others were students enrolled in a class dedicated to the Project. In a few cases, the writers were working journalists, called on an emergency basis after the end of the semester, when the Project was trying to meet a looming production deadline.

The journalism students who wrote those original stories were provided a videotaped interview, as well as any accompanying documentation, such as discharge papers or certificates. The stories were rigorously edited in individual side-by-side sessions with either the Project director or one of the guest editors. The stories then went to military fact-checkers, and afterward, to the Interview Subjects, for pre-publication review.

The value of the original stories in preparing this volume cannot be overstated: the *Legacy* writers were able to read those newspaper stories and find the essence of it before summarizing. In many instances, exact wording from those original stories was used. In preparing this volume, the previously published stories were resent to the Interview Subjects for any additional corrections, revisions and information.

Ana Cristina Acosta	Karin Brulliard	Juan de la Cruz	Ruben Alí Flores
Sarah Adams	Emily Burgess	Krystal De Los Santos	Yasemin Florey
Vanessa Adams	Luisito Caleon	Erin Dean	Sandra Freyberg
Cynthia Agnew	Bianca Camaño	Anjali Desai	Jennifer Gallo
Trinidad "Tito" Aguirre	Antonio Cantú	Christa Desimone	Marisa Galvan
Monica Jean Alaníz	Cindy Cárcamo	Cliff Despres	Guillermo X. Garcia
Jonathan Alexander	Edna P. Carmona	Alicia Dietrich	Irma Garcia
Scott Allison	D.J. Carwile	Violeta Dominguez	Ernie Garrido
Sparkle Anderson	Miguel A. Castro	Fernando Dovalina	Raquel C. Garza
José Araiza	Denise Chávarri	Shelby Downs	Eric Garza
Alyssa Armentrout	Kristen Clarck	Nicole Dreyer	Barbara Gibbon
Stephanie Babb	Ashley Clary	Shan Dunn	Katie Gibson
Mario Barrera	Adrienne M. Cody	Kaz Edwards	Antonio Gilb
Elisa A. Batista	Leigh Cole	Elizabeth Egeland	Jeffrey Gilbert
Habib Battah	Jacob Collazo	Rebecca Eng	Therese Glenn
Amy Baur	Francisco Cortés	Natalie England	Betsy Glickman
Allison Baxter	Andrea Couch	Claudia Farías	Mayella Gonzalez
Nathan Beck	Cheyenne Cozzalio	Ellie K. Fehd	Karla E. González
Lindsay Blau	Amanda Crawford	Rachel Finney	Brian Goodman
Melanie Boehm	Lisa Cummings	Emiko Fitzgerald	Lindsay Graham
Deborah Bonn	Heather Cuthbertson	Monica Flores	Tammi Grais

Emma Graves-
　Fitzsimmons
Alyssa Green
Brandi Grissom
Lucy Guevara
Clint Hale
Cari Hammerstrom
Peggy Hanley
Ann Harbour
Matt Harlan
Minette Hernandez
Shelley Hiam
Connor Higgins
Heather Hilliard
Ashley Hitson
Rachel Howell
Sandra Ibarra
Andria Infante
Robert Inks
Sarah Jackson
Elizabeth James
Melanie Jarrett
Valerie Jayne
Callie Jenschke
Ruchika Joshi
Erin Keck
Darcy Keller
Alison Kelley
Katie Kennon
D'Arcy Kerschen
In-Young Kim
Maureen King
Sarah Kleiner
Meridith Kohut
Melanie Kudzia
Sara Kunz
Mark LaVergne
Gillian Lawlor
Yazmin Lazcano
Justin Lefkowski
Joshua Leighton
Yvonne Lim
Jennifer Lindgren
Angela Macias
Marisela Maddox
Lynn Maguire-Walker
Courtney Mahaffey

Gabriel Manzano
Erika Martinez
Nicolas Martinez
Ismael Martinez
Ryan Martinez
Desirée Mata
Catherine Mathieson
Karen Matthews
Robert Mayer
Kendra Mayer
Jason McDaniel
Marta McGonagle
Hannah McIntyre
Leslie McLain
Brooke Meharg
Sofia Mena
Sylvia Mendoza
Henry Mendoza
Rhonda Miller
Susan Miller
Elaine Mingus
Ayesha Mirza
Whitney Mizer
Allison Mokry
Wesley Monier
Robert C. Moore
Celina Moreno
Haldun Morgan
Nicole Muñoz
Jenny Murphy
Donetta Nagle
Jennifer Nalewicki
Christopher Nay
Carrie Nelson
Stacy Nelson
Sonia Nezamzadeh
Beth Nottingham
Jane O'Brien
Veronica Olivera
Caren Panzer
Noelle Pareja
Helen Peralta
Javier Perez
Doralís Pérez-Soto
Unity Peterson
Christine Pev
Lindsay Peyton

Will Potter
Christine Powers
Naomi Price
Emily Priest
Anne Quach
Chandler Race
Kristina Radke
Laura Radloff
Nora Ramírez
Alicia Rascon
Brandon Rawe
Rajesh Reddy
Anita Rice
Brandi Richey
Alexandra Ritchie
Maggie Rivas-Rodriguez
Dionicia Rivera
Dennis Robbins
Maro Robbins
Misty Roberts
Elizabeth Robertson
Erika Rodriguez
Gina Ross
Christina Rucker
Israel Saenz
Veronica Sainz
Xochitl Salazár
Joanne Rao Sanchez
Katherine Sayre
Chris Schulz
Aryn Sedler
Melissa Sellers
Andrea Shearer
Rachna Sheth
Brasher Sierra
Jane Slater
Lori Slaughenhoupt
Benjamin Smith
Lauren Smith
Cheryl Smith
Otto Smith-Goeke
Ginny Snyder
Anthony Sobotnik
Gilbert Song
Stacie Schutze
Kristin Stanford
Meredith Stencil

Whitney Sterling
Stephen Stetson
Darcie Stevens
Jamie Stockwell
Courtney Stoutamire
Kelly Tarleton
Michael Taylor
Sandra Taylor
Stephanie Threinen
Ashley Tompkins
Shelby Tracy
Amanda Traphagan
Frank Trejo
Christopher Trout
Yolanda Urrabazo
Andrea Valdéz
Karina Valenzuela
Joe Myers Vasquez
David Vauthrin
Liliana Velazquez
Valerie Venegas
Brian Villalobos
Angela Walker
Melissa Watkins
Heather Watkins
Joanna Watson
Jason Weddle
Joel Weickgenant
Brooke West
Kimberly Wied
Tara Wilcox-
　Ghanoonparvar
Elizabeth Wilder
Andrea Williams
Brent Wistrom
Anna Wong
Katie Woody
Nathan Wyman
Jennifer Yee
Ronnie Zamora
David R. Zavala
Paul R. Zepeda
Anna Zukowski
Julia Zwick

Index

Tenorio, Arthur "Chavalito," 98, 102
Thomas, María Isabel Solis, xxix, 217
Tijerina, Pedro "Pete" Jr., xxx, 258, 272
Tijerina, Reies, 266
Todd, William Henry, 141
Torres, Antonio Aurelio Martínez, 251
Torres, Gilberto, 51
Tovar, Rudolph, 144, 148
Towns, David Pineda, 48, 52
Trejo, Juan Concepción Dominguez, 251
Treviño, Domingo, 160, 169
Treviño, Felix, 304
Tripodi, Dominick, 52
Trujillo, Antonio, 142, 325
Trujillo, Charles, 325
Truman, Harry S., 86

U

Unanue, Joseph, 289, 304
Uranga, Charles, 305
Urias, José Jesús "Chuy," 76, 83
Urias, Leova Tellez "L.T.," 67
Uriegas, Joe Moreno, 36, 53

V

Valades, Gabriel, 86, 90
Valades, Salvador, 83
Valderas, Harold, 305
Vara, Manuel Castro, 170, 327
Vasquez, Edward, 325
Vasquez, George S., 56, 67
Vasquez, Refugio Miguel "Mike," 22
Vasquez, Wilhelmina Cooremans, xxix, 211, 212, 217
Vazquez, Anna Torres, 183, 189
Vazquez, Roberto, 272
Vega, Lauro, 35, 53
Vega, Martín, 54
Vega, Raymond, 306
Velázquez, Ángel Antonio, 151, 153, 154
Venegas, Francisco, 84
Vidaurri, Edelmiro Treviño, 326
Vidaurri, Martha Ortega, 222, 242
Villanueva, Gonzalo, 22
Villarreal, Oscar, 118
Villarreal, Raul Cantú, 84

W

White, Mark, 311
Wood, William "Bill" Raymond, 306

X

Ximenes, Vicente, 287, 307

Y

Ybarra, Andres, 54

Z

Zamudio, Esequiel, 128
Zaragoza, José R., 170
Zatarian, Domingo, 90
Zenizo, Jaime, 131
Zepeda, Daniel, 204, 205
Zepeda, Elías, 204-205
Zepeda, Isaac, 204-205
Zepeda, Paul R., 193, 204
Zepeda, Roberto, 204
Zuniga, Alejandra Rojas, 289, 307

Mexican Americans & World War II

Up to 750,000 Mexican-American men served in World War II, earning more Medals of Honor and other decorations in proportion to their numbers than any other ethnic group. Mexican-American women entered the workforce on the home front, supporting the war effort and earning good wages for themselves and their families. But the contributions of these men and women have been largely overlooked as American society celebrates the sacrifices and achievements of the "Greatest Generation." To bring their stories out of the shadows, this book gathers 11 essays that explore the Mexican-American experience in World War II from a variety of personal and scholarly perspectives.

The book opens with accounts of the war's impact on individuals and families. It goes on to look at how the war affected school experiences; how Mexican-American patriotism helped to soften racist attitudes; how Mexican Americans in the Midwest, unlike their counterparts in other regions of the country, did not experience greater opportunities as a result of the war; how the media exposed racist practices in Texas; and the role of Mexican nationals in the war effort through the Bracero program and the Mexican government's championing of Mexican Americans' rights.

Contributing Writers: Luis Alvarez; María Eva Flores; Erasmo Gamboa; Lynne Marie Getz; David Montejano; Julio Noboa; Naomi Quiñonez; Maggie Rivas-Rodriguez; Rita Sanchez; Dionício Valdés; Emilio Zamora—*Published by University of Texas Press, 2005.*

A Legacy Greater Than Words and *Mexican Americans & World War II* are available through University of Texas Press, or ask for these titles at your local bookstores.

U.S. Latino & Latina WWII Oral History Project • *Austin*